THE ANGLO-SAXON WORLD

THE
ANGLO-SAXON
WORLD

NICHOLAS J. HIGHAM AND MARTIN J. RYAN

YALE UNIVERSITY PRESS
NEW HAVEN AND LONDON

For information about this and other Yale University Press publications, please contact:
U.S. Office: sales.press@yale.edu www.yalebooks.com
Europe Office: sales@yaleup.co.uk www.yalebooks.co.uk

Set in Minion Pro by IDSUK (DataConnection) Ltd
Printed in China through Worldprint

Higham, N. J.
  The Anglo-Saxon world/Nicholas J. Higham and Martin J. Ryan.
    pages cm
  Includes bibliographical references.
  ISBN 978-0-300-12534-4 (cl : alk. paper)
1. Great Britain—History—Anglo-Saxon period, 449–1066. 2. Anglo-Saxons. I. Ryan, Martin J. II. Title.
  DA152.H528 2013
  942.01—dc23

                                                                                          2013005724

Library of Congress Cataloging-in-Publication Data

A catalogue record for this book is available from the British Library.

10 9 8 7 6 5 4 3 2 1

For Cheryl and Rosa

Contents

Illustrations

Acknowledgements

Over the course of researching and writing this book we have accumulated countless debts to friends and colleagues – happily, not mutually exclusive categories. They cannot all be named in the space we have, but we offer to everyone our most sincere thanks.

Some particular debts need to be specifically acknowledged, however. We are most grateful to the University of Manchester for granting Nick a sabbatical in 2009–2010 and to the Leverhulme Trust for awarding him a Leverhulme Research Fellowship in 2010. We have benefited enormously over the years from the unstinting aid and advice of colleagues past and present at the University of Manchester including the late Jeff Denton, the late David Hill, Kate Cooper, Paul Fouracre, Conrad Leyser, Stephen Mossman, Gale Owen-Crocker, Stephen Rigby, Alex Rumble and Donald Scragg. We would also like to thank the numerous members of the Manchester Centre for Anglo-Saxon Studies and the Centre for Late Antiquity at the University of Manchester. Generations of students at Manchester have been unwitting guinea pigs for many of the ideas in this book and we thank them for this and for the stimulus they have provided through their questions, suggestions and comments.

Paul Fouracre generously read and commented on chapters 1, 2, 3 and 8, Steve Rigby chapters 3 and 8, and Rosa Vidal chapters 4, 5, 6 and 7. Paola Fumagalli of the Bridgeman Art Library provided invaluable assistance with securing images. David Matthews shared his expertise on national identity in Britain in the later Middle Ages to the benefit of the introduction. Martin Richards helped with the archaeogenetic content of chapter 2, correcting draft text, Kevin Leahy assisted with cremation, the archaeology of the East Midlands and Sources and Issues 3b (the Staffordshire Hoard), which he corrected, and provided illustrations 2.8 and 2.11. The late Richard Hall, Mike Andrews, Lesley Collet and Christine Kyriacou provided valuable assistance with Sources and Issues 7a, on Viking Age York, and sourced 7a. 1–5 illustrations, and Richard in particular very kindly corrected draft text. Paul Bennett, Andrew Richardson and Andrew Savage were most helpful regarding Canterbury and Kent's archaeology, supplying numerous illustrations and advice quickly and expertly. Dominic Powlesland very kindly discussed many issues regarding early settlement and landscape with us, and provided illustrations 2.17, 2.20, 2.21, 2.22 and 2.23. Ian Riddler generously provided illustration 5b.4 and advised regarding Hamwic; Gabor Thomas provided pictures from his excavations at Lyminge (2.16, 6a.3); Tom Green kindly discussed the early history of Lindsey and provided illustration 2.27a and we thank Murray Cook for providing information about the Viking-Age burials at Cumwhitton and for supplying us with notes from a symposium on the burials. Jonathan Jarrett, and Allan McKinley have generously shared their expertise in early medieval diplomatic, and much else, on numerous occasions, as well as allowing us to read material not yet published that has assisted greatly with numerous chapters. Discussions with Morn Capper on the kingdom of Mercia have likewise improved many of the chapters. Luca Larpi provided invaluable assistance with Latin and palaeography, as well as sharing his extensive knowledge of Gildas and the *De excidio*.

Chapters 2 and 3 benefited enormously from meetings with Helen Geake, Helena Hamerow, Catherine Hills and Sam Lucy, Howard Williams, and Catherine and Sam also most kindly corrected Sources and Issues 2a, on Spong Hill, and helped source the illustrations, which were ultimately provided by Tim Pestell and Alison Yardy. Christopher Loveluck most helpfully corrected Sources and Issues 4b, on Flixborough, the illustrations for which were sourced by Rose Nicholson. Nick's doctoral student Erik Grigg very kindly provided text from which were précised passages on dykes on pp. 52-4, and supplied illustrations 1.25, 1.26. Sources and Issues 2b, on Prittlewell, has benefited enormously from input by Elizabeth Barham, Lyn Blackmore, Ian Blair, Andy Chopping and Nicky Powell, while Daniel Pett assisted with illustration for Sources and Issues 3b, the Staffordshire Hoard. Bob Higham and Michael Rouillard were generous with illustrations relating to the excavation of Hen Domen (8.23), and Andrew Birley kindly provided illustrations 1.13 and 1.27. Pauline Stafford kindly shared with us her considerable expertise on the *Anglo-Saxon Chronicle*, particularly the *Annals of Æthelflæd*.

James Gerrard very helpfully discussed several issues regarding the fifth century and in particular late Roman Bath and Southwark, and Gary Brown generously supplied illustration 1.20. Gundula Müldner very helpfully corresponded with us regarding isotopic research, Rosemary Cramp regarding Jarrow, Ailsa Mainman regarding Riccall, Sam Moorhead regarding coin loss in late Roman Britain, Tania Dickinson regarding the 'cunning Woman' from Bidford-on-Avon and Eastry, and Alan Lane regarding fifth-century Wroxeter. Alison Telfer very kindly discussed her research around St Martins-in-the-Fields, providing illustration 1.21, and Keith Fitzpatrick-Matthews the excavations at Baldock, providing illustrations 1.18 and 1.19. Philippa Walton very kindly provided illustration 1.14 prior to publication in her own work and we are grateful to Vanessa Straker for illustration I.9. Mike Baillie generously corresponded to update us on recent work regarding climate change. Maggie Kneen provided the beautiful reconstruction of St Mary's Deerhurst that is illustration 5.13. Ellen Heppell kindly supplied the photograph by the late Ron Hall of the fish trap on the Nass that is illustration 4.13.

We are grateful to Bryan Sitch for the opportunity to view the skeletal remains from early excavations at Heronbridge held by Manchester Museum and provision of illustration 2.10. Jon Newman very generously discussed Anglo-Saxon Suffolk at some length, and Tom Williamson his recent work on Anglo-Saxon landscapes and rural settlements. Thames Valley Archaeological Services kindly granted permission to reproduce illustration 7.8. We must also thank the St Edward Brotherhood at Brookwood, Surrey for permission to photograph the shrine of St Edward and for their kind hospitality when visiting.

All errors of fact, misconceptions and mistakes, however, remain solely our responsibility.

We also thank Heather McCallum, the rest of the staff at Yale University Press – in particular Tami Halliday, Katie Harris, Steve Kent, Jessica Lee and Rachael Lonsdale – our illustrator, Martin Brown, and our copy-editor, Richard Mason, for the considerable effort and care they have put into this volume and for the assistance they have given us at all stages of the process.

Our greatest debt, as ever, is to our families, particularly Cheryl and Rosa: this book is for them.

Introduction

NICHOLAS J. HIGHAM AND MARTIN J. RYAN

English history opens with the Anglo-Saxons. For our own convenience, we generally divide history into periods: for England the Anglo-Saxon period is the first, therefore, the starting point. Running from the fifth century through to the eleventh, it is also the longest. From a twenty-first-century viewpoint, though, there can be a feeling that it all happened a very long time ago. Since the last Anglo-Saxon monarch, King Harold II, fell at the Battle of Hastings some 40 generations have been born and died, great plagues and wars have come and gone, and the pace of technological change has been such that the world we live in now is very different.

Given all that, do the Anglo-Saxons still have relevance? Do they really matter? A little surprisingly, perhaps, there are many indications that they do. In important ways, the Anglo-Saxons were the first English; they gave their name to England (ultimately, 'land of the Angles'), and the adjective 'Anglo-Saxon' is used today to describe a vast array of cultural phenomena, ethnic markers and character traits believed to be partic-ular to Britain, the United States and other parts of the English-speaking world. It is

I.1 **Opposite page**
Photographer and publisher Richard Keene makes notes at the foot of the Anglo-Saxon cross in the churchyard of St Lawrence, Eyam (Derbyshire). The photograph was taken by John Alfred Warwick in July 1858

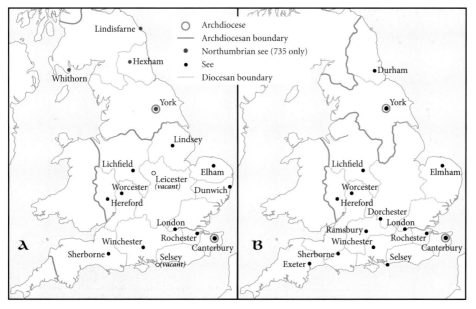

I.2 Archdioceses and dioceses of the Anglo-Saxon Church: (a) in 735; (b) in 1066

clear that for many people now living in England, and, indeed, elsewhere, the Anglo-Saxons are still recognised as an historic form of 'us' or 'we' in ways that other historic groups simply are not. Beginnings matter.

There are numerous dimensions to this assertion. Modern English, one of the most important and widely used languages in the world, began with and developed from the speech of the Anglo-Saxons, which we call Old English or Anglo-Saxon. That does not mean to say that Old English is easily understood in the modern day, for it is not, but nonetheless the English we speak today is its direct descendant.

So, too, was England unified, or created, in the Anglo-Saxon period. The English monarchy dates back to the tenth century and the shape of England has changed comparatively little since. English Christianity dates back even earlier, beginning with

1.3 Internal structure of England: (a) English shires as designated in Domesday Book, 1086; (b) **Opposite page:** English counties before the major re-organisation of 1974

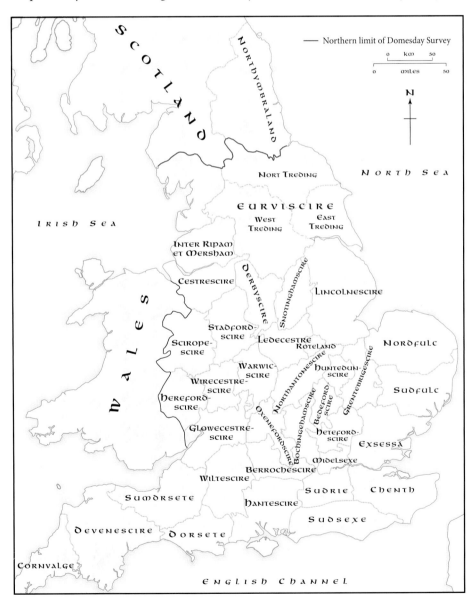

a process of conversion in the late sixth and seventh centuries, with key centres of authority established at Canterbury (rather than London) and York. Though there are today many more dioceses than there were in the Anglo-Saxon period, the oldest, such as Rochester, Lichfield and Winchester, all began in the seventh century, supplemented by others, including Durham, Dorchester-on-Thames and Wells, added after the Viking Age. Even many local churches were founded by the eleventh century with their parish boundaries already in place; indeed, some retain structural details centuries older than that.

The whole system of English regional government, through shires and hundreds, originated in the Anglo-Saxon period. Look at the shires of the Domesday Book entries for 1086 and you see very much the same structure as lasted up to the

re-organisation of local government in 1974. Even much of the settlement pattern of England derives from the Anglo-Saxon period. It is tempting to look back to the Romans for the foundation of Britain's pre-industrial towns, but the major centres of Roman Britain had fallen into ruin and were deserted by AD 500. They were only revived as urban nodes in the later Anglo-Saxon period, when they were refortified against the Vikings. Many reused old Roman walls but plenty more, like Hereford and Shrewsbury, were built from scratch. And the relationship between towns and shires dates to this period, with particular centres linked to the running of the wider county and sharing the name, hence Buckinghamshire, Bedfordshire, Cheshire (Chestershire) and Herefordshire.

Not only the towns but also many villages and dispersed townships date back to this period and many English manors or country estates originated then. Study a map and look up local parish or township names in the Domesday Book and, like as not, you will find them listed, discover who held them in 1066, how much land there was, of what kind, and how much tax was owed. England is an old country, therefore, and many of its basic structures and its local geography were sketched out, at least, in the Anglo-Saxon period.

But there is more to it than that. There are issues around national identity, that sense of social cohesion and belonging centred on a shared history and perspective on the world, which rest on Anglo-Saxon foundations. In November 2005 the British government introduced a written test for those applying for citizenship or for indefinite leave to remain in the UK. The test consisted of twenty-four multiple-choice questions, to be answered in forty-five minutes, and covered aspects of British society, culture, government and law. When the test was first mooted a few years earlier, there was debate as to whether it should include a section on British history and various possible historical questions circulated, including 'When was Britain last invaded?' The 'official' answer to this question was 1066, when Duke William of Normandy ('the Conqueror') defeated and killed King Harold II at the Battle of Hastings, in other words the date which we use to close the Anglo-Saxon period. Predictably enough, newspaper columnists and correspondents countered with a range of objections and alternative answers – 1940 when Germany occupied the Channel Islands; 1797 when the French attacked Fishguard in south Wales; the Jacobite Rising of 1745; the 'Glorious Revolution' of 1688 when William of Orange overthrew King James II, and so on. Perhaps partly in response, historical questions were dropped from the test.

Nevertheless, when a study guide was compiled to aid those sitting the test, entitled *Life in the United Kingdom: A Guide to Citizenship*, it included a survey of British history which begins with the construction of Stonehenge and concludes with the late twentieth century. The description of events in the fifth and early sixth centuries is as follows:

> As the Roman Empire gradually became weaker, new tribes invaded [Britain] from Northern Europe looking for better land. These were called the Jutes, Angles and Saxons. These people spoke dialects which later became the basis of English. The people of Britain fought against these new invaders and were led for a while in the

sixth century by the legendary King Arthur. Eventually, however, the invaders took over all of southern and eastern Britain, setting up their own kingdoms and pushing the Britons to the west and to the north.

The people whose origins are described here are, of course, the Anglo-Saxons and they dominated what is now England and parts of lowland Scotland until the battle in 1066 that may or may not have marked the last time Britain was invaded. The British government in the early twenty-first century considered that this was needful for British citizens to know.

It is these Anglo-Saxons, then, and their interactions with the wider world of which they were a part, who are the subjects of this book. Most of the individuals featured in the following pages would recognise the story told in the guide – with the exception of its reference to King Arthur – and many would certainly feel comfortable that it offered the story of their own origins. Indeed, the description quoted rests very heavily on the account written in the early eighth century by the Venerable Bede.

Yet this passage is noteworthy less as a witness to the longevity of one particular vision of the fifth century than for what it tells us about modern ideas and attitudes towards the Anglo-Saxons. The Anglo-Saxons are, the guide implies, important in a way that, say, the Beaker Culture of the Bronze Age is not; the Anglo-Saxons are therefore included whereas the Beaker Culture is excluded. Their presence in a brief and very general guide to upwards of five thousand years of British history marks the perceived significance of the Anglo-Saxon period and the continuing interest it holds for modern audiences.

This interest was spectacularly confirmed with the discovery in 2009 of a vast cache of Anglo-Saxon gold in a field in the English Midlands – the Staffordshire Hoard. Not only did reports of its discovery dominate the news media but members of the public queued sometimes for upwards of four hours to see the hoard when elements were first displayed at Birmingham Museum. The amount and quality of the material discovered

I.4 The queue for entry to Birmingham Museum to view the Staffordshire Hoard when first exhibited

no doubt in part explain this fascination, but such public enthusiasm also reflects a more general interest in the Anglo-Saxons. Numerous societies devoted to the study or re-creation of the Anglo-Saxon Age have been founded in Britain, the United States and elsewhere. Novels set in the period, such as Bernard Cornwell's series *The Saxon Stories*, are routinely best-sellers. The popular London-based satirical magazine *Private Eye* even features a character called Athelstan (an Anglo-Saxon name), who boasts of one thousand years of 'Anglefolc blood' running in his veins and a diet consisting solely of mead and pottage.

Present-day interest in the Anglo-Saxon period is widespread, therefore, and it takes many forms, ranging from the studiously academic to the playfully anachronistic. But such interest has been by no means a historical constant. The current idea – as reflected in *Life in the United Kingdom* – that the Anglo-Saxons are worth knowing about would have been vigorously contested if not flatly denied at numerous points in the past: 'Let them lie in dead forgetfulness like stones' as one Elizabethan scholar, Richard Harvey, wrote. Such can seem strange to a modern audience, for the significance of the Anglo-Saxons might on the face of it appear self-evident.

It is not the purpose of this book to assess the extent to which we see the Anglo-Saxons as 'us' in the past, nor to estimate the debts modern societies owe to the Anglo-Saxon period. Thinking about such questions, however, and in particular how they have been answered in the past is a useful and necessary preparation for any study of the Anglo-Saxons. Despite the often-invoked image of academics working away in ivory towers, in reality most scholars do not operate in a rarefied environment,

1.5 Migration into and out of Britain, 400–600

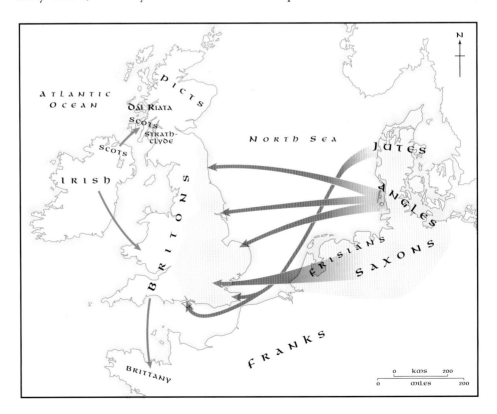

free from external influences. 'Popular' images of the past impact on scholarly reconstructions – how many have come to the study of the Anglo-Saxons through Tolkien's *The Lord of the Rings*, for example. Nor do scholars approach their sources in a neutral, disinterested way, free from preconceptions. The questions scholars ask of the past, the way they interpret the evidence, even the particular pieces of evidence they select and the weight they give to them are all shaped by the concerns of earlier scholarship. Such influences are inescapable; although an awareness of them does not remove their effect, exploring previous interpretations can at least help to situate modern accounts within the scholarly traditions of which they are a part.

On Being Anglo-Saxon

To begin with terminology: a book with the title *The Anglo-Saxon World* makes at the outset a central assumption, namely that the Anglo-Saxons constitute a meaningful and discrete object of study. That is, the Anglo-Saxons were, in sufficiently significant ways, distinct and different from the other inhabitants of, say, the island of Britain or the Atlantic Archipelago in the Early Middle Ages. The application of ethnic labels – such as 'Anglo-Saxon' – to peoples and groups in the Early Middle Ages is fraught with diffi-culties, and the nature of early medieval ethnicity today remains the subject of intense debate. To apply any label to the past is necessarily to simplify and to homogenise, emphasising similarity and continuity at the expense of difference and complexity. Yet it is clear that the people we now label Anglo-Saxons were seen by themselves and by others as representing, in important ways, a distinct and identifiable group.

Such did not preclude competition, enmity or rivalry between different groups of Anglo-Saxons – far from it. Nor did it mean that Anglo-Saxons would necessarily be hostile to the other peoples of Britain; indeed, Anglo-Saxons and Britons would some-times ally against other Anglo-Saxons or against other Britons. Likewise, it should not be assumed that this shared identity was fixed or stable, meaning the same thing at all times. One of the recurring themes in this book is the way in which collective identi-ties have been refashioned and reactivated in numerous different contexts and for multiple purposes. Nevertheless, despite such qualifications and complexities, 'Anglo-Saxon' remains a meaningful, albeit imperfect, label.

'Anglo-Saxon' is, however, a modern label and one that would not have been easily understood, if understood at all, by many of those to whom it is now applied. The compound noun 'Anglo-Saxon' and variants thereof were first used by writers on the Continent in the mid-eighth century, seemingly to distinguish Germanic-speaking peoples living in lowland Britain from the Saxons (sometimes called the Old Saxons) living in northern Continental Europe. By the end of the ninth century, 'Anglo-Saxon' was being used by King Alfred the Great to describe the extent of his power; he was 'king of the Anglo-Saxons'. In this context, the term signified Alfred's rule over his own kingdom of the West Saxons (including 'Saxon' Sussex and Essex and 'Jutish' Kent) and also Mercia, a kingdom supposedly founded by Angles. It did not include Northumbria, beyond the Humber, but in the mid-tenth century Alfred's successors took over much of this more northerly Anglian realm as well. They still employed the royal style 'king of the Anglo-Saxons', but the term gradually fell out of use and was used only sparingly of kings in the eleventh century. It was only in the sixteenth century that the term 'Anglo-Saxon' was again routinely employed, being used in roughly its modern sense to describe the inhabitants of England, or what would become England, before the Norman Conquest.

Contemporaries, however, employed a number of different terms to describe the people we would now call Anglo-Saxons. Roman writers used the term 'Saxon' to refer to the barbarian peoples of northern Europe who attacked Britain by sea in the fourth and fifth centuries, and this terminology was similarly employed by the British writer Gildas in his account of the recruitment and rebellion of Germanic mercenaries in Britain. Gildas's usage seems to have influenced subsequent references in Welsh, Irish and Scottish sources, where the Anglo-Saxons are most commonly referred to as 'Saxons', though 'Angles' does occur on occasion. The usage persists to this day as Celtic languages use 'Saxon' to refer to the English, witness 'Saeson' in Modern Welsh or 'Sasanaigh' in Irish Gaelic. Other writers employed different ethnic terminology. In the mid-sixth century the Byzantine author Procopius of Caesarea described the island of Britain as being inhabited by three peoples, the Angles, the Frisians and the Britons, while at the end of the sixth century Pope Gregory I ('the Great') employed the term 'Angles'.

Gregory's use of 'Angles' was perhaps what encouraged Bede's adoption of the term in his magnum opus, *The Ecclesiastical History of the English People* (*Historia ecclesiastica gentis Anglorum*, completed 731). Though Bede recorded the story of the settlement in Britain of three tribes, the Angles, the Saxons and the Jutes, when referring to these people collectively he tended to label them 'Angles' and their language, despite different dialects, as 'English'. Bede's terminology would prove highly influential.

At the end of the ninth century, King Alfred and the scholars close to his court were experimenting with ideas of a unified English people, employing the term '*Angelcynn*' to designate this group, whilst Alfred's tenth-century successors would increasingly claim to be kings of the English ('*rex anglorum*'), with the word 'Englalonde' (whence, ultimately, 'England') in use by the late tenth or early eleventh centuries. Though 'Angle' or 'English' eventually emerged as the preferred term, there was no simple linear progression from the vocabulary of Bede to the vocabulary used in the tenth and eleventh centuries. Nor was usage even consistent at the time. Bede's near contemporary, Stephen of Ripon, described Wilfrid of York as 'bishop of the Saxons', despite his diocese being in what Bede termed 'Anglian' Northumbria. Likewise, a Canterbury scribe writing in the late 820s could describe the participants at an English church synod as having come from various parts of Saxony, meaning not Continental Saxony but the Anglo-Saxon kingdoms in Britain. Even during the reign of Æthelstan (d. 939), the first ruler routinely to use the royal style '*rex anglorum*', a poet could describe the king's realm as 'this *Saxonia* now made whole'. The Englishness of the English was, therefore, only one of a number of possible identities that were in circulation across the Anglo-Saxon period.

Similar complexities surround the use of geographical or territorial terminology, including England itself. Though something resembling the modern divisions of Britain into England, Scotland and Wales had emerged by the end of the Anglo-Saxon period, there was nothing natural or inevitable about their geographical extent or focus. A unified English kingdom stretching from the River Tweed to the Channel and from the North Sea to the Dee and Severn estuaries, with its political, cultural and governmental foci in the south, was only one of several possible configurations. Throughout the Early Middle Ages other polities and groupings were imaginable and, indeed, in some cases actively pursued. Nor were what now seem obvious natural barriers – the Irish Sea or the English Channel, say – necessarily thought of as such by the early medieval inhabitants of the Atlantic Archipelago. Both Britons and Anglo-Saxons settled in Continental Europe, and there were considerable Irish settlements in western Britain which retained strong links with their homelands for many generations.

By the 630s, the Anglo-Saxon kingdom of Bernicia (eventually incorporated into Northumbria) extended to the Firth of Forth, in what is now lowland Scotland. In the mid-seventh century Northumbrian kings ruled south-west Scotland and Fife and were pushing ever northwards until a disastrous defeat in 685 put paid to their ambitions. On at least one occasion a Northumbrian army crossed the sea into what is now County Meath in Ireland, taking hostages and causing much destruction. A kingdom embracing territory from the North Sea to the Boyne Valley and from the Humber to the Moray Firth may have seemed achievable at the Northumbrian court in the early 680s.

Similarly, the boundary between Wales and the English Midlands was far from constant. English Mercia expanded at the expense of both English and British kingdoms across the seventh century, then late eighth and early ninth-century Mercian kings pursued widespread conquest of their western neighbours. English armies right up to the 1060s were intervening decisively in Wales. In practice, the modern boundary lies further east than at any period between 700 and 1066.

The creation of a kingdom of England was likewise less about the unification of all the English people than the use and promotion of a supposed common English identity to justify the territorial ambitions and achievements of West Saxon kings. Significant 'English' areas could be found outside later Anglo-Saxon England: Lothian, for example, an area that had long been under Anglo-Saxon control and even in the twelfth century would be recognised as a region peopled by the English, passed under the kings of Scotland in the later tenth century and was never recovered; northern Cumbria (Cumberland) lay outside England until after the Norman Conquest despite its inclusion in pre-Viking Northumbria, and such 'Northumbrian' regions as Galloway, Cunningham and Kyle were never recovered by a unified England centred predominantly south of the Thames.

Older identities could also prove resilient even within England. Cornwall came under Anglo-Saxon control over the course of the ninth to (probably) eleventh centuries, but the Cornish language continued in use as did the sense that the Cornish were a people separate from the English. In the sixteenth century the Italian scholar Polydore Vergil could write of Britain being divided into four parts, one inhabited by the English, another by the Scots, the third by the Welsh and the fourth by the Cornish ('*Cornubienses*'); today such groups as Mebyon Kernow continue to campaign for greater political autonomy for Cornwall and to promote its distinct cultural heritage and history.

1.6 Northumbrian expansion, seventh century to 685

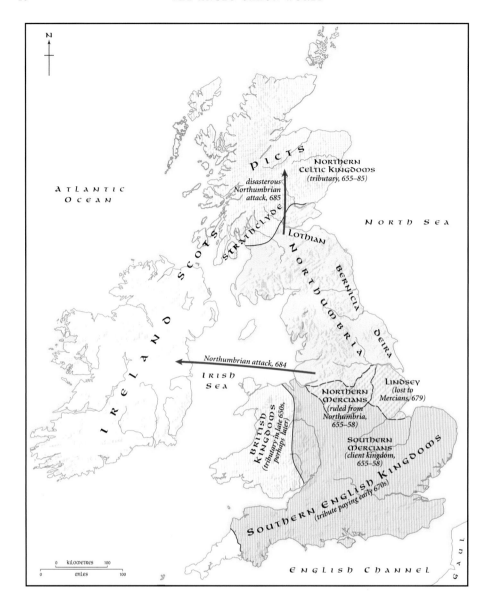

Nor was the emergence of a single 'English' kingship obligatory, or even always very likely. Even given the impetus provided by resistance to the Vikings, it was in part at least a series of dynastic accidents that led across the tenth and eleventh centuries to the repeated re-imposition of a single monarchy over a land which otherwise showed strong signs of regional self-determination. While it is fair to say that the English saw themselves as bound together in a single polity in the mid-eleventh century, England had been divided between rival political claimants to the throne in 924 (Ælfweard, Æthelstan), 955 (Eadwig, Edgar), 1016 (Cnut, Edmund), and as recently as 1035 (Harthacnut, Harold I). Had such divisions at any point persisted, they could easily have set down strong roots.

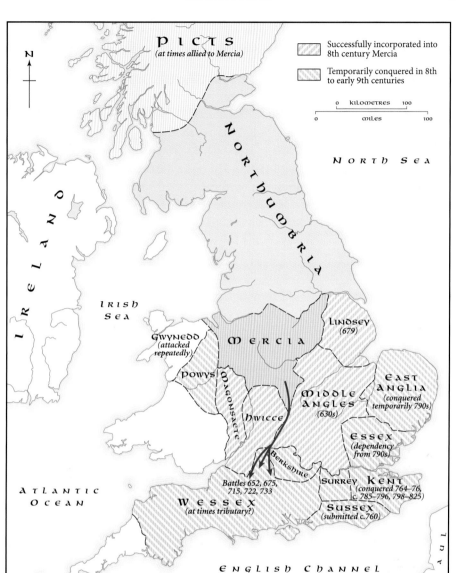

1.7 Mercian expansion to the 820s

Studying the Anglo-Saxons

The nature of the long-term changes wrought by the Norman Conquest in 1066 remains the subject of intense debate. Initially at least, however, the conquerors had good cause to stress continuity between Anglo-Saxon and Anglo-Norman England. Among other reasons, Duke William's title to the English throne was based on his claim to be the acknowledged heir of the late Anglo-Saxon ruler Edward the Confessor (d. 1066), and Edward's status was later enhanced by confirmation of his sanctity. The Conquest likewise initiated a flurry of legal scholarship as the Normans sought to understand the governmental, administrative and tenurial arrangements operating in England. Numerous Anglo-Saxon legal and governmental documents were collected and compiled, with some law codes translated from their original Old English into Latin.

Such legal activities also included the creation or at least confection of new texts purportedly of Anglo-Saxon origin or describing pre-Conquest conditions, most notably the so-called *Laws of Edward the Confessor* produced in the mid-twelfth century.

The Anglo-Saxon past more generally was a subject of considerable interest to succeeding generations. In the twelfth century several Anglo-Norman writers, most notably William of Malmesbury and Henry of Huntingdon, produced histories of Britain that devoted considerable attention to the Anglo-Saxon period and drew extensively on such pre-Conquest sources as the *Anglo-Saxon Chronicle* and Bede's *Ecclesiastical History of the English People*. These Anglo-Norman historians undoubtedly had access to many more sources from the Anglo-Saxon period than have survived to this day. Indeed, many current interpretations rely heavily on material included at earliest by these authors. As will be readily apparent, however, there are some significant dangers with such an approach and the validity of any material so used has to be carefully assessed.

Alongside these broad-ranging histories, accounts of individual religious institutions founded or believed to have been founded in the pre-Conquest period included much Anglo-Saxon material. Given the role that kings played in the foundation and endowment of religious houses, these accounts often focused on the deeds of such supposed royal patrons as Offa of Mercia, even including the texts of purported royal grants. In some cases, such as the history of St Augustine's Abbey, Canterbury, compiled by Thomas of Elmham in the fourteenth century, a significant number of the documents included are authentically Anglo-Saxon; yet, in other cases, such as the fifteenth-century *Chronicle of Croyland* of Pseudo-Ingulf, the majority are forgeries.

The Anglo-Saxon past, therefore, retained some value after 1066. Nevertheless the Norman Conquest led gradually to a very different vision of the past, which marginalised the Anglo-Saxons, questioned their importance and challenged their value. The extraordinary success of Geoffrey of Monmouth's *History of the Kings of Britain*, completed in the 1130s, popularised the legendary Trojan origins of the British, that is of the Welsh and Cornish. According to this story, Britain had been founded by refugees from Troy after the end of the Trojan War and was named for their leader, Brutus. Geoffrey's narrative gave a history of Britain from the time of Brutus to the abdication of the last of the kings of Britain, ending with a very late Anglo-Saxon conquest and settlement. One of the great heroes of this account was King Arthur and it is Geoffrey's narrative that first introduces many recognisable features of the Arthurian stories, which had hitherto circulated only in Wales, Cornwall and Brittany.

Perhaps surprisingly, given the well-founded factual criticism it attracted from some of his contemporaries, Geoffrey's *History* became the basis for most subsequent medieval accounts of the history of Britain. A Trojan and Arthurian past came, therefore, to displace and to devalue the Anglo-Saxons, marking them down as pagan, wicked and other. Across the rest of the Middle Ages, the inhabitants of Britain, even eventually the English included, saw themselves as descendants of the Trojans; national pride centred on stories about Brutus and Arthur far more than on figures from the Anglo-Saxon past.

Beyond all else, it was the Reformation and establishment of the Anglican Church in the sixteenth century that led to a revival of interest in the Anglo-Saxons and a belief in the centrality of the Anglo-Saxon period to the history of Britain. Protestant reformers saw themselves as purifiers of a Church that had been fundamentally corrupted. They looked to the past, therefore, almost as much as to the Bible, to find evidence for the pure, primitive faith that they sought to restore. For the English this meant looking to the Anglo-Saxon past. Though stories such as Joseph of Arimathea's foundation of Glastonbury Abbey or the conversion of the second-century British king, Lucius, were widely believed, actual sources for the pre-Anglo-Saxon Church in Britain were very few indeed. Many later texts that appeared to provide information, much like Geoffrey of Monmouth's *History*, were ill-equipped to stand up to the critical scrutiny of Renaissance Humanism and were increasingly recognised as largely fictions.

Though the Anglo-Saxon Church had been founded from Rome, sixteenth-century English reformers believed traces of a primitive, uncorrupted Church could be found in texts from the Anglo-Saxon period. Thus such scholars as Archbishop Matthew Parker (d. 1575) looked to Anglo-Saxon texts for confirmation of central tenets of Anglican doctrine, including the denial of transubstantiation and rejection of clerical celibacy. Scholars therefore began to publish editions of texts which they believed, often erroneously, justified their positions.

The dispersal of monastic libraries resulting from Henry VIII's Dissolution of the Monasteries in the late 1530s helped this work, making Anglo-Saxon texts more readily accessible. Some scholars assembled extensive manuscript collections. Parker's own library, now held by Corpus Christi College Cambridge, contains some of the most important surviving Anglo-Saxon manuscripts, including the earliest extant version of the *Anglo-Saxon Chronicle*.

In response, Catholics also quarried the Anglo-Saxon past to argue their cause. In 1565 the Catholic theologian Thomas Stapleton translated Bede's *Ecclesiastical History* into English to demonstrate to Queen Elizabeth, and her subjects, 'in what faith your noble Realme vvas christened, and hath almost these thousand yeres continvved', namely Catholicism. And even despite these renewed appeals to the Anglo-Saxon past, the Arthurian and Trojan story still had its defenders; Richard Harvey's 1593 work *Philadelphus: or A Defence of Brutes and the Brutans History* rejected the importance of the Anglo-Saxons (his opinion that they should 'lie in dead forgetfulness' has already been quoted) and reasserted the Trojan origins of the inhabitants of Britain.

It was the seventeenth and eighteenth centuries that witnessed the gradual but almost total eclipse of the Arthurian and Trojan past in historical and other scholarly writings, though those versions continued to be powerful sources of inspiration for storytellers, poets and artists. Now, discussion of the Anglo-Saxon past moved away from the religious to focus instead on politics and governance. Just as religious reformers in the sixteenth century had looked to the Anglo-Saxon past to buttress their positions, so seventeenth-century Parliamentarians turned to the Anglo-Saxons once again to justify their attempts to limit the powers of the Crown. They were able to draw on an increasing body of antiquarian scholarship that explored the origins of key institutions, customs and laws.

Some authors, such as the great jurist Sir Edward Coke (d. 1634), believed that English institutions dated back to even more ancient times. Over the course of the seventeenth century, however, most scholars came to the view that Parliament, the Common Law, trial by jury and numerous other aspects of English governance had their origins in the Anglo-Saxon period. At the same time Continental scholars were depicting the Germanic peoples of the Early Middle Ages as uniquely committed to liberty and popular representation. Under their influence English writers portrayed the Anglo-Saxons as the freedom-loving founders of primitive but effective democratic institutions that were ancestral to those they sought to defend and promote in the present. The Norman Conquest had undermined these institutions, they argued, replacing freedom and liberty with tyranny and oppression. Whether or not this 'Norman Yoke' had ever been fully removed from English necks was much debated.

A belief in the superiority of the Anglo-Saxons and their institutions was not restricted to English writers. Over the course of the eighteenth and nineteenth centuries such notions would also be voiced increasingly by writers in the American Colonies and, following the Revolutionary War, the United States. In 1776 the Philadelphian author 'Demophilus' held up the Anglo-Saxon system of governance as a blueprint for the authors of the Pennsylvania Constitution, describing the former as 'the best model, that human wisdom, improved by experience, has left them to copy'. Around the same time, Thomas Paine warned the American people of the consequences of being under British rule; with the colonial masters so distant what was to stop some 'desperate adventurer' taking control, leaving 'ourselves suffering like the wretched Britains under the oppression of [William] the Conqueror'?

By far the most ardent enthusiast in this period for the Anglo-Saxons was Thomas Jefferson. For him, the systems of law and governance that had existed in the eighth century were 'the wisest and most perfect ever yet devised by the wit of man'. The Anglo-Saxon past offered both a model for emulation and a historical precedent for the American experience. Jefferson's suggested design for the Great Seal of the United States had on one side Moses and the Israelites following the pillar of flame and on the other a depiction of Hengest and Horsa, the legendary leaders of the Anglo-Saxons migrating into Britain. Such parallels between the Anglo-Saxon conquest of Britain and the foundation of America would only multiply in the nineteenth century as the United States expanded westwards from the original thirteen colonies, much as the Anglo-Saxons had progressively expanded westwards in Britain.

The nineteenth century represented the high point of scholarly and popular Anglo-Saxonism, with national pride and confidence in Britain inextricably intertwined with a belief in the importance and significance of the Anglo-Saxon past. Britain's greatness and stability were seen in large part as the products of its Anglo-Saxon heritage. At the same time, in both Britain and the United States, Anglo-Saxon scholarship became progressively more racial in outlook. There had always been a racial element in Anglo-Saxon studies – Richard Verstegan's 1605 work *Restitution of Decayed Intelligence in Antiquities*, for example, presented the English as a purely Germanic people. Attention had, however, tended to focus more on institutions, laws and customs. But in the later nineteenth century it was the supposed racial superiority of the Anglo-Saxons, as much as the superiority of their (supposed) institutions, that was lauded by scholars. The Anglo-Saxon settlement in Britain became something akin to ethnic cleansing, with the Anglo-Saxons sweeping away whatever they found remaining of the British people and replacing it with their own superior bloodlines and culture. Even subsequent conquests had not diluted the racial purity of the English (or their American cousins); the Vikings and Normans, it was claimed, came from the same pure Nordic stock as the Anglo-Saxons themselves, so served to reinforce, rather than dissipate, their presence.

Popular enthusiasm for the Anglo-Saxon period tended to coalesce around particular figures, none more so than King Alfred the Great. Though Alfred had for centuries been held up as a model of good kingship – in some ways replacing the legendary figure of King Arthur – it was in the Victorian and early Edwardian periods that his cult peaked. The celebrations at Winchester in 1901 marked what was believed, albeit erroneously, to be the millennial anniversary of his death (which actually occurred on 26 October 899). They included public lectures and festivities. The high point was the unveiling of a statue by Hamo Thornycroft of Alfred (which still domi-nates the Caves end of Winchester High Street), accompanied by an address from Lord Rosebery, the Liberal statesman and former prime minister (1894–5), that described Alfred as 'the highest type of kingship and the highest type of Englishman' and 'the embodiment of our civilisation'. To better prepare the public for these celebrations, a selection of essays edited by Alfred Bowker, formerly the mayor of Winchester, was

1.8 Bronze statue of King Alfred the Great on the Broadway, Winchester. Designed by Hamo Thornycroft and commissioned by the City Corporation, the statue was unveiled in 1901 as part of the misdated millenary celebrations of Alfred's death

published in 1899. The eulogising of King Alfred therein reached dizzying, even some-what ridiculous heights. Frederic Harrison claimed Alfred to be widely acknowledged, in Britain and abroad, as 'the only perfect man of action recorded in history', while Sir Clements Markham even hailed the king as 'the founder of the science of geography in this kingdom'. In 2001 the centenary was again celebrated, but in a lower key and without the hyperbole.

It was only in the late nineteenth and early twentieth centuries that many of the long-cherished tenets of Anglo-Saxon scholarship – such as the Anglo-Saxon origins of Parliament or the Common Law – were fully and finally disproved, with legal histo-rians establishing the post-Conquest period as the real beginnings of the history of English law. Popular belief in the racial superiority of the Germanic peoples dissipated, largely as a result of two world wars. Alongside this there was widespread rejection of racial theories of history. This was accompanied, especially after the Second World War, by renewed interest in the non-Anglo-Saxon history of early medieval Britain, with a resurgence of both scholarly and popular works investigating King Arthur and the sub-Roman period. Alongside such changes, however, the study of the Anglo-Saxon past continued to flourish, with works such as Sir Frank Stenton's *Anglo-Saxon England* (first published in 1943) and Dorothy Whitelock's *The Beginnings of English Society* (1952) deservedly reaching a wide audience, both inside and outside academia.

The second half of the twentieth century saw significant changes in approaches to the Anglo-Saxon period. Scholars in disciplines such as archaeology, landscape history and place name studies have increasingly been able to challenge the centrality of written sources to the reconstruction of the Anglo-Saxon past. Attention has switched instead to previously neglected aspects and opened up new and hitherto unexpected vistas, into trade links, for example, fields and villages, mills and fisheries, and wood-land and heaths.

Scientists have also turned their attention to the Anglo-Saxon past and we now understand the environmental backdrop in ways beyond the reach of scholars only two generations ago. Victorian writers assumed that fifth-century Angles and Saxons entered a Britain still largely covered with virgin forest, pushing into the great river estuaries of the east coast to find lands to clear and settle. The newcomers, were, there-fore, as much colonial frontiersmen (and women) equipped as lumberjacks, as warriors exterminating the Britons.

Such assumptions were eventually overturned by new environmental sciences. First among them was palaeobotany – the study of plant remains, particularly pollen, preserved in chronologically ordered strata in peat bogs. This began in Denmark but was taken up in Britain pre-Second World War. There followed Carbon 14 dating, begun in the US in the 1940s. Carbon 14 provides a much needed method of dating strata within columns of peat, dating which had hitherto to rely on recognition of common horizons, such as the 'elm decline', used to mark the start of the 'Neolithic Revolution' around five thousand years ago. Carbon 14 became increasingly accurate and widely used across the later twentieth century, to the great benefit of Anglo-Saxon studies.

These breakthroughs heralded a scientific revolution. Pollen diagrams reveal the sequence of plant colonisation in the post-glacial era, from the initial appearance of tundra-type vegetation, juniper and birch through the deciduous forest climax of c. 5000 BC. Human interference began with hunting and gathering, then grew with the inception of agriculture and domesticated animals. The focus was initially on prehistory, and research methods were best suited to the *longue durée* approach, but the past three decades have witnessed far greater attention given to the first millennium AD. The concentration of suitable sampling sites in the north and west of Britain has caused problems, but in recent years there has been a concerted effort to access pollen data from more sites in lowland Britain, often using quite small deposits of peat. While the results from such sites tell us less about the wider area than samples taken from the centres of much larger wetlands, they are beginning to provide data more relevant to Anglo-Saxon England as a whole. Although the spread of sample sites remains patchy, the overall pattern now offers a body of evidence broadly representative of England and its several regions.

Across the first millennium AD, we now realise that woodland was far less widespread than Victorian scholars imagined. Indeed, it is often said that tree cover in the Roman period, when population probably peaked, was no more than at the outbreak of the First World War in 1914. By 400, there was little if any Wild Wood left.

I.9 Glastonbury Relief Road. Overlapping monolith tins inserted into a vertical face of peat to extract the full sequence from this substantial deposit

That trees are the oldest living things on Earth leads naturally to ask of the British Isles, 'Are there still trees standing that were growing before 1066?' We generally think of the oak as the oldest of our trees, but its natural span of years is less than this. When pollarded, though, with the upper branches harvested, or coppiced, so cut down at ground level and allowed to regrow, the oak's life is extended; some of the very largest today just might be candidates. A few surviving 'champion trees' are massive in circumference; these may date back to the Viking Age, among them several in Sherwood Forest and Windsor Great Park but also including examples at Bishop's Castle (Shropshire) and the Marton Oak (Cheshire), which is over 13 metres in girth.

The oldest surviving trees are, however, yews, which are markedly slower growing. A few are silent witnesses to the Anglo-Saxon period. Most such have survived in churchyards, sometimes apparently pre-dating the church. Examples are concentrated in western England, with one at Ashburton (Somerset) 11.5 metres in circumference and a concentration in and around Shropshire, with examples such as those at Church Preen and Acton Scott. Ancient yews are not exclusive to England, with examples occurring widely in both Wales and Scotland – a particularly impressive example which is often claimed to be the oldest living thing in Britain is at Fortingall (Perthshire), near Loch Tay. With these you can actually touch something dating back over one thousand years.

I.10 Silent witness. A pollarded yew, already a substantial tree by 1066, in the churchyard of St John the Baptist's, Church Preen, present girth 6.8 metres

Anglo-Saxon scholarship has broadened out, therefore, from the political and constitutional focus that dominated earlier research, embracing the environment, the economy, society at large, culture, religion and gender. New work has increasingly sought out a past less centred on the court and the archives preserved by a few churches, seeking rather to explore the crowded workshops of Anglo-Saxon towns, the wharves of trading settlements, the highways and byways of the countryside, rural settlements, local churches, the artistic achievements of the past and its graveyards, all alongside the scriptoria of its major monasteries, where so many of our surviving texts originated.

Today the study of the Anglo-Saxons comprises a rich dialogue between scholars from numerous disciplines. Numismatists – specialists in coins – for example, have brought to the table previously unknown kings and new understandings of the birth, growth and use of currency. Archaeologists offer insights into the wealth of newly discovered settlements, changing material culture, trade links and occupational evidence. Art and architectural historians explore the intellectual achievements, cultural values and aesthetics of both pagan and Christianising Anglo-Saxon England. A range of scientists pursue new insights into the origins of the Anglo-Saxons, their diets and the world in which they lived, based on data of types unthinkable only a half-century ago. Particular mention should here be made of the effects of the Treasure Act 1996, which established the Portable Antiquities Scheme to log, identify and interpret a veritable host of new finds as these have arisen, largely through the activities of metal detectorists. It is fair to say that as a result the material evidential base for Anglo-Saxon England has been drastically rewritten in recent years.

All these specialities inform the chapters that follow, though none is as fully explored as one might wish – there is simply insufficient room in such an introductory work to open out every disciplinary approach to the full light of day. For those wishing to take their understanding of the Anglo-Saxon world beyond this introductory stage, there are bibliographies offered specific to each chapter and each section of sources and issues, which are designed to help the reader along this route, as well as offer access to the many and varied discussions and debates that underlie and underpin this work.

The Organisation of this Book

It is in this spirit that our book offers a new introduction to the Anglo-Saxons and the Anglo-Saxon period. The approach taken here is interdisciplinary and we have sought to draw on evidence and insights from all fields of historical enquiry. For some periods or debates, particular forms of evidence are foregrounded – archaeology for the Anglo-Saxon Settlement or written sources for the West Saxon conquests of the tenth century, for example – but we have attempted to approach events from as many perspectives as is feasible. The book is divided into chapters that explore the main events, processes and persons of the Anglo-Saxon period, running chronologically. Between them short essays, entitled 'Sources and Issues', introduce particular pieces or forms of evidence or set out key debates and issues. Though the formal chronological divisions of the chapters frequently reflect key political changes, this is purely for authorial convenience and we have moved outside such boundaries where it has proved necessary.

A Note on Spelling and Nomenclature

In addition to the letters of the Roman alphabet, in their writings the Anglo-Saxons employed a number of characters derived from the runic alphabet, namely Æ (ash), Ð (eth), Þ (thorn) and Ƿ (wynn). Except when quoting directly from texts, eth, thorn and wynn have been replaced in this volume by their modern equivalents, 'th' for Ð and Þ and 'w' for Ƿ; ash has been retained. The spelling of personal names was not standardised in this period, so the name of a single individual could be spelled in numerous different ways. Where possible we have used the spellings as given in the *Oxford Dictionary of National Biography* and have been guided by its conventions for individuals not included therein. Place names are given in their modern forms and spellings – so Whitby rather than Streanæshalch, for example. Where two or more places with the same name exist or confusion is possible, we have given reference in brackets to the historical county (i.e. pre-1974) in which they are located. Where a recorded place name can no longer be located with confidence, it is set in italics (e.g. *Clovesho*).

CHAPTER 1

Britain in and out of the Roman Empire

NICHOLAS J. HIGHAM

The Venerable Bede opened his *Ecclesiastical History of the English People*, completed in AD 731, with the Roman conquest of Britain. Without the benefit of archaeological scholarship, Bede knew far less than we do about Roman Britain, but he had access to many of the same literary texts and the landscape with which he was familiar was scattered with Roman-period ruins in ways that we can only imagine. Close to Bede's own monastery at Jarrow just south of the River Tyne, Hadrian's Wall loomed large, with its attendant vallum, road, forts and milecastles. He knew it well. And when he visited York he would have seen the massive fortress walls and great buildings within, some still even roofed, towering over the bishop's church. The masoned stones from which the great monastic churches were built came from Roman ruins, such as the bridge abutment at Corbridge on the Tyne, which Bishop Wilfrid quarried for stone to build Hexham.

The bishops of Rome loomed large, too, in Bede's world: here the Western Church was centred, its authority preserved and orthodoxy defended; from here had come Augustine of Canterbury, spearheading the English conversion. Late seventh- and eighth-century English clerics saw themselves as champions of this 'Roman' Christianity, suppressing heresy and re-establishing the 'Roman' Church in Britain. For Bede, therefore, Roman Christianity in the present coloured that time when Britain had been part of the Roman Empire.

Today, albeit for different reasons, the Roman period remains a natural starting point for any book focused on Anglo-Saxon England. Just what sort of Roman Britain we envisage, how we depict its ending, and what type of sub-Roman Britain then followed, conditions any discussion of – and attitudes to – the 'Anglo-Saxon' period that came after. And attitudes to Roman Britain have changed dramatically across the past century. Early twentieth-century Britain was in awe of Rome, seeing it as a civilising force in a Britain otherwise given over to barbarism. More recently the Roman Empire has been viewed less favourably, as an institutionalised military dictatorship exploiting the peoples and lands which it had conquered. As Britain's own empire disintegrated, so did attitudes to the Roman World begin to change.

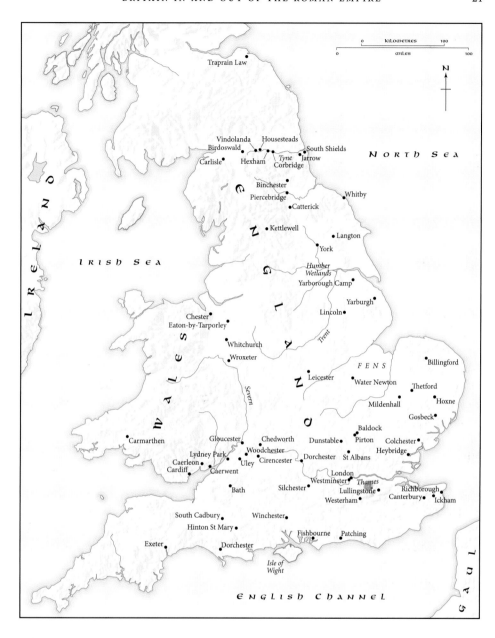

1.1 Places named in Britain in chapter 1

Roman Britain

The main outline of Britain's provincial history is easy to summarise: the island lay on the edge of Julius Caesar's conquests in Gaul (58–51 BC). He crossed the Channel in force in the summers of 55 and 54 BC, but Britain was not permanently annexed until the next century, following invasion in AD 43 by the armies of the emperor Claudius. Conquest took several generations but gradually brought under control the resources of an island which the Roman author Tacitus, for one, considered rich. In fact, it was probably a drain on imperial resources for a century and more.

1.2 The later Roman Empire. Stretching from Cumbria in Britain to Upper Egypt on the Nile, the Roman Empire was vast. By the late fourth century it was divided between the Latin West and the Greek East. Britain stands out in being separated by the Atlantic from the remainder of the Roman World, and as the most northerly of the twelve dioceses

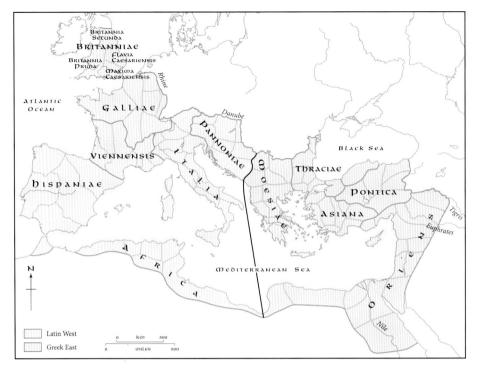

Although several British products were highly valued – such as pearls, hounds and tin – the island was economically marginal. In terms of its agricultural climate, it lay on the very edge of the Roman World. The north and west were incapable of supporting wide-scale arable farming. High rainfall, impervious soils and low temperatures meant that here even most low-lying areas were ill-suited to the sort of agrarian regimes characteristic of more southerly climes. Many standard crops of the Empire, such as olives, simply could not be grown in Britain; others, such as vines, were only established in particularly favourable localities in the south and east of the island.

Difficulties of the topography had consequences for the expansion of Roman political power. Despite periodic efforts to conquer the whole island and even threaten Ireland, successive land frontiers were established on Hadrian's Wall (122–38) and then the Antonine Wall (141–58), which excluded the more northerly, mountainous areas. In the second half of the second century the Hadrianic frontier was re-occupied and would henceforth provide a northern boundary. Scotland would not be conquered and incorporated into the Empire, albeit Roman influence there was considerable; Ireland too stayed outside. In that sense, the Roman conquest of the British Isles remained an unfinished project.

Frontier Society

In the mid-second century about 10 per cent of the entire Roman Army, some 40,000–55,000 troops, were stationed in Britain, giving a very 'military' character to the province. The troops were not distributed evenly, with hardly any stationed east of the Severn or south of the Humber. The largest concentrations were at the three great

1.3 Relief and rainfall: defining the upland/lowland divide in Britain. Contours are at 123 and 246 metres (400 and 800 ft). Rainfall is below 762 millimetres (30 in) in eastern England, rising to two and three times this level in the north and west

legionary fortresses of Caerleon (south Wales), Chester and York, each capable of accommodating some 5,500 soldiers though only rarely were more than a fraction present. Stretching across Wales and the north of Roman Britain lay a network of auxiliary forts, each holding 500–1,000 men. Following the withdrawal from southern Scotland, auxiliaries were concentrated along the Hadrianic frontier from the Solway to the Tyne estuary, and in its hinterland. In Wales and northern England a distinctive, 'frontier' society evolved. At its core was an economy centred on soldiers, whom the imperial government paid and supplied. Markets at the gates of most forts gradually became permanent settlements, known as *vici*, dominated by shops and trading booths. Outside lay parade grounds, small temples, shrines and cemeteries, many with stone memorials. The army controlled extensive grazing lands, made numerous demands on local communities, and exercised authority over the tribes of the north and west.

1.4 Hadrian's Wall. Milecastle
39 at Steel Rigg looking east

The military garrisons were in some respects, however, only small islands of
governmental influence within the wider landscape. Rural settlements lay scattered
across the better drained lowlands, valley sides and hill slopes up to around the
300 metre contour. The indigenous population lived in enclosed settlements that
changed little in consequence of Roman occupation beyond the appearance of a few
pots, small items of metalwork and cheap jewellery. Such settlements retained pre-
Roman characteristics throughout much of the period, with roundhouses still in use,
for example, and enclosures and small fields with clear debts to the Iron Age. Military
garrisons in their stone forts seem somewhat isolated amidst a settlement pattern
which otherwise consisted almost entirely of extended family farms and without much
in the way of towns (Carlisle, Corbridge and Carmarthen were small-scale exceptions), rural shrines or villas. Local elites are barely visible archaeologically, very few

1.5 Auxiliary fort and *vicus* at
Old Carlisle, Cumbria

coins were lost in the countryside and there was little indigenous investment in Roman culture, perhaps because the pressure of taxation and requisitioning by or on behalf of the army left little surplus in the hands of the local population.

Within this 'upland' or 'military' zone, the army was dominant, with its own cultural apparatus, epigraphic and religious traditions, expertise in masonry and metalworking, and appetite for foodstuffs, drink and leather. Comparatively high levels of literacy have been revealed by writing tablets from around AD 100 excavated at Vindolanda just south of Hadrian's Wall. The army was initially drawn primarily from Gaul, with some units from more distant parts of the Empire and on occasion from outside, although recruitment became far more local in the third century. Similarly, prominent members of the civilian community servicing the army's needs in the *vici* seem to have been in large part incomers, such as Barathes from Palmyra (in Syria), who buried his British wife outside the fort at South Shields. The contribution of the local community was mostly in the form of labourers, recruits to the army (early generations of whom were sent to the Continent), slaves and prostitutes.

Part of what had driven the Roman conquest of Britain was its mineral wealth, and therefore extractive industries were active from the early years, particularly in upland areas. Tin in Cornwall, gold at Dolaucothi (Wales), lead (and silver) in eastern and north-eastern Wales, the Peak District and the northern Pennines, salt at Droitwich, in Cheshire and on the coasts, coal in the East Midlands and iron in the Weald and south-east Midlands – these were all exploited, although none developed into major industries by Continental standards. Management was largely via imperial monopolies or concessions, so the profits from these activities rarely fed back into local communities, but they probably helped to offset the considerable costs to the imperial government of garrisoning the island province.

The Lowland Zone

The British lowlands developed in rather different ways to the uplands, although still much affected by the unusually heavy Roman army presence. A network of roads was constructed, centred on London which rapidly became the principal port through which trade and supplies for the army entered Britain. London (*Londinium*) emerged as the provincial capital in the aftermath of the Boudiccan revolt in AD 60–1. Before the Roman Conquest there were no towns in Britain, though there were some coastal trading sites and quite numerous *oppida* – massively ditched and embanked settlements of high status. Three colonial towns (*coloniae*) were quickly established by the settlement of retired soldiers at Colchester, Gloucester and Lincoln; York and London were later accorded comparable status in recognition of their size and roles as provincial capitals. As the conquest proceeded and the military zone pushed northwards and westwards, civil government was gradually transferred to newly constituted tribal territories (*civitates*) and the towns which developed as their centres. These were very variable in size: the provincial capital London was by far the largest, covering some 128 hectares, but most *civitas* centres were only about 40 hectares and northern or western examples, such as Carmarthen, as small as 6 hectares.

1.6 Roman roads in Britain.
Initially built for military
purposes, increasingly they
connected the towns, both
major and minor, as lowland
forts were abandoned

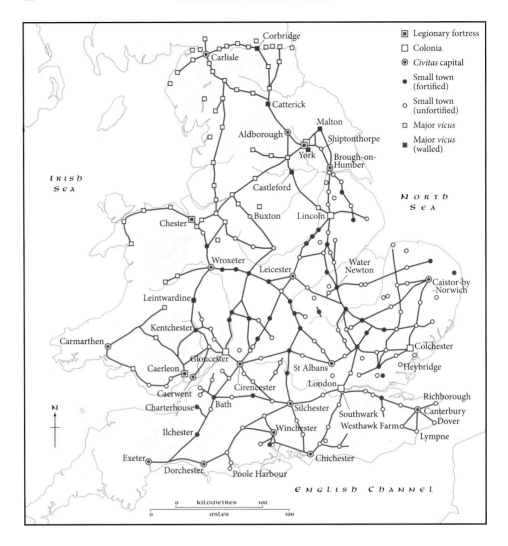

Most of these towns lie beneath later cities that have obscured the Roman levels. Since the late 1960s, however, excavation has achieved new understandings of the Roman towns of Britain, nowhere more so, perhaps, than at London itself. London was unusual in not being a tribal centre but bordering several *civitates*. It developed rapidly as a trading port around a mid-first-century fort guarding the river crossing, then, following the destruction caused by the revolt in AD 60, was rebuilt as a planned town with large-scale public buildings. By the late first century, an auxiliary fort had been constructed at Cripplegate and there were impressive concentrations of buildings. Emperor Hadrian's visit in AD 122 boosted civic construction and London had become a major city by the mid-second century, with perhaps 50,000 inhabitants. A substantial complex beneath Cannon Street station has been interpreted as the governor's palace. The largest forum north of the Alps lay at the centre of the city and several temples have been identified. This is the only site in Britain exhibiting extensive use of imported high-quality Roman building stone.

London's wealth and magnificence reflected its administrative functions and its role as the principal centre of Continental trade via extensive harbour facilities that have been excavated on both sides of the Thames around London Bridge. The city lost momentum, however, in the later second century – declining trade and/or plague have been blamed. London entered a recession from which it never fully recovered in this period, with continuing shrinkage in the number of buildings and a drop in population, although claims that it shrank to a mere 'administrative village' are exaggerated. London was walled on the landward side, probably by the imperial usurper Clodius Albinus, before his death in civil war in AD 197. London Wall is massive: at around 3 kilometres long, 6 metres high and 2.5 metres thick it was the largest stone structure in Roman Britain barring only Hadrian's Wall. It was extended along the river front in the second half of the third century, perhaps to counter seaborne raiders.

London was by far Britain's grandest urban settlement, but others which were not later built over have much better preserved archaeology, particularly *Verulamium* (St Albans), Silchester (Hampshire) and Wroxeter (Shropshire), where excavation over many decades has revealed much of their complex history. Street grids were fundamental to the early towns, with central provision for a forum and basilica where government and trade were centred. Although early digs focused exclusively on stone foundations, timbered or half-timbered buildings predominated throughout, with utilitarian structures giving way to civic buildings in stone in the second century, accompanied by the construction of numerous townhouses, also increasingly in stone (or with stone foundations). Compared to other Western provinces, however, urban development was slow. Major towns are more thinly distributed, building inscriptions far fewer and bath suites, piped water and facilities for entertainment more modest. The only circus identified in Britain, albeit the largest so far discovered outside Italy, lies outside the early capital, Colchester, and was clearly part of the imperial project. Similarly, Britain's only front-ranking classical temple is there. Elsewhere the Romano-Celtic temples typical of northern Gaul were copied both in town and country, although Bath itself, where the indigenous cult of Sulis was conjoined with that of the Roman goddess Minerva, is an exception.

Towns were, however, walled unusually early in Britain, some being equipped with earthwork circuits with a stone facia even in the late first century AD. This style was unusual in Gaul, where only the grandest towns were fortified before the third century. It is unclear why this occurred in Britain and why so early. One might suppose that walls were built primarily to provide defence against raiders from outside Britain or protection against rebellion within, but this may be too simplistic. The emphasis on gateways may best be explained as a means of self-advertisement to compete for trade and status. The suggestion that walls appeared particularly early close to tribal boundaries would support such a view if we had a clearer grasp of where such divisions lay. Perhaps urban defences served multiple functions to do with the separation of urban and rural spaces, policing, defence, security and civic status, though it is difficult to see this as any different from towns in Gaul. Excepting London and the other *coloniae*, walls were paid for by local subscription, so they were necessarily something which local communities wanted. A 'British' impulse is suggested by the similarity between some town walls and the defences of the great pre-Roman *oppida* which preceded several such walls (as at Colchester). The impulse to equip new towns with walls is one of many factors which differentiate Britain from its Continental neighbours.

The urge to build defences is visible too at many minor towns. Small towns were quite numerous and differed in size (but consistently under 20 hectares). The factors encouraging their development varied widely. They provided accommodation and facilities for travellers, offered markets to local industries (as salt extraction, pottery production or mining), served the needs of the military (as Catterick), and provided local markets. Small towns are often difficult to differentiate archaeologically from large villages or villa complexes but generally have some extra dimension not found elsewhere. Many small towns, such as Bath, Gosbeck and the newly discovered Elms Farm, Heybridge (Essex), developed around a temple complex which attracted numerous visitors, so supporting the hotel and catering trades and stimulating the sale of local goods and services. The presence of stone buildings was highly variable in these settlements, with some, such as Heybridge, almost entirely timber-built.

Along the roads emanating from the major towns well-ordered cemeteries developed. The rather disparate burial practices of the late pre-Roman Iron Age gave way in the first and second centuries to Roman-style cremation with commemorative grave markers. The dominant rite shifted in the late second and early third centuries to inhumation, often in new cemeteries. Coffins were common and wealthy graves might include decorated stone sarcophagi. Large-scale excavations at Bath Gate (Cirencester), Poundbury (Dorchester) and Lankhills (Winchester), and in extra-mural cemeteries at York and Leicester, have revealed how well regulated these were. The scarcity of recutting suggests that graves were well marked and managed long term. Even so, the cemeteries so far identified were never sufficiently extensive to accommodate more than a small proportion of the dead from Roman Britain. Many sectors of society, particularly in the countryside, were disposing of bodies in ways which are far less accessible to archaeology than these suburban burial grounds.

Despite the comparatively modest scale of urban development in Roman Britain, the major towns were both foci of Roman culture and central to the administration. London had emerged as provincial capital by AD 100. Around AD 200, Britain was divided into two provinces. London remained the capital of the larger, southern province, *Britannia Superior*, with a governor of senatorial rank, while York was the centre of the more northerly, smaller *Britannia Inferior*. Further subdivision in the fourth century created a diocese with four, then ultimately perhaps five, provinces. Predictably, London was the capital of *Maxima Caesariensis* and housed the diocesan administration. It was renamed *Augusta* in the mid-fourth century, an honorific title confirming its centrality to the government of Britain. It long housed a mint, although that ceased production in the later Roman period. London also served as the principal focus of taxation, with the substantial bureaucracy which that involved. York retained its status in the north and Cirencester and Lincoln are the strongest candidates for provincial capitals elsewhere. *Civitas* centres were responsible for local government and the administration of justice and taxation, holding voluminous records.

The assumption has long been that Britain was Celtic-speaking prior to the Roman Conquest, using local dialects of a language shared across Gaul and parts of Spain which then developed into medieval and modern Welsh, Cornish and Breton. That significant regional differences existed seems plausible: lowland British Celtic was more influenced by Latin and should perhaps be distinguished from highland British Celtic, though the evidence is thin.

An alternative view is that only the highland zone spoke Celtic by the Roman period and that contacts with tribes collectively known as the Belgae in France and Belgium north of the Seine had encouraged the spread of a Germanic language in lowland Britain. The great advantage of this model is that it helps explain the ease with which the lowlands became English-speaking in the next half millennium. However, this proposal goes well beyond the evidence. There is no certainty that the Belgae were Germanic speakers – they are at least as likely to have spoken Celtic Gaulish; while there was clearly some contact, resulting in the tribal names Parisi in eastern Yorkshire and Belgae and Atrebates in the south, these are not Germanic names, and cross-Channel contacts are also well evidenced between Celtic Lower Normandy and Dorset, the Isle of Wight and Hampshire, and Celtic Armorica (Brittany) and the south west of Britain. Place names in eastern Roman Britain are as uniformly Romano-Celtic as in the west, with little trace of Germanic, and Celtic name development continued at least into the fifth century, demonstrating that British Celtic was a living language. The case for a substantial Germanic linguistic presence in Iron Age and Roman Britain is best, therefore, set aside.

1.7 Curse tablet from Uley. Honoratus appeals to the god Mercury to punish the theft of two wheels, four cows and various unspecified items from his house. Latin in Roman cursive script on a lead sheet folded to provide a degree of security

Just how widely Latin spread in Roman Britain is unclear. All surviving inscriptions on stone and writing on other materials are in Latin. This suggests that Latin was the language of the army, of administration, of trade and of elite discourse. It is even the language of graffiti in Romano-British towns, as well as on the vast majority of the more than three hundred curse tablets of lead or pewter sheet found at temple sites (predominantly Bath and Uley). Many of these were written not by professional scribes but by the supplicants themselves, implying that both Latin and literacy were widespread; indeed, some authors took steps to obscure their meaning, using simple codes (for example Greek lettering) or folding or rolling them and driving a nail through, which implies that they were nervous of others reading them. Stylus finds suggest widespread literacy in towns, at temples and villas.

By the fourth century, Latin may have been well on the way to replacing British Celtic across the lowlands, as occurred in Gaul, but the evidence only need reflect a minority of the British population. Some curse tablets were inscribed by semi-literates or illiterates, who may have struggled equally with Latin. The traditional Roman education evidenced by British priests and writers in the sub-Roman period was probably the preserve of the elite. Some place names surviving into Anglo-Saxon England reflect sound changes in Brittonic later than AD 400, which confirms that the language was spoken alongside Latin even in the south east.

Personal names may provide a clue. Outside London the standard Roman *nomen* and *cognomen* are virtually absent from inscriptions; instead provincials generally bore Latinised versions of Celtic names and distinguished themselves in the 'peregrine' fashion, if at all, by reference to a parent. Immigrants, soldiers and officials probably played a dominant role in many towns, both socially and economically, and were responsible for a significant proportion of the inscriptions that have survived (about three thousand), which are far fewer than in most other provinces (compare North Africa with about sixty thousand). The bulk of the population, however, was British and many still spoke British Celtic even in the late Roman period.

The Economy

If we turn to the rural landscape, much has been made of the changes which the Roman period witnessed. New villa residences were characterised by novel styles of architecture, hypocaust heating systems and painted wall plaster. New roads bisected the landscape, along which small towns sprang up, villages and farms grew and spread, rural shrines and markets emerged, and new crops were introduced (including carrots, cabbage and grapes). However, villas only developed in a tiny minority of settlements and in most areas there was a high level of continuity in patterns of land use from later prehistory. Centuriation of land into new rectilinear units characterises Roman land allocation across much of the Empire's Western provinces but has proved elusive in Britain, suggesting that the conquest was not accompanied by wholesale land re-organisation. Overall, the countryside of Roman Britain represents a progression, not a revolution.

The ubiquitous roundhouses of the Iron Age continued as the commonest type of vernacular building throughout most of the Roman period and their inhabitants worked land in ways that changed little. Since the 1950s there has been a dramatic rise in the number of Iron Age and Roman-period settlements which have been located, leading to an upward revision of the population of Roman Britain. Whereas estimates in the 1930s centred on 1 million, scholars in the 1980s and 1990s preferred 2–4 million, with some going even higher. More recently, opinion has fixed on the lower end of this range, but whatever the precise figure offered, all now agree that the Romano-British population stood at or above 2 million. Though small by modern standards, this approximates to the population in 1086, then again at the start of the Tudor period, around 1500.

Roman Britain was, therefore, extensively and, in places, densely settled. Farming accounted for the bulk of production and was both the principal source of wealth for the elite and the bedrock of taxation. Villas provide a measure of the success of landowners, although the term is an elastic one used of any rural complex built in the Roman style in stone or brick. They varied enormously in size and architectural complexity: at one end of the scale palatial residences had as many as 50 rooms, many with sumptuous mosaics, as Chedworth and Woodchester (both Gloucestershire) or

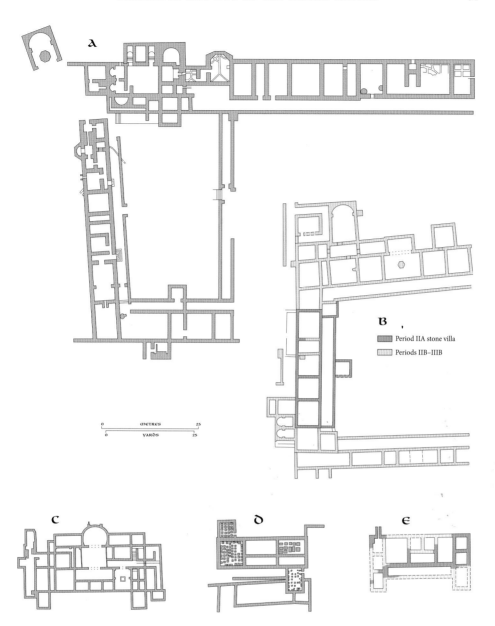

Period IIA stone villa

Periods IIB–IIIB

Bignor (West Sussex); at the other were small farmhouses with no more than perhaps five rooms, as Langton (North Yorkshire) or Eaton-by-Tarporley (Cheshire). Some were the residences of Romanised Britons of high status, as most conspicuously Fishbourne (West Sussex), but many of the grander type were probably built for incomers – officials, army officers, displaced landowners, or 'foreign' merchants, agents or businessmen. Very occasionally an owner can be identified: Lullingstone (Kent) was probably the rural retreat of the governor Publius Helvius Pertinax (185–7), who went on to become emperor, albeit briefly, in AD 193. The vast majority of such residences, however, are anonymous and we are left to surmise who commissioned and inhabited them.

1.9 Lullingstone Roman villa. Aerial view reconstruction of the central building in the later fourth century

1.10 Fourth-century mosaic in the dining room of Lullingstone Roman villa. The abduction of the princess Europa by Jupiter, disguised as a bull, with two cupids. The inscription makes allusions to the works of Virgil and Ovid, suggesting the villa-owner was a Classically educated sophisticate

The distribution of villas illustrates the variability of the Romano-British rural landscape. A recent listing identified 2,342 candidates, although these include a few examples which should arguably be interpreted rather as small towns, villages or shrines. Even so, the totals for each county are revealing: just five counties – Cambridgeshire, Northamptonshire, Norfolk, Lincolnshire and Wiltshire – contain over 40 per cent of the total, while over half the 46 modern counties have fewer than 30 villas per county, and some (Cumbria, Gwynedd, Powys and Lancashire) only one candidate apiece. This variability is greater than environmental factors and different rates of discovery can explain – compare Suffolk's 28 villas with Norfolk's 217, for example. It probably reflects, therefore, complex social and economic factors, differences between neighbouring farming regions and differing relationships between local communities and the government. There may well have been extensive imperial estates in some areas where villas are few.

Roman manufactures of all sorts streamed into Britain in the first century, but the province became progressively less reliant on imports and more self-sustaining economically across the second century, with the development of local pottery industries, for example. Potteries were workshop-based and used the potter's wheel and purpose-built kilns, but they were not massive in scale by Roman standards, although products such as Oxford colour-coated ware had an extensive distribution south and east of a line from Bristol to Hull. There were other major kiln groups, at Poole Harbour (Dorset), in the New Forest, at Alice Holt (Hampshire) and in the Nene Valley, but pottery manufacture was uncommon and never more than short-lived outside the lowland zone. While imports continued, finds dwindle and are numerically insignificant for the fourth century, when quantities of incoming amphora, holding olive oil and fish sauce, diminished.

Many industries focused heavily on local markets. For example, third-century mosaicists based in or near Cirencester worked in elite residences in both town and country but rarely outside a small group of adjacent tribal territories. Some two thousand mosaics have been recovered in Britain, mostly bearing geometric designs but with increasing numbers of motifs from Classical literature and mythology used in the third and fourth centuries, most probably copied from standard pattern books. Similarly, masons and sculptors worked mostly with locally quarried stone to respond to both public and private commissions.

Later Roman Britain

Events both in Britain and elsewhere in the Roman Empire affected this huge super-state's management of its most northerly diocese. In the East, the rise of Persia in the third century necessitated a large-scale redeployment of troops and resources, which weakened the Western Empire and made it less capable of resisting barbarian invasion. This gradually precipitated a shift in the balance of power in north-western Europe, resulting in episodic outflows of bullion from the Empire to neighbouring barbarian groups as diplomatic gifts, payments to mercenaries or booty. Increasing barbarian inroads in the third century created a long-term crisis, worsened by

1.11 The defences of late Roman Britain. Note the forces on both sides of the English Channel, intended to stop North Sea raiders attacking the rich lands in Britain south of the Wash and on the Atlantic coasts of Gaul

currency inflation, as hard-pressed governments repeatedly diluted the precious metal content of the coinage. The result was a breakdown in central Roman government of the Western Empire, with separate regimes in Gaul for substantial periods, which only ended with Emperor Diocletian's re-unification of the Roman state at the end of the third century. Although technically one Empire, there was a mounting tendency for separate governments to control the East and the West throughout the fourth century.

These changes affected communities beyond the Rhine. Within Germanic society, sections of the adult male population increasingly opted for warfare as a career, either in Roman armies or in the retinues of tribal elites. Raiding was endemic along and beyond the northern frontiers of the Empire, and ever more embedded in social structures. Behind the frontier peoples, a western migration of the Huns on the Steppes had considerable repercussions, triggering two waves of barbarian migration into the Empire, the first in the 370s and the second in the first decade of the fifth century. These included large bodies of warriors capable of confronting and even routing

1.12 Pevensey Saxon Shore fort. The lower courses are late Roman, the castle walls above medieval

Roman armies, as occurred at the Battle of Adrianople in 378, when the Eastern emperor, Valens, was vanquished by the Goths. Even with peace restored, the Empire was forced to accommodate semi-autonomous barbarian peoples within its frontiers. Although the Huns did not actually cross the frontier until Attila's invasion in the 450s, their push westwards had devastating consequences for the Roman World much earlier and began the long process of disintegration which afflicted the Western Empire. Governments were unable to call on the resources of manpower, supplies and money necessary to rebuild the armed forces sufficiently to re-establish the frontiers. By the last quarter of the fourth century, Roman authorities were ever less able to respond to crises in Britain.

As an outlier of the Empire, Britain was particularly vulnerable to these growing weaknesses, and as an island it was open to barbarian attack on all sides. A substantial garrison was therefore needed to guard both the land frontier to the north and exposed coasts elsewhere. By the mid-fourth century, Roman army numbers had been reduced to perhaps half or a third of those of the second century. Successive troop withdrawals were made in response to Continental emergencies: Chester's barracks were largely demolished by 300; *Legio* II *Augusta* departed Caerleon in South Wales before 400; the only legion still in its second-century base by the end of the fourth century was VI *Victrix* at York. Alongside, many auxiliary units were reduced in numbers by anything up to 80 per cent. Declining manpower was accompanied by a shift in strategies regarding neighbouring communities – a rise in gift-giving and the payment of subsidies is one possible explanation for such late Roman hoards as that found on Traprain Law (East Lothian, Scotland), which was one of several defensive strongholds emerging in southern Scotland. That virtually no Roman material was reaching the Pictish heartland of north-east Scotland may signal imperial caution regarding a people who had proved dangerous in the third century. However, such a policy may have stimulated Pictish raids down the east coast when Roman defences were weak.

Declining army numbers and the low pay of frontier forces reduced the buying power of the garrisons, causing shrinkage of occupation in, and even abandonment of, the *vici*. In the short term, the lessening burden of requisitioning may have benefited Romano-British landowners, allowing resources to be switched to building villas, as well as late urban development at such sites as Carlisle in the hinterland of Hadrian's Wall. This may have been one stimulus underpinning the late flourishing of British villas, many of which reached their maximal size and sophistication in the early fourth century, but the evidence is patchy, at best, and signs of affluence dissipate by the mid-century. There are some signs of economic retrenchment already in the third century and real decline in the fourth in levels of activity of many kinds.

Despite the dropping troop numbers, there is no reason to suppose that the defences of fourth-century Britain were dangerously weak. Except in exceptional circumstances, such as the so-called 'Barbarian Conspiracy' of 367, they were effective and the British diocese enjoyed extended periods of external peace. Evidence is thinner for the later period, but a surviving list of late imperial commands, the *Notitia Dignitatum*, provides skeletal information on garrisons in Britain, probably relevant to the late 390s, which archaeology both confirms and supplements.

In the south, the 'count of the Saxon Shore' (*comes litoris Saxonici*) commanded the remnants of the second legion, formerly at Caerleon but now at Richborough (Kent), plus units stationed along the coast – some 12 in all (the *Notitia* names 8) with perhaps 3,500 men. The forts with which they were associated had emerged over a century and a half: Dover on the south coast of Kent was fortified early in the second century, with the forts of Brancaster (late second) in Norfolk and Reculver (early third) on Kent's eastern coast then added; in the third quarter of the third century these were supplemented to create a string of coastal forts from the Wash to the Solent. From this point these fortifications begin to look like an integrated system of defence.

The later forts differed from second-century types, with rectangular, trapezoidal or occasionally oval ground plans and thick, high walls supplemented by projecting towers and ditches. There was normally only one gateway, unlike the earlier fort design with four. Many forts seem to have been used somewhat haphazardly, perhaps even on occasion by civilians, but the scale of the walls demonstrates that they were designed to resist enemy attack. Poor integration with the road system confirms that these forts were intended primarily as bases for ships. This is borne out by the appearance of a fleet detachment named from Roman Pevensey, the *classis Anderetianorum*, which is evidenced in Gaul in the *Notitia Dignitatum*.

The Saxon Shore was one of several coastal commands on the Channel, operating in tandem with forces stationed in similar fortifications along the coasts of Belgica Secunda (northern France and the Rhineland) and Armorica (Brittany). Earlier suggestions that the 'Saxon' designation of the command derived from Roman use of Saxon mercenaries here has been set aside. Rather, it was named for the enemy it was expected to confront, not the troops stationed there. These commands were for a long time effective at keeping Germanic raiders out of the Channel and away from the coasts of southern Britain and Atlantic Gaul beyond.

In the north, frontier forces were still stationed along Hadrian's Wall and along the roads southwards. These lay under the command of the *dux Britanniarum* stationed at York. Many forts along the Wall, such as Housesteads, Vindolanda and Birdoswald, were occupied, but normally by only 200–300 men, and in some cases perhaps by fewer than 100. There is far less evidence for major new construction than on the south coast, but there were some refurbished or rebuilt forts: at Lancaster the Wery Wall was part of a coastal stronghold equipped with corner turrets on the Saxon Shore model, while elsewhere existing forts, such as Maryport (Cumbria), had corner towers added. Roman scouts (*areani*) are referred to in the account of the attack of 367, suggesting a strategy of intelligence-gathering along the frontier. The late Roman writer on military affairs, Vegetius, may have been referring to Britain when he described coastal scout ships painted green as camouflage.

Along the North Sea, a fort at South Shields commanded the Tyne while Brough-on-Humber oversaw the approaches to York. Between the Tees and the Humber a system of coastal signal stations was constructed, probably post-368, in association with a fortlet now within the medieval castle at Scarborough. A naval station at Whitby is a possibility; finds exist but no fort has been located. North British or Pictish seaborne raids seem the likeliest threat here, skirting the Hadrianic frontier to strike down the coast.

In the west similar precautions were taken: a mid-third-century fort at Cardiff is similar to those on the Saxon Shore; a fortlet and watchtowers overlooking the seaways around Anglesey policed those seaways against Irish pirates. Excavation has demonstrated occupation of several forts in Wales into the second half of the fourth century. Although these go unremarked in the *Notitia*, it seems likely that the listing is defective in this respect and that a further minor command existed in the west of Britain, guarding against raiders from Ireland, Man and/or western Scotland.

All the units commanded by the *dux* at York and the *comes* on the Saxon Shore were *limitanei* – the lower-grade frontier forces of the Empire. There were perhaps 12,000–13,000 in late Roman Britain. There is no evidence of a permanent field army

1.13 Vindolanda. Late Roman buildings in the north-west quadrant of the fort

present in the 360s, but the *Notitia* does list a *comes Britanniarum* at the head of a mixed force of three infantry *numeri* and six cavalry units, perhaps totalling in all 3,000–6,000 men. These were *comitatenses* – the better paid and equipped field army units, present in Britain most likely in the late 390s.

By the fourth century, the use of barbarian troops was commonplace throughout the Roman Empire, and Britain was no exception. When Constantine I launched his bid for empire at York, in 306, a Germanic king, Crocus, with a force of *Alamanni*, was part of his army. Another group of *Alamanni* is known to have been sent to Britain in 372. It has often been suggested that the sub-Roman presence of Irish in western Wales began with the settlement of federate troops in the fourth century. Although such barbarians provided only a minority of the garrison, the names of the commanding officers in 367 – Nectaridus and Fullofaudes – look suspiciously Germanic. It is quite possible that some or all of the *comitatenses* in the 390s were barbarians.

Overall, therefore, Britain's defences were comparatively effective through to the late fourth century. Recruitment to the frontier forces at least was largely local, with sons following their fathers into service. Responsibility for the army fell more heavily on the insular population than had been the case earlier, when the Roman army was supplied predominantly via long-distance networks. From Diocletian's reign in the late third century onwards, military provision was increasingly via taxation in kind, with civilians carrying produce directly to the fort gate. British supplies were also used to feed the army of the Rhine in the later fourth century.

Pottery continued to reach the Hadrianic frontier from southern Britain into the late fourth century, probably as small-scale consignments of trade goods carried alongside official supplies. Other kinds of goods, and in particular military equipment, were increasingly manufactured in state-run factories. An imperial weaving mill supplying army uniforms was located in Britain; the procurator responsible was mentioned in the *Notitia*. Military units in Britain also received manufactures from comparable factories on the Continent, as well as coin from the imperial mints.

One way of monitoring the decline of the exchange economy of Roman Britain is through changing patterns of coin loss. By 2010 some 70,000 Roman coins were known from Roman Britain, with rapid increases due to the Portable Antiquities Scheme. Although some areas were already under-represented, there was widespread coin deposition in the early fourth century suggesting a dynamic exchange economy. A

1.14 Rural sites in Roman Britain with above average coin loss: (a) late third to early fourth centuries; (b) mid-fourth century; (c) late fourth century

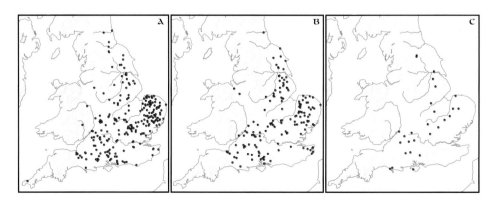

1.15 Second-century baths at Wroxeter (*Viroconium*), the fourth largest town in Roman Britain with perhaps 15,000 inhabitants in its heyday. The baths were no longer in use in the fourth century, with part turned over to grain storage

decline in the number of sites exhibiting high rates is noticeable by the mid-century. By the late 370s coin loss is concentrated in a band running from East Anglia through the Thames Valley and central southern England. This pattern prevails to the end of the century, with the exception of Richborough, where some 22,000 copper coins were deposited in the last decade.

The heyday of Roman Britain's provincial towns lay in the second century, when local landholders built numerous townhouses and invested heavily in urban lifestyles. Thereafter they experienced shrinkage and retrenchment. Fewer inscriptions on stone and new sculpture reflect changing tastes, associated perhaps with a shift of power towards career soldiers from the frontier regions or beyond. By the fourth century the provincial elite were absenting themselves in favour of their rural estates. Increasing numbers of *basilicae* and/or *fora* in Britain's towns were falling into disrepair, being demolished, or converted to other uses, as at Silchester (Hampshire) where the central spaces were used for metalworking from the late third century onwards. The amphi-theatre was perhaps still in intermittent use in the mid-fourth century, but rubbish was being dumped on the ramparts post-350, suggesting diminishing civic control. While some public buildings clearly remained foci of urban life, numberous theatres, amphi-theatres, water conduits, aqueducts and public baths fell into disrepair across the fourth century or were converted to new purposes. The extensive public baths at Wroxeter (Shropshire) offer one of many examples.

A number of such complexes may have had pagan associations, so it is possible that growing commitment to Christianity lay behind some at least of these changes. An imperial decree in 341 banned urban temples, and paganism was effectively outlawed in the 390s, although the longevity of temple complexes at Bath, Lydney (Gloucestershire) and elsewhere suggests that implementation of such legislation was at best inconsistent.

1.16 Lead font from Icklingham (Suffolk), with Chi-Rho monogram on the side, probably used for baptism

Christianity is difficult to identify archaeologically even in the later fourth century and the Church in Britain may have been comparatively low-key in comparison with Gaul. Only a handful of British bishops or their representatives attended the Church Council at Arles in southern Gaul in 314, suggesting that they represented the provinces rather than individual *civitates*; one, Restitutus, was probably the metropolitan bishop of London and the senior churchman in Britain. Archaeology has so far identified few urban churches with any certainty. A substantial building excavated at Silchester, close by the forum, was initially interpreted as a church, but doubts have crept in that it may originally have served some other purpose. At Lincoln the church of St Paul in the Bail in the Roman forum began life in the late fourth century, was rebuilt on a larger scale in the fifth century, and was probably only demolished in the later sixth century. Late Roman churches are otherwise comparatively small structures, such as that excavated at Richborough. However, lead tanks apparently used for baptism occur with some frequency, particularly in East Anglia and Lindsey (Lincolnshire), and several hoards reflect Christian ritual, such as the Water Newton Treasure (Cambridgeshire). Finds such as these imply that not all Christian communities were poor, and further churches presumably await discovery. The overtly Christian wall painting at Lullingstone Roman villa (Kent) and the Chi-Rho monogram at the centrepiece of a mosaic at Hinton St Mary (Dorset) corroborate elite patronage of the new religion, although the head featured in the latter owes as much to imperial portraiture as to Christian iconography.

Just how far the British had adopted Christianity by 400 is unclear. Bishop Victricius at Rouen seems to have assumed in the 390s that St Alban was well known among his primarily Continental audience, but otherwise British saints are not well attested. In practice, the progress of Conversion was probably highly variable, concentrated particularly in the towns, among officers and administrators, and the families of the landholding elite.

The End of Roman Britain

It is often said that the Romans left Britain in or about 410. In practice, this makes no sense, since the Britons in some manner at least were Romans. The ending of Roman Britain was a far lengthier and more complex phenomenon than is often realised. It is best explored over a period of perhaps sixty or seventy years.

The so-called 'Barbarian Conspiracy' of 367 overran the defences of Roman Britain and brought widespread raiding by Saxons, Picts and Scots, but the situation was quickly rectified. It is unclear how significant these events were, since the reporting was highly political – given that Ammianus Marcellinus, who is our only source, dedicated his *History* to Emperor Theodosius I, whose father had mounted the rescue, Marcellinus probably exaggerated the scale of the crisis. Though much is made of Count Theodosius's success, therefore, the fact that his expeditionary force was just 2,000 men suggests only a minor crisis.

Another imperial general, Magnus Maximus, campaigned successfully beyond Hadrian's Wall and then had himself proclaimed emperor in 383, taking the British garrison to the Continent. He secured Gaul and a degree of recognition from rival rulers of the Roman World but was defeated and killed in 388, when he invaded Italy. His failure brought to an end hands-on imperial management of the Rhine frontier, which fell henceforth to the Franks. Roman control of Britain was only re-established belatedly, but further troop withdrawals followed in the 390s to counter barbarian threats elsewhere.

Maximus re-established the mint at London, but that ceased once more at his death, leaving Britain dependent on coin imports. British coins came predominantly from mints at Milan, Trier and Lyon, but these were in steep decline by the 390s and virtually ended production c. 413. The last substantial influx of coin to pay the garrison reached Britain around 400, after which soldiers went unpaid. This precipitated a revolt in 404, the centenary of Constantine I's successful coup at York. There followed the successive elevation of three usurpers to the purple. The last of these, the soldier Constantine III, led troops from Britain to Gaul c. 407 to secure the Western Empire, both against the established authorities and new barbarian forces that had crossed the Rhine. Despite some initial successes, his cause disintegrated under the pressure of internal revolts, barbarian demands and imperial resistance. He was captured by forces loyal to Emperor Honorius and put to death at Arles.

Constantine's evacuation of a majority of the Saxon Shore forts brought about the final collapse of Roman control of the western seaways. A devastating Saxon raid c. 410 was recorded by Gallic chroniclers. Thenceforth the coasts of both Gaul and Britain were open to attack. Commenting on this raid, the early sixth-century Eastern historian, Zosimus, later claimed (in Greek) that

> they [the Saxons] reduced the inhabitants . . . to such straits that they revolted from the empire, no longer submitted to Roman law, and reverted to their native customs. The Britons, therefore, armed themselves and ran many risks to ensure their own safety and free their own cities from attacking barbarians.

With the Saxon Shore command no longer operative and with no field army in post, the Saxons struck at the richer south of the diocese. Without military help from the Continent, the Britons were forced back on their own resources. In practice, all parties surely anticipated the restoration of imperial control, as had always happened over the previous three and a half centuries. Zosimus noted elsewhere that Emperor Honorius 'sent letters to the cities in Britain, urging them to fend for themselves', but 'Britain' here is likely to be a mistake for Bruttium in Italy, with which the remainder of the passage is concerned. He never revised this section of the work, which is strewn with errors.

Broadly contemporary was a steep decline in most aspects of the Romano-British economy. There was little if any further building in stone, no new mosaics, little maintenance of existing buildings, and a sharp reduction in trade and manufacturing. The seminal study, by Simon Esmonde Cleary, argues that the late Romano-British economy rested on a cycle of economic activity driven by taxation: agricultural produce was sold for bronze coin, which was then exchanged for the silver and gold in which taxes were paid and manufactured goods purchased. By this reckoning the failure of the coin supply c. 400, then the ending of Roman governance c. 410, destroyed Britain's economic cycle, bringing down urban markets, trade, manufacturing and the villas which had been centres of both production and consumption. While there were Britons in the fifth century, therefore, they should no longer be termed Romano-British. Rather, the whole structure of Roman life and the provincial hierarchy failed, very suddenly and irrevocably.

Certainly, at settlement after settlement, it becomes increasingly difficult to find evidence of Roman-style activity. Numerous sites reveal what has been termed 'squatter' occupation, denoting the end of a Romanised lifestyle, with elite residences no longer maintained and/or converted to agricultural functions, then abandoned altogether. Occupation of many towns seems to have shrunk across the late fourth century to the point where large parts of the walled area were unoccupied.

There are difficulties, however, with the underlying assumptions on which this case is based, for taxation is normally a brake on enterprise rather than a stimulus, making economic collapse as a consequence of the breakdown of tax collecting somewhat implausible. That new coin was no longer available from imperial mints did not affect the large quantities already in circulation. In practice, the evidence requires a more complex explanation. Decline in various manufacturing processes had been a factor since the 360s, if not before, and the number of sites that reveal vigorous activity was already in steep decline in the later fourth century, even before the collapse of Roman government. It is worth questioning whether the crisis that archaeologists identify in the early fifth century might have occurred even had imperial control been restored.

Coin evidence is significant here, for the Roman government did not stop supplying coin just to Britain but to all the north-western provinces. In this respect Britain was similar to the Rhineland, though there the reduction in manufacturing and trade was less acute. The crisis of the early fifth century was not just a result of the collapse of imperial government but of a culmination of changes visible across many aspects of material culture which now intensified as the political crisis bit deep. Given the scarcity of dateable evidence, it is unsurprising that occupation is difficult to identify in the early fifth century, but a lack of evidence of occupation is not necessarily evidence of a lack of occupation. We need a more nuanced view of the whole continuity/ abandonment debate.

Written sources may help us here. St Patrick was probably a child in the early fifth century. His father was Calpornius, a provincial landowner, decurion and deacon of the church, and his grandfather the priest Potitus, both of them associated with an unlocated settlement called *Bannavem Taburniae*. All three personal names are Latin, the place name is a Latin/Celtic hybrid, the household was Christian, and Patrick was undergoing a traditional Roman education until at the age of 16 he was captured by pirates. He spent six years as a slave in Ireland, then, following his escape, eventually returned there as a missionary. His two surviving works, the *Confession* and *Letter to Coroticus*, demonstrate that Latin remained in the mid-fifth century the standard medium in which to communicate; indeed, Patrick expected others to have a more fluent command of it than he had himself. Reference to the sale of his status as a nobleman should probably be interpreted as selling his family estate, which implies that a land market still existed in mid-fifth-century Britain. Patrick was operating, therefore, in a world still with its roots deep in Roman provincial culture.

Constantius's *Life of St Germanus*, probably written 460–80, included two visits to Britain by his hero (the first can be dated to 429). Germanus preached against the heresy of Pelagianism, whose original proponent was the British Pelagius, who taught in Rome very early in the fifth century. Germanus must have preached in Latin and he allegedly met several individuals of high status, among whom one, Elafius, had a name of Greek origin (as did Pelagius). Germanus supposedly baptised the British soldiers who were given into his command, suggesting that many common folk at this date were either pagans or herectics, then journeyed inland to the shrine of St Alban (presumably that outside *Verulamium*), from which he took relics home. This implies that the roads remained passable two decades after Constantine's death, here at least. That Germanus supposedly took back with him to the Continent on his second visit the leading advocates of Pelagianism suggests that sufficient civil authority still existed in Britain to enforce the exile prescribed by Roman law. This second visit has, however, been challenged as unhistorical.

The later British writer Gildas also used Latin. He had enjoyed a traditional Roman-style education and his had not been disrupted as Patrick's had. Rather his writing displays a sophistication and erudition the equal of anything coming out of late fifth- or early sixth-century Gaul. He referred in the present to compatriots selling up to fund travel to the Continent for ordination, which likewise implies the existence of a British land market but at an even later date.

The literary evidence therefore seems to indicate that aspects of Roman Britain long survived 410. On this basis we should see sub-Roman Britain as part of Late Antique Christian Europe, for several generations at least. There is something of a contrast, therefore, between the collapse of material culture revealed by archaeology and the literary evidence for on-going Roman behaviours. Continuing elite culture in turn implies the survival of the social hierarchies by which the landowning classes were sustained.

To an extent the problem is one of poor dating evidence. Pottery is the key dating material of Roman Britain but potteries were in decline from the 360s onwards, producing diminishing quantities of pottery with less and less product development, so that many fifth-century vessels are virtually indistinguishable from those produced c. 370. While wheel-turned pottery manufacturing reduced dramatically across the first half of the fifth century, some still occurred: for example, four wheel-turned cremation urns displaying Roman techniques were found in the Anglo-Saxon crema-tion cemetery at Cleatham (Lincolnshire), which did not operate until the second half of the century. Some areas reverted to metal or wooden vessels, others produced hand-made pottery without the use of the potter's wheel. Distribution of such vessels was comparatively localised. For example, a handmade jug and pedestalled cup in a sandy fabric found in a fifth-century grave at Baldock (Hertfordshire) are typical of the vessels from around St Albans at this date. That one late Romano-British potter was attracted by the style of early Anglian cremation urns is suggested by a vessel found at Pirton, less than 10 kilometres away.

These are experimental pieces, made by craftsmen who were rediscovering the art of making pottery by hand and perhaps manufacturing also in part for a new, Anglo-

1.17 Part of an early fifth-century, furnished inhumation from a Romano-British pagan cemetery at Baldock, showing just the pelvis and upper legs. Note the jug and pedestalled cup, made without use of the wheel but reminiscent of earlier Roman pottery

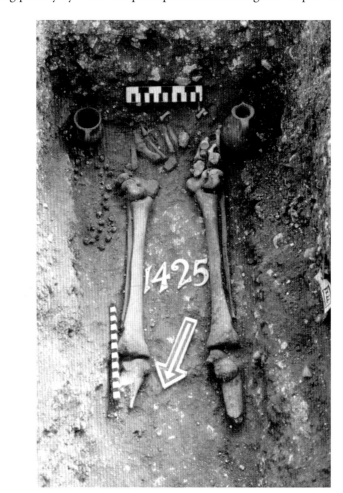

1.18 Late Romano-British hand-made vessel from Pirton (Hertfordshire). The fabric is typical late Romano-British, but the style is similar to some early Anglo-Saxon vessels

Saxon clientele. Fourth-century vessels were also being deposited in fifth-century contexts, demonstrating that older vessels were still in use.

The quantity of metalwork of probable British manufacture from the fifth century is comparatively small. The difficulty of finding it may to an extent be a consequence of changing patterns of deposition: a significant number of British pieces come from Anglo-Saxon graves – including the quoit-style brooches which are clearly rooted in late Roman chip-carving techniques. The British, Type 1 pennanular brooches are more widely dispersed, with concentrations particularly around the Severn estuary and in south-east Scotland, but there are concentrations in parts of Anglo-Saxon England, particularly Lindsey, where again they mostly come from Anglo-Saxon cemeteries. Other items include rings cut down from recycled late Roman bracelets, highly decorated spindle whorls, and a variety of such mundane objects as hairpins, which are difficult to categorise and/or date. A few sites offer a richer picture. At

1.19 Late Roman/sub-Roman watermill at Ickham, Kent. Reconstruction drawing

Ickham in Kent, a series of watermills has been excavated, powered by leats diverting water from the Little Stour estuary. These continued into the fifth century, as evidenced by the deposition of dress accessories, horse trappings and glass vessels and beads. The bulk of the pottery was manufactured post-370 and the water channel associated with the fourth mill was recut in the fifth century. Numerous small finds, mostly of bronze, seem to have been manufactured on site, suggesting a workshop supplying both the military at Richborough and the *civitas* capital of Canterbury into the sub-Roman period.

Urban deposits of this period pose particular difficulties. For decades archaeologists just cleared away everything above the stone foundations of the central Roman period, so much evidence has been lost. The upper levels of sites tend in any case to be the worst affected by later damage, so attention has of necessity to focus on those which were not rebuilt as medieval towns. At Wroxeter, the bath complex was abandoned in the fourth century. Excavation revealed deposits which were interpreted as a complex of poorly dated timber-framed buildings resembling a villa. However, very few artefacts are associated and much of this post-Roman phase may relate less to 'Dark Age' occupation than to later Anglo-Saxon stone robbing for the church. The extent of post-Roman occupation is therefore currently in question.

Canterbury has timber-framed buildings built in the ruins of earlier stone structures, standing at least through the 420s, perhaps later, but control of urban space declined to the point where humans and animals were buried in a pit in Stour Street and the city seems to have been virtually abandoned. At *Verulamium* attention has focused on *Insula* XXVII, where a masonry building constructed c. 380 was redeveloped to incorporate corn-dryers early in the fifth century, then replaced by a barn. That in turn had its foundations cut by a well-constructed water pipeline post-450. The dating of this sequence has been challenged on the basis that the mosaic of the primary building is likely to have been earlier than initially suggested, but a coin sealed beneath does corroborate the original dating. The cult of St Alban developed outside the town walls, though no burial church has so far been discovered. A scatter of finds suggests continuing activity across the fifth and sixth centuries; Bede believed that worship had continued uninterrupted to his own day.

Upper levels at Silchester have been severely affected by later ploughing, but on the basis of imported pottery, a glass bead and an ogham inscription, occupation continued into the later fifth century. The town seems eventually to have been intentionally abandoned, with the wells sealed deliberately. Occupation cannot, however, be described as 'urban' after around 450, at the latest.

These examples suggest decline, certainly, and the demise of urban lifestyles, but not sudden or dramatic abandonment in the early fifth century. Rather, there are signs of continuing organisation and management of urban space. Nor are these sites the only ones still in use; occasional finds of coins of Valentinian III dating to the 420s or 430s suggest that such sites as Caerwent (Monmouthshire) and Dunstable (Bedfordshire) were still occupied; Bath and Chester certainly feature post-Roman activity and at Whitchurch (Shropshire) it seems likely. Such signs of life stand beside the lack of archaeological evidence of a barbarian sack of British towns, such as Gildas later envisaged. The so-called 'black earth' which has repeatedly been found covering Roman deposits on urban sites has been explained variously as evidence of decayed buildings, agricultural soils and/or the result of refugees taking sanctuary within the walls. It likely originates from human and animal waste that has been allowed to accumulate, so it indicates continuing activity alongside the collapse of civic control. We should probably envisage fifth-century occupation of many towns but an absence of a Roman-style town-life. The distinction may, however, be clearer today than it was in, say, 430.

Across Britain, graves provide further insights into fifth-century activity, although 'British' cemeteries have so far received much less attention than their 'Anglo-Saxon' equivalents. Where alignment is very varied and grave goods are prevalent, paganism probably survived; though Christianity did not rule out grave goods, they do generally diminish with conversion and west–east alignment was the Christian norm. The late Roman-period cemetery at Lankhills, Winchester, for example, reveals a predominant west–east alignment to numerous graves, with low levels of recut suggesting a well-organised graveyard. Many bodies had footwear, evidenced by nails; a minority were associated with grave goods but these largely consisted of belts, knives and crossbow brooches, which may indicate the presence of a military and/or official segment of the local population. This was probably a predominantly Christian cemetery.

Elsewhere, though, pagan complexes continued to attract burial. At Baldock numerous graves with grave goods have been identified alongside successive repairs to

1.20 Late Romano-British inhumation with grave goods at Trinity Street, Southwark. The cemetery, which is typically pagan, is coin-dated after 388 and associated with a Romano-Celtic temple still in use in the late fourth century

1.21 Late Roman sarcophagus from St Martin-in-the-Fields; one element of a Christian cemetery which continued well into the fifth century

the road surfaces; a strong case has been made for occupation stretching into the sixth century. A large cemetery continued in use for some time outside the Roman small town at Billingford, in Norfolk. Recent excavations at Southwark in south London have revealed a temple complex constructed in the second century but still in use in the late fourth. An associated large cemetery revealed grave goods and a multiplicity of alignments and burial styles which suggest paganism. That such continued into the fifth century so close to the diocesan capital suggests that non-Christian religion was widely practised and accommodated by those in charge.

In Gaul, where Christianisation was perhaps a generation or two further advanced, extramural churches constructed in the later fourth or fifth centuries within or even beyond urban cemeteries became important centres of the Christian cult, with burial and a variety of ritual activities attracted to them. St Martin's grave outside Tours, for example, quickly developed as a basilica and Germanus was similarly buried outside Auxerre. We can assume a comparable church at St Albans, though as yet undiscovered. Elsewhere such sites have proved elusive in fifth-century Britain, but St Martin-in-the-Fields, Westminster, has revealed an elite burial ground lasting into the fifth century, when a tile kiln was also in use. This site continued to attract burials into the early Saxon period and may represent a successful extramural church associated with late Roman London.

Hoards of metalwork have long been viewed as an important form of evidence for the late fourth and early fifth centuries in Britain. The more spectacular, such as the Thetford Hoard and the Mildenhall Treasure (both discovered in East Anglia), centre on precious metal items sometimes of quite exceptional workmanship. The Thetford Hoard consisted largely of silver cutlery and gold jewellery. Clearly, very high-quality pieces were finding a market in fourth- and early fifth-century Britain. Not all the hoards being deposited, however, were of precious metal: the Drapers' Garden Hoard, found down a well in the City of London, was of 20 bronze, pewter and iron vessels.

Compared with other parts of the Western Empire, late Romano-British metalwork hoards are exceptionally numerous. Since other areas also suffered equivalent barbarian invasions, collapsing security may not provide a sufficient reason for so many depositions and opinion is tending towards ritual as an explanation. The Drapers' Garden Hoard, for example, seems to have been part of a complex process of sealing the well. This may again suggest that non-Christian religious practices remained popular. A

1.22 An onyx engraved with a figure of Mars set on a plain but very large gold ring, part of the Thetford Hoard. This hoard, buried around 400, is unusual both in the strength of its pagan content and in the quality of the jewellery, much of which probably came from a single workshop, perhaps even one in Britain

1.23 Irregular, imitation silver siliqua from the Hoxne Hoard. The inscription reads 'D N HONO-PIUS AUG', a garbled attempt at the name Honorius, emperor of the West, 395–423

disproportionate number of hoards, characterised by particularly rich finds, come from East Anglia. This apparent concentration of wealth does not map onto earlier distributions, for example of mosaics or other indicators of high-status occupation.

The largest hoard of Roman precious-metal objects so far found in Britain was discovered in 1992 in a field near Hoxne (Suffolk) and includes 580 gold *solidi* and around 15,000 silver coins. The hoard was buried in a wooden chest, within which 29 pieces of gold jewellery and 124 silver table utensils had been carefully stowed away, after which the coins were just poured in. Over 5,000 from the imperial mints were dated 395–402, and only 102 were later, the date range closing at 407/8. This is one of some seventy-six hoards of about this date so far discovered, at least a third of which were deposited later than 407/8 but within the first third of the fifth century. Whether this hoard should be interpreted in terms of ritual deposition is unclear, but the possibility certainly exists.

An important aspect of this hoard is the presence of 428 irregular imitation silver coins which were not produced at imperial mints. A few of these were criminal forgeries, but most were accurate copies replicating the official coinage in both weight and metal content, so they were locally made imitations issued for governmental purposes. Most replicated fourth-century coins so were probably made then, but 184 post-dated the last substantial importation of coin into Britain.

A total of 98.5 per cent of the whole coins had been clipped. Coin clipping is a particular characteristic of British finds. It was undertaken to extract silver while leaving the coin still in circulation, so care was taken not to cut away the central image. All eight coins minted in 407/8 had been clipped, so both coin use and coining necessarily continued thereafter. Some coins had been clipped repeatedly, reducing their weight to perhaps a third of the original, suggesting that the practice was long lived.

We have here, therefore, evidence for management of the coinage in Britain post-407/8. Silver coins were both in use and being clipped to provide bullion. This silver probably provided the silver ingots which appear in the archaeological record at this stage, as in the Coleraine Hoard in Ireland (deposited no earlier than 407–11) and at Vindolanda. Such ingots could be used as diplomatic gifts, for ransoming captives and/or payments to soldiers, including mercenaries. Their worth depended on their weight and purity. Alongside, the clipped coins for a time continued to circulate, with a growing mismatch between their face and bullion values.

Imperial taxation was in gold, not silver. Occasional individual finds demonstrate that gold coins continued both to enter Britain and to circulate, albeit not in great

1.24 Gold tremissis minted in either Merovingian or Burgundian Gaul, found on the shore of the Isle of Wight. Like other barbarian coins of the period this is modelled closely on Roman coinage; the bust is of the Roman emperor Valentinian III (425–55) and probably dates from his reign. A thin scatter of such coins from across Britain may imply circulation there as well

numbers. Without the pressure of imperial tax collection, however, these may not have been used as coins; rather it is tempting to see them as units of bullion or collectable items in their own right. Across the fifth century some gold coins were adapted as pendants and are found in Anglo-Saxon graves.

It is only the silver coins, therefore, that imply some sort of sub-Roman authority even after the collapse of Constantine III's regime and militate against a short/sharp collapse of Roman Britain. When coin-clipping ended is unclear: a hoard was deposited at Patching in Sussex, c. 470, which included five imported *siliquae* that had not been clipped, so coin-clipping had apparently ceased by then, but the coinage probably collapsed decades earlier than this, and with it any pan-British authority.

The ending of Roman Britain in the early fifth century was therefore neither so absolute nor so abrupt as is often imagined. For a generation, Britons surely anticipated the re-establishment of imperial control, if only because such had always occurred previously. One should envisage, therefore, some sort of interim government negotiating with the authorities in Gaul, and with various barbarian groups. This is reflected both in the British appeal which prompted Germanus's arrival in 429 and in Gildas's reference to a British plea to Aëtius, who was the dominant military leader in Gaul between 430 and 454, and who was indeed 'thrice consular', as Gildas remarked, from 446.

Gildas provides the only surviving account of the next generation, and his has been the basis of all later reconstructions, from Bede onwards, but this is an extraordinarily difficult text for a modern reader to use. Gildas viewed developments from an overall British perspective, lamenting the fate of fellow citizens of a fatherland which probably consisted of the old Roman diocese. Barbarian attacks were against the Britons in their totality, not just one particular local group, and the response of the British 'proud tyrant' (later named as Vortigern) was agreed in council with advisors whom Gildas termed 'silly princes of Zoan' advising pharaoh. This allusion to the great Egyptian pharaoh in the Book of Isaiah reads easiest as a ruler of an extensive territory, perhaps even the whole diocese. Gildas asserted that Britain in the present 'has her *rectores* ["governors"], she has her *speculatores* ["watchmen", or perhaps "bishops"]'. He was familiar with the Roman language of government, at least. Comparable terms recur on inscribed memorial stones from western Britain of around this date.

Gildas refers to civil conflict across the recent past and to British tyrants in the present, but he indicates that transformation from the Roman governmental framework of the early fifth century to the petty British kingships of the sixth was comparatively recent. Fundamental change came with warfare between the Britons and the Saxon warriors whom those governing Britain had hired as mercenaries. The literary evidence, therefore, implies a degree of governmental continuity across the ending of imperial control of Britain rather than a rapid and wholesale collapse of late Roman Britain into petty kingships soon after 410.

That said, some shift of power from the diocese to the provinces and *civitates* does seem likely after 410, given the collapse of imperial authority and of centrally administered army units. Henceforth, the British diocese was always a rather ramshackle affair. Local divergence is visible archaeologically in the pattern of deposition of different styles of sword-belt fitting, which suggest several regional workshops.

1.25 Tor Dyke, near Kettlewell (North Yorkshire), one of many enigmatic but massive running earthworks thought to date to the fifth and/or sixth centuries

The implication is that different styles were favoured by different provinces, *civitates* or elite families, all of whom may have employed militias in the late fourth and fifth centuries.

More significant must be the linear earthworks, or dykes, which have been ascribed to this period or later (the last and greatest are from the eighth century). Their dating is notoriously difficult, but those that cut Roman remains are obviously not prehistoric. They usually consist of one ditch and one accompanying bank, and the larger are some of the biggest man-made structures in Europe before the Industrial Revolution. Scholars have used various terms to describe them, 'travelling earthworks' or 'linear earthworks' for example, but the word 'dyke' (or *dic* as it is in Old English) is the most commonly used, both today and in the Anglo-Saxon period. Archaeologists utilise scientific advances such as radiocarbon dating and Optically Stimulated Luminescence to distinguish the prehistoric from the post-Roman, but some (such as Combs Ditch in Dorset) are prehistoric earthworks which were refurbished at the end of Roman Britain. Their distribution is intriguing, but it is unclear what the pattern is trying to tell us. They are absent from western Wales, the Highlands of Scotland, north-west England, most of central England, Lincolnshire, Sussex, Essex and Devon; some lie on their own, others, as in Cambridgeshire, form parallel groups, while those in Norfolk seem to face each other.

Thanks to good excavation evidence historians are fairly certain that the long dykes running parallel to the Anglo-Welsh border, Offa's Dyke, Wat's Dyke and Rowe Ditch, are Anglo-Saxon; scientific dating makes it very probable that Bokerley Dyke and West and East Wansdyke, as well as three of the Cambridgeshire dykes (Bran's Ditch,

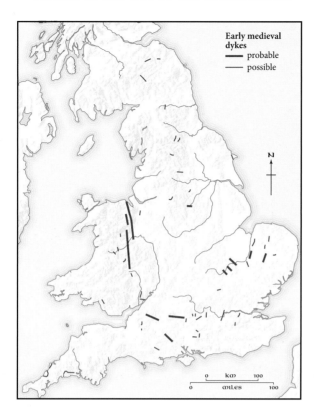

1.26 Dark Age dykes: probably or possibly in use c. 400–800. Numerous dykes were constructed in prehistory but only those that are thought to have been re-used at this date are included

Fleam Dyke and Devil's Ditch), date from around the time of the Anglo-Saxon arrival, but in many regions the evidence is far more problematic. Contradictory results from the excavation and survey of Norfolk's many dykes suggest that, like the Devil's Ditch near Garboldisham, many were refurbished prehistoric monuments. In Cornwall a series of unexcavated dykes cuts off large peninsulas; that they are named after giants (the Giant's Hedge or the Giant's Grave, for example) simply compounds our ignorance regarding their origins. In Hampshire, Berkshire, Surrey and Kent there are dykes recorded in Anglo-Saxon charters, but it is impossible to know how old these were when first recorded.

Dykes vary massively in length; some of the East Hampshire dykes are barely 100 metres while Offa's Dyke is at least 112 kilometres long. Those dating from the Anglo-Saxon period invariably consist of a single bank at least 2 metres high with no sign of a palisade atop it and a single ditch at least 2 metres deep. None provides clear evidence of gateways, nor of forts along their length.

Scholars are divided as to why dykes were built. Concentration on the larger monuments has encouraged them to ascribe rather grander meanings to them than if they had studied the numerous smaller examples. Traditionally, post-Roman dykes were thought to have been built by Britons against Anglo-Saxon invaders, or by Saxons to consolidate gains against British counter-raids. During the late twentieth century, however, this simplistic division of early medieval people into Britons on one side and Anglo-Saxons on the other locked in a fight to the death became discredited, and with it theories of hostile ethnic groups neatly divided by defensive dykes. The lack of garrisons and the ease with which many could be circumvented make it unlikely that most were military frontiers.

Seminal studies in Cambridgeshire in the 1920s, then of Offa's Dyke, Wat's Dyke and Wansdyke, concluded that Wansdyke and the Cambridgeshire examples were defensive, but Offa's and Wat's were border markers. That dykes might merely mark borders was taken up by later scholars, but they never explained why kings only felt the need to mark one side of their kingdoms. One of the odd features of Anglo-Saxon dykes is that they are rarely contiguous with parish or county boundaries (though there is an unexcavated dyke still marking the Surrey–Kent border near Westerham), whereas prehistoric earthworks were often reused as administrative borders. Historians have long tied themselves in knots trying to match the known borders of early medieval kingdoms with dykes. More recently, dykes have been interpreted more symbolically, built by kings to unite their heterogeneous kingdoms, alongside the idea that the Romano-British/Anglo-Saxon divide was more 'cultural' than 'racial'. But while it seems fair to view Offa's Dyke in terms of royal display, no other dyke is named after a known king (many are named after the Devil) and, despite being full of the great deeds of hero kings, nowhere in Anglo-Saxon literature does a writer boast that a king ordered any other dyke to be built.

An alternative is to view dykes as a deterrent to raiders at a time when raiding was endemic. Perhaps dykes, especially the shorter ones, were intended to stop hit-and-run raids. Many bisect major routeways that might have been used by raiders, and as they seem set back from the known frontiers of kingdoms they would be places where local defenders could gather once the border had been breached. Dykes were undoubtedly built or rebuilt at different times and probably had various functions, but closer analysis is currently beyond us. Whatever their immediate purpose, dykes provide us with important evidence of the ability of sub-Roman society to marshal considerable resources of manpower. It seems likely that regional hierarchies were responsible for managing these great building works. Indeed, Gildas's comments on the Antonine Wall may reveal an awareness of how dykes were being constructed around 500.

Additionally, there are signs of re-occupation of numerous Iron Age hillforts, particularly in western Britain, during the fifth and sixth centuries. The best known examples are in the south west, including South Cadbury where there was large-scale rebuilding of the inner rampart and occupation of substantial new buildings in the interior. However, they also include sites in the east of Britain, such as Yarborough Camp, north of Lincoln, where late Roman material has been discovered, and perhaps also Yarburgh near Louth. Occupation of such fortified sites suggests a flight from undefended settlements to take refuge behind the reconstituted ramparts of much older defensive sites. Some had served religious functions in the interim, so their reuse in the fifth century may owe something to a continuing awareness of their protective value. Such re-occupation implies a breakdown in security and reliance on local solutions, separate from government.

It was this problem of security that lay at the heart of events across the fifth century. When Constantine III took with him to the Continent the British field army and around half the Saxon Shore units, Britain was left with defences that were disproportionately located in the north, with much richer areas now vulnerable to sea-raiders in

1.27 RIACUS inscription at Vindolanda, from the later fifth century and commemorating a Romano-British name. Such inscriptions testify to the survival of Latin literacy on the extreme northern edge of Roman Britain

the south. Numerous forts in the north show signs of continuing activity. One of the granaries at Birdoswald (Gilsland, Cumbria) was levelled and a great timber hall built over it in the fifth century; at Binchester (Bishop Auckland, County Durham) the Commandant's House had a bath suite added in the second half of the fourth century and subsequently extended, then with the building falling down it was used for butchering cattle and metalworking and the metal-fittings of the bath suite were robbed out, all before the mid-sixth century when a burial was inserted. At Vindolanda (Northumberland), a church was constructed at the commanding officer's residence and the Riacus inscription and Brigomaglos memorial stone indicate literacy, Christianity and a continuing ability to work stone. Close by, Housesteads was still occupied. At Piercebridge (County Durham), new drains suggest continuing use of the bath suite into the fifth century and at Catterick (North Yorkshire) timber buildings were being erected post-400.

In the fifth-century lowlands, in contrast, social, economic, religious, administrative and legal power rested predominantly in the hands of a civilian, landholding elite. That elite lacked the military protection which had hitherto provided security. Beneath the landowning class was a provincial society that was comparatively localised in many respects and less 'Roman' than were most provincials on the Continent. Paganism was still widespread, even dominant in the countryside, and present even in London's suburbs, and British Celtic had survived the pressure of Latin. Roman culture had been centred in towns, which were now in terminal decline, and in the households of the landed elite, which could no longer be maintained in the traditional style. The 'Roman-ness' of Britain was decaying and the diocese lay exposed, lying as it did on the outer edge of the Empire, open to land attackers to the north and seaborne raiders on all sides. Even Bishop Germanus reportedly ended up leading British forces against barbarian raiders. Insecurity was the fundamental problem which Britain's leaders faced and which underlies Gildas's later description of the 'ruin' of Britain.

With Britons unable to provide for their own defence, they tried to call in Roman aid. When that was not forthcoming, they hired one set of barbarians to counter the attacks of others. That this was a typically 'Roman' response to such difficulties is reinforced by Gildas's use of terms characteristic of the late imperial employment of barbarian mercenaries, as the *hospitium* (hospitality) via which they were billeted and the *annona* (supplies) and *epimenia* (provisions) to feed them. The British authorities were following imperial precedents.

There was a comparatively 'Roman' elite still running Britain, therefore, in the early to mid-fifth century, but they were presiding over a community that was decreasingly Roman. For a generation or so the situation was recoverable, but the necessary imperial intervention never arrived. Roman Britain changed in one sphere after another, with progressive devaluation then failure of the coinage, the collapse of building, trade and manufacturing, and an upsurge in piracy and raiding.

If there was one event that finally brought the old diocese to an end, then it was the failure of British attempts to shore up security by hiring barbarian mercenaries. The latest estimate of when Roman Britain ended has to be when the Britons failed to bring to a successful conclusion the war against their rebellious Saxon troops. Of course, British leaders retained control of many localities, even in lowland areas where their authority interleaved with the new Saxon settlements, but the integrity of Roman Britain was irrecoverable. In key respects, Roman Britain was over.

GILDAS

NICHOLAS J. HIGHAM

In this letter I shall deplore rather than denounce, the style may be vile, nevertheless my intention is benign, what I have to deplore with tearful complaint is a general loss of good, a heaping up of bad, but no one should think that anything I say is said out of scorn for humanity or from conviction that I am superior to others, rather I sympathise with the difficulties and miseries of my country and rejoice in remedies to relieve them.

So begins Gildas's *De Excidio Britanniae (On the Ruin of Britain)*, which is by far the longest insular text available to us prior to 600. It is framed as a letter, as the New Testament epistles, but obeys many of the conventions of Classical authorship. For example, it offers as preface a brief, 'geographical' introduction, which owes much to Orosius's in his early fifth-century *Seven Histories against the Pagans*, but it is also surprisingly original. The bulk of the work is a condemnation of the behaviour of five contemporary rulers and the British clergy en masse; Gildas considered that their sins had fractured the relationship between God and His British people, causing Him to withhold His protection. The work is an impassioned plea for repentance, moral reform and a return to the ways of the Lord.

Despite Gildas's own focus, however, scholars down the ages have paid more attention to the schematic review of Britain's history down to the year of Gildas's birth which prefaces his main complaint – the so-called 'historical' section which forms chapters 4–26 of this 110-chapter work. These passages provide the only extant near-contemporary insular account of the ending of Roman Britain and the settlement of the Anglo-Saxons.

But Gildas never set out to write history as we would understand it today; he offered no dates and his story is so hemmed around by his condemnation of the British leaders as to be close to incoherent. His historical section was designed to establish that there was an inescapable relationship throughout history between sin and divine punishment. Gildas's history was the story of a new chosen people, a 'latter-day Israel' as he put it, and their relationship with God. The logic that sustained this account derived from the Old Testament. It is the moral imperative that dominates, therefore, as his introductory remarks suggest.

1a.1 Page from the earliest surviving copy of Gildas's *De Excidio Britanniae*, an eleventh-century manuscript in the Cotton collection. The collection was severely damaged by a fire at the family home in Westminster in 1731; the opening line of chapter 57 appears in the least smoke-affected section at the centre of image, reading (in translation from the Latin) 'Have regard next to the words of the chosen prophet Zachariah, son of Iddo..', introducing a quotation from the Prophet Zaccharias, I, 3-4 in the Old Testament

This may be the only history that we have from the period, but the historical section is clearly mistaken or ill-informed in important respects. Gildas misplaced the reign of the emperor Tiberius (AD 14–37) after the revolt of Boudicca (or Boadicea: AD 60–1). He assumed that the persecution of Christians by the emperor Diocletian impacted on Britain, an impact that is otherwise unattested and seems improbable. He made the usurper Magnus Maximus responsible for the final exodus of soldiers from Britain, omitting any clear reference to Constantine III a generation later. And he placed the building of the Saxon Shore forts and both the Hadrianic and Antonine Walls later than 388, despite all of these being constructed in the second and/or third centuries.

To an extent, such errors can be explained as a consequence of a lack of sources, for Gildas tells us that he had no British texts to draw on as they had either been destroyed by 'the enemy' (presumably, the Saxons) or taken abroad by emigrants. The 'foreign' works Gildas accessed will not have offered dating for the Saxon Shore forts or the northern walls, so he inserted these as best suited his needs. That said, Gildas had read Orosius and so would have known about the usurpation of Constantine III. His omission therefore seems to have been deliberate, to keep historical examples and, in particular, names to a minimum. Again, this is not history as we would know it. Instead of a continuous historical narrative, Gildas presented episodes chosen in accordance with his own religious imperatives and often in so generalised a form as to be almost unrecognisable.

It is when, in the fifth century, Gildas is our only guide that these problems threaten to overwhelm us. Following two putative Roman expeditions to Britain to chase out Scottish and Pictish raiders, he portrays the Britons as so pressured by barbarian attackers and shortages of food that they appealed for the third time to the Continent for aid, this time to 'Agitius, thrice consul'. Ever since Bede in the eighth century, 'Agitius' has been identified with Aëtius, the Roman commander in Gaul from around 430 to 454, who was made consul for the third time in 446. The only alternative is to identify him with an even later Roman general in fifth-century Gaul, Aegidius, whose lack of consulships and late chronology effectively rule him out. According to Gildas, after their request for assistance had been turned down, the Britons hired Saxons who then revolted and ravaged Britain. The resulting war between Britons and Saxons ran up to Gildas's own birth in the year in which the Britons scored pretty well their last victory, the siege of Mount Badon. Thereafter external peace was established – though not freedom from civil wars, which lasted up to the present.

If, as most scholars have assumed, Gildas was here describing the first significant arrival of Saxons into Britain, there are some real problems with his chronology. The earliest appearance of Saxons post-446 is at odds with archaeological evidence for their presence by the 430s and perhaps a generation earlier. Additionally, the *Gallic Chronicle of 452* independently records Britain as largely under Saxon rule in 441. Clearly there is a difficulty here. Perhaps Gildas was referring to an appeal in the 430s to Aëtius before his third consulship, in which case he adjusted the wording of the appeal. Alternatively, the Britons may have been seeking aid against the Saxons after their rebellion, and not against the Picts and the Scots. The trouble is that historical accuracy, as a modern reader would perceive it, was of less interest to Gildas than his general thesis of sin and divine punishment, and he was quite capable of manipulating his material so as to fit best with the logic of his work. Parallels have been noted between Gildas's history and the proto-martyr Stephen's speech before the Sanhedrin in Acts 7: 1–51, which likewise subverted literal historical truth for rhetorical purposes.

Despite the central importance of *On the Ruin of Britain* to our understanding of the events of the sub-Roman period, the work itself clearly presents considerable problems, which are compounded by our relative ignorance about the author. We know very little regarding Gildas beyond what can be learned from his own works: alongside *On the Ruin of Britain* we have only a handful of letter fragments and a brief penitential. His reputation was, however, high among the generation or two following his death. His authority on ecclesiastical and monastic discipline was invoked c. 600 by the Irishman Columbanus (at that time active in Frankish Gaul) in a letter to Pope Gregory the Great, and Gildas was cited approvingly on 12 occasions in the *Collectio canonum Hibernensis*, an Irish canon collection compiled around 700. Bede used *On the Ruin of Britain* extensively in the first book of his *Ecclesiastical History*, referring to Gildas as the Britons' own historian and to his work as 'a tearful sermon'. By 800, Gildas was revered as a saint in Ireland and probably soon afterwards in Anglo-Saxon England,

1a.2 Church of Gildas de Rhus, Morbihan, southern Brittany. The monastery claimed Gildas as founder and patron saint and parts of his reputed skeleton are encased in medieval silver and kept as relics

though his cult was never widespread. By the early eleventh century, the Breton monastery of St Gildas-de-Rhuys was claiming to possess his relics, and a *Life* written there described him as of royal birth, from the Clyde Valley (in Scotland), and educated by St Illtud in south Wales before emigrating to Gaul in his thirtieth year. Gildas subsequently appeared in various guises in a number of Welsh hagiographies produced in the late eleventh and twelfth centuries and was the subject of a second *Life*, written by Caradog of Llancarfan in the twelfth century (in this one, Gildas ends his days at Glastonbury rather than Rhuys). These eleventh- and twelfth-century texts are, however, pure fiction. While medieval authors viewed Gildas as a figure of some prestige and authority, they had access to very little reliable information about him.

The *Welsh Annals (Annales Cambriae)*, compiled in the 950s, date Gildas's death to 570. On this basis, *On the Ruin of Britain* has traditionally been dated to the 540s. Recent scholarship has, though, rightly cautioned against reliance on a mid-tenth-century text which appears to have had few if any near-contemporary sources for the sixth century. The *Annals* are, in any case, internally inconsistent. They offer a date of 516 for the Battle of Mount Badon, to which Gildas refers as occurring in the year of his own birth, some 43 years and 1 month before the time of writing. The resulting date of 559/60 for authorship of *On the Ruin of Britain* conflicts with the obit of 547 given in the *Annals* for King Maelgwn of Gwynedd, who is Maglocunus, one of the five tyrants Gildas condemns and clearly still alive when *On the Ruin of Britain* was composed.

Given these problems in the *Welsh Annals*, recent commentators have attempted to establish the date of authorship from the sequence of events recounted in the historical section. Gildas, however, offered no dates at all and provided only the vaguest of chronological parameters. The last event he mentioned which can be dated with any confidence is the third consulship of Aëtius in 446, but that may well be misplaced in his sequence. The assumptions that have to be built into estimates of any chronology are so great as to undermine its credibility, leaving the traditional dating of authorship, in the 540s, still widely accepted. Given that Gildas clearly received a traditional Roman-style education, and that there are parallels between his style and that of a number of late fifth-century Gallic authors, it is possible that Gildas could have been writing as early as 500; majority opinion, however, still favours the first half of the sixth century.

It is also unclear where Gildas was writing, although it is generally agreed that he was voicing an insular British perspective and so probably composed the work within Britain. In the 1970s the case was made for a northern Gildas, based perhaps in the Chester region, but since then most have preferred to place him, if anywhere, in southern Britain, somewhere in the region stretching northwards from Dorset. Certainly, the five tyrants whom he castigated seem to have been located in the south west and Wales, which may imply that Gildas was close to but outside these areas.

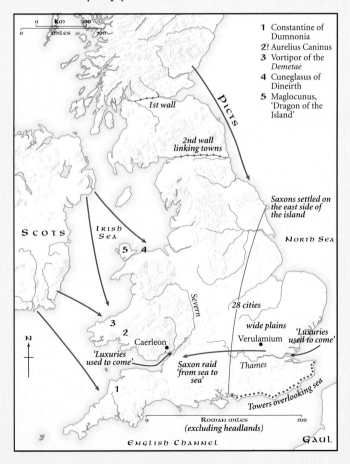

1a.3 The geography of *On the Ruin of Britain*. The dimensions and other basic information in the introduction derive from the *Natural History* of Pliny the Elder, but Gildas followed Orosius in giving a breadth of 200 miles in error for Pliny's 300, adding 'excepting various large headlands' to correct this

Whilst Gildas cannot be precisely dated or located, his writings nevertheless offer important evidence regarding what one man of this generation thought about his own past and he is a valuable guide to insular culture in his day. He considered the employment then revolt of Saxons as a terrible blow to his people, far worse even than the attacks of the Scots and Picts that they were intended to remedy. The Saxons are likened by Gildas to wolves, dogs, lions and other savage beasts, and he claimed 'nothing more destructive, nothing more bitter has ever befallen the land' than the coming of the Saxons. We also learn a great deal about literary culture from Gildas's works. He had clearly benefited from a traditional Roman-style education and had evidently had training at the hands of a rhetor; he refers to such a figure also having educated King Maglocunus. To the elite at least, therefore, a high-quality Classical education was still available in parts of Britain when Gildas was young. There are indications that Gildas himself was sympathetic to the nascent monastic movement in Britain but his was clearly an episcopal Church, ruled by bishops. Although he apparently considered international trade a thing of the past, there were various current contacts between Britain and the Continent, for Gildas wrote of the accessibility of Belgic Gaul in the present. He may have had some awareness of the doctrinal controversies currently engaging Christians across Europe, and is likely to have been in touch with Ireland and the British mission there.

A powerful message emanating from the works of Gildas is just how very 'Roman' he and his contemporaries were. Of course, he identified himself and his fellow countrymen not as Romans but as Britons, but these were very 'Roman' Britons still. The system of law he defended against the tyrants, the religion in which he had immersed himself, the biblical texts he quoted at length, the language he used, the rhetorical skills he deployed, the elitist values to which he adhered, all derived from the Roman Empire. Even a century or so after Britain had slipped from under imperial protection, the social, cultural and religious values of parts at least of the British elite remained keenly aligned with those of their contemporaries on the Continent. The 'Britishness' to which Gildas was giving voice in his work was, beyond all else, modelled on Israel in the Old Testament, but it was a very 'Roman' type of Israel nonetheless.

KING ARTHUR

NICHOLAS J. HIGHAM

If asked to name a Dark Age ruler in Britain, most people think first of Arthur, but it is extremely difficult to demonstrate that he actually existed. Most of what we today think we know about King Arthur derives from writings of the central and later Middle Ages, in particular from Geoffrey of Monmouth in the 1130s to Sir Thomas Malory (d. 1471). These works are essentially fictional. If we are to assess the evidence for a 'real' King Arthur, we must search out the earliest literary evidence available.

What may be the earliest literary reference to Arthur appears in *The Gododdin*, an Old Welsh collection of elegiac stanzas, parts at least of which were written in commemoration of a failed attack by the war-band of a king of Edinburgh on *Catraeth* (most likely Catterick in North Yorkshire). *The Gododdin* was probably originally composed around 600 but was revised successively before being written down in two different versions in the second half of the thirteenth century. Arthur occurs in verse 38 of the 'B' version only, which in A.O.H. Jarman's translation reads:

> He charged before three hundred of the finest,
> He cut down both centre and wing,
> He excelled in the forefront of the noblest host,
> He gave gifts of horses from the herd in winter.
> He fed black ravens on the rampart of a fortress
> Though he was no Arthur.
> Among the powerful ones in battle,
> In the front rank, Gwarddur was a palisade.

The similarity between the two names (Welsh 'dd' is pronounced 'th') is presumably what prompted Arthur's appearance here. Clearly he was considered a paragon of military valour, but the language of this stanza includes both archaisms and later accretions so there is no guarantee that the reference pre-dates the tenth century, particularly since it appears in only one of the two extant versions.

Other 'early' mentions suggest a spate of personal naming around 600: an Arthur occurs in the genealogy of the kings of Dyfed (south-west Wales); Bishop Adamnan of Iona in the late seventh century referred to an *Arturius*, son of King Aedan of Dál

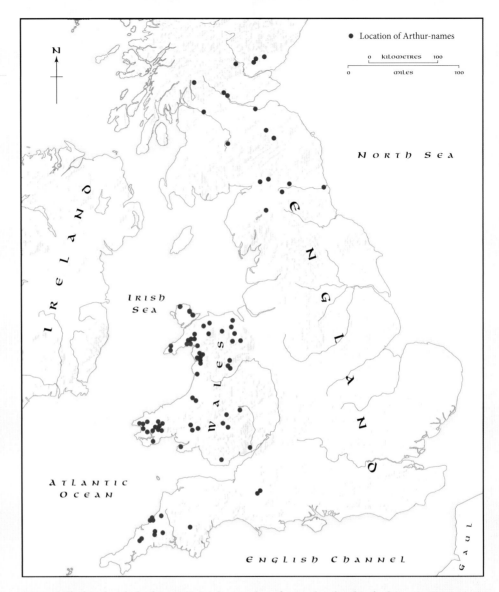

Riata, killed in battle before 597; Irish annals refer to the death of a king in Kintyre at the hands of an Arthur in the 620s, and an Irish legal document of the late 690s mentions an Arthur as grandfather to Feradoch. That the name was popular in Ireland and the Irish colonies in Britain does not require, however, the existence of an earlier British hero-figure of that name, fighting against incomers; indeed, it might even suggest the opposite.

A more convincing scenario derives from the recent revival of a view which first circulated in the later nineteenth century, that Arthur originated as a mythological figure associated with wild places and great deeds, who was then historicised by writers of Latin. The name certainly lends itself to this interpretation. Modern Welsh *arth* (Old Welsh **arto-*) combined with *gwr* (OW **wiros*) gives the name 'bear-man'. Bears were edging towards extinction in Britain in the first millennium AD, so were a suitable association for an elusive spirit of the wilderness. Literary references are exclusively to the Latin name *Artorius*, but the ambiguity of a Brittonic origin myth would not have been lost on a British audience used to Latinised forms of Welsh names.

Supposing this to be the starting point, the man responsible beyond all others for the historicisation of Arthur was the author of the *Historia Brittonum (History of the Britons)*. This work, later but not necessarily accurately attributed to the Welsh priest Nennius, was written in the fourth regnal year of Merfyn, King of Gwynedd, 829/30. The *History* championed the Britons as a martial people of the Lord and as the rightful occupiers of all Britain. This is, therefore, a polemical work, written just a few years after Mercian pressure on Wales had dramatically reduced in 825 and the Mercians had been forced, albeit briefly, to acknowledge the West Saxon King Ecgberht as their ruler, and he had also received the submission of the Welsh kings. Neither Ecgberht nor the West Saxons are mentioned, suggesting a degree of caution regarding contemporary politics, but this work is in other respects nationalistic and anti-English. It explains that much of Britain had been lost to the Saxons through the stupidity and wickedness of a ruler named Vortigern, who appears sporadically across chapters 31 to 50, despite the presence of the good Bishop Germanus, the Christian virtues of the Britons as a whole and the valour of Vortigern's own son Vortimer. Hope for the recovery of Britain is offered prophetically via the boy Emrys/Ambrosius, a legendary figure apparently based on that Ambrosius to whom Gildas referred as the Britons' leader against the Saxons.

The prophecy which Emrys interprets centres on the combat of two worms, one red (for the Britons) the other white (for the Saxons: think of rugby), taking place on a cloth floating on an underground lake. Three times the red worm was driven back to the edge of the cloth, three times it rallied and drove the white back. Finally the red triumphed, pursuing its opponent across the lake. Victory of the red signified the expulsion of the English from Britain.

1b.2 Arthur's Stone, a Neolithic burial chamber at Dorstone in the Golden Valley (Herefordshire) to which Arthur's name has become attached

Three episodes were included in the work as having occurred previously, but the
final triumph was still to come, presumably under the leadership of Merfyn himself,
whose nickname 'Frych', meaning 'the freckled one', suggests red hair. The red worm
was probably intended therefore as a metaphor for King Merfyn – worm here may be
read as a metaphor for a dragon, a legendary beast which Gildas also used to represent
a British king.

The first triumph over the Saxons was their expulsion from Thanet by Vortimer
(chapters 43, 44), the third, mentioned only briefly, was Urien's siege of the Northumbrian
king on Lindisfarne (63), but the second was a highly stylised and biblically inspired
treatment of Arthur as a type of Old Testament Joshua (56), to which the author built
up via treatment of St Patrick as a Moses figure (50–5). Arthur is the *dux bellorum*
('commander of battles') of the Britons, an uncommon phrase paralleling the reference
to Joshua as *dux belli* ('commander of battle') in the opening lines of the Book of Judges;
his 12 victories recall the disciples of Christ (the names Jesus and Joshua are identical in
Hebrew), the 12 pebbles which Joshua collected from the Jordan when crossing into the
'Promised Land', and the 12 tribes into which he then formed the Israelites.

Although the twelfth battle was the historical one to which Gildas had referred as
the siege of Mount Badon in *On the Ruin of Britain*, the remainder look to have been
culled from a variety of literary contexts and include British defeats as well as victories.
These have no validity as a list of victories won by a British champion in the years
following Patrick's death. This is a highly contrived British hero-figure, therefore,
whose battles were of ideological rather than historical value, and whose role as a
paragon of Christian martial virtue was developed to inspire Merfyn in the present,
rather than to profile a true figure of the past.

That this author found his inspiration for Arthur in folk stories is sustained by his reappearance in the list of miraculous phenomena (the *mirabilia*: 67–75). The *mirabilia* serves to prove the continuing presence of God as an active force in territories controlled or recently controlled by British rulers. In 73 there are two 'Arthurian' miracles: the first refers to the hunting of the great boar, *Twrch Trwyth*, which is a tale best known from the group of stories that came to focus on *Culhwch and Olwen*, but this version originates as an attempt to explain the place name Carn Gafallt ('Horse Cairn'), near Rhayader in the Upper Wye Valley, by reference to Arthur's dog. That a warrior whose name recalls the bear has a hound named 'horse' used in the hunting of 'the essential boar' places this story firmly in the realm of the mythical. The second tale is another local wonder-story devised to explain the name of what was probably a prehistoric monument, called *Llygad Amr*, as the resting place of Arthur's son, Amr, whom he had slain and buried there in a grave the dimensions of which were forever shifting. Both *Llygad* and *Amr* mean 'eye', in the sense of a source of tears, serving as a metaphor for the spring at the head of the River Gamber (sic) nearby. Superficial similarity of the names 'Arthur' and 'Amr/Gamber' had arguably brought this explanation into existence.

Both these stories demonstrate that there were folk tales about Arthur associated with specific features of the countryside of western Britain around 800 which our author had come across (he specifically recalls visiting *Llygad Amr* and trying the grave for size), and it seems highly likely that the Arthur of chapter 56 was inspired by such pre-existing stories. Arthur continues to be associated with a wide variety of landscape features in western and to a lesser extent northern England, some of which are natural features and some prehistoric monuments, in ways entirely consistent with his origin in folklore.

1b.4 Tintagel, the north Cornish promontory site under excavation in 2000. The site was associated with King Arthur's birth by Geoffrey of Monmouth in the 1130s, though there is no way of knowing how much earlier the connection was made; large quantities of imported Mediterranean pottery imply the site was of high-status around 500

1b.5 The Winchester Round Table: this quintessentially 'Arthurian' piece of ceremonial furniture reflects the value of the cycle of Arthurian stories to the medieval English court. It was probably made in the thirteenth century for Henry III, then refurbished on behalf of Henry VIII in the sixteenth

Once Arthur had been historicised in the *History of the Britons*, later authors sought to include him too. In the mid-tenth century, the author of the *Welsh Annals (Annales Cambriae)* inserted an extended entry on the Battle of Mount Badon under the year 516, then notice of Arthur's death in 537. The similarity of the language used suggests that the author based both on the *History* but adapted the martial Arthur whom he found there for his own audience. The *Annals* were written in Dyfed (south-west Wales) in the mid 950s when its king, Owain, was locked in a struggle against his cousin the king of Gwynedd, and in need of English protection. That this work plays down conflict between Britons and Saxons, preferring to adopt a far less nationalistic approach than the *History*, is a function of the politics of the time. Arthur appears in the maternal lineage of Owain, so the author probably assumed that he was a local figure and portrayed him very differently so as to avoid any offence to the English court of the day. His 'Arthur carried the cross of our Lord Jesus Christ for three days and three nights on his shoulders . . .', contrasts dramatically with the warrior responsible for 12 victories over the Saxons listed in the *History*, instead invoking the figure of Simon the Cyrenian, who in Luke 23:26, carried the cross for Christ. There is little reason to suppose the dating is accurate or the entry historical.

Thereafter, Arthur appears in several saints' *Lives* written in Wales in the central Middle Ages. To this point, Arthur had been depicted as a warrior, a *miles*, but now he emerges as a figure of royal authority. This developed out of the logic of the *History of the Britons*, where he is depicted as the leader of the Britons despite the presence of kings. To later generations this read in terms of superior kingship.

Scenes reminiscent of the old figure of a warrior associated with the wild still surface on occasion, but the Arthur of the saints' *Lives* was generally a king who could be juxtaposed with the saint being commemorated. He might appear as a relative or associate; alternatively and more commonly he could be represented as a powerful wrongdoer, to be corrected, humbled and forced to do penance, so enhancing the authority of the saint. As such, Arthur was being used as an exemplar of arbitrary lordship and warrior-kingship in a world in which the behaviour of kings was frequently offensive to the clergy. These stories feed into the later medieval cycle of Arthurian literature but have nothing whatsoever to tell us about the sub-Roman period, being composed for contemporary purposes in the tenth–twelfth centuries.

It is Geoffrey of Monmouth who then took up these stories in the 1130s and reimagined British history around the figure of Arthur, who dominates a substantial section of his extraordinarily popular *History of the Kings of Britain*. It is his King Arthur, 'both upright and generous' and a mighty warrior, who underlies the irruption of the icon of chivalric insular kingship into which Arthur metamorphosed across the centuries that followed. Geoffrey made the connection between Arthur and various sites in the south west, including Tintagel, where he placed his birth and the court of the rulers of Cornwall. And it was Geoffrey who popularised the 'once and future' king for the Anglo-Norman elite and so began the reconciliation of Arthur with the English. The Round Table is perhaps the greatest surviving relic of the Arthurian revival in the Plantagenet era, which was then 'improved' on behalf of Henry VIII to impress his new Hapsburg relatives. The whole story had become firmly entrenched in England by the fifteenth century, when Malory wrote his *Morte d'Arthur*.

Arthur had become, then, a media success long before the modern era. Malory's work was printed by Caxton in 1485 and achieved far greater circulation than any previous Arthurian text. Tennyson recycled Malory's epic for a nineteenth-century audience, achieving huge popularity with his *Idylls of the King* in the 1850s. The work offered Tennyson the opportunity to comment on a range of modern issues in the safety of a Romantic genre set in a pseudo-historical past. His success only underlines the probability that all the many Arthur figures offered ever since the ninth century have been fictional constructs developed on the basis of non-historical sources to serve present political and ideological needs. If that is true for the *History of the Britons*, then it is equally so for every later appearance of Arthur, since all can be traced back ultimately to the inventiveness of one Welsh cleric, writing for and probably at the court of Merfyn Frych in the third decade of the ninth century.

CHAPTER 2

The Origins of England

NICHOLAS J. HIGHAM

In his *Agricola*, written at the end of the first century AD, the Roman historian Tacitus speculated about the origins of Britain's inhabitants. The southern Welsh, he suggested, so resembled the Spanish that they were probably descended from immigrants from the peninsula. Similarly the Caledonians of Scotland were likely to be descendants of Germans, while on the same grounds lowland Britons perhaps derived from Gaul. Ultimately, though, he dismissed the whole matter as unworthy of the attention of his aristocratic Roman audience: 'Who the first inhabitants of Britain were, whether indigenes or incomers, remains unknown; do remember, we are dealing with barbarians.'

Today broadly similar questions focus on Britain in the immediately post-Roman period, c. 430–570. At issue are the dramatic cultural changes that occurred primarily in the south and east and which mark the ending of a 'Roman' and 'British' past and the opening of something new and 'Anglo-Saxon'. Both the Latin and Brittonic (Celtic) languages died out across lowland Britain to be replaced by Old English, Christianity was displaced as the dominant religion by Germanic paganism, material culture and architecture changed dramatically, and to the archaeologist the whole society looks very different indeed.

What really changed, and what caused these dramatic shifts? Should we look to population replacement as the key, with the British population overrun by German incomers en masse in the aftermath of Empire? Or should we suppose that the existing population, with just a leavening of new settlers, underwent such wholesale linguistic and cultural change that they 'became English'? And why was this process so extreme compared with other parts of the Western Roman Empire where Germanic warriors settled? The whole of France, Italy and Spain had Germanic immigrants, after all, but retained Latin, and Christianity was not seriously challenged in the first two, at least, and in Spain only by Islamic conquest. To understand how and why the south-eastern core of the old British diocese changed so profoundly we need to explore evidence from a diverse range of disciplines – historical, archaeological, genetic and linguistic. But these questions also call for a comparative approach, so we will compare Britain's experience with that of other communities across the Channel, to see how and why it differed.

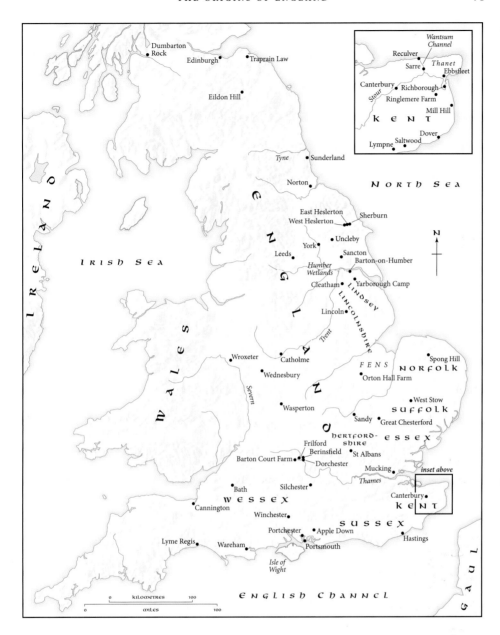

2.1 Places named in chapter 2

History and the 'English Settlement'

Across the nineteenth and much of the twentieth centuries, a mass Germanic migration into lowland Britain in the fifth century, the 'English Settlement', was celebrated as the starting point of English history. John Richard Green wrote in 1892, 'It is with the landing of Hengest and his war-band at Ebbsfleet on the shores of the Isle of Thanet that English history begins. No spot in Britain can be so sacred to Englishmen as that which first felt the tread of English feet.'

Although bolstered both by place name studies and burial archaeology, belief in this event rested primarily on the *Anglo-Saxon Chronicle* and the writings of Bede. The

2.2 Early Germanic society in the Victorian imagination. Pastoral scene from *Illustrated History of the World*, c. 1884

late ninth-century *Chronicle* provided Victorian writers with a skeletal history in which they placed absolute faith. 'Arrival' stories therein featured Hengest in Kent (in 449), Ælle in Sussex (477) and Cerdic in Wessex (495), each leading tiny squadrons of ships (three, three and five respectively). The archetype of such stories was, though, Gildas's account of the arrival of three shiploads of Saxon mercenaries, repeated by Bede, which Anglo-Saxon writers then adapted as origin myths for different kingships.

Interplay between personal names and place names demonstrates that the late ninth-century chronicler had no reliable sources for the fifth century. West Saxon history opens with entries detailing the arrivals by sea of first Cerdic and his son Cynric, both British names, then later Port – from the Latin *Portum Arduni* (probably Portchester, near Portsmouth) – and his two sons, one at least of whom, Mægla, likewise has a Celtic name. This is highly improbable. In fact, the West Saxons were earlier called the *Gewisse* and probably originated in the Upper Thames Valley, only refocusing south of the Thames under pressure from the Mercians.

Bede, writing in the early eighth century, was closer in time than the chronicler but still far too late to be a useful primary source. However, the origins of the English interested him, and his works reveal something of what was believed at the time; additionally, he so influenced all later history writing that his views merit our attention. Bede considered 'the arrival of the English' (the *adventus Saxonum*) foundational to English history. He was aware of dating from the Creation (which he used in his *The Reckoning of Time*) and from Rome's foundation (the standard Roman method). In the same way he occasionally used years since the *adventus*: so, for example, Gregory was pope 'about 150 years following the arrival of the English'. In the 'Lesser Chronicle' (in 703) Bede offered only two 'English' entries: firstly 'The race of the Angles comes to Britain', and then their Conversion to Christianity. He included far more material in his 'Greater Chronicle' (c. 725):

> The people of the Angles or Saxons were conveyed to Britain in three long-ships. When their voyage proved a success, news of them was carried back home. A stronger army set out which, joined to the earlier one, first of all drove away the enemy they were seeking [the Picts and Scots]. Then they turned their arms on their allies [the Britons], and subjugated almost the whole island by fire or sword, from the eastern shore as far as the western one on the trumped-up excuse that the Britons had given them a less than adequate stipend for their military services.

Bede had clearly by now discovered Gildas, but was struggling with the latter's lack of chronology: this entry comes before Bishop Germanus's visit to Britain in 429. Gildas's account then served again as the basis for Bede's next comment on the matter:

> Under the leadership of Ambrosius Aurelianus – a man of modest means who alone of the mighty Romans had survived slaughter by the Saxons in which his parents, who had worn the purple, had been killed – the Britons goaded the victors to battle and defeated them. And from that time, first one side then the other gained the victory, until the incomers, being the stronger, gained possession of the whole island for a long time.

Bede did not glorify the English but left the moral high ground to the Roman Ambrosius. Nevertheless he recorded a universal Saxon conquest of Britain.

A second version of this story then occurs in the first book of the *Ecclesiastical History* (in 731). Again Bede followed Gildas but now at greater length, telling the moralising story of the problems besetting a decadent British people deprived of Roman military protection. Chapter 12 closes with the Britons suffering brutal Irish and Pictish raids. Their appeal for aid to the Roman commander Aëtius in Gaul failed and they determined (in chapter 14) to call in Saxon aid 'from across the seas'. To Gildas this was an act of blind stupidity, but Bede reinterpreted it as 'ordained by the will of God so that evil might fall upon those miscreants [the Britons]'. He then focused on the arrival of the English in chapter 15, emphasising their martial qualities.

Although he returned to it later, in mid-chapter Bede abandoned Gildas's account, offering a passage describing the 'Anglo-Saxon Settlement':

> They came from three very powerful German peoples, the Saxons, Angles and Jutes. The people of Kent and the inhabitants of the Isle of Wight are of Jutish stock and also those opposite the Isle of Wight, that part of the kingdom of the West Saxons which is today still called the nation of the Jutes. From the land of the Saxons, that is the

region now called the land of the Old Saxons, come the East Saxons, the South Saxons [and] the West Saxons. And besides, from the land of the Angles, that is that homeland which is called *Angulus*, between the provinces of the Jutes and the Saxons, which remains deserted from that time right up to the present, came the East Angles, Middle Angles, Mercians and the whole race of the Northumbrians. . . . Their first leaders are said to have been two brothers Hengest and Horsa, and later Horsa was killed in battle by the Britons and in the eastern part of Kent there is a monument bearing his name. They were the sons of Wihtgisl, whose father was Witta, whose father was Wecta, whose father was Woden, from whose stock the royal families of many kingdoms claimed descent.

2.3 The geography of Bede's description in *The Ecclesiastical History* (I, 15) of the foundation of Anglo-Saxon England. Boundaries equate with those thought to be in place in the later seventh/early eighth centuries but are necessarily approximate

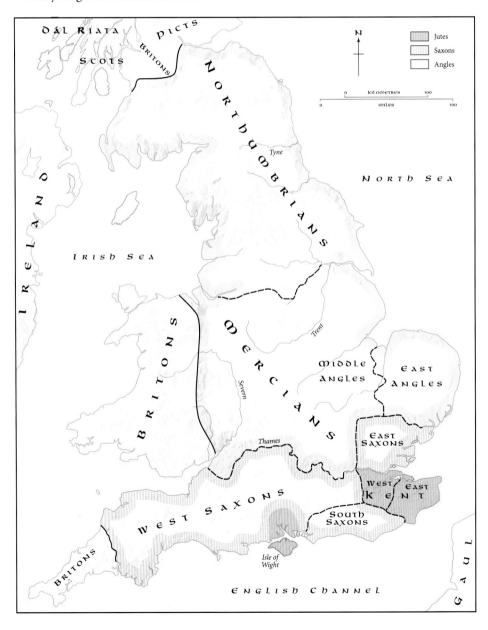

This was added late in the writing process. Since Kent opens and closes the account, the work probably derives from Canterbury. The political geography is that of the early eighth century; the *History* contains repeated references to the present and the closing genealogy owes debts to the Jutish settlement story at the beginning – the names Wihtgisl and Wecta derive from vernacular and Latin names for the Isle of Wight. This reads, therefore, as an early eighth-century reimagining of the settlement history of the English, framed according to the geopolitics of the present. It has little historical validity.

Bede then reverted to Gildas, developing his notice of a second, larger force into a vast horde of incomers, then followed through Ambrosius's leadership of the Britons to close with the siege of Mount Badon where 'the Britons gave not the least slaughter to their enemies'. The next five chapters of the *Ecclesiastical History* are based on Constantius's *Life of Germanus*, written at Lyon c. 460–480, from which Bede took Germanus's two visits to Britain and his 'Alleluia' victory won over the Saxons and Picts. Bede's focus here is, however, primarily on the moral failings of the Britons. The ultimate chapter, prior to introducing Gregory's mission to the English (in I, 23), then reverts to Gildas's account. There is external peace but civil war, the continuing ruin of cities, the collapse of 'truth and justice' and wholesale moral meltdown. Bede closes with the comment that to Gildas's complaints against the Britons should be added the crime of never preaching the faith to the English, but God had appointed worthier 'heralds of the truth' as missionaries, so prefacing Augustine's arrival in the next chapter.

There are differences, therefore, in the ways that the 'Anglo-Saxon Settlement' was portrayed in the 'Greater Chronicle' and the *Ecclesiastical History*. These are not just a consequence of Bede having additional material in 731 but reflect his changing purposes. In 725 he was weaving insular material into a universal chronicle intended to provide a chronologically framed Christian understanding of the passage of time, within which the English claimed Britain by conquest. In 731 the early passages in the *Ecclesiastical History* explained to a wider audience that the moral failings of the Britons had led to their abandonment by God and consequent loss of Britain, a cautionary tale for a Northumbrian audience whose territory had shrunk significantly since 685. Bede's purposes required that these two peoples be entirely separate, each having an independent relationship with the Lord. An English 'arrival' which featured large-scale folk movement was therefore essential in the *Ecclesiastical History*. Of Bede's several versions of the settlement story, though, this is the furthest removed from his sources and has no independent value.

If we focus instead on Bede's sources, it is striking just how few these are and how little they say. Gildas's account clearly provided the backbone, but was adapted differently in these two works. Constantius's *Life of Germanus* offers only one passing mention of Saxons. Focusing on Gildas has the advantage of using a nearer-contemporary account than Bede's, but the *Ruin of Britain* is problematic as regards its chronology, its geography, the characters involved, and the actual outcome of the war between Britons and Saxons. That said, Gildas clearly had an abiding hatred of the Saxons; he portrayed them as dangerous warriors, slave-takers and raiders, who both controlled territory and were a force to be feared at the time of writing.

The other main 'British' texts of the period are Patrick's *Confession* and *Letter*, probably both written in Ireland in the mid-fifth century, but neither mentions Saxons, though they do reveal a chaotic world of slave-raiding on both sides of the Irish Sea. A letter of the Gaulish bishop Sidonius Apollinaris around 480 to one Namatius, who was employed by the Visigoths in Aquitaine on 'half military, half naval duties' refers to Saxon pirates. Before leaving the Continental coast, they would, he alleged, sacrifice a tenth of their captives by drowning. These may have been Britain-based Saxons, shipping slaves back to England.

One other source, the so-called *Gallic Chronicle of 452*, refers to Saxon success in Britain in 441:

> The British provinces even at this time have been handed over across a wide area through various catastrophes and events to the rule of the Saxons.

This was written in southern Gaul, almost certainly by a cleric not personally acquainted with Britain, so there are issues regarding its reliability, but it was probably composed in the early 450s, making it near contemporary. Overall, the *Chronicle* records major events in the Western Empire, with Britain mentioned several times from the 380s onwards. The author was writing for a clerical audience, but provided an outline of the career of Aëtius, the major 'Roman' military leader in Gaul until his death in 454. Even if we cannot have complete confidence in it, this remains the nearest-to-contemporary comment now available and should be accepted with some caution. What constituted these 'catastrophes and events' is not explicit, the author merely acknowledging that the story was more complex than he was recording. The one overriding 'fact' here was the fall of the old diocese ('the Britains') 'widely' to the Saxons barely a decade before this chronicle was written. That Saxon 'rule' in Britain should be a matter of record a mere 12 years after Bishop Germanus's first visit reflects the shift of military power to the raiders. It likewise makes a mockery of Constantius's remark that Germanus left Britain 'a most wealthy island', 'secure in every sense'.

Archaeology

In areas such as the Middle Thames Valley and Somerset, British-style burials continue to 500 and even beyond. At Poundbury, Dorchester, a settlement, perhaps a monastery, developed on the well-used Romano-British extramural cemetery. Some urban sites also show signs of continuing occupation to the mid- or even late fifth century. But overall, archaeologists struggle to identify distinctively British material culture by the 430s. In eastern England and the Upper Thames Valley, we see instead new burial practices associated with novel types of artefacts and different styles of architecture. We use the term 'Anglo-Saxon' to distinguish this new and distinctive archaeology. It will be used here but it must be stressed that archaeology provides insights into material culture and behaviours, not race.

Anglo-Saxon archaeology has a long history. Seventeenth-century writers described ploughed-out burials. Purposeful digging began in the late eighteenth, with the campaigns of Bryan Fausett and James Douglas on Kentish barrow cemeteries. Douglas was the first to identify his finds as Anglo-Saxon, as opposed to Roman or British. His interpretation finally prevailed in the mid-nineteenth century, when scholars connected finds from graves with Bede's description of the Anglo-Saxon Settlement. They linked such distinctive artefacts as saucer brooches with 'Saxon' areas, and cruci-form brooches with 'Anglian' ones. The resultant framework has long structured the whole subject, with 'Saxon' archaeology in the Upper Thames Valley and across much of southern England distinguished from 'Jutish' in Kent, the Isle of Wight and Hampshire, and 'Anglian' in the east. Similarities in pottery and metalwork from England and north-west Germany/southern Denmark and Lower Saxony confirm that the English were connected with or had come from this part of the Continent.

Archaeologists experience problems with dating their finds which they address by developing relative chronologies of manufactured goods, based on the stylistic changes to which they were subject – a method known as typology. Typologies are anchored by grave assemblages on the Continent, where coin-dating is possible much later than in England, but even so the chronology of the later phases is weak. Not only do styles overlap chronologically as well as geographically but also the age of artefacts when they were consigned to the ground varies widely, with some freshly made and some already generations old.

Initially archaeologists working on Anglo-Saxon sites viewed their role primarily in terms of elaborating and illustrating an 'English Settlement' story reaching them from historians. This 'migrationist' or 'culture-historical' approach is well illustrated by J. N. L. Myres, who updated his original pre-war study in 1986, remarking (p. 24):

> Much can certainly be learnt of the course and character of the invasions from the distribution pattern of cemeteries and settlements in relation to the geography and geology of those parts of the country where they are found. Even more significant does that distribution pattern appear when superimposed on that of Roman towns, forts, villas, and villages and of the roads that connected them.

By the 1970s, however, many archaeologists were less accepting of this dependence on history and keen to take control of their own agenda. They focused increasingly on broad, social and economic processes, and abandoned invasion as the principal expla-nation of change. The resulting 'processual' archaeology was anti-historical, reinter-preting the early Anglo-Saxon period as prehistoric and focusing on social structure, exchange mechanisms and access to resources, with little more than a passing wave to migration. But late twentieth-century scholars in turn challenged this 'processual' approach as too functionalist, inclined to generalities and overly simplistic, and advanced instead more nuanced, complex and theoretical explanations of the data. They imported cultural theory from other disciplines and embraced the diversity of material that characterises the evidence. Rapid technological developments and the far more detailed recording of recent excavations have enabled use of powerful computing packages capable of sorting massive data sets more quickly, effectively and sensitively than previously. In recent years this has allowed archaeologists to set aside the some-

2.4 Highly ornamented copper-alloy belt buckle plate from an early Anglo-Saxon grave at Mucking, Essex, with silver foil and wire detailing. Of late Romano-British manufacture in the style of late-Roman belt fittings, burial in an Anglo-Saxon grave may imply employment in early fifth-century Britain

what subjective categorisations of specific items that earlier prevailed in favour of analysis of whole assemblages.

The date at which Anglo-Saxon settlement began has long been a bone of contention. In the mid-twentieth century, Myres argued that a particular style of pottery, which he termed 'Romano-Saxon', was manufactured by Romano-British potters for a market consisting of Saxon troops garrisoning the forts of the Saxon Shore. This had the potential to push the *adventus* back into the fourth century, but his thesis collapsed when it was recognised that this 'Romano-Saxon' pottery shared patterns of deposition with other styles from the same kilns, so had been made for and used by the same assortment of customers as other contemporary styles.

Attention then focused on late Roman-type sword belts, found in graves across western Germany and the Rhineland as well as Britain, on the assumption that these represented barbarians who had served in the Roman army. In Britain, some belt fittings were locally made, but others came from the Continent. They are generally found in the lowland zone, at Richborough in Kent for example, where a late Roman military presence seems highly plausible, and at Dyke Hills, Dorchester-on-Thames. However, these may be Roman burials as easily as Germanic. More certainly barbarian are those found in early Anglo-Saxon cemeteries alongside more typically 'Anglo-Saxon' metalwork, such as the three from Mucking (Essex), from among the earliest graves.

Another possible indicator is the quoit-brooch style of metalworking. This fifth-century style originated in late-Roman belt equipment but was translated by British artisans into a unique style of chip-carved brooch. Examples are concentrated in England south of the Thames, but occur also in Gaul. Although items are not numerous, a high proportion were buried in early Anglo-Saxon graves and so may indicate use by Germanic mercenaries. Early examples are characteristically 'late-Roman' in style but later ones are increasingly 'Germanic', suggesting stylistic change under the influence of barbarian users. They were probably used as cloak fasteners, replacing the military 'crossbow' types of the late Roman period. Some eventually became female dress accessories, so final deposition could be a world away from their purpose when first made.

Burials

Anglo-Saxon cemeteries are characterised by two very different styles of deposition, inhumation – burial of the whole body in a grave, and cremation – the deposition of cremated remains, generally in a pottery urn. Cremation was a common rite across northern Germany in the fourth century, but furnished inhumation also occurred on both sides of the imperial frontier. There is a very strong connection between 'Anglian' areas and cremation, and 'Saxon' regions and inhumation, though this has become less marked as the number of cremations discovered outside the primary 'Anglian' areas has risen.

Different rites imply divergent ways of mourning the dead and perhaps also reflect differing social organisation. Cremations are the more obviously Germanic and are sometimes viewed as evidence of immigration; since cremation was very rare in fourth-century Britain, it is difficult to see the fifth-century rite owing anything to local practices. There are, however, also significant differences between Anglo-Saxon inhumations, a proportion of which are accompanied by weapons, jewellery and other material, and the Romano-British rite, which was rarely associated with anything more than the nails from boots, knives and/or coffin fittings.

Continuity in the use of a cemetery across the Romano-British/ Anglo-Saxon divide does occur (as Wasperton in Warwickshire, Sandy in Bedfordshire and Frilford I in Berkshire), but is rare. Most Romano-British cemeteries of any size were associated with towns and urban decline rendered them obsolete. Deposition therefore eventually ceased.

The number of early Anglo-Saxon graves so far identified runs to perhaps 25,000 in around 1,100 cemeteries, with discoveries still continuing. That this exceeds the number of known Romano-British graves suggests that overall population density was not the key factor in determining the numbers. Clearly, only a proportion of the population was buried in cemeteries in either period. To an extent inclusion in early Anglo-Saxon cemeteries depended on age. Although there are burial sites where numerous infants and foetuses occur (as Great Chesterford, Essex), they are generally few, suggesting that the very young were disposed of elsewhere. Other under-represented groups were probably the un-free and 'un-English', including Britons. Given the scarcity of burials found for this period in the great swathes of western and northern Britain which lack Anglo-Saxon archaeology, their low incidence across much of the lowland zone should not surprise us.

2.5 Silver quoit brooch, parcel-gilt, 68 mm in diameter, with bands of animals and masks. From grave 13 in the Anglo-Saxon cemetery of Howletts, Kent

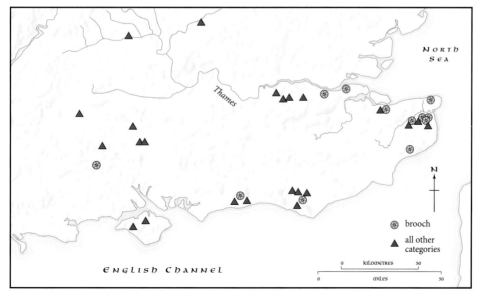

2.6 Distribution of the quoit style of fifth-century metalwork in Britain

2.7 Insular distribution of
furnished Anglo-Saxon
cemeteries. Main picture: all
furnished Anglo-Saxon
cemeteries; (a) 'Anglian'
cruciform brooches; (b)
'Anglian' square-headed
brooches; (c) 'Saxon' saucer
brooches

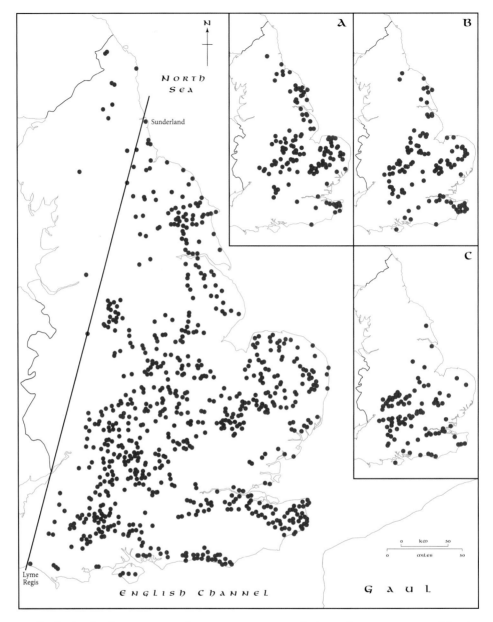

Early Anglo-Saxon cemeteries were concentrated along the east coast and in the Upper Thames Valley, later spreading across England east of a line from Lyme Regis (Dorset) to Sunderland (Tyne and Wear). In many areas they are comparatively dense, but there are gaps: some, such as the Weald of Kent and Sussex, can best be explained as seasonally used terrain, from which the dead were returned to cemeteries in core territories to north and south; others are areas where extensive marine inundation occurred at this date, such as the Fens and Humber wetlands. There remain, however, significant breaks, for example in Hertfordshire, parts of Essex, much of Suffolk and parts of Yorkshire, which suggest local variability in burial preferences that goes beyond the choice of inhumation versus cremation. Whether or not some of these represent 'British enclaves' is debated. Negative evidence offers only weak indications on which to judge, but the distribution links, for example, with literary evidence for British kingship in Elmet east of Leeds into the early seventh century.

Cemeteries were often laid out in or around some pre-existing monument. The commonest are prehistoric barrows (as at Uncleby, Yorkshire, or Millhill, Buckland (Dover) and Saltwood, in Kent), but numerous others are represented, from Neolithic henges through to Roman ruins, and also natural hillocks apparently mistaken for old burial mounds. Cemetery founders favoured landmarks on which to orientate burials, and particularly monuments already associated with the dead. The intention may have been to assert claims on the landscape, its management and its produce, as successors to those buried earlier.

Of known cemeteries, only perhaps 3 per cent are recorded sufficiently well for modern statistical analysis, and it is this data set on which modern scholarship principally concentrates. Around eight hundred cemeteries are broadly dated, however, with perhaps 60 per cent being fifth/sixth century and 33 per cent sixth/seventh, with only some 7 per cent running across both periods. The composition varies considerably, with 70 cremation-only and 175 exhibiting both rites (although this latter figure seems likely to rise as more are excavated), the rest being inhumation-only. While cremation was predominantly early, inhumation occurred across the whole period. With only a few early inhumations which could be of immigrants, cremations represent the initial horizon of Anglo-Saxon evidence. The earliest were deposited in the first half of the fifth century. Small numbers of un-urned cremations occur in late Roman cemeteries, such as Lankhills outside Winchester (Hampshire), and the two urned cremations of early Anglo-Saxon type from Wasperton are Carbon-14 dated to around 400.

Cremations occur across much of southern and eastern England, but large cemeteries are concentrated in Norfolk, Lincolnshire and eastern Yorkshire. The largest, such as Spong Hill (Norfolk), Sancton (Yorkshire) and Cleatham (Lincolnshire), each contain more than 1,500 burials, which implies user populations in excess of 500, arguably spread across a district. Such a cemetery served as a focal point on which groups periodically converged. Although Continental parallels suggest that pyres normally burned within cemeteries, such are rarely identified in England; rather, cremation seems to have taken place elsewhere and the burnt remains were then transported for interment. Burial was a public spectacle laden with symbolic meaning. Correlations between the age, sex and wealth of the dead person and the size, ornamentation and shape of cremation urns suggest that those responsible commissioned vessels appropriate to the individual.

Some cemeteries have structures associated with interments, as the four-square posts set around burials at Apple Down, Sussex, interpreted as 'cremation-houses'. Urns were often grouped and 'family plots' can sometimes be discerned. At Cleatham the use of small plots to bury individual pots successively in intercut pits revealed the relative chronology of such burials. Most urns, though, come from pits which were not intercut.

Most cremation urns contain no grave goods, but perhaps 10 per cent have at least one piece of toiletry equipment, such as tweezers, razors or bone or antler combs.

2.8 Seven intercut cremation urns at Cleatham. Suggestive of a family group, all were covered by large stones, one of which is visible in the foreground

These occur in the graves of the young as often as of adults. Some had gone through the cremation process, others were added post-cremation. Cosmetic equipment may have had particular value in the context of a funeral. Other goods often accompanied the body to the pyre or were added later, and a minority of urns contain glass beads, small vessels, combs, brooches and/or spindle-whorls. Larger items, such as swords, spears or shields, only appear very rarely but may have been on the pyre.

By the end of the fifth century a secondary, generally undecorated vessel (or even two), containing the cremated remains of a horse, frequently accompanied the primary urn. These burials were neither age nor sex specific. The horses were not necessarily riding animals. Unlike the far rarer horse burials in inhumation cemeteries these were not status-related, but were perhaps symbolic of a particular social or religious grouping. That the traditional leaders of the first Saxon settlers both had names meaning 'horse', Hengest and Horsa, may reflect this animal's significance. Later objections by papal emissaries to the English 'mutilation' of horses may be linked.

Anglo-Saxon cremations exhibit close similarities with cemeteries in the 'Elbe-Weser triangle' of northern Germany and the German-Danish border regions of Schleswig, Holstein, Mecklenburg and Fyn, with 'Saxon' types of decorated vessel relating particularly to the first and 'Anglian' styles to the second. However, these styles were already mixing on the Continent by the late fourth century, and the degree of regional conformity in England is less than was once suggested. Such is the diversity of artefacts that to date no Anglo-Saxon cemetery has been definitively tied to a specific place of origin in Germany as if the result of migration en bloc to Britain. Material culture seems to have altered as a consequence of both migration and colonisation; additionally non-migrants assimilated the new material in unpredictable ways. Some English cemeteries reveal multiple associations across their periods of use. Communities may even have cultivated differences in the use of material culture as a means of distinguishing themselves from their neighbours.

Inhumations provide us with very different information, offering fuller skeletal and artefactual evidence, with occasional fragments of fabric and other furnishings. Very large inhumation-only cemeteries do not occur; graves number from a score or so to a few hundred, so most probably they represent settlements of perhaps 20–60 individuals. Cemeteries seem to have been well organised, with just one or two main orientations of the graves and intercutting so rare as to suggest surface-markers. West/

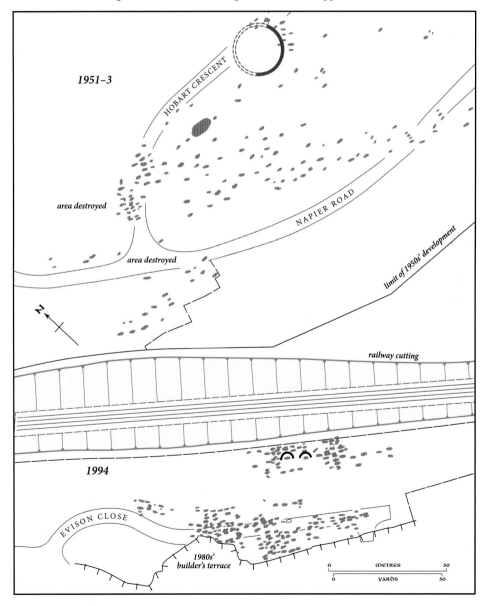

2.9 Plan of the fifth- to sixth-century inhumation cemetery at Buckland, near Dover. The northern part was excavated by Vera Evison in 1951–3, the southern by the Canterbury Archaeological Trust in 1994. The area between was destroyed by a nineteenth-century railway cutting

east burial is common and differs little from Romano-British practice, although at some cemeteries, as Castledyke South, Barton-upon-Humber, orientation is more variable than for late Roman-period graves. Most burials consist of a single individual face-up (supine) and extended, although legs are sometimes flexed or the body crouched. Multiple burials are found occasionally, with more than one body sharing a grave, but most have a single adult and child, probably a mother and her offspring.

Skeletal condition varies: while little bone survives in cemeteries dug into sand, gravel or clay, on chalk or limestone skeletons are often well preserved. Burials in good condition can be aged (although determination is imprecise beyond about 45) and sexed (although this is problematic below 20). Overall health generally appears to have been good, particularly as regards tooth decay, which, without refined sugar, was less than in modern populations, and some individuals can be shown to have survived serious illnesses, broken limbs or even surgery. Occasionally the cause of death is clear, particularly when that was violent, although injuries likely to have resulted from warfare are rare.

The determination of sex biologically can be compared to indications of gender in the grave goods. In a small number of cases males are found with jewellery, which is otherwise characteristically female. The number of males buried with annular brooches at West Heslerton, North Yorkshire, for example, suggests that here this was normal. Elsewhere, as at Buckland (Dover), women were occasionally buried with weapons. Where sex has not been biologically determined, therefore, there is a small risk that determining gender solely by artefacts is inaccurate. Overall, though, grave goods generally fluctuate in quantity and type according to the age and sex of individuals,

2.10 One of several skulls showing clear signs of sword slashes excavated from a cemetery at Heronbridge, Cheshire. It is likely that this individual was one of the casualties of the Battle of Chester, c. 600

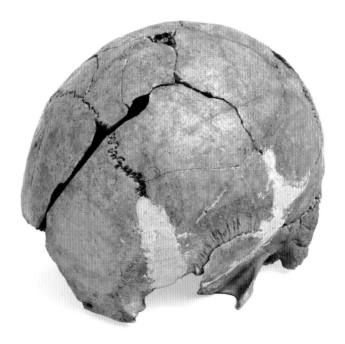

with masculinity and femininity determining clothing and associated artefacts. Perhaps half of both sexes were buried with none. Young children were generally associated with gender-neutral objects, then between the ages of 7 to 12 artefacts deposited were increasingly gendered, although often having the appearance of hand-me-downs. Such individuals were treated as young adults.

As yet only a few warrior graves have been found dating from the early to mid-fifth century, but these rise as a proportion of adult male graves to peak in the mid-sixth century at close to 50 per cent. By far the commonest weapon is the spear, occurring in 80 per cent of weapon burials, with shields in around 50 per cent, and other weapons (including axes, arrows and swords) in only 10 per cent. Weapons were the preserve of a warrior caste, defined most probably by birth, since a proportion of such burials were of juveniles or men too old or incapacitated to fight. The presence of board games in some warrior graves suggests that these individuals had leisure time, implying that weapons signified social rank. Other males were buried with knives, tweezers and/or shears, generally found at the waist as if they had hung from a belt. Bodies were buried clothed in day-to-day attire, in belted trousers with a tunic, some additionally wearing a coat and/or cloak.

The characteristic artefacts found in female burials are brooches of various kinds, strings of beads, sleeve-clasps (in Anglian areas), knives and items hung from a belt, most of which were in some sense functional. Brooches secured clothes, though they might be more decorative than utilitarian, so indicative of status and wealth. Brooches are central to the recognition of regional difference across early England. In 'Anglian' areas, annular, small-long, square-headed and cruciform brooches predominate, the full set having one on each shoulder and one on the chest, alongside girdle-hangers and sleeve-clasps. In 'Saxon' areas, disc, button, saucer and applied brooches outnumber other styles, often in pairs on the shoulders but on occasion in a row down the upper body, with pendants made from Roman coins and strings of beads worn across the pelvis. In 'Jutish' Eastern Kent and Hampshire, styles varied again, signifying different costume preference.

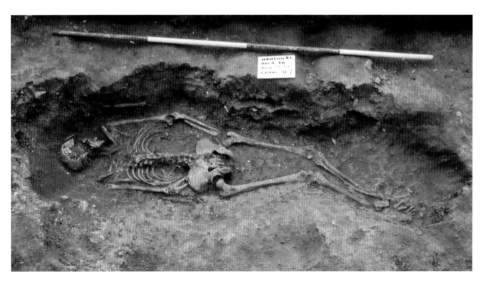

2.11 Cleatham grave 31, a prone male burial accompanied by spearhead (visible above the far arm) and several other metal artefacts including a buckle, all by the near hip. Good preservation of the bones reflects a comparatively deep grave cut into limestone

We can, therefore, identify regional patterns of brooch-wearing and variations in female dress, but some cemeteries reveal either more than one dress style in use at the same time or mixed styles, suggesting that 'Anglian', 'Saxon' and 'Kentish' fashions were far from exclusive. Indeed, East Kent exhibits 'Saxon' and 'Anglian' influences as well as the southern Scandinavian element characterised as 'Jutish', and there was additionally Gallo-Roman and Frankish material arriving. The unique 'Kentish' material culture developed, therefore, out of a rich cultural admixture of neighbouring styles in the maritime environment delimited by the English and Wantsum Channels. Numerous gold bracteates, many bearing images deriving ultimately from Roman emperors, mark an important distinction between this community and its neighbours.

The origins of these various different types of brooch are highly variable. Some derive from northern Germany/Scandinavia. Indeed, some early square-headed and small-long brooches were manufactured on the Continent and imported, though insular manufacture quickly took over. However, close attention to the location in the grave of even early imports or copies of imports suggests that their use was often unorthodox when compared with contemporary Continental usage. Only a selection

2.12 Some brooch types in Anglo-Saxon England: (a) square-headed brooch from West Stow; (b) cruciform brooch, and (c) annular brooch, both from Empingham II; (d) small-long brooch from Cleatham; (e) applied saucer brooch from Beckford

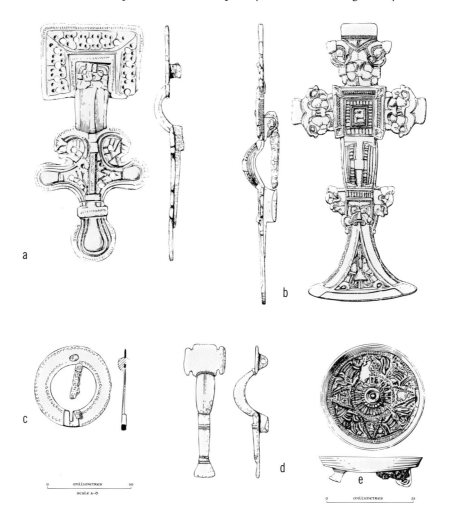

of the full range of artefacts available was introduced, making it uncertain whether such graves were those of immigrants. Other styles, such as disc, annular and applied saucer brooches, do not have close Continental parallels but actually originated in Britain, developing from late Romano-British metalworking traditions. Such traditions of working can even be identified on some insular examples of more 'Germanic' styles of brooch. Annular brooches – the commonest type of brooch in eastern England – lack close Continental parallels. Even these, then, may reflect 'British' influence in even that part of Britain most open to Germanic migration, though their appearance no earlier than the late fifth century undermines arguments in favour of continuity from late Roman Britain.

As in cremations, inhumations do appear to differentiate status within communities, although other interpretations remain possible. Those of lowest status, whether because of age, ethnicity or social standing, were probably excluded altogether. Those buried without grave goods were likely to be of lower status than those with, while the artefacts associated with a minority suggest a degree of affluence. The mid-sixth century witnessed a steepening of the social gradient visible in grave goods, with increasing concentration of brooches, for example, in fewer graves. These can cluster, as at Alton (Hampshire), perhaps signifying a small number of wealthier families. Even the richest burials, however, are dispersed across the cemetery, associated spatially with graves with poorer assemblages. These arguably represent leading figures within extended households rather than chieftains. As at Norton (Cleveland), there are sometimes comparable numbers of weapon-burials and women with full brooch sets, which may indicate high-status couples. Where groupings of graves suggest that there are household plots in use, there is a broad similarity in terms of scale and wealth from one to another, with status differentiated within the plot rather than between plots.

The Early Anglo-Saxons and the Laboratory

Scientific developments offer new methods of examining the 'English Settlement'. The longest established of these is palaeobotany. Human impact on vegetation varies with population size, among other factors, and it is interesting to note that across most of England there is little evidence from pollen diagrams of the large-scale reforestation that might have been expected had significant population decline occurred in the fifth century. Indeed, some diagrams even suggest increasing pressure on the environment. There are, of course, several ways to interpret this, one of which is to argue for large-scale immigration coupled with and alongside the displacement of comparable numbers of the indigenes. Certainly, there is literary and linguistic evidence of Britons emigrating, particularly to Armorica/Brittany, but the fluidity of population replacement required to avoid widespread abandonment seems implausible. The simplest explanation is to assume comparatively little disruption of farming, so of the farming population.

Another area of research has long been the investigation of physical anthropology in an attempt to distinguish incoming Germans from the indigenes, working on both ancient people and their living descendants. This began in the nineteenth century with

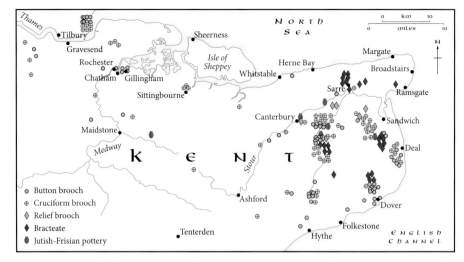

2.13 Finds in Kent indicative of Jutish and Continental North Sea coastal areas

experiments on the basis of cranial measurements (phrenology) and/or skin colour (nigrescence) to establish the extent of post-Roman migration. Racial stereotyping lost favour as a consequence of the Second World War but has since revived, in conjunction with its use in forensic science. However, cranial measurements reveal less variation between Romano-British and Anglo-Saxon populations than between Anglo-Saxon and medieval. Burials at Cannington, Somerset, for example, show so little change in measurements from Romano-British to Saxon that the populations were almost certainly the same.

Larger-scale study of selected Anglo-Saxon cemeteries has indicated that male burials accompanied by weapons tended to be of taller men than burials without. The conclusion drawn was that weapon burials were predominantly 'Saxon' while the remainder were more likely to be 'British'. That height might be indicative of race is plausible, but such factors as nutrition can equally cause stature to vary. There is less height variation correlated with material wealth in female graves. Given the apparent differences between regional groups of Romano-Britons and the presence of incomers

2.14 Copper alloy Anglo-Saxon button brooch from Harham Hill, Wiltshire. At the centre is a chip-carved face-mask and the brooch has traces of gilding. The decoration is derivative of quoit-style

from all over and outside the Empire, plus the polyglot nature of Anglo-Saxon immigration, detecting race archaeologically by such means remains fraught with difficulty.

An alternative is to focus on a particular part of the skeleton, in the expectation that systematic variations can be identified. Study of teeth irruption across populations identified on archaeological grounds as either 'Roman' or 'Saxon' has suggested that locality had more influence than burial styles. Skeletal similarities suggest that contiguous but culturally dissimilar cemeteries, such as Berinsfield and Queenford Farm, Dorchester-on-Thames, may have been used by the same population across the period, simply abandoning one burial practice in favour of the other.

Another approach is isotopic investigation of an individual's diet and lifetime mobility. Isotopes are atoms of the same element but with different atomic masses, the abundance of which varies systematically. They have long been used to explore what individuals ate but can also serve as markers of a particular environment. Oxygen isotopes vary with temperature and strontium with geology, so a study of these in teeth – where they are fixed from a comparatively early age – may distinguish locals from immigrants. To date, the best results come from Roman Britain. Late Roman cemeteries at York reveal a minority of individuals with exotic eating habits, from Central Eastern Europe, the southern Mediterranean and/or North Africa, confirming the heterogeneous population of this northern outpost of the Empire. At Lankhills, Winchester, excavations published in 1979 identified a group of burials which paralleled 'Pannonian' graves on the Danube, and these were interpreted as immigrant. More recently a further 350 burials have been examined. Isotopic testing has shown that the burial rite used is a weaker than expected indicator of geographical origin, with most of the 'Pannonian' skeletons exhibiting local characteristics. Further, a minority of those previously thought indigenous actually came from overseas.

So far, the extent to which such techniques have been applied to fifth- or sixth-century burials is very limited. A small-scale study on skeletons from the 'Anglian' cemetery at West Heslerton suggested that most of the sample had either grown up locally or came from western Britain, with only a very few from the Continent. Similarly, sampling of the less well-preserved Roman-to-Anglo-Saxon skeletons at Wasperton, Warwickshire, was consistent with the majority from both periods having been children locally, with immigration from western Britain and the Mediterranean but not from northern Europe. At Ringlemere Farm, East Kent, isotopic analysis of 8 out of 51 inhumations suggested that some of those buried had migrated from Frisia. Material evidence linked to Merovingian France and northern Germany and consistent with deposition in the mid- to late fifth century suggests that we are here seeing incomers. These are comparatively small data sets, however, and more confident interpretations must await further investment in this technology.

Another post-Second World War arrival is the sub-discipline of archaeogenetics, the study of aspects of the human past, including the dispersal of populations, by means of the analysis of genetic variation. Although there is hope that ancient DNA may eventually provide significant evidence, other than studies on Neanderthals and the Mesolithic/Neolithic transition the bulk of research so far has been conducted on modern populations, working back from the present to explore migrations in the past. This introduces a range of complexities not all of which have so far been resolved, including issues regarding the rate of the accumulation of genetic variation as a means of dating. At the level of Eurasia, significant patterns in the distribution of genetic variations have been identified across the past 40 years, which encourage the view that this technique has considerable potential for the study of history. Research on mitochondrial DNA, inherited exclusively from the mother, suggests only gradual genetic variation across Europe, but examination of the Y chromosome, inherited from the father, distinguishes an Atlantic Zone in western Europe, stretching northwards from the Basque country to include western parts of the British Isles, which contrasts with a Central European Zone including most of England.

The interface of these two zones was explored by sampling a series of small towns on a transect from Norfolk to Anglesey. Results in 2002 suggested comparative uniformity across England but significant differences from Wales, which researchers explained in terms of large-scale (50–100 per cent) replacement of the population of lowland Britain by incomers from Friesland, where similar genetic patterning was identified. Faced with widespread scepticism, one member of this team, with two new collaborators, suggested in 2006 that the same results could have been achieved through the operation of an apartheid system; if incoming males making up only an initial 10 per cent of the adult male population enjoyed a significant reproductive advantage, then they could have contributed as much as 50 per cent towards the gene pool. Whether such an initial advantage would continue over the several centuries required seems improbable, and basic assumptions regarding the underlying homogeneity of the 'British' and 'Germanic' populations are in any case implausible. But this second paper does open the door to new ways of interpreting such data.

A more detailed study of Y-chromosome variation, published in 2003, suggested similarities between all the different regions of Britain and the Basque country. Continental influence was strongest in East Anglia, the north east and the Thames Valley, and least in Wales, the south west and south eastern England. The study estimated Continental admixture averaging 38 per cent for England but only 13 per cent for Wales, yet assumed a uniform population prior to Continental migration and did not suggest any dating for the Continental intrusion(s). The English emerge from this work as less homogeneous than previously supposed, with data from parts of central/eastern England virtually indistinguishable from data from Scandinavia/North Germany but those for other regions differing more or less significantly. It is impossible to distinguish

2.15 The second dimension of Y-chromosome diversity in western Europe, derived from classical gene frequencies. Note similarities between the western British Isles and northern Spain, while eastern Britain conforms to the nearer Continent, to which it was joined in prehistory

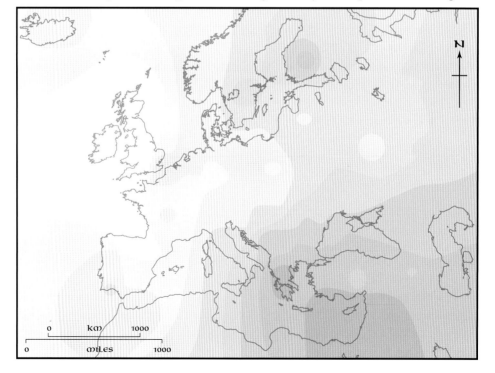

Anglo-Saxon from Danish genetic influence, making it likely that successive prehistoric, migration-period and Viking Age colonisations have magnified the effect in eastern England. By contrast, genetic evidence from southern England was comparatively unlike that from Scandinavia/North Germany, as it was also for southern Scotland.

A new synthesis of the data in 2006, on the basis of published work, concluded that the Y chromosome data from England had most in common with Belgium. If this proves a valid comparison, then the lack of any known migration from Belgium to England since the Roman period must cast doubt on the assumption that Germanic immigration had much impact on lowland Britain. This study concluded that the principal genetic traits visible within the British population were to a large extent established ten thousand years ago by recolonisation after the last Ice Age. However, while assumptions regarding rates of genetic mutation do vary from one study to another, the one used here was to date the slowest, which will have privileged early prehistoric migrations over those of the historic period.

Another recent overview does not favour dramatic population change in the migration period. While accepting that in this respect parts of eastern England are virtually indistinguishable from Scandinavia/north-west Germany, this stresses that the connection is not yet effectively dated, nor the numbers involved quantified. This study postulates a genetic admixture deriving in part at least from colonisation following the last Ice Age, when much of the North Sea was dry land, but then strengthened in the Neolithic and across later prehistory, as well as in the Migration Period and Viking Age.

Overall, therefore, while archaeogenetics undoubtedly offers an important new method of exploring the nature of the 'Anglo-Saxon Settlement', work in this area has not so far established the agreed parameters and common methodologies necessary to compare one study with another to best effect. Late Palaeolithic and Mesolithic communities were arguably highly mobile, but there is a very real possibility that once farming was established then tribal geographies would have tended to limit genetic exchange to comparatively well-defined regions. Tacitus's remarks on several tribes, as regards hair, skin colour and stature, suggest long-lived differences visible around AD 100, which may have survived to the fifth and sixth centuries. Modern studies need therefore to compare regional communities one with another, as well as with others outside Britain, so as to build up a better picture of local tribal differences as well as of transnational migration in the fifth and sixth centuries.

Settlement Archaeology

Although quarrying revealed the first buildings in the 1920s, early Anglo-Saxon settlements only became the object of systematic scholarly attention in the post-war period. The nature and quantity of artefacts deposited and the type of buildings found distinguish them from late Romano-British sites. All were timber-built, with roofs of thatch or wooden shingles, and structures generally fall into just two types, *Grubenhäuser* or 'Sunken-Featured Buildings' (SFBs), and 'post-hole buildings', 'houses' or 'halls', which appear in various combinations. While there are some sites where Roman-Saxon continuity can be postulated (as at Barton Court Farm, Oxfordshire, and Orton Hall

2.16 Sunken-Featured
Building under excavation at
the early monastic site at
Lyminge, Kent

Farm, near Peterborough), in no case is this certain and these are a small minority of places excavated to date; most early Anglo-Saxon settlements were established on sites which were previously unoccupied, but not necessarily unused.

Grubenhäuser, which were the first building type to be identified, are characterised by a shallow flat-bottomed pit of roughly oval or rectangular shape and less than 1 metre deep, which defines the bulk of the interior; most are comparatively small, measuring rarely more than about 8 metres × 5 metres. Set around the pit, some feature two, four, or six paired post-holes which supported a superstructure, with dwarf walls perhaps of turf. Entrances are rarely identified. The pit base has often been viewed as the floor of the SFB (as at Mucking, Essex), but examination of those excavated at West Stow (Suffolk) concluded that suspended wooden floors spanned the pit. Both views have found support, but recent study favours suspended floors.

SFBs were initially interpreted as 'pit dwellings', but the discovery of larger post-constructed halls led to a rethink. The frequent presence of loom weights has encouraged interpretation as weaving sheds, as was assumed at Catholme (Staffordshire), but in practice weaving is more likely to have occurred outside or in post-hole buildings. Many *Grubenhäuser* may have been grain stores, which are not otherwise evidenced. Loom weights in the pit-fill derive mostly from later rubbish disposal. Given literary evidence for sleeping accommodation being separate from the hall, an alternative would be to see some fulfilling this function, and there are clearly other options. The pits stand out on aerial photographs or ground surveys, making SFBs a defining feature of many early Anglo-Saxon settlements, but they are not always present.

'Halls' are larger but less clearly visible, since they are defined only by the post-holes marking their walls. They are almost uniformly rectangular in plan with soft corners, generally measuring 6–11 metres long and approximately half as wide. The majority provided only a single room but some had an internal wall dividing the interior into unequal spaces. Entrances are generally at the centre of the long sides, facing each other, in a style reminiscent of Bede's description of King Edwin's hall in the *Ecclesiastical History*. Evidence of a hearth is rare; structural evidence at West Heslerton (North Yorkshire) suggests that these buildings commonly had timber floors supported by the external walls. Halls are less obviously Continental in origin than are SFBs: excepting a recent excavation at Eye (Suffolk), the great aisled buildings shared with animals which are common in western *Germania* barely occur in England. These post-hole buildings have as much in common with late Romano-British timber-framed buildings as with the lesser buildings found on German, Dutch and Danish settlements, and it seems reasonable to assume a degree of input from both traditions.

These settlements generally lack boundaries, sprawling across the landscape in ways that make them difficult to excavate in totality. Similar settlements on the Continent have been interpreted as 'shifting' or 'wandering'. In England, however, the degree of 'shift' varies considerably. Mucking (Essex) has been interpreted in terms of long-running settlement mobility. Excavation revealed a multi-period landscape including Romano-British enclosures and a cemetery abandoned in the later third

2.17 Loom weights at the base of an SFB at West Heslerton. Such finds have encouraged the view that Sunken-Featured Buildings were often used for weaving but in most instances they form part of the refuse thrown in after structural use had finished, when they became rubbish tips

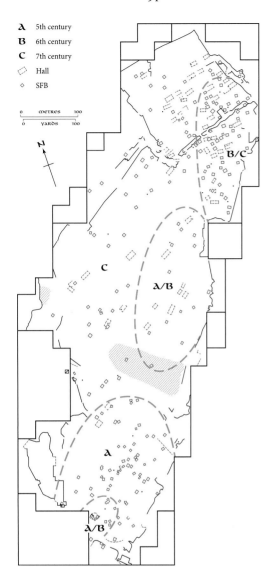

5th century
6th century
7th century
Hall
SFB

metres 100
yards 100

N

B/C

C

A/B

C

A

A/B

2.18 Plan of the Anglo-Saxon
settlement at Mucking, Essex.
Phasing from the fifth century
through to the seventh

century, after which the Anglo-Saxon settlement was established, with in total 53 post-hole buildings and 203
Grubenhäuser. The settlement began in the early fifth century
and had perhaps 100 persons at any one time using at least 10
halls and 14 SFBs. Although the size of buildings offers little
evidence of social differentiation, the wealth of artefacts in
some graves does imply a degree of hierarchy. This was interpreted as a shifting settlement made up of households whose
principal figures were distinguished by the weapons and
jewellery deposited with them.

West Stow (Suffolk) similarly suggests successive
replacement of the buildings, but it retained a more stable
location: 14 halls were associated with 69 SFBs, interpreted as
perhaps 4 households. Each had a substantial hall and several
SFBs, all of which were occasionally rebuilt across the fifth–
seventh centuries. Finds from the settlement were not
numerous, but the associated cemetery (dug in the nineteenth
century) yielded weapons and a variety of brooches. Such
artefacts imply that households were comparatively large and
hierarchically organised.

Some sites, however, reveal more static occupation over
centuries. Catholme is a substantial settlement that evolved
from the fifth to the ninth centuries and saw numerous structural replacements on the same location. Another example is
West Heslerton, in the Vale of Pickering, where excavation has
revealed a 22.5 hectare settlement of some 80–90 timber-
framed buildings and 140 *Grubenhäuser*, and its cemetery.
The Anglo-Saxon settlement replaced Romano-British road-
side occupation slightly lower down the valley slope, where
increasingly wet conditions led to abandonment around 400.
The new settlement developed upslope from a major Roman
site, interpreted as a shrine, which was well used across the fourth century and seems
to have been respected thereafter. The cemetery was focused on an older ritual landscape featuring a henge and round barrow. The new settlement was occupied for more
than four hundred years.

Unlike the situation at West Stow and Mucking, where *Grubenhäuser* generally
cluster around post-hole buildings, part of the West Heslerton village was dominated
by SFBs, suggesting that this was a craft or processing area where metalworking, textile
manufacturing, butchery and malting all occurred at some distance from the accommodation. The whole community was perhaps 75 individuals at any one time, organised within 10 households, each centred on one of the halls, which were constructed
very largely of timber, rather than wattle and daub, and benefited from high-quality
carpentry. Around 9,000 pieces of Anglo-Saxon pottery were found, although that very
large total is dwarfed by the 30 kilos from the Roman period, mostly from the shrine.

2.19 Reconstruction of hall-type buildings excavated at West Stow, Suffolk

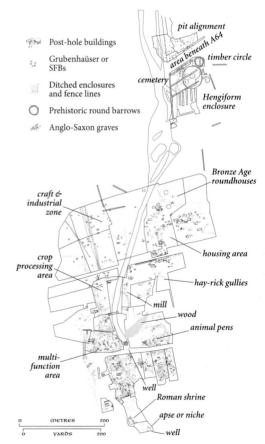

2.20 Plan of the large Anglo-Saxon settlement at West Heslerton

To set West Heslerton in context, the largest and most intensive campaign of aerial and ground survey ever attempted in Britain has explored an area of the Derwent Valley 8.5 kilometres long and 2 kilometres wide (at its widest), and discontinuously beyond that. This has revealed even larger settlements than West Heslerton at East Heslerton and Sherburn, identified by clusters of SFBs. Along the edge of the valley wetlands, and immediately above the Roman-period 'ladder' settlement system, a small Anglo-Saxon settlement has been identified approximately every 800 metres with a larger one every 2.5 kilometres, with some 1,300 *Grubenhäuser* identified in total. All these settlements seem broadly contemporary, implying intensive land use. Collectively, they mark the last phase of a period of landscape utilisation, stretching right back to the Bronze Age, which ended in the ninth century when the settlement was abandoned and the site ploughed.

Despite the comparative uniformity of building types across early Anglo-Saxon England, there are therefore different interpretations of the density of occupation and the structuring, use and management of occupied areas. Debates regarding the comparative mobility of settlement may reflect regional differences, but equally they may result from the comparative paucity of modern excavations and the problems of scale involved in tackling such extensive remains.

Language and Place Names

In 410 the inhabitants of the old diocese spoke either Latin or British Celtic (Brittonic) or both, with Latin most prevalent in the lowland zone. Similarly, early fifth-century

2.21 Half-excavated Sunken-Featured Building at West Heslerton. Large numbers of these in one part of the site suggest a workshop, storage and/or crafts area

2.22 Post-hole defined halls, as yet un-excavated, intermixed with SFBs at West Heslerton

personal names are either Latin or Celtic, with occasional Greek. Sub-Roman, Latin inscriptions found in Wales but with outliers in south-west England, south-west Scotland and northern England confirm that the higher-status language of Roman Britain survived as the standard medium of Christianity, but it otherwise died away. Although there are no inscriptions on stone in British Celtic, poetry was certainly being composed in the vernacular by the sixth century. British Celtic had adopted

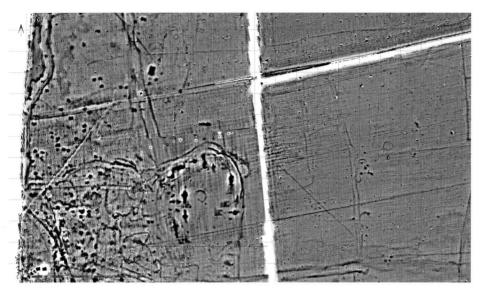

2.23 Detail from the geophysical survey of the Derwent Valley. The dark patches predominantly on the left are SFBs, indicating a large settlement at Sherburn, seen here against the backdrop of complex earlier archaeological enclosures

hundreds of Latin loanwords during the Roman period, when that was the more prestigious language, but borrowing reduced steeply thereafter as Latin's status declined. However, contact with Latin or Latin-affected Celtic caused sound changes in Highland Brittonic (the ancestor of Welsh, Breton and Cornish), apparently stimulated by an influx of Latin-speaking lowlanders. These migrants were numerous but eventually adopted Highland Brittonic, importing sounds and structural features from Latin which others found sufficiently attractive to copy. The result was rapid language change, from which emerged medieval Welsh.

German was probably heard occasionally in late Roman Britain but only became common after the Saxon seizure of power across the lowland zone. By 570, Old English was widely spoken and already driving other languages out of lowland Britain. Setting aside a handful of scratched, usually single-letter or word inscriptions on metalwork, we have no written Old English earlier than c. 600 (and that only in much later texts), so discussion of its initial impact and historical significance necessarily rests on later place names and language.

English is a Germanic language in origin, which adopted fewer than 20 words now still in use from either British Latin or Brittonic before c. 600. The vast majority of England's place names are no earlier than Old English. While considerable energy has been poured into identifying pre-English names, new discoveries are too few to affect the overall pattern. Place name scholars have been among the most committed supporters of mass migration as an explanation of cultural change in the fifth and sixth centuries, arguing for sufficient incomers to overwhelm the local indigenes and swamp or marginalise their languages. This case is persuasive and of long standing.

There can be little argument with the data presented here, but there are issues regarding its interpretation. Taking language first, contact linguistics leads us to expect that loanwords are normally adopted by speakers of a substrate, low-prestige language from a superstrate, high-prestige one, and speakers of a low-prestige language become competent in the use of a high-prestige language far more often than the reverse.

Lengthy continuance of substrate status often leads to language extinction, as, for example, Latin's replacement of Gaulish in France, or Gaelic of Pictish in Scotland. Few borrowings pass in the opposite direction. The Roman conquest of Britain led to significant language replacement and/or bilingualism in the lowlands, and wholesale adoption of Latin loanwords into Highland British Celtic. If a Saxon military conquest rendered Old English the high-prestige language in mid-fifth-century lowland Britain, then we should expect English to have replaced pre-existing languages with only a low take-up of loanwords. That is precisely what occurred.

Evidence of contact should be sought more in the area of phonology. If British Celtic had already given way to Latin to an extent in south-eastern Britain during the

2.24 Celtic and Latin place names in England, excluding Cornwall. For simplicity, the symbols do not differentiate between probable and possible examples. Note the general west–east contrast

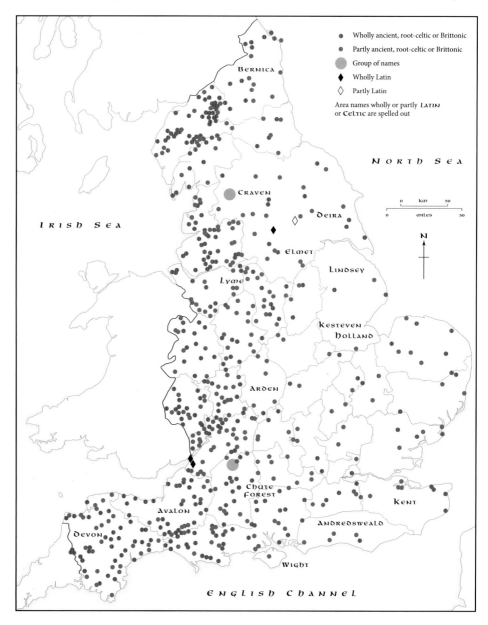

Roman period, then early Germanic incomers would have encountered both Latin and Celtic. There have been several attempts to show that British Celtic affected Old English structurally but these are contentious, occur mostly in the outer edges of England and are predominantly late, associated with the spread of English into the Pennines and western England. Earlier, contact with British, Celtic-influenced Latin may have caused phonological shifts as Old English separated from Old German, though these sound changes are fewer and less pronounced than occurred in British Celtic under the influence of Latin in the same period. It seems likely that the social interface was very different. While it was probably fashionable for Highland Britons to adopt a Latin-accented Celtic, Saxons are unlikely to have favoured a British-Latin, let alone a Celtic, accented Old English. Bede implies that language was a key marker of ethnicity in Britain. The low-key sound changes which Old English experienced as a consequence of contact with insular languages suggest that Britons seeking to anglicise found it necessary to learn the language of their conquerors very well indeed.

Place names provide important evidence of spoken language. The place names of Roman Britain seem to have been predominantly Latinised British Celtic, with a scatter of purer Latin. However, outside Cornwall (and to a much lesser extent northern Cumbria), comparatively few current place names in England were formed prior to the spread of Old English. Although there is a gradient of sorts from east to west, there is no other county in which pre-English names are even a significant minority. To take a north-western example, where more might be expected, Cheshire's four hundred or so township or parish names include barely 2 per cent which are Brittonic and none which are Latin (there is one possibly Latin-originating regional name, Lyme), along-side a very thin scatter of pre-English elements in minor names. Such eastern counties as Hertfordshire, Leicestershire and Suffolk have even fewer. Clearly, there has been a near complete replacement of the place names present in the Roman period in England (excluding Cornwall), far more so than in neighbouring regions across the Channel.

Large-scale Germanic immigration could have had this effect. However, Romano-British place names exhibit no better survival rates in Wales and Cornwall than in eastern England. In fact, one of the greatest densities of Romano-British names in continuing use lies along the south-east coast (Reculver, Sarre, Richborough, Canterbury, Thanet, Dover, Lympne). Clearly, name loss was a Romano-British phenomenon, not just one associated with Anglo-Saxon incomers. Research in this area is hindered by our ignorance of so many Romano-British place names – fewer than 250 are now known. Although there are major exceptions, such as London and Lincoln, many survivors, such as *Aquae Sulis* (Bath), are not now used. But there are also English place names which contain Latin words, such as *fons* ('spring': as Bedfont), *vicus* ('settlement': as Wickham, Nantwich), *campus* ('field' or 'plain': as Campsey) and *portus* ('port': as Portland), which may reflect the early adoption of Latin terms into the Old English lexicon across southern England. These borrowings demonstrate language contact, but they are noticeably few.

The lack of early written material means that we know very little about English place names before c. 670. Around 1900, it was assumed that place names containing references to pre-Christian religious practice or gods (as Wednesbury, West Midlands) and those with the element *-ingas* (meaning 'followers of-', as Hastings, Sussex) were early. This chronology of place name formation was overturned, however, in the 1960s. Pagan names now belong no earlier than to the late Conversion period and *-ingas* names are unconnected with pre-Christian cemetery sites so probably later than the Settlement period. Hitherto neglected groups, such as topographical names formed with such elements as -wood, -ford, or -hill, have at least as much claim to early formation as do habitative names.

Early literary sources imply that names have been replaced or adapted over a long time period. The number of pre-English names as a proportion of the whole data set recorded up to 731 is as high as 26 per cent, despite these being in the writings of Anglo-Saxon churchmen. Bede allows us an insight into the process of name-changing in the case of *Verulamium*, which was called by contemporaries in English either *Uerlamacæstir* or *Uæclingacæstir*. All three were eventually abandoned in favour of the saint's name, so St Albans, though *Uæclinga* survives in Watling Street.

The sequence Romano-British *Eburacum* – Anglo-Saxon *Eoforwic* – Scandinavian *Jorvik* – modern English 'York' provides a comparable example in which the modern name has changed so dramatically that had the several stages not been documented the connection would now be lost. Clearly place names were comparatively fluid across the early Anglo-Saxon period, with phonological changes occurring, different names or versions competing for currency, and non-English options the most easily lost. There is a strong bias in favour of major places in these texts; minor Brittonic place names were probably numerous to a later date and replaced gradually and not always very efficiently, leaving us sporadic evidence of early pre-English elements in later documentation for names of places, hills or minor settlements. Only river names seem to counter this trend, displaying a noticeable east/west bias with only major rivers retaining the earlier names in the east but more minor ones in the west.

It is perhaps worth challenging the assumption that it was necessarily speakers of English who inhabited places named in that language. Welshmen lived in some marcher manors with Old English names in Domesday Book, and such names may have occurred widely across England in the early Anglo-Saxon period, as speakers of British Celtic or Latin were slowly absorbed into Anglo-Saxon England and places were given new names under English patronage. Pre-English and English names were probably often in use at the same time, as Bede's comment on St Albans implies. The ninth-century *History of the Britons* provides alternative names for several places in England, which may still have had some currency locally among more conservative language users.

Finally, widespread evidence of rural settlement shift across the Anglo-Saxon period may help explain the high rate of name-changing. What we have in most cases is the name given in the last phase of this process, as recorded in the period c. 800–1100, in late Anglo-Saxon charters or Domesday Book (1086). Even some Old English names recorded by Bede are among those lost in the process. As relocation occurred, tied in with changes of ownership, social context and use, there was a high incidence of new naming. In this sense, name replacement reflects low levels of literate estate management and was arguably a natural corollary of other changes in the countryside. Most English place names are either possessive, so naming a landholder, or descriptive of

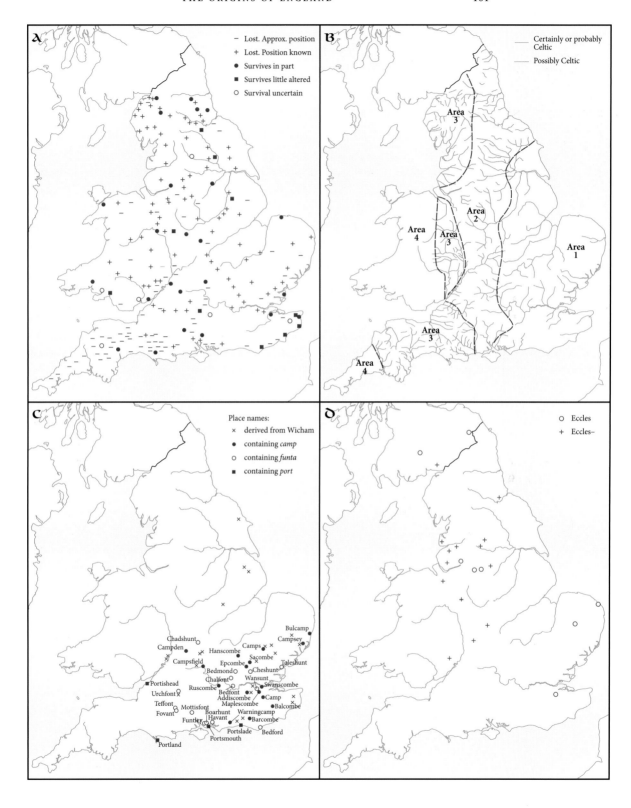

the topography in some way. That new generations of names were coined in Old English rather than Latin or British Celtic merely reflects settlement change occurring alongside language replacement.

Language and Social Structure

The early history of the Old English (OE) language affords some insights into aspects of migration-period social structure, value systems and religion. Although difficulties arise from the lack of dating prior to Anglo-Saxon becoming a written language, comparison with other Germanic languages allows an exploration of their collective roots, and Roman ethnography provides an anchor of sorts. Recent discussions foreground kinship, the assembly, lordship and the war-band as core social features. Kinship (OE *cyn*) was identified by Tacitus at the end of the first century AD as the basis of tribal armies, but large-scale warfare seems improbable in migration-period England. More importantly, kinship, as the first major social unit, provided protection to the individual, offering support in the assembly, in pursuing a feud, paying compensation (*wergild* or 'man-value') to avoid it, and finding oath-helpers. A kinless man was highly vulnerable. Feud was the principal mechanism for maintaining law and order and its threat the only meaningful disincentive to violence, pushing families towards negotiation and compensation. Maintenance of the kindred as a collective capable of action on behalf of its members was therefore a core responsibility of freemen.

Early Germanic society was largely structured around warfare, in the context of the kindred (feud), the war-band (feud/raid/mercenary service) or the tribe (tribal warfare). It is the war-band that provided the second major organ of society, headed by a leader who was the 'ring-giver' (OE *bēahgifa*) to his followers. Generosity required plunder or tribute, so a state of near-constant warfare. The war-band was held together not by discipline of the kind instilled in a Roman army unit but by personal loyalty to the leader, which might cut across tribal or kindred boundaries, as Bede remarked of the warriors gathered around King Oswine of the Deirans.

Tacitus portrayed the Germanic tribal assembly (the *thing*) as both a legislative and decision-making body which was attended by freemen in arms, who showed their support of proposals by clashing their weapons. This was, therefore, a military assembly, in which freemen had decision-making rights, even though led by nobles and those more skilled in the law. In OE the word denoting 'law', *áé*, is cognate with terms denoting 'custom', 'habitual practice' and 'religious ritual'. In pre-migration Germany, Tiu seems to have been the god of both war and law until displaced from the former role by Woden (whom Tacitus implied was earlier a Mercury-figure, the messenger of the gods), arguably in the process of migration. An assembly of those with the right to bear arms, bearing them in proof thereof, was central to Germanic society; the right to attend was a prerogative of the free-born, in contrast with un-free dependants.

At its lowest level, what we might term 'lordship' was invested in this class of freemen with the right to carry weapons. The OE term *frēa* can denote the lord of a household, which included dependants, and one who exercised authority over the household's land, as well as figures of higher rank, so 'chieftain' or later 'king'. OE *dryhten*, paralleling Old High German (OHG) *truhtin* ('war-band leader'), appears in *Beowulf*, for example, to denote 'war leader', so 'king', but *cyning* eventually proved the more popular term. This signified a chieftain in pre-migration Germany, but eventually denoted small-scale kingship in early England. The language of kingship reflects a shift from chieftain/petty king to large-scale kingships in the Frankish and Gothic worlds, when heredity gradually replaced election as the principal mechanism of appointment.

While such linguistic evidence is poorly dated, it has the potential to help us interpret other categories of evidence and aid our understanding of the migration period more generally.

Modelling the *adventus*

First of all, the broad context: Roman defence of the Empire's Atlantic and North Sea coasts collapsed progressively across the late fourth and early fifth centuries, leaving Britain open to raiders crossing the North and Irish Seas. That trade between Britain and the Mediterranean dwindled implies that piracy was endemic, as suggested in contemporary written sources. Raiding helps explain the appearance of late Roman material in Ireland, southern Scotland and coastal Germany, but diplomatic payments and the employment of mercenaries may also have played their part. Insecurity may have been another factor leading to high concentrations of late Roman hoards deposited in southern and eastern Britain, though interpretation of this phenomenon remains contentious.

Irish raids led to immigration into south-west Wales, in particular, attested both by ogham inscriptions (using an Irish alphabet of twenty characters) and Irish names in the genealogy of the Demetian kingship; an ogham inscription implies that at least one Irishman was buried as far east as Silchester in Hampshire. Units of Attacotti, from

2.26 Dumbarton Rock, stronghold of the British kingdom of Strathclyde

Ireland, appear on the Continent in the *Notitia Dignitatum* but may initially have been recruited in Britain. In Scotland late Roman material is concentrated particularly at Traprain Law, Edinburgh, Dumbarton Rock (near Glasgow) and Eildon Hill (above Melrose), all elite sites in the fifth century; similar deposition was restricted to Edinburgh and Dumbarton Rock in the sixth.

Without Roman oversight, the British diocese was reliant on its own resources. Short of military units and beset by raiders, British authorities employed barbarians, much as Roman leaders had long been doing on both sides of the Channel. Gildas's story of Saxons employed, reinforced, then in revolt is in broad terms plausible. Our early written sources suggest a military conquest, as opposed to mass migration, and this seems consistent with the comparatively small-scale archaeological evidence for Anglo-Saxons pre-450. The Saxons were initially, in essence, the field army of sub-Roman Britain. This would have numbered in the hundreds, perhaps even the low thousands, but not tens of thousands. When this force rebelled, it proved impossible to counteract and Saxons seized power. The nearest contemporary source available, the *Gallic Chronicle of 452*, points to Saxon 'rule' over large parts of the old diocese established in 441. Archaeologists date the earliest Anglo-Saxon burials at latest to the second quarter of the fifth century, and British employment of Saxons seems broadly to coincide with the career of Aëtius in Gaul, from the 430s through to 454. Gildas's Saxon revolt, the Gallic *Chronicle*'s Saxon 'rule', the collapse of British taxation and coin-clipping, and the start of recognisably Anglo-Saxon burial probably all happened across this one generation. Collectively they mark the beginnings of Anglo-Saxon England.

The problem still remains as to why Anglo-Saxon material, ideological and linguistic culture attained such dominance in the British lowlands, compared, for example, with the Frankish impact on Gaul, where the incomers gradually acculturated, adopting Gallo-Roman Latin and Christianity and establishing little more than their name. One solution is to assume that cultural impact was proportionate to the numbers migrating, necessitating unusually high levels of immigrants settling England. Critics of this model in the late 1980s and early 1990s argued that this was overly simplistic. They developed alternative models featuring acculturation, 'anglicisation' and elite dominance or emulation. These models supposed that the culture of comparatively few Germanic incomers had eventually been adopted by the whole community, much as Romanisation worked previously.

Looking across the several disciplinary approaches explored here, there is clearly still a long way to go before we are able to comment authoritatively on the whole issue of migration into and out of Britain. Overall, however, the evidence favours large-scale population continuity alongside significant migration. This is the simplest means of interpreting the palaeobotanical evidence, which is the most mature of the scientific data sets. Small-scale isotopic research has identified immigration from both northern Europe and western Britain into eastern England, but alongside far more evidence for continuity. The small number of tests, however, means that this can currently be no more than straw in the wind. Presently the evidence for Continental migrants is greater for the Roman period than for later.

Scholars have interpreted archaeogenetic research in different ways, but the case for a mass influx across the North Sea into Britain in this period is currently unproven and probably illusory. On balance, scientific approaches tend to favour an 'English Settlement' characterised as much by acculturation as migration, and with a majority of the population indigenous.

Considerable difficulties remain, however, for if elite dominance is invoked to explain dramatic cultural change in Britain, then why does it not occur elsewhere, for example in Gaul? Clearly we need a more sensitive model of cultural change than has previously been offered, capable of explaining the shift from a late Roman and British cultural milieu to the very different Anglo-Saxon one. This needs to take account of the particular circumstances in Britain and draw comparisons with neighbouring regions where the Roman–barbarian transition had dramatically different outcomes. What follows is no more than a preliminary, outline sketch.

Britain was conquered comparatively late, it was Rome's only substantial island territory outside the Mediterranean, it always remained a frontier province, to an extent at least dominated by the army, and Britons were never anything like so well integrated into the Empire as were other Western provincials. Unlike for Gaul and Spain, we know of no British individual who rose to imperial status prior to 400, attained a significant military command, held office as a provincial governor, rose to leadership in the Church or founded a major aristocratic lineage. Britons were despised and ridiculed by Roman literati, including Gallo-Roman authors. We should view Britons, therefore, as socially and culturally substrate within the Empire. Uniquely, Gildas's work acknowledges the divide: his provincial community is 'British' and he saw the Romans as different – and superior. What we have in later Roman Britain, therefore, is a 'Romanised' form of 'Britishness', rather than full *Romanitas*.

The collapse of coin imports perhaps triggered the final crisis. Successive rebellions led to a new effort by the leadership of the Roman garrison to emulate the achievements of Constantine I and secure the Western Empire, but this ended in disaster, leaving Britain under attack from raiders. The bulk of the British units guarding the south east went to the Continent in 407 but did not return. Britain's separation from the Empire occurred earlier and more completely, therefore, than in neighbouring dioceses, once Honorius's regime had failed to reclaim the island post-410. In this respect the Channel mattered. Although Continental authorities retained some influence, Britain was left in a no-man's-land, without military protection or legitimate governance.

By the 430s, many of the more 'Roman' attributes of British culture were falling away. There were no imperial appointees in authority. The towns were poverty-stricken and depopulated, with many buildings derelict and others in changed use. Alongside, coin use was in decline and the currency undergoing rapid devaluation, taxation was in difficulties, markets were ceasing to function, and many industries and trades had collapsed.

This contrasts with Gaul, where Roman garrisons survived and Roman leaders played a key role through to the late fifth century. Towns there retained populations within smaller walled circuits of citadel-type capable of withstanding siege, now refocused around cathedrals and under the oversight of bishops. In Britain, excepting Lincoln, there is little evidence of fifth-century cathedral building. Black earth deposits in many towns may imply their use as refuges by nearby country-dwellers but their wall-circuits dated from centuries earlier, when their population was at its height. Towns were increasingly indefensible.

Some scholars have suggested that the diocesan and provincial system collapsed immediately post-410, giving way to a multitude of small-scale societies. Such thinking rests on the assumption that larger and more centralised polities would have stood up to the Saxons more effectively. However, this is to compare two very different types of society, of which only the Saxon was organised for war. New evidence of fifth-century coin-clipping suggests the survival for a while of comparatively Romanised civil authority. On balance, our limited literary evidence implies that provincial society retained Roman forms at least until the Saxon revolt, but sub-Roman Britain arguably always had rather an interim look to it. The British polity overthrown by the Anglo-Saxons was far weaker ideologically, militarily and economically than Roman Gaul.

Nor were the Saxons much like the Franks, whose entry into Roman territory occurred across several generations, giving time for acculturation. Though they were numerous, the Franks remained predominantly on the periphery of the Empire, close to the frontier. Frankish kingship emerged across the later fifth century, and Clovis's conquests rapidly made this large-scale, providing a central organ capable of negotiating with provincial representatives and taking over imperial responsibilities. Like their Gothic counterparts, Frankish kings acted as diocesan authorities, collecting taxes, for example, minting coins and appointing governors. Critically, Clovis's military success provided a target for conversion. His adoption of Christianity offered the Gallo-Roman clergy protection and a role in the new polity. Frankish/Gallo-Roman cooperation rested on mutual self-interest.

In contrast, the Saxons were feared pirates then federate troops, then a rebellious army looting the diocese, all in the space of a comparatively short period. Success brought them wealth and overwhelming social power. The rebellious warriors cannot have been very numerous, but other war-bands were probably soon operating alongside them and we should envisage a comparatively chaotic scene in the mid-fifth century, with raiding parties and settlers but without the sort of coordination which Frankish kingship came to provide. Kingship had made little progress in northern Germany/ southern Scandinavia and the Continental Saxons still managed without kings in the eighth century. There is an important contrast between the low levels of social hierarchy evidenced within early Anglo-Saxon England and increasingly king-centric Francia. The British elite had less to bring to the table than their Gaulish counterparts by the mid-fifth century, lacking effective taxation, a sustainable coinage, major markets or defensible towns. There was not the same scope for cooperation as in Gaul, so little opportunity to negotiate a modus vivendi.

Early Anglo-Saxon cemeteries reveal a society gaining access to various metals, particularly silver, which do not occur naturally in eastern England. Some came from Continental Europe but most was recycled from the stock of silver in late Roman Britain. Whereas the Franks settled the frontier provinces of Gaul, leaving the heartlands below the Loire little affected, Germanic incomers to Britain seized the most productive British lowlands, taking control of the short sea crossings to the Continent and cutting communication between the most Romanised region of Britain and the Roman World. Later fifth- and sixth-century finds are concentrated in the newly 'English' areas, suggesting that the incomers increasingly drew down the residual wealth of Roman Britain. Plunder and tribute underpinned the early Anglo-Saxon economy, therefore, with a flow of goods and persons from British communities to Anglo-Saxon. This may help explain the presence of individuals apparently from western Britain buried in Anglo-Saxon cemeteries.

Circumstances in Britain and much of Gaul were therefore very different. The lowland British elites were less able to engage with barbarian military domination than their Gallo-Roman neighbours. Gildas refers to psalm-singing Britons fleeing over-seas. These well-educated Christians were probably members of the elite. Likewise some lowland Britons took refuge in the upland zone, again probably mostly the better off.

This does not mean that the lowlands were deserted. Archaeogenetics, palaeo-botany and landscape archaeology all suggest considerable continuity across the Romano-British/Anglo-Saxon divide. Numerous medieval field systems developed from Roman-period ones. That the archaeology of this community is elusive should not surprise us, given the collapse in deposition of recognisable artefacts in the late

2.27 The geography of the Anglo-Saxon Settlement: (a) distinctively Anglian, cremation dominant cemeteries and Saxon brooches of the second half of the fifth century plotted onto the late Roman provinces; (b) the division of southern Britain into different provinces based on river drainage. Correlations between these two maps suggest that the drainage pattern influenced both Roman territorial organisation and Anglo-Saxon settlement

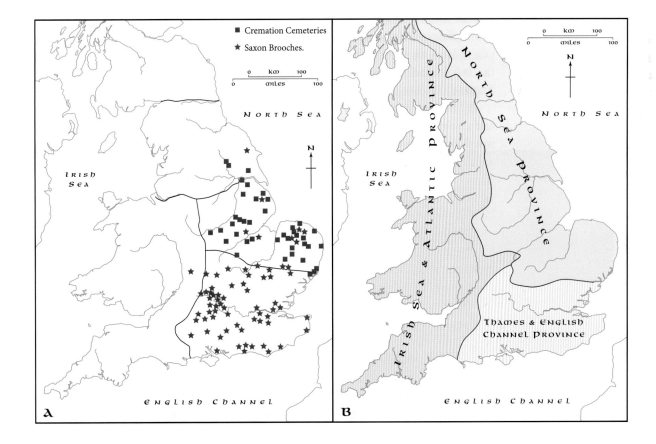

but enjoyed a wergild ('man-value') only half that of equivalent 'Saxons'. Interpretation of such a racially defined legal system bears comparison with Apartheid in late twentieth-century South Africa. Recent exploration of that parallel suggests that the disparity at law would eventually have led Britons to lose the bulk of their assets. Comparable differentials are also a feature of some Continental law codes, providing lower wergilds for Romans than barbarians.

As Bede later implied, language was a key indicator of ethnicity in early England. In circumstances where freedom at law, acceptance within the kindred, access to patronage, and the use and possession of weapons were all exclusive to those who could claim Germanic descent, then speaking Old English without Latin or Brittonic inflection had considerable value. The leaders of Anglo-Saxon households therefore had a vested interest in resisting the adoption of Celtic or Latin loanwords, structural influence and/or phonetic change, and even the use of non-English names for their own settlements, in case such might imply 'British-ness' in the occupants. Self-interest therefore probably reduced the impact of earlier insular languages on Old English. By adopting unaccented English, lower-status individuals gradually established themselves as 'Anglo-Saxon', and opened up opportunities for themselves and their descendants.

This is not to suggest that the fabric of late Romano-British society collapsed instantaneously or uniformly across the whole of the lowland zone. The very lack of large-scale hierarchies within early Anglo-Saxon society suggests that the takeover of land was comparatively piecemeal, affecting some localities even while leaving others comparatively unscathed. Kinship groups operated at a local level, creating small-scale tribal polities, even while war-bands ventured further afield. This was, therefore, the creation of small groups of peoples each consisting of a group of household units centred on assembly and burial sites, but early Anglo-Saxon communities were not ubiquitous: the absence of early Anglo-Saxon finds in some areas may indicate that the immediate impact was comparatively localised. 'British' carved stones at Wareham (Dorset), concentrations of pre-English place names in, for example, Wiltshire, Lancashire and West Yorkshire (the Pennine Wales), and the survival of pre-English cults at St Albans and elsewhere all point to very different local histories.

Such shreds of evidence imply that some 'British' communities and indeed whole districts escaped Anglo-Saxon land seizures for a while, but they are unlikely to have escaped tribute. Place names in *walh* (as Walton, Wallasey) may reflect settlements headed by Britons at a late date, when their scarcity made them distinctive, though this element does also occur in OE personal names and some place names may reflect this. Inter-regional contact and the growth of chieftaincies eventually encouraged even such local communities as remained distinctively 'British' to adopt 'Anglo-Saxon' cultural and social norms, including language.

This model of small-scale social transformation helps to explain the low levels of territorial integrity discernible across the fifth and sixth centuries. In Gaul, the basic units of the Frankish kingdom were the *civitates* of the Roman period, which were also the early medieval bishoprics and enjoyed a high incidence of name survival. In England, of all the tribal names of the early Anglo-Saxon period only Kent (the

Cantwarena) is recognisable as a direct descendant of the Romano-British *civitas* name (*Cantium*), with Lindsey (*Lindes Farona*) and the *Wrocensæte* of the north-west Midlands carrying forward the names of provincial or tribal capitals (Lincoln and Wroxeter respectively). Some tribal names derive from British Celtic, as Elmet and *Deira* in Yorkshire, but these may be post-Roman in date, contemporary with the new creations in Old English. All these names relate primarily to the people and only secondarily to the space where they were settled, again emphasising that it was the network of free tribesmen, articulated by assemblies, kin groups and war-bands, that was focal. When writing about northern England in the 1980s, I saw the sub-Roman period very much in terms of a 'Return of Tribalism' in both English and British versions. This sense of a shift from the administered Empire of Rome to a fundamentally 'tribal' Britain has since been endorsed more widely and provides us with a useful model.

Early Anglo-Saxons probably owned multiple social identities. At the bedrock of society lay the free-status family, with its claim to Germanic descent, presiding over an extended household, its dependants and its hide(s) of land. Working outwards this leads us to that family's ties of kinship comprising patrilinear and matrilinear connections. Another sense of belonging came from male membership, either present or past, of a war-band, and so links with that leader. Ceorls were involved too in communal management of the landscape, and this was probably a key aspect of local tribal identity. Above that there was membership of supra-tribal groupings and finally overall there was Germanic identity, with links back into Continental society and a major fault line vis-à-vis the Britons.

In late Roman Britain, citizenship, religious identity and legal status were all individual. The establishment of Anglo-Saxon England involved a significant shift in favour of the family, with personal status subordinated to that of the lineage and kindred. The centrality of the kin in early Anglo-Saxon society contrasts with the emphasis on the individual enshrined in both Roman law and Christianity. While on the Continent Germanic kings adopted both comparatively early, in England kinship remained central. Written law, when it began c. 600, was in the vernacular and still bounded by tribal custom. The closest parallels to early Anglo-Saxon England on the Continent come not from Gaul or Spain but the Balkans, where the Slav takeover similarly replaced the language of Empire with a new vernacular. There too we have a society devoid of steep hierarchies and equipped with a simpler technology than the Roman World which it replaced, without the minting of coins, without professional classes and without trading sites or officialdom, lay or secular.

THE ANGLO-SAXON CEMETERY AT SPONG HILL

NICHOLAS J. HIGHAM

Spong Hill, in central Norfolk, lies at around 40 metres above sea level on the southern end of a low gravel ridge above the valley of the Blackwater river, which at this point marks the southern boundary of North Elmham parish. Two Roman roads are thought to intersect nearby, suggesting that the site was easily accessible. Reports of cremation urns begin in 1711, when a local antiquarian wrote to the Royal Society on the subject, and an unknown number were dug out in the eighteenth and nineteenth centuries without being recorded adequately. Small-scale excavations occurred in the 1950s, then trial excavation and survey in 1968 established the risk of wholesale destruction from deep ploughing cutting into the subsoil. The Department of the Environment funded a series of annual excavations between 1972 and 1981 under the overall direction of Dr Catherine Hills, which has led to total excavation of the cemetery.

Spong Hill proved to be a mixed cemetery containing both cremations and inhumations but the vast majority were the former and this is best viewed as a cremation cemetery which for a period late in its life also attracted some inhumations. The original number of cremations is unknowable: 2,284 individuals have been identified from the bone evidence recovered from recent excavations but the original number deposited was probably 2,500–3,000 or perhaps even greater. This is the largest Anglo-Saxon cemetery so far explored, representing a burying population of perhaps 750 individuals at any one time across a period of 150 years. The size of the cemetery is such that it seems most unlikely that it could have been used only by the inhabitants of a single settlement; rather, it probably served as a place of burial for several communities across a wide district. One settlement contemporary with the latest phase of the cemetery has been excavated immediately to the west, consisting of 6 or 7 SFBs and 5 post-hole buildings, and others have been identified or are suspected in the area. It is as yet uncertain how extensive the territory may have been of those choosing to bury their dead here, but the location of a small Roman town nearby at Billingford and the later Anglo-Saxon diocese at North Elmham both suggest that over the long term this part of the valley of the River Wensum served as the focus of a significant area.

Prior to burial, cremation of the dead body occurred on a pyre made up of both logs and brushwood capable of reaching temperatures as high as 1200°C. The body was laid out on the top of the pyre fully clothed, most probably supine and extended.

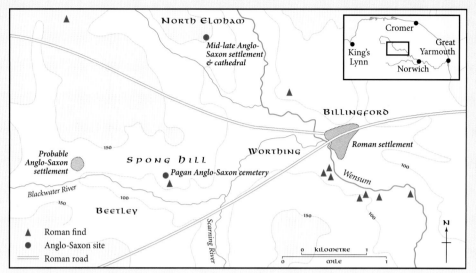

2a.1 Spong Hill. Location map of the cemetery's relationship with pre-existing Romano-British occupation sites and roads, as well as with Anglo-Saxon settlements

Together with the body, food and drink were often placed on the pyre, including joints of meat and/or suckling pigs, and some also had a horse or dog cremated with them. Grave goods perhaps reflect the status of the deceased and their family, as well as age, wealth and sex. The cremation rite was used for both sexes and all age groups. Where this occurred, however, is unclear: the intense burning that would have been indicative of a pyre was not found within the cemetery, suggesting that the actual fire occurred elsewhere, perhaps at or close to the settlement in which the dead person had lived. After the pyre had burned out, bones were collected. Although all parts of the body are normally represented in the burial urn, all the bones were never present, suggesting that sampling occurred at the pyre site. The cremated remains were then brought to the cemetery for public deposition in an urn, perhaps at a particular date in the calendar.

There is no simple correlation between the number of urns deposited and the number of individuals buried. While the vast majority of urns contained the remains of only one individual, in a small minority of cases two or more were represented, most often an adult with a child. In other cases two pots deposited as a pair were associated with only a single individual. In such instances, one pot was generally highly decorated while the other was plain. The undecorated vessel normally contained bones from a cremated animal; this is termed an 'animal accessory' vessel. However, division between the two of human and animal bones was often less than clear cut; a decorated pot might contain mostly human bones but some animal, paired with an undecorated vessel containing predominantly animal bones but with just a small number of human. Horses were the commonest animals involved in such deposits, occurring in around a third of instances and representing around 227 individual horses, with sheep/goat the next most common.

Two-thirds of the cremation urns contained grave goods. This is a much higher proportion than has been identified on most other English cremation sites, suggesting that excavation here has been unusually thorough. Grave goods included both items which had been burnt with the corpse and others which had been added to the fill of

2a.2 Plan of the cemetery.
Phase A cremations are
indicated in red, illustrating
the early distribution of deposition

● Phase A cremations (Total 485)

the pot at a later stage, perhaps even as late as the process of deposition. Manicure sets were particularly common in this context.

From the beginning, deposition was scattered across the whole site, with only a minor concentration identifiable at the core. This perhaps suggests that individual families or households established burial plots which they then maintained over a period of anything up to a century. During the final phase, though, deposition was concentrated particularly in the north of the site, along with the inhumations, perhaps reflecting a partial breakdown in previous patterns of behaviour.

Precisely when the cemetery first came into use is an issue currently receiving close attention. Excavation occurred before computing developed adequately to carry out complex analyses but recording of the finds was sufficiently detailed, burial by burial, for new techniques to be applied as they became available. Correspondence analysis of finds from the individual burials has since been used to explore the different combinations of artefacts found so as to build up a complex picture capable of telling us a great deal more about the chronology of and practice at this cemetery. Comparison of the various categories of finds with the vessels which contained them has suggested that the cemetery began early in the fifth century, since both combs and brooches deposited here parallel types known on the Continent across the later fourth and fifth centuries. Spong Hill has revealed copious evidence of Roman-period occupation. The back-fill of a late-Roman ditch contained fourth-century material but this feature then served to an extent as a boundary for the early cemetery, suggesting

2a.3 Cremation urns under excavation illustrating the density of finds in some parts of the site. A variety of styles and sizes is visible; some were sealed by stones, but plough damage has removed many, disturbing and/or breaking the urns

that its inception was not that much later and that the late-Roman boundary was still visible.

Analysis of the pottery has revealed three successive phases, termed A, B and C. Of these B – often characterised by lavish stamping, bosses and linear designs – can be dated by analogy with similar sites to the middle of the fifth century. Phase C pottery typically has comparatively little decoration but often features pendant stamped triangles; this begins c. 480 and runs into the first half of the sixth century. Phase A is very simple, with little decoration, and dates to the first half of the fifth century. Phase B is the earliest that is easily recognisable as 'Anglo-Saxon' in terms of decoration and style. This analysis demonstrates that the bulk of the cremations (1,500–2,000 individuals) were deposited during the fifth century, with the rite losing popularity and the cemetery eventually being abandoned at some stage around the mid-sixth century.

Phase C vessels generally occur on the periphery of the cemetery, along with the remains of glass vessels and ivory, which only appear in any quantity late in the sequence. Use of the same stamp tool on more than one of the more highly decorated vessels – predominantly of phase B – has allowed some progress to be made in establishing the relative chronology of manufacturing, with in all some 67 groups so far identified. Heavily bossed vessels are paralleled particularly well by examples found at Issendorf, near Stade on the Lower Elbe, but both Spong Hill and closely comparable Continental sites then continued to be active in parallel across the fifth century. These similarities therefore suggest ongoing contact between communities on both sides of the North Sea, and the repeated sharing of material culture and depositional behaviours, rather than a single migration event at the start of the fifth century.

Other parts of the assemblage also reveal debts to Continental material but from a variety of different areas. Three equal-armed brooches have close parallels in northern

2a.4 Cremation urn number 1564, belonging to the middle phase of deposition, B. Note the wealth of stamped decoration

Germany. The numerous miniature artefacts at Spong Hill are best paralleled in Denmark rather than around the Elbe while arm-clasps derive from Scandinavia and around 100 cruciform brooches derive from late Roman Nydam-type brooches from Jutland. While there are clearly very strong connections between the material culture found at Spong Hill and parts of Scandinavia and North Germany, this regional community in East Anglia seems to have been able to pick and choose the material they wished to adopt and/or copy, taking ideas from numerous different sources.

Whether he founders of the cemetery were Germanic immigrants remains in question, though it is difficult not to assume that there were some incomers. What is clearer, though, is that these communities were led by groups who looked to northern Germany and Scandinavia for the inspiration behind their material culture. However, they also deposited significant numbers of Roman objects, including small pieces of pottery of no practical value. It is unclear whether these were strays deriving from earlier occupation of the site or incorporated as markers of a valued material culture which was ancestral to this community.

Towards the later period of use, cremations overlapped with the use of the same site for inhumation burial. All but one of these took place in a distinct group on the northeastern periphery of the cemetery, with deposition occurring alongside cremation

2a.5 'Spong Man'. A unique clay urn lid, featuring a seated figure, probably male, probably of phase B. Whether this was intended to represent the dead person, a deity or some other figure is unclear

2a.6 Inhumation 40 fully
excavated, cut into the natural
ground surface at the centre of
an area marked by a slight
circular ditch, perhaps
originally limiting a barrow,
and flanked by further inhumations (right)

burial. Both rites then continued in parallel until the cemetery was abandoned. In all there were only about 57 inhumations, most of which were orientated approximately east–west, with the head towards the west. One linear arrangement of several graves was identified, with another possible. Most graves contained a single extended burial in a wooden coffin without metal fixtures, although a minority contained crouched burials. Of those that could be sexed biologically, 27 were female and 16 male but this leaves 14 unsexed, which probably includes some children. Biological sexing coincided closely with sexing via artefacts but a dozen graves with very few or no grave goods could have been male, which would render the numbers of males and females approximately equal.

A proportion of the metalwork finds were broken, repaired or very worn, while others were in very good condition and appeared comparatively new. Taken together these suggest everyday objects in normal use. Some burials were accompanied by pots or parts of pots containing food or drink but in others pots were represented by small shards which may have been token deposits, or had been deliberately broken. Elsewhere the finding of metal repair clips suggested that wooden bowls may have been present, perhaps in numerous instances. There were clear disparities in wealth between graves but none was exceptional: there was no gold at all and only three graves contained any silver objects. Exotic items tended to be deposited together with comparatively rich assemblages: for example, the only imported bronze bowl was found in a female burial with numerous other objects including a large gilt brooch and an iron weaving batten.

Two inhumations were particularly distinguished, each occurring in a wood-lined chamber with a timber and turf cover within a circular ditch, which may once have marked a low barrow, with numbers of large uncut flints used as packing. One of these, grave 40, has been interpreted as a founder burial marking the inception of inhumation here: this individual was buried with a sword in its scabbard, a spear and a shield, plus a bronze-bound wooden bucket but there was no trace of any coffin within the chamber.

Why a small group of inhumations should have been inserted into this large cremation cemetery is unclear. However, the cremations themselves show no signs of having been organised spatially in terms of sex, wealth or gender (as sometimes occurred on the Continent), implying that their organisation is most likely to have derived from social ties and family membership. It seems probable, therefore, that the inhumations represent a particular household or very small group of households that had for some reason adopted a different burial practice. Whether this was a group with pretensions to greater status and power than neighbours who were practising cremation is unclear but it is certainly one possibility.

Here cremation and inhumation ended at approximately the same time but regionally cremation gave way to inhumation across the sixth and early seventh centuries. Inhumations were generally deposited in smaller cemeteries more likely to have been exclusive to particular settlements, so perhaps we should anticipate a number of inhumation cemeteries beginning in the general area during the later fifth and early sixth centuries, when Spong Hill phase C starts to look rather more like a range of other mixed cemeteries which belong to this period.

THE PRITTLEWELL CHAMBERED GRAVE

NICHOLAS J. HIGHAM

Railway construction in the 1880s first revealed the presence of a late-sixth/early seventh-century Anglo-Saxon cemetery at Prittlewell, on the northern edge of Southend-on-Sea (Essex). Excavation in advance of road building in 1923 revealed 19 weapon-burials (exceptionally including six swords), 3 burials with female jewellery and other unaccompanied inhumations. In 2003 planned road-widening led Southend-on-Sea Borough Council to commission the Museum of London Archaeological Service (MOLAS) to undertake new archaeological investigations.

Initially, this team found just a few more inhumations in the flat-grave cemetery, including a new weapons-grave, but at the south end of the site they identified a 4-metre square demarcated by wood stains. When excavated, this proved to be a real rarity, a previously undisturbed burial chamber. The chamber – one of the largest ever found and the first to be excavated using modern techniques – had been lined with timber and covered with a roof of planks, then covered with an approximately 10 metre diameter mound of sandy soil. As the planking slowly decayed, highly acidic, sandy soil trickled into the chamber, burying the body with its entire assemblage still in situ. Unlike those at Sutton Hoo in Suffolk, this mound seems to have been so damaged, firstly by collapse and then probably by medieval ploughing, that it quickly became unrecognisable, so disguising the presence of a rich deposit and leaving it untouched by later grave robbers.

Excavation was necessarily from the top down, keeping within the internal faces of the now decayed walls. Several items had been hung on the walls, and these were found still suspended from their iron hooks, the first being an elaborate copper-alloy hanging bowl, with inlaid enamel mounts and cruciform strips decorating the exterior. Other copper-alloy vessels followed, including a Byzantine flagon, a large Coptic bowl and a cauldron with an iron handle. On the chamber floor the body had been deposited in a coffin set away from the walls and surrounded by one of the richest grave assemblages ever found, laid around the edges of the chamber.

The body itself has not survived, due to the acidity of the soil, but copper-alloy shoe buckles, a magnificent gold belt-buckle, gold braid from clothing found in the chest area and tooth enamel identified in the laboratory all suggest that it was buried supine, feet to the east. Two gold tremisses from Merovingian Francia were found in the

2b.1 Location map for
Prittlewell

vicinity of the chest and below the waist, one of which suggested deposition in the
early seventh century while the other belongs to a less precisely dated sequence of
coins. Two small, thin and delicate gold-foil crosses of a type otherwise only found at
this period in Alpine regions came from the head area, where they may have been laid
on clothing or perhaps a veil – although the absence of the usual attachment holes
could indicate that they had simply been placed over the eyes of the deceased. Although
biological sexing is not possible, the finds and the layout all suggest an adult male,
which conforms with other 'princely burials'.

   At his head, at the west end of the coffin, was found an iron folding stool of a kind
familiar to a modern audience from camping or fishing. This is the only example of its
kind so far found in Anglo-Saxon England, though comparable items have come from
Roman graves and from post-Roman burials on the Continent. To the south on the
chamber floor lay his sword, the iron fittings from his shield and two spearheads that
had fallen from the wall. In the south-west corner, a wooden box contained smaller
objects including a lidded copper-alloy cylinder and a silver spoon of sixth-century
Byzantine manufacture with an inscribed cross on the inside of the bowl added later,
along with a brief inscription beneath which starts 'FAB' . . . . On the southern side a
lyre signified entertainment. To the east wooden and horn drinking vessels, embel-

2b.2 Prittlewell Burial Chamber under excavation. Vessels mark the wall; within, the body area inside the wooden coffin and the iron sword are receiving attention; in the foreground are the remains of the folding stool

lished with intricate and ornate metal trim, and two pairs of matching glass jars with external applied decoration, one pair blue and the other green, reflect the feasting and drinking culture of the great hall, much as attested by the poem *Beowulf*. Iron-bound wooden stave buckets stood in the south-east corner, while a massive copper-alloy cauldron lay at the foot end of the coffin, on edge against the eastern wall.

In the north-east corner, an iron stand 1.33 metres high was discovered still upright, resting on its four curving feet each welded to a main shaft which is occasionally twisted along its length. At the apex it tapers to a point but has at least two short branches to the side. The function of this object is still being debated but it may have had some 'official' purpose or have held a torch to provide light. That illumination mattered to those making this deposition is demonstrated by the discovery in the laboratory of an iron lamp from the vicinity of the cauldron, containing a yellow material which may, on parallels from Sutton Hoo, have been beeswax.

A set of bone gaming pieces, along with two large dice made from antler, had been deposited, probably in a bag, near the north-east corner. With 57 individual pieces, this gaming set is one of the largest of the period ever found in England.

In the north-west corner a very large iron-bound wooden tub or bucket was located, which was almost half a metre in diameter and would have held over 80 litres when full. The interior was excavated in the laboratory due to the excessive compression which had distorted it; inside a small, lathe-turned, copper-alloy bowl and an iron scythe blade were discovered, which may indicate that this part of the assemblage was related to the food supply to the hall.

The nature and size of the burial chamber suggest an individual of exceptional status and this impression is confirmed by the wealth and quantity of grave goods, which are second only to the finds in the chamber within the ship under mound I at Sutton Hoo. The gold-foil crosses suggest a strong Christian influence, which is reinforced by the orientation of the body with its feet to the east and the presence of what may well have been a baptismal spoon, with Roman lettering and a cross inscribed on the upper side (although the cross need not necessarily have Christian connotations). The hanging bowl is likely to have been of Celtic manufacture, though as in other instances provenance is unclear. The flagon and bowls imply trade or diplomatic contacts with the eastern Mediterranean, whether direct or indirect.

Like Snape (Suffolk) but unlike most other 'princely burials' and the great mounds at Sutton Hoo in particular, the Prittlewell chambered grave was clearly part of a larger inhumation cemetery, and one of high status at that. If some of the weapon-burials prove to be demonstrably earlier than the chambered grave, this would mean that it was added to an existing cemetery, but this matter is still under consideration. There are parallels here with practice in Kent, where rich early seventh-century burials normally occur in large cemeteries, sometimes in some numbers each under its own barrow. There are other connections also with Kent, including the glass vessels that

2b.3 Copper-alloy Byzantine flagon found hanging on the north wall. The flagon was cast in a mould, the handle added separately, attached by bands, the lower one ornamented by three embossed medallions of horsemen; the lid is secured to the ornate handle by a chain. The only example of its kind so far found in an archaeological context in England

2b.4 Gold-foil crosses found in the burial in the face area. These delicate Christian symbols are unique in Anglo-Saxon England, only paralleled in the lands around the Alps in the decades around 600

2b.5 Two pairs of squat glass jars, one blue, the other green, found against the east wall. The blue pair have applied plaitwork around the body; the green ones are smaller, with decoration at the base and neck. The jars are probably Kentish products of the early seventh century

were probably manufactured there and the evidence of Christianity, which was particularly associated with Canturbury in Kent at this date.

Given these connections, it is tempting to see Prittlewell as the final resting place of the East Saxon king Saberht, the only Christian ruler of the East Saxons known to us before the 650s. His story is comparatively well known in outline from Bede's *Ecclesiastical History*. Saberht was the nephew of the powerful Kentish king Æthelberht through his sister Ricula, and his closest political and dynastic ally. He accepted baptism from Kent at the beginning of the seventh century and a bishop, Mellitus, established at London. Bede did not date Saberht's death precisely but implies that it was no later than that of Æthelberht in 616, at which point Saberht's three sons rejected Christianity and made demands on Mellitus which he felt unable to satisfy, leading to his withdrawal from London back to Canterbury.

Certainly, several features of the burial would suit that context. If these pagan sons influenced the actual burial process, as one might expect, then the failure to bury in a Christian cemetery or in association with a church is understandable. Burial in an inhumation cemetery in current use perhaps implies their commitment to traditional practices, within a cemetery which already had strong associations with the elite, perhaps even with their own kin. Such a rich chambered burial indicates a desire to emphasise the wealth and power of the individual via mechanisms which are familiar to us from other late pagan graves, using a burial style which owed much to Merovingian Gaul but was not associated specifically in contemporary England with Christianity. The assemblage speaks of the widespread connections of the individual interred, so to his fame and fortune, and in that respect there are close parallels with the ship burial under mound 1 at Sutton Hoo, which has a similarly diverse range of artefacts. That was, however, arguably buried slightly later and marked the burial of an individual of even higher status if it was that of Rædwald, who was an *imperium*-wielding king – a king with power over other kings – at his death.

Such interpretations are, of course, more supposition than established fact. Whoever was buried in the Prittlewell chambered grave, he was clearly an individual of very considerable wealth and political power, living on the cusp of the Christianisation

2b.6 Ornate copper-alloy and gold mount on the rim of one of the drinking horns found at the east end of the chamber, close to the glass jars

of parts at least of south-east England. The quality of workmanship on display, the number of items of gold, the sheer quantity of goods, and the presence of several rare or unique pieces which are likely to have kingly significance, all point to very high status indeed. As the only 'princely grave' so far found undisturbed and excavated under modern conditions, this is an extremely important find, from which research will eventually provide important new insights into Anglo-Saxon England in the early seventh century.

Such questions as 'Was he a Christian? Was he a pagan?' are natural but ultimately unlikely to be very helpful in moving forward the interpretation, since this is a burial which occurred in a period stretching from the late sixth century through to about 630, which is characterised by both ideological experimentation and religious syncretism. This period sees by far the richest burials that we have from Anglo-Saxon England, alongside growing numbers of virtually artefact-free inhumations. The assumption that this reflected a steepening of social hierarchies at this date seems apt. At Prittlewell, it does seem likely that we have the burial of a historically identified East Saxon king, but certainty continues to elude us.

CHAPTER 3

From Tribal Chieftains to Christian Kings

NICHOLAS J. HIGHAM

For Bede, English history was primarily a story of Conversion to Christianity and the establishment of Catholicism in Britain. The coming of St Augustine and his Italian fellow missionaries to Kent in 597 was the moment when he shifted his attention decisively from the Britons to the English. His 'Greater Chronicle' captures this moment:

> [Gregory] sent to Britain Mellitus, Augustine and John with many other God-fearing monks alongside, to convert the Angles to Christ. And when Æthelberht was quickly converted to the grace of Christ, together with the people of Kent over whom he ruled and together with those of neighbouring kingdoms, he gave him Augustine to be his bishop and teacher, as well as other holy priests to become bishops.

It is Bede's perspective that dominates most later histories. Indeed, it was often exaggerated, and spiced with a hostility towards pagans that he rarely showed – R. H. Hodgkin in 1935, for example, wrote that 'their heathen customs were often ugly enough and reeked of blood'. But today scholars are increasingly challenging the dominant role of religion in this story. While the Conversion remains important, it is better viewed as part of a bigger history stretching back a generation before Augustine's arrival and on into the early eighth century. Alongside Conversion, this larger story encompasses broader cultural changes, the emergence of kingships and kingdoms, questions about ethnicity, social developments, the re-emergence of coining and the revival of trade.

This is the very start of English history. Before this point, the Anglo-Saxons are anonymous; from the last third of the sixth century near-contemporary written evidence begins to offer a faint sketch of what was going on, at the highest levels of society at least. But it is also a period with an exceptional wealth of archaeology. The scarcity of written sources means that material evidence must lead us initially, bringing in other disciplinary approaches as these become available. We will start by exploring the changes which were occurring in the burial record from the mid-sixth century onwards, moving on from there to settlement archaeology and ultimately to the written record.

Burial and the Material Record

Well-established methods of disposing of the dead across the later fifth and earlier sixth centuries began to break down in the mid-sixth century, with cremation declining in popularity. It virtually ceased in the mid-seventh. Destruction of the body by burning was incompatible with the Christian focus on the body and expectations of the Day of Judgment; this may eventually have discouraged cremation. However, its initial decline was too early for Conversion to have been the cause. Whether or not the reason was in any sense 'religious' is unclear; one might otherwise point towards social changes, or the suggestion that Anglo-Saxons were shifting away in the sixth century

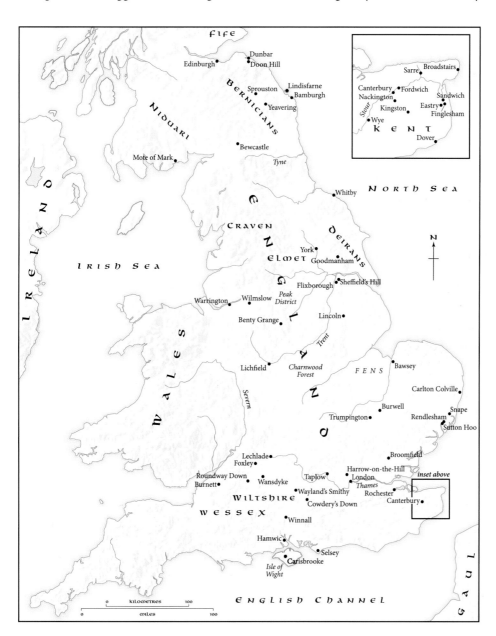

3.1 Places named in chapter 3

from portraying themselves as 'Germanic', adopting instead more 'Frankish' and/or 'Roman' behaviours in various aspects of their lives, burial included.

Furnished inhumation, rather than cremation, therefore dominated disposal of the dead by the later sixth century. At the same time this spread to such new areas as Wiltshire, the north east and the Derbyshire Peak District. The spread of Anglo-Saxon burial practices into what had hitherto been 'British' areas reflects new regions being conquered or drawn into unequal partnerships with Anglo-Saxon elites. Western and northern England had so far retained much from the British past, in terms of material culture and language, but these regions were now increasingly coming into prolonged contact with English culture. Research in the Peak District suggests land-taking by Anglo-Saxon warriors to which indigenous leaders responded by themselves adopting forms of 'English-ness', in particular the furnished burial. The small number and comparative wealth of these graves, and continuing traces of 'British' material culture within them, all imply acculturation.

Significant changes occurred in the material being deposited in graves in the late sixth century, but the cause is debated. Numerous existing types of artefact continued, including handmade pottery, swords, spears, amulets, shears and double-sided combs. Others, such as annular brooches, finger rings and claw-beakers, display a degree of selection as regards the characteristics which continue, with significant stylistic changes coming in. Alongside, deposition ceased of such well-established artefacts as long strings of amber beads and several brooch types, implying that they were no longer manufactured. Exotic goods imported from Francia and the Eastern Empire increasingly marked high status. In tandem there was a revival of insular Roman culture, with the widespread deposition of elaborate hanging bowls of British manufacture. Remains of the Roman period were still very much in evidence and Roman sites attracted the new Christian centres – Canterbury, Rochester, London, Lincoln and York were among the new church sites adopted across the early seventh century.

The inhumation rite also exhibits differences around 600 which suggest significant social change. By c. 550, weapons occur in perhaps half of all male graves, suggesting those responsible were focused on the social and legal status that weapon-ownership conferred. Within the weapon-bearing sector of society, however, some individuals and families had higher ambitions. Such men may have experienced success as the leaders of war-bands or as figures wielding influence in the assembly.

Barrows were associated with a small minority of burials throughout the early Anglo-Saxon period and many cemeteries were located at or around pre-existing monuments. But they became noticeably more popular from the mid-sixth century onwards, with some cemeteries virtually given over to small barrows or burial within a penannular ditch. Even many flat graves were now more carefully structured, exhibiting a greater input of both skill and labour, and wooden coffins with metal fittings proliferated. Although the connection is far from predictive, there is a higher incidence of exotic grave goods under barrows than in flat graves, and textiles were increasingly employed to display the dead during internment.

These changes were earliest and most pronounced in East Kent, at such cemeteries as Finglesham, St Peters Broadstairs and Updown Eastry. From there they spread

3.2 Bronze hanging bowl of 'Celtic' type from the ship burial at Sutton Hoo; the focus is on one of three external circular escutcheons from which it would have hung. The escutcheon was decorated with red and blue enamel and is stamped with repousse ornament. Such 'Celtic' finds from high-status Anglo-Saxon graves suggest elite patronage of British craftsmen and an attempt to engage with Britain's Roman heritage

across Anglo-Saxon England, replacing both 'Anglian' and 'Saxon' styles of burial. Outside Kent, early seventh-century graves are less easily identified than for other periods, creating something of a hiatus in the evidence, but regional distinctiveness as regards clothing, metalworking and burial practices certainly diminished.

Excluding barrows, the deposition of grave goods fell away rapidly in the early seventh century, with more and more bodies interred with few or none. In particular, weapons-graves become far less common. In 1936 Edward Leeds coined the term 'Final Phase' for cemeteries producing very few grave goods. His study began with excavations at Burwell (Cambridgeshire) in the 1920s and 1930s. Leeds initially viewed such cemeteries as the burial places of poor pagans but eventually reinterpreted them as Christian. Since then, we have learned to understand 'Final Phase' burials rather better. They are characterised by the Christian associations of some artefacts (including crosses), the regularity of west–east orientation, an absence of cremation, frequent lack of artefacts beyond a knife, the changed appearance of clothing and ornamentation, and the scarcity of weapons. On occasion sixth-century cemeteries were replaced,

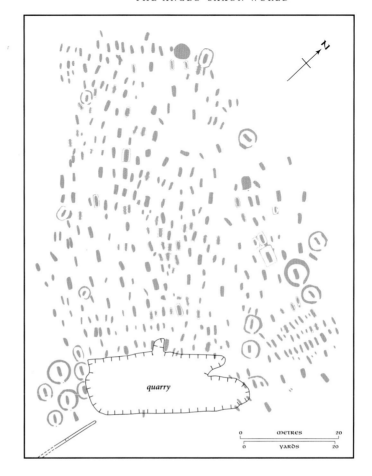

3.3 St Peter's Tip, Broadstairs, Thanet (Kent). Part of a large sixth- to eighth-century inhumation cemetery, probably initially aligned on Bronze Age barrows, it features rows of graves, aligned north west/south east, a minority of which are surrounded by annular or penannular ring-ditches

resulting in such paired cemeteries as Winnall I and II (Hampshire) and Sheffield's Hill (Lincolnshire). The later cemetery was often closer to the settlement, as at Bloodmoor Hill (Carlton Colville, Suffolk), where a small seventh-century cemetery among the halls and SFBs replaced one on the hill nearby. Even so, some cemeteries continued in use right through, as did that at Butler's Field, Lechlade (Gloucestershire), which, like many others, centred on an Early Bronze Age monument. Butler's Field has revealed the wealthiest graves so far excavated in the Upper Thames region, so its continuing use may have related to a particular, dominant settlement.

Although 'Final Phase' cemeteries broadly coincide with Christian Conversion, it is difficult to establish a causal link; contemporary Christian texts do not condemn burial goods. Rather, this trend may mirror other shifts within contemporary society, such as changing dress styles, an awareness that Frankish burial practices had moved in the same direction, and a growing disinclination within the middling ranks of society to lock away expensive items under the earth.

Alongside such changes to the use of cemeteries, small numbers of distinctive individual burials occurred, accompanied by grave goods that were exceptional as regards both their quality and quantity. These are generally marked by particularly prominent features, including barrows, and on occasion contained in a timber-built chamber. Their exploration began on 5 August 1771, when labourers employed by the Reverend Bryan Faussett, curate of Nackington, dug into a sizeable mound within the extensive barrow cemetery on Kingston Down (Kent) and found beneath it an unusually large grave containing a wooden coffin. Inside they found the skeleton of a small woman. A gold pendant hung from her neck and the most intricate Anglo-Saxon brooch ever discovered gathered her clothes, which were fastened by two delicate silver safety pins at her waist. At her feet lay two imported bronze vessels, a wooden casket and a pot. Outside the coffin lay the remains of a child and a glass cup. The finds suggest the burial of an exceptionally wealthy woman in the early seventh century, a period when spectacular metalworking and particularly brooch manufacture had taken off in Kent under Frankish influence.

Weapons-graves declined in number but became richer and grander, incorporating chamber and barrow burial. Burial chambers sealed by a barrow occur in both southern Scandinavia and territories peripheral to northern Francia in the late sixth century. There were barrow burials in England from the fifth century onwards, utilising existing mounds as well as constructing new ones, and chamber burial occurs very occasionally. But the combination of rich burial in a chamber under a large barrow was something new. It was probably triggered by Frankish influence, even though the Frankish elite had abandoned the rite before it was taken up in England, turning to forms of Christian interment instead. Comparable chamber burials have been excavated at Morken and Krefeld-Gellep in Westphalia, but most famously in the richly accoutred, late fifth-century burial of King Chilperic, at Tournai in Belgium. The practice reached

3.4 The Kingston Brooch. The finest so far found of the composite brooches made in Kent under Merovingian influence early in the seventh century, it features intricate use of gold and cloisonné, with inlaid panels of garnet, white shell, glass and gold filigree set in concentric circles

3.5 Slender claw-beakers from the high-status barrow-burial at Taplow (Buckinghamshire). These intricate glass drinking vessels were imported from northern Francia for an elite market

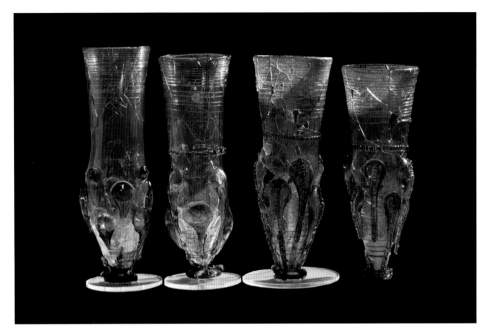

south-east England via the same networks as brought Coptic bowls, Byzantine spoons, glassware, silks and wheel-turned pottery, and was adopted primarily in the first few decades of the seventh century.

Such exceptional graves are often found in prominent locations visible from a distance, either alone or in small groups. It has long been suggested that early Anglo-Saxon boundaries utilised prehistoric burial mounds as markers, which in turn attracted English burials to the edges of territories, but the new wave of exceptional graves involved monuments of a scale hitherto rarely achieved. These new barrows might be 4 metres or more in height, with the body either inserted into a substantial but pre-existing prehistoric monument or laid beneath a newly erected mound. They bear witness to grandiose ideas about the setting appropriate to the final resting place of a select few. Such rites entailed far greater costs in terms of skill, labour and more valuable objects taken out of circulation than did anything previously.

Although female burials are occasionally found under new barrows (as mound 14 at Sutton Hoo), most were inserted into pre-existing monuments and more, again, into flat graves. The majority of newly erected barrows cover male burials distinguished by the range and quality of accompanying finds. In Germany, the social status implicit in the combination of monument and find assemblage has led to the term *Fürstengrab* – literally 'princely grave'. The individuals buried were members of families with aspirations, at least, to royal status. In England the term 'princely burial' serves the same purpose. Although these are less rich than Continental examples, they still represent a significant shift of scale compared to earlier practices and reflect comparatively complex funeral arrangements.

Well-known examples of 'princely burial' include a coffin excavated in 1883 more than 6 metres below the apex of a great barrow in the churchyard at Taplow (Buckinghamshire), accompanied by weapons, glass beakers, vessels, fabric and other equipment, the quality and craftsmanship of which were exceptional. Likewise a male skeleton was found at Broomfield (Essex) in a sub-surface burial chamber made of timber, associated with a plethora of finds which included a bronze bowl, fragments of two drinking horns, various vessels and weapons. In 1862 a ship burial was excavated at Snape (Suffolk), under a barrow built within a Bronze Age cemetery which had been reused in the early Anglo-Saxon period. The ship was 14 metres long and 3 metres wide. Fragments of a wealth of grave goods were recovered, including spearheads, blue glass, a glass claw-beaker and a gold ring.

This discovery has since been overshadowed by the famous ship burial excavated beneath mound 1 at Sutton Hoo, just over 15 kilometres to the south. Mound 2 also had a ship burial but this had been robbed. The great ship under mound 1 lay undisturbed other than by decay. The ship was 27 metres long and buried in a trench cut to accommodate it 3.5 metres below the natural ground surface. The ship contained the greatest burial hoard ever discovered in Britain, which is now on permanent display in the British Museum. At the centre of the ship rich textiles in red and yellow had lined a timber chamber filled with goods befitting a king, including precious weapons, a unique mail-coat and helmet, and a purse containing Frankish coins, alongside gaming pieces, drinking horns and silver table vessels. This may have been the grave of the East Anglian king Rædwald, known to us from written sources, since the coins are consistent with a date in the 620s when he is thought to have died and his status as an 'over-king' might warrant the display of such wealth. Other elite burials occurred on the same site, with mound 17, for example, yielding a young nobleman accompanied by a full set of weapons of high quality and a riding horse with decorated bridle. Only

3.6 The ship under mound 1, Sutton Hoo, during excavation in 1939

3.7 The Sutton Hoo helmet. This elaborate and highly ornamented helmet is derivative of late Roman parade ground styles but the closest near contemporary parallels come from southern Sweden. Note the facing dragons' heads meeting above the forehead, and the way that the eye- and nose-guards form elements of the applied animal decoration. Helmets are so rare in pre-Viking England as to imply exceptional status

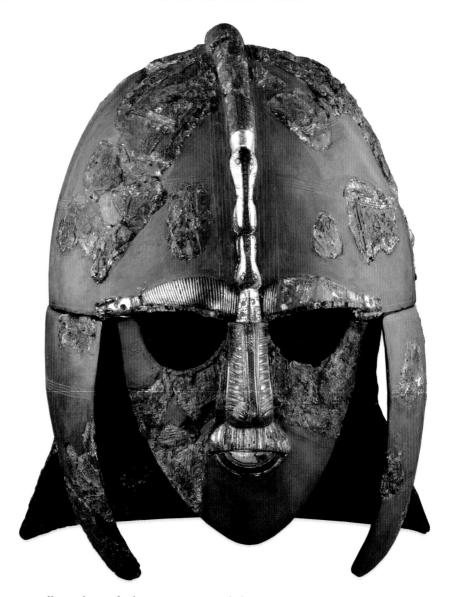

very small numbers of inhumations in English cemeteries are accompanied by horses. These date to the later sixth and early seventh centuries and are generally males with rich grave assemblages. Other barrows covered cremations, several accompanied by rich accessories.

The princely burials at Sutton Hoo did not occur in a vacuum. Excavation previous to the erection of the National Trust visitor centre 500 metres from the great barrows revealed an earlier mixed cemetery, focused in part at least on a prehistoric burial mound, with numerous small barrows erected over inhumations. Beginning in the second quarter of the sixth century and lasting into the early seventh, this comparatively wealthy burial ground featured numerous warrior burials and perhaps plots the rise of a particular kin or family to wider power. Once the elite burial ground came into use, though, these lesser burials ceased.

3.8 Purse-lid from the ship burial at Sutton Hoo. The gold and ivory surface is decorated with jewelled plaques featuring garnets and millefiori; the outer pair of plaques show men standing spread-eagled between two rampant animals, probably wolves; the interior plaques each have a bird of prey swooping onto a duck. The purse contained 37 Merovingian gold coins, 3 blank flans and 2 plain gold billets. The workmanship is of exceptional virtuosity

At Sutton Hoo, archaeology and history come almost close enough to touch, but elsewhere the pre-Christian burial record is entirely anonymous, unless the names given to individual tumuli, such as Taplow (Buckinghamshire), which means 'Tæppa's mound', or Wilmslow (Cheshire), meaning 'Wilma's mound', actually identify the individual buried. As in Francia, the very richest burials coincide with the first few decades of Christianisation, suggesting that these represent a protest against Christianity. After the 620s, however, elaborate 'princely burials' died away in Britain. Across the next generation, Christian habits of disposing of the dead spread, region by region, and gradually drove out alternative expressions of social rank.

Elaborate princely burials have barely been discovered outside the south east. While Northumbrian cemeteries have yielded a high proportion of well-furnished burials, there is nothing indicative of exceptional status. The helmet found at Benty Grange (Derbyshire) implies a very high-status warrior burial, but otherwise the burial practices of the pre-Conversion elite in Mercia and Wessex remain obscure. This suggests that, to an extent at least, princely burials were a product of direct Continental contact; regions more heavily influenced by British ideas about kingship did not invest in this strategy. Indeed, there may even be a link between the presence of British names in a royal dynasty and the absence of princely burial. Rich female graves carry on longer than male, certainly into the late seventh century and do occur in the far west, as at Roundway Down (Wiltshire) and Burnett (Somerset). None, however, even approaches the wealth on show at Sutton Hoo, Prittlewell or Taplow.

Settlement Archaeology

Anglo-Saxon settlements of the mid-sixth century display very little evidence of social rank. Most carry on in very much the same way across the seventh century. Around 600, however, a minority display changes consistent with the emergence of new hierarchies, in the form of buildings of exceptional size and unusual architectural form. Evidence is so far limited to Yeavering (Northumbria), Cowdery's Down (Hampshire), Foxley (Wiltshire) and Dover (Kent).

At Yeavering, crop marks photographed from the air led to excavation of what should be viewed as a palace site dating to the first half of the seventh century. The excavator interpreted the site with the assistance of passages in Bede's *Ecclesiastical History* referring to a palace complex called *Ad Gefrin* (Yeavering: 'the hill of goats'), which was abandoned after King Edwin's death in 633 and replaced by *Mælmin* (probably Millfield; aerial photography has revealed similar remains there). In its setting, the site had exceptional claims on the past; a massive Iron Age hillfort and an earlier prehistoric henge dominated the immediate landscape. A late sixth-century group of buildings was developed into a prestigious complex, probably by the great pagan king Æthelfrith (d. c. 616), whose deeds Bede lauded. A hall which features numerous ox skulls has been interpreted as a pagan temple, with a kitchen alongside. This lay near an 'assembly' structure built of massive timbers which seems to have been modelled on a Roman theatre, even though none are known so far north. The complex was then reconstructed by King Edwin (616–33), with a great timber enclosure capable of holding very large numbers of cattle, two halls connected by an enclosed courtyard, and a timber-framed church with associated cemetery. Later, the site was redeveloped once more, with the church and fenced graveyard relocated eastwards, the assembly structure rebuilt and a new range of halls with large annexes constructed outwards from the gable ends.

By any standards, this complex can only have been commissioned and then rebuilt successively by powerful individuals capable of mobilising a large workforce. This speaks of kingship, despite the minimal quantities of pottery and other artefacts recovered.

3.9 Palace complex at Yeavering: (a) later sixth century; (b) late sixth to early seventh century, with pagan temple, associated kitchen and assembly structure; (c) early seventh century, great enclosure, a range of massive halls and first church with cemetery; (d) halls and assembly structure was rebuilt with a church and cemetery on a new site. The sequence suggests that ritural activity dominated the early layout giving way to re-orientation on the great halls in the later phases

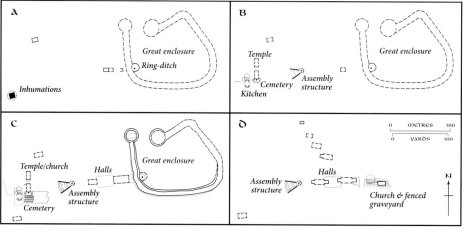

Neither Cowdery's Down nor Foxley is the equal of Yeavering, but both sites have yielded large timber-built halls, associated with annexes built out from the gable end and with regular, fenced enclosures, dominating a range of other buildings. The major halls had ancillary timbers around the exterior to serve as flying buttresses to help support the weight of the roof. Cowdery's Down lies close to Basing, which takes its name from the *Basingas*, a group making up part of the seventh-century West Saxons. Perhaps these halls represent an early centre of that people. The halls at Dover are on a scale comparable with Yeavering. They are seventh-century or later, probably part of a royal monastery which provided accommodation for the king and his retainers.

Elsewhere it seems quite possible that the emerging elite pressed existing sites into use to serve the functions which the assembly building performed at Yeavering. The Roman theatre at Canterbury could have been in service in the reign of Æthelberht, Æthelfrith's contemporary in Kent, who was probably responsible for reoccupation of the old *civitas* capital as a high-status site. Such buildings had considerable value in terms of large-scale assemblies, public tribute-paying and speech-giving.

In the far north, Sprouston (Borders) offers comparable aerial photographic evidence to Yeavering and Millfield. Elsewhere the Northumbrians were notable for taking over defensive sites previously used by their Celtic neighbours, occupying such strongholds as Bamburgh (Northumbria), Mote of Mark (Dumfries), Edinburgh, Dunbar and Doon Hill (near Dunbar), where a 23-metre long hall was built inside the palisaded enclosure. There is no sign of the use of defences of this kind, however, outside Northumbria. In the south, some of the sites identified through concentrations of metalwork finds – so-called 'productive sites' – may have been elite settlements. Rendlesham, for example, is just such a site and appears in Bede's *History* as a royal palace of the East Angles, but seems not to have been defended.

Archaeological evidence from both burials and settlements therefore suggests the development of social hierarchies in the late sixth and early seventh centuries. This indicates that kingship was emerging at this date. Further evidence comes from written sources, to which we will now turn.

The Origins of Kingdoms

Bede's description of the settlement of the Anglo-Saxons, people by people, in the *Ecclesiastical History* (I, 15) implies that he believed that the major kingships of the seventh century had their origins in the settlements of different Germanic tribes in the fifth century. However, his occasional references to smaller tribal units, termed 'regions' or 'provinces', suggest that processes of kingdom formation were still very much ongoing across the seventh century. Today there are two competing views on how Anglo-Saxon kingdoms came into being. One assumes a degree of territorial continuity across the Roman/Saxon divide and that some of the *civitates* and/or territories associated with Romano-British centres were taken over by warrior bands as going concerns. The second posits a catastrophic breakdown of Roman territorial structures, with Anglo-Saxon society then developing without respect to earlier territories. According to this second scenario the seventh-century Anglo-Saxon kingdoms derived not from pre-existing territories but from small tribal units coalescing to form regional kingdoms.

Both options have some value. The first is relevant to parts of the south east and to England's western and northern peripheries. Kent emerged with its Roman name of *Cantium* virtually unchanged and centred on Canterbury – Roman *Durovernum Cantiacorum*, then English *Cantwaraburg*, 'the stronghold of the Kentish people', though there was probably a hiatus in its use as a high-status site. Less convincing claims for continuity have been made for the Romano-British *Trinovantes* re-emerging as the East Saxons, and for the *Regni* reappearing as the South Saxons. In neither case did the urban centre retain a role, though Chichester re-emerged later as an English bishopric. That several seventh-century Anglo-Saxon kingdoms seem to map on to the *civitates* of Roman Britain with some precision at least invites speculation regarding continuity, even while it proves little.

Further west and north, where British polities survived longer, the case is more robust. The *Dumnonii* became Anglo-Saxon Devon (*Defnas*: the name is cognate). The *Cornovii* of the extreme south west became Cornwall. Wroxeter, Roman *Viroconium*, was the capital of the other Romano-British tribe named the *Cornovii*; the first element of the city's name is shared with The Wrekin, a prominent hill overlooking the site. That name re-emerged as the early English tribal name, the *Wrocensæte*. In the east, a similar case can be made for Lindsey, the area focused on Lincoln from which it took its name, though this was not the tribal capital but that of the province. The Old English name, *Lindisfarona*, incorporates an early post-Roman, British one. The *Deiri* of eastern Yorkshire similarly evolved out of a British tribal territory, centred on the Yorkshire Wolds and the valleys of the Derwent and Rye, and the *Bernicii*, the *Niduari*, Craven and Elmet are all pre-English.

Above the level of the *civitas*, seventh-century Northumbria closely resembles the late Roman province of *Britannia Secunda*, based on York, where the bishopric was re-established in the 620s. The western province of Roman Britain, *Britannia Prima*, retained its identity well through the fifth century if not the sixth; while the province's eastern lowlands were conquered, the more westerly highland region eventually became Wales and Cornwall. Lindsey similarly represented that part of the late Roman province of *Flavia Caesariensis* which adhered longest to the old provincial capital. 'Mercians' means 'border-people' and this may derive from the frontier region of these two late Roman provinces – we simply do not know. And the boundary between *Flavia Caesariensis* and *Maxima Caesariensis* cannot have been very different from that between the East Angles and East Saxons. There is a case of sorts, therefore, for the

3.10 The Wrekin. The hill dominates the landscape around Wroxeter and is visible as far away as Lancashire and Staffordshire. On the top is a substantial Iron Age hillfort, the original *Uriconio*, from which Roman Wroxeter took its name and which was the focus of the late pre-Roman *Cornovii*. The early Anglo-Saxon *Wrocensæte* reflect a degree of continuity with the Iron Age and Roman tribe

continuing influence of provincial structures as well as *civitates* over the mid-Anglo-Saxon kingdoms.

That said, the names of many kingdoms are late formations, coined to give expression to new social and political realities and reliant on similar names for their meaning. The East Saxons require the existence of the West Saxons, and vice versa; similarly the East Angles are unlikely to have been named without an awareness of Angles further west. Bede knew that the West Saxons had earlier been called the *Gewisse*. The name 'Northumbrians' was only just coming into being in the early eighth century, with reference to an important frontier – the Humber. Few if any of these names are likely to have been common parlance in 570, even if some of the groupings to which they applied were already in being.

The second option directs attention away from these larger tribal kingdoms towards the scatter of obscure, minor peoples who were being absorbed into larger neighbours in the Middle Anglo-Saxon period. Some certainly had substantial territories and their own dynasties, as the *Hwicce* and *Magonsæte* in the west and Lindsey in the east. Others were smaller and less clearly ruled by kingly families, though the South Gyrwe, in the Fens, had a 'prince' in the 660s. These smaller groups may represent survivals of the fundamental building blocks from which the historic kingdoms were constructed. Many were topographically defined, such as the *Cilternsæte* (the Chiltern dwellers) the *Arosæte* (the people of the Arrow Valley) and the *Pecsæte* (the people of the Peak District), so perhaps they originated in social groupings sharing access to particular environments which they needed to manage collectively.

The last three of these names appear on the Tribal Hidage, a much debated list of tribute payments which survives in Old English in a copy of around AD 1,000 but was probably written initially in the seventh century. The Tribal Hidage provides a whole melange of small-scale peoples in the region of the Wash, such as the *Spalda* (cognate with the place name Spalding) and *Hicce* (Hitchin). Agglomeration occurred here when Penda, king of the Mercians, reconstituted them as the Middle Angles to provide a kingship for his son Peada. Other minor 'people' names can potentially be recovered from later regional or hundred names, such as the *Blythingas* ('people of the Blyth valley': Suffolk) and the *Beningas* ('people of the Bean valley': Hertfordshire), who gave their name to Benington and Bengeo respectively.

Local names such as these may mark the dawn of kingship in Anglo-Saxon England. The seminal argument is that propounded by Steven Bassett, who, somewhat tongue-in-cheek, viewed the Tribal Hidage as if illustrative of a late stage in a sporting knock-out competition, such as the fifth round of the F.A. Cup (1989, p. 26):

> Most of the little teams have long gone, there are a few potential giant-killers left – the Spalda, the Arosætna, the East and West Willa – survivors only because they have so far avoided being drawn against the major teams. But the next round will see them off; they have had their brief moment of glory . . . .

There are assumptions underlying this analysis, however, which warrant further attention. One is that kingship originated specifically in the context of territorial

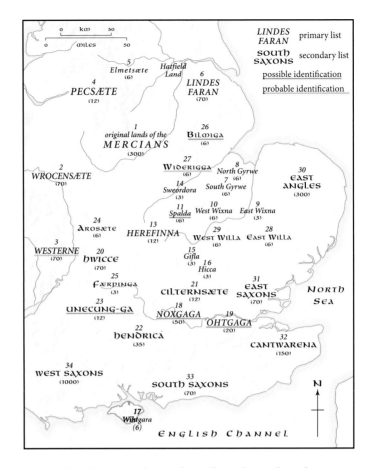

3.11 Map of the Tribal Hidage, a probable seventh-century tribute list of unknown origin. Often thought to be Mercian because it begins with 'the original lands of the Mercians', but their inclusion may imply it is Northumbrian. Written in two parts, with a (correct) total for the first list after 19 entries, then an (incorrect) grand total after the secondary list, this structure implies the final list follows dramatic expansion of tribute-taking from the Midlands across southern England. Entries are numbered 1–34; dubious identifications are distinguished; those omitted from the map are un-located; the number of hundreds of hides allocated to each name is given in brackets and some names have been modernised

organisation. Another is that only warfare allowed one kingdom to expand at the expense of another. In practice, the 'knock-out' analogy is probably not sufficiently flexible to accommodate the complexity of early, intertribal relations. If the Tribal Hidage is correctly viewed as a tribute list, all the names listed are equal in the sense that all paid tribute, but differences in the scale of payments show that some were clearly 'more equal' than others. It is unlikely that the smaller peoples were in any real sense autonomous; rather, each was dependent on more powerful figures to protect them from expansionist neighbours. Take the Isle of Wight, for example, which had been protected by the Mercians under Wulfhere (658–75) and his clients the South Saxons, but was invaded and conquered by the West Saxons in the 680s.

A close reading of Bede's *Ecclesiastical History* reveals that he referred to kingdoms not by a territorial name but by their peoples (the Mercians, East Angles, and so on). Bede was clearly aware of the location of such peoples, and that they were not somehow detached from the land. But it was social relationships, rather than occupation of space, which lay at the heart of kingship formation. Even the word from which 'king' derives belongs to a group indicative of 'kinship', not of Roman concepts of territorial governance. The emphasis should be more on tribal kingship than spatial kingdom, therefore, centred on those acknowledging the leadership of a particular 'royal' family and membership of a shared identity.

The relationship between a king and his people involved their support for him and his protection of them. The king's war-band therefore lay at its heart. While this war-band would normally include near neighbours and kindred, it also contained men with no connection to its leader's tribe beyond service to him. Although most aspirant kings probably had dependants within the tribal territory, this was clearly not necessary. The West Saxon prince Cædwalla first emerged in the 680s as a claimant to royal power while an exile in the Weald. There he assembled a force sufficient to invade the land of the South Saxons and kill their king, then take over the West Saxons. Aspirant royals often returned from exile to press their claims, with both internal and external support but without current control of estates.

Kingship originated, therefore, out of the relationship between tribal communities and successful war leaders, some of whom were able, from the late sixth century onwards, to acquire a following, wealth and influence sufficient to give permanence to the pre-eminence which they or their predecessors had gained. It is surely those individuals, and their close families, who are represented in the south east by the increasingly elaborate 'princely burials'.

Such individuals were not constrained by their own tribal origins to limit their claims on power and status. Rather, in a world characterised by small-scale tribal elites, a successful war-leader may well have established his influence from the beginning over several peoples, through family connections, patronage, negotiation, marriage, the widespread recruitment of followers and/or intimidation. In fact, the classic statement of kingship formation is one already alluded to, when Penda of the Mercians created the kingship of the Middle Angles for his son out of a dozen or so small fenland peoples. In this sense, we should not envisage kingship formation as a linear process in which the 'proto-kings' of small-scale tribes fought local rivals to achieve larger agglomerations. Instead, leading figures attained kingship through their ability to negotiate protection and support both internally and externally; the coalescence of contiguous tribal units was surely part of the process of kingship formation from the beginning.

To take the East Anglian kingship as an example, the close proximity of the royal palace site at Rendlesham to the boat burials at Snape and Sutton Hoo suggests an early concentration of kingly power in south-east Suffolk on the north bank of the Deben river. The absence of any rival centres visible in the archaeology of the late sixth and early seventh centuries suggests that this family networked effectively and reconciled potential rivals from an early date. Similarly, the Kentish kingship originated in East Kent, east of the Wantsum Channel. Its expansion westwards into West Kent, Surrey and London is visible archaeologically in the spread of distinctive artefacts in the later sixth century. Likewise, the Northumbrian kingship began at and around Bamburgh, expanding through processes of patronage, cultural imperialism, military conquest and intermarriage to take in the peoples of a territory at its greatest from Fife to the Wash.

A key factor missing from this account of kingship formation is the notion of 'over-kingship', or *imperium* as Bede put it. Although he sometimes made little distinction between *regnum* ('kingly rule') and *imperium* ('imperial rule'), Bede understood that 'kingship' was tiered and that some kings had influence or authority over others. The West Saxons, for example, had not just one single king but numerous sub-kings who on occasion ruled without a superior leader, and 'overkingship' existed above this level as well. In his famous list of *imperium*-wielding kings in the *Ecclesiastical History*, (II, 5), Bede named Æthelberht of Kent as the third to have wielded 'overkingship' over the southern English. Æthelberht reigned probably from the 580s to c. 616, and he was pre-eminent by 596. Since Bede names Ælle of the South Saxons and Ceawlin of the West Saxons before Æthelberht in this list, then 'overkingship' probably existed by the 560s, at least, so before 'princely burials' had entered the archaeological record. 'Overkingship' obviously cannot precede kingship. Still more challenging is the comment of Procopius in the mid-sixth century:

> The island of *Brittia* is inhabited by three very numerous nations, each having one king over it. And the names of these nations are *Angili*, *Frissones* and *Brittones*, the last being named from the island itself.

One might just dismiss Procopius as an unreliable witness; he wrote in the distant Eastern Empire and relied for his information on Frankish ambassadors to the imperial court. That he included stories about the souls of the dead being shipped over from Gaul clearly undermines his credibility, but these remarks are not so far distant from those of Bede. Both imply that Anglo-Saxon kingship began earlier than 'princely burials'. If so, then the new burial rite was perhaps reflective more of reactions to Christianity than of the inception of kingship itself. In that case, Anglo-Saxon kingship may have originated earlier than is sometimes supposed.

While it is inadvisable to push this evidence too far, Bede's notice of *imperium* in the late sixth century emphasises the transient nature of political power, for all those whom Bede named were from different dynasties and kingdoms. Clearly, there was nothing institutional about it, rather *imperium* shifted from one leader to another according to military strength, reputation and the chances of warfare. There are other aspects of kingship that come into play, for a fundamental part of 'overkingship' in the seventh century was the management of relations between one people and another. Penda's army on his invasion of Northumbria in 642 consisted of 30 war-bands led by royal or noble lords, among them the rulers of client kingdoms. Acknowledging another king's leadership in war was, therefore, one manifestation of an unequal relationship between rulers. The payment of tribute and accepting guidance regarding royal marriage were others. Lesser kings of the seventh century conceded power to overlords in other ways as well, including the involvement of the superior in granting estates, the protection of individuals (particularly exiles), and following their lead on matters of religion. The separate recognition of the *Spalda*, for example, in the Tribal Hidage, reflects less their avoidance of conflict with major kingdoms than their retention of the protection of successive 'overkings'. War was a threat to local elites and failure on the battlefield could have disastrous consequences, with those not killed forced into exile. Some dynasties suffered violent deaths in successive generations. The extreme case is the Northumbrian, in which Theobald (603), Æthelfrith (c. 616),

Edwin (633), Osric (634), Eanfrith (634), Oswald (642), Ælfwine (679) and Ecgfrith (685) all died in battle, and additionally Hereric and Oswine were both assassinated; only Oswiu (670) certainly died in his bed.

Royal genealogies and lists of kings provide another means of exploring the origins of kingship. They survive in the work of Bede and in separate lists, at the earliest from around 800. While the Kentish kings claimed descent from Hengest, supposedly the leader of the Saxons in the mid-fifth century, the claim appears to have been made comparatively late; Oisc, reputedly Hengest's son, was the figure from whom the Kentish kings were named the *Oiscingas*, suggesting that he was earlier seen as the founder. The Kentish list has three generations before Æthelberht which look historical: his father Eormenric, grandfather Octa and great-grandfather Oeric Oisc. This dynasty's roots could therefore date to the first half of the sixth century. Kent's close links with the Merovingian world may account for the early appearance of kingship here.

Other lineages look fictional earlier than around 550: the Mercians claimed descent from Icel, so called themselves *Iclingas*, but the historical threshold comes with Penda son of Pybba, who lived in the first half of the seventh century. Their names proved popular in place name formation in the south-west Midlands, which suggests they originated there. Bede identified Ida as the founder of the Bernician kingship, dating his reign 547–59, and the East Anglian kings, the *Wuffingas*, claimed descent from Wuffa, grandfather of the earliest East Anglian king known to history, Rædwald, who died c. 624.

The names in sixth- and seventh-century sections of these genealogies are highly heterogeneous: Eormenric suggests a borrowing from Gothic while Æthelberht and the East Anglian Sigibert reflect Merovingian naming practices, though none is likely to have had parents from either group. There are also British or Celtic names. These include Cerdic, the founding figure of the West Saxon dynasty, other West Saxons including Cædwalla, who died at Rome in 688, and Penda (d. 655) and his father, Pybba, of the Mercians. Comparable British naming occurred in apparently noble families referred to by Bede (as bishops Chad, Cedd and Tuda), reflecting the cross-cultural pattern of elite naming practices. Genealogies that have British names may reflect the convergence of petty Celtic kingship and the protective role of an Anglo-Saxon warrior leader, perhaps through marriage.

There are dangers in this analysis, of course, since it rests on a conjunction of archaeological evidence, which is contemporary but difficult to interpret, with written comment which is predominantly later. But it does allow us to begin, at least, the process of exploring how and when Anglo-Saxon kingship emerged. While the picture is far from clear, kingship seems generally to have originated in the sixth century, particularly the middle decades. In Kent it was probably early and heavily influenced from Francia. Elsewhere it grew out of changing relationships between the leaders of successful war-bands, the tribal communities to which they belonged, and local British leaders with whom they interacted. But the idea of kingship clearly came from neighbouring peoples who already lived under kings, including the Franks, the Eastern Empire and Celtic neighbours.

coining by producing their own silver penny, or *sceatta* coinages. The far greater quantities than hitherto reflect the ease of access to silver, as opposed to gold.

Coin finds occur scattered across southern and eastern England but are particularly numerous at the *emporia* (or *wics*), where some at least were minted. These sprawling trading and manufacturing centres developed from the mid-seventh century. Hamwic on Southampton Water is perhaps the best known, but others lay at Ipswich and on the western approaches of London at Aldwych (literally, 'the old *wic*'). All extended over 40–60 hectares. These *emporia* exhibit peak coin loss in the early eighth century, which may indicate heightened trading activity. Hamwic was refounded on a new site at this date, with a planned layout. This was a unique international trading hub for the West Saxons, as were Ipswich for the East Angles and London for the Thames basin – coming under the control variously of Kent, Essex, Mercia and the West Saxons. On the Humber, coin finds imply a *wic* at North Ferriby by 700, but Fishergate outside the walls of York was also beginning about then.

Away from the main *wics*, 'productive sites' characterised by significant coin loss are also relevant to discussion of trade. Some were arguably elite residences or reli-

3.13 *Wics*, or *emporia*, and 'productive sites': large solid circles signify the main trading and manufacturing sites on both sides of the Channel; small hollow circles are 'productive sites', here only mapped consistently for England

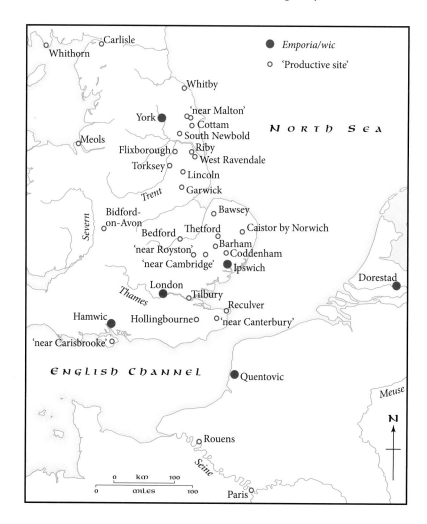

gious sites which attracted both exchange and manufacturing, others may have been markets or collecting points on trade networks emanating from the *emporia*. Bawsey (Norfolk), Barham and Coddenham (Suffolk), Carisbrook (Isle of Wight) and Flixborough (Lincolnshire) were all sites where exotic trade goods were in use: at Flixborough, wheel-thrown pottery from the Seine Valley and other burnished wares from northern France and the Rhineland were present in the late seventh century, and porpoise, dolphin and larger whale bones indicate marine resources reaching the site via the lower Trent.

Trade was increasing by c. 700, encouraging new industries. The cooking vessels and decorated pitchers termed 'Ipswich Ware' and fired near the modern city were traded into East Anglia and around south-east England, while stamped pitchers of the same type travelled up the east coast. Traded items or goods reaching a consumer via gift exchange could come thousands of kilometres. At his death Bede famously gifted pepper, from southern India, and incense, from Arabia or the Horn of Africa, to his fellow priests. Archaeological finds from similarly exotic locations include cowrie shells from the Indian Ocean, silks from China and Byzantium, elephant and walrus ivory, and metal vessels from Byzantium and the eastern Mediterranean.

The bulk of these goods presumably flowed through the *emporia* and commodities were necessarily passing the other way as well. The number of loom weights found on rural settlements may imply cloth production at near-industrial levels. Many crafts occurred at the *wics*, including comb manufacture using bone and antler. Metalworking was recovering from its slump in the fifth century. The frequent finding of buckles, strap ends and other mundane metal objects suggests that smiths were numerous. Aside from manufactured goods, ores, slaves and agricultural produce of various kinds could all have been exported from Anglo-Saxon England to finance exotic imports.

Around 600, 'Anglian' and 'Saxon' regional styles in clothing and jewellery began to give way across England to fashions which had developed in Kent under Frankish influence. This took place when Kentish hegemony extended across much of southern

3.14 Ipswich Ware of the mid-Anglo-Saxon period from excavations in Canterbury, demonstrating the coastal trade in pottery from East Anglia

3.15 Brooches from a woman's grave in the Buckland (Dover) cemetery. A pair of high-quality, radiate-headed silver brooches with garnet inlays, imported from Francia, and a quatrefoil brooch, with ivory inlay and garnet set in a cloisonné cell, over mercury-gilded, patterned silver foil

England and may have been politically driven. Change embraced all of material goods, styles of dress and funerary practices. Salin Style I metalwork gave way to Style II at this point, distinguished by more fluid forms, delicate gold filigree and the use of garnet, as seen to good effect at Sutton Hoo (Suffolk) and in the Staffordshire Hoard. New cultural impulses came both from the old Roman Empire on the Continent and insular traditions, such as the often beautifully ornamented, bronze hanging bowls found in Anglo-Saxon graves, particularly in the early seventh century. These derive from Celtic traditions of metalworking, though where remains a mystery. Frankish cultural influence on Kent and Sussex is well evidenced and occasional references in Continental writings suggest that Frankish kings might on occasion have thought of the peoples of the south east as their political dependants.

In the period 575–81 Bertha, daughter of the deceased Frankish king Charibert, was married to Æthelberht of Kent when he was still only 'the son of a certain king in Kent', as Gregory of Tours put it. The marriage was probably brokered by King Chilperic, who dominated north-west France between 574 and his death in 584 and who would have been using the daughter of his deceased half-brother to extend his own influence across the Channel. Bertha was a member of the most powerful family in western Europe, therefore this marriage would have helped the Kentish king to gain 'overkingship'. Now, for the first time (as far as we know), a Christian had influence at the heart of a powerful English kingship. Bertha brought with her a familiarity with mechanisms for state-building. In her entourage was a bishop. At this point we must turn our attention away from issues of kingship and the elite economy to explore religious affiliation and the English Conversion to Christianity.

English Paganism

Archaeology provides little direct information regarding Anglo-Saxon paganism. Gold bracteates, which are concentrated in sixth-century eastern Kent, may have been associated with a northern Germanic religious cult; certainly they remind us of Kent's 'Jutish' connection with Scandinavia. Some stamps cut into cinerary urns may be religious symbols, including the swastika, for example. There is a total absence so far in England of the carved wooden idols found in Danish and German peat bogs, but small metal figurines occasionally occur in cemeteries.

The lack of literacy before the Conversion to Christianity and distaste among Christian writers thereafter for pagan practices mean that we know little about pre-Christian religion. Bede, in *The Reckoning of Time*, provides the traditional English calendar of months: *Eosturmonath* (April) already contains the English name of Easter and may indicate a goddess and/or seasonal festival; *Blodmonath* (November) signifies the culling of livestock as winter approached; *Giuli* (both January and December) recalls Yuletide; Bede also noted that the English New Year began on 25 December, called *Modranecht* ('night of the mothers'), implying that the winter solstice marked the depths of winter, with the new year reflecting the lengthening days thereafter. In English, days of the week retain the names of the gods Tiu (Tuesday), Wutan/Woden (Wednesday) and Thunor (Thursday), and the goddess Freia (Friday), alongside the Moon, Saturn and the Sun.

Anglo-Saxon paganism encompassed a hierarchy of divine powers, from gods and goddesses to elves, spirits and ghosts. Central was the desire to gain divine approbation, or good luck – in Old English *hál* (giving us 'hale', 'healthy'). Animal sacrifice was used to earn divine favour, but references also to human sacrifice occur in the letters

3.16 Gold bracteates from Buckland (Dover), used as pendants in richly furnished sixth-century women's graves. The bracteates were probably all made in Kent but the Kentish group are outliers of a distribution otherwise centred on Norway, Denmark, northern Germany and southern Sweden. In Kent, therefore, they reflect Scandinavian, as opposed to Frankish, connections; the use of gold underlines their cultural value

of Sidonius Apollinaris; the display of King Oswald's head and hands on stakes in 642 by the pagan king Penda could be interpreted similarly. Auspices were important, with priests responsible for foretelling whether or not a proposed course of action might be attended by good fortune. Some burials were accompanied by balls of crystal, which were probably considered to have 'magic' power. Similarly, occasional female burials, such as one excavated at Bidford-on-Avon (Warwickshire) dating from the sixth century, were accompanied by numerous amulets of one kind or another, perhaps for use in telling fortunes. The behaviour of birds was observed to predict events, as noted both by Procopius and the anonymous author of the Whitby *Life of Gregory*. Little has come down to us concerning pagan priests beyond their existence, but the role was probably inherited, as it was in later Iceland. Bede's comments on the Deiran 'chief priest', Coifi, imply that priests neither used weapons nor rode stallions. Both taboos would have distinguished them from others of the elite.

While archaeologists have proposed several temple sites, only Yeavering has so far been generally accepted. Temple building may well belong predominantly to the Conversion period, appearing in reaction to churches. Germanic religion traditionally favoured groves or woodland glades. Old English *hearg*, which appears in place names as 'harrow' (hence Harrow-on-the Hill, Middlesex), is generally translated as 'temple'. 'Harrow' names regularly occur at a distance from Roman roads and may represent

3.17 Place names relating to possible pre-Christian temple sites. Some *hearg* names may reflect the presence of temples specific to particular peoples or communities, while the distribution of *wēoh* sites implies that these were more wayfarers' shrines

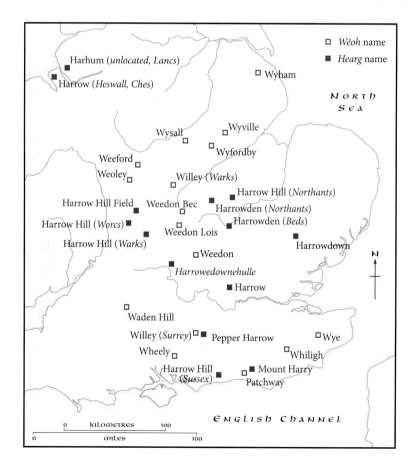

tribal ritual sites, attendance at which may even to an extent have defined that people. Recent research suggests that some 'harrow' place names identify sites connected with Romano-British and/or prehistoric rituals, throwing up the possibility that Anglo-Saxon paganism may be rooted in earlier cult practices, though this may have been entirely coincidental. Old English *wēoh* ('idol') also occurs in place names (as Wye, Kent), probably indicating pagan sanctuaries. Since *wēoh* names are commonly close to a Roman road, they perhaps marked a different type of sacred place, accessible to travellers and distinguished from *hearg* sites in terms of rites, participants and perhaps the deities involved.

The names of gods also occur in place names, with Woden (as Wednesbury, Staffordshire, and Woodnesborough, Kent) and Thunor (as Thundersley, Essex) the commonest. Stories of the deeds of gods and heroes were an important part of pagan culture and some proved long-lived: scenes from a tale about the smith-god, Wayland, appear carved on the front panel of the whalebone Franks Casket, which is arguably of late seventh-century manufacture, perhaps in southern Northumbria. A scene depicting the story of Wayland's brother Egil decorates its only surviving lid panel. Such scenes remind us that much that was pagan retained value and familiarity in Conversion-period England, providing a richness and depth to a newly Christianised culture.

Gods were also invoked as a means of naming and interpreting the landscape, as Wayland's Smithy (a Neolithic long barrow on the Berkshire Downs), or Wansdyke (literally 'Woden's dyke'). They were replaced in that role in the Christian era by the Devil – as Devil's Dyke (Cambridgeshire).

3.18 The Franks Casket, a lidded rectangular box made of whale bone carved in relief with scenes from Roman, Jewish, Christian and Germanic traditions, accompanied by carved texts in Old English and Latin. This front panel features both a composite scene (left), representing the legend of Weland the Smith and (right) the Adoration of the Magi

3.19 Devil's Dyke, Newmarket. The Dark Age dyke with the highest bank and deepest ditch in England, this was one of a series cutting the Icknield Way between East Anglia and Middle Anglia. Clearly it was named, perhaps re-named, in the Christian era

Harrow (Middlesex) and Wednesbury ('Woden's fortress') are both elevated sites which later attracted Christian churches. At Harrow sufficient traces of early activity have been found to justify interpretation as a pagan complex. The shrine mentioned by Bede at Goodmanham on the Yorkshire Wolds could likewise have been on the site of the later parish church. Pope Gregory's letter to Bishop Mellitus while en route to England in 601 urged that pagan sites be ritually purified and reused as churches, and that is a possibility in such instances. However, pagan-type names are commonest on estate boundaries and only rarely associated with sites of later churches. Indeed, many are only known from boundary clauses in later charters. Overall, place names that refer to pagan religion are thinly scattered across southern and central England, east of Dorset and predominantly south of a line from Lichfield to Ipswich. The distribution correlates poorly with early Anglo-Saxon burials – there are noticeable gaps in East Anglia, East Yorkshire and the north east, and only a single example in Lincolnshire. It seems most unlikely that surviving 'pagan' place names provide a reliable guide to the distribution of shrines in, say, 600; rather, such names say more about patterns of name-survival, suggesting that names indicative of pagan practices were more likely to survive on the margins, distant from mission stations.

Paganism centred not on faith but on rituals designed to bring benefits to the individual or the community. Pagan sacred sites, intercession and priestly status were all probably older than Anglo-Saxon kingship, and traditional religion was embedded in many aspects of Anglo-Saxon life, including warfare, story-telling, the assembly, legal practice, medicine and the agricultural calendar. As kingly power developed, so analogy with other convert societies encourages us to expect tensions between kings and the priestly class. Conversion to Christianity offered kings influence over religious affairs, with priests under their own protection and operating at sites of their own choosing. Unsurprisingly, therefore, the Christianisation of the English looks to have been sponsored largely by kings.

Conversion to Christianity

Bede's *Ecclesiastical History* dominates the English Conversion story. He wrote for his own contemporaries, focusing initially (book I, 23–33) on Pope Gregory's responsibility for and efforts to support the Augustinian mission, quoting papal letters to England at length. Augustine reached Kent in 597, rapidly baptised the king and was established by him at Canterbury. Early success led to the foundation of further bishoprics at Rochester and London. After the deaths of Gregory, Augustine and King Æthelberht of Kent, however, the mission experienced difficulties. It was rescued by Paulinus's conversion of King Edwin of the Northumbrians, in the 620s, and from this point Bede's focus shifts northwards. Edwin's death in 633 brought renewed crisis, but a new style of Christianity was introduced by King Oswald in the mid-630s from the monastery of Iona where he had been in exile, leading to the foundation of Lindisfarne as a monastery and bishop's seat. This northern Irish/Scottish form of Christianity then spread across Northumbria and central England, as far as Essex. The story of Northumbria and the Scottish mission dominates Bede's book III and he promoted the memory of its heroes, particularly King Oswald and Bishop Aidan. He then tells how the English Church was reunited under Canterbury through the actions of King Oswiu of the Northumbrians at the Synod of Whitby in 664.

In the late 660s the elderly Greek Theodore was appointed by the papacy as leader of the newly unified English Church, bringing with him another distinguished émigré, the African Hadrian, as abbot of the monastery at Canterbury. There was a need to unify and reorganise since the Church was in disarray. There were precious few bishops in post and several dioceses were excessively large. Theodore imposed order, split dioceses, clarified doctrine, and provided leadership to a Church which had been divided since the 630s. In Bede's view the early years of Theodore's episcopacy (668–90) were a golden age for both English Christianity and kingship, from which a decline later occurred, marked most particularly by King Ecgfrith's death in battle against the Picts in 685. Bede was himself a child of this era (b. 672/3) and the twin monasteries at which he resided were founded then, Monkwearmouth c. 673 by the much travelled Northumbrian nobleman Benedict Biscop, a close associate of Theodore and temporarily abbot at Canterbury, and Jarrow c. 681. Both were established under the patronage of Ecgfrith, Northumbria's fiercely Catholic king.

Bede had much invested, therefore, in the age of Theodore and so too had Abbot Albinus at Canterbury, Bede's principal informant regarding the Gregorian mission and a graduate of Abbot Hadrian's school there. Theodore's rule led naturally to renewed interest in Rome and the Gregorian mission among the English: Pope Gregory's earliest *Life* was composed in England at Whitby c. 700, his cult disseminated across England, and a growing trickle of English travellers found their way to Rome, on business or as pilgrims. Stephen's *Life of Wilfrid*, written shortly after 710, records his hero's three trips to Rome and sets great store by the authority of the papacy. Bede's work was, therefore, influenced by a considerable revival of interest in Gregory and Rome since the 670s, as well as his own admiration for Gregory's writings.

However, Bede's story of an English nation eager for conversion by Roman missionaries is both simplistic and overly optimistic. In fact, Augustine's mission had lost the little impetus it had ever had by c. 616, when King Æthelberht died and Bishops Mellitus and Iustus withdrew from London and Rochester, leaving Canterbury isolated and on the verge of failure. While the conversion of King Edwin's court in the north provided temporary relief, York also had to be abandoned c. 633, leaving just a deacon, James, to care for Rome's converts. Although Pope Honorius (d. 638) sent Bishop Birinus to Britain as a missionary, this was independent of Canterbury. Papal interest in the Kentish mission waned and communication with Rome collapsed between the 630s and 660s. The death in 653 of Archbishop Honorius, the last survivor of Gregory's missionaries, brought on what could easily have been the mission's final crisis, with the succession at Canterbury unresolved for eighteen months.

Recent scholars have questioned Bede's focus on Rome for the English Conversion, arguing for a greater Gaulish/Frankish contribution. Irish missionaries have also been credited with more success as preachers than the Romans. Other voices have argued for a British input. King Æthelberht's preference for Roman missionaries may imply that they were seen in Kent as less beholden to Frankish kings at a date when there was a danger of subordination to Francia. The uniformity with which Gregory's Romans then monopolised episcopal authority at Canterbury suggests a deliberate policy, but in practice even the papal missions had a strong Frankish element, and all should be viewed against the ever-shifting backdrop of Merovingian dynastic politics. The first recorded bishop in Kent was the Frankish Liudhard, who reached Canterbury with

3.20 The west interior end wall of St Martin's Church, Canterbury. According to Bede, this was used by Bertha and her bishop prior to Augustine's arrival. Bede asserted that the church dated back to Roman Britain and the architecture parallels known buildings from that period. Additionally, its location outside the walls may indicate a Late Antique extramural church

Æthelberht's bride, Bertha, probably in the period 575–81. Liudhard's name appears on a gold medalet recovered from the vicinity of St Martin's at Canterbury, where Bede tells us that he ministered to his flock. The church dedication reflects Bertha's close association with Tours. That a bishop accompanied the princess implies the intention to baptise. His letter to her demonstrates that Pope Gregory viewed Bertha as capable of furthering the mission, but her advocacy of Christianity surely pre-dated Augustine's arrival.

When it did come, Gregory's mission was a collaborative venture undertaken in partnership with one branch of the Merovingian royal house working against another. The sudden and unexpected death of Gregory's ally, the powerful King Childeberht, precipitated Augustine's return to Rome in 596. Sent back with new letters of introduction, Augustine engaged Childerberht's mother, Brunhild, and his heirs, the boy-kings Theudeberht and Theuderic, as allies and recruited Frankish clergy to aid him, later returning to Francia to be consecrated. Gregory's remark in a letter to Alexandria in 598 that 10,000 of the English had been baptised the previous Christmas suggests that Æthelberht and the Kentish elite had accepted Christianity within months of Augustine's arrival. In that case the king was very much behind the conversion process.

Little more seems to have occurred, however, beyond the baptism of Æthelberht's nephew, Saberht of the East Saxons, until Theudeberht and Theuderic defeated their rival Clothar in 600 and took over Gaul's Atlantic coast. With the balance of power in Francia overturned, the Canterbury mission sent back to Rome in 601 for the priests, books and vestments which would enable expansion outside eastern Kent. Churches and bishoprics were established at Rochester and London, but the baptism of King Rædwald proved less successful, with the East Anglian king reverting to paganism on his return home. By 605, relations between Theudeberht and Theuderic were deteriorating and open warfare broke out in 610, leading to both their deaths. This enabled Clothar II to secure the throne of a newly reunited Francia. That senior figures from the Canterbury mission attended his Church Council at Paris in 614 indicates that Æthelberht was keen for reconciliation with the new Frankish superpower. Francia loomed large, therefore, in the early history of the Church at Canterbury, and Frankish dynastic politics were a major factor affecting even papal missions.

Frankish interest was not confined to Kent, for Continental missionaries spearheaded the conversion of the East Angles around 630, then that of the West Saxons. The senior representative of the Roman Church at the Synod of Whitby in 664 was the Frankish Agilbert, recently bishop of the West Saxons and soon to be bishop of Paris. Employing missionaries direct from overseas allowed kings greater independence than working through the metropolitan. Although it was always Catholic, West Saxon Christianity in particular displayed considerable independence. The desire to harness alternative sources of divine authority encouraged Oswald and the Bernicians to adopt Scottish Christianity from Iona in the 630s, in opposition to King Edwin's recent patronage of Roman missionaries and the continuing paganism of the Mercians. There were Irish foundations in other parts of England, including a monastery established by Fursa in East Anglia and the small house of Irish brethren noted by Bede at Bosham in West Sussex.

The whole issue of a British input is more contentious, particularly since Bede denied it so vigorously in the *Ecclesiastical History* (I, 22):

> To other abominable wickedness which their historian Gildas lamented in a sermon they [the Britons] added this that they never preached the faith to the Saxons or Angles who inhabited Britain with them . . .

In the West Midlands, however, the lack of an English Conversion story and the combination of a dominance of English place names alongside a scarcity of pre-Christian burials suggest a different story. Here the Britons may well have converted incoming Angles, allowing elements of the pre-existing British Church to survive. In reality, many 'Anglo-Saxons' in the west and north were probably in origin British Christians. The Scottish mission, which established itself throughout Northumbria and Mercia, would have had no difficulty accepting such groups as Christians. In the later seventh century, however, Theodore presided over a Catholic Church that treated both Britons and Scots as heretics. Its adherents stamped out the British Church wherever they could. In so doing they were probably responsible for a dramatic rise in Anglicisation, as Britons became far less easy to distinguish from Anglo-Saxons.

Prior to this religious cleansing, a substantial indigenous contribution to English Christianity is likely, particularly in western Britain, from Galloway, where the British church at Whithorn became an Anglo-Saxon episcopal church, via Cumbria, Lancashire and the Welsh marcher counties down to Somerset, Dorset and Devon. A very few Celtic church dedications remain, as St Elphin's at Warrington. Even in eastern England a few British Christian centres survived down to the seventh and eighth centuries. Bede believed that the cult of St Alban had a continuous history of miracles from the Roman period through to his own time. Pope Gregory referred in a letter in 601 to the pre-existing, so presumably British, cult of St Sixtus, and that same letter addressed issues which imply that Augustine had contact with British Christians. *Eccles* place names (from Latin *ecclesia* 'church' via Celtic *eglwys*) probably reflect the presence of British churches, and archaeological evidence from such sites as Lincoln suggest a Christian cult lasting into the sixth century, at least. Catholic writers had every reason to overlook the British origins of some English church sites, so this evidence is all the more convincing. There is a case for British Christianity having survived comparatively well to the seventh century in western and northern England, and in pockets, at least, even in the east and south.

What attracted English kings to Christianity in the late sixth and seventh centuries was clearly not its British-ness, since Britons were considered subordinate in Anglo-Saxon society. Rather, it seems to have been the political utility of Christianity, plus a new interest in and desire for *Romanitas*. Church foundation and burial in Christian cemeteries were taking place in Francia in the late sixth century and reached England early in the seventh. Conversion, however, offered further advantages to kings beyond the cultural or religious. The presence of strangely dressed and spoken religious professionals with exotic patterns of behaviour and equipped with books, wine and oil offered a new dimension to a royal court and distinction to its king.

Christianity was, first and foremost, a religion of the book. The Old Testament presented a style of kingship which was divinely ordained and quasi-sacral, while the imperial government of the New Testament had law-making and tax-raising powers. Patronage of a literate clergy enabled kings to claim law-enacting powers, encode what had hitherto been traditional laws, and introduce changes commensurate with the growing authority of kingship. The missionaries wrestled with the difficulty of representing the unfamiliar sounds of Old English in an alphabet adapted to Latin, but somehow they succeeded. Although only extant in a twelfth-century manuscript – the *Textus Roffensis* ('Rochester text') – Æthelberht's law code is the earliest surviving document in English, written down while Augustine was still alive.

Letters made it possible for a king to communicate at a distance, and monastic foundation provided a means of establishing a permanent royal presence in contested territories. Christianity ensured that identical religious rituals would be replicated at all churches throughout the kingdom, with prayers said for the king. In key ways, therefore, Conversion restructured religious life around the royal family.

Christianity also provided rituals capable of underwriting unequal relationships within the elite, to the benefit of powerful kings. For example, King Oswald acted as godfather at the baptism of the West Saxon King Cynegils, whose daughter he had just married, thereby underlining his superior status. Æthelberht probably had a comparable role when King Rædwald was baptised at the Kentish court, and this was certainly the position taken by Oswiu at the baptisms of several subordinate kings conducted deep inside Northumbria. Oswiu also used monastic foundation as expiation of his responsibility for the murder of a kinsman, King Oswine of the *Deiri*, and to elicit divine aid before battle against Penda of the Mercians in 655.

That kings and their advisors were consciously engaged in rethinking Britain as a Roman space was suggested above. That impulse finds echoes in Bede's *Ecclesiastical History*, which offers a Roman Britain with obvious debts to Anglo-Saxon England. His presentation of the English as if latter-day Romans is particularly noticeable in the context of their respective relations with the Britons but is never quite explicit. Such impulses connect with royal pretensions to imperial status. Bede actually described Æthelberht's law code as written 'after the Roman manner', despite it having little particularly 'Roman' about it beyond being written down. The ship burial under mound I at Sutton Hoo included an object sometimes interpreted as a standard and another that resembles a sceptre, the style of which owes much to Celtic work. When referring to King Edwin of Northumbria, Bede wrote:

> So great was his majesty in his realm that not only were banners carried before him in battle, but even in time of peace riding between his cities, rural estates and provinces with his thegns a standard-bearer would always precede him, when walking anywhere through public open spaces the type of standard which the Romans call a *tufa* and the English a *thuuf* would be carried before him.

Kings were, it seems, reinventing themselves in terms of their understanding of Roman political culture. Such strategies proved comparatively successful across the seventh century, allowing the greater kings both to distinguish themselves from their own tribal elites and to pressurise and slowly extinguish lesser kingships. The declining ability of the kings of the *Hwicce* to grant land without Mercian approval provides one of the better documented examples of this process.

The establishment of dioceses in subordinate kingdoms enabled powerful rulers to place individuals on whose loyalty they could rely in kingdoms ruled by powerful sub-kings. Æthelberht achieved this at London, and the establishment of a bishop at Rochester put in place an agent through whom he could oversee the more distant and recently acquired parts of his own territory. Oswiu later achieved something similar on a larger scale through bishops appointed under his protection for the East Saxons, Middle Angles and Mercians.

Within their own kingdoms, church and monastic foundations provided opportunities for kings to establish new institutional foci of royal authority, around which to reorientate local society. By the late seventh century, numerous families, both royal and noble, were investing in family monasteries, often vesting authority in female kin. Whitby is a prime example, ruled successively by female members of the Northumbrian royal family from its foundation in the 650s into the early eighth century. Many such sites were intended as places of elite burial, for Oswiu in this instance though King Edwin's remains were also reinterred there. The monastery at Canterbury became a mausoleum for the Kentish kings, but in many kingdoms individuals established their own foundation, generating numerous royal churches linked to different branches of the royal family.

3.21 Stone sceptre or ceremonial whetstone found in the ship-burial at Sutton Hoo in 1939. The apex of the stone has human masks, all slightly different, on each of its four faces, perhaps signifying universal authority as befitting an 'overking'. Above, an iron ring surmounts the stone, on which a bronze stag is set. An enigmatic object, the sceptre seems emblematic of power and may have mythic or religious connotations. The style suggests Celtic influences

Conversion to Christianity therefore provided a new institutional framework which offered cohesion to kingdoms, opportunities for powerful kings to influence the less powerful, and novel mechanisms for elite patronage. Oswiu followed the Continental precedent, presiding in person over a church council in 664, the Synod of Whitby. It was Christianity, above all else, that enabled powerful kings to establish themselves across the seventh century and to institutionalise their own pre-eminence. After Penda's death in 655, Northumbrian and Mercian 'overkings' vied for influence over the Church and for power over neighbouring communities. Despite the initial advantage going to Oswiu and his son Ecgfrith, the Mercians emerged as the more powerful in the 680s. By the end of the seventh century, influence was unevenly divided between them, with the Mercians dominant south of the Humber and the Northumbrians to the north.

Conversion also brought opportunities to other sections of the elite. Christianity offered an alternative career to that of warrior which might lead to a position of high status, wealth and even political power – such as Cuthbert and Wilfrid both enjoyed. Some noble families clearly saw the Church as their preferred means of advancement. For individuals, entry to a monastery or nunnery provided an opportunity to avoid marriage or difficult political circumstances, or to retire from family commitments in later life. Senior clergy, including Bishop John of Hexham and York and Bishop Earconwald of London, often founded monasteries (in John's case Beverley) to which they retired, having laid aside episcopal responsibilities. Earconwald, who may have been a member of the East Saxon royal dynasty, founded a house for himself, at Chertsey (Surrey) where he was abbot until elevated to the episcopacy, and another for his sister, Æthelburh, at Barking (Essex). Most inmates of such foundations seem to have come from the secular elite; Earconwald himself was clearly a member of a very wealthy family.

Patronage of the Church was, however, expensive. While warriors expected maintenance at court, prestige objects and ultimately grants of land for life, part at least of these resources eventually reverted to the Crown at their death. Additionally, the support of an armed following generally encouraged the inflow of wealth to royal coffers. In contrast, the foundation of churches and monasteries required the permanent alienation of land as well as treasure to fund the necessary buildings, books, vestments, wine and oil, and support the community. Estates granted to the Church were measured in hides, so in units of productive land capable of supporting a household of free status.

Grants could be large: Bede said of Æthelberht that

he gave many gifts to the bishops of each of these churches [London and Rochester] and that of Canterbury and he also added both lands and possessions for the maintenance of the bishops' retinues.

In 655, Oswiu gave land to found 12 monasteries, each with 10 hides, in thanks for his victory over Penda; Cædwalla of the West Saxons promised Wilfrid a quarter of the Isle of Wight, valued at 300 hides, and a quarter of the spoils of his war of conquest. The *Penitential* attributed to Theodore stipulated that a third of plunder should come to the Church. Great monasteries, such as Monkwearmouth (Sunderland), were endowed with scores of hides, were the recipients of numerous gifts and supported hundreds of brethren. Although other sections of elite society founded monasteries from the later seventh century, the earliest houses were the responsibility of kings, who provided a degree of stability for their new foundations by having records made of their land-grants in the form of the charter. This 'booked' land to the Church, creating 'book-land' which was exempt from traditional inheritance practices.

The speed of conversion has occasioned considerable debate. Bede wrote as if baptism of the king and his immediate associates equated with the Christianisation of an entire people, but the last pagan Anglo-Saxon king – Cædwalla of the West Saxons – only received baptism, at Rome, in 688. In reality royal baptisms only started the process and Christianisation of the rest of society may have taken generations. The active suppression of paganism seems only to have begun late in the seventh century, and monastic foundation on a large scale likewise only took off about then. Assessing progress is problematic and the results are not entirely consistent. Clearly the Church was wealthy by the early eighth century, but Bede considered that this had come at a cost and the quality of its personnel and practices was at risk.

One measure is the length of time before the English Church was self-sustaining. The foundation of schools to train clergy was an essential aspect of establishing

Christianity. Augustine presumably founded one at Canterbury and Bede tells us that Felix did so in East Anglia in the 630s, but there is little evidence that either prospered. Ithamar, at Rochester (Kent), is often seen as the first bishop to have been trained in England, but his Old Testament name is typical of British practices, not Roman, so he may have been British trained. Another candidate is Thomas, Felix's deacon and then his successor as bishop of the East Angles in the late 640s. He had probably served what amounted to a clerical apprenticeship combined with attendance at Felix's school. The West Saxon, Deusdedit, was the first English archbishop of Canterbury, in 655. Wigheard, one of Deusdedit's clerics, was despatched to Rome in 664 for consecration and was considered by Bede well fitted to be archbishop at Canterbury, but he died in Italy.

In the north such figures as Cuthbert were educated in the Scottish monastic tradition and many travelled to Ireland to further their education, while Wilfrid and Benedict Biscop went to Gaul and Rome. Southern English training only really took off in the 670s under Abbot Hadrian's oversight at Canterbury. It is the scholarship of such figures as Aldhelm (d. 709/10), abbot of Malmesbury and bishop of Sherborne, and Bishop Wilfrid (634–710), that attracted Bede's praise. It was this generation and the next, with such figures as Bede himself, Abbot Ceolfrith of Monkwearmouth/ Jarrow (d. 716) and Bishop Tobias of Rochester (d. 726), that permanently established Christian learning among the English.

Clearly, Monkwearmouth/Jarrow lay at the forefront of the new English learning, with its magnificent library and Bede's own vast output of exegesis and school books. The making of three massive Bibles under Abbot Ceolfrith's direction perhaps marks this progress most clearly. One, the *Codex Amiatinus*, survives at Florence. Its 2,060 pages, made from parchment processed from around 1,550 calf hides, are a monument to the wealth at Ceolfrith's disposal, the scale of literary production of which the greatest Anglo-Saxon monasteries were by then capable, and the skills of its scribes. Other magnificently illustrated books were made elsewhere, including the *Durham*, *Echternach* and *Lindisfarne Gospels*, all of which arguably date from the late seventh or early eighth centuries. According to an interlinear gloss added when they were at Chester-le-Street around 970, Eadfrith, bishop of Lindisfarne from 698, was the author of the *Lindisfarne Gospels*.

Even at lesser monastic sites, literacy was probably widespread in the early eighth century, but the production of large-scale and highly ornamented texts was centred on very few houses. Except for a small minority of individuals, such as King Aldfrith of the Northumbrians (685–707) who had trained in Ireland for a career in the Church, neither reading nor writing is likely to have spread very far within secular society. However, the monastic community was substantial by the early eighth century. Although there were clearly illiterate monks, particularly those who took vows late in life, literate clerks were numerous and their skills well understood. Additionally, such bishops as Wilfrid also educated the children of the elite in their own households. Some houses were double foundations in which communities of monks and nuns both resided, including Whitby and Coldingham in Northumbria and Barking in Essex. Some nuns were literate, corresponding with Bede, for example, and the Anglo-Saxon

3.22 Front cover of the *Lindisfarne Gospels*. This sumptuously illustrated Gospel Book, written c. 690-721, was originally bound in richly decorated and bejewelled leather but the binding was lost in the Viking Age. This replica, made in the mid-nineteenth century, probably gives a realistic impression of its original splendour

missionaries in Germany; the erudite abbot (later bishop) Aldhelm addressed letters to communities of nuns.

Sculpture offered another form of literacy, not just via inscriptions but also through relief sculpture used to convey religious ideas and motifs, often brightly painted. The inception belongs to the second half of the seventh century, with such figures as Bishop Wilfrid introducing carved ornamentation of a type he had encountered on the Continent to his magnificent new churches at Hexham and Ripon. Scenes from the Bible, portraits of the saints and various styles of ornamentation proliferated, sometimes resulting in works of considerable sophistication, carrying subtle Christian messages. The cross shafts at Ruthwell (Dumfries) and Bewcastle (Cumbria) offer sophisticated examples which were very much in tune with contemporary liturgy at the start of the eighth century.

Written evidence that pagan practices survived the Conversion is not substantial, though this may be due as much to bias as to anything else. Evidence of apostasy suggests continuing knowledge of and respect for paganism in some regions. King Ealdwulf of the East Angles (d. 713) reputedly used to recall seeing Rædwald's pagan temple still standing when he was a boy, suggesting that this was a substantial building through the 630s and 640s. Bede remarked in his *Life of Cuthbert* that many still took refuge in incantations and amulets to ward off the plague while his hero was active (d. 687). In the *Ecclesiastical History* he noted that some of the East Saxons restored derelict temples in the 670s for similar reasons. Severe epidemics in the 660s and 680s clearly posed considerable challenges to society to which neither religion had effective answers, despite the various efforts made to write miracle cures into several hagiographies. Bishop Daniel of the West Saxons wrote to Boniface in Germany proffering

3.23 The Bewcastle Cross. At 4.4 metres high, this incomplete cross shaft is one of the finest pieces of pre-Viking Age Northumbrian sculpture. The west face, here, shows relief panels featuring (from top) St John the Baptist, Christ treading the beasts, and St John the Evangelist, with his eagle. Runic inscriptions appear on three sides and seem to commemorate kings Ecgfrith (d. 685) and Aldfrith (d. 705), suggesting that the cross was carved and erected no earlier than c. 710–30

advice on how best to persuade pagans to accept Christianity in terms which suggest that he was practised in the art as late as the 720s. Written evidence for pagan practices comes from the *Penitential* attributed to Archbishop Theodore, written after his death in 690, although section I, 15, headed 'Of the Worship of Idols', is very short:

1. He who sacrifices to demons in trivial matters shall do a year's penance, but in serious matters ten years' penance.
2. If any woman puts her daughter on the roof or into an oven to cure a fever, she shall do seven years' penance.
3. He who causes cereals to be burned where a man has died, for the health of the living and the house, shall do five years' penance.
4. If a woman performs diabolical incantations or divinations, she shall do a year's penance or the three forty-day periods, or forty days according to the offence . . . .
5. In the case of one who eats food that has been sacrificed and later confesses, the priest should consider the person, his age, how he had been brought up and how it had happened. So also the priestly authority shall be modified in the case of a sick person. . . .

Some of these practices had little religious significance but were perhaps alien to Theodore and so interpreted as pagan survivals. Others are unmistakeable. Overall, they imply that pagan rites retained a following but were increasingly associated with the elderly, who had been pagans from birth. Others were healing rites practised by women, who may have felt excluded by the male-centred nature of ritual within Christianity, which cut across the 'cunning-woman' role that is evidenced occasionally in pre-Conversion burials. While mixed houses and nunneries offered positions of power and influence to a minority of well-connected women, all were excluded from priestly functions. Furnished burial shows a female bias in the later seventh and early eighth centuries, perhaps for similar reasons.

Contrasting the law code of Æthelberht (c. 600) with that of Wihtred (695) illustrates the extent to which Kentish kings embraced Christianity by the close of the seventh century. While the earlier code merely fitted the clergy into the existing compensation system, a century later we find pagan sacrifice prohibited, the enforcement of Christian marriage and the Sabbath, and a ban on eating meat during prescribed fasts. By the end of the seventh century, therefore, parts at least of England were well on their way to becoming a Christian land.

Conversion-Period England: A Conclusion

Across the later sixth, seventh and early eighth centuries, Anglo-Saxon society was transformed. The tribalism implicit in mid-sixth-century burials proved incapable of accommodating growing inequalities of wealth, status and power. Cremation gave way to inhumation across the period and the inhumation rite became more variable. 'Final Phase' burials appear, provided with very few grave goods and often in a new cemetery. In the south east 'princely burials' in the very late sixth and early seventh centuries reflect the emergence of new social hierarchies and the rise of kingship; they also probably reflect opposition to Christianity. That opposition died away thereafter and progressively the elite abandoned traditional burial rites in favour of church-centred inhumation with ever fewer grave goods, while the remainder of the population increasingly used field cemeteries. Richly furnished inhumations are rare by the late seventh century, and many, like the female bed-burial at Trumpington (Cambridgeshire), are accompanied by Christian symbols, in this case a pendant cross. By 730 this transformation was virtually complete, with no more than an occasional scatter of furnished burials thereafter until the Viking Age. The rise of kingship was accompanied by significant cultural change which reflected a shift away from Scandinavian influence in favour of Francia and the Eastern Empire, combined with a growing reinvestment in the insular Roman heritage. Fashions in dress, styles of ornamentation and of metalwork were all affected.

Under Frankish influence, coining in gold revived in the seventh century, spreading outwards from Kent alongside the Conversion, with larger-scale minting of silver pennies in evidence from c. 675. From the later seventh century, new *emporia* or *wics* gave access to external trade and became important centres of small-scale manufacturing, minting and crafts. In the south and east smaller 'productive sites' developed in their hinterlands, as centres of consumption, production and/or dissemination.

Alongside these developments, missionaries from Italy, Francia, the Britons and Scottish Dál Riata introduced Christianity to the Anglo-Saxons, converting all the English courts by the close of the 680s and establishing literacy, a bookish set of rituals, new forms of record-keeping and a political ideology which embraced kingship. Kings, and particularly powerful kings, sponsored the mission and supported it with substantial grants of land and material wealth, gaining in return a valuable set of state-forming mechanisms. The development of kingship and the process of Conversion went hand in hand.

We began this chapter with the Anglo-Saxon community as pagan. By the 730s paganism was extinguished as a separate cultural force, if not entirely dead, and Christianity was firmly established, with growing numbers of monastic houses and churches and a sufficient flow of educated clerics to maintain an English Church. The Romanists had won the contest with Iona, secured the framework of a Christian Church in England and even persuaded Iona to adopt Roman practices. It would be false to suppose that Christianity had swept away all aspects of paganism, but it had become the dominant intellectual paradigm, affecting how the Anglo-Saxons saw themselves, their past, their future and their role on earth.

A single archbishop presided over the English Church from 669 until the archbishopric at York was recreated in 735. Theodore began the task of breaking up the massive early dioceses, so that Mercia and Northumbria both had as many as four bishops and the West Saxons and East Angles two each, though pre-existing tribal groupings clearly influenced these dioceses. This chapter ends, therefore, with the Anglo-Saxons Christian and organised under kings. While there had been perhaps 30 or 40 small-scale tribal kingships when the Tribal Hidage was written, by the 730s the more powerful kings had successfully reduced this to perhaps seven, converting many smaller communities to provinces in their own extended kingdoms. By the standards of Francia, even the greatest Anglo-Saxon kingships appear small; the contest for supremacy between Mercia and Northumbria across the seventh century had brought neither total success. The most powerful kingships were Northumbria, which dominated northern England and southern Scotland but had failed in its bid to conquer the entirety of Scotland, and Mercia, which dominated central England. Wessex remained Mercia's largest rival in the south but the East Angles, East Saxons, Kentings and South Saxons still retained separate kingships, even when tributary to the Mercians.

State-formation had not kept up with cultural or religious contexts in terms of the creation of an English people. Reference to the Angles, Saxons, Jutes and Frisians tends to emphasise regional identities. Tribes seem to have formed at the local level, despite a common 'English' language which had only dialectical differences between regions. The increasing homogeneity of burial rituals and artefact assemblages implies a growing sense of 'English' identity across the seventh century. By the close of the century, a universal religious framework and the rhetoric of the *ecclesia Anglorum* – the 'Church of the English' – provided a stronger sense of Englishness than hitherto. In particular, the collapse of the British Church throughout English-dominated areas removed the last major barrier to integration and the British become ever harder to identify within England, becoming absorbed into English society. A sense of collective

3.24 Chapel of St Lawrence, Bradford-on-Avon. Reputedly founded by St Aldhelm early in the eighth century, the chapel was only re-discovered in the mid-nineteenth century. While we cannot be certain, the small nave and chancel may well be largely original

English-ness was growing, therefore, but even so identity was layered and important loyalties remained local and/or regional. Despite their collective Christianity, the political classes do seem to have divided very much along the lines of the major kingships. Bede's unwillingness to include information from Mercia demonstrates the gulf that separated Northumbrians from their southern neighbours, despite their common adherence to a single Church.

THE VENERABLE BEDE

MARTIN J. RYAN

Lo, the mouth of Britain, which once only knew how to gnash its barbarous teeth, has long since learned to sing the praises of God with the alleluia of the Hebrews.

The Northumbrian monk Bede (c. 673–735) took these lines from Gregory the Great's *Morals on the Book of Job* to refer to the conversion of the Anglo-Saxons initiated by Augustine. Whether or not this is what Gregory meant by his words – and it seems unlikely – they reflect the common medieval motif of the transformative and civilising power of Christianity spreading to the farthest and most barbarous regions of the Earth.

There can be no better microcosm of this process than Bede himself. His grandparents would most likely have been pagans, perhaps converting to Christianity as adults, and Bede would have been 12 or 13 when the final Anglo-Saxon kingdoms embraced Christianity. His life was spent in the north east of England, far distant from the great Christian centres of the world. Yet Bede became – and remains – a towering figure in the Christian tradition. He is now best known for his *Ecclesiastical History of the English People* (c. 731), a work that is the paramount source for Anglo-Saxon history of the seventh and early eighth centuries, but his scholarly output was far broader, encompassing biblical commentary (exegesis), orthography, figures of speech and tropes, metrics, geography, cosmography, poetry, the reckoning of time and hagiography.

Even during his own lifetime, Bede's learning and expertise were recognised, and his works were in considerable demand within a few years of his death. Manuscripts soon began circulating on the Continent; Anglo-Saxon missionaries to northern Europe wrote to religious houses in Northumbria requesting copies of Bede's writings and by the beginning of the ninth century he was being cited by Carolingian authors as an authority on a par with the Church Fathers.

One of the earliest surviving copies of the *Ecclesiastical History*, the 'Moore Bede' (Cambridge University Library Kk. 5.16), was for a time held by the court library of Charlemagne, perhaps brought there by Alcuin, a graduate of the cathedral school at York. Further copies of the *History* and other of Bede's works found readers in many of the monastic and cathedral libraries across Francia, as witnessed by surviving manuscripts and book-lists. In England, the *Ecclesiastical History* was translated and adapted into Old English in the late ninth century, perhaps by a Mercian with connections to King Alfred's court, and was also one of the sources used by the compilers of the *Anglo-Saxon Chronicle* for the period up to 731.

Bede's reputation continued to grow throughout the Middle Ages. Anglo-Norman historians in the twelfth century, such as William of Malmesbury or Henry of Huntingdon, explicitly took Bede as their model and presented themselves as restarting and reinvigorating the tradition of historical writing that he had initiated. Likewise, the central work of biblical commentary in the high and later Middle Ages, the so-called *Glossa ordinaria* or *Ordinary Gloss*, drew extensively on Bede's exegesis, as did St Thomas Aquinas's *Catena aurea* or *Golden Chain*, a collection of Patristic and medieval commentary on the four Gospels. Such was Bede's reputation that Dante even featured him in his *Paradiso* – the only Englishman included.

Despite Bede's importance, relatively little is known about his life and the majority of the information that survives comes from his own writings. He closed his *Ecclesiastical History* with a short autobiographical statement, describing himself as 'servant of Christ and priest in the monastery of St Peter and St Paul which is at Wearmouth and Jarrow', and recounting how at the age of seven he was placed in the monastery by his kinsmen. He describes how he subsequently spent the rest of his life there, studying the Scriptures, performing the liturgy, and delighting in the opportunities given to him to learn, to teach and to write. He became a deacon at 19 – a young age and perhaps an early acknowledgement of his abilities – and a priest at the canonical age of 30. Bede appended to this autobiography a list of the books he had written, running to well over thirty entries, implying that it was as an author and teacher that he wished to be remembered.

3a.1 St Paul's Church, Jarrow. The tower is Norman, but the chancel is substantially that of the seventh-century monastic church

The circumstances of Bede's death, on 26 May 735, are recorded in a letter by his pupil Cuthbert, later abbot of Wearmouth and Jarrow, to an otherwise unknown Cuthwin. According to the letter, Bede spent his final days praying and teaching, dictating a translation of the Gospel of St John and making extracts from a work by Isidore of Seville. Shortly before his death, he distributed among his brethren some of his possessions, namely pepper (a high-status commodity), incense and liturgical cloths.

The monastic community of which he was a part is in many ways better documented than Bede himself. The twin-sited monastery of Wearmouth-Jarrow is known through Bede's own writings – particularly his *History of the Abbots of Wearmouth and Jarrow* – and an anonymous biography of one of the abbots, Ceolfrith, probably produced in the second decade of the eighth century.

There survives considerable Anglo-Saxon fabric in the churches currently standing on the two sites and, in addition, archaeological excavation has revealed much about the layout of the two monasteries and the kinds of activity that took place there. Decorative details such as the stained glass windows, the red-brick floors and the turned balusters, as well as the layout and arrangements of the buildings, all speak of monastic architects and craftsmen consciously emulating Roman models.

Wearmouth-Jarrow was in many respects atypical of Anglo-Saxon monasteries. Its founder, the Northumbrian nobleman Benedict Biscop, had undertaken numerous pilgrimages to Rome and spent two years as a monk at the island monastery of Lérins, off the coast of Marseilles, before he was persuaded by King Ecgfrith of Northumbria to found a monastery at Wearmouth, around the year 674. Benedict returned to the Continent to recruit stonemasons and glaziers who could build a church for him in the Roman style, and he ensured through this and subsequent trips to Rome and else-where that Wearmouth, and later Jarrow (founded in 682), were well-stocked with relics, paintings and books. Such were the activities of Benedict and his successor Ceolfrith that the library of Wearmouth-Jarrow possessed at least two hundred volumes and was one of the most extensive in England.

Wearmouth-Jarrow was one of a number of so-called Romanising centres in Northumbria, that is, monasteries and religious institutions that sought to demonstrate their special links with and allegiance to Rome and the Mediterranean world. Such links and ideals could be expressed in numerous ways. The stone churches and monastic precincts of Wearmouth and Jarrow would have been the most visible signs of these affinities, but forms of the liturgy would likewise have underscored Roman connections – from one of his trips to Rome, Benedict brought back John the Archcantor of St Peter's to teach Roman chant to the monks of Wearmouth – as would artistic and cultural output.

The most famous of the cultural productions of Wearmouth-Jarrow is the so-called *Codex Amiatinus*, one of three single-volume Bibles – pandects – produced at the monastery in the early eighth century. The *Codex* was intended as a gift for the pope, though it is unclear whether he ever received it, and it eventually ended up in a monastery in Monte Amiato (hence the name). Such was the debt of the *Codex* to late antique and Italian exemplars in terms of its script and decoration that it was only in the nineteenth century that its Anglo-Saxon provenance was recognised. Whether or not Bede took any part in the production of the *Codex* is unknown, indeed his apparent surprise at the departure of Abbot Ceolfrith with it on his way to Rome may suggest that he had been left undisturbed to continue with the exegesis on which he was then engaged. On the other hand, a work as intellectually demanding and ambitious, not to mention as spiritually meaningful, as the production of the *Codex* and its sister-pandects would have held considerable appeal for Bede and it seems likely that he must have had some input into the project.

That the *Codex Amiatinus* remains one of the most important witnesses to the Latin text of the Bible is an indication of the intellectual resources of Wearmouth-Jarrow, resources that Bede utilised fully in his own studies. His writings draw extensively and often verbatim on the works of earlier authors – indeed, he even devised a system of marginal annotations to demonstrate which authority he was utilising at any

3a.2 Christ in Majesty from the *Codex Amiatinus*, one of the three pandects produced at Wearmouth-Jarrow in the early eighth century. The debt of the *Codex Amiatinus* to Late Antique Italian exemplars is unmistakeable

given point. Yet it would be a mistake to see him as merely a compiler or copyist. His writings show an intelligent and creative mind at work, carefully selecting and shaping his source material, adding to it and correcting it where he felt necessary. Moreover, a number of Bede's biblical commentaries, such as that on the construction of the Tabernacle or on the Books of Ezra and Nehemiah, are sustained explorations of particular themes or particular books of the Bible not otherwise tackled by Late Antique or medieval writers.

Bede was not unaware of his own abilities or the merits of his writings. His oft-repeated statement that he was following in the footsteps of the Church Fathers is less a claim to be a humble imitator and transmitter of Patristic wisdom and more an assertion of being part of that same tradition, of following the same bearings. Bede could even be stirred to anger if his learning and wisdom were challenged. In his first work, on time, Bede offered a radical recalculation of the age of the world. Bede's study of the earlier books of the Old Testament led him to the conclusion that the world was some 1,200 years younger than the influential calculation by Eusebius of Caesarea suggested. Bede's revised reckoning necessitated redating the incarnation of Christ and set him at odds with those who believed that the Six Ages of the World were each of one thousand years' duration. Bede's critics misrepresented his arguments – wilfully or otherwise – and he was accused, in his absence, of heresy by members of the household of Bishop Wilfrid. Bede's response was to label his accusers drunken and lewd yokels before offering a detailed explanation as to why they were wrong.

Though Bede's works were intended to serve a range of different immediate purposes – some were designed for the monastic classroom, some commissioned by

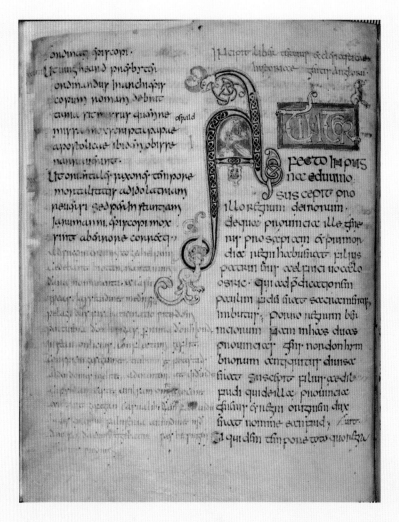

3a.3 The opening of book III of the *Tiberius Bede*, describing the events following the death of King Edwin of Northumbria. The work is an early ninth-century copy of Bede's *Ecclesiastical History*, possibly produced at Canterbury

other churchmen, some seemingly Bede's own initiative – they nevertheless show particular concern with a number of issues that were obviously of especial interest to him. Most notable among these, and apparent across the largest range of Bede's writings, was the need for reform of the Church in Northumbria. Such concerns are made most explicit in Bede's last surviving work, a letter to Bishop Ecgberht of York dating to 734. In it he laments the problems of an avaricious yet pastorally negligent episcopacy, detailing how numerous villages and hamlets do not see their bishop from one year to the next and yet are not exempt from rendering payment to him. Likewise, Bede complains of countless monasteries in Northumbria founded not out of genuine religious devotion but in order to gain land and privileges.

Such concerns are adumbrated by his exegesis. Especially in his later biblical commentaries, Bede put forward a model of the ideal Church leader – ascetic, educated and pastorally active – drawing on language and concepts taken from the writings of Gregory the Great. Bede likewise explored such ideas in his other writings. His prose biography of Cuthbert, for example, recast the saint as the exemplary Gregorian-style pastor, an embodiment of the reforming ideals which Bede espoused.

This specific reforming agenda in part underlies Bede's most widely read work, the *Ecclesiastical History of the English People*. In the preface Bede emphasises his explicitly hortatory intentions:

3a.4 Reconstruction of stained glass from Jarrow. Excavations of the monastic complex uncovered a number of fragments of pre-Viking stained glass. This is a recreation of glass found in the building that may have served as the monastic guesthouse

> Should history tell of good men and their good estate, the thoughtful listener is spurred on to imitate the good; should it record the evil ends of wicked men, no less effectually the devout and earnest listener or reader is kindled to eschew what is harmful and perverse.

Though Bede provided numerous exemplary religious figures in the text – Gregory the Great, Aidan, Wilfrid, Hild, Cuthbert, Æthelthryth, amongst others – and did, indeed, record the evil ends of less pious churchmen and women, his attention was clearly on the laity as well. The *Ecclesiastical History* is the only one of Bede's works dedicated to a secular patron, King Ceolwulf of Northumbria, and some of the greatest heroes of the text are secular figures, kings in particular. What Bede offered in the *Ecclesiastical History* was an all-encompassing vision of the reform of Christian society. Numerous episodes in the text emphasise the message that peace and prosperity result when kings and the Church, particularly bishops, act in harmony and in accordance with God's laws. Such a message had an immediate, contemporary relevance; the eighth century had witnessed considerable political and dynastic upheaval in Northumbria and Ceolwulf was himself deposed, albeit briefly, in 731.

If the *Ecclesiastical History* spoke to a particular historical moment, Bede nevertheless conceived of his narrative in much broader terms. The text situated the English

3a.5 A mid-twelfth-century manuscript of Bede's commentary on the Gospel of Luke, produced in southern England. This page shows the preface to the work, including Bede's address to Bishop Acca of Hexham, one his main patrons

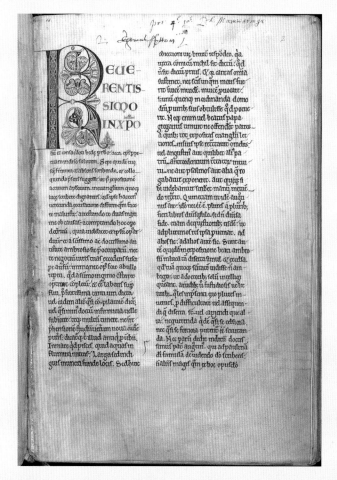

people within the grand sweep of salvation history and staked their claim to be a part of the wider Christian world. Bede undoubtedly took as his model the *Ecclesiastical History* of Eusebius of Caesarea – known to Bede in the Latin translation and continuation made by Rufinus of Aquileia in the late fourth century – a work that detailed the history of the first centuries of Christianity, showing the growth and spread of the early Church and the conversion of different peoples, most notably the Romans. This model provided Bede with a methodology and technique – Eusebius included extracts from numerous documents and sources in his work – and a sense of the underlying driving force of history, the relationship between man and God. Thus, though Bede's *History* can often read like a modern work of history – he cites his sources and quotes directly from other texts – his work is intended less to reconstruct history for its own sake and more to show how the past reveals the unfolding of Divine will and the lessons that should be drawn from this. In this sense, it is important that the *Ecclesiastical History* be read very much in the context of Bede's wider output and his overall aims as a scholar, a priest and a monk within one of the most 'Roman' centres of contemporary Northumbria.

THE STAFFORDSHIRE HOARD

NICHOLAS J. HIGHAM

On 21 July 2009, Terry Herbert was running his metal detector across a field a few kilometres south-west of Lichfield when he came across hundreds of Anglo-Saxon metal objects: the Portable Antiquities Scheme quickly became involved and an excavation and geophysical surveys were undertaken. More than 3,571 objects have now been recovered totalling over 5 kilograms of gold and 1.4 kilograms of silver. This is by far the largest quantity of Anglo-Saxon gold objects ever found in one spot – to give the obvious parallel, the gold from Sutton Hoo mound 1 totals less than 1.7 kilograms. The whole assemblage was declared Treasure on 24 September at a coroner's inquest. It was then valued by the Treasure Valuation Committee and purchased by the Birmingham Museum and Art Gallery and the Potteries Museum and Art Gallery, Stoke-on-Trent, following a successful campaign of public subscription topped up by grants from the Art Fund and the Heritage Memorial Fund.

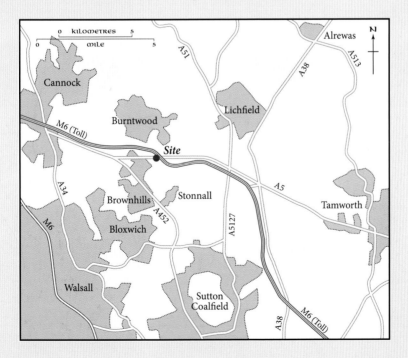

3b.1 Map showing the find spot of the Staffordshire Hoard. This part of Mercia was probably still very 'British' at least until the eighth century

3b.2 High-quality gold filigree work, though still unwashed, on one of over 90 highly-decorated sword pommels from the hoard

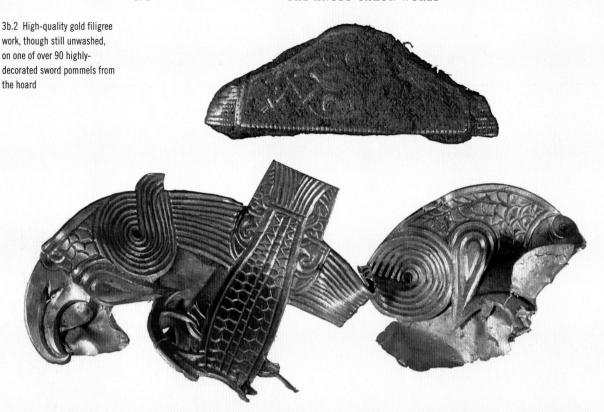

3b.3 Sheet-gold incised plaque, probably from applied decoration on a shield, featuring two stylised birds of prey grasping a large fish in their talons

What was actually found? The bulk of the hoard consists of sword fittings, with over ninety pommel caps so far identified, some in a fragmentary state, over 350 decorative plates which had been removed from the hilts of swords, knives and daggers, and smaller numbers of pyramids, pommel rings and buttons, all probably accessories to sword and scabbard. There are also fragments from one or more helmets, including decorated cheek fittings and an animal head comparable to those on the Sutton Hoo helm. Any one of several hundred of these items would have been a major find, but the discovery of an entire collection on this scale sent shock waves through the archaeological community and engaged the wider public in ways that we rarely see: the temporary exhibition staged at Birmingham Museum from September to October 2009 attracted over forty thousand visitors, many queuing outside for over four hours to see it.

Many pieces display decorative techniques of the highest quality. A beautiful sheet-gold incised plaque featuring two stylised birds of prey grasping a large fish in their talons probably derived originally from applied decoration on a shield owned by a king or nobleman, and bears comparison with the gilt-bronze plaque featuring a similar hawk or eagle from the shield from mound 1 at Sutton Hoo. The commonest decorative style on the Staffordshire Hoard pieces is gold filigree work, often with three-strand bands of beaded wire on raised back-plates, but a substantial minority have cloisonné decoration utilising garnet, niello and occasional millefiori inlays. Taking the sword pommel caps as a sample, some 60 per cent are decorated with gold interlace but about a quarter feature garnets set in gold cloisonné of a type which finds parallels at Sutton Hoo on the sword fittings, although the hoard contains no workmanship as fine as the Sutton Hoo purse and shoulder clasps. A few are of silver or copper alloy. The cloisonné work reveals a delicacy comparable to the finest pieces so far excavated, including examples where garnet inlays have been used to create patterns featuring animal figures, as opposed to the commoner geometric designs; these align with the Salin Style II interlaced animal ornamentation to be seen carved lightly on numerous gold surfaces. In all, almost thirty pieces exhibit Salin Style II decoration, making this by far the largest collection ever found and substantially increasing the total number of such items known. Garnets are a particular feature of this collection, despite their more normal association with 'female' objects. They occur on around 150 separate pieces, such as pyramids, pommel caps and hilt plates, in association with both filigree and cloisonné techniques. Analyses already carried out by a team in Paris suggest that most Continental garnets came from India; the team will include stones from the Staffordshire Hoard in ongoing study to determine their origin.

The largest single item is a gold cross weighing 140 grams, which has been folded inwards on itself to form a ball, presumably for ease of transport. The gold arms feature flowing but carefully regulated and balanced animal interlace of the highest quality, leading towards round mounts for decorative stones at the ends of each arm and the

3b.4 Garnet-decorated gold cross, originally serving as a rich facia to a wooden cross. There are clear signs of repair but it had been folded up prior to deposition, presumably to fit into a bag for ease of travel

3b.5 Cross fragment bearing a biblical inscription from either Numbers or Psalms. A rougher version, probably a trial attempt, is on the reverse, which would not have been seen had this piece too fronted a wooden cross

ascender, with another at an equal distance down the base, with the largest, oval in shape, at the crux. One mount still retains a garnet in its original position, which had been chipped, cracked and then mended with a small strip of gold even before deposition. This crucifix would originally have been fitted on a wooden cross. Another two possible cross fragments were discovered, one of which carries a Latin inscription which translates: 'Rise up, Lord, and may thy enemies be dispersed and those that hate thee be driven from thy face', a biblical quotation from both Numbers (10: 35) and the Psalms (variously listed 67 or 68). The context suggests that it was the latter which the author had in mind for what was probably the arm of a processional cross: again a mount for a decorative stone lies at the extremity, this time with beaded gold wire as a border. The inscription occurs on both faces of the gold strip, with what looks like a trial piece on the inside which was then concealed when the strip was nailed to the wood – the nail holes survive. However, spelling mistakes occur even in the finished text on show, suggesting that the person responsible was barely literate. The text would have been very suitable to a processional cross being carried into battle against pagans or heretics, and in this sense the crosses fit with the military focus of the bulk of the hoard.

There are, however, other objects that are less obviously military in style, prominent among which are several gold-wire serpents, bent in the characteristic looping shape of a snake in motion and with the head formed distinctively but quite subtly. These are not obviously brooches since they are without pins or fasteners of any kind and there are very few parallels indeed for them, although a comparable example in silver has come from Faversham (Kent).

What was this assemblage intended for, when was it deposited and in what circumstances? Answers to such questions may become clearer as work continues, given that many pieces are now (2012) only just being cleaned of soil, but overall the assemblage seems distinctly unbalanced. There is a total absence of iron, for the hilt fittings had

3b.6 Gold wire serpent, one of several in the hoard, for which there are very few parallels elsewhere in Anglo-Saxon England

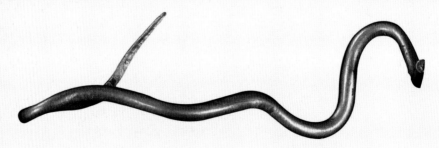

been stripped from the sword blades; there are no knives, spears, horse fittings, gaming pieces, vessels or coins, no belt buckles (although there are two small buckles which may have come from a helmet), and none of the female dress fittings and accessories which would be expected were this a cemetery site. Rather, this is a highly gendered hoard made up entirely of objects with male associations and particularly linked to warfare, but without the actual weapons: only the valuable, precious-metal accessories are included. To find these categories of artefact in such numbers is remarkable. The frequent absence of sword pommels, for example, from graves, even 'princely burials', indicates that they were often handed down across the generations, or perhaps even returned to the patrons who had given them. To find so many present here may suggest they were reclaimed from the sword when that went out of use (for example, through burial with a body) and recycled. Swords of the period were comparatively easy to disassemble, with the fittings coming away from the iron blade and the hilt, but in addition to the weapon fittings the hoard contains a range of fine garnet-inlaid plates and strips the function of which is, as yet, unknown.

The date of the deposit is somewhat conjectural. Not all the material is of one date: parallels suggest that some items could be of late sixth-century workmanship, with other pieces clearly deriving from the seventh century or potentially the eighth, the problem being that dating by comparison does not necessarily offer close parameters. The inscription necessarily dates from the Christian era but experts are currently in disagreement, with some being comfortable with the seventh century whereas others argue that it is later. On the whole archaeologists are inclined to the view that the hoard was deposited in the later seventh century but contained items which were anything up to three-quarters of a century old at that point.

The social context of the assemblage is even more contentious. Given that the predominant content is the precious-metal accessories to war gear – or 'male gangland bling', as the historian David Starkey remarked in January 2010 when exhorting public donations – one explanation must be that this was the spoils of war resulting from a victorious army having stripped the precious metal from the equipment of their dead opponents. The pagan Penda's victory over the Christian Oswald in 642 has been mooted as one possibility, though this was probably too early to fit with the material in its totality. But an objection to this explanation would be that Anglo-Saxon society valued the weapons themselves at least as much as the precious metals that were attached, as evidenced for example in the poem *Beowulf*. The will of Prince Æthelstan in 1014 bequeathed to his brother Edmund Ironside what he described as King Offa's sword, which would already have been well over a century old at that date. The Bayeux Tapestry's lower border shows swords being collected from the fallen in their totality. An alternative would be to see the assemblage as tribute rather than booty, offered perhaps *in extremis* by an inferior force to purchase the right to depart or the favour of a powerful figure. There again, similarly unbalanced hoards in southern Scandinavia and northern Germany dating to the Roman Iron Age have been termed 'war booty sacrifices' and interpreted either as material donated to the gods or as war trophies. Although there is no hint otherwise that this location was a sacred site, it seems quite possible that this was a deposit made in a ritual context.

The finds came from the end of a low hill immediately beside Watling Street, which was probably then heath or woodland. There was no trace of a mound or pit; the material came from the plough soil and was exposed by ploughing. All the archaeological features identified by excavation were ephemeral, without clear association with the metalwork. The soil is patchy, with sand, pebbles and glacial till. The assemblage came from a localised area of clay which was probably distinguished by surface vegetation, suggesting that the hoard was buried shallowly with the intention of retrieval. All of the material could easily have fitted into a single bag, so a substantial pit would not have been necessary. The gold was equivalent in weight to perhaps 800 *solidi*, so the value of about eight hundred riding horses, which implies substantial value but less than one might expect from a royal treasury, for example.

Another factor is the township name on the edge of which the hoard was discovered, which is Hammerwich. 'Wich' – from Latin *vicus* – was used variously of a dependent settlement, a centre of specialised production or a place where trading occurred, while the first element of the same is Old English *hamer* ('hammer'), perhaps suggesting a metalworking centre. Deposition so close to a Roman road implies that it had recently been moved. The area probably had a very low population indeed and was used mostly as summer pasture. One possibility must be that the assemblage related less to warfare itself than to metalworking, in which case this may have been a consignment for use in ornamenting new weapons, which for some reason was buried, rather than being delivered, then not retrieved.

Finally, we should consider the sociopolitical context of the hoard. The Mercians – 'the people of the frontier' – are perhaps the least understood of the major Anglo-Saxon kingships: the predominant archaeological material comes from cemeteries further east, and there is a lack of written evidence. Stylistic parallels link the material discovered here to Kent, East Anglia and/or Northumbria, but it is equally possible that parts of the hoard, at least, were manufactured in Mercia: several different workshops appear to be represented, but smiths were probably itinerant so we cannot easily establish the geography of manufacture. Though this is in material cultural terms a very 'Anglo-Saxon' hoard, western Mercia in the seventh century was culturally ambiguous, with British linguistic and religious culture only giving way slowly to Anglo-Saxon and with plentiful signs of continuity across the period. Penda's own name is British in origin as are those of other family members, and the population of this region was probably biologically very largely British. The Staffordshire Hoard is thereby rendered the more enigmatic, though its social connections are surely exclusively with the elite: in some sense, it seems reasonable to suppose that the hoard is less representative of the local population around Cannock and Lichfield at this date than of kings and ealdormen, retainers and priests, who thought of themselves as in some sense 'Anglian' or 'Saxon' and were in the process of forging a new 'English' identity. Gold served as the social capital on which hierarchies were built and it lubricated the interfaces that were central to the royal court, patronage and status. It is that milieu on which the Staffordshire Hoard sheds new light.

CHAPTER 4

The Mercian Supremacies

MARTIN J. RYAN

> When I consider the deeds of this person, I am doubtful whether I should commend
> or censure. At one time, in the same character, vices were so palliated by virtues, and
> at another virtues came in such quick succession upon vices that it is difficult to
> determine how to characterise the changing Proteus.

So William of Malmesbury, writing in the twelfth century, described the difficulties he
faced accounting for the character of Offa, king of Mercia from 757 to 796. A modern
audience can only sympathise with William here. Offa, and, indeed, the eighth century
as a whole, continue to present formidable problems of interpretation.

The difficulty is not a lack of sources, for in comparison with the preceding centuries the eighth is richly documented, both through texts and, increasingly, archaeological excavation. Rather, what is lacking is a coherent narrative, such as that supplied
for the seventh century and early eighth century by Bede's *Ecclesiastical History*. Bede's
work provides a means of making sense of the seventh century, a way of understanding
the relationship between different events and of comprehending something of their
wider significance. Though we may now question the motives behind Bede's selection
of material or challenge his overall picture, we can do so precisely because his writings
have given us the wherewithal to unravel many of the complexities of the seventh
century. For the eighth century, by contrast, although the sources permit us to establish the overall shape of things and even shine a bright light on certain episodes, the
relationship between different events and their meaning and importance is far harder
to determine.

Since the nineteenth century at least, the eighth and early ninth centuries have
been characterised as the period of the Mercian supremacy. That is, this period saw the
political, military, economic and, perhaps, also the cultural dominance of the Midlands
kingdom of Mercia. Successive Mercian rulers extended their authority over much of
southern England and in the process brought to an end the independence of a number
of the Anglo-Saxon kingdoms.

For scholars in the first half of the twentieth century – particularly Sir Frank
Stenton – the Mercian hegemonies of this period brought the Anglo-Saxons to within
touching distance of political unity. The extensive overkingships of Mercian rulers

4.1 Places named in chapter 4

such as Æthelbald and Offa were, like those of their seventh-century Northumbrian counterparts, staging posts on the path to the united England that would be achieved under the West Saxon kings in the tenth century.

Such visions of the Mercian supremacy have by now, rightly, receded. The Mercian overlordships of the eighth century need to be understood, as much as is possible, on their own terms, not as trial runs or failed attempts at English unity. The distinctive and idiosyncratic nature of the successive Mercian overkingships and, indeed, of the Mercian polity as a whole, needs to be appreciated. Mercia remains central to any account of the eighth and early ninth centuries but labels such as 'Mercian supremacy' or 'Mercian hegemony' may obscure considerable complexities. Mercia's influence over its neighbours was both fluctuating and frequently contested. The danger lies in viewing all events through the lens of an assumed, continuous Mercian pre-eminence.

Whatever the extent of their authority in this period, the power and wealth of the Mercian kings were due in large part to their ability to harness the changing economy of Anglo-Saxon England from the late seventh to mid-ninth centuries. International trade expanded exponentially and *emporia*, such as those at York, Ipswich, Southampton (Hamwic) and particularly London, increased both in size and in organisational complexity in this period.

The rural landscape was likewise exploited with mounting intensity. Settlements and their associated field-systems were restructured and reorganised. Some settlements shifted location to heavier, more fertile soils; others moved from subsistence agriculture to specialised – and perhaps market-orientated – production. The control and management of natural resources were intensified. Archaeological excavation has, for example, revealed an abundance of fish-traps and weirs in rivers and estuaries while the written sources describe an increasing investment in such activities as the extraction of salt from brine springs.

The rising wealth of Anglo-Saxon England was, however, not only exploited by the royal dynasties. The most obvious beneficiary and perhaps the main driving force of this growing economy was the Church. The late seventh to mid-eighth centuries was a period of monastic foundation and endowment on a vast scale. Rich and powerful monasteries now commanded extensive landed resources – in some cases on the scale of small kingdoms – and were the foci of economic and cultural innovation.

Yet the very success of such monasteries and the rapid integration of the institutional Church into Anglo-Saxon society brought problems. The perceived worldliness of some monasteries and their apparent embrace of the world view and values of aristocratic society caused consternation in some ecclesiastical circles. Leading churchmen pursued vigorous programmes of reform, with varying degrees of success. Moreover, the wealth and importance of some institutions were such that they could not avoid becoming part of wider struggles for power and influence. As kings sought to exert a closer control over monasteries and their landed resources and manpower, so churchmen (bishops in particular) sought to check this encroachment and to exercise and extend their own power, with the interests of individual monasteries often taking a back seat. Such contests culminated in the early ninth century in a bitter struggle between King Cenwulf of Mercia and Archbishop Wulfred of Canterbury for control of a number of key monasteries in Kent – a struggle from which neither man emerged with much credit.

Mercia in the Eighth Century

The centrality of Mercia to modern accounts of the eighth century is in many ways at odds with the surviving source materials. Apart from charters, Mercian rulers seem to have commissioned remarkably few written texts. If works comparable to Bede's *Ecclesiastical History* or to the *Anglo-Saxon Chronicle* were composed by Mercian authors, they have not survived. Mercian kings may have produced law codes, for King Alfred of Wessex in the ninth century claims to have drawn on a code of King Offa when composing his own. None, however, is now extant, unless by Offa's law code Alfred meant the report of the papal legates who toured England in the 780s.

It is a distinctive feature of the Mercian hegemonies, therefore, that many of the key events of the reigns of such kings as Æthelbald or Offa are documented only in sources produced in other kingdoms. Our understanding of the character and personality of these rulers is therefore shaped by the views of external writers, such as the West Saxon Boniface or Northumbrian Alcuin. Whilst such non-Mercian witnesses were by no means universally hostile, they would necessarily have had a perspective different from those inside Mercia and from those closer to its rulers.

It is tempting to look to better documented kingdoms and time periods – such as Northumbria in the seventh century or Wessex in the ninth – for insights into eighth-century Mercia. Offa might more closely resemble Alfred the Great had but the texts produced at his court survived.

Given the vagaries of the preservation and transmission of texts, not least the deleterious effects of Viking raiding in the ninth century, such an approach is an eminently reasonable one. Yet the very absence of source materials may tell us something important about the nature of the kingdom of Mercia and the Mercian hegemonies. Royal power and authority could manifest themselves in a multiplicity of ways, not all of which need to have generated the same amount or same types of written evidence. Likewise hegemony could take many forms and the intentions behind the extension of overlordship could vary significantly. The structure and organisation of the Mercian kingdom may have differed considerably from other, better documented kingdoms.

Mercian domination of large swathes of southern England was not in any case a new phenomenon in the eighth century. For lengthy periods of the preceding century, Mercian kings such as Penda (d. 655) or Wulfhere (d. 675) exerted considerable influence over their neighbours. The true extent of Mercian power in this period is probably obscured by Bede's Northumbria-centred narrative. Charter evidence shows that the Mercian kings of the early eighth century – Æthelred (abdicated 704), Coenred (d. 709) and Ceolred (d. 716) – continued to exercise some form of overlordship over the kingdom of the *Hwicce*, parts of Middlesex (including London), Surrey and possibly Essex.

The significance of the Mercian hegemonies of the eighth and early ninth centuries is, then, more about the duration and nature of Mercian power than its extent. The reigns of Æthelbald (716–57) and Offa were amongst the longest of any Anglo-Saxon ruler; indeed, Æthelbald has a claim to be the longest-reigning Anglo-Saxon monarch. The contrast with Northumbria is particularly marked: some 12 kings ruled there during the reigns of Æthelbald and Offa in Mercia.

The Mercian overlords of the eighth century were also very different rulers from their seventh-century counterparts. The enhanced importance of international trade has already been noted, and *emporia* and other trading centres were resources that could be managed to advantage by ambitious kings. Though land remained the key source of wealth in this period, the pre-eminence of Mercian rulers in southern

England may have owed much to their control of the key port of London and its rural hinterlands. The geographical focus of Mercian rule also shifted to reflect these new sources of power. Though the traditional Mercian heartlands in the Trent Basin retained their importance, with Lichfield, Repton and Tamworth being particularly prominent, charters show Mercian kings increasingly active in the region that is now Greater London.

Christianity likewise had transformed the exercise and ideology of kingship. Literacy allowed for the more carefully organised – and hence more intensive – exploitation of royal resources and facilitated the delegation of royal authority. If the physical presence of the king remained enormously important, the written word could nevertheless act as an extension and reinforcement of the royal will, and a means of shaping and controlling perceptions of the king and his rule. Yet Christianity also heightened the demands and expectations placed upon rulers. Anglo-Saxon monarchs governed as Christian kings and could draw on all the ideological apparatus that such a status brought with it, but the morality of their conduct was now judged according to Christian principles, with the Church presenting itself as the arbiter of royal behaviour. Kingship was no longer – if, indeed, it ever had been – simply about leadership in battle or the taking of plunder and the imposition of tribute. Kings were expected to uphold justice, to promote learning and wisdom, to patronise the Church and to further Christianity.

The Reign of Æthelbald

Penda's son, Æthelred, finally retired in 704 after 29 years as king of the Mercians, becoming a monk at Bardney (Lincolnshire). He was succeeded first by his nephew Coenred then his son Ceolred. Æthelbald descended from a distant branch of the royal family and was in exile during the latter's reign, at least. The *Life of St Guthlac*, written by the otherwise unknown Felix for Ælfwald, king of the East Angles (713–49), depicts the exiled Æthelbald in close contact with Guthlac, who was likewise a Mercian royal but living as an anchorite near Crowland (Lincolnshire). Guthlac had allegedly prophesied Æthelbald's ascent to the throne, perhaps indicating political endorsement by the saint and the East Anglian court.

Ceolred's death in 716 enabled Æthelbald to gain the throne, but it was arguably the death of Wihtred of Kent (725), then the abdication of Ine of Wessex (726), that allowed him to emerge as the most powerful of the southern English kings, leading Bede, in the penultimate chapter of his *History*, to term him the 'overking' of England south of the Humber. This comment may reflect or may even have inspired statements of authority that can be found in some of Æthelbald's own charters, most famously the 'Ismere Diploma' of 736. In this, Æthelbald is styled 'king not only of the Mercians but also of all the provinces which are called by the general name "South English" [Sutangli]', while in the witness list he is styled more simply but more grandiosely 'king of Britain'. It is difficult to know what to make of such titles. King of Britain surely represents aggrandisement, though whether Æthelbald himself, his advisors, or the scribes of the charters were responsible is unclear. 'King of the South English' may

4.2 The *Ismere Diploma*. The charter records a grant of land made by King Æthelbald to his follower Cyneberht for the purposes of founding a monastery. One of the earliest Anglo-Saxon documents dated using the Anno Domini system – the year 736 can be read in the final lines of the body of the charter – the charter includes a subscription by Æthelbald as 'rex Britanniae'

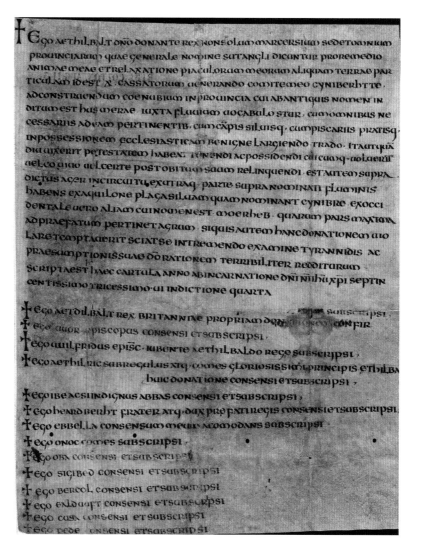

confirm or echo Bede's assertion of a south Humbrian overlordship, but might equally mean specifically southern Anglian peoples rather than all those south of the Humber. At any rate, such royal styles are rare in Æthelbald's reign – indeed, they only occur in texts originating from Worcester – and charters most frequently title him simply 'king of the Mercians'.

The overall impression of Æthelbald's rule south of the Humber is that he sought to exercise concerted control over a relatively restricted area. Beyond the Mercian heart-lands, Æthelbald exerted greatest influence and power in an area running roughly south-east from the Trent Basin towards London, following very approximately the line of Watling Street. He had direct control over the *Hwicce*, with its royal dynasty appearing in charters as sub-kings or lower rather than as fully independent rulers. Æthelbald similarly exercised direct control over Middlesex and London – the latter traceable particularly through a series of toll exemptions granted to various religious institutions. Economic interests – chiefly, though not exclusively, the great trading centre at London – were carefully exploited. Some territorial expansion took place, particularly into the frontier regions of Berkshire, Wiltshire and Somerset, at the expense of the West Saxon kings.

For large parts of southern England, however, Æthelbald must have been at most a distant overlord whose authority, such as it was, impinged little. The kings of Kent continued to grant land in their own names without reference to the consent or witness of the Mercian king. Æthelbald's own involvement was indirect, consisting chiefly of grants to religious houses in Kent, either of toll exemptions or of land outside Kent. Successive archbishops of Canterbury – Tatwine (d. 734), Nothhelm (d. 739) and Cuthbert (d. 760) – were either from religious houses in Mercia or in regions under Mercian control, which may have been a result of Æthelbald's influence in Kent, though not necessarily.

Conclusive evidence of Æthelbald's direct involvement in South Saxon, East Anglian or East Saxon affairs is likewise lacking, though his annexation of Middlesex and London was ultimately at the expense of the East Saxon kings. Æthelbald's relationship with the kings of Wessex seems more complex, though this may be because more evidence survives from Wessex than from other kingdoms. Æthelbald clearly gained territory at West Saxon expense, and Cuthred of Wessex (r. 740–56) fought against him on a number of occasions. However, the two kings also mounted at least one campaign together, in 743 against the Britons – probably the Welsh. In practice, then, there is only limited evidence of Æthelbald's south Humbrian hegemony as suggested by Bede, and in many areas it probably amounted to little more than the recognition of superiority and perhaps some taking of tribute.

North of the Humber, Æthelbald's interventions were even more limited, restricted to two raids on Northumbrian territory in 737 and 740. The latter, significantly, took place while King Eadberht of Northumbria (r. 737–58) was away fighting the Picts. The evidence for Mercian involvement in Wales is equally exiguous. Welsh sources record destructive Mercian raids on the Wye Valley in this period – perhaps the result of the campaign of 743 – and the ninth-century Pillar of Eliseg records the Mercians being driven from Powys in the middle of the eighth century, but beyond this it is difficult to go.

Contemporary assessments of the nature of Æthelbald's rule create an impression of periodic violence lapsing into despotism. Æthelbald granted land to a Mercian abbess in recompense for murdering her kinsman, while a monk had a vision of Æthelbald being tormented by demons after his death. Such negative depictions of Æthelbald loom largest in a letter sent to him around 746 by the Continental missionary Boniface. Though the letter noted Æthelbald to be 'very liberal in almsgiving' and 'famed as a defender of widows and of the poor', the bulk of it is a sustained assault on Æthelbald's moral failings and his ill-treatment of the Church. Æthelbald was accused of violating church privileges and treating monks 'with greater violence and extortion than any Christian kings have ever done' – the import of which is explored below. Moreover, Boniface asserted that Æthelbald had never taken a lawful wife and instead committed fornication with nuns and virgins dedicated to God.

In the absence of comparable Mercian sources, Boniface's characterisation of

4.3 Later eighth-century silver-gilt finger ring, recovered from the Thames near Chelsea. The animal interlace decoration has affinities with the later 'Trewhiddle Style'

Æthelbald and others like it have largely won the day. There may, however, have been further perspectives and other interpretations of Æthelbald's behaviour. His sexual relationships clearly fell short of appropriate Christian unions – at least in the eyes of Boniface – but Christian marriage was only one of a number of reproductive strategies that could be pursued by Anglo-Saxon rulers. Though Æthelbald's liaisons attracted condemnation they need not necessarily have been the product of unbridled lust. Marriage or monogamy meant the elevation of one woman to a position of prominence and the concomitant increase in her own power and influence as well as that of her family. Rejecting marriage or stable unions may have been one way in which Æthelbald sought to negotiate the complexities of Mercian politics, even if it risked ecclesiastical censure. If so, he would not be the only Christian Anglo-Saxon king to follow such a policy.

However such charges against Æthelbald ought to be understood, they indicate at least that his rule was divisive and aspects of his power resented. Such an impression is confirmed by the manner of his death. Æthelbald's long reign came to an end in 757 when he was murdered – treacherously at night by his bodyguards, according to one source. He was buried in the church at Repton (Derbyshire), perhaps in the crypt that had been constructed during his reign and which subsequently served as a royal mausoleum.

The specific reasons for Æthelbald's murder are unknown. Perhaps his lengthy reign had been in part his undoing; the witness lists of his charters suggest that he had outlived his early supporters. Whether his successor, Beornred, was implicated in his murder is likewise unknown. At any rate, Beornred's own reign lasted only a few months before he was driven out by Offa, a cousin of Æthelbald and grandson of Eanwulf, a man who had enjoyed extensive patronage during Æthelbald's reign.

Offa clearly took some time to establish himself securely on the Mercian throne. One set of annals has Offa attempting 'to conquer the Mercian kingdom with sword and bloodshed' after driving out Beornred, while a charter from later in his reign suggests Offa became king only in 758. In such circumstances, Offa can have inherited little of Æthelbald's southern hegemony. It is likely to be in this period that King Cynewulf of Wessex (r. 757–86) temporarily regained control of Berkshire and parts of the Thames Valley, and that the Welsh reasserted themselves in Powys.

The Reign of Offa

In certain respects, Offa's reign closely resembles that of Æthelbald. The geographical concentration of his power was similar: he appears most active and his authority most secure in the Mercian heartlands and the corridor stretching south-east to London, with Chelsea an especial focus of his activities by the 780s. Similarly, international trade and its royal oversight retained their importance. These are illuminated particularly in a letter from the Frankish ruler Charlemagne (r. 768–814) encouraging Offa to control the quality of English exports and promising protection of English merchants in Francia.

In other ways, however, Offa appears a very different ruler from Æthelbald. He attempted to harness more fully the ideological apparatus offered by Christianity and the Church, seeming to draw particular inspiration from ideas about Christian kingship and rule being developed in the courts of the Carolingian monarchs of Francia. Likewise, Offa's power and influence over other Anglo-Saxon kingdoms were greater and more extensive than Æthelbald's and he sought to exercise them in a more direct way. By the 780s, Offa had effectively brought to an end the independent royal dynasties of Kent, the South Saxons and the *Hwicce*. In the latter two kingdoms, members of the dynasties may have survived as non-royal leaders – ealdormen – operating under Offa's control. In Kent he seems to have preferred to place Mercian nobles in positions of authority.

By the final decades of his reign, Offa had become the ruler of a kingdom stretching from the Midlands down to the south-east coast – a vast territory by Anglo-Saxon standards. That Offa and those around him conceived of this territory as a uniform kingdom, an enlarged Mercia, is clear. In his charters and on his coinage he appears, almost without exception, simply as the king of the Mercians, adopting no grander or more expansive royal style. Offa was not attempting to unify the English – even assuming such a concept was meaningful in the eighth century – but simply to expand Mercian authority.

The extent of Offa's power outside this territory is less clear. East Anglia may have come under Offa's authority by the 790s, for coins were minted there in his name. His rule there was, however, resisted: in 794, King Æthelberht of East Anglia was beheaded on Offa's orders. Even less is known of Offa's relationship with the kings of the East Saxons. London and Middlesex remained under Mercian control, as they had been in Æthelbald's reign, but Offa does not appear to have exercised any authority in the East Saxon kingdom itself.

Offa's relationship with King Cynewulf of Wessex is likely to have been strained, for Offa reasserted Mercian authority over the Thames Valley by defeating the West Saxons at Bensington in 779 and subsequently gained control of territory on the south bank of the Avon. Whether or not Offa exercised a meaningful overlordship over the West Saxons remains unclear. Relations with Cynewulf's successor, Beorhtric (r. 786–802), appear more cordial, for he married one of Offa's daughters, Eadburh, and the two kings cooperated in exiling Ecgberht, a man who would later become king of Wessex. Another of Offa's daughters, Ælfflæd, married King Æthelred of Northumbria in 792, but this may have been the limit of Offa's involvement in affairs north of the Humber. The turbulent political situation in Northumbria in the latter decades of the eighth century must have made a consistent Mercian policy difficult.

Discussion of Offa's relationship with the different kingdoms that made up Wales is inevitably dominated by the great linear earthwork that bears his name: Offa's Dyke. This attribution rests on an assertion by the Welsh cleric Asser in the late ninth century that 'Offa [. . .] had a great dyke built between Wales and Mercia from sea to sea'. Whilst Asser's words have been almost universally accepted, the purpose of Offa's Dyke and its true extent remain much debated. The extensive excavations and surveys of the Dyke

4.4 Section of Offa's Dyke near
Clun, Shropshire

led by David Hill in the 1970s–1990s suggested that it extended only from Treuddyn in the north to Rushock Hill in the south, a distance of just over 100 kilometres. Its purpose was less to provide a barrier between Mercia and the whole of Wales than to reinforce a frontier with a newly resurgent Powys. The Dyke was intended rather to impede the easy movement of people back and forth – cattle rustlers and small-scale raiding parties, for example – than to act as a defensive barrier, capable of repelling full-scale attack.

The southern extent of this truncated Dyke has, however, not received universal support and a case can be made for the Dyke having originally extended as far south as Sedbury Cliffs in Gloucestershire. It does seem clear, though, that the Dyke never extended as far as the sea in the north. Though not the earthwork 'from sea to sea' of Asser's account, Offa's Dyke was nevertheless a formidable undertaking. Estimates of the labour involved diverge greatly – figures have ranged from 5,000 men to over 125,000 men – and much depends on whether the Dyke was constructed in a few years or over a longer period. Even to maintain the lowest estimate of 5,000 men would have been an exacting task, requiring not just the recruitment and organisation of the labour force but the provisioning and housing of these workers and, perhaps, their protection from attack. It is a testament to the organisational ability and, indeed, administrative sophistication of Offa's regime that such a task would even be contemplated let alone achieved. The Dyke must also have been a powerful ideological statement, inviting comparisons between Offa and Roman rulers of the past who had undertaken similarly grand construction projects – the Hadrianic and Antonine Walls being the most obvious insular examples.

However imposing Offa appeared within Britain, his relationship with Charlemagne shows clearly both his ambitions and, ultimately, the limitations of his power. Some modern scholars, such as Dorothy Whitelock, have suggested that Offa could aspire to – even achieve in some areas – an equality with Charlemagne. Given that Charlemagne laid claim to being the most powerful ruler in Europe at this date, such would be a remarkable endorsement of the extent of Offa's authority.

If Offa did entertain such thoughts, his contemporaries on the Continent viewed things very differently. When Charlemagne sought the hand in marriage of Offa's daughter for his son, Charles, Offa demanded a reciprocal marriage: Charlemagne's daughter Bertha for his son Ecgfrith. For Charlemagne, such a request was an insult, reportedly making him 'somewhat angry', and he imposed a trade embargo on English merchants in Francia. Offa responded in kind with an embargo on Frankish merchants, but the significance of the episode was clear: a marriage alliance between Francia and Mercia was not one between equals, whatever Offa might have thought.

Relations – and trade – had been restored by the mid-790s, when Charlemagne sent two letters to Offa concerning a number of different issues. Again, though Charlemagne might address Offa as 'beloved brother' and 'dearest brother', the language of diplomacy should not be mistaken for the language of equality. The royal titles used in the letters – Charlemagne 'by the grace of God, king of the Franks and Lombards and Patrician of the Romans' and Offa 'King of the Mercians' – make clear, probably deliberately so, their very different statuses.

Even the gifts accompanying the letters could underline this point. With one letter, Charlemagne sent Offa a 'Hunnish' sword, part of the spoils of his campaigns against the Avars in Pannonia. This was undoubtedly a prestigious gift, but of the kind that a lord gave his retainer. Indeed, Frankish sources record that Charlemagne distributed the plunder from the Avar treasury among his leading churchmen and nobility as well as other faithful men; presumably this last category included Offa. In his dealings with Offa, Charlemagne undoubtedly saw the Mercian king as an important figure and one to be treated with some respect and, at times, flattery, but he was in no sense an equal. Charlemagne's power and his ambitions, as realised in his imperial coronation in 800, were of a far greater magnitude than Offa could hope to achieve.

If his claims to equality with Charlemagne cannot be sustained, nevertheless Offa does seem to have been inspired by Carolingian concepts of the nature of royal authority and government. Direct influence is, however, difficult to trace. The wealth of material emanating from Charlemagne's court, exploring the nature of kingship and exalting his rule, finds only the faintest echo in Offa's Mercia. Such similarities as there are may well derive from shared traditions rather than self-conscious emulation. Scholars from Ireland and from Anglo-Saxon England played a vital role in shaping Carolingian ideologies, and Offa's court could easily have drawn on similar resources.

One area where emulation seems clear is in the adoption of the ritual of royal anointing. In 787 Offa had his son, Ecgfrith, anointed as co-ruler probably by

4.5 Gilded-silver sword-grip and pommel, dating from the later eighth century, found at Fetter Lane, London. Its use of precious metals and complex decorative schemes make this one of the finest examples of Middle Saxon weaponry; its owner was clearly of high status

Hygeberht, bishop of the newly established archdiocese of Lichfield (Staffordshire; see below). Ecgfrith was the first Anglo-Saxon ruler so consecrated, and the inspiration would seem to be the papal anointing of Carolingian monarchs and their heirs, which began in the 750s. Such rituals drew on Old Testament images of kingship – Samuel anointing Saul, for example – and presented the ruler as in some way Christ-like, for Christ (Greek Χριστός) means simply 'the anointed one'. The ceremony must also have called to mind the post-baptismal anointing with chrism, emphasizing the transformative qualities of the rite.

In other areas direct Carolingian emulation is less clear. On a number of his coins, Offa is shown with a distinctive curled hairstyle that has its closest parallels in contemporary depictions of King David. Such may have been inspired by the identification of Charlemagne with David in Frankish circles, but the Old Testament king had long been held up as an exemplar of Christian kingship in Anglo-Saxon literature and insular inspiration may be more probable.

What seems clear is that Offa, like the Carolingians, sought to mobilise the possibilities afforded by Christianity for the legitimation of kingship and to bring into sharper relief the moral underpinnings of rule. As with royal anointing, such ideas are most visible in the strategies Offa adopted to ensure the succession of his son. Though these were long in the making, they come to the fore in the mid-780s.

In 786 two papal legates, George of Ostia and Theophylact of Todi, toured Anglo-Saxon England, meeting with leading churchmen and with various kings, Offa included. They sought, as their report put it, 'to uproot completely anything harmful', promulgating a series of decrees designed to check such abuses as they had found. Though these were presented as solutions to problems that beset all of the Anglo-Saxon kingdoms, certain of them would have had particular value for Offa. Canon 12 emphasised the status of kings as 'the Lord's anointed', the full import of which would manifest itself in the following year when Ecgfrith received unction.

The same canon also declared that rulers were 'not to be those begotten in adultery or incest'. This would, likewise, have served Offa's interests well. In marked, and perhaps deliberate, contrast to Æthelbald, Offa had adopted a policy of conspicuous

4.6 Silver penny of King Offa of Mercia, produced by the moneyer Eadhun. Offa's distinctive hairstyle has affinities with depictions of King David

monogamy. His wife, Cynethryth, regularly witnessed his charters, appearing as 'queen of the Mercians' in a number of them, and coins were issued in her name, one of only a handful of women so marked out in the early medieval west. Cynethryth's prominence no doubt reflected her importance at court – in one letter Alcuin suggests she is too busy with the king's business to read correspondence and in another he describes her as 'mistress of the royal household' – but it also stressed the legitimacy of her union with Offa and so the legitimacy of her offspring and their suitability to rule. Given Æthelbald's rejection of monogamy, such a strategy must have undermined the claims of a number of potential rivals as well as strengthening Ecgfrith's own claims.

4.7 Silver penny of Queen Cynethryth of Mercia, wife of Offa, produced by the moneyer Eoba

If Offa exploited developing ideas about Christian kingship in his promotion of Ecgfrith, he nevertheless also pursued other strategies perhaps less becoming of a pious king. In a letter to a Mercian nobleman, Alcuin wrote of 'how much blood the father shed to secure the kingdom for his son', implying the brutal suppression of rivals. Such actions led, as Alcuin saw it, to divine judgment. When Offa died in July 796 – apparently of natural causes – he was, as he had hoped, succeeded by his son. Ecgfrith, however, reigned for only a matter of months, dying – likewise, apparently of natural causes – in December of that year. As Alcuin put it in a letter to Bishop Unwona of Leicester, 'you know well how the illustrious king prepared for his son to inherit his kingdom, as he thought, but as events showed, he took it from him. [. . .] Man plans, but God decides.'

Mercian Hegemony in the Early Ninth Century

Ecgfrith was succeeded by Cenwulf (r. 796–821), a distant cousin from another branch of the royal dynasty. If Æthelbald and Offa dominate historical accounts of the Mercian supremacy, nevertheless Cenwulf's power and authority were as extensive, perhaps more so in some regards, as his predecessors'. The kingdom of Essex finally succumbed to Mercian domination, with the East Saxon King Sigered (c. 798–825) witnessing Cenwulf's charters first as king, then as sub-king and finally simply as an ealdorman.

Cenwulf was also able to mount a series of devastating raids on Wales, killing the king of Gwynedd in one and annexing part of what is now the county of Conwy in another.

Perhaps during the brief reign of Ecgfrith or more likely in its aftermath, Kent and East Anglia broke free from Mercian control. In East Anglia, coins were minted for a time in the name of King Eadwald, a member of the native ruling dynasty of that kingdom. Cenwulf soon reasserted control over the East Anglian mint and so, presumably, over the kingdom itself. In Kent, Eadberht 'Præn' (r. 796–8) claimed the throne, driving out the Mercian-appointed archbishop, Æthelheard, and probably sacking Canterbury. Eadberht had been forced into exile during Offa's reign and had spent time at the court of Charlemagne. In connection with his exiling, Eadberht had taken holy orders. Such would, in theory, have disqualified him from kingship and, indeed, Pope Leo III, ultimately at the instigation of Cenwulf, excommunicated him as an 'apostate cleric' in 798. The same year, whether emboldened by papal judgment or finally secure on the Mercian throne, Cenwulf invaded Kent. Eadberht was dragged away to Mercia in fetters and subsequently blinded and maimed. Perhaps in recognition both of the importance of Kent and the difficulty of controlling it, Cenwulf installed his brother, Cuthred, as king there under his authority.

It is in Cenwulf's reign, however, that the problems and tensions that seem ultimately to have undermined Mercian hegemony south of the Humber appear in sharp relief. The death of King Beorhtric of Wessex in 802 and the succession of the previously exiled Ecgberht (r. 802–39) marked the beginnings of a reversal in the fortunes of Mercia and Wessex, a shift adumbrated by an unsuccessful Mercian raid into West Saxon territory in the immediate aftermath of Ecgberht's accession.

The rising power and ambitions of Wessex certainly impinged on Mercian activities, but the attitude of Mercian kings to client kingdoms contributed to the problems. Even with his brother Cuthred installed as sub-king, Cenwulf had little direct involvement in Kent, preferring to rule it from a distance, a pattern that continued after Cuthred's death in 807. Cenwulf did not appoint another king in Cuthred's place, and though a series of charters records grants by Cenwulf to Kentish recipients, they tend

4.8 Gold coin of King Cenwulf of Mercia, produced in London. Gold coins were minted only very infrequently in the Anglo-Saxon period – this example seems to have been intended for use in international as well as internal trade, while other examples may have served as diplomatic gifts

to have been issued outside Kent. One charter shows a grant to Archbishop Wulfred of Canterbury being witnessed first by Mercian nobility and churchmen at Croydon in Staffordshire, and then at a separate ceremony in Canterbury some time later by the nobility of Kent.

The impression gained from this and other charters is of a distant ruler, operating in Kent not through the local nobility but through a select group of churchmen and women – particularly Archbishop Wulfred, Abbess Selethryth and his own daughter, Abbess Cwenthryth. All of these are likely to have owed their positions, in some way, to Mercian influence. Though such an approach mirrors the policies adopted by Offa, the dangers of it were made clear in the disputes that arose between Cenwulf and Archbishop Wulfred over the control of a number of monasteries in Kent (see below). The disputes were all the more protracted because such monasteries were clearly key economic assets, and Cenwulf's limited involvement in Kent had facilitated Wulfred's build-up of a substantial powerbase. Similarly, because Cenwulf had not directly patronised the Kentish nobility, and so failed to establish a broad base of clients and alliances, he had fewer options available for dealing with Wulfred and could count on only limited local support.

The rich source materials from Kent allow the essential features of Cenwulf's over-lordship there to be reconstructed in some detail and underline its potentially fragile nature, but it is likely that such patterns were repeated in other, less well-documented, kingdoms. The difficulty for Mercian rulers was not so much in establishing hegemony, hard though this was, as in making such gains permanent. It was to be the very different model of overlordship practised by the West Saxon kings in the ninth century that would prove to be the more durable form of hegemony.

Economy and Society in the 'Long Eighth Century'

The past two decades have witnessed a near-revolution in our understanding of the Anglo-Saxon economy in the late seventh to early ninth centuries. It is above all archaeological evidence that has transformed our perceptions. Such evidence allows us insights into the vibrancy of the economy in this period, the emergence of new settlement types, and a fundamental reorganisation of the Anglo-Saxon landscape. Though the great trading centres, the *emporia*, at Southampton, London, Ipswich and York, remain central to any understanding of the economy in the long eighth century, it is clear that they were only one aspect of far wider networks of exchange and production that criss-crossed the Anglo-Saxon landscape.

As has been outlined above, the *emporia* originated in the seventh century, with a number of small-scale settlements engaged in a limited level of trading activities that then expanded. At London, for example, by the late 670s there was limited settlement in the areas around present-day Charing Cross and the church of St Martin-in-the-Fields. Archaeological evidence points to timber-revetted embankments on the Thames and there are documentary references to the pulling-up of ships. In the final decades of the seventh century, settlement spread inland, with new buildings across an area formerly used for burial and several new roads running north-south to connect these new-built areas with the Thames. Both Southampton and Ipswich show similar expansion from small groups of settlements. At York, by contrast, a site at Heslington Hill that was engaged in limited long-distance trade seems to have declined by the mid-seventh century and activity shifted to Fishergate on a tributary navigable from the River Ouse.

The first half of the eighth century saw the *emporia* expanding to their maximum extent, with evidence for carefully planned and organised layouts and effective maintenance of such infrastructure as roads, trackways, wells and drains. This period also sees the maximum levels of coin loss at *emporia*, suggesting the most intense phase of economic activity. The trading centre at London – Lundenwic – grew to some 55–60 hectares, stretching from modern-day Seven Dials down to the River Thames, at what is now The Strand and Aldwych.

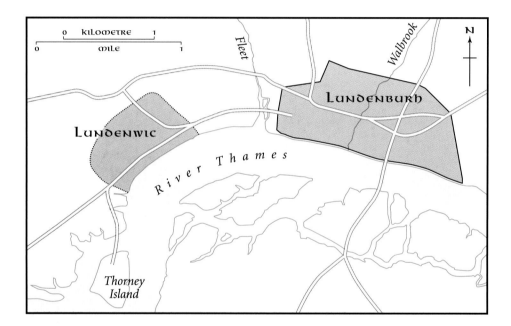

4.9 Location of the Middle Saxon trading settlement at Lundenwic

The most extensive excavations of Lundenwic took place at the Royal Opera House in Covent Garden. After a rapid expansion of the site in the late seventh and early eighth centuries, the period c. 730–70 witnessed what the excavators described as a period of consolidation and prosperity. The site was by now covered with a network of efficiently maintained roads and alleyways. The main road, running north–south through the site, was repaired and resurfaced on numerous occasions using gravel from quarries on the edges of the main settlement. Timber drains lined each side of the road and it was cambered to facilitate the run-off of surface water.

Many of the buildings constructed during this phase had street frontages, aligned on the north–south road, and were separated by small streets and alleyways. Some had enclosed open-air yards at the rear, where various activities such as butchery and the preparation of raw materials took place. At the north-eastern edge of the site were a number of pits used for the preparation and tanning of hides. Finds from the buildings

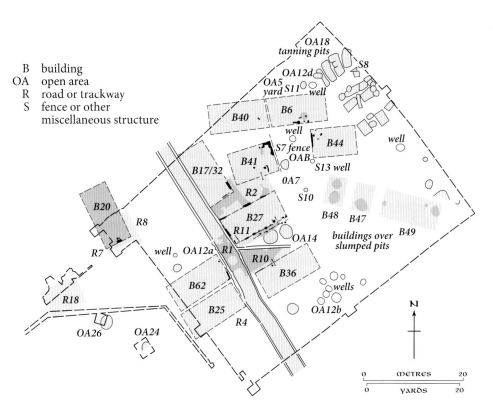

B   building
OA   open area
R   road or trackway
S   fence or other
        miscellaneous structure

4.10 Layout of the site at the
Royal Opera House, Covent
Garden during the eighth-
century heyday of the trading
centre at Lundenwic

themselves suggest that a range of craft and manufacturing activities took place, including metalworking, weaving and textile production, and bone- and antler-working. Many buildings saw a range of small-scale craft activity while others seem to have served more specialised purposes. One building, for example, occupied until the middle of the eighth century, was probably a smithy, with a brickearth hearth and a circular clay furnace that was found to contain significant quantities of slag. Hearth bottoms and dense slag were also recovered from the open area or yard to the north of this building. Materials recovered from across the site as well as elsewhere at Lundenwic point to trading links with areas in what are now northern France, the Low Countries and the Rhineland, with lava quernstones, pottery, glass and wine amongst the commodities imported.

At Ipswich in East Anglia, manufacturing perhaps played a more significant role in the economy, with industrial-scale production of Ipswich Ware pottery from around the second decade of the eighth century, alongside trade and more limited levels of other manufacturing and craft production. The wheel-turned and kiln-fired Ipswich Ware can be found on sites throughout much of Anglo-Saxon England, from Yorkshire to the south coast and as far west as the Upper Thames Valley, and was virtually the only pottery used in East Anglia.

These major *emporia* were dominant in overseas trade but settlements in other coastal areas maintained more limited contacts, with such beach-trading sites as Meols on the Wirral serving specific hinterlands. Small-scale trading places persisted in

complains of the poor quality of imported English cloaks, claiming them to be too short, perhaps suggesting that if Offa dealt promptly with this issue he would expedite despatch of the black stones. The earlier breakdown in the relationship between Offa and Charlemagne, which resulted in a trade embargo between Francia and Mercia, likewise indicates the extent to which rulers were both involved with and profiting from international trade – an embargo was both achievable and damaging to those targeted.

Understandings of the relationship between the *emporia* and their hinterlands have been transformed over the past generation by the discovery of significant numbers of so-called 'productive sites' – named for the large quantities of coinage and non-ferrous metalwork recovered. Most have been discovered by metal detectorists but few have been fully excavated by archaeologists, though this situation is now improving.

Alongside their method of discovery and their levels of coinage and metalwork, these 'productive sites' share a number of other characteristics. Their distribution is largely concentrated in the south and east of England, particularly towards the coast but with some in the Middle and Upper Thames Valley. They are generally close to main routes of communication, either navigable rivers or roads and trackways, be these prehistoric or Roman. There are nevertheless significant differences between the various 'productive sites', both in terms of levels of material recovered and the range of activities undertaken. Some, such as Flixborough or Brandon (Suffolk) were clearly major settlements, yielding imported goods and evidence of crafts, industry and literacy (particularly in the form of styli). Others were more minor, producing lower levels of coinage and metalwork, and they show less evidence of being multifunctional settlements.

Given the high levels of coinage recovered, it seems clear that many, if not all, the 'productive sites' were involved at some level in commerce and trade; this would explain their presence on major routes and the frequent finds of imported pottery and other goods. Some may have emerged simply as places where traders or merchants congregated, at seasonal fairs or markets. Such may be the case with South Ferriby (Lincolnshire), a probable terminus for ferries across the Humber and for the difficult crossing of the Ancholme floodplain, so an obvious focus for travellers. At other sites, there is evidence, both contemporary and later, for ecclesiastical functions. Flixborough (Humberside), for example, may have been a monastery for at least parts of its lifespan, while the discovery of styli and a gold plaque with a representation of John the Evangelist (perhaps part of a book cover) at Brandon similarly suggest an ecclesiastical community of some kind. Likewise, significant numbers of 'productive sites' in East Anglia were later the sites of monasteries or churches, or formed parts of the endowments of such institutions.

Given the role of monasteries and churches in international trade, as highlighted by the toll exemptions referred to above, it is not surprising that religious communities may have been stimuli for networks of exchange and production at the local and regional level. The liturgical life of such communities necessitated access to imported goods, particularly wine and olive oil; written sources as well as archaeological excavations of known religious sites demonstrate that they could be centres for industrial production and craft-working, as at Whitby (North Yorkshire) and Lyminge. Given that the written evidence points to the close supervision of traders and merchants by royal officials, some of the 'productive sites' may also have been secular administrative centres, where the need to pay tolls and taxes and have goods inspected also provided an opportunity for trade and commerce.

Below the *emporia* and 'productive sites' in the economic hierarchy was a large number of settlements – harder to detect archaeologically – that supplied them with raw materials and foodstuffs but were otherwise outside the networks of international trade and exchange that developed over the course of the seventh and eighth centuries. There is evidence that certain settlement sites in this period were moving from general subsistence farming to more specialised and, probably, market-orientated production. Such seems to have been but one part of a much wider intensification of rural production and exploitation of landed resources that took place across the Middle Saxon period. By the seventh century, the nature of Anglo-Saxon settlements was changing, with a move away from the scattered farmsteads of earlier periods to more structured and carefully organised layouts, with trackways, enclosures and other internal demarcations. There is also evidence of a more general relocation of settlements, a 'Settlement Shift', away from lighter, and in some cases more marginal, soils to heavier and more productive soils, beginning perhaps in the middle of the seventh century or slightly later and continuing for at least a century. This type of process is thought to lie behind the abandonment of such sites as Mucking (Essex) and Chalton Down (Hampshire).

The period also witnessed a marked growth in the area under cultivation, with increasing acreages particularly of wheat, and wider use of floodplains for pasture, as witnessed around the lower Severn. Natural resources were likewise being exploited

4.13 Middle Saxon fish-weir on the Nass, Essex

with burgeoning intensity, with both archaeological and documentary evidence for the construction of numerous fish-traps and weirs on rivers and estuaries, such as those on the Blackwater Estuary in Essex or the River Thames at Chelsea. There was similar investment in the processing of raw materials, with watermills such as those at Kingsbury (Berkshire) and, probably, Tamworth (Staffordshire) being constructed in this period, and evidence for a late seventh-century tidal mill at Ebbsfleet (Kent).

The driving force behind much of this agricultural intensification and development is likely to have been the Church. The monastic boom of the later seventh and eighth centuries resulted in an increasingly wealthy Anglo-Saxon Church, with extensive landed endowments. In addition, the growth of the Church meant the growth of a static and, in agricultural terms, relatively unproductive population whose ritual life nevertheless consumed significant resources. The expansion of such a population would have increased demand on the agricultural surplus and perhaps required new methods for its collection and redistribution. At the same time, the stability of land tenure created by the introduction of bookland – effectively, land free from the usual norms of inheritance and intended in the first instance to allow for the permanent endowment of religious institutions – rewarded long-term investment in agricultural production and the exploitation of wider landscape resources. Such intensification of production was made more profitable and probably was stimulated further by the networks of long-distance trade centred on the *emporia* and other sites.

If the Church played a central role in these developments, it is nevertheless clear that kings were also making increasing demands on their subjects and undertaking ambitious projects – the already-cited Offa's Dyke being the most obvious case in point. Coinage offers another example of the increasing demands and ambitions of kings in the eighth century. From the 670s to the 740s, a coinage of silver pennies – known as *sceattas* – was in circulation in England and, indeed, elsewhere in northern Europe. Few of these coins bear inscriptions, and debate continues as to the level of royal oversight in their minting; some are likely to have been royal issues, whereas others may have been ecclesiastical or private issues.

By the 730s, the silver content of the *sceattas* circulating in England had declined significantly, mirroring the debasement of coinage elsewhere in Europe and suggesting a general shortage of bullion. This decline seems to have been the trigger for a currency reform, with the issuing of a new type of coin containing a higher precious metal content, of a more uniform weight and, crucially, bearing an inscription recording the king in whose name the coinage had been issued. Eadberht of Northumbria was the first to undertake such a reform, probably in the 740s, and he was followed by King Beonna of East Anglia in the 750s and Offa of Mercia and Heahberht of Kent in the 760s, with the latter two rulers inspired also by a reform of the Frankish coinage undertaken by Pippin III. Offa would initiate a further reform of coinage, with larger, heavier pennies being produced from the early 790s, probably in response to a similar reform by the Frankish ruler Charlemagne.

These heavy pennies would quickly become the standard form of coinage in the south Humbrian kingdoms, though in Northumbria the lighter, thinner type of penny, introduced by Eadberht, would persist. These reforms were also accompanied by a

4.14 Silver 'sceat' of King Eadberht of Northumbria

contraction in the number of mints in operation in England, with coins being minted only at York, London, Canterbury, Rochester, in Wessex (probably at Winchester or Southampton) and in East Anglia (probably at Ipswich).

Though rights to issue coinage were granted to a small number of bishops, chiefly the archbishop of Canterbury, from the middle of the eighth century coinage in the Anglo-Saxon kingdoms became, effectively, royal. The level of direct royal oversight is likely to have varied significantly. Uniformity of design and royal style across mints could sometimes be enforced or achieved, such as during the early years of Offa's light coinage or after his introduction of the heavy coinage, but at other times there existed considerable variety.

The mechanisms by which kings profited from the production of royal coinage are likewise obscure. Moneyers may have paid kings a fee for the right to mint coins, either at a flat rate or as a proportion of the value of coins minted, and rulers may similarly have claimed a percentage of the value of foreign coins or bullion brought to moneyers to be melted down and made into coins. It was perhaps the very idea of an explicitly royally controlled and guaranteed coinage that was significant in the eighth century rather than any level of actual royal involvement. It speaks of an increasing desire by kings to assert their authority over all aspects of life in their kingdoms and to manage more carefully the resources that were available to them.

Such processes can also be seen in the demands kings made of those who held lands in their kingdom. The end of the seventh century saw the first royal privileges freeing church lands from the payment of taxation and other burdens. Both Wihtred of Kent and Ine of Wessex issued general decrees to that effect, and Wihtred included a similar statement in his law code. The precise details of the burdens from which the churches and monasteries were being freed are not spelled out by any of these documents. In addition, despite such general statements of immunities, church lands, at least in Kent, still owed some royal service. A charter of Æthelberht II, Wihtred's son, freed the land granted from all royal rights except those – left otherwise undefined – that were generally known to be owed by all church lands in Kent. Even during the reign of Wihtred, there is evidence that the religious institutions of Kent could be subject to sometimes onerous burdens. Around 720 a Kentish abbess, Eangyth, complained in a letter to the Continental missionary Boniface that she and her

4.15 The *Durham Liber Vitae*. A 'Book of Life' contained the names of individuals connected to a religious community – inmates, patrons, friends and so forth – who were to be remembered in the liturgy. This example was begun in the first half of the ninth century, probably at Lindisfarne or perhaps Wearmouth-Jarrow, and the entries on this page are the names of abbots of priestly grade. The first named is Ceolfrith, abbot of Wearmouth-Jarrow

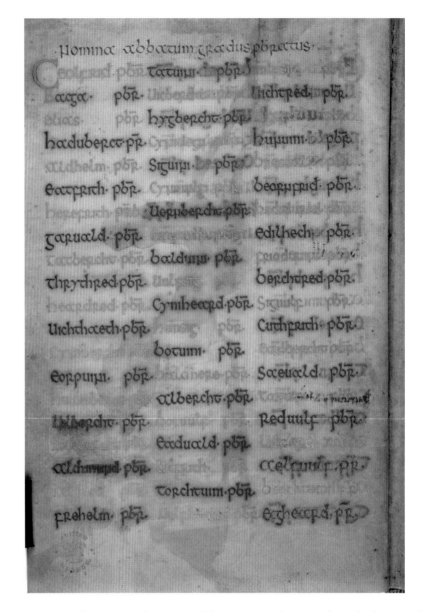

community were facing ruin because of the services they owed to the king and the queen, the bishop and various secular officials.

As has been noted, Boniface himself wrote a letter to Æthelbald of Mercia condemning the violence and extortion the king inflicted on monks in his kingdom. Soon afterwards, in 749, Æthelbald issued a decree at a council at Gumley (Leicestershire) freeing all churches and monasteries in Mercia from royal taxation and tribute except for those burdens that fell on the whole population by royal edict and which could not be excused, namely the construction of bridges and the maintenance of fortifications. The decree also stated that Æthelbald would ensure that churches and monasteries could enjoy without encumbrance the produce of their lands and that they were free from making gifts to the king and to other secular powers, unless these were made voluntarily and from affection. The possibility that gifts might not, in the past, have been made freely gives some substance to the exactions that Abbess Eangyth so complained about.

Æthelbald's decrees at Gumley might represent, then, the king's response to accusations of unjust exactions placed on monks and clerics. The freeing of Church lands from all royal dues, with the exception of what have become known as the 'common burdens', represents a statement of precisely what rights the king and the secular powers could and could not claim from church lands. In exchange for the Church accepting certain military burdens, Æthelbald pledged to protect the churches and monasteries of Mercia from further taxation and burdens. After the council at Gumley, the military obligations or common burdens appear also in documents from the kingdom of the *Hwicce*, from Kent and Sussex, and eventually Wessex. By the end of the eighth century a third burden, to provide men to serve in the army, had been added. Although personal loyalty and the expectation of reward continued to be of vital importance in the raising of royal military retinues, the second half of the eighth century thus saw the beginnings of a shift away from military service as a personal obligation to one's lord to an expectation attendant on the holding of land, a vital stage in the development of royal power.

Christianity and the Church

By the end of the seventh century, the Conversion period, in the strict sense, was over. Though there had been setbacks, the Conversion of England had been achieved remarkably quickly and with very few problems. Within a century of the arrival of the first missionaries, the Anglo-Saxons were, nominally at least, Christian. All of the kingdoms were governed by rulers who professed the Christian faith, monasteries and churches had been established, and a network of dioceses covered England. Aspects of Christian ritual and morality such as infant baptism, observation of the Sabbath, monogamy and regular marriages were legally enforced. Bede writes as if paganism, in the sense of a widely supported religion or cultural force, had effectively come to an end by the first few decades of the eighth century. Practices identified as pagan continue to be referred to – and condemned – by ecclesiastical writers over the course of the eighth century (and, indeed, later) but in a context of Christians lapsing into error rather than of pagans living alongside Christians.

If the period of formal missionary activity was at an end by the beginning of the eighth century, it was succeeded by a longer, more drawn-out and far more obscure process of what we might term 'Christianisation'. Over the course of the eighth century, therefore, the Anglo-Saxons moved from being a converted people to being a Christian people. The new religion filtered through to all levels of Anglo-Saxon society, leaving few areas untouched. As with the Conversion process, Christianisation is best seen as a dialogue – challenging, but productive and dynamic – between the Anglo-Saxons and their new faith. As Christianity transformed and reshaped Anglo-Saxon society, so the Anglo-Saxons transformed and reimagined Christianity, inflecting it in the light of their own cultural needs.

If the eighth century ultimately saw the triumph of the processes first set in motion by missionaries before 600, it is a triumph that seems to have left only the faintest echo in the surviving sources. The Anglo-Saxon Church of the eighth and early ninth centuries appears as one beset by problems: declining standards of monasticism, secularisation, lay lordship of religious institutions and inadequate provision of pastoral care. Such a picture is, to an extent, a product of the surviving sources. Most of our information concerning the Church in this period comes not from narrative sources, as was the case for the seventh-century Church, but from documentary sources – charters, records of litigation and dispute settlement, and the decrees of ecclesiastical synods, such as the councils that met at *Clovesho* (location now unknown) or Chelsea in 816.

Such sources tend to focus on perceived abuses and controversies, but in so doing they also provide eloquent testimony to the success of Christianity within Anglo-Saxon England. The elite in particular seized upon the possibilities presented by Christianity and its attendant institutions, and the new faith was rapidly integrated into the lives and outlook of the Anglo-Saxon aristocracy. To certain ecclesiastical writers – writers whose voices, inevitably, dominate the surviving sources – this integration could look like the exertion of undue secular influence on the Church, but this perspective should not be allowed to disguise the very real success of Christianity. Moreover, in responding to this perceived secularisation, church councils of this period reveal an increasingly assertive episcopacy, looking to resist secular encroachment and to extend their power and influence into all areas of the religious life of their dioceses.

Condemnations of monasteries and churches as excessively wealthy and worldly reflect the growing importance of the institutional Church in the economic and cultural life of the Anglo-Saxon kingdoms. As has been explored above, religious institutions played a central role in long-distance trade and commerce and could be centres of craft-working, production and manufacturing. The Anglo-Saxon Church of the eighth and early ninth centuries undoubtedly faced significant problems, but a straightforward narrative of decline and decay is a gross oversimplification. If Bede and a number of his Northumbrian contemporaries articulated through their writings the idea of a Golden Age of Anglo-Saxon Christianity in the seventh century, Alcuin of York, writing in the 790s, could find, with equal confidence, a Golden Age in the mid-eighth century.

From the 670s onwards there was a rapid growth in monastic foundation and endowment. First kings and then, increasingly, the nobility founded and endowed a large number of monasteries, gifting some of the most important houses extensive landed patrimonies. The result of this patronage was that the Church was massively enriched over the course of just one or two generations. Monasteries founded in this period drew on a range of different influences – Irish, Frankish, Italian – and in the absence of a single, standard monastic Rule the patterns of life and religious observance at these houses would have varied considerably. While some monasteries were large, with numerous inmates and vast landed resources, others were smaller, consisting of a handful of individuals and possessing only very limited estates. Nor were monasteries in this period necessarily detached from the wider world; as will be seen, some were also active among the laity.

The wide variety of forms of monastic life in this period and their varied personnel – priests, bishops and minor clergy as well as monks and nuns – have led some scholars, such as Sarah Foot, to champion use of the term 'minster' to describe religious communities in this period. Such a term has the benefit of avoiding some of the anachronistic connotations of the word 'monastery' but, inevitably, carries its own set of connotations, not all of which are helpful. In this chapter the term 'monastery' will be used but should be understood in this wider sense, as a word embracing a varied range of different types and sizes of community.

For Bede, the extraordinary enthusiasm for the monastic life in the early eighth century might be counter-productive, or at best mischannelled. In a letter to Bishop Ecgberht of York in 734 he bemoaned the numerous monasteries in Northumbria ruled by men with no knowledge of the true monastic vocation, and vociferously condemned the countless noblemen who had gained lands on the pretext of establishing monasteries but instead lived lives of debauchery and sin, spending their days in the monastic enclosures and their nights in bed with their wives. Others had apparently gained lands under false pretences, receiving grants for the foundation of monasteries only to avoid military service or to gain hereditary control over such lands.

Bede's solution to these sham monasteries was a simple one: tear up the charters that established them and put their lands to better use, either secular or ecclesiastical. Whether all the nobles Bede so described would have recognised themselves in his account seems unlikely. If some had less than pious motivations, others must have been inspired by a genuine devotion, but the form their religiosity took did not meet with Bede's approval. His criticisms stem at least in part from competing and conflicting ideas about the correct observance of communal religious life. Moreover, in seeking to stamp out one perceived abuse, Bede opened the door to another. In the mid-750s, Pope Paul sent a letter to King Eadberht of Northumbria and Ecgberht, now archbishop of York, demanding the restoration of three monasteries. These had been seized from a certain Abbot Forthred and given to a nobleman called Moll. It is tempting to read this letter in the light of Bede's advice. Yet if Eadberht and Ecgberht had liquidated estates they believed were held by a nobleman-abbot of the type Bede had condemned, nevertheless Forthred had been able to convince the pope, at least, that he was a true religious. The differences between reform and secular encroachment and between royal support of the Church and the unjust appropriation of ecclesiastical resources could be, in part at least, a matter of perspective.

By the mid-eighth century, other voices joined Bede's in asserting that something had gone fundamentally wrong with Anglo-Saxon monasticism and, indeed, with the Church as a whole. In a letter of c. 747, Boniface described to Archbishop Cuthbert of Canterbury the steps he had taken to reform the Frankish Church and suggested Cuthbert take similar measures to reform the Anglo-Saxon Church. Monks ought not to wear luxurious clothes, drunkenness among the clergy – a specifically English vice according to Boniface – should be stamped out, and laymen who controlled monasteries ought to be excommunicated.

In the same year and probably in response to Boniface's letter, a council of the archdiocese of Canterbury met at *Clovesho*, issuing canons that condemned the secularisation of monasteries and churches and criticised, among other things, displays of excessive luxury, drunkenness and debauchery. The problem of lay lordship of monasteries was mentioned and such institutions were condemned, but the council stopped short of implementing Boniface's policy of excommunication against transgressors. Instead, the council decreed that bishops ought to inspect and to supervise the monasteries in their dioceses to ensure standards were being maintained.

The canons promulgated at *Clovesho* were, however, less about resisting the encroachment of lay culture on religious life than about trying to define, potentially in new ways, where the boundaries between the secular and ecclesiastical spheres should be drawn. How far should the mores of aristocratic culture suffuse religious institutions? How far could Christianity and its ritual life be reshaped and reimagined by the Anglo-Saxons? The creative dynamism of Anglo-Saxon England in the eighth and early ninth centuries owed much to just this kind of cultural fusion and dialogue, but for the bishops at *Clovesho* limits urgently needed to be put in place.

Other equally pressing problems also occupied the council at *Clovesho*. Scurrilous rumours were circulating of rivalry between the secular aristocracy, kings included, and the Church. Kings and their nobilities, it was said, accused the Church of being insincere in its affections for them and envious of the wealth that they possessed. To

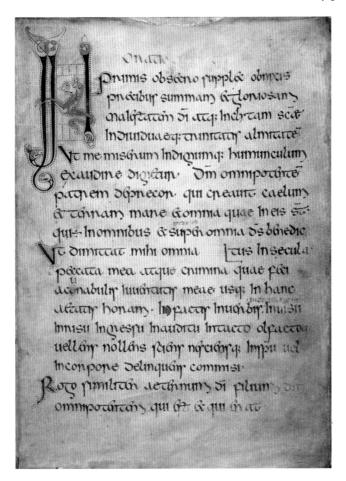

4.17 The *Royal Prayerbook*. The manuscript is one of a number of prayerbooks produced in the later eighth and early ninth centuries and shows the influence of the 'Tiberius Style' in its decoration. The contents of this volume are especially concerned with matters of illness and healing

end such rumours, ecclesiastics and monastics were enjoined to pray not just for themselves but also for kings, nobles and all Christian peoples.

There is certainly evidence of growing tensions surrounding the Church in the later eighth and early ninth centuries, but it would be wrong to draw a sharp divide, as this canon does, between the secular aristocracy and the Church. Most, if not all, of the leading churchmen and women were members of the nobility and a significant number were royal. Furthermore, as the canons of *Clovesho* themselves made clear, there was often little difference between the atmosphere of the aristocratic hall and that of the monastic precincts. Individuals could move relatively freely between the two.

Equally, it would be wrong to present the Church in this period as a monolithic whole. For Mercian overlords, powerful churchmen and women, above all the archbishop of Canterbury, could represent a focus for local resistance and revolt, accumulating powerbases that could threaten their own. The fluctuating political situation also meant that such individuals could owe their positions and, perhaps, their loyalties to previous regimes and so were often figures of suspicion to their new overlords. Yet monasteries and other religious houses in client kingdoms could attract extensive patronage from kings such as Offa and Cenwulf. They became very powerful and wealthy institutions, nominally under the authority of the diocesan bishop and archbishop but in practice largely beyond their control. Such may have been the case with the Kentish monasteries of Minster-in-Thanet and Reculver in the ninth century. Tensions thus existed not only between the secular aristocracy and the Church but also between different parts of the Church and between different institutions. Loyalties cut across any simple lay and ecclesiastical divide.

Such growing tensions are made manifest in a series of disputes in the later eighth and early ninth centuries. Mercian control of Kent under Offa was much resented and

4.18 Detail from a frieze at St Mary and St Hardulph, Breedon on the Hill. The birds, beasts and chimeras of this and other friezes at Breedon owe a clear debt to Coptic and Byzantine artistic traditions

sparked a successful revolt in the 770s. Offa regained control by the mid-780s, but probably only by comparatively brutal means, and his relationship with Archbishop Jænberht suffered accordingly. As an ex-abbot of St Peter's and St Paul's, Canterbury, Jænberht was almost certainly of Kentish extraction and although he had been elevated to the archiepiscopate during Offa's first overlordship of Kent, and so presumably with his consent, it is likely that the Mercian king now doubted Jænberht's loyalty. Certainly, Offa seized lands that had been granted to Jænberht's kinsman Aldhun by the Kentish King Ecgberht II during the brief period of native rule in the late 770s and 780s.

Hostility between Offa and Jænberht may also explain the Mercian king's establishment of a new archdiocese. A synod at Chelsea in 787 stripped Jænberht of part of his province, creating a new archdiocese centred on Lichfield, in the heartlands of Mercia. Such proved highly contentious and was, of course, bitterly opposed at Canterbury. Jænberht died in 792 and was succeeded by the abbot of Louth in Lincolnshire, Æthelheard, presumably under Mercian pressure. With Canterbury now neutralised as a centre of Kentish resistance, once Archbishop Hygeberht of Lichfield died in the early ninth century, the archdiocese was dissolved and the traditional sphere of influence of Canterbury restored.

Disputes between Mercia and Canterbury also took other forms. A papal privilege from Pope Hadrian I makes it clear that Offa of Mercia and his wife Cynethryth had substantial interests in several religious houses. Cynethryth herself retired to take charge of Cookham (Berkshire) after her husband's death in 796, but also retained control of the church at Bedford where her husband was buried. The monastery at Cookham had originally been granted by King Æthelbald to Christ Church, Canterbury, but had been seized first by King Cynewulf of Wessex and then subsequently by Offa. Despite numerous requests from successive archbishops of Canterbury, Offa retained control of the monastery, presumably in part because of its location in the disputed frontier zone between Mercia and Wessex. In 798 Cynethryth reached an agreement with Archbishop Æthelheard, giving up Bedford and a number of estates in Kent in exchange for Canterbury surrendering its claims on Cookham.

These two problems – tension and distrust between the archbishop of Canterbury and Mercian kings, and disagreement over the control of monasteries – come together in a protracted dispute between Archbishop Wulfred (d. 832) and King Cenwulf. Before his elevation to the archiepiscopate, Wulfred had been a member of the Christ Church community at Canterbury, though his roots were probably in the Middlesex region and he retained significant landholdings there. As such he must have been a candidate attractive to both Christ Church and King Cenwulf. Nevertheless by around 808, there were clearly tensions between the archbishop and the Mercian king, for Pope Leo III noted in a letter to Charlemagne that a dispute between the two had still not been resolved.

The causes of these tensions are unknown and the two enjoyed better relations after this date, with Cenwulf making a number of grants to Wulfred in the period 809–15, albeit often in exchange for money or other estates. In 816 Wulfred held a council at Chelsea that sought, amongst other things, radically to extend the power of bishops over monasteries in their dioceses. Bishops were given the power to elect abbots and abbesses and, if institutions were threatened by secular rapacity, the right to take control of monastic properties. Such effectively inverted the existing relationship between bishops and monasteries, despite the council's claim to be following the judgments of the Council of Chalcedon of 451.

If the council at Chelsea was intended to check the spread of lay lordship in general, nevertheless it seemed designed specifically to strengthen Wulfred's hand in his struggles with Cenwulf. By this date, the two were in dispute over control of the monasteries of Reculver and Minster-in-Thanet. This dispute is known only from a record drawn up in 835 when, with Cenwulf dead and Reculver and Minster-in-Thanet in the hands of his daughter, Cwenthryth, the matter was resolved in Wulfred's favour by the Mercian ruler Beornwulf.

The record of this dispute is frustratingly opaque in places and it is not clear precisely what rights over the two monasteries Wulfred thought he had been denied. The matter was of such seriousness that in the aftermath of the Council of Chelsea Cenwulf had driven Wulfred into exile. Both men sought to buttress their positions in other ways. Cenwulf himself had secured a privilege from Pope Paschal confirming his authority over the monasteries in his possession, while Wulfred forged a number of royal privileges, from both Kentish and Mercian rulers, granting him extensive powers over the religious institutions in Kent. A reconciliation between the two was achieved at a meeting in 821 at which Wulfred agreed to hand over to the king an estate of 300 hides and the sum of £120 – a vast sum – apparently in return for the restoration of certain rights over Reculver and Minster-in-Thanet, though the document is vague on this point. Whatever agreement was reached, Wulfred felt it had been broken by Cwenthryth and he subsequently appealed to King Beornwulf, eventually gaining control of Minster-in-Thanet.

Disputes of this kind were also played out at a local level, between bishops and the nobility. It was not only royalty who treated religious houses as in some sense their own private property. Over the course of the eighth and ninth centuries, lay lords of monasteries increasingly treated them as resources to be exploited in whichever way they saw fit. In the early 820s, for example, Wulfheard, the lay owner of the monastery at Inkberrow (Worcestershire), constructed a residence for himself within the monastic enclosure. The canons of the Council of Chelsea likewise suggested that impoverishment due to secular rapacity was a danger facing many monastic institutions.

That lay owners were asset-stripping monastic communities or progressively encroaching on their landed resources would explain the gradual shift away from large communities of monks to the smaller communities of clergy evidenced in the early to mid-ninth century. Charters from Kent, for example, suggest that religious communities there were being staffed increasingly by priests and members of the secular clergy instead of monks. Small communities comprising perhaps a handful of priests and members of the minor orders would require far less extensive resources to support them than a large monastic community but would, nevertheless, be able to meet most of the pastoral and liturgical needs of their lay patrons.

In some cases the efforts of bishops to defend standards within their own dioceses led them to take over smaller monasteries to protect them from secular encroachment

4.19 Figure of the Virgin or an abbess from St Mary and St Hardulph, Breedon on the Hill

and lay lordship. The process is best seen at Worcester, where numerous small houses and their property came into the hands of the diocesan Church during the eighth and early ninth centuries, marking a significant improvement in its resource base. At Worcester such processes were facilitated by pre-existing ties between the founders or owners of many of the monasteries so taken over and the episcopal see. The owners and patrons of these smaller houses would also have benefited from being part of a wider, more extensive and better resourced network of monasteries and churches.

Nevertheless, episcopal oversight and ownership need not always have been welcomed. If bishops could be motivated by a desire to uphold standards and prevent lay lordship, episcopal avarice could also play a part. The acceptance of lay lordship may have been one means by which monasteries hoped to escape the unwanted attentions of their diocesan bishop. Certainly, Wulfred was remembered at Minster-in-Thanet not as the person who had rescued the monastery from the dangers of lay control but as a despoiler of monastic property. Monasteries therefore risked finding themselves caught between the ambitions of their lay patrons and the designs of bishops.

If the patronage of the elite could bring problems, it nevertheless enriched the Anglo-Saxon Church, facilitating the development of a remarkable and productive intellectual and artistic culture. The *scriptoria* of several important institutions were clearly active in copying major works, including those of Bede, for which there was considerable demand across the mid- and later eighth century from Continental Europe. Leading churchmen, such as Abbot Cuthbert of Wearmouth-Jarrow and Archbishop Ecgberht of York, were in correspondence with their counterparts on the Continent, where Anglo-Saxon missionaries were heavily involved in the Frankish efforts to convert their neighbours to the north. Anglo-Saxon churchmen such as Alcuin of York were active at the court of Charlemagne and provided significant intellectual underpinning for the Carolingian Renaissance. From being a major importer of texts and scholarship across the seventh century, eighth-century England took its place within the Western Church as a fully participating province, able to export texts and learning as well as draw them in.

Alongside learning and scholarship can be placed the flourishing artistic culture of the Anglo-Saxon Church. In Northumbria, illuminated manuscripts such as the *Lindisfarne Gospels* (?720s) extended and refined the so-called Hiberno-Saxon style that had developed across Britain and Ireland in the seventh century. The combining of decorative motifs from Celtic La Tène style – peltae, triskeles and trumpet-spirals – with animal interlace deriving particularly from Germanic metalwork and interlace and step-patterns from Mediterranean traditions first occurred on metalwork but was subsequently translated to other media, reaching its creative peak in the illuminated manuscripts of the late seventh and eighth centuries.

In the south Humbrian kingdoms a different style of illumination developed across the mid-eighth to early ninth centuries. Hiberno-Saxon elements were deployed but the tradition drew more extensively on Classical and Italo-Byzantine motifs with a greater use of gold and purple pigment. The beginnings of the development of this so-called 'Tiberius Style' can be seen in the *Vespasian Psalter*, produced in the 720s or 730s, perhaps at Canterbury. It was subsequently used for a series of de luxe manuscripts such as the *Stockholm Codex Aureus* and the Canterbury *Royal Bible*, as well as for a collection of personal prayer books, including the *Book of Nunnaminster* and the *Royal Prayerbook*.

The eighth century also saw the development of new types of sculpture in Northumbria, most notably free-standing crosses, often decorated with vine-scroll and interlace and sometimes featuring complex and allusive iconographic programmes executed in high relief. There is little surviving sculpture from the south until the mid- to late eighth century when in eastern Mercia in particular there was a flourishing of architectural sculpture such as ornamental friezes and figural panels. As with manuscripts, the southern style of sculpture was more Classicising, though it still employed certain insular decorative motifs and schemes. Some of the best examples are preserved in the church of St Mary and St Hardulph at Breedon on the Hill (Leicestershire), with other important works preserved at Wirksworth (Derbyshire), Peterborough ('the Headda Stone') and Lichfield (the recently discovered 'Lichfield Angel').

If manuscripts and sculpture redeployed existing artistic traditions in a new,

Christian context, so Anglo-Saxon vernacular poetry was pressed into the service of Christianity. Bede records how Cædmon, a member of the Whitby community during the time of Abbess Hild (d. 680), was divinely inspired to compose Christian poetry in Old English, a feat none had accomplished before him. Though little vernacular poetry from this period survives – only a few lines of Cædmon's verses are extant, for example – the recasting of the Christian story in Old English poetic diction and imagery was clearly of considerable cultural importance. This led to a reimagining of key Christian events and characters, with episodes such as the spreading of the Gospel by the Apostles being seen through the lens of the secular heroic ethos. Whilst the achievements of poets such as Cædmon could be praised by ecclesiastical writers and vernacular poetry was probably of vital importance in spreading the message of Christianity to the laity, some churchmen, as has been seen, sought to place limits on such cultural fusion. The council of *Clovesho* condemned those who recited in church in the manner of secular poets, decreeing that the pronunciation of Holy Scripture should not be mutilated and disfigured as if it were heroic verse.

Religion and the Laity

The extent to which the religious lives of the laity were transformed by Christianity depended to a large degree on the effectiveness of provisions for pastoral care – that is, the activities carried out by the Church to meet the spiritual needs of the laity. In the eighth century this embraced a range of activities from administering the sacraments – such as baptism, confirmation, communion, confession and the imposition of penance, and the Last Rites – to preaching, teaching and more general religious advice and guidance.

Though clearly of vital importance to the religious life of the Anglo-Saxon kingdoms, there is surprisingly little evidence for how the pastoral needs of the laity were met. Much of the evidence that survives is normative – setting out what ought to happen but not necessarily what was happening. Other evidence comes from sources stressing the inadequacy of current arrangements and the need for reform, such as Bede's aforementioned letter to Bishop Ecgberht in 734. Ultimate responsibility for pastoral care lay with the bishops, and the sources repeatedly stress the need for bishops to tour their dioceses annually to educate and to exhort the laity. Bishops were also the only churchmen who could administer the full range of sacraments, including confirmation, the ordination of clergy and the consecration of churches. The bulk of pastoral work must, however, have fallen to priests and to the minor clergy.

While the surviving sources emphasise the role of priests in the provision of pastoral care, it is less clear how such provision was organised: what areas did priests administer to, for example, or at what kind of institutions were they based? On the Continent in this period and in England at a later date, pastoral care was provided by small, local churches staffed by one or two priests and under direct diocesan control. Such churches are largely absent from the written sources of late seventh- and eighth-century England and their apparent scarcity makes it unlikely that they could have been the basis for an effective system of pastoral care. Instead of these small, local

4.20 All Saints, Brixworth. One of the finest surviving examples of Anglo-Saxon architecture, the nave is substantially late eighth- or early ninth-century and was originally flanked by a series of porticus that probably acted as oratories. The original narthex subsequently formed the base of the tower, the upper sections of which were built in the eleventh century at the same time as the turret. The spire and the Lady Chapel date to the thirteenth or fourteenth century

churches pastoral care in this period may have been administered by religious communities – monasteries, in the loose sense of the word discussed above. These communities had responsibility for extensive 'parishes' far larger than the parishes of later periods.

This so-called 'Minster Model' of pastoral provision has been particularly championed by John Blair. Though it accords well with the surviving evidence, the problem is that the written sources are dominated by monastic writers and by texts relating to monasteries and their landed endowments. Such may provide an overly monastic vision of Anglo-Saxon Christianity in this period, emphasising the role of monasteries at the expense of smaller churches. Given the small number of clergy staffing such institutions and the very limited landed resources they would have needed to support themselves, it is not surprising that these houses are mentioned only infrequently in the written sources.

However pastoral care was provided, not all religious communities would necessarily have been engaged in formal pastoral activities; indeed, some of the smaller monasteries are likely to have lacked priests. Even for those communities with clergy and active in the provision of pastoral care, meeting the needs of the laity still presented significant problems. The extent to which the liturgy was intelligible to the laity was

4.21 The Wirksworth Slab. Grave-cover or monument from Wirksworth, Derbyshire, with scenes from the life of Christ and the early Jerusalem community. Though less accomplished than the sculpture from Breedon on the Hill, this piece exhibits a similar range of Mediterranean and Byzantine stylistic influences

limited, with many of the rituals conducted in Latin, a language very few lay people would have learned. Comprehension of Latin was a problem for priests, too. The council of *Clovesho* in 747 noted that there were many priests who did not understand the meaning of the words of the Mass or the Lord's Prayer, presumably having learned their part by rote. Vernacular translations needed to be made, the council decreed, to ensure that both priests and their congregations understood the meaning and significance of the liturgy.

Even where there was adequate provision of pastoral care, the involvement of the laity in the ritual life of the Church was limited. As discussed, infant baptism was assumed by the law codes and presumably would have taken place throughout the year rather than at specific Christian festivals such as Easter. At the other end of life, very few of the laity in this period would have been interred in the burial grounds of monasteries or churches, for such privileges were restricted to the elite. Nor did the adult lay population routinely receive communion. Sources stress the need for a period of sexual abstinence before communion and, aside from chaste couples, only children, young adults and old people were encouraged to take communion routinely, presumably because they were not sexually active. For the rest of the adult population, communion may have been at most an annual event. The *Dialogue* of Ecgberht of York, dating to the mid-eighth century, records that the laity were accustomed to fast, abstain from sexual intercourse, offer up alms and visit their confessors in the 12 days before Christmas that they might receive communion on the day of the Lord's nativity.

Some of the laity may, however, have attended church more frequently than this. The council of *Clovesho* instructed priests to invite the laity to church on Sundays and feast days to hear the word of God, listen to sermons, and be present at the sacrament of the Mass (though presumably few of them would have been able to receive it). A number of the surviving homilies by Bede suggest these may have been written for

4.22 Grave marker from the monastery at Hartlepool; just visible are the letters 'UGUID', probably part of a personal name. Numerous stone grave markers of this type have been found at various Northumbrian religious sites; their decoration and layout have affinities with contemporary illuminated manuscripts

such an occasion; for example, his homily for Holy Saturday refers to those in the congregation who had not yet received baptism, suggesting he was addressing an audience of both monks and laity.

The cult of saints offered another mechanism through which the laity could express their devotion and take some part in the religious life of the Church. Numerous figures were venerated in this period, ranging from universal saints such as the Apostles to minor, local saints about whom nothing, save their names, is now known. Most churches would have possessed at least one relic and some had extensive collections. Shrines such as the tomb of St Cuthbert on Lindisfarne became the focus of pilgrimages, attracting crowds seeking the saint's intercession or blessing, as well as beggars looking for charity, and other less savoury characters.

Outside the formal structures of the Church other outlets for lay piety developed, often perceived by ecclesiastics as of dubious spiritual worth. Lay people collected relics, in some cases carrying them about their person, for in the late eighth century Alcuin complained about the custom of wearing amulets and charms, stating 'it is better to copy the examples of the saints in the heart than to carry bones in bags'. In the same letter Alcuin also condemned those who left churches and travelled to the hills 'where they worship, not with prayer, but in drunkenness'. Another of Alcuin's letters from the same period made reference to meetings or assemblies of those who had sworn pacts of brotherhood, describing such things as unpleasing to God and most certainly incompatible with the Christian religion.

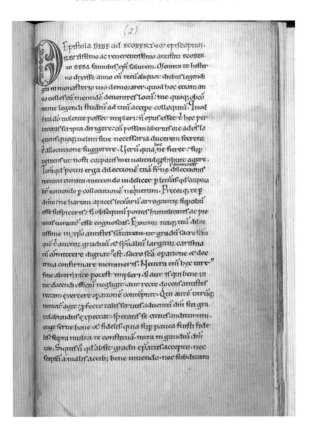

4.23 Opening of twelfth-century manuscript of Bede's letter to Bishop Ecgberht. The names of Ecgberht and Bede can be seen in the first and second lines of the letter proper

What Alcuin was condemning in these letters was not the survival of pagan practices, but the existence of patterns of Christian lay religiosity that did not meet with his approval. Christianity had moved beyond the confines of the Church, quite literally in some cases, and outside the ritual structures of organised, institutional religion. Such practices might meet with condemnation but they are testimony to the penetration of Christianity into Anglo-Saxon society and its acceptance by the laity and incorporation into their wider lives.

THE 'CONTINENTAL MISSIONARIES'

MARTIN J. RYAN

Have pity on them, for even they themselves are wont to say; 'We are of one blood and one bone'; remembering that the way of all the earth draws near, and no one shall confess to the Lord in hell, nor shall death praise, and the way of all the earth draws near.

So the Anglo-Saxon churchman Boniface (d. 754) wrote in a letter of 738, appealing to the English for aid, both spiritual and material, for his mission to bring Christianity to the Old Saxons. Boniface is the best known of countless Anglo-Saxon churchmen and women who were active in the mission fields of northern Europe from the late seventh to ninth centuries – the 'Continental Missionaries' as they are known collectively.

Their religious and cultural impact was significant and long-lasting; Boniface, for example, has been called 'the Apostle of the Germans', albeit with little justification, while some of the religious institutions founded by these missionaries came to be amongst the most prestigious and important in Europe. They also played a central role in spreading insular artistic and scribal traditions to the Continent. Manuscripts originating from England and elsewhere in the Atlantic Archipelago served as the inspiration for new works, either emulating insular decorative schemes or fusing them with Continental traditions. Insular artists and scribes themselves also found homes in the scriptoria and ateliers of these new foundations. Such was the extent of intellectual and cultural exchange that it is the treasures of these Continental houses that provide the best insight into the now largely lost riches of the pre-Viking Anglo-Saxon Church.

The motivations for Anglo-Saxon churchmen and women to travel to the Continent varied significantly. Boniface would stress the kinship between the Anglo-Saxons and the Old Saxons as a factor, at least in the contexts of letters to England. General biblical injunctions to spread the word of God must have provided the inspiration for many, regardless of ethnic affiliations. The Irish, who had brought Christianity to parts of Anglo-Saxon England and were also active on the Continent, offered another source of inspiration. Their idea of voluntary exile from one's homeland for the sake of God ('*peregrinatio pro amore dei*') was particularly influential. Thoughts of personal advancement may have motivated some, whereas ties of kinship may have drawn

4a. 1 Religious foundations in Northern Europe in the age of the Continental missionaries

others. The monastery at Echternach in Frisia founded by Willibrord (d. 739), for example, was ruled subsequently by two of his brothers, Aldberct and Beornrad, while Abbess Leoba of Tauberbischofsheim (d. 782) was a kinswoman of Boniface and was put in charge of the foundation by him.

This outward flow of people, ideas and objects was facilitated by the growth in long-distance trade of the later seventh and eighth centuries. Boniface, for example, is known to have travelled from the trading settlement at London to Frisia on a merchant's ship that was returning to its home port, the *emporium* at Dorestad. He undertook another similar journey from London to the *emporium* at Quentovic. The successes of the missionaries were also closely tied in with the rising power of the Carolingian dynasty, with figures such as Pippin II (d. 714), Charles Martel (d. 741), Carloman (d. 754) and Pippin III (d. 768) actively supporting their work and through military

4a.2 The *Calendar of St Willibrord*. The marginal annotation details the arrival of Willibrord and his companions in Frisia in 690 and may have been penned by Willibrord himself

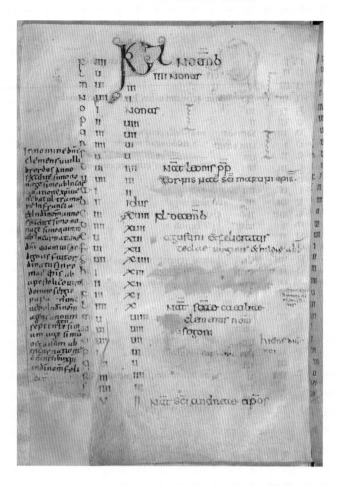

expansion and political influence bringing some stability to the often turbulent areas of the mission fields.

Much is known about the lives of some of the key missionaries. Boniface was the subject of a number of biographies, with three alone being produced within a century of his death. There also survives a substantial body of correspondence between Boniface and a wide range of recipients in England and on the Continent. Among the most interesting of these letters is one by Bishop Daniel of Winchester setting out the methods he recommends that Boniface employ when attempting to convert pagans; it is unclear whether Daniel was offering the fruits of his own dealings with Anglo-Saxon pagans or simply suggesting the kinds of strategies he felt likely to bring results.

Other missionaries were likewise the subjects of hagiographies. The deeds of Willehad (d. 789), a Northumbrian active in Frisia and Saxony, who became bishop of the newly established diocese of Bremen, were recorded in a biography written in the mid-ninth century, probably on the occasion of the translation of his body to the new cathedral. Likewise, Leoba of Tauberbischofsheim was the subject of a biography written in the 830s by Rudolf, a monk at Fulda, the monastery where she was buried.

Though these biographies and numerous others like them focus attention on the major figures and leading individuals, other written sources throw light on the

4a.3 The martyrdom of St Boniface as depicted in a tenth-century sacramentary

communities surrounding them, giving a sense of the large number of people involved in this missionary activity, as well as of the pull that charismatic figures like Boniface could exert.

The earliest Anglo-Saxon to achieve any real successes in missionary work on the Continent was the Northumbrian Willibrord. Bede includes an account of Willibrord's activities in his *Ecclesiastical History of the English People* and he was also the subject of biographies in both verse and prose written in the later eighth century by his kinsman, Alcuin of York.

Willibrord first entered the monastic life at Ripon in Northumbria under the abbacy of Wilfrid – a figure who would himself make an abortive attempt to bring the Frisians to Christianity in 679. Willibrord subsequently travelled to Ireland to join the monastic community at *Rath Melsigi* (probably Clonmelsh, County Carlow). There he came under the influence of another expatriate Anglo-Saxon, Ecgberht, who had already developed plans for missionary work among the Germans. It was Ecgberht who eventually dispatched Willibrord and 11 companions to the Continent – the number must surely be significant here.

Rather than head directly for Frisia they landed first in Francia in 690. This date is known from an entry in the margin of a liturgical calendar – a note possibly written by Willibrord himself. It was only some two years later, having secured the backing of the Carolingian Pippin II, that Willibrord travelled to Frisia. Later that same year he journeyed to Rome to gain papal backing for his mission.

Willibrord was subsequently made archbishop by Pope Sergius I and, eventually, established his see at Utrecht, having been granted lands there by Pippin, following successful military campaigns against the Frisians. Willibrord also founded the monastery at Echternach, on lands granted by the noblewoman Irmina. This last institution was subsequently the focus of significant patronage by the Carolingian family and came to house an important and influential scriptorium.

It was probably at Echternach that Willibrord spent his final days. He died on 7 November 739 and was buried in the church there some three days later. Outside his

4a.4 The symbol of St Matthew the Evangelist from the *Echternach Gospels*. The provenance of this manuscript is much debated — it may have been produced in Britain or Ireland or by a Continental scriptorium under insular influence

ecclesiastical institutions, it is less clear what impact Willibrord's missionary activities actually had in Frisia. Nevertheless, Willibrord is remembered as the patron saint of the Netherlands and Luxembourg, and his tomb at Echternach is still the site of veneration.

Willibrord is overshadowed by his younger contemporary Boniface, a man who likewise began his Continental career among the Frisians. Boniface was born in Devon in the mid-670s, entering the monastery at Exeter as a child and eventually becoming the head of the monastic school at Nursling near Southampton. In 716, at around the age of 40, he chose to leave Anglo-Saxon England to evangelise the Frisians. Political turmoil in Frisia forced him return to England, but in 719, having first visited Rome and received papal approval for his missionary work, he travelled again to Frisia where he worked alongside Willibrord at Utrecht for a few years.

It was in Thuringia and Hesse that Boniface was most active, founding several monasteries – the most important of which was that at Fulda – and establishing a number of dioceses. Boniface formed strong ties with the papacy, travelling to Rome on a number of occasions and remaining in close correspondence with successive

4a.5 Alcuin of York (centre), alongside Hrabanus Maurus (left) and Bishop Otgar of Mainz (right) from a ninth-century Fulda manuscript

popes. Such ties culminated in Boniface's elevation to archiepiscopal status in 732. Initially Boniface had no fixed diocese but eventually his metropolitan see was established at Mainz.

As already noted, the progress of Boniface's work was much tied up with the spread of Carolingian power. It was Charles Martel's military campaigns against the Old Saxons in 738 that were the trigger for Boniface to launch what was ultimately an abortive attempt at missionary work in that region. In the 740s Boniface was active in reforming the Frankish Church, holding a series of councils and, as has been seen, encouraging reform of the English Church through letters to various recipients.

In the 750s Boniface again turned his attention to missionary work, setting off for Frisia in 753. On 5 June the following year he met his death at the hands of a band of robbers. His body was eventually buried at Fulda, where a cult soon developed and he was venerated as a martyr. One of the relics associated with his cult is a book, now known as the *Ragyndrudis Codex*, that Boniface is said to have used to fend off his attackers; the cuts made by swords and axes are still visible.

Despite his subsequent reputation and, indeed, the way he sometimes presented himself in his own letters, Boniface was only infrequently a missionary amongst pagan peoples. Most of his Continental career was spent in Hesse, Thuringia and Bavaria, regions that had had a Christian presence for a considerable time. Here Boniface was engaged more in the reorganisation and restructuring of the Church than in formal missionary work. Nevertheless, Boniface was a potent figure of authority both in his own lifetime and after his death – the numerous accounts of his life that were written were in part the product of competing attempts to claim his legacy and to determine the meaning of his life and his death. In some of his correspondence he can come across as a stern, austere and unyielding character, scornful of those who opposed his plans or disagreed with his actions. In other letters he displays a lightness of touch and a surprising wit and he was also able to inspire considerable affection in his disciples and contacts, with his passing provoking much sadness and displays of grief amongst his correspondents.

The Continental missionaries were but one part of a more general outward flow of churchmen and women from Anglo-Saxon England across the seventh to ninth centuries. Numerous individuals undertook pilgrimages to Rome – Boniface's letters include responses to requests for information by those undertaking such journeys – and some travelled to more distant sites such as those in the Holy Land. One of the most detailed accounts of such a pilgrimage is the so-called *Hodoeporicon* – more correctly the *Life of Willibald and Winibald* – written by the nun Huneberc of Heidenheim. This tells of Willibald's journeys and adventures around the Mediterranean and the sacred sites of the Holy Land, including his imprisonment by Saracens and the smuggling of balsam in a calabash. Having toured the Holy Land, Willibald would subsequently spend time at the monastery of Monte Cassino before joining Boniface to undertake missionary work.

Perhaps the most influential and significant of these other Anglo-Saxon travellers to the Continent was Alcuin (d. 804). Having been educated at the cathedral school in York, he was recruited by Charlemagne to join a growing circle of scholars at the royal court. There Alcuin would become one of the principal intellectual architects of the Carolingian Renaissance.

The missionaries of the seventh to ninth centuries, as well as other Anglo-Saxon Christians active on the Continent, are eloquent testimony to the rapid success of Christianity within Anglo-Saxon England. Within only a few generations of the coming of Christianity, the Anglo-Saxon Church was confidently looking outwards, seeking to spread the faith to other regions and peoples, with individual churchmen and women prepared to risk hardships, suffering and even death in order to gather souls to God.

MID-LATE SAXON SETTLEMENT AT FLIXBOROUGH

NICHOLAS J. HIGHAM

Timber-built and lacking major earthworks, most Anglo-Saxon rural settlements have been badly damaged by later activity. At Flixborough (Humberside), however, excavations revealed not only an extensive stratigraphy, including structures occupied across a period stretching from the seventh century to the early eleventh, but also middens and rubbish dumps on a scale never previously uncovered on a site of this kind. On the whole, digging at Anglo-Saxon settlements reveals comparatively low levels of occupation debris, the assumption being that refuse was collected into heaps which were later carted off as manure onto adjacent farm land. This had not occurred to the same extent at Flixborough. High levels of finds label this clearly as a 'productive site', so excavation here also provided an opportunity to examine why some sites produce exceptional quantities of finds. Although the habitation sequence is complicated by successive rebuilding, often on the same site, then levelling and dumping leading to large-scale re-deposition of material, the site does offer a unique opportunity to explore the footprint of the inhabitants of this rural settlement across more than four centuries. This has, in turn, provided an opportunity to revisit the ways in which rural settlements have been interpreted in recent years and to suggest a more complex and time-sensitive approach, exploring comparatively short-term variations as regards both settlement status and the secular/ecclesiastical divide.

The site lies in historic Lincolnshire, north of Scunthorpe in the parish of Flixborough but some 600 metres south of the modern village, on a north–south ridge of wind-blown sand just above the floodplain of the Trent (to the west). Settlement seems to have been attracted to this interface between wetlands along the river and the good-quality agricultural soils which were easily accessible along Lincoln Edge, to the east. Medieval occupation nearby is well attested: immediately east of the Anglo-Saxon settlement is the graveyard of All Saints Church (now demolished), beyond which lie the deserted medieval village (DMV) of North Conesby and a late medieval or early modern moated platform. Iron Age and Roman material was found during the excavations, suggesting that occupation had occurred in the general vicinity for most of a millennium and a half, with easterly settlement drift towards the better agricultural soils across the Anglo-Scandinavian and Anglo-Norman periods.

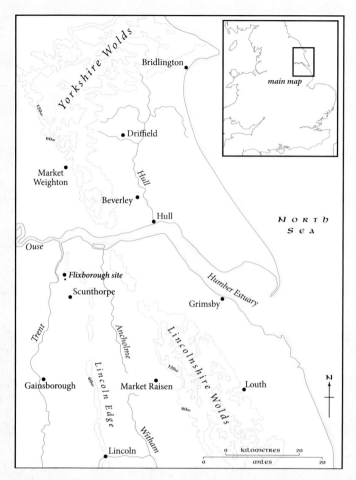

4b.1 Location map for Flixborough

Planning consent for sand quarrying led to excavation in 1988 south-west of the grave-yard, directed by Kevin Leahy, which revealed 11 badly damaged Anglo-Saxon east-west inhumations, probably of the seventh to ninth centuries, and possible building foundations. Larger-scale, open-area excavation was then funded by English Heritage and undertaken by Humberside Archaeological Unit (now Humber Field Archaeology), primarily in 1989–91, under the direction of Christopher Loveluck. Excavation, however, has to date revealed only part of the site. Survey work both north and west of the church suggests that further extensive remains are waiting to be excavated, including the Anglo-Norman settlement around the church itself and the DMV beyond.

The 1989–91 excavation focused on a section of the sand belt where a shallow valley ran in from the west between two spurs of sand; around 40 structures were identified, primarily on the sand spurs but straying into the valley as the level rose due to dumping of rubbish. In the seventh century the area excavated seems to have lain on the periphery of a large early Anglo-Saxon settlement, of which successive post-hole-founded buildings were located on the southern spur. Imported lava fragments from quernstones and small numbers of pottery vessels plus some high-quality metalwork of English manufacture suggest that the site was already then a wealthy one. New building plots on either side of the shallow valley then came into use in the decades around 700, in both cases with post-hole-based structures in two phases running from the seventh century into the eighth. These levels continued to produce residual fifth- and sixth-century dress accessories indicative of a large settlement and cemetery which has not so far been otherwise explored.

From the late seventh to the early ninth centuries (phases 2 and 3), however, the nature and range of the artefacts and faunal remains deposited changed. Significant quantities of fine tableware were used, broken and thrown away. This was mostly high-quality glass, including palm cups, a funnel-beaker, a possible claw-beaker and glob-ular bowls and beakers, but also included various copper-alloy vessels which were damaged and discarded. Many of these artefacts had been imported from the Rhineland and/or north-western France, signifying the inhabitants' continuing capacity to attract exotic items as trade goods. These were excavated not just from a single part of the site but from most of the buildings in use at this time, suggesting a spread of use of such vessels rather than their concentration, for example, in a single banqueting hall. Beef consumption also peaked at this time, with cattle slaughtered as adults or 'sub-adults' representing around half the animals consumed on site. Study of the skeletal remains suggests that cattle may have reached Flixborough in part at least as specially selected beasts delivered as food renders from subordinate settlements. Many animals were of exceptional size by English standards, opening the possibility that stock may have been imported. Alongside, an exceptional range of wild species, including cranes, wild geese, duck, black grouse, roe deer, pine marten and hare, suggests that hunting and falconry were contributing to the menu. Combined, the evidence points to conspicuous consumption on the part of some at least of the inhabitants, who were enjoying an aristocratic lifestyle focused particularly on the dining table and elite outdoor leisure activities. Sixteen Continental silver *sceattas* found on site from the first half of the eighth century are indicative of trading contacts with the Rhineland and eastern England, perhaps associated with the export of wool. In the late seventh and early eighth centuries, pottery was reaching the site as part of a broad riverine and coastal trading network spanning the East Midlands. Thereafter, shelly wares made in Lincolnshire tended to drive out their competitors, with a predominantly overland pattern of distribution. It seems likely that the pottery found on the site was used predominantly for less ostentatious purposes than the glassware or copper-alloy vessels, in the kitchens and workshops.

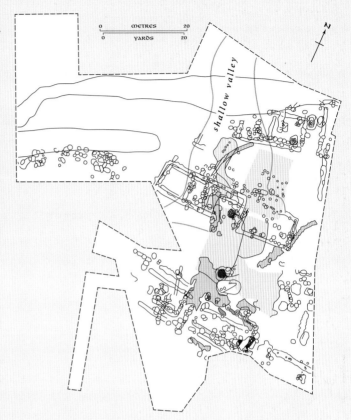

4b.2 Plan of the excavated area of the site, all periods, showing the construction of successive buildings in parallel over the line of a shallow natural valley, with ditches to the north

It was in the mid-eighth century that the shallow valley began to be used for the dumping of refuse on a systematic scale, drawing in material from outside the excavated area. This may indicate a shift in the balance between the production of waste and its disposal off-site. A rather more sophisticated timber-framed building was constructed at about this time, some 14 metres by 6 metres and equipped with internal subdivisions, which became the focus of a series of four inhumation graves cut through the floors inside and another two close by outside. This structure may well have served as a church or chapel, such as are widely referred to in the literature of the period in association with rural estate centres. The second burial area, further south, excavated in 1988, which was probably broadly contemporary, suggests variable degrees of inclusion in the disposal of the dead, with perhaps aristocratic family members being given preferential access to a church or mortuary chapel whereas others were deposited further away.

4b.3 The excavations of 1981–91 showing the spurs, and buildings and refuse dumps in one central shallow valley

It was at this period that buildings constructed with continuous foundation trenches first appeared, used alongside post-holes and limestone post-pads supporting a minority of the structural uprights. Some of these more sophisticated buildings were fitted with window glass set in lead cames, both of which occur very rarely away from stone ecclesiastical architecture. Again, an aristocratic context is requisite. Alongside, craft skills identified include woodworking, blacksmithing, textile manufacturing and some non-ferrous metalworking on a scale at least sufficient to support an elite house-hold and provide for the needs of those who were working the estate. Numerous pieces of querns made from Eifel lava from the Rhineland suggest the ready availability of imports despite the easy accessibility of good-quality sources of grindstones from the region.

Profound changes occurred on site in the early ninth century through to the 860s. While settlement clearly continued unabated and established building plots survived, new buildings were constructed in the central and northern zones, and the range and quantity of specialist crafts undertaken on site rose significantly, alongside changes in animal husbandry and the appearance for the first time of significant evidence of literacy. Whereas the site in the eighth century had been characterised by an excess of consumption over production, drawing in goods and foodstuffs from outside the immediate area, in the ninth century such evidence of conspicuous consumption died away. Instead, it seems likely that the products of craftsmen and women based here were being exported locally. Large numbers of clay loom weights were discovered, including some of a new, lighter type, and spinning and weaving was one area in which production seems to have risen dramatically, manufacturing finer quality cloth than hitherto. It seems possible that we are witnessing a shift from the export of wool to cloth. The back-fill of a ditch to the north-west of the site yielded heckle teeth, implying that fibre processing was going on nearby, but weaving-related artefacts were largely confined to the shallow valley area, suggesting that different processes were being undertaken in different areas. Non-ferrous metalworking also increased and lead began to be worked here for the first time, rapidly becoming the commonest metal being crafted on site. There is an obvious link between lead-working and ecclesiastical demand for its products, which may imply a new religious interest in activities here. A substantial hoard of iron tools, largely relating to woodworking, was found in 1994 outside the excavated area and contained in two large lead vessels, perhaps buried ritually following their use to construct a sacred building.

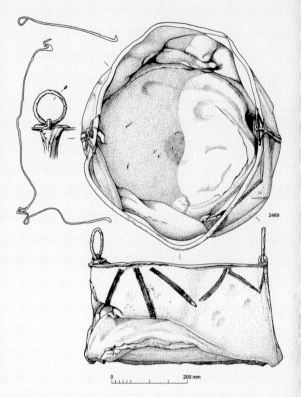

4b.4 Larger of two lead vessels containing the tool hoard

The clerical flavour of ninth-century Flixborough is reinforced if we turn to the over 20 styli of different types found, which make up roughly one-fifth of the total number so far from Anglo-Saxon England. These suggest that writing on waxed tablets was a fairly commonplace activity among some at least of the inhabitants. Several inscriptions were found, including a lead plaque with seven Old English names, all male bar one. This evidence for a dramatic rise in literacy has encouraged some scholars to interpret Flixborough as a monastic site, but this may be to harbour too close a correlation between literacy and clerics or monks. Such ignores evidence for the wider dissemination of literacy among parts at least of the secular elite, some of whom had enjoyed the benefits of a monastic education, and also perhaps supposes too rigid a divide between those who were and those who were not literate, these two in practice merging into one another to an extent via various shades of reading and/or writing. Clearly sections of the population at ninth-century Flixborough were accustomed to writing, but this does not require us to suppose that the site had necessarily been converted to a monastery. It is equally possible that the estate had been granted to a major church, or even that a great aristocratic family had installed literate estate management. What is clear, though, is that the type of elite occupation which was characteristic of the eighth century had either ceased or declined dramatically in the ninth. The consumption of beef fell sharply as did that of wild animals, and the breakage of high-quality tableware virtually ceased. If this was still an estate in the hands of the secular elite, then it had lost favour as a place of residence and had become, instead, a centre which was expected to provide revenues to a household normally based elsewhere. Significant numbers of Northumbrian *stycas* of the period c. 837–55 may have been in use as small change at Flixborough, reflecting the inflexibility of the southern silver coinage.

Following the demolition of the period 4 buildings, a set of new, smaller structures was built, varying between 3 × 3 and 3.5 × 4 metres. On parallels with West Heslerton and elsewhere, these were interpreted as probable granaries, so still very much in keeping with the changed use of the site. Associated with them were a number of fired-clay and stone ovens, which underscore the utilitarian character of the settlement at this date. Coins are virtually absent from the period and the appearance of weights implies that a bullion economy was present, in the later ninth century, reflecting disruption of the North Sea trade routes by Viking activity.

From the early tenth century, however, conspicuous consumption and ostentatious display returned to Flixborough, with feasting again in evidence but this time without the breakage of expensive tableware imported to the site that had been such a feature of the eighth century. Instead, the new owners constructed the largest buildings so far seen on site: building 7 had continuous foundation trenches some 0.5 metres deep and a floor area of 19.7 × 6.5 metres. This new occupation represented a significant discontinuity with what had gone before, which was reflected in the layout, with signs that the settlement was shifting eastwards towards the church. This period experienced peak consumption of wild animals and birds, suggesting that the new elite were throwing themselves into hunting and hawking. There was virtually no evidence, however, of trade goods coming from any distance. It was this period of occupation in the Viking Age which is likely to have led to creation of the place name Conesby – *Kunings-byr* ('king's settlement'), which implies a new owner of the highest status. Given that Scandinavian incomers do seem disproportionately to have taken over ecclesiastical estates, this may provide some slight support to the notion that Flixborough had passed to clerical or monastic ownership in the early ninth century, but that remains no more than a possibility. For a royal residence, it is noticeable that the household adopted a very 'rural' lifestyle, without the trappings of the great hall despite the growing presence of trading centres in the region, which may imply that this was used in some sense as a hunting lodge. That said, Flixborough was in receipt of the full range of East Midlands pottery from the late ninth century onwards,

4b.5 Inscribed lead plaque with names of seven individuals, both male and female, found in a refuse dump

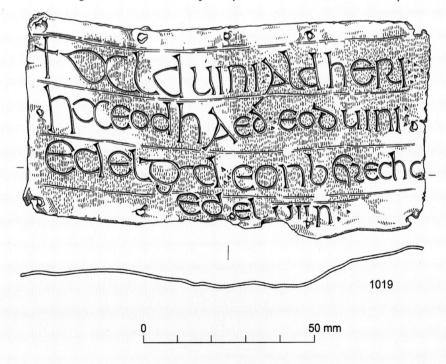

including the new wheel-thrown wares emanating from York, Torksey, Lincoln and Stamford, suggesting that the kitchens at least were functioning efficiently with the best equipment available.

Overall, what comes out of the excavation of Flixborough is the mutability of settlement through time. Here we have strong evidence of the continuous occupation of the same site, with some sideways movement admittedly, across a very long period indeed. Within the lifetime of the settlement, it has been possible to identify a series of comparatively short episodes which differ quite fundamentally one from another: the extensive occupation of the seventh century gave way, probably before 700, to an elite residence at the heart of a substantial estate, but with authority and spending power even beyond that estate sufficient to bring in large quantities of beef cattle, trade goods from the east coast and imports from across the North Sea. This in turn led to a phase across the ninth century when elite consumption was largely absent and the settlement was given over to craft production, storage and the exporting of goods into the hinterland. This all changed in the tenth century when once again the site became an elite residence but occupation appears subtly different, without evidence of imports despite the clear emphasis on status provided by the new place name and the exceptional scale of the buildings. It has been the unparalleled stratigraphic sequence coupled with the vast rubbish deposits present on site that have provided the opportunity to tell the story of this settlement and its inhabitants across time. Throughout, the inhabitants appear to have been relatively profligate in their willingness to discard artefacts, even metal tools such as are rarely thrown away on site elsewhere: clearly recycling was not much of an issue here even in the absence of an elite household. The lessons learned need to be carried forward into the interpretation of sites without these unusual features to assess their wider applicability. Across the later Middle Ages few English rural settlements retained elite status for as long as two centuries, and it is a mistake to assume that change was any less common in the early Middle Ages. Instead, we should expect rural settlement to have been dynamic, with the fortunes of individual places rising and falling according to a whole matrix of factors, most of which are beyond archaeological recall. Flixborough, therefore, provides us with a very valuable object lesson in the interpretation of settlement history and the wider landscape of which it was a central part.

CHAPTER 5

The Anglo-Saxons and the Vikings, c. 825–900

MARTIN J. RYAN

Introduction

In the mid-ninth century a Kentish noblewoman called Ealhburg made a grant to the monastery of St Augustine, Canterbury. From an estate at Brabourne, the monastery was to receive annually a bullock, 4 sheep, 20 hens, 240 loaves, a wey of lard, a wey of cheese, 40 'ambers' of malt (perhaps around 160 bushels) and 4 cartloads of wood. In return, the community was to remember Ealhburg and her husband, Ealdred, in their daily round of prayers.

This grant is one of a remarkable series of ninth-century documents that allows us to see something of the activities of a pious and prosperous local nobility in Kent. The documents record them endowing favoured religious houses, exchanging lands, petitioning the king, preparing for foreign pilgrimages, feeding the poor and the destitute, and generally making provision for the health of their immortal souls through displays of considerable largesse. Written primarily in the vernacular, these documents shed light on a world that is largely hidden in the more formal Latin charters of the period – women like Ealhburg play active roles in these documents, appearing alongside their menfolk as landowners and testatrices.

Ealhburg's own family, of some significant local standing, features prominently in these texts, with Christ Church Canterbury a particular focus of their benefactions. Ealhburg's estate at Brabourne – sitting at the foot of the North Downs, an easy day's journey from Canterbury along the old Roman road, Stone Street – lay in the heartlands of her family's power, the south and east of Kent. Her brother, Ealhhere, held land at Finglesham, while another brother, Æthelmod, had land at Little Chart, and Ealhburg herself owned another estate at Bishopsbourne.

Ealhburg's donation to St Augustine's fitted into long-established patterns of lay piety and was but one part of a more extensive network of familial religious patronage. Yet the final clause of the grant hints at the changes that were taking place and the troubles that were to come. If, because of disruptions and panic caused by 'heathen invasion', the annual render could not be paid, double was to be paid the next year. If three years went by in which the render could not be paid, the estate itself was to pass to St Augustine's. The heathens whose depredations so concerned Ealhburg were the Vikings.

Scandinavians had first targeted the Anglo-Saxon kingdoms in the late eighth century and the frequency of their attacks and the destruction they caused increased steadily over the course of the ninth century. By the end of the 870s, the Vikings had overrun nearly all of the Anglo-Saxon kingdoms. Ealhburg's own family felt directly the impact of these attacks: her brother, Ealhhere, was killed in battle against the Vikings in 853; indeed, he may already have been dead when she made her grant to St Augustine's.

The Vikings loom large both in contemporary sources and in the modern popular imagination and the near-total defeat of the Anglo-Saxon kingdoms at their hands casts a shadow over the whole of the ninth century. It is easy to see all events in that century as leading up to that defeat and to construct a narrative of decline and decay, presenting the ultimate collapse of the Anglo-Saxons as inevitable. Yet, if the Vikings were a significant and meaningful threat throughout the ninth century, nevertheless it was only in the 860s, with the arrival of a 'Great Heathen Army', that they began seriously to undermine the security of the Anglo-Saxon kingdoms. Even then, some form of normal life was still possible. For all Ealhburg's concerns about the Vikings and the grief she must have felt at her brother's death, the estate at Brabourne continued to pay the annual render to St Augustine's without significant disruption, despite intense Viking activity in Kent.

5.1 Places named in chapter 5

But as Ealhburg's donation makes clear, even before the arrival of the Great Army, the Viking threat could not be ignored: allowances and accommodations had to be made. Within the text of Ealhburg's grant there is continuity and change, old established patterns of behaviour and new responses to shifting circumstances. If the whole of the ninth century bears the imprint of the Vikings, nevertheless they were not the only agents of change. The century was one of dramatic, even revolutionary, changes, but it would be wrong to present all this as driven only by the Viking attacks or by Anglo-Saxon responses to them. Though it can be difficult to disentangle the two, both internal and external forces shaped the development of the Anglo-Saxon kingdoms in the ninth century. The societies and peoples whom the Vikings conquered and colonised in the 860s and 870s were very different from those they had first attacked in the later eighth century.

From the mid-820s, the century-old Mercian hegemony over the south of England began to come apart and Mercian pre-eminence gave way before the growing might of

5.2 The Lindisfarne Stone, a ninth-century grave marker depicting a band of warriors. Though often described as of the Viking sack of the monastery, it is more likely a depiction of the End of Days and the Last Judgment

Wessex. West Saxon rulers extended their power and influence east and west along the southern coasts, taking control of Sussex, Kent and Essex, consolidating their hold on Devon and pushing further into Cornwall. East Anglia and Northumbria offered their submission and even Mercia itself was, for a brief time, ruled directly by the West Saxons. By the middle of the ninth century, Wessex encompassed nearly all of the lands south of the Thames and also those east of the Lea.

Under the leadership of King Alfred, this 'Greater Wessex' would survive the Viking raiding and conquests of the ninth century relatively intact. Elsewhere, the political and ethnic map would be fundamentally redrawn. Large areas of East Anglia, the East Midlands and Northumbria came under Viking control and their native ruling dynasties were permanently extinguished. Though West Saxon kings would progressively roll back these Scandinavian conquests over the course of the tenth century, Viking occupation and settlement would have an enduring impact on language, culture and society.

The political changes of the ninth century were accompanied by a no less dramatic economic upheaval. The great trading centres – the *emporia* – that had so character-ised the economy of the late seventh and eighth centuries declined and eventually failed, taking with them many of the smaller centres of trade, exchange and produc-tion that formed their hinterlands. By the end of the ninth century, the focus of urban life had shifted from the *emporia* to the network of fortified centres established by King Alfred – centres known today, with scant regard for the niceties of Old English spelling, as *burhs*. In addition to their military functions, these *burhs* would come to hold a central position in the governmental, economic and cultural developments of the later Anglo-Saxon period.

Anglo-Saxon commentators were, however, struck most forcibly by the religious and intellectual changes that occurred across the ninth century. In the 890s, King Alfred would lament the decline in education and the near-extinction of learning in southern England. Likewise, in the tenth century monastic reformers would set out to renew a Church that had, they believed, been stripped of its wealth and vigour by the rapacity of kings and nobles as well as by the savagery of the Vikings.

The dramatic changes of the ninth century are, however, now seen predominantly through West Saxon eyes. Texts from Wessex, particularly from the later years of the reign of King Alfred (d. 899), dominate the record. The main witness for the events of the ninth century is the *Anglo-Saxon Chronicle*, probably compiled at the court of King Alfred in the 890s. The narrative of the *Chronicle* centres on the rise of Wessex and on the dynasty of which King Alfred was a part. It offers an essentially West Saxon perspective on political developments and the Viking raids and settlements.

The *Chronicle* is not necessarily hostile to other Anglo-Saxon kingdoms – unsurprising, given the cosmopolitan nature of Alfred's court – but rather the history of these kingdoms is of secondary concern. Events in Northumbria in the ninth century are barely noted other than the fall of York to the Vikings in 867, with East Anglia and Mercia likewise seriously under-reported. Even for Wessex and King Alfred, the *Chronicle* does not offer a comprehensive account. The Viking attack on Southampton in 842, known from Continental sources, is not recorded in the *Chronicle*, nor are the apparently devastating raids that took place throughout Britain in 844. Alfred's campaigns in Surrey, known from charters, are similarly omitted.

Other written sources do allow us to round out the picture and, on occasion, to challenge directly the account offered by the *Chronicle*. Likewise, other forms of evidence – particularly archaeology and numismatics – permit insight into areas about which the *Chronicle* is largely silent, such as economic change and development. Nevertheless, such evidence tends to be understood and interpreted in a context provided by West Saxon sources. For good or ill, it is the vision of the past current at the court of King Alfred in the 880s and 890s that serves as the master narrative for the ninth century.

The Beginnings of the Viking Age

Sometime during the reign of King Beorhtric (786–802) three Danish ships landed on the coast of Wessex, probably near Portland in Dorset. The king's reeve, a man called Beaduheard, came to escort the new arrivals to the royal residence thinking, it seems, that they were foreign traders who needed to pay the required tolls. Beaduheard's error was soon made clear to him, for the Danish mariners slew him. The significance of this incident was underlined in the *Anglo-Saxon Chronicle*: 'those were the first ships of Danish men which came to the land of the English'.

This first Viking attack had little wider impact; it was the raid on the island monastery of Lindisfarne in 793 that attracted most contemporary comment. The 'Northern Recension' of the *Anglo-Saxon Chronicle* records a series of ominous portents –

whirlwinds, lightning and fire-breathing dragons – followed on 8 June by the sacking and plundering of Lindisfarne by heathen men. The shock and horror of this disaster were felt well beyond Anglo-Saxon England. At the court of Charlemagne in Francia, the expatriate Northumbrian, Alcuin, wrote a series of letters to recipients in Northumbria expressing his sorrow and disquiet. These letters detail the violence that accompanied the Viking attack, the desecration of the altar and the shedding of the blood of saints. Alcuin turned to the language of the Old Testament to describe and to understand what had taken place: 'in us is fulfilled what once the prophet foretold: "From the North evil breaks forth, and a terrible glory will come from the Lord"'.

For Alcuin, the Viking assault was both a punishment and a warning. A punishment for sins that had already been committed in Northumbria – Alcuin lists fornication, adultery, incest, greed, robbery, violence and vanity in one of his letters – and a warning to the Church and nobility of Northumbria to examine more closely their own moral conduct. Alongside calls for reform, Alcuin offered more immediate help. When Charlemagne returned from campaign, Alcuin would see whether anything could be done about those carried off from Lindisfarne as hostages.

Contact with Scandinavia was nothing new in the eighth century. The Anglo-Saxons had maintained trading and cultural links since the Migration Period. Indeed, Alcuin chastised the Northumbrian nobility for copying Scandinavian hairstyles and beards. Yet the raid on Lindisfarne was clearly seen as something new. Alcuin's letters express surprise at the nature of the onslaught; such a sea voyage, he claims, was not thought possible nor had the Anglo-Saxons ever witnessed such an atrocity in Britain.

The following year brought another raid. The *Anglo-Saxon Chronicle* records an attack on Northumbria and the looting of a monastery at the mouth of the River Don. If post-Conquest sources can be relied upon, Vikings plundered two further Northumbrian religious sites, Hartness and Tynemouth, in the year 800. The *Chronicle*, however, notes no further raids on the Anglo-Saxon kingdoms until 835, when the Vikings raided the Isle of Sheppey. From that date onwards, Viking attacks are detailed for almost every year until the 880s.

The Viking attacks on the Anglo-Saxon kingdoms were part of a much larger Scandinavian diaspora across the eighth to eleventh centuries. To the west, Scandinavians raided and established settlements and trading networks in Britain, Ireland and the surrounding islands. They colonised the Faroes, Greenland and Iceland and ultimately reached the Atlantic seaboard of North America, founding a short-lived settlement in what is now Newfoundland. Continental Europe likewise saw extensive raiding and settlement with violent incursions into the Carolingian Empire and Iberian Peninsula. Eventually, substantial territories were ceded to Scandinavians, most notably the region that would later become the Duchy of Normandy. To the east, the Scandinavians set up extensive trade routes and settlements throughout what are now the Baltic States, Russia and the Ukraine, with the river systems of that region providing them access to the Caspian Sea and thence to the wealth of the Middle East, as well as to the Black Sea, Constantinople and the Byzantine Empire.

The term 'Viking' is often applied to all Scandinavian activity in this period and, indeed, the period itself is frequently labelled the 'Viking Age'. Given the connotations

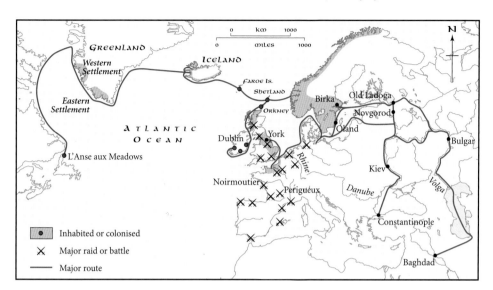

5.3 Scandinavian activity in the Viking Age

of violence and savagery that the word 'Viking' still bears, this may be misleading: not all interactions between Scandinavia and the wider world were at the point of a sword (or the blade of an axe). Indeed, since the seminal work of Peter Sawyer in the late 1950s and 1960s, scholars have increasingly stressed the positive contributions of Scandinavians to early medieval Europe in this period. They have foregrounded the role of Scandinavians in international trade and in cultural development while emphasising that their reputation as a violent, pagan 'Other' is largely a product of the Christian sources that record their activities. The absence of written sources by the Vikings themselves meant that for too long they had been viewed only through the eyes of their victims.

The question of whether the Vikings were especially or distinctively violent remains a vexed one and will be touched on again below. Nevertheless, it is clear that the late eighth century saw the beginnings of new, and at times violent, relationships between Scandinavia and the wider world. The Viking Age witnessed Scandinavians involved in a complex network of activities – maritime exploration, trade, raiding, piracy, military conquest, settlement and colonisation – over extensive areas of Europe, the Atlantic and Asia. Any attempt to account for this set of interrelated activities – to attempt to 'explain' the Vikings – is necessarily doomed to failure, but it is clear that the outflow of people and ideas from Scandinavia was bound up with a range of other developments and changes.

Economic growth and the rise in international trade are likely to have made parts of north-western Europe attractive targets for Viking raiding, with moveable wealth now more readily available. Trading links between Scandinavia and the rest of Europe would likewise have spread knowledge about clusters of wealth – and so potential foci for raiding – as well as information about political weaknesses and dynastic conflicts which Vikings seem to have exploited opportunistically.

That said, the earliest Viking raids did not target the *emporia* and other trading centres, though such sites would eventually be subject to attacks. Instead, monasteries and churches seem to have been particularly singled out – though some of these did, of course, play a central role in trade and exchange. For Christian authors such as Alcuin, attack on monasteries and churches represented a pagan people desecrating sacred sites, but it is unlikely that the Vikings themselves saw these activities in religious terms. Rather, religious institutions were simply wealthy but poorly defended sites, many of them occupying coastal or riverine locations that were easily accessible by boat. The members of such institutions were often of high status and made useful hostages or prisoners who might attract a sizeable ransom, as may have been the case with the raid on Lindisfarne. Even books could be ransomed, as happened to the set of Gospels now know as the Stockholm *Codex Aureus*.

5.4 The Stockholm *Codex Aureus*. An early example of the 'Tiberius Style' this manuscript was seized by Vikings and then ransomed by Ealdorman Alfred and his wife, Werburh. A note at the top of the page records these events and the subsequent presentation of the book to Christ Church Canterbury

By the late eighth century, Vikings were able to target the increased wealth of north-western Europe, but change within Scandinavia itself also played a role in promoting raids and settlement. The eighth century witnessed increasing political centralisation in Scandinavia, with concomitant dynastic infighting and struggles for power and influence. To stake a claim to power in this period of centralising authority – either to resist the encroachment of others or to extend one's own dominance – required access to wealth in order to attract and maintain the loyalty of warriors and to take part in diplomatic and status-enhancing exchanges of gifts. Trade offered one source of wealth, raiding and plunder another. Some losers in the processes of political centralisation – rival royal dynasties or cadet branches of the successful ones – may have been driven into exile and so sought land and power elsewhere. Others may have left voluntarily to establish powerbases abroad in preparation for another bid for rule in Scandinavia.

The Anglo-Saxon Kingdoms

Whatever their causes, the Viking attacks of the first half of the ninth century took place against a backdrop of profound political change. The death of King Cenwulf in 821 was the beginning of the end of nearly a century of Mercian dominance in southern England. Though Mercia remained a significant power for some decades, by the close of the ninth century it had been partitioned by the Vikings and the area remaining in Anglo-Saxon hands was under West Saxon overlordship. Mercia's place as the dominant Anglo-Saxon kingdom was taken by Wessex, with the central decades of the ninth century witnessing something approaching West Saxon pre-eminence.

Even contemporaries were struck by the sense that Cenwulf's death represented more than simply the passing of one king. A charter of 825 recorded that after Cenwulf's death there arose much discord and numerous disputes between kings and bishops, with many churches despoiled of their lands. The reign of Cenwulf's brother, Ceolwulf, was certainly short-lived and ended badly: the *Anglo-Saxon Chronicle* records that he was deprived of the kingdom in 823, though it gives no further detail. Nevertheless, he was able to maintain much of his brother's southern hegemony. There may have been a brief, successful bid for East Anglian independence after Cenwulf's death, but Mercian dominance there was quickly re-established. Similarly, Ceolwulf's control of Kent initially may have been tentative and contested but by 822 he was more secure in his power and was consecrated king by Archbishop Wulfred of Canterbury. Ceolwulf also campaigned in Wales, destroying the fortress at Deganwy in the north and invading Powys in the east.

In some respects, then, Ceolwulf's reign continued long-established patterns of Mercian activity – hegemony over parts of southern England and periodic military expeditions into Wales – but the brevity of his reign and the manner of its ending hint at underlying problems. The turmoil occasioned by Ceolwulf's removal from the throne continued into 824, with the killing of the ealdormen Burghelm and Muca, the latter having been a leading figure in Ceolwulf's regime.

The following year the Mercian hegemony began to unravel. According to the *Chronicle*, the East Angles, motivated by fear of the Mercians, appealed to Ecgberht of

Wessex 'for peace and protection'. In the same year, 825, in the aftermath of defeat by the West Saxons at the Battle of Wroughton (Wiltshire), Mercia lost control of Kent to Wessex and the East Angles killed Ceolwulf's successor, Beornwulf. In 827 Beornwulf's successor Ludeca was himself killed, an event that post-Conquest sources place in the context of an attempted retaliatory invasion of East Anglia. Though numismatic evidence does indicate Ludeca briefly ruled East Anglia, internal disputes within Mercia seem a more likely reason for his death. Whatever the context of Ludeca's death, from the late 820s East Anglia remained an independent kingdom; the East Anglian mint subsequently produced coins only in the name of its native kings. Though nothing else is known, this independence is in itself significant, implying a kingdom able to resist both the reimposition of Mercian overlordship and the establishment of a West Saxon one.

This dismantling of the Mercian hegemony in the late 820s put considerable pressure on the resources of Mercian kings, forcing them to seek out new strategies of benefaction and new – sometimes acquisitive – relationships with the religious institutions in their kingdom. Though there survive numerous grants by Mercian kings to religious institutions and to the laity, they tend to be exemptions from certain royal rights rather than outright grants of land and often such grants were made in exchange for money or leases of land. Thus in 866 King Burgred granted land at Seckley (Worcestershire) to one Wulferd in exchange for a life's lease of a larger estate, a payment of 400 silver *sicli* as well as various livestock and crops. In addition, several charters from this period make reference to the seizures of ecclesiastical estates by Mercian kings and their subsequent regranting to royal followers.

The other marked feature of Mercian rule in this period is dynastic instability. With the exceptions of Cenwulf and, probably, Berhtwulf (d. 852), no Mercian ruler was succeeded directly by a close relative. Rather, repetition of certain letters and elements in the names of kings and members of the Mercian nobility suggests the existence of perhaps three separate dynasties vying for control of the Mercian throne. The so-called 'C' dynasty included Kings Cenwulf and Ceolwulf, as well as their brother Cuthred, sub-king of Kent, and a number of other important noblemen. The 'B' dynasty probably included Kings Beornwulf (d. 825), Berhtwulf and Burgred (d. 874), while the 'W' or 'Wig' dynasty controlled the throne only during the reign of King Wiglaf (d. 839), although its members occupied prominent positions in Mercia in the late eighth and ninth centuries.

If Mercian political power and stability waned in the ninth century, the kingdom nevertheless remained a significant force and an ally to be cultivated. Æthelswith, daughter of the West Saxon ruler Æthelwulf, married King Burgred in 853, and Alfred, later king of Wessex, married Ealhswith, daughter of the Mercian nobleman Æthelred Mucel, in 868. Mercia also maintained ties with the Continent. A charter of 848 for the monastery at Breedon-on-the-Hill (Leicestershire) noted the obligation to support envoys coming from overseas, as well as those from Northumbria and Wessex. Mercian overlordship of parts of Wales or at least ambitions of such also continued: the *Chronicle* records that in 853 Burgred called on West Saxon aid to further his successful campaign to subdue the Welsh.

5.5 Penny of King Eanred. This coin, despite being minted in the name of a Northumbrian king, has closest stylistic affinities with south-Humbrian issues. The reasons for its production are unknown; tribute payment is one possibility

Despite continuing Mercian influence, it was Wessex that dominated the Anglo-Saxon kingdoms across the middle decades of the ninth century. In 802 Ecgberht gained the West Saxon throne and founded a dynasty that would eventually rule a united England and be eclipsed permanently only by the events of 1066. Little is known of the first decade or so of Ecgberht's reign but his subsequent focus was initially on westward expansion. The *Anglo-Saxon Chronicle* records him as ravaging Cornwall from east to west in 815 and describes a battle between the men of Devon and the Cornish at Galford in 825. A charter of the same year has Ecgberht campaigning against the Britons, presumably meaning the Cornish, at *Criodantreow*. The campaigning season of 825 also saw the battle between the West Saxons and the Mercians at Wroughton, Wiltshire. Given the location, the Mercians were the likely aggressors, but Ecgberht was victorious 'and a great slaughter was made there' according to the *Chronicle*.

Following his victory at Wroughton, Ecgberht sent an army into Kent, with his son, Æthelwulf, Bishop Ealhstan of Sherborne and Ealdorman Wulfheard at its head. This army drove out King Bealdred – probably a Mercian-appointed sub-king – and received the submissions of Kent, Surrey, Sussex and Essex. This collapse of Mercian authority over the south was more protracted than West Saxon sources imply – a Kentish charter of 826 is dated by reference to the reign of Beornwulf of Mercia – but it was also more comprehensive than the loss of client kingdoms. In 829 Ecgberht deposed the Mercian ruler Wiglaf and conquered his kingdom, ruling as king of Mercia. Subsequently, Ecgberht led his army to Dore where he received the submission of the Northumbrians.

At this stage, Ecgberht was undoubtedly the most powerful Anglo-Saxon king. The *Chronicle* marked this occasion by adding his name to Bede's list of the seven most powerful overkings and by describing Ecgberht as *brytenwalda* ('wide-ruler' or 'mighty-ruler'). The significance of the term *brytenwalda* (or *bretwalda*, 'ruler of Britain' as version 'A' of the *Chronicle* has it) has been much debated by scholars, for it is used in no other Anglo-Saxon source. It seems best understood not as a title or a specific office but simply as an attempt by the compiler of the *Chronicle*, or its source, to celebrate and to magnify the power of Ecgberht in a single laudatory sobriquet.

Ecgberht was at the apogee of his power and a year later, in 830, he campaigned in Wales, reducing the Welsh to submission according to the *Chronicle*. The same year, however, Wiglaf regained his Mercian throne. In charters from the 830s, Wiglaf appears as a fully independent ruler clearly of some prestige, yet there are signs he did

5.6 Penny of King Ecgberht of
Wessex as 'king of the
Mercians' ('rex m') minted at
London

5.6 Penny of King Ecgberht of Wessex as 'king of the Mercians' ('rex m') minted at London

not regain the totality of his royal authority. No coins were minted in Wiglaf's name after 829 or if they were it was as a brief and small single issue soon after his restoration. Such may reflect the declining economic importance of London in this period – see below – or suggest that Wiglaf's control of the Mercian kingdom was not as extensive or as complete as in his first reign. Whether Wiglaf regained his throne in the face of West Saxon resistance or took advantage of an overstretched or overambitious Wessex is not clear, and a negotiated restoration is certainly also a possibility. There is no indication of continued hostility between Mercia and Wessex and, indeed, the succeeding decades witnessed increasingly close cooperation between the two kingdoms. Such even included a brokered transfer of power: in the middle of the ninth century, Berkshire passed peacefully from Mercian to West Saxon control, even retaining its Mercian ealdorman, Æthelwulf.

Whether Northumbrian submission to Wessex continued beyond 829 is equally uncertain. Northumbrian history in this period is frustratingly opaque and its kings are now little more than names. In contrast to the later eighth century, Northumbrian kingship in the ninth century appears relatively stable, with a single dynasty dominating the first half of the century. This family's dominance probably owed much to its Continental connections. In circumstances that remain obscure, King Eardwulf (r. 796–806; 808–?) was driven into exile in 806. He fled to the Continent, seeking aid from Emperor Charlemagne and from Pope Leo III. Letters from the pope to the emperor describe a flurry of diplomatic activity and show something of the wider context of Eardwulf's expulsion; Cenwulf of Mercia, a nobleman called Wado and Archbishop Eanbald of York were all implicated in the plotting. Eardwulf was eventually conducted back to his kingdom – and perhaps to his throne – by legates of Charlemagne and of Leo, the latter a deacon called Aldwulf who was an Anglo-Saxon by birth.

This episode demonstrates the considerable concern of emperor and pope for Eardwulf's fate and their willingness to intervene directly in Northumbrian affairs. Such intervention would have been a source of considerable and enduring prestige and a product of long-established links between Eardwulf and the Continent, which may explain the longevity of the reign of Eardwulf's son, Eanred: post-Conquest sources assign him a reign of over thirty years, a duration that receives some support from the surviving numismatic evidence.

Little further is known of Eanred's reign. He must, presumably, have led the

Northumbrian submission to King Ecgberht at Dore in 829 and this event may have been the occasion for the production of the unique silver penny of Eanred, found at Trewhiddle in the eighteenth century. This coin, more closely resembling contemporary south Humbrian issues than Northumbrian ones, may have been part of a larger diplomatic gift or tribute payment by Eanred to Ecgberht. Though the *Anglo-Saxon Chronicle* makes no mention of any payment, post-Conquest sources claim tribute had been imposed by Wessex and such would be unsurprising in this context.

If the events of the 820s had dragged it into the power struggles of the south Humbrian kingdoms, Northumbria was soon entangled also in power struggles in the north of Britain. The *Chronicle of the Kings of Alba* – probably written in the tenth century – records that Kenneth (Cináed mac Alpin), king of Dál Riata from 840, attacked Northumbria some six times, burning Dunbar and Melrose. Such may have been in the context of Kenneth's conquest of Pictavia, for John of Fordun, writing in the 1380s, reported that the Northumbrians had aided the Picts against Kenneth. Little more is known of the political history of Northumbria until the 860s and the arrival of the Viking 'Great Army'. If Northumbria continued under some form of West Saxon overlordship, the *Anglo-Saxon Chronicle* makes no mention of it. It seems likely that the submission at Dore in 829 represents the entirety of Ecgberht's dominance of Northumbria, and only in the early decades of the tenth century would Wessex again wield similar power over the north.

Whatever Wessex's continued influence over the kingdoms of Northumbria and Mercia, it maintained its hold over Kent, Surrey, Sussex and Essex. This hegemony would survive the Viking attacks of the later ninth century largely intact and subsequently formed the basis of a united kingdom of England. Ecgberht was succeeded by his son Æthelwulf, and Æthelwulf succeeded in turn by his sons Æthelbald, Æthelberht, Æthelred and Alfred, with Alfred's grandson, Æthelstan, becoming the first king of the English (927–39). West Saxon hegemony endured in a way that the earlier Mercian hegemony did not.

Part of the explanation for this persistence of West Saxon power may lie in differing structures of rule. Ealdormen, exercising governmental, judicial and military functions over particular areas – called variously *regiones*, *prouinciae*, shires and ealdordoms – are known from all the Anglo-Saxon kingdoms. Yet the similarity of terminology conceals important differences between the kingdoms, much as, say, the office of sheriff differs greatly in modern Britain and the United States. The *regiones* of Mercia look much like formerly independent peoples or polities, with the ealdormen the appointed leaders of these peoples or, perhaps, members of their former royal dynasties. The sources make reference to such ealdormen as Hunberht of the *Tomsæte* or Æthelred of the *Gaini* – rulers of people rather than regions. Mercia may have been more a loose confederation of peoples than a tightly controlled and centralised kingdom, with its king less a figure of paramount authority and more *primus inter pares*.

In Wessex by contrast, ealdormen appear much more like royal officials, appointed by the king and exercising delegated royal

5.7 Gold finger ring, inlaid with niello, bearing the inscription 'King Æthelwulf' ('ETHELVVLF RX'). The ring is more likely to have been a gift to a follower than something worn by the king himself. The peacocks and Tree-of-Life motifs may suggest a connection with baptism

authority. Though some of the West Saxon shires were formerly independent kingdoms – such as Devon or, later, Sussex – other shires look like governmental subdivisions based on royal centres – thus Dorset was centred on Dorchester, Wiltshire on Wilton. The impression is of greater political centralisation in Wessex than in Mercia, of the king and his court as the hub of the West Saxon political order.

Such continued lower down the political scale. Below the ealdormen in authority – though not necessarily in importance – was a class of royal followers most commonly called king's thegns or *ministri*. These occupied a diverse range of positions: some acted as reeves, appointed to manage and maintain royal estates; some fought in the king's immediate military retinue; others served in the king's household supervising his table as cup-bearer or butler, maintaining his stables or guarding his wardrobe and treasure. The closeness to the king that such positions brought was much sought after, a source of considerable prestige and a marker of dignity and superior status rather than servility.

Though *ministri* do feature in Mercian sources they are much more prominent in West Saxon ones. Charters show the West Saxon king as attended on by a relatively stable body of *ministri*, and the careers of a number of these can be traced in some detail. Attendance on the king as a *minister* seems to have been the most important – perhaps only – route to the office of ealdorman. Thus Æthelmod, the brother of Ealhburg, was ealdorman in Kent in the mid-ninth century but earlier had served Æthelwulf of Wessex as a *cellerarius*, a butler or steward. Moreover, though the body of noble families from which the West Saxon *ministri* – and thus ealdormen – were drawn was tight-knit, it was also comprehensive and encompassing. All prominent families enjoyed a share of power and the expectation of royal office, a state of affairs that made rebellion costly: the political status quo served the interests of all significant players. What rivalry there was among the nobility took the form of competition for plum appointments or career advancement. It was competition for royal service and for the delegation of royal power, not for the throne itself.

West Saxon rulers also took a different approach to conquered territories from their earlier Mercian counterparts. Where Mercian kings had been distant overlords of Kent, organising their interactions with the kingdom from outside and largely marginalising the Kentish nobility, West Saxon kings intervened more directly, making regular visits and promoting members of the Kentish nobility to positions of power, as happened with Ealhburg's family. Ecgberht was also able to secure the support of the archbishop of Canterbury, Ceolnoth, for the succession of his son, Æthelwulf, and for his dynasty as a whole. Ecgberht similarly reached an agreement with Ceolnoth that recognised the right of monasteries in Kent to seek out the protection and lordship of Ecgberht and Æthelwulf, while at the same time guaranteeing the status of bishops as the spiritual lords of these monasteries. Such agreement effectively ended the decades-old dispute between the archbishop of Canterbury and successive overlords of Kent about the control of Kentish monasteries.

5.8 Gold finger ring, inlaid with niello, inscribed inside 'Queen Æthelswith' ('EAÐELSVIÐREGNA). Like the ring in the name of Æthelswith's father, Æthelwulf, this is likely to have been a gift, perhaps in the context of her marriage to King Burgred of Mercia

5.9 Items from the Trewhiddle Hoard. Probably buried in the mid-860s, the hoard was discovered in the eighteenth century and included both coins and precious metalwork. Many of the items feature geometric motifs and stylised zoomorphic figures and vegetal ornamentation picked out in niello – hence the name 'Trewhiddle Style' for decoration of this type

Where West Saxon overkingship did resemble earlier Mercian practice was in the use of sub-kings. Ecgberht and then Æthelwulf appointed sons to govern Kent and the eastern regions of 'Greater Wessex' on their behalf. Indeed, it seems that Æthelwulf's ultimate intention was for the kingdom of Wessex and the eastern regions of Sussex, Surrey, Kent and Essex to become separate kingdoms, with separate but related royal dynasties. It was only the early death of Æthelwulf's first two sons that allowed Æthelberht, his third son, to reunite Wessex and the eastern regions into a single king-ship in 860. Even this occurred only after Æthelberht had secured the consent of his younger brothers, Æthelred and Alfred. Though in part due to the careful cultivation of conquered regions, the establishment of an enduring 'Greater Wessex' stretching along the southern coast owed much to chance, early deaths and, perhaps, to the growing recognition of the need for unity in the face of an increasing Viking threat.

Urban Life and the Economy

As the Mercian hegemony was coming apart in the second quarter of the ninth century, the economic conditions that had allowed that kingdom to prosper were similarly undergoing significant changes. The volume of coinage circulating in the south Humbrian kingdoms declined dramatically in the middle decades of the ninth century – more than halving. In Northumbria the situation differed, with debasement leading to a dramatic increase in coinage. From the end of King Eanred's reign (r.c. 810–?840) the Northumbrian currency was progressively and substantially debased and by the mid-ninth century it was a base-metal currency. Such made it eminently suitable for low-value transactions, indeed, debasement may have been a deliberate economic decision by Northumbrian kings. Whatever the reasons for debasement, the volume of

5.10 Copper alloy bucket, found at Hexham. It contained some 8,000 Northumbrian coins from the late eighth to mid-ninth centuries

Northumbrian coinage increased exponentially between the 830s and 840s. In certain areas south of the Humber – particularly East Anglia and Lincolnshire – Northumbrian coins from this period have been found in some numbers, suggesting that here, too, the economic utility of a low-value currency was recognised.

Levels of coinage do not map straightforwardly onto economic growth or decline. There are no indications that the Anglo-Saxon kingdoms were substantially poorer in the ninth century than they had been in the eighth. Indeed, the ninth century is noteworthy for the amount of precious metalwork that has been recovered. Silver strap-ends – often with ornate niello decoration – are near-ubiquitous in this period and some of the finest examples of Anglo-Saxon jewellery date from the ninth century. Likewise, charters and wills make repeated reference to bullion and to precious metals. Nevertheless, the fluctuating levels of coinage in circulation must indicate both a change in the nature of coin usage and a change in the nature of the ninth-century economy.

Such a change is most notable at the *emporia*. In London, the trading settlement on the Strand – Lundenwic – had been contracting in size since the later eighth century. The excavations at the Royal Opera House, Covent Garden, found only three new buildings constructed after c. 770 as well as a general decline in the upkeep of the site and the maintenance of its infrastructure. A number of alleyways fell into disrepair and the main north–south road through the site was not resurfaced in the ninth century, though it probably remained passable for some time. One of the alleyways between the buildings was resurfaced over the course of the late eighth to ninth centuries, but before the mid-ninth century refuse was no longer being cleared from it and it became a dumping ground.

Manufacturing and industrial activity did continue on the site but at levels considerably reduced from their eighth-century high. The remains of a smithing hearth were found in one of the ninth-century buildings, along with scrap iron and slag. Small scale bone- and antler-working took place in the same building, and loom weights and a spindle whorl were also recovered. Another building had evidence for a similar range of industrial and craft activities, including two sword-hilt fittings that point to the continued manufacture of high-status items. The tanning pits at the northern edge of the excavated site fell into disuse in the ninth century and the area was used instead for dumping. Textile production continued to be an important activity, with most of the dumps and middens on the site containing loom weights and spindle whorls, but, again, the level of activity was significantly lower than in the eighth century. The early ninth century also saw a shift in the geographical focus of trading activity and a reduction in its levels. There is a preponderance of Ipswich Ware pottery in the later phases of the site and some indication of an intensification of trade links with the Rhineland at the expense of regions further to the south.

In the early ninth century a large defensive ditch, over 55 metres long, was constructed at the northern edge of the site, passing through a number of earlier abandoned buildings. Traces of similar ditches have been found during other excavation in the area of Lundenwic, such as those at Maiden Lane or Bruce House, and it is possible that the entire area of Lundenwic was enclosed by a ditch to the north and the river to the south. By the mid-ninth century, Lundenwic had been effectively abandoned and the site largely reverted to agricultural uses. The area around and inside the Roman walls, downstream from Lundenwic, subsequently became the focus of Anglo-Saxon London. The decline of Lundenwic affected nearby settlements as well, with the high-status complex upstream at Whitehall being similarly abandoned by the mid-ninth century.

Though the precise chronologies and trajectories differ, for the other *emporia* the basic pattern is the same. At Hamwic (Southampton), no new buildings were constructed from the mid-ninth century onwards, and there was a general decline in all activity on the site until it was all but abandoned in the last decades of the ninth century. As with Lundenwic, a more defensible site close by – Southampton – became the focus of urban life in the later Anglo-Saxon period. At York, extramural activity continued into the tenth century and beyond, but even here the middle decades of the ninth century saw the shifting of trade and production away from the existing site at Fishergate to new locations.

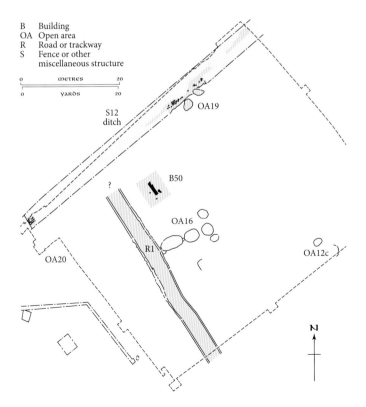

5.11 Final phase of activity on the site at the Royal Opera House, Covent Garden. Note the defensive ditch at the north-west edge of the site

B   Building
OA   Open area
R   Road or trackway
S   Fence or other
      miscellaneous structure

Only at Ipswich is there evidence of continuing occupation and activity on the site of the eighth-century *emporium*, with new buildings being constructed in the late ninth and tenth centuries. The East Anglian mint, probably at Ipswich, increased in productivity across the middle decades of the ninth century, accounting for over a third of south Humbrian coin finds. Across the same period, East Anglia itself was the most highly monetarised of the Anglo-Saxon kingdoms outside of Northumbria. The circulation of coinage in the kingdom also suggests an economy that diverged somewhat from its neighbours. Though coins from other southern mints did circulate in East Anglia, by the mid-ninth century locally minted coins account for nearly three-quarters of all finds there. If Ipswich's decline was not as precipitous as that of the other *emporia*, nevertheless the cessation of the production of Ipswich Ware pottery around 850 does imply a significant alteration in the nature of the site. Pottery manufacture did continue, with the sand-tempered Thetford Ware first produced at Ipswich in the later ninth century, but its distribution was not as extensive as that of the earlier Ipswich Ware nor, at least initially, was its production on the same scale.

Beyond the *emporia* there is evidence for similar changes taking place at smaller-scale trading centres and sites of local exchange and production. At Sandtun (West Hythe, Kent), activity at the seasonal trading and manufacturing site declined in the second half of the ninth century, with a marked reduction in quantities of pottery, coins and metalwork. The site was almost totally abandoned by the end of the century, with only a few potsherds from the later Anglo-Saxon period recovered.

Other coin-rich and metalwork-rich 'productive sites' were similarly being abandoned or changing in nature in this period. At Cottam (East Riding, Yorkshire), finds associated with the sub-rectangular enclosure at the southern end of the site cease in the mid-ninth century and the area seems to have been abandoned at the same time. Focus subsequently shifted to the north of the site, where a new enclosure complex, with a rampart and probably a gatehouse, was constructed. Activity in this new area continued for fifty years or so before settlement shifted again to the now deserted villages of Cottam and Cowlam (East Riding, Yorkshire). The productive site at Wormegay (Norfolk) underwent similar changes, with activity shifting in the later ninth century to a short-lived enclosure complex. Some 'productive sites', such as that near Carisbrooke on the Isle of Wight, seem simply to have been abandoned in the ninth century; others, such as those at Congham or Rudham (both Norfolk), continued in use into the later Anglo-Saxon period, though probably with some change in function.

The ending of 'productive sites' may be part of a more widespread and thoroughgoing reorganisation of the rural landscape. Over the course of the Middle Saxon period, settlements shifted in location, with settlement patterns in the later Anglo-Saxon period differing significantly from those that had gone before (see chapter 4). Activity on the 'productive site' at Bidford-on-Avon (Warwickshire), for example, seems to have ended around the same time as the nearby settlement shifted focus to its current site. The evidence from Cottam and Wormegay also points to the development of new types of elite settlement that may have acted as foci for exchange and production as well as for local and regional governance. Cottam and Wormegay probably represent residences of the lesser nobility, but a number of high-status sites of similar layout were constructed in the later ninth century. At Goltho (Lincolnshire), two earlier farmsteads were cleared and a large sub-rectangular enclosure, some 48 x 48 metres, bounded by a rampart and ditch, was constructed. Within the enclosure was a complex of buildings including a large bow-sided hall – a place for the public display and practice of lordship – and a smaller bower, providing private accommodation for the lord and his family. The complex also included a weaving shed, a separate kitchen, complete with clay floor, and a garderobe or latrine pit.

For the *emporia*, and perhaps sites like Sandtun, it is tempting to invoke the Vikings as the cause of change and decline. Certainly, Vikings targeted London in 842 and 851 and Hamwic in 840 and 842. The ditch constructed at Lundenwic also suggests a concern for safety, with the Vikings seeming the obvious threat here. The Vikings also sacked Continental *emporia*, such as Quentovic (near Étaples, France) and Dorestad (near Utrecht, Netherlands), on a number of occasions. Viking activity must also have threatened merchant ships and other maritime transport. Viking fleets had been active in the English Channel since the early 790s, when Offa of Mercia had made provisions for the protection of the coasts of Kent and Sussex. Similarly, around 800, Charlemagne established a naval force to combat piracy off the northern Frankish coasts. Aldwulf, the papal legate who accompanied Eardwulf back to Northumbria, was kidnapped by pirates when returning to the Continent and was freed only when ransomed by one of King Cenwulf of Mercia's men.

Yet the chronology of the decline of the *emporia*, both in the Anglo-Saxon kingdoms and on the Continent, does not fit well with the Vikings being the primary cause: the *emporia* were already in decline when first targeted. No wholly satisfactory explanation has been advanced for this decline. London is known from written sources to have suffered serious fires in 764, 798 and 801, and these may have contributed to the retrenchment of trading activity and production at Lundenwic. At Dorestad, environmental factors such as the silting up of the river and changing sea levels may account for its eventual abandonment. Numerous smaller trading centres that had sprung up in Dorestad's hinterlands also challenged its pre-eminent role in commerce, with some of these centres subsequently forming nuclei for new urban development in the later ninth and tenth centuries. Given the interconnectedness of the *emporia*, decline and change in one is likely to have had a knock-on effect on the others, with the Vikings supplying only the *coup de grâce*.

Anglo-Saxon kings made some attempts to revive trade and commerce over the course of the ninth century. At some point between 844 and 852 the Mercian king Berhtwulf confirmed the exemption from toll at London granted to the bishopric of Rochester by King Æthelbald in 733. A few years later, in 857, Berhtwulf's successor, Burgred, granted to Bishop Ealhhun of Worcester 'a profitable little estate in the town of London … which is situated not far from the west gate' together with the right 'to use freely the scale and weights and measures as is customary in the port'. Both documents suggest that Mercian kings were endeavouring to re-establish trade at London at a new site, away from Lundenwic. Given the description of Ealhhun's estate, this alternative site lay within the Roman walls, and Berhtwulf's confirmation of the toll privilege may have been designed to show that it applied to the newer trading site.

5.12 Lunette-type penny of
King Burgred of Mercia

Berhtwulf's reign also saw the re-establishment of the Mercian mint at London after an interruption during the final years of Wiglaf's reign. This earliest coinage of Berhtwulf drew on expertise from the mint at Rochester, with either dies cut there or moneyers active there transferred to London, suggesting that Berhtwulf lacked the necessary craftsmen in his own kingdom. After this initial revival under Berhtwulf, the London mint once more went into decline, being revived again only in the 860s during Burgred's reign. The later 860s also saw the establishment of a shared coinage between Mercia and Wessex. This lunette-type coinage was produced first for King Burgred at London but was minted subsequently also in the names of the king of Wessex at the West Saxon mints. The reasons behind this monetary cooperation are unclear but it is possible that the creation of a larger zone of single currency was intended as an economic stimulus.

Though the *emporia* were in decline in the ninth century, evidence from elsewhere in the Anglo-Saxon kingdoms suggests urban life was in many respects flourishing. Most is known of ninth-century Canterbury, where material from the archives of Christ Church provides an unparalleled window onto urban life in this period. The eastern parts of the walled city contained a number of streets lined with narrow burgage plots. Charters reveal the existence of a set of local customs or bye-laws stipulating a minimum distance between buildings in this location – 2 feet (60 centimetres) of 'eavesdrip' to allow the run-off of rainwater – suggesting a densely populated area with space at a premium. Many of these plots had appurtenant agricultural lands outside of the city and were particularly valued assets, worth up to ten times as much as equivalent land elsewhere, and there was a flourishing market in general for properties in Canterbury. The western parts of the city were, by contrast, given over to agricultural uses – probably because the land here was prone to flooding and so less suitable for intensive building – with larger estates owned by a number of religious communities.

Already by the ninth century, the citizens of Canterbury were organised into fraternities and corporations. There was a guild of *cnihtas*, or retainers, probably those charged with managing the urban properties of important landowners. The purpose of the fraternity of *mycle gemettan* is obscure, but the name 'the many guests' or 'many food sharers' suggests poorer inhabitants who depended on others for their sustenance or perhaps workers entitled to food as part of their wages. There were also groups of *innan* and *utan burhware*, burgesses who lived, respectively, inside and outside of the city, the latter perhaps living in the immediate extramural environs of Canterbury.

The evidence from Canterbury is exceptional and the city itself may be a special case – having been a royal centre and an archiepiscopal see since the very early seventh century. Canterbury was also the most important and most productive of the south Humbrian mints, accounting for up to half of the coins found in that region. Given the volume and wide distribution of its coinage, Canterbury must have occupied a privileged position in the south Humbrian economy, and the decline of Lundenwic and Hamwic can only have magnified Canterbury's importance.

If Canterbury was exceptional, nevertheless there are hints of urban growth and renewal elsewhere. Parts of Rochester, for example, were probably divided into burgage plots by the middle of the ninth century. As at Canterbury, the presence of an episcopal see and a mint, albeit on a smaller scale, may have stimulated urban development and growth here. At Winchester, if an early tenth-century poem can be trusted, Bishop Swithun had a bridge built outside the east gate of the town in 859. Such may have been designed to facilitate the flow of increasing traffic into the town, and by the early tenth century this route across the River Itchen and through the walls had become the principal market street in Winchester. It is possible that Swithun's bridge-building was part of a more general redevelopment of Winchester undertaken at this time by the bishop and King Æthelbald of Wessex, perhaps in response to the decline of Hamwic. How extensive such redevelopment was is unclear and the greater part of the reconstruction of Winchester, particularly the laying-out of its grid of streets, probably belongs to the later ninth century.

Whether the flourishing of urban life at Canterbury and elsewhere was a new phenomenon in the ninth century is not clear. Viking attacks must, though, have made walled cities attractive propositions, and the high price of urban properties is likely to reflect in some ways the protection that towns such as Canterbury could offer. Certainly Abbess Selethryth and her community at Lyminge were granted land in Canterbury in 804 to act as a refuge in times of need, and the community at Minster-in-Thanet may have been granted a similar refuge in the city. It may also be significant that the first West Saxon charters to impose specifically the obligation of fortress-work belong to the 850s.

Religion and the Church

At the end of the ninth century, King Alfred looked back to the days of his youth. Though monasteries and churches had been full of books and treasures accumulated by earlier generations, little profit was gained from them. By the time of Alfred's accession to the throne of Wessex in 871, learning and the love of wisdom had declined to such an extent that no one south of the Thames could understand the liturgy or translate Latin into English. North of the Thames things were little better. King Alfred's vision of a materially wealthy but moribund Church was echoed by his biographer, Asser. As the Welsh cleric saw it, though there were many monasteries in Alfred's kingdom they did not follow a proper monastic rule, either because of Viking attacks or because great wealth had caused the monastic life to fall into disrepute. Knowledge of the declining state of the Anglo-Saxon Church had even spread beyond Britain. Writing to King

Alfred in the 880s, Archbishop Fulco of Rheims added the ending of regular Church councils and synods to the list of problems besetting Anglo-Saxon Christianity.

It is not difficult to find evidence to confirm such gloomy assessments. Book production in Anglo-Saxon England ceased almost entirely in the years between 835 and 885 – only three manuscripts survive that are likely to have been written during this period. Though charters and other legal documents continued to be produced, declining standards in Latinity and script are apparent. The evidence from the scriptorium at Christ Church Canterbury has become infamous. By the 870s its principal scribe was aged, with failing eyesight, and even had he been able to see properly the texts he was copying, his comprehension of Latin was almost non-existent. Nor were the other scribes at Christ Church any better. The vernacular may to some degree have taken the place of Latin, whether through necessity or by design, for in the ninth century there was a dramatic increase in the number of documents – land grants, memoranda, wills and other bequests – written in Old English, particularly at Canterbury.

Outside of Canterbury and the south east, there is some evidence that standards of Latinity were better maintained. A separate tradition of West Saxon charters continued into the early 870s. Produced in the heartlands of Wessex and with their own distinctive formulae, these charters show little of the calamitous decline evidenced at Canterbury. Continental influence may have played a part here, for King Æthelwulf of Wessex is known to have had a Frankish secretary, Felix. Western Mercia similarly may have maintained better standards of Latinity and education, for when King Alfred sought to revive learning in his own kingdom Bishop Werferth of Worcester was one of those he called on for assistance. Nevertheless, that Canterbury – the most important see in England – was unable to find a competent Latin scribe by the middle decades of the ninth century suggests that, though it can be qualified, Alfred's gloomy assessment was far from inaccurate. Similarly, as Archbishop Fulco had claimed, Anglo-Saxon Church councils did come to an end in the mid-ninth century: the last recorded synod of the south Humbrian province was held in London in November 845.

If far from flourishing, the Anglo-Saxon Church was by no means moribund in all areas. Ties with the wider Christian world were maintained or revived across the ninth century and evidence points to a continuing concern with religious orthodoxy and right behaviour. In the 830s Bishop Ecgred of Lindisfarne wrote a letter to Archbishop Wulfsige of York concerning heretical beliefs surrounding a letter said to have fallen from heaven – the so-called 'Sunday Letter'. Such ideas were being spread by an Anglo-Saxon called Pehtred, who obtained his information and probably a text of the letter from the Irish deacon and visionary, Nial.

More profitable contacts between the Anglo-Saxon Church and other Christian communities are evident in the correspondence of Lupus, abbot of Ferrières. In the early 850s Lupus wrote to Archbishop Wigmund and Abbot Ealdsige, both of York, seeking to renew ties of prayer and friendship first established in the time of Alcuin. Lupus also requested Ealdsige to send him works by Jerome, Cassiodorus, Quintillian and Bede that the scribe Lantramm – who was apparently known personally to Ealdsige – might copy them at Ferrières. Even in the 870s, at the height of the Viking attacks, the papacy maintained contact with the archbishops of Canterbury and York.

Papal letters reminded them of the need for priests to wear proper clerical vestments, and the archbishop of Canterbury was warned especially to uphold ecclesiastical discipline and to enforce Christian marriage.

Decline in Latin learning likewise need not have meant a decline in religious enthusiasm or lay devotion. Though the level of activity did not compare with the eighth century, a number of churches and religious institutions were constructed or enlarged across the middle decades of the ninth century. At Repton (Derbyshire), the crypt was extensively remodelled, with the construction of a stone vault supported by four pillars and the digging out of two new entrances in the north-west and south-west corners. This remodelling is likely to have been necessitated by the burgeoning cult of the Mercian royal saint Wigstan (Wystan), who was murdered in 849. At Deerhurst (Gloucestershire), the existing church was fundamentally rebuilt in the first half of the ninth century and was decorated with extensive painted and sculptural programmes. According to eleventh-century traditions, the episcopacy of Ecgred of Lindisfarne (830–45) saw the construction or remodelling of a number of churches in Northumbria such as those at Billingham or Norham, and certainly ninth-century sculpture has been recovered from both sites.

The religious benefaction of lay magnates in Kent was referred to at the beginning of this chapter and the evidence shows a continued enthusiasm among the laity for the opportunities offered by Christianity and the Church. Such went beyond the patronage of religious institutions or making provisions for liturgical commemoration. The

5.13 Reconstruction of the church at Deerhurst, Gloucestershire, as it may have appeared in the ninth century

5.14 The crypt at St Wystan's Church, Repton. Constructed in the eighth century, the crypt was extensively remodelled in the ninth with the addition of vaulting, columns and new entrances

Opposite

5.15 Cross shaft, St Peter's Church, Codford, Wiltshire, late eighth to late ninth century. Various interpretations have been suggested for the lively dancing figure including a representation of the sense of taste, King David dancing before the Lord and the faithful partaking of the Eucharist

charters show nobles making arrangements for the disposal of their properties should they go on pilgrimage to Rome or putting in place protection for their dependants when they themselves entered a religious institutions.

Whether the pious activities of the Kentish nobility were given greater stimulus or urgency by the Viking attacks is unclear. Certainly King Æthelwulf of Wessex sent at least one of his sons on pilgrimage to Rome in 853, a trip that may have had a penitential dimension and been designed to gain divine favour. Æthelwulf himself undertook a similar pilgrimage two years later, an indication perhaps of the need to escalate attempts at divine placation in the face of a continued Viking threat.

That Æthelwulf's pilgrimage was intended as something more than personal devotion is hinted at by his actions before setting off. In what has become known, confusingly, as the 'Second Decimation', Æthelwulf freed a tenth of certain lands in the kingdom from all royal tribute and service. The charters recording this Decimation present it as an act designed to benefit the whole of the kingdom, and in response members of the Church were to recite psalms and Masses for the king, the ealdormen and the bishops. The Decimation and the pilgrimage that followed were thus part of a campaign of prayer and religious devotion, encompassing the whole of the West Saxon kingdom. If this campaign was not directed explicitly at the Viking threat, such must nevertheless have been uppermost in the mind of Æthelwulf and his counsellors.

Assessing the impact of the Vikings on the Anglo-Saxon Church itself is not easy. For later Anglo-Saxon and medieval writers, the Vikings were a convenient mechanism to explain the termination or interruption of religious life at particular ecclesiastical sites. Stories of Christian fortitude in the face of extreme violence or of divine punishment of pagan raiders (often at the instigation of a particular saint) also made for engaging and edifying reading. The thirteenth-century author Roger of Wendover, for example, described the 'admirable deed' performed by the abbess of Coldingham in cutting off her nose and upper lip ('unto the teeth') with a razor to make herself unappealing to Viking raiders. Though the abbess and her nuns were, according to Roger, thus spared ravishment, the Vikings nevertheless burnt Coldingham to the ground, making martyrs of its inmates in the process.

Despite such stories, it is difficult to find conclusive proof for Viking destruction of religious institutions. Part of the problem, as Asser and Alfred understood, was that the vitality of aspects of religious life in Anglo-Saxon England had been under threat even before the Viking attacks. By the end of the eighth century, monasteries and religious houses were increasingly being seen as economic assets to be exploited by their owners – whether lay or ecclesiastical – and the landed patrimony of some institutions had been diminished to the point of impoverishment.

At the same time, there had been a shift away from religious monastic life, with former monasteries instead housing small numbers of clerks rather than monks or nuns. Such processes, rather than the depredations of Vikings, may explain the disappearance of particular religious institutions over the course of the ninth century. Likewise, when tenth- or eleventh-century sources record a small community of priests on the site of a once prosperous pre-Viking monastery, the owner of the former monastery and not the Vikings may have been responsible for its changed state and impoverishment.

The monastery at Medehamstede (Peterborough) is a case in point. Post-Conquest sources describe the monastery as having been burnt and destroyed by a Viking army in 870 and all its inmates killed. Yet ninth- and tenth-century evidence suggests instead a formerly rich and powerful monastery that had come under lay lordship, with parts of the monastic enclosure becoming a fortified complex and its estates supporting only a small community of clerks. Likewise, the nunnery at Nazeing in Essex is known from archaeological evidence to have been abandoned in the ninth century, but the cause here seems to have been the ending of royal patronage as the East Saxon kingdom lost its independence rather than Viking violence.

This is not to suggest that Viking raiding and settlement did not seriously disrupt religious life in Anglo-Saxon England nor that some institutions did not suffer badly, even fatally, at their hands. The point of Alfred's reminiscences about the parlous state of learning and education was that things had been bad before the impact of the Vikings, not that the Vikings had had no impact. Indeed, he writes of everything being 'ransacked and burned', a reference, surely, to Viking destruction on a significant scale. The nadir of Latin charter production at Canterbury coincided with the period of most intense Viking activity in Kent, and the scarcity of mid-ninth-century manuscripts must in some way be the result of looting and burning of libraries and scriptoria. It is also difficult to explain the absence of charters and other muniments from the religious institutions of pre-Viking Northumbria, East Anglia and the East Midlands except by reference to the Vikings. In addition, a number of episcopal sees in Northumbria and East Anglia vanish from the record over the course of the ninth century or have extended gaps in their episcopal succession, suggesting significant upheaval and disruption.

Even if Vikings did not directly destroy an institution, their activities or Anglo-Saxon responses to them could put serious strain on the resources of religious houses. Charters from the early tenth century make reference to lands that had been despoiled of crops and cattle by the Vikings and describe the efforts that had been made to restock them. The bishops of Worcester and Winchester were forced to lease out their estates in order to meet their share of payments made to buy off the Vikings. Religious institutions also had to help meet the increasing demands placed on the existing military infrastructures of the Anglo-Saxon kingdoms. As early as 811 a grant to Archbishop Wulfred of Canterbury imposed not only the obligation to repair fortifications and bridges but also to destroy fortifications used by the Vikings – the first time such structures are mentioned in an Anglo-Saxon context. Even in the early 790s, Offa of Mercia imposed additional military burdens on churches in Kent and Sussex in the event of Viking attacks.

Kings may have been driven to more extreme lengths in order to meet the Viking threat. When the pope wrote to the archbishop of Canterbury in the 870s, although he made oblique reference to the troubles facing the archbishop and his Church, it was the king's violation of ecclesiastical privileges that the pope referred to explicitly. One interpretation would be that the king – Alfred – was expropriating Church lands and resources to aid military initiatives against the Vikings. Such may explain why, in the twelfth century, Alfred was remembered at Abingdon as a Judas-figure who despoiled Church lands.

Far harder to quantify, though no less significant, was the fear that the Viking attacks provoked and the sense of the loss of safety and peace. Alcuin's letter on the sack of Lindisfarne made this point clearly: 'never before has such a terror appeared in Britain as we have now suffered from a pagan race, nor was it thought that such an inroad from the sea could be made'. Likewise, asked Alcuin, if Lindisfarne, the fount of Christianity in Northumbria, could be attacked, what hope was there for less venerable institutions?

5.16 Seal die of Bishop Æthelwald. This Æthelwald is probably to be identified as the mid-ninth-century bishop of *Dummoc* (?Dunwich) in East Anglia. *Dummoc* was one of the sees destroyed or left vacant following the Viking conquests of the later ninth century

Churches and monasteries had been the victims of violence long before the arrival of the Vikings, but such violence was comprehensible to members of the Anglo-Saxon Church. It was the product of motives and mechanisms that could be understood and sometimes anticipated – political rivalry, dynastic infighting, invasion by neighbouring kingdoms and the like. Moreover, methods, not least ecclesiastical censure, existed for the diminution of violence and for the amelioration of its effects. Viking attacks, by contrast, seemed from the outset savage and unpredictable, and susceptible to few of the established remedies: such raids were a new and terrifying form of violence. Vikings need not have been inherently more brutal than their Christian counterparts for their brutality to appear more shocking and for their attacks to seem savage and their consequences more severe.

Exposed coastal or island monasteries must have felt particularly vulnerable to Viking attacks and some institutions sought safety elsewhere. The refuge in Canterbury granted to Abbess Selethryth has already been noted and her community at Lyminge occupied a site lying only a few kilometres from the coast. This need for security and protection may have accelerated secularisation and the growth of lay lordship as monasteries and churches sought out patrons capable of offering protection against the Viking threat. Similarly, as the focus of institutions shifted to new locations, their ability to maintain their hold on existing estates may have declined, with such lands passing instead into lay hands.

Such problems are underlined by the activities of the community of St Cuthbert on Lindisfarne. In the mid-ninth century the community relocated inland, eventually settling at Chester-le-Street before moving to Durham in the late tenth century.

Twelfth-century Durham sources depict Cuthbert's community as a pathetic band of refugees being driven hither and yon by the Vikings. Yet the places visited by the community in the course of their wanderings suggest more a tour of their estates and landholdings, intended perhaps to ensure that the community retained control of them during a period of extensive upheavals and Viking colonisation.

The Viking Attacks and the 'Great Heathen Army'

Between 794 and 835 the *Anglo-Saxon Chronicle* records no Viking raids on the Anglo-Saxon kingdoms. It is clear that such a hiatus reflects the concerns of the *Chronicle's* compilers and the particular story they are telling rather than the reality of Viking attacks in England and the surrounding seas. When the *Chronicle* does return to the subject of Vikings in the 830s, raids are still recorded – such as that on Sheppey in 835 – but the focus is predominantly on military engagements between the Vikings and the West Saxons. Battles are mentioned at Carhampton (836, 843), Hingston Down (838), Southampton (840), Portland (840), Romney Marsh (841) and the mouth of the River Parret (845). Whether this represents a change in the nature of Viking attacks or simply a desire by the compilers of the *Chronicle* to present the West Saxons as actively resisting Viking depredations is unclear – the *Chronicle* is certainly selective in its account of Viking activity in this period.

The 850s witnessed a change in the scale and nature of the Viking attacks recorded in the *Chronicle*. Whereas the raids of the 830s and 840s were made by forces of around 30–35 ships, the army that attacked Canterbury and London in 851 is said to have comprised 350 ships. If this figure seems high, nevertheless the basic veracity of the account is confirmed by Continental sources: fleets of up to 260 ships are recorded in the 860s and even as early as the 840s fleets of 120 ships are reported. The year 851 was noteworthy for other reasons as well. This was the first year that Vikings overwintered in England – in this case on Thanet – rather than returning home in the autumn. Again, this reflects a wider change in Viking activity across western Europe: Vikings first overwintered in Ireland in 840 and in Francia in 843.

Though the size of Viking armies was growing and their activities were increasing in intensity and duration, the *Chronicle* was still able to record Anglo-Saxon, and particularly West Saxon, successes. The force of 350 ships in 851 was met by King Æthelwulf and his son, Æthelbald, who inflicted upon the Vikings 'the greatest slaughter on a heathen army we have ever heard of until this present day'. The same year also saw another of Æthelwulf's sons, Æthelstan, and Ealdorman Ealhhere, brother of Ealhburg, defeat a great army at Sandwich on the east coast of Kent. Not all encounters resulted in West Saxon victory – after his success at Sandwich, Ealhhere was killed in battle on Thanet in 853. Yet the impression created by the *Chronicle* is that up to the 860s the Vikings were a manageable if ever-present threat.

The turning point in the *Chronicle's* narrative was the arrival in the winter of 865 of a 'Great Heathen Army'. It was to be this army – reinforced by the arrival of a 'Great Summer Army' in 871 – that would come close to overrunning the whole of Anglo-Saxon England. Previous Viking attacks seem to have been about plunder and wealth,

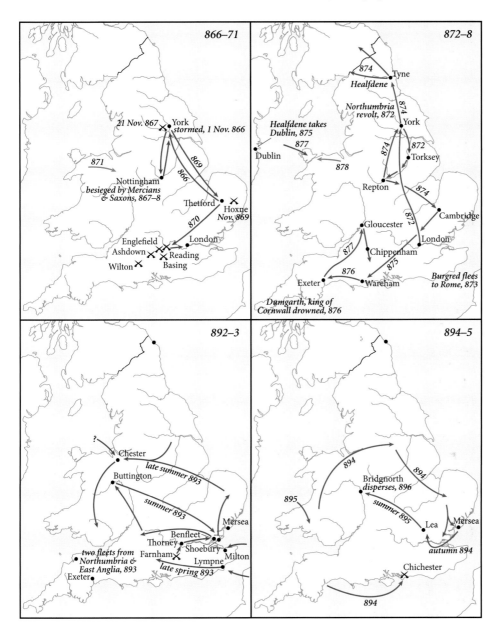

5.17 Movements of the Viking armies in England in the later ninth century

but this army was intent on settlement and conquest, or at least would quickly become so. Rather than coming directly from Scandinavia, this force appears to have been a loose confederation of groups already operating in Britain, Ireland and Francia temporarily united in the pursuit of common goals. One of its leaders, Ívarr, is known to have been active in Ireland in the 850s and early 860s, and the army contained a number of different kings as well as numerous earls. As the Anglo-Saxon kingdoms would discover, such an organisation in no way impeded the efficiency and capabilities of this army.

The army first made peace with the East Angles, receiving horses and supplies from them, and in the autumn of 866 it turned its attention to York and Northumbria.

The *Anglo-Saxon Chronicle* describes a state of disunity and civil unrest: the Northumbrians had deposed their king, Osberht, and replaced him with Ælla, despite the latter having 'no hereditary right' to the throne. Though later Northumbrian sources describe Ælla and Osberht as brothers, they nevertheless confirm the disunity and unrest in the kingdom. Having seized York and killed both claimants for the throne in battle, by 867 the Vikings had control of Northumbria. Post-Conquest sources describe the army subsequently plundering as far as the River Tyne and appointing an Anglo-Saxon, Ecgberht, to act as king over at least part of Northumbria.

East Anglia was the next kingdom to fall. In the winter of 869 the Vikings rode over Mercia into East Anglia and took up winter quarters at Thetford. The East Anglian king, Edmund, fought against them but was ultimately defeated and killed. The army then took over all of East Anglia – the first time the *Chronicle* refers explicitly to an Anglo-Saxon kingdom being conquered by the Vikings. Edmund was soon venerated as a martyr, killed at the hands of the pagans. A coinage bearing the inscription 'sce eadmund rex' ('O, Saint and King Edmund!') was circulating in East Anglia by the final decades of the ninth century, and by the mid-tenth century the church at Beadricesworth (later Bury St Edmunds) was dedicated to the king and claimed his relics.

Mercia had first been targeted by the Viking army in the autumn of 867, when it took up winter quarters in Nottingham. Despite calling on West Saxon aid, the Mercians were unable to drive out the Vikings and made peace with the army – presumably at a price. The Mercians again bought peace when the army overwintered in London in 871 and Torksey (Lincolnshire) in 872. Though the terms of the agreement were sufficiently onerous to put a strain on the resources of Mercia, the real crisis came in the following year when the Vikings overwintered at Repton, in the heartlands of the Mercian kingdom.

The Viking army took control of the royal mausoleum and cult site of St Wystan's church. As well as its symbolic and spiritual importance to the Mercian regime, the site occupied a commanding position overlooking the River Trent and, farther away to the north west, the Icknield Way. The Viking force constructed a heavily ditched defensive enclosure between the river and the church, with the latter acting as a gatehouse. Within the enclosure itself, the army buried a number of their dead and more burials were made in the disused mortuary chapel to the west of the enclosure. At the same

5.18 St Edmund memorial penny, minted in East Anglia in the late ninth or early tenth century

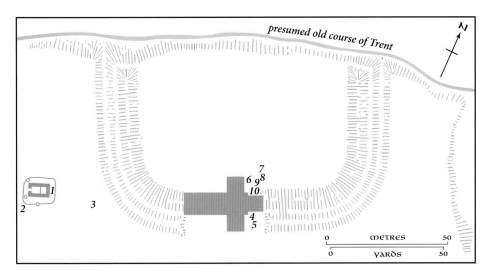

5.19 Base of the Great Army at Repton. Numbers on the plan mark the sites of burials

time as this activity at Repton, another group of Vikings, probably also members of the army, were cremating their dead and burying them under mounds in Heath Wood, Ingleby – a site clearly visible from Repton.

During this time, the Vikings forced King Burgred into exile. From Mercia, he travelled to Rome where he died soon after, being buried in the church of Santa Maria in the English quarter. In place of Burgred, the Vikings gave the Mercian throne to Ceolwulf, a man described contemptuously in the *Chronicle* as 'a foolish king's thegn'. If such ideas were current in the 890s, contemporaries in Mercia nevertheless accepted the legitimacy of Ceolwulf's rule. He issued charters independently, without reference to Viking overlords, and his grants were witnessed by the Mercian clergy and nobility, including two ealdormen who had served under Burgred. When the Vikings returned to Mercia in 877, they divided the lands between themselves and Ceolwulf, leaving him as the sole ruler of western Mercia – 'English' Mercia as it is sometimes labelled – a position he occupied at least until 879.

Like Mercia, Wessex was targeted repeatedly by the Viking army in the 870s. Though there were some West Saxon victories, for the most part the army had the better of the exchanges. Soon after he succeeded to the throne in 871, King Alfred was defeated at Wilton (Wiltshire) and after a series of subsequent battles he was forced to make peace with the Vikings, on condition they left Wessex. When the army returned in 876, Alfred again made peace, receiving hostages and securing oaths. The events of the following year would see large parts of Wessex effectively conquered by the Vikings and the West Saxon royal dynasty come close to being permanently extinguished.

After Twelfth Night, the army came to Chippenham (Wiltshire) and, according to the *Chronicle*, occupied the land of the West Saxons, driving some to flight and accepting the submission of others. Alfred escaped, travelling with a small band of followers through the remote places of the kingdom – 'the woods and the fen-fastnesses' as the *Chronicle* has it. By Easter 878, Alfred had established a fortification on the island of Athelney on the Somerset Levels, from where he launched a series of raids against the Vikings.

Eventually, Alfred was able to gather together the men of Somerset, Wiltshire and part of Hampshire and engage the Viking army at Edington (Wiltshire) in May 878. Alfred's forces put the Vikings to flight and then laid siege to a Viking stronghold, where the survivors of the battle were holed up. After two weeks the Vikings surrendered, offering Alfred oaths and hostages and pledging that their leader, Guthrum, would accept baptism. Three weeks later, Guthrum and 30 of his leading men were baptised near Athelney. Guthrum and his army subsequently withdrew from Wessex, passing through Mercia, and ultimately returned to East Anglia, where Guthrum became king. At a later date – precisely when is unclear – Alfred and Guthrum agreed a treaty, drawing a boundary between their two realms up the River Thames, along the River Lea and thence up the River Ouse to Watling Street.

Alfred is popularly remembered as the king who saved England from the Vikings. Yet such a reputation is misleading. There existed no England to be saved – England, in a political sense, would be the creation of Alfred's grandsons and great-grandsons. What Alfred's victory at Edington secured was the immediate safety of the kingdom of Wessex. Neither did Alfred defeat *the* Vikings but rather one particular Viking army. Alfred's claims to greatness rest less on his victory at Edington – Anglo-Saxon kings had enjoyed victories against Vikings before – and more on the steps he took subsequently to strengthen his kingdom.

In the year following Edington a new Viking army encamped at Fulham, and though it subsequently moved to Francia the following year it would eventually return to Wessex in 892, its progress on the Continent having been carefully tracked by the *Chronicle*. For the next four years this army would play a cat-and-mouse game with Alfred and his allies, but by the summer of 896 it was largely a spent force, with the *Chronicle* noting 'by the grace of God, the army had not on the whole afflicted the English people very greatly'. The very different fortunes of the great Viking army of 865 and the Viking army active in the early 890s are one indication of the real achievements of Alfred.

Alfred the Great

If the scarcity of sources means that the great Mercian kings of the eighth century remain shadowy figures about whom little can be known, for Alfred the problem is almost reversed. Alfred and his reign are far better documented than any previous Anglo-Saxon king, and very few of his successors generated a comparable level of written sources. Alongside the *Anglo-Saxon Chronicle* can be placed the biography of King Alfred written by the Welsh cleric Asser in the early 890s. Fewer charters survive from Alfred's reign than from those of his immediate predecessors but Alfred alone issued a law code, the first West Saxon king to do so since Ine (d. 726).

To these texts can be added a number of works, mostly translations and adaptations from Latin into Old English, produced at Alfred's court or under his sponsorship. Most remarkably, a good case can be made that four of these works – translations of Gregory the Great's *Pastoral Care*, Augustine's *Soliloquies*, Boethius's *Consolation of Philosophy* and the first 50 psalms – were produced by Alfred himself. Ultimate certainty about Alfred's role here is impossible, but linguistic analysis suggests these to

5.20 The Alfred Jewel. This is likely to be a pointer or *æstal* – now missing its rod – used to follow words on a page. Alfred is known to have distributed such pointers with copies of the translation of the *Pastoral Care* and a number of objects similar to the Alfred Jewel have survived. The inscription around the edges of the setting reads 'AELFED MEC HEHT GEWYRCAN', 'Alfred ordered me to be made'. The enamel figure is probably a representation of the sense of sight, intended here as more than simply the physical sense. In Alfred's writings, sight and the eyes are connected with the pursuit and attainment of wisdom. The eyes on the Alfred Jewel also may represent the eyes of the mind – an image frequently encountered in Alfred's translations – that are the path through which wisdom may enter

have been the work of the same author-translator. Similarly, there is a consistency of ideas and concepts across the texts that speaks of a shared authorial agenda.

The comparative richness of the written record for Alfred's reign means that far more can be known about him than about earlier Anglo-Saxon kings. Moreover, his own writings seem to offer an insight into his mind and character that cannot be replicated for any other Anglo-Saxon ruler. Such is the level and the nature of the surviving information that Alfred cannot but look exceptional, cannot but look great. Unsurprisingly, some modern scholars – most notably Michael Wallace-Hadrill and Ralph Davies – have urged caution in our assessments of Alfred. The wealth of written sources – almost all, moreover, associated with Alfred's court – conspires to over-emphasise Alfred's differences from other rulers and to magnify, perhaps deliberately so, his achievements.

Yet this caution must be balanced by an appreciation of what was exceptional about Alfred. The survival of sources may owe something to the vagaries of chance, but this cannot explain everything. Even allowing for such random factors, it is clear that more than any other Anglo-Saxon king before him, Alfred sought to rule through the written

5.21 'Cross-and-lozenge' penny of King Alfred

word and to shape the image of his own kingship and authority through the production of texts. In this way, Alfred more closely resembles Continental kings of the ninth century, such as Charlemagne or Charles the Bald, than other Anglo-Saxon rulers. Indeed, it seems likely that Alfred drew direct inspiration for his cultural activities from these and other Carolingian rulers.

Alfred's achievements in the final decades of the ninth century are all the more surprising given his family circumstances. At his birth, it must have seemed highly unlikely that he would ever become king, let alone achieve all that he did. Alfred was the youngest son of King Æthelwulf and three of his older brothers were kings of Wessex before him. At least one of these, Æthelred, is known to have produced male heirs, though not of an age to succeed their father on his death. Nor was succession always straightforward and uncontested. If West Saxon kingship in the ninth century was monopolised by the line of Ecgberht, nevertheless there were clear tensions within this narrow ruling dynasty.

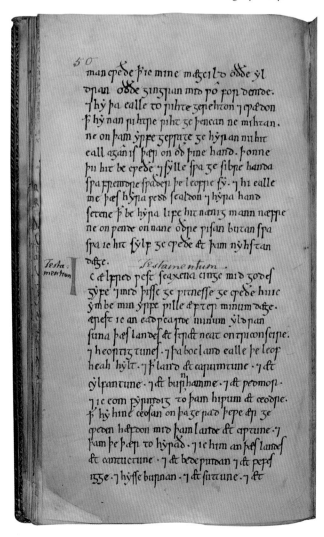

5.22 The opening of King Alfred's will as preserved in the eleventh-century *Liber Vitae* of the New Minster, Winchester

When his father Æthelwulf was on pilgrimage, Æthelbald rebelled and seized the West Saxon throne in 856. On Æthelwulf's return from the Continent, the kingdom was divided, with Æthelbald ruling the western parts – the traditional West Saxon heartlands – and Æthelwulf ruling the eastern parts – the territories gained in the ninth century. The reasons for Æthelbald's rebellion are unclear, though he had the support of some powerful figures, among them the bishop of Sherborne and the ealdorman of Somerset. Æthelwulf's marriage to Judith, daughter of the Frankish ruler Charles the Bald, may have been the catalyst. Certainly, she was consecrated queen, an act that would have raised her status above that of Æthebald's mother and was, according to Asser, contrary to existing West Saxon practice. A son from this union would clearly pose a threat to Æthelbald's own ambitions. That Æthelbald wed Judith on his father's death – a marriage that was contrary to Canon Law – underlines the prestige that such a union could bring.

Tensions did not end with the deaths of Æthelwulf (858) and Æthelbald (860), nor with those of Æthelberht (865) or Æthelred (871). Alfred's own will includes lengthy sections, defensive and justificatory in tone, about properties he had inherited from his father and brothers. On at least one occasion when king, Alfred was forced to defend publicly his possession of these estates and his disposal of others. Certain of Alfred's kindred clearly felt aggrieved about the distribution of family resources and had sufficient support to challenge him. Even after Alfred's death in 899, his own son Edward was challenged for the throne by his cousin Æthelwold, the son of King Æthelred.

Given his status as youngest son, it is possible that Alfred was intended for a clerical or monastic career rather than secular office. Certainly, Asser records a youthful Alfred learning the Divine Office, enthusiastically visiting churches and shrines to engage in extended sessions of prostrate prayer, and collecting psalms and prayers in a book which he kept about his person. Though an intended ecclesiastical career is possible, such activities may be better understood as showing the influence of Carolingian ideas about lay religiosity. These stressed the heavy moral obligations and burdens that Christianity placed upon even the secular nobility and emphasised the need for constant prayer and meditation on Sacred Scripture.

Such demands brought into sharp relief the apparent tensions between aspects of the lifestyle of the warrior elite – in particular sex and violence – and the ideals of Christian behaviour. Like others, Alfred may have found such tensions unbearable. Asser describes a young Alfred fearing he would be unable to restrain his carnal urges and seeking, and receiving, from God an illness that would strengthen his resolve. Though this youthful malady – probably piles – was subsequently removed by God, it was replaced by another, more serious illness – plausibly identified as Crohn's disease – that afflicted Alfred throughout his adult life.

This sickly, suffering Alfred, beset with sexual anxieties, seems at odds with the warrior king of Edington, which has encouraged some, most notably Alfred Smyth, in the belief that Asser's biography is a later Anglo-Saxon monastic forgery. Such doubts are exacerbated by the problems with manuscript transmission. The sole manuscript witness to the text was totally destroyed by fire in 1731 and the work now survives only in early modern editions and transcripts, often with unwarranted additions and alterations.

Yet most scholars would accept that the work is genuinely ninth-century and that Asser's Alfred, however strange he appears to a modern audience, is the genuine Alfred. Sex, lust and sin were dangers that preoccupied Alfred every bit as much as did the Vikings and were potentially as damaging. In Alfred's own writings, lustful thoughts appear as forces that upset the balance of the mind and the body's equilibrium: such things mattered to ninth-century kings. Alfred's religiosity is best understood not as the invention of a monkish forger but as the response of a man always destined for secular office but all too aware of the moral compromises and pitfalls of such a path.

That Alfred was intended from a young age for high secular office, even for king-ship, is suggested by the *Anglo-Saxon Chronicle*. This describes how in 853 King Æthelwulf sent the infant Alfred to Rome where he was consecrated king by Pope Leo IV, information that is repeated by Asser. Though the *Chronicle* does not note this, Alfred was probably accompanied by one of his brothers, Æthelred, for their names are included together in the *Liber Vitae* of San Salvatore in Brescia.

That Alfred did meet the pope is confirmed by a fragment surviving from a letter from Leo to Æthelwulf. In contrast to the *Chronicle*, this notes only that Leo decorated

Alfred 'as a spiritual son, with the dignity of the belt and the vestments of the consulate, as is customary with Roman consuls'. Whether the *Chronicle*, or perhaps Alfred himself, misinterpreted, deliberately or otherwise, the events in Rome is unclear. It may be that Alfred's encounter with Leo was but a minor aspect of the visit whose significance was later magnified. Alternatively, Æthelwulf may have been trying to ensure that Alfred, and, perhaps, Æthelred also, were not excluded from possible royal succession and saw papal blessing as a means of furthering this goal.

Whatever the significance of the events of 853, Alfred did, of course, succeed to the West Saxon throne in 871 and would remain king until his death, of natural causes, in 899. The early 870s would seem an inauspicious time to gain the kingship of Wessex. Two Anglo-Saxon kingdoms had already fallen to Viking armies, and Mercia and Wessex were both hard pressed. Yet even before his victory at Edington in 878, Alfred's actions mark him out as an ambitious and capable ruler.

Around 875, Alfred initiated a reform of the West Saxon coinage, introducing the so-called 'Cross and Lozenge' type. This reform restored the weight and fineness of the coinage as well as introducing new designs that more closely imitated Classical Roman models. Particularly noteworthy is that a number of these coins were minted in Alfred's name at London, as well as at mints in 'Greater' Wessex. One of Alfred's earliest 'Cross and Lozenge' coins produced at London even bears the royal style 'rex sm', presumably to be understood as 'king of the (West) Saxons and Mercians'. Sometime after the expulsion of King Burgred in 873/4, Alfred had clearly been able to extend West Saxon influence into parts of Mercia, London included.

If Alfred had influence over London, he was not the only ruler there. His reform of the coinage was carried out in tandem with King Ceolwulf II, continuing a tradition of monetary cooperation between Mercia and Wessex. Alfred appears the senior partner in this relationship: as well as the 'Cross and Lozenge' type both kings also issued the 'Two Emperors' type, but where Ceolwulf's simply styled him 'rex' ('king'), Alfred is described on his as 'rex anglorum' ('king of the Angles' or perhaps 'king of the English').

Alfred's authority over Mercia increased following the death or deposition of Ceolwulf in the late 870s. Ceolwulf was succeeded as ruler of 'English' Mercia by a certain Ealdorman Æthelred, whose antecedents are unknown. By the early 880s, Æthelred had recognised the authority and overlordship of King Alfred and governed 'English' Mercia as an ealdorman, never claiming for himself the title 'king'. This relationship with Alfred was confirmed in the late 880s when Æthelred married Alfred's daughter, Æthelflæd. Alfred clearly enjoyed a close and productive relationship with Æthelred. In 886 Alfred bestowed on him authority over London, sharing with him the task of rebuilding and restoring areas within the old Roman walls and establishing new settlements. Similar authority seems to have been granted in other parts of Mercia, including Gloucester and Worcester.

From the mid-880s, Alfred increasingly employed the royal style 'king of the Anglo-Saxons', indicating his authority over both Saxon Wessex and Anglian Mercia. There are some indications that Alfred or those at his court experimented with more expansive notions of identity. The *Anglo-Saxon Chronicle* describes all the English people – the 'anglecynn' – except those under Danish rule submitting to Alfred in 886.

Similarly, Alfred's treaty with Guthrum was made with 'the councillors of all the English race'. Such ideas of a single English people are, however, muted and fleeting in the Alfredian corpus. The same is true of more expansive royal styles. Asser describes Alfred on one occasion as 'ruler of all the Christians in the island of Britain'. Such may reflect the submission of various Welsh kings to Alfred's overlordship – Asser lists the kings of Dyfed, Glywysing, Gwent and Brycheiniog – as well as Alfred's own piety. Yet there are no indications such titles were used routinely; Alfred was, until the end of his reign, simply king of the Anglo-Saxons.

As the return of a large Viking army in 892 demonstrated, despite Alfred's gains in the 870s and 880s the survival of his kingdom of the Anglo-Saxons was far from secure. What victory at Edington in 878 had bought was breathing space and time for Alfred to strengthen his kingdom. In the preface to his translation of Gregory the Great's *Pastoral Care*, probably produced in the early 890s, Alfred looked back to better days:

> there were happy times then throughout England and . . . the kings, who had authority over this people, obeyed God and his messengers; and how they not only maintained their peace, morality and authority at home but also extended their territory outside; and how they succeeded both in wisdom and in warfare.

Such a statement summarised well Alfred's own aims for his kingdom – success in wisdom and in warfare. The two goals were interconnected and success in one would be meaningless and transitory without success in another. To strengthen his kingdom, Alfred needed to put in place both military and educational reforms.

Taking military reforms first: Alfred clearly understood that Viking victories over the Anglo-Saxons were less the result of any inherent military superiority than of the particular tactics and strategies the Scandinavians adopted. Above all, their armies relied on their mobility, making raids and plundering and then moving on quickly before they could be engaged. Where Anglo-Saxon forces were set up for pitched battles and open warfare, the Vikings actively avoided such encounters, preferring the element of surprise and favouring hit-and-run tactics. By the time an Anglo-Saxon army had been raised and mustered, their enemy had already done much damage and had often moved on elsewhere or retreated behind fortifications, necessitating lengthy and often futile sieges.

5.23　The Abingdon Sword. Recovered from the River Ock in Oxfordshire, this sword features detailed Trewhiddle Style decoration in silver and niello, including the Evangelist symbols on the upper guard – suitable ornamentation for a Christian warrior facing a pagan foe

Alfred's response was to divide his army in two. As the *Anglo-Saxon Chronicle* put it, this ensured 'that always half its men were at home, half on service'. This effectively created a permanent standing army that could be deployed immediately when needed. At the same time, all areas of the kingdom retained some defensive capabilities when the army was on campaign. This approach was not always effective – on one occasion, West Saxon forces laying siege to a Viking army returned home when their period of service was over, even though they had not yet been relieved by a new contingent – but it did allow Alfred's army to respond more rapidly to any Viking threat.

Of greater long-term significance was the establishment of a network of fortified centres – *burhs* – throughout Alfred's kingdom. Though written evidence shows that Anglo-Saxon kings had long made use of fortifications, with archaeological excavations uncovering the remains of defensive ramparts around a number of Mercian centres, what was innovative about Alfred's burghal system was the idea of a network of such centres covering the whole of the kingdom. The siting of the fortifications ensured that nowhere was more than a day's ride from a *burh*. Moreover, the location of many of them on navigable rivers, Roman roads or other important nodes of transport significantly reduced Viking freedom of movement.

Yet the construction, maintenance and garrisoning of such a network placed a considerable burden on Alfred's subjects. The figures from the *Burghal Hidage* suggest that over 27,000 men would have been required to maintain and defend the *burhs*. To these must be added the expense of constructing the network in the first place. No wonder that Asser could write of Alfred's need to cajole and chastise his subjects to do his bidding, and that the Welsh cleric would complain 'of fortifications commanded by the king which have not yet been begun, or else, having begun late in the day, have not been brought to completion'. Alfred's military reforms were making hitherto unheard-of demands on his people, and this after decades of Viking raids and plundering had already strained the resources of Wessex.

Yet, as Alcuin had seen many decades earlier, the Viking raids on Christian peoples were possible only because God had withdrawn his protection. Military responses alone could not hope to counter the Viking threat. Divine favour and divine support needed to be regained if any successes were to be permanent.

For Alfred, the greatest failing of the Anglo-Saxons was their laziness and indolence in pursuing wisdom and promoting education. His comments about the parlous state of learning in England have already been noted. In order to revive learning and wisdom, Alfred gathered at his court scholars from throughout Britain and the Continent: Asser himself was recruited from St David's in Wales, Bishop Werferth from Worcester, John from Continental Saxony and Grimbald from St Bertin (now in Saint-Omer, France).

Latin was the primary language for the diffusion of Christian knowledge in western Europe and competence in Latin was the ultimate, if very distant, goal of Alfred's educational reforms. Yet such was the decline of learning in the Anglo-Saxon kingdoms that most of Alfred's efforts were directed at translations from Latin into Old English. Some were produced by scholars patronised by Alfred – such as Bishop Werferth's translation

5.24 The Fuller Brooch. One of the finest examples of Anglo-Saxon jewellery, the central roundel features representations of the five senses, with sight in the middle. Like the Alfred Jewel, the brooch is probably a representation of the Alfredian search for wisdom

of Gregory the Great's *Dialogues* – but others, as already mentioned, are presented as the work of Alfred himself, aided and assisted by his advisors.

Central to Alfred's educational reforms was the idea that the need to pursue wisdom and learning was not simply an obligation for clergy or monks. What the writings produced at Alfred's court stressed was that all who held positions of authority, whether secular or ecclesiastical, needed to seek after knowledge and wisdom. Indeed, such a pursuit was not secondary to the appropriate and effective exercise of power but an essential precondition of it. Alfred's translations were, in his own words, 'those works men most needed to know'. They were those works that would both educate readers and further inculcate in them the desire to seek for wisdom and spiritual guidance.

Such lofty aims were backed up with cajoling and threats. Asser recorded how Alfred threatened to remove from office those of his nobles 'who neglected the study and application of wisdom'. As a result almost all of his ealdormen and thegns 'who were illiterate from childhood, applied themselves in an amazing way to learning how to read, preferring rather to learn this unfamiliar discipline (no matter how laboriously) than to relinquish their offices of power'. The extraordinary demands Alfred made of his subjects concerning military matters were matched by the demands he made about learning.

Alfred's vision of his own rule, as well as the contribution he made to the development of Anglo-Saxon kingship, is underlined by his law code. Alfred presented this code as the summation of previous Anglo-Saxon legal activity. He had extracted from the codes of his predecessors – he names explicitly Æthelberht of Kent, Ine of Wessex and Offa of Mercia – those laws which he found most pleasing and just; Ine's law code

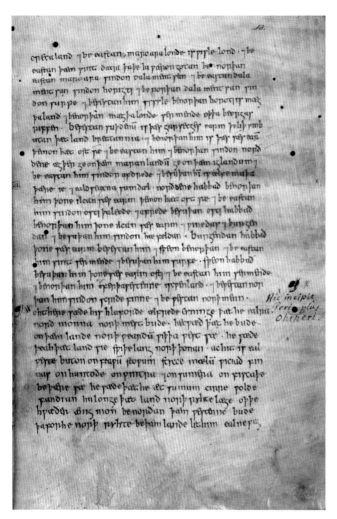

5.25 Page from the *Tollemache Orosius*, a tenth-century manuscript of the Old English version of Orosius's *Seven Books of History against the Pagans*, one of the translations associated with Alfred's court. The page features one of the additions made to Orosius's text, an account of the travels of a Norwegian, Ohthere, as told to King Alfred

was even included in its entirety after Alfred's own laws. There is certainly little in Alfred's laws that appears innovatory – a notable exception is a reference to what might be a universal oath of loyalty sworn by all his subjects, perhaps following a Carolingian precedent.

What was innovatory was the context in which Alfred placed his laws. The preface to the code sets out the history of Christian law-giving, from the *Decalogue* and the laws of Moses, to Apostolic letters and Church synods, ending finally with Alfred's own legal activities. The effect is to make royal law, Alfred's law, part of the continuum of Christian law-giving, presenting it as standing in direct lineal descent from the laws of Moses and the judgments of the Apostles. Even the number of chapters in Alfred's code underlines this. The entirety of the code, Ine's laws included, is divided into 120 chapters. Such not only corresponds with the reputed age of Moses at his death but is also the number of people on whom the Holy Spirit descended at Pentecost.

Anglo-Saxon kings before Alfred had been Christian, some had even harnessed the tools and ideology of Christianity to further their own rule. Yet it is with Alfred that we see for the first time in England the development of a fully Christian kingship.

THE *ANGLO-SAXON CHRONICLE*

MARTIN J. RYAN

He caused a book to be written in English
Of adventures and of laws,
And of battles in the land,
And of kings who made war.

So Geoffrey Gaimar wrote of King Alfred in his *L'Estoire des Engles*, a poem outlining the history of England up to the reign of William Rufus (d. 1100). The book that Gaimar was describing was almost certainly one of the manuscripts of the *Anglo-Saxon Chronicle*, perhaps that now known as the *Parker Chronicle* (Cambridge, Corpus Christi College, MS 173), a compilation that does indeed include both a version of the *Anglo-Saxon Chronicle* and the laws of King Alfred. The *Chronicle* exceeds in importance any other written source for Anglo-Saxon England. Not only does it supply the chronological framework for much of the period, providing details of characters and episodes not otherwise recorded, but it also sheds valuable light on how the Anglo-Saxons approached their own history, how they retold, reinterpreted and reconfigured past events in order to shape and to make sense of their present. Even after the Norman Conquest, the *Anglo-Saxon Chronicle* continued to be read, updated and edited, and it served as one of the key sources of information for Anglo-Norman historians such as Henry of Huntingdon, William of Malmesbury and, of course, Geoffrey Gaimar himself.

As is often recognised, the title the *Anglo-Saxon Chronicle* is in many ways unhelpful, even misleading, for the *Chronicle* is not a single text but a set of separate yet related annals, mostly in Old English, produced at various centres in England throughout the Anglo-Saxon and Anglo-Norman periods. There survive some seven different manuscripts of the *Chronicle* – assigned the letters 'A' to 'G' by scholars – and a fragment from an eighth – H – but these represent only a fraction of those that must have originally existed. In the late tenth century, for example, the ealdorman Æthelweard produced a Latin chronicle that drew extensively on a now lost version of the *Anglo-Saxon Chronicle*. Asser, likewise, made considerable use of another version, which is no longer extant, in his late ninth-century biography of King Alfred.

Determining the relationship between the different surviving versions presents formidable complexities and the history of individual manuscripts can be equally

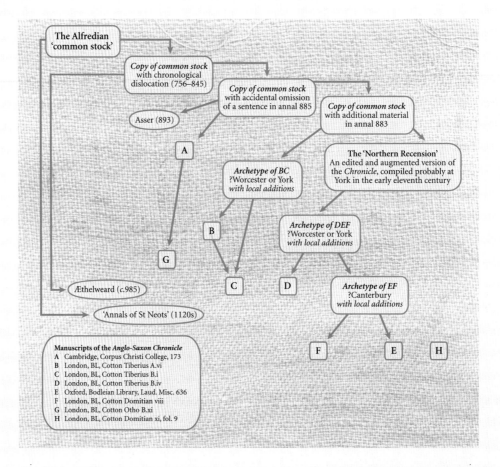

The Alfredian 'common stock'

Copy of common stock with chronological dislocation (756–845)

Copy of common stock with accidental omission of a sentence in annal 885

Copy of common stock with additional material in annal 883

Asser (893)

A

The 'Northern Recension'
An edited and augmented version of the *Chronicle*, compiled probably at York in the early eleventh century

Archetype of BC
?Worcester or York
with local additions

Archetype of DEF
?Worcester or York
with local additions

B

G

C

D

Archetype of EF
?Canterbury
with local additions

Æthelweard (*c*.985)

'Annals of St Neots' (1120s)

F   E   H

Manuscripts of the *Anglo-Saxon Chronicle*
A Cambridge, Corpus Christi College, 173
B London, BL, Cotton Tiberius A.vi
C London, BL, Cotton Tiberius B.i
D London, BL, Cotton Tiberius B.iv
E Oxford, Bodleian Library, Laud. Misc. 636
F London, BL, Cotton Domitian viii
G London, BL, Cotton Otho B.xi
H London, BL, Cotton Domitian xi, fol. 9

involved, with material being added, amended, erased and reordered on numerous occasions. The different versions of the *Chronicle* all ultimately descend from one produced in the early 890s, most probably at the court of King Alfred. Though this original is no longer extant, its contents and form can be reconstructed in large part from the surviving versions of the *Chronicle* and from other early witnesses such as Asser's *Life of Alfred*. The original version – sometimes referred to as the *Alfredian Chronicle* or the *Common Stock* – comprised entries from 60 BC to, probably, the end of 891, and may well have been prefaced by both a list of kings and an extended genealogy of the West Saxon kings, since that precedes annalistic entries in the *Parker Chronicle*.

In parts, the story told by this original version of the *Chronicle* was of the rise of Wessex and the emergence of its dynasty as the pre-eminent and eventually sole surviving Anglo-Saxon royal lineage. To that extent the text might be termed dynastic propaganda, but the narrative of the *Common Stock* and its aims are far more complex and subtle than this and its scope wider. If, as seems likely, the text was part of the literary projects initiated and sponsored by King Alfred – or at the very least it owed its wide circulation to him – then it might be seen as responding to the particular needs of his kingship and his kingdom in the early 890s. The immediate context of the production of the *Common Stock* may have been the return to England of a great

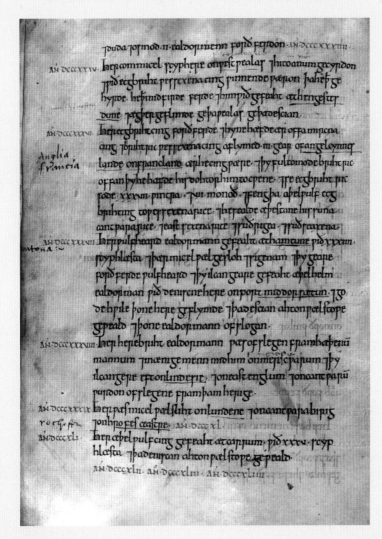

5a.2 Version C, the so-called 'Abingdon Chronicle'. This page features entries from the years 835–41 (recte 838–43), describing the Viking attacks on southern Britain

Viking army in 892 and the need for unity in the face of this renewed threat. The *Chronicle* provides a shared history for the peoples under Alfred's rule, particularly those of the 'Greater' Wessex that stretched along the southern coast, uniting them and their different traditions and stories in a single narrative, just as they had been united under the rule of a single dynasty over the course of the ninth century. Whether the articulation of this shared history should be seen as seeking to celebrate or as seeking to convince is difficult to determine.

Very soon after the compilation of the original *Chronicle*, copies were being made of it and material added to it at a number of different locations. The mechanisms for the dispersal of the *Chronicle* are not known but, following the model of other texts associated with King Alfred, it was presumably sent to various religious centres to be copied, with further manuscripts being made from these. Certainly, none of the surviving versions is a direct copy of the original *Chronicle* for they all display a chronological dislocation in their annals between 756 and 845, meaning events are dated at least two years too early.

5a.3 Version D, the 'Worcester Chronicle'. This page shows the preface to the Chronicle, describing the island of Britain and its inhabitants

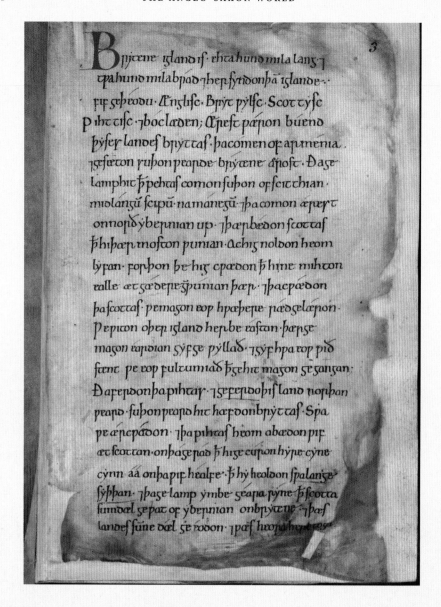

Periodic 'updates' to the *Common Stock* seem to have been issued by the West Saxon court. Versions 'A', 'B', 'C' and 'D' all contain near-identical batches of annals for the years 893–6 (on the campaigns of King Alfred), 901–14 (on the campaigns of King Edward the Elder) and 934–46 (the reign of King Æthelstan and King Edmund). Such may have continued into the eleventh century, for versions 'C', 'D' and 'E' likewise contain near-identical annals for the reign of King Æthelred II, suggesting similar semi-official dissemination of information or texts from a central source.

The *Parker Chronicle*, Manuscript 'A', is the earliest of the extant versions, with entries up to the end of 891 written in a single hand in the late ninth or early tenth century, probably at Winchester. Additions were made by several different scribes in the tenth century – it has a particularly detailed account of the reign of Edward the

Elder – and at some point in the early eleventh century it was taken to Canterbury but not before a copy of it had been made, either manuscript 'G' or the exemplar for it.

Manuscript 'B' was completed in the late tenth century – its final entry is for 977 – and it contains significant Mercian elements, such as the account of the activities of Æthelflæd of Mercia in the 910s known as the *Mercian Register* or the *Annals of Æthelflæd*. Manuscript 'C' was written in the middle of the eleventh century, and up to 977 is in large parts a copy of manuscript 'B'. It contains a stratum of material that relates to Abingdon and its production has often been assigned to that abbey, but this may be to place too great an emphasis on these entries. Production at a religious house somewhere in Mercia is probably the most that can be claimed.

Manuscripts 'D' and 'E' derive in large part from a version of the *Chronicle*, no longer surviving, known as the 'Northern Recension'. This version, dating to the tenth or early eleventh century, added significant material relating to Northumbria and the north of England, derived from such sources as Bede's *Ecclesiastical History* and annals produced at York in the eighth century. Despite the name, the 'Northern Recension' need not have been written in the north of England, but its creation probably stems from the desire to write Northumbria into the story presented by the original *Chronicle* at a time when West Saxon kings were establishing their control over the north. Some of the entries from the later tenth century, such as the account of the aftermath of the death of King Edgar under the year 975, were written by Archbishop Wulfstan of York (d. 1023), but it is unlikely that the entirety of the compilation of the 'Northern Recension' was his work.

Manuscript 'D' was probably compiled in the mid- to late eleventh century, perhaps at York during the archiepiscopate of Ealdred (1060–9). The exemplar for manuscript 'E' was at St Augustine's Abbey, Canterbury, around the time of the Norman Conquest, but E itself was written at Peterborough in 1121 and continued there until 1154. Manuscript 'F' is a bilingual version of the *Chronicle*, with entries in both Old English and Latin, and was put together by a scribe in Canterbury c. 1100, using a number of different versions of the *Chronicle*. The same scribe was also responsible for making some alterations and additions to manuscript 'A' after comparing it with the exemplar of manuscript 'E', suggesting significant scholarly investment in the texts of the *Chronicle* at this point in time. The fragment 'H' contains entries for the years 1113 and 1114 and may have had some connection with Winchester, but it is now impossible to determine its relationship to other manuscripts of the *Chronicle*.

Taken as a whole, the different versions of the *Anglo-Saxon Chronicle* cover the period from the attempted invasion of Britain by Julius Caesar in 60 BC to the death of King Stephen and the accession of Henry II in 1154. The chronological range of each version differs, however, with only 'E' and 'H' containing twelfth-century material. The basic format of each annal is the year expressed using the *Anno Domini* dating system – though, curiously, 'B' does not include dates after its entry for 652. The year is then followed usually by the word '*her*' ('here', i.e. 'at this time' or 'in this year') and then the events recorded for that year. Not every year has an entry and chronological coverage is patchy. Entries across the middle decades of the tenth century tend to be short and few in number, and the coverage of the reign of King Cnut (d. 1035) is equally thin.

The length of entries can vary from the simple record of a death or a battle or some-times a noteworthy natural phenomenon – such as the death of Bishop Daniel of Winchester in 745 or the great mortality of birds recorded in 671 – to lengthy extended entries detailing a series of events – such as the campaigns of the West Saxon kings against the Vikings in the ninth century. The vast majority of the entries are in prose but a number of poems are included, such as the description of King Æthelstan's victory at the Battle of *Brunanburh* in 937 or King Edmund's conquest of the Five Boroughs in 942. As well as the annals, different versions of the *Chronicle* include a range of prefatory material. Manuscript 'A' has already been mentioned in this regard; 'C' begins with a metrical calendar and a series of proverbs or aphorisms; 'D', 'E' and 'F' include a description of the island of Britain and the origins of the Britons, Picts and Scots.

Despite the similarities between the various versions of the *Chronicle*, it is their differences – local references, chronological dislocations, corrected or reordered entries, additional or unique information – that are most significant and most useful, and not only for determining a place of origin. Though the *Chronicle* remains central to reconstructing events of the Anglo-Saxon period, it is important less as a repository of facts than as a record of the varying uses made of the past by different individuals and groups at different times and places. For the period 1035–66, for example, versions 'C' and 'E' present divergent and often conflicting accounts of events, probably reflecting the different factions competing for power and influence at this particularly turbulent time. Manuscript 'E', for example, tends to favour Earl Godwine of Wessex and his descendants, whereas C shows marked sympathies for the family of Earl Leofric of Mercia, and was probably written by a member of his affinity. Similarly, the account of the reign of King Æthelred II in versions 'C', 'D' and 'E' seems to have been composed by a single author writing in the aftermath of the conquest by Cnut. Æthelred's reign, seen by the author in the light of this ultimate defeat, is presented as a period of inevitable and inexorable decline and decay, hastened on by the king's evil deeds and bad judgements.

The various versions of the *Chronicle* make clear that the past mattered to the Anglo-Saxons and that control of its meaning and significance through the production of texts and the maintenance of records was of fundamental importance. The past was, however, flexible and able to be reshaped and reinterpreted to serve better the needs of particular individuals and groups. The texts of the *Chronicle* preserve the traces of these activities, with some manuscripts showing repeated scribal interventions over time. In some cases such versions of the past have proved immensely powerful and influential – King Æthelred's reputation, for example, has never quite recovered from the damage done to it by 'C', 'D' and 'E'. Other reconfigurations have proved more temporary and fleeting, albeit they may have achieved their immediate contemporary aims.

THE REBIRTH OF TOWNS

NICHOLAS J. HIGHAM

Britain's Roman towns ceased to function in the fifth century, although both ruined towns and forts remained highly visible and were often reused thereafter as royal and/or church sites. A revival of trade in the later seventh and early eighth centuries focused on a few undefended *emporia* or *wics* on the coasts and tidal rivers of the major kingdoms: at Ipswich in East Anglia, on the Strand west of London, at Hamwic near Southampton and at Fishergate outside York. Hamwic, lying between the Rivers Itchen and Test, is probably the best understood. Large-scale excavation on the Six Dials site revealed a grid of streets laid out around 700 with 68 Middle Saxon structures scattered across several properties divided by pit and stake-hole alignments. Numerous crafts were practised: iron, bronze, lead and gold were all worked plus glass-making, textile manufacturing, bone-working, pottery-making, leather production and wood-working. Hamwic was probably the sole West Saxon mint and seems to have had a regional monopoly on trade with Continental Europe across the eighth century and into the ninth, with a network of lesser trading sites inland and on the Isle of Wight. However, by the third quarter of the ninth century traders had abandoned these open sites in favour of more defensible locations.

Defended royal and/or ecclesiastical centres had long been a feature of Anglo-Saxon England. In Northumbria examples go back to the sixth and seventh centuries, with small but heavily fortified settlements at Bamburgh, Dunbar, Edinburgh and the palisaded enclosure at Yeavering, as well as the Roman walls at York. In Mercia, royal charters from the 740s onwards include clauses requiring a contribution to the construction of 'necessary defences'. Precisely where is unclear but excavations at Hereford, Tamworth (Staffordshire) and Winchcombe (Gloucestershire) all revealed substantial banks and ditches constructed by at latest the mid-ninth century. At Hereford on the Welsh borders the primary defences consisted of a gravel rampart and an external ditch on the west of the city combining with the River Wye to defend the area around the cathedral. Later work augmented the bank with turf and clay and extended it eastwards, probably in the late ninth century, then provided a new breast-work and fronted it with stone. The tenth-century defences enclosed the cathedral, St Guthlac's, and an urban community centred on Broad Street. Tamworth was a focus of Mercian royal government, almost certainly centred on a palace complex. In the

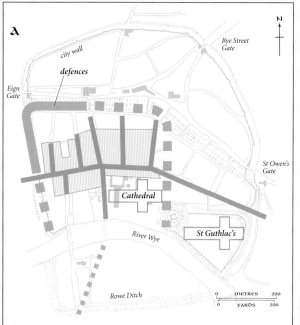

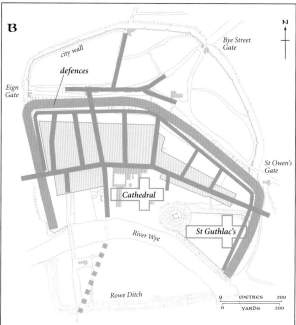

5b.1 Development of ninth-century Anglo-Saxon Hereford. (a) mid-ninth-century gravel and clay rampart built on the north and west sides of the core of the town around the cathedral; (b) a timber-faced turf and clay rampart replaced earlier defences in the late ninth century, extending to enclose St Guthlac's in the eastern part of the town

eastern Midlands the *Anglo-Saxon Chronicle* implies that Nottingham and Repton also had meaningful fortifications by the 870s and many others gained them either under Viking occupation or in the course of the West Saxon conquest of the Danelaw.

West Saxon charters only began to require contribution to defences in the mid-ninth century. There were, however, some defences earlier: the *Anglo-Saxon Chronicle* makes reference to Merton (?Devon) as a defensible settlement in the 750s; Asser's *Life of Alfred* refers to existing fortifications at Shaftesbury, Canterbury and Rochester (both the latter had Roman walls), and there are scattered references in the *Chronicle* to walls at, for example, Chippenham and Chichester, which may well pre-date Alfred's reign. Clearly though, Alfred, his daughter Æthelflæd and son-in-law Æthelræd (in Mercia), and his son Edward the Elder (899–924), were responsible for numerous new fortifications, the garrisoning of the whole network and the expansion of this West Saxon system of *burhs* north of the Thames. Warfare turned into a succession of sieges, punctuated by the construction of new defences; it is difficult to overestimate the connection between West Saxon royal government and fortified towns.

The *Anglo-Saxon Chronicle* provides an account of some at least of the new foundations, starting with Alfred's building of Athelney (Somerset) in 878 and running through Æthelflæd's *burhs* in the West Midlands and Edward the Elder's at Manchester and further east. A document known as the Burghal Hidage lists 33 places and provides the number of hides associated with each. Appended to this list is a set of calculations which establishes the relationship between the length of wall and the number of hides required to man it:

> For the establishment of a wall of one acre's breadth, and for its defence, 16 hides are required. If each hide is represented by 1 man, then each pole [of wall] can be

furnished with 4 men.

    Then for the establishment of a wall of 20 poles there is required 80 hides; and for a furlong, 160 hides . . . for 12 furlongs, 1920 hides.

The West Saxon *burhs* are listed in clockwise order starting in East Sussex, running west to Lydford (Devon) and then back through northern Wessex to Southwark, crossing the Thames to include both Oxford and Buckingham en route. Omission of Kent and London implies that this was a working document rather than one intended to describe the whole system. It probably belongs to the second decade of the reign of Edward the Elder, although most of the places named were fortified significantly earlier.

    David Hill divided the places named in the Burghal Hidage on the basis of size, interpreting the larger as towns and the smaller as campaigning forts. Many of the new towns developed from pre-existing royal and ecclesiastical centres. Winchester is the classic example of a new town: lying among late pre-Christian burials suggestive of early claims on authority, from the seventh century a bishopric was centred within the old Roman walls, the church (the Old Minster) surviving little altered until 971. A royal palace probably lay alongside. Alfred and his father had both been to Rome and were keen to stress this connection. In consequence the very 'Roman' practice of town foundation was core to Alfred's policies; this was the single most important example. Excavation has revealed a grid of streets orientated on High Street, accompanied by a series of channels to supply water for drinking and to power mills. The Roman walls and gateways were retained but, excepting High Street, the earlier internal layout was obliterated. Almost 9 kilometres of new roads were laid using some 8,000 tonnes of cobbles. The interior was divided into substantial plots on which incomers constructed residences and churches, and subdivided areas as tenements. The original religious complex was expanded by the construction of the New Minster (founded by 901) and Nunnaminster, later St Mary's Abbey, taking up the south-eastern quarter of the walled

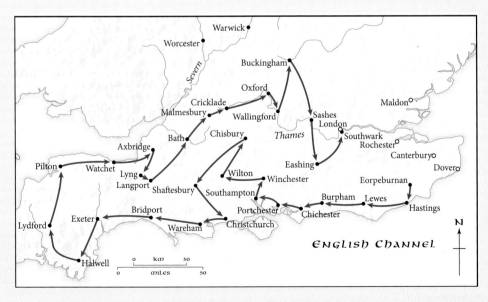

5b.2 The Burghal Hidage. This enigmatic early tenth-century document lists the towns indicated on the map (solid circles); most are in Alfred's Wessex but even there not all contemporary towns are included; other towns of the period in Kent and Essex are also shown (hollow circles)

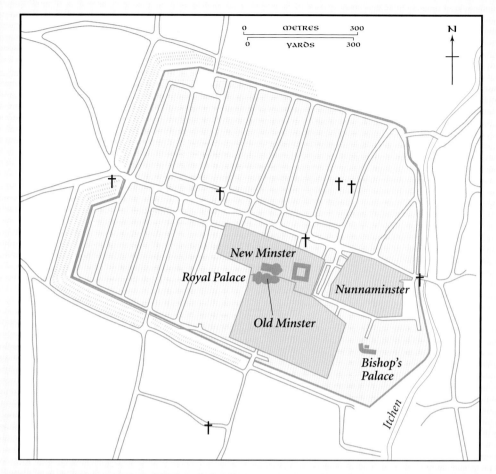

5b.3 Winchester. A new capital for the West Saxon kingdom in the late ninth and early tenth centuries, Alfred and Edward re-used the Roman walls but reorganised the interior

area. A mint was operating from the 870s onwards. High Street experienced rapid commercial development across the tenth century, to the point where the monastic quarter had to be enclosed to insulate it from the townsfolk.

By the eleventh century Winchester was home to a large urban community, with specialised markets for meat and fish and general markets at each of the landward gates. The cult of St Swithun attracted pilgrims. In the 970s the Old Minster was substantially extended and a great new western tower was added to the New Minster. The churches played an important role in the life of the town: many of England's kings were buried in the Old Minster and it had one of the most productive scriptoria in later Anglo-Saxon England, creating a market for hides, inks and colouring materials. There was also a permanent royal establishment, including the treasury. Members of the royal family were often present, or on their estates nearby.

Winchester has rightly been called 'the heart of the Old English Kingdom'. The new *burh* should be thought of very much in terms of a partnership between king, church and townsfolk. Its prosperity rested both on redistribution of revenues derived from the countryside and on manufacturing and trade; there were at least four guilds serving the townsfolk in the later Anglo-Saxon period. The city was omitted from Domesday Book, but a survey compiled for Henry I around 1110 listed royal rents and services

dating from the reign of Edward the Confessor, when there were around 1,130 tenements, placing Winchester on a par with Lincoln in terms of population. The king's
tenancies were held variously by shoemakers, moneyers, reeves, beadles, herring-
mongers, blacksmiths, hay-merchants, 'wet-mongers' and goldsmiths. Medieval street
names refer to the working of gold, silver and leather. This was, then, a substantial and
successful urban settlement.

Winchester's economic development was, however, limited by its inland position.
On the coast to the south Hamwic gave way to a new, defended settlement built on
slightly higher ground just a kilometre away at Southampton. This served as a port for
Hampshire and boasted a mint in Æthelstan's reign, but the defences were in-filled by
the mid-tenth century and settlement was dispersed across a wide area. The port had
links with Flanders and coastal France but it was always comparatively small.

Although the road system was clearly well used by traders in later Anglo-Saxon
England, bulk cargoes travelled predominantly by water, around the coasts and along
navigable rivers. The Graveney boat, excavated on the marshes of north Kent and
dated to the late ninth–early tenth centuries, reveals the type of vessel in use. Originally
some 13.6 metres long and 4 metres broad, it was capable of carrying 6–7 tonnes of
cargo. Recent loads had included both lava quernstones, for grinding grain, and hops.
The quernstones were blanks imported from Mayen, in the Eifel region of Germany,
implying passage of the Rhine via Utrecht then the Channel crossing, then to be
finished in England prior to sale. Such blanks are a key indicator of long-distance trade
in early medieval Europe, also found in wrecks at Lüttingen and Salmorth in Germany.
Their presence on this vessel may suggest its use on the Channel crossing, as well as
around the English coast.

London was far larger than either Winchester or Southampton and combined the
advantages of both sites, as both a major port and a key political and religious centre.
Alfred and Æthelred's 're-foundation' of London in 886 should be associated with
relocation of the trading community to the riverbank at Queenhithe within the walled
city, where the bishopric was already located. This expanded dramatically in the
second half of the tenth century, particularly around Cheapside and Eastcheap, 'cheap'
deriving from Old English *cēap*, 'to barter'. The city became as a major industrial
centre, with metalworking particularly active, as the most prolific mint in late Anglo-
Saxon England and England's premier trading site. By the end of the tenth century,
London was emerging as a quasi-capital city and was of real political importance in its
own right.

Numerous other centres also developed significant commercial and craft facilities,
often around pre-existing elite centres of royal and/or ecclesiastical power. Many of the
most successful incorporated Roman walls, as at Chester, for example, or Lincoln,
where the old legionary fortress retained its pre-existing ecclesiastical and political
functions while trade and manufacturing developed in the Lower City, spreading
uphill in the later tenth century. The shiring of the Midlands clearly advantaged those
settlements selected as the administrative centres. Some in the east, such as Derby,
were Viking fortifications; others, such as Warwick and Stafford, were new English
burhs. Some ancient centres were marginalised in the process; Tamworth was down-

graded on purpose, one suspects, by Edward the Elder to prevent its serving as a centre for Mercian separatism after his imposition of direct rule on the Midlands following his sister's death.

The minting of coins was a core function of these new towns, to lubricate the workings of their urban markets. Before 850 there were only some six mints in operation in England, but by the mid-tenth century there were between 35 and 40. Æthelstan's second law code, the 'Grately Code' dated 926–30, ordered that minting should occur only in towns (the term used was 'port') and stipulated the number of coiners per centre in southern Wessex: seven in Canterbury (four for the king, two for the archbishop and one for the abbot); three in Rochester (two for the king, one for the bishop); eight in London; six in Winchester, and in other places just one or two.

How successful were the new towns of later Anglo-Saxon England? In comparative terms the answer must be 'very successful indeed'. Their walls provided critically important defensive capabilities across the second Viking Age (the 990s to 1042). Additionally, a range of manufacturing processes has been found in one after another of the new towns, working bone, antler, various metals and wood and manufacturing a range of different types and qualities of cloth. Minting occurred very widely indeed, and trade was clearly encouraged, bringing economic specialisation and increased wealth. There was no comparable urban development elsewhere in the British Isles, with the partial exception of Viking Dublin and a handful of lesser sites along the eastern Irish seaboard. English towns were denser on the ground and better established than comparable settlements across most of Francia and Germany. Although a proliferation of small boroughs occurred under Norman patronage in the twelfth and thirteenth centuries, the basic network of urban centres remained the same as pre-

5b.4 Viking Age bone comb from excavations in Ipswich

1066. That said, many eleventh-century towns do seem to have been oases of urbanity. In the north there was very little urban development outside the shire towns before the Norman period: Chester, for example, was the only town worthy of the name in north-west England in 1066.

Even in the south, where a market economy was more deeply entrenched, urban development was patchy. In Berkshire, all the new towns lay on the shire border along the Thames; in Surrey only the shire town of Guildford and the London suburb of Southwark can really claim urban status, and there were no towns west of Bodmin in Cornwall. In some regions, however, urban markets were becoming increasingly accessible. Wareham, in Dorset, is among the best preserved Anglo-Saxon *burhs* today. Walls are still upstanding on three sides, with a fronting ditch, forming a rectangular plan encompassing some 34 hectares on the banks of the River Frome, with access to Poole Harbour. An irregular grid of streets is based upon three landward gates and the river crossing. Some 285 houses in 1066 plus further burgesses associated with estates nearby suggest a prosperous town. This was a shire where no one urban settlement was predominant: the Domesday account opens with a survey not just of Dorchester but also Bridport, Wareham and Shaftesbury. Even Bridport, with 120 houses in 1066, was not much smaller than a shire town such as Stafford, with 154 houses, or Hertford with 146. Dorset, therefore, along with Somerset, Kent and Sussex, had a network of urban centres such that most farmers were within 15 to 30 kilometres of market facilities. Town life was well established by 1066 across much of England and urban centres provided a variety of functions. The rise of towns in later Anglo-Saxon England made possible the increasingly specialised economy which emerged across southern England in the twelfth and thirteenth centuries, but it would be a mistake to suppose that commerce and industry were the key drivers of urbanism around 900; rather, urbanism developed out of the need to bolster royal power, provide defences and re-energise resistance to the Vikings.

5b.5 Western defences of the late Anglo-Saxon town of Wareham

CHAPTER 6

Conquest, Reform and the Making of England

MARTIN J. RYAN

In midwinter 878, as Alfred took refuge from the Viking assaults at Athelney in the Somerset marshes, Anglo-Saxon kingship was virtually extinguished. Yet within sixty years, Alfred's grandson Æthelstan would control a territory corresponding, to a large degree, to modern England. Alongside these extensive conquests, Æthelstan and his successors would establish new methods of governance and administration and new means of controlling the vast territories now at their disposal.

This process of West Saxon conquest looms large in the contemporary sources and dominates modern accounts of the tenth century. The danger, as always, is hindsight. That a unified England would emerge over the course of the tenth century does not mean that such unity was inevitable nor that there had long existed the idea of or the desire for political unification, an England waiting impatiently to be born. To assume that successive kings had in mind this ultimate goal of unification and to interpret their activities in this light – or, worse still, to assess the success or failure of their reigns by this yardstick – is unhelpful and presumptive. Nor was the process of unification one way: territory was gained and lost repeatedly by Alfred's descendants over the course of the tenth century. The underlying tendency, if there was one, was political fission as much as political fusion. Old identities and loyalties died hard and could be easily reactivated as circumstances changed and ambitions fluctuated.

West Saxon territorial gains came at the expense of the communities and kingdoms in the north and the east that had emerged in the wake of the Viking conquests of the ninth century. Our knowledge of these new polities is frustratingly limited. The written sources offer an essentially West Saxon perspective on events and, as so often, the north is seen not on its own terms but through southern eyes. Though it is clear that the Viking conquests resulted in Scandinavian settlement across large areas of northern and eastern England – the so-called Danelaw – much about this settlement remains obscure. Its impact can be traced through place names, material culture and, increasingly, genetics. Though such data have most often been mined for information about numbers of settlers and settlement, they may actually tell us more about the development of new identities and the responses of those in the Danelaw to the new circumstances of the tenth century.

The tenth century also witnessed far-reaching religious changes. The written record is dominated by the so-called Benedictine Reforms of the later tenth century.

Anglo-Saxon churchmen inspired by Continental developments as well as by their own idiosyncratic readings of works such as Bede's *Ecclesiastical History* sought to reform and to renew communal religious life in England, privileging the monastic Rule attributed to St Benedict of Nursia. Particularly during the reign of King Edgar (d. 975), these reformers enjoyed considerable royal support and their newly founded or reformed communities attracted lavish patronage. These reforming centres were then instrumental in promoting the use of standardised forms of Old English and in the propagation of particular styles of art and manuscript decoration.

Yet if the Benedictine Reforms dominate the sources from this period, their wider impact should not be overstressed: large areas of England were affected only minimally, if at all. It was the emergence of small local churches and the development of new systems of pastoral care – processes only imperfectly documented – that would have the more enduring impact and more thoroughgoing effect on religious life in England.

6.1 Places named in chapter 6

Scandinavian Settlement

Tracing the nature and impact of the Scandinavian settlement that accompanied the conquests of the later-ninth century remains acutely difficult and the subject of intense and ongoing debate. As with the Anglo-Saxon takeover of lowland Britain in the fifth century, work has traditionally focused on the question of numbers and density of settlement, with estimates ranging from a limited number of high-status settlers to something approaching a mass migration of low-status Scandinavian farmers. The types of evidence drawn on are, likewise, similar to those used to chart the Anglo-Saxon settlement: place names, mortuary and settlement archaeology, material culture and, increasingly, archaeogenetics and other scientific data.

The idea that all or any of these can offer a simple index of levels of Scandinavian settlement has by now given way to an appreciation of the complexities of ethnic identity and affiliation in the Early Middle Ages. Material culture or language does not passively reflect ethnic identity, much less personal origin. Rather, such identities are actively shaped and constituted material culture as well as social interactions, political affiliations and other mechanisms. The

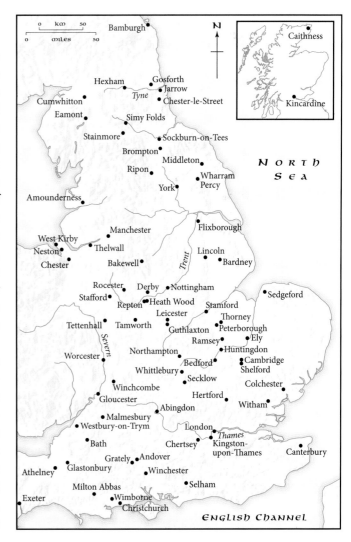

6.2 A selection of coinage from the Danelaw. From left to right: King Guthrum/Æthelstan, minted in East Anglia (late ninth century); King Siefred, probably minted in York (late ninth to early tenth century); King Olaf Guthfrithsson, York (mid-tenth century); King Sihtric II, York (940s); King Eric, York (mid-tenth century)

identities so constructed in eastern and northern England in the tenth and eleventh centuries did not seek simply to claim Scandinavian ethnicity. They did not represent the straightforward transplanting of Danish or Norwegian identities to an English context but rather should be seen as distinctively Anglo-Scandinavian. Much as Anglo-Saxon identities developed in situ in Britain rather than being imported from the Continent, so Anglo-Scandinavian identities were constructed to meet the particular needs of the inhabitants of the Danelaw, not all of whom, not even a majority of whom, need have been of Scandinavian descent.

The multiple identities that developed in the Danelaw reflect the complex circumstances of the establishment of Scandinavian control. The Viking armies of the ninth century were heterogeneous in composition, representing the amalgamation of numerous different war-bands and groups, operating in Britain, Ireland and on the Continent for many campaign seasons at a time with only limited contact with Scandinavia. Behind the simple 'Danish' identity attributed to the Viking armies in Anglo-Saxon sources lay a complex mix of nationalities, ethnicities and loyalties.

The Viking armies that had conquered the Anglo-Saxon kingdoms in the ninth century were not the only source of settlers. Though debates continue about whether there were subsequent migrations directly from Scandinavia in the wake of the Viking Conquest – a scenario that seems highly likely – north-west England certainly did see further migration. Welsh and Irish sources record the expulsion of Vikings from the Dublin area in the early tenth century with some at least of these crossing the Irish Sea and settling on the Wirral, in Cumbria and in Lancashire. These settlers are sometimes described in modern accounts as 'Hiberno-Norse', that is Irish-Scandinavian or Irish-Norwegian, and distinguished from the Danes who settled elsewhere in England. Though there is some limited place name evidence for a significant Norwegian element in the Scandinavian settlement of the north west, to draw sharp distinctions between 'Hiberno-Norse' and Danes or to posit political factions and allegiances on the basis of these identities is unhelpful. Ethnic boundaries were more fluid than this and alliances more pragmatic.

The surviving written sources offer little information about the process of Scandinavian settlement or the political structures such settlement put in place. The

Anglo-Saxon Chronicle, for example, describes how in 876 the Viking leader Healfdene 'shared out the land of the Northumbrians [among his followers] and they proceeded to plough and to support themselves', but provides no further details. Likewise, the *Chronicle* includes references to numerous Scandinavian kings and earls, as well as other nobles called *holds*, active in the Danelaw, but includes insufficient information to reconstruct the political circumstances or to determine who was subordinate to whom.

In general, the *Chronicle* presents settlement outside of Northumbria as focused on urban centres or *burhs*, such as Northampton or Leicester, with each of these centres having their own army. Beyond this it is difficult to go. The existence of larger political groupings or collective identities is suggested by references in the sources to the 'Five Boroughs' – namely Leicester, Lincoln, Nottingham, Stamford and Derby – but what such identities meant in practice is uncertain. It is possible that the compilers of the *Chronicle* were themselves unable to reconstruct fully the political structures of the Danelaw in the period of the West Saxon conquests. Shifting allegiances, temporary alliances and fluctuating levels of power and authority characterise this period. The numismatic evidence adds to this picture of political complexity. Coins were issued in the names of a vast array of rulers, some of whom are otherwise unattested, and a number of new, often short-lived mints emerged, such as those at Shelford (Cambridgeshire) or Rocester (Staffordshire).

The written sources give little indication of the interactions between the incoming Scandinavians and the native Anglo-Saxons or the extent to which existing political and administrative structures were retained. The tenth-century *History of St Cuthbert* offers a story in which a king, Guthred, was raised from a Viking army through the visionary intercession of Cuthbert. In gratitude, Guthred granted Cuthbert's community, then based at Chester-le-Street, control over all the lands between the Rivers Tyne and Wear. Stripped of its miraculous elements, such a story looks like the leader of a Viking army acknowledging the power and influence wielded in the north by Cuthbert's community and coming to an agreement with them about mutual spheres of influence. In return, Cuthbert's community offered its allegiance to, as well as saintly approval of, Guthred's accession to the throne. Other accommodations of this type must have been reached elsewhere. Numismatic evidence suggests cooperation between the archbishop of York and the various Scandinavian rulers of that city in the late ninth and early tenth centuries. At least one of these rulers, Guthfrith (d. 895), is known to have been buried in the York Minster.

Moving beyond the written sources, place names offer one of the largest potential data sets for Scandinavian settlement in England. Place names that include elements from the Scandinavian languages are concentrated in northern and eastern England. While a range of such names exists the most common are the so-called 'Grimston Hybrids', place names that combine a Scandinavian specific with the Old English generic *-tun* ('farmstead', 'settlement'); those in which an Old English or Scandinavian specific is compounded with the Scandinavian generic *-bý* ('settlement' – hence, 'town' in modern Danish); and those containing the Scandinavian generic *-thorp* ('secondary settlement').

6.3 Distribution of
Scandinavian place names in
Britain

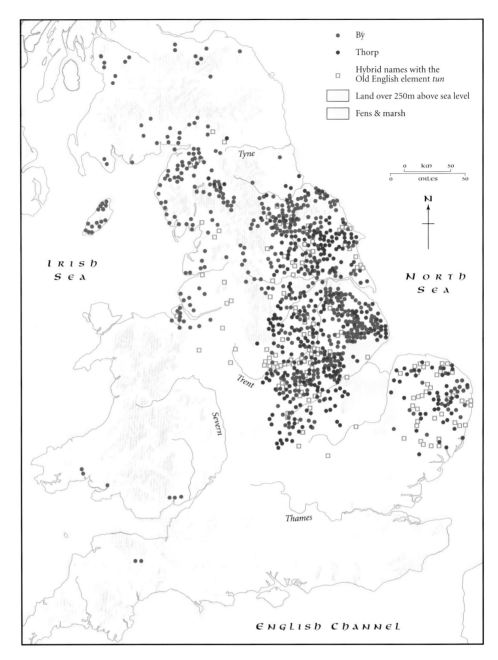

There remain formidable problems in interpreting the significance of these place names. Firstly, a site with a Scandinavian place name need not have been named or settled by Scandinavians. The Scandinavian language had a significant impact on Old English and many words were borrowed. Some place names with Scandinavian elements undoubtedly just reflect this linguistic borrowing. Secondly, the majority of Scandinavian place names are recorded for the first time only in the Domesday Book of 1086. They could, in theory, have been coined at any point between the late ninth and the late eleventh centuries and need not provide any evidence for the initial circumstances of settlement. Likewise, numerous Scandinavian place names may have been coined across this period only to drop out of usage after a time, making no impact on the documentary record. Distribution maps of Scandinavian place names are, for the most part, simply showing such place names as were in use in the later eleventh century.

Given the significant changes in landscape and settlement patterns in the later Anglo-Saxon period, most notably the fragmentation of the large 'multiple' estates into smaller landholdings, many Scandinavian place names may have been coined only in the mid–late tenth century. Such would explain why Scandinavian place names are largely absent from those areas conquered early in the tenth century by West Saxon kings. If these regions were in the hands of Anglo-Saxon lords when estate fragmentation occurred, Old English rather than Scandinavian place names would probably have been coined for the new landholdings.

This model of Scandinavian place name formation would accord well with analyses based on the underlying drift geology of different regions. Analysis of this kind allows the most agriculturally productive areas to be distinguished from more marginal zones and Scandinavian place names to be mapped onto these. In general, Grimston hybrids tend to be located on prime agricultural land, whereas names in -bý or -thorp occupy more marginal positions. Such may suggest that Grimston names belong to the earliest phase of Scandinavian settlement, representing the takeover by incomers of existing Anglo-Saxon sites already occupying the best lands. Names in -bý or -thorp would represent later, secondary colonisation of poorer quality land either by new waves of migrants or as a consequence of the dividing up and fragmentation of existing estates.

Despite the attractions of such a model, it cannot fully explain the situation on the ground. Straight divisions of land into more and less agriculturally productive regions are too simple to deal with the complexities of the early medieval landscape. The wetlands of Amounderness in Lancashire, supposedly a marginal area, were nevertheless a valuable and productive region, whose resources were carefully cultivated. Moreover, the majority of names in -bý look to have been coined in a Scandinavian-speaking environment – some preserve Scandinavian inflectional endings, for example. This would suggest that such names belong to the earliest phases of settlement rather than a period of secondary colonisation. If so, this would also be evidence against Scandinavian place names being predominantly the product of later estate fragmentation.

It is unlikely that any single model of place name formation will be able to explain fully the situation on the ground. Place names are the product of a varied range of social, economic and political processes, and stem from interactions between different language groups and contacts between native and incomer. If place names are not a simple index of initial settlement density, nevertheless they cannot be explained fully as the result of the later restructuring of landholdings.

Material Culture and the Scandinavian Settlement

Though less pronounced than the impact of place names, the Scandinavian settlement had an undeniable effect on certain aspects of the material culture of northern and

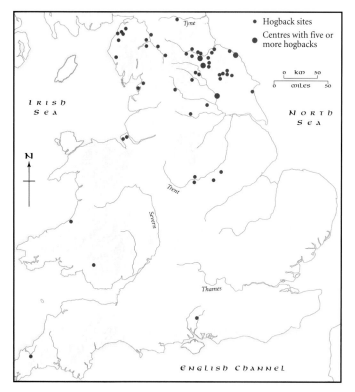

6.4 Distribution of hogbacks

eastern England. Such is most notable in stone sculpture. Not only was there a marked increase in the production of sculpture in the tenth century but also new iconographies and new decorative motifs were utilised. In some cases, this new decorative repertoire was employed on existing types of sculpture, in particular the free-standing cross. Alongside existing types, a new form of monument, the hogback, developed. These were curved, house-shaped grave-covers, frequently with bears or other beasts at either end. They are distributed throughout northern England and parts of lowland Scotland, though there are particular concentrations at sites such as Brompton (North Yorkshire) and Sockburn on Tees (Durham). Though hogbacks represent a new monument type, their producers may have drawn inspiration from existing insular sculpture or metalwork, particularly 'house reliquaries', such as the Bamberg Casket or Ranvaik Casket, or stone grave-covers, such as the Headda Stone at Peterborough.

Some of this sculpture employs iconography and imagery deriving from Scandinavian paganism, such as the figure standing by the open jaws of a vast creature on the Gosforth Cross (Cumbria) likely to represent the god Víðarr battling the wolf Fenrir. Much of the sculpture has a markedly secular air, with numerous depictions of armed warriors, such as that on the cross at Middleton (North Yorkshire), or other aspects of elite lay culture, such as the hunting scene on the cross at Neston (Cheshire). Despite such imagery, much, if not all, of this sculpture was produced in an ecclesiastical milieu. The Gosforth Cross, for example, also has a depiction of the Crucifixion, while a cluster of sculpture in South Yorkshire and Lincolnshire seems to have had links with the archiepiscopal see at York.

Despite the presence of Scandinavian iconography and decorative schemes, this sculpture cannot be seen as the straightforward assertion of Scandinavian identity. Stone sculpture is largely absent from Scandinavia in this period and the use of Anglo-Saxon motifs and forms points to the continuation of native traditions and tastes. This new sculpture of the tenth century is best seen as reflecting the ambitions and pretensions of an Anglo-Scandinavian elite, mediated through the ecclesiastical workshops likely responsible for its production. The presence of pagan iconography may represent attempts to make central tenets of Christianity comprehensible to newly converted Scandinavians, drawing parallels between pagan stories and characters and events from the Bible and the life of Christ. On the other hand, such decoration may simply represent sculptors and patrons secure in Christianity

6.5 Hogback from St Bridget's Church, West Kirby, a relatively plain example featuring *tegulae* (roof tiles) and interlace decoration

and content to embrace a range of designs and subjects, whatever their ultimate origin.

Unlike the Anglo-Saxon takeover of lowland Britain, there is very limited evidence in settlement archaeology for the impact of Scandinavian colonisers and settlers. In urban centres, above all York, there are clear indications of significant trading and industrial activities, as well as the expansion of areas under occupation and the further development of infrastructure. Yet the trajectory of towns inside the Danelaw is not appreciably different from those outside it. Towns under Scandinavian control do seem to have developed more extensive international trading links – such as the important York–Dublin axis – earlier than their southern counterparts. Until the later tenth century, trade in London, for example, was dominated by links to Oxfordshire and the Thames Valley rather than further afield. Nevertheless, the overall development of urban life in England in the tenth century effectively follows the same course, whether the towns were under Anglo-Saxon or Anglo-Scandinavian control or passed from one to the other.

The impact of Scandinavian settlement in rural areas is equally exiguous. Part of the problem lies in disentangling the consequences of Scandinavian colonisation from wider changes in the structure of settlements and the landscape across the later Anglo-Saxon period. Settlement shift, the nucleation of villages and the fragmentation of larger estates into smaller manorial-style holdings all took place alongside Scandinavian conquest and settlement.

Some sites have been claimed as specifically Scandinavian settlements, most notably Simy Folds, a group of three farmsteads on Holwick Fell in County Durham. Here each of the three farmsteads includes a long, narrow building with rounded corners and turf and boulder foundations – features characteristic of dwellings in Scandinavian settlements in the north Atlantic region. Carbon-dating of material from hearths in two of the buildings produced a date range from the seventh to eleventh centuries. Such a range does include the period of Scandinavian settlement in the

6.6 Engraving of the Fenrir
scene from the Gosforth Cross

north but is not sufficiently narrow to prove definitive. Likewise, though the shape and construction of buildings at Simy Folds correspond with those from other Scandinavian sites, the overall layout of the farmsteads reflected local, Pennine traditions.

It is similarly difficult to find evidence for a distinctively 'Scandinavian Phase' in settlements occupied continuously across the middle and later Saxon periods, except in a chronological sense. Certain sites have produced material with Scandinavian affinities, such as the metalwork featuring Borre-style motifs recovered from Wharram Percy (North Yorkshire), yet other continuously occupied sites, such as Flixborough (Lincolnshire) or Sedgeford (Norfolk), have not yielded material of this type nor provided evidence of significant change or disruption.

Mortuary archaeology presents similar problems. The corpus of burial sites so far identified as Scandinavian remains very limited, particularly in comparison with early Anglo-Saxon burials, and amounts to no more than forty sites. As with settlements, the difficulty is determining what range of features or what types of evidence can be considered diagnostic of Scandinavian presence or Scandinavian influence. Cremation is a clear marker but beyond the cremation cemetery at Heath Wood, Ingleby (Derbyshire), there are very few unquestionable examples of cremation burial from the ninth and tenth centuries.

Furnished inhumation has long been considered another marker, but the case is by no means compelling. Part of the problem is the considerable range and diversity of burial practices in the middle and later Anglo-Saxon periods. Though furnished burial had declined significantly by the eighth century, examples continue across the Anglo-Saxon period, with grave goods ranging from simple dress fittings and jewellery to knives, toilet implements and even the bodies of animals. Similarly, there existed a varied range of mortuary practices in Denmark and Norway in this period – there was no distinctively 'Scandinavian' rite. The Scandinavian settlers in England had a wide repertoire of practices to draw on and were disposing of their dead in regions that had pre-existing traditions of complex and varied burial rites.

Even when a site can reasonably by identified as containing the graves of Scandinavian migrants or their descendants, burial rites may be indicating something other than simple personal identity or ethnicity. At Cumwhitton in Cumbria, for example, some six richly furnished inhumations, four male and two female, buried over perhaps twenty-five years in the early tenth century, have been excavated following metal-detector finds. One of the female burials was accompanied by two domed oval brooches of a form typical of the late ninth to early tenth centuries and found commonly in areas of Scandinavian settlement.

Three of the four males were buried with swords, with one of these graves also including a bridle and spurs and featuring a curved ditch to its north-east that may once have enclosed the whole grave. Male inhumations of this type, furnished with weapons and other military equipment and showing signs of significant investment in grave construction or layout, are a common feature of many purportedly Scandinavian burials of the late ninth to mid-tenth centuries.

Such burials may, however, tell us less about the ethnic identity being claimed by or for the deceased and more about social status and ambitions. As with the 'princely burials' of the early Anglo-Saxon period, these burials seem to represent an attempt to underline warrior and aristocratic status in a time of intense competition for power and influence. The ending of such distinctive burial practices by the mid-tenth century may point less to a declining emphasis on warrior status than to a more stable social order and heavier investment in other arenas of competitive display, such as the commissioning of sculpture or the foundation and endowment of churches.

The focus thus far has been primarily on material culture as a reflection of high-status identities. Increasingly, however, evidence is being found showing that the creation of an Anglo-Scandinavian identity went beyond a relatively narrow and restricted elite. Metal detectorists, in particular, have turned up increasing quantities of dress fittings, jewellery and other personal accessories employing Scandinavian decorative motifs whose form derives from Anglo-Saxon metalworking traditions or which feature motifs from both the Scandinavian and Anglo-Saxon stylistic repertoire. For example, a number of disc brooches featuring Scandinavian-derived Borre-style decoration have been recovered

6.7 Cross-shaft from St Mary's and St Helen's Church, Neston

from the Norfolk region, but whereas Scandinavian disc brooches tend to have a convex profile, these disc brooches are flat in form, like earlier and contemporary Anglo-Saxon disc brooches. Given the large numbers of such items that have been found and the fact that many are made from base metals, cultural interaction and artistic borrowing were clearly taking place across nearly all levels of society in the Danelaw.

6.8 Ivory-handled knife, used in leather-working, featuring animal interlace and Scandinavian borre-style decoration. Found at Canterbury, it was probably manufactured in the Danelaw – an example of the portability of Anglo-Scandinavian artistic culture

Genetics and the Scandinavian Settlement

Alongside well-established disciplines and data-sets, archaeogenetics and related techniques have also made a contribution to the debates surrounding Scandinavian settlement. After the collapse of the crude racial forms of anthropology of the nineteenth and early twentieth centuries, the first studies to explore Scandinavian migration through the physical characteristics of modern populations concentrated on the evidence of blood groups. The results of such studies were largely ambiguous, but more recent studies exploring a greater number of genetic systems and markers have produced more positive results.

A 1998 study of 18 genetic systems (blood groups, serum proteins and red-cell enzymes) in individuals in the East Midlands suggested that the region could be divided geographically into five separate sub-populations and that such groupings represented the impact of immigration. For example, the study found north-east Derbyshire to be genetically distinct from neighbouring regions but to have close links with populations in Denmark. Such genetic variance mapped well onto the place name evidence: Scandinavian place names survive from north-east Derbyshire but are largely absent from the north-west of that county.

A 2003 study looked at Y-chromosomes from individuals in 25 small towns and cities across Britain and Ireland. These were then compared with Y-chromosomes from Norway and Denmark, representing Viking settlement, from Schleswig-Holstein for the Anglo-Saxon contribution, and Castlerea in Ireland, representing the indigenous population of Britain and Ireland. The Danish and Norwegian input could not be easily distinguished from that from Schleswig-Holstein but such groups only made a significant genetic contribution to areas formerly in the Danelaw. Southern England appeared to be predominantly 'indigenous', suggesting that the Scandinavian settlement of the ninth and tenth centuries had a greater demographic impact than the Anglo-Saxon one.

One of the most recent genetic studies concentrated on the Wirral and west Lancashire and was carried out between 2002 and 2007. This study compared the DNA of men with surnames traditional to that region – that is, ones that had been attested in the medieval and early modern periods – with those who bore non-traditional surnames. The study found that the 'traditional' or 'medieval' population and 'modern' population were in some ways genetically distinct, though both populations were closer to each other than they were to populations in North Wales and Cheshire. Moreover, the 'medieval' population had an increased genetic affinity with Norway, suggesting that the Wirral and west Lancashire had seen significant migration from that region before the modern period.

Studies of modern populations do have the potential to shed light on historic migrations, but there remain significant difficulties in disentangling the effects of these population movements from more recent ones. Likewise, such studies may say less about initial settlement and migration and more about the subsequent success of immigrant populations. As discussed above (pp. 89–91), debates still continue about appropriate methodologies and there remains much discussion about what kinds of questions genetic studies of this type can actually answer.

6.9 Pre-Viking Anglo-Saxon sculpture from All Saints' Church, Bakewell. Though little is known of Bakewell prior to King Edward's construction of a *burh* there, the sculptural remains show it was the site of an important ecclesiastical community with links to other centres in the Peak District

The study of the skeletal remains from ninth- and tenth-century graves themselves is one way in which such problems can be minimised. Though DNA can be successfully extracted from ancient bones, it continues to be very difficult and the potential for contamination is still high. A more promising technique is stable isotope analysis. Isotopes of elements such as oxygen, lead and strontium preserved in tooth enamel

6.10 Building-type penny of King Edward the Elder, by the moneyer Wulfgar. A number of different Building-type coins were minted in Edward's name by various moneyers. The reverse design may commemorate the construction of *burhs* or the foundation of churches – this example certainly resembles a front view of a basilica-style church

can indicate where an individual grew up, as such elements are taken in with drinking water and are retained in the enamel as the teeth develop.

Only a small number of studies has so far been undertaken and on a limited number of sites, but these indicate well the potential of such work. At Repton, Derbyshire, for example, three of the burials associated with the Viking occupation of the site in the 870s were analysed. The individuals in two of these, graves G511 and G295, could have been from the west coast of Denmark, though locations in western Britain or the Low Countries are also possible. The third individual, G529, looks to have been from south-eastern Sweden – a further reminder of the cosmopolitan nature of Viking armies.

Though the question of the number of Scandinavian settlers has long dominated discussions, the surviving evidence can offer only limited answers. Yet if the question of numbers is largely intractable, it is mostly only of secondary importance. The processes by which the distinctive cultures of the Danelaw came into existence and the purposes that these identities served are bound up with a range of wider phenomena and developments, of which migration, on whatever scale, was but only one element.

The Grandchildren of Æthelwulf

On 26 October 899, King Alfred died. He was succeeded by his eldest son, Edward, known since the end of the eleventh century as 'Edward the Elder'. Given Alfred's victories over the Vikings and the reforms he initiated, it is easy to assume that the succession of his son and the subsequent dominance of his grandsons and great-grandsons were inevitable and assured by 899. Yet it remains unclear whether Edward inherited to the fullest extent the royal power wielded by his father – Edward's precise influence over 'English' Mercia is particularly difficult to determine. Moreover, in the person of his cousin, Æthelwold (c. 868–903), son of Alfred's older brother King Æthelred (d. 871), Edward faced a serious rival for the throne and one able to command considerable loyalty and support. Even Alfred himself may not have intended Edward to succeed him: some evidence suggests that he increasingly favoured Edward's son, Æthelstan, towards the end of his reign. Behind the simple story of succession recorded by the *Anglo-Saxon Chronicle* lies a far more complex situation and one that now can be only partially reconstructed.

Soon after the death of Alfred, Æthelwold, with a band of followers, seized two residences, in Wimborne and Christchurch (Dorset), only departing when Edward camped with an army at nearby Badbury Rings. Though his behaviour is presented by the *Anglo-Saxon Chronicle* as a rebellion against Edward's royal authority, Æthelwold was every bit as eligible for the throne as Edward and clearly had support in Wessex. Given that Edward had not yet been crowned when the 'rebellion' took place, Æthelwold's actions may have been a play for a throne not yet securely controlled rather than a revolt against well-established and widely accepted royal power.

The significance of the threat Æthelwold posed is underlined by his actions on fleeing Wessex: immediately he travelled to the Danish army in Northumbria, who submitted to him and accepted him as their king. Perhaps the Danes envisaged Æthelwold would make a pliable client king in Wessex, much as Ceolwulf had been in Mercia or perhaps the support Æthelwold was able to call on in Wessex was more extensive than the account of the *Anglo-Saxon Chronicle* would suggest. At the very least, Æthelwold and the Danes believed they had overlapping interests.

In the autumn of 901, Æthelwold landed with a fleet in Essex and by 903 he had persuaded the Danish army in East Anglia to break peace with Edward. Æthelwold then harried parts of Mercia and Wessex and in response Edward ravaged parts of what is now Cambridgeshire, though he did not directly engage Æthelwold in battle. When Edward left East Anglia, for reasons that are unclear, some of his army remained behind and were attacked by Æthelwold and his supporters. Though the Danish army won the battle there were severe losses on both sides. Æthelwold was killed, as was Eohric, probably king of East Anglia, and Brihtsige, probably a scion of one of the ruling dynasties of Mercia.

What is striking about Æthelwold's 'rebellion' is the level and the range of support he was able to draw on: he could call on allies from Wessex, Northumbria, East Anglia and, probably, Mercia and Essex. For a time Æthelwold had a claim to be the most powerful ruler in England. Edward's apparent reluctance to engage him in battle may have been well founded. The extent of Edward's own power in the early tenth century is difficult to reconstruct with any certainty. In his charters, Edward employed the royal style 'king of the Anglo-Saxons' or similar, suggesting he had inherited authority over 'greater' Wessex and 'English' Mercia – that is, the kingdom of the Anglo-Saxons – largely intact from his father. How far Edward's authority extended in practice remains problematic, as does his relationship with the rulers of Mercia, his brother-in-law Æthelred and sister Æthelflæd (Alfred's eldest daughter).

This Æthelred had submitted to the overlordship of King Alfred in the early 880s, a relationship that was acknowledged in the charters issued in Æthelred's name. After Alfred's death, however, Æthelred's charters and those of his wife make no reference to the consent of any overlord. Indeed, a number of them come very close to describing Æthelred and Æthelflæd as king and queen, employing such circumlocutions as 'holding, governing and defending the sole rule ['*monarchia*'] of the Mercians'.

Likewise, the late tenth-century *Chronicle* of Æthelweard describes Æthelred as the king of Mercia, while a number of near-contemporary Welsh and Irish sources describe Æthelflæd as queen.

There also survives in some versions of the *Anglo-Saxon Chronicle* a set of entries known as the *Mercian Register* or, perhaps better, the *Annals of Æthelflæd*. These provide a distinctively Mercian perspective on the events of the early tenth century, offering particular insight into Æthelflæd's actions against the Vikings and the Welsh after the death of her husband in 911. These annals present Æthelflæd as a strong ruler, pursuing her own policies and strategies against the enemies of Mercia. In this way, she stands in a long line of powerful Mercian women, with the political traditions of that kingdom arguably giving her greater scope for action than would have been possible in her native Wessex, where the status of the king's wife was considerably lower.

Yet coins produced in Mercia in this period were issued solely in the name of Edward as king, and Æthelred and Æthelflæd appear in a number of Edward's own charters as accepting his royal authority over them and Mercia. By 909 at least, Edward was also able to command the armies of both Wessex and Mercia, sending them into Northumbria to ravage and plunder. If Edward's rule over the kingdom of the Anglo-Saxons was in some way acknowledged by Æthelred and Æthelflæd, nevertheless they enjoyed considerable freedom of movement within Mercia and to outside and later observers there was clearly something regal about their power.

Other recorded activities enhance this impression. Æthelred and Æthelflæd established a new church at Gloucester – now known partly from standing ruins and from archaeological excavation – which they richly furnished and decorated. In 909 the relics of St Oswald were translated to Gloucester from Bardney (Lincolnshire) – where they had been placed by Osthryth, Oswald's niece and, perhaps significantly, a powerful Mercian queen in her own right – and both Æthelred and Æthelflæd were later buried there. It is tempting to see this new foundation at Gloucester as something like a royal mausoleum, intended to replace the one at Repton (Derbyshire) that had been destroyed by the Vikings.

In the last resort, it may be best to see English government in the early tenth century in terms of a tight-knit family arrangement. Edward's brother-in-law and, increasingly, his sister had a considerable but ultimately subordinate share of royal authority in that part of the family's realms which they managed within the distant but overall superiority of King Edward.

The Expansion of Wessex

On the death of his brother-in-law Æthelred in 911, Edward gained direct control over London, Oxford and the surrounding regions, while his sister Æthelflæd became ruler of what remained of 'English' Mercia. From this point onwards until their deaths in 918 and 924 respectively, the recorded activities of Æthelflæd and Edward are dominated by campaigns against the Vikings in East Anglia, the East Midlands and Northumbria. The *Anglo-Saxon Chronicle* details these campaigns almost exclusively in terms of the construction of *burhs* at key sites, often followed by the submission of the Viking army in that region and of the people from the area who had previously been under Viking rule.

Though the *Chronicle* focuses on these *burh*-building activities, Edward had earlier pursued other strategies against the Vikings. He made reference to peace agreements with the Vikings in his law codes, and one version of the *Anglo-Saxon Chronicle* records Edward making peace, 'from necessity', with the armies of East Anglia and Northumbria. Similarly, a number of charters dating from of the reign of his son, King Æthelstan, record how Edward and Æthelred encouraged thegns to purchase lands in Viking-controlled territories – examples are known from Bedfordshire and Derbyshire – presumably as a means of spreading influence into those regions.

By 909, Edward had adopted more aggressive strategies, sending the armies of Wessex and Mercia to ravage Northumbria, for reasons that are now unclear. Presumably in response to this aggression, in the following year the army in Northumbria ravaged parts of Mercia but was overtaken and defeated by the armies of Wessex and Mercia at Tettenhall, with the *Chronicle* recording the deaths of two Viking kings, two earls, five *holds* and many thousands of men.

A change in emphasis came in 911, when Edward constructed a *burh* at Hertford, presumably intended to check Danish advances from East Anglia and the East Midlands. The following year, Edward constructed another *burh* at Hertford, this time on the south bank of the River Lea, and one at Witham in Essex, to block raids from Colchester along the Roman road to London. The following years saw the construction of further *burhs*, with Edward pushing deeper into Danish-controlled territory and moving from a defensive to an offensive strategy.

The *Mercian Register* records similar activities by Æthelflæd, strengthening the northern and western frontiers of Mercia to combat Danish attacks from the East Midlands, Vikings active in the Irish Sea and the Wirral and, probably, the Welsh from the west. By the death of Æthelflæd in 918, all the Danish armies south of the Humber, with the exception of those based at Nottingham and perhaps that at Lincoln, had submitted either to Edward or to Æthelflæd. Edward received the submission of Essex, East Anglia, Northampton, Bedford, Huntingdon and Cambridge, while Æthelflæd had accepted the submission of Derby and Leicester. North of the Humber, the people of York had offered their submission to Æthelflæd, but she died soon after this agreement was reached and it was never put into effect. The submission of York was probably motivated as much by fear of the Scandinavian leader Ragnald, active in Ireland and northern Britain in this period, as by the threat of Mercian military expansion.

What such submissions actually meant is problematic. For the years from 910 until his death in 924 – precisely the period he was most active against the Vikings – Edward issued no charters or, at least, no authentic charters survive. If his conquests were accompanied by the redistribution among his followers of lands previously controlled by Vikings, such grants were not recorded in writing. There is also evidence that some Viking landowners managed to retain control of their estates, or at least received them back from Edward. Certain Viking leaders, such as Earl Thurferth of Northampton, even maintained something of their status after their submission. Moneyers who had produced coins in Viking-controlled *burhs* also subsequently minted coins in Edward's name, suggesting he was unwilling or unable to dismantle such governmental and administrative structures as were already in place.

The activities of Edward and Æthelflæd were clearly complementary – establishing a line of fortified centres running from the south east to the north west of England – and it is likely that their actions were in some sense coordinated. Nevertheless, some rivalry existed. The *Mercian Register* is careful to present Æthelflæd as acting independently, receiving submissions directly from Danish armies, with no indication that such actions also implied submission to Edward; indeed, he is not mentioned until 921. By contrast the 'A' version of the *Anglo-Saxon Chronicle*, probably being compiled at Winchester at this time, includes no mention of Æthelflæd until her death, with the focus exclusively on the activities of Edward.

When Æthelflæd died in 918, Edward's response was telling. He occupied Tamworth (Staffordshire), where she had died, and according to the main text of the *Anglo-Saxon*

6.11 Castlefield, Manchester. Site of the Roman fort and *vicus* of Mamucium and probably location of the Edwardian *burh*

Chronicle 'all the nation in the land of the Mercians, which had been subject to Æthelflæd, submitted to him'. Three Welsh kings, Hywel, Clydog and Idwal, also submitted to Edward on the same occasion. The *Mercian Register* describes how in the same year Ælfwynn, the daughter of Æthelred and Æthelflæd, was 'deprived of all authority in Mercia and taken into Wessex'. Whether Ælfwynn had enjoyed the same level of authority as her mother or whether someone, presumably Edward, was seeking simply to remove a potential focus of resistance, is unclear, but from 918 onwards Mercia was under the dircct authority of Edward. Had Æthelred and Æthelflæd been survived by a son it is by no means sure that Edward would have been able to establish direct rule anything like as easily as he did, and Mercian independence, albeit ultimately under West Saxon overlordship, may have continued for some time.

In the same year that he accepted the submission of 'English' Mercia, Edward received the surrender of the *burh* at Stamford (Lincolnshire) and captured the *burh* at Nottingham, ordering it to be manned by both Englishmen and Danes. The following year Edward directed his attention northwards, establishing a *burh* at Thelwall (Cheshire), close to the River Mersey, and occupying Manchester, which he repaired, perhaps restoring the Roman fort located in what is now the Castlefield district of the city. In 920 Edward travelled to Bakewell (Derbyshire) in the Peak District and ordered the construction of a *burh* there. At the same time, according to the *Anglo-Saxon Chronicle*, 'the king of the Scots and all the people of the Scots, and Ragnald, and the sons of Eadwulf and all who live in Northumbria, both English and Danish, Norsemen and other, and also the king of the Strathclyde Welsh and all the Strathclyde Welsh chose him [namely Edward] as father and lord'.

This event need not have been the simple submission presented by the *Anglo-Saxon Chronicle*. Other participants may have seen it more as the negotiation of a peace treaty, recognising and confirming a recently redrawn political map – alongside Edward's newly acquired power in Mercia and parts of Northumbria, Ragnald had gained control of York in 919. Whatever the events of 920 meant, the achievements of Edward over the course of little over two decades of rule remain impressive.

The Conquest of Northumbria

Edward died in June 924 and was succeeded in Wessex by his second son, Ælfweard. In Mercia, Edward's eldest son, Æthelstan, succeeded to the throne. It remains unclear whether Edward had planned such a division. There is no reason to assume he would necessarily have been committed to continuing a unified kingdom of Wessex and Mercia, particularly after the gains made in his reign. On the other hand, this division may represent the reassertion of local loyalties. Certainly Æthelstan had campaigned in Mercia with his uncle and aunt, Æthelred and Æthelflæd, and he may have been a more attractive candidate to the Mercians than his younger half-brother. In any event, Ælfweard died soon after his accession and Æthelstan succeeded to a newly reunited kingdom. Nevertheless, he faced some resistance in the heartlands of Wessex, particularly Winchester, and was crowned only on 4 September 925, perhaps significantly on the borders between Mercia and Wessex at Kingston-upon-Thames.

Æthelstan's conquest of Northumbria was achieved with apparent ease. In 926 he negotiated a marriage between his sister and Ragnald's successor as ruler of York, Sihtric. That the negotiations were sealed at Tamworth, deep within Æthelstan's kingdom, suggests the alliance was not one between equals, though no other details of the agreement survive. When Sihtric died the following year, Æthelstan 'succeeded to the kingdom of the Northumbrians', according to the 'D' version of the *Anglo-Saxon Chronicle*. Such may have been in the face of competition from other Scandinavian leaders. The 'E' version of the *Chronicle* records that in the same year Æthelstan 'drove out King Guthfrith', a figure who had been active in Britain and Ireland in previous years and had links to both Sihtric and Ragnald.

Subsequent to his taking of Northumbria, Æthelstan 'brought under his rule all the kings who were in this island . . . and they established peace with pledges and oaths in

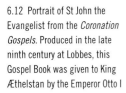

6.12 Portrait of St John the Evangelist from the *Coronation Gospels*. Produced in the late ninth century at Lobbes, this Gospel Book was given to King Æthelstan by the Emperor Otto I

the place which is called Eamont', according to the *Chronicle*. Post-Conquest sources record that Æthelstan then bestowed treasures on his followers and destroyed the Scandinavian fortifications at York.

The significance of Æthelstan's achievements in the late 920s are underscored, perhaps magnified, in a poem composed by Peter, probably a member of the community of New Minster in Winchester, attendant on the king in the north. The poem, known after its opening lines as 'Carta dirige gressus' ('Letter, direct your steps') sends a report of Æthelstan's achievements back to his queen and the rest of his court in Wessex. Æthelstan is described in it as ruling 'this England [*Saxonia*] now made whole' and as 'glorious through his deeds'.

Yet the peace brokered at Eamont did not last. In 934 Æthelstan ravaged Scotland with a land and naval force, attacking by land as far north as Kincardine and by sea Caithness. His reasons for these expeditions are uncertain, but it is surely significant that in 937 Æthelstan met in battle at *Brunanburh* – location unknown – a combined force of Scandinavians from Dublin, under Olaf Guthfrithsson, Scots under King Constantin I, and Britons from Strathclyde, under Owain. Despite the forces arrayed against him, Æthelstan won the day, a victory recorded by a poem entered into the *Anglo-Saxon Chronicle*. The poem praises the martial valour of Æthelstan and his brother, Edmund, describing the vast numbers of the enemy dead, the battlefield soaked in blood, and how the surviving Scandinavians fled by sea and returned to Dublin.

If *Brunanburh* looked at the time like a definitive victory, nevertheless West Saxon control over Northumbria was far from secure. The political situation in Northumbria made it particularly volatile. Along with Scandinavians, based in Northumbria, Ireland and elsewhere, Æthelstan had to contend with the growing power and ambitions of the kingdom of Scotland. Other powers active in Northumbria were the archbishop of York, the influential community of St Cuthbert, with extensive landholdings between the Tyne and Wear, and in the far north of Northumbria the quasi-regal rulers of Bamburgh.

If these last three may be classed as 'English' or 'Anglo-Saxon', there is no reason to assume their loyalties naturally lay with the West Saxon kings. Indeed, when Ealdred of Bamburgh was driven from his lands by Ragnald sometime around 918, he sought sanctuary and assistance from King Constantin I of Scotland; likewise the cooperation between the archbishop and various Scandinavian rulers of York has already been noted and it was to continue into the mid-tenth century. Those seeking to rule in Northumbria had to find ways to balance these factions and to ensure the loyalties of the different groups and powers. Æthelstan, for example, carefully cultivated the support of the community of St Cuthbert, visiting the saint's shrine, probably in 934, where he presented lavish gifts to the saint, including two illuminated manuscripts.

Æthelstan's brother, Edmund, succeeded him in 939 but soon lost control of Northumbria, when in 940 Olaf Guthfrithsson returned there from Ireland and was accepted as king. That same year Olaf invaded Mercia, aided in some way by Archbishop Wulfstan of York, and took control of the 'Five Boroughs'. Though Edmund laid siege to Olaf and Wulfstan at Leicester, he was unable to drive the former out and was forced

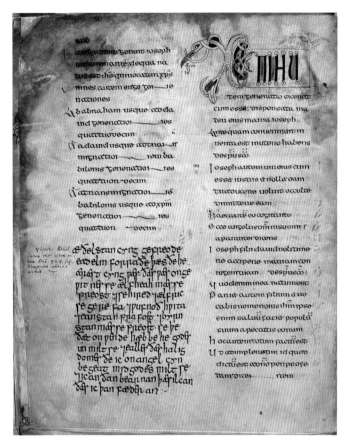

6.13 Opening of the Gospel of Matthew from an eighth-century Northumbrian Gospel Book. At the bottom of the left column, a tenth-century hand has recorded the freeing of the slave Eadhelm by King Æthelstan – the earliest surviving Anglo-Saxon manumission

to acknowledge Olaf's control of this region. In 942, after the death of Olaf, Edmund reconquered the 'Five Boroughs', a victory that was, like Æthelstan's at *Brunanburh*, celebrated in the *Anglo-Saxon Chronicle* in verse. The poem presents Edmund as redeeming the 'Danes who were previously subjected by force under the Norseman' – another reminder of the complexities of ethnic identities and loyalties in this period.

In 944 Edmund then reconquered Northumbria, driving out Olaf Sihtricsson and Ragnald Guthfrithsson, the brother of Olaf Guthfrithsson, who had established themselves there as kings. The difficulties continued under Edmund's successor, Eadred (r. 946–55). The succession of events and their chronology are difficult to determine now, but Eadred had to deal with the return of Olaf Sihtricsson to Northumbria and, more problematically, with the seizure of the Northumbrian throne by a certain Eric, probably to be identified with the Eric Bloodaxe whose legendary exploits are known from later sagas. Eadred's control of the north was finally secured only when Eric was driven out by the Northumbrians, perhaps in 954, and according to post-Conquest sources subsequently murdered by an Earl Maccus at Stainmore in Cumbria.

It is tempting to see Eadred's reign as marking the end of the process of West Saxon conquest and of the 'unification' of England. Yet the kingdom would be divided again in the late 950s, with Edmund's son Eadwig ruling south of the Thames and his younger brother Edgar reigning in Mercia and the north. Though Eadwig's death in 959 allowed Edgar to reunify the kingdom, it would again be divided along similar lines in 1016 and the 1030s. Moreover, it is clear that well-established local identities could prove enduring: when Eadric was appointed an ealdorman in 1007, his sphere of authority was described by the *Anglo-Saxon Chronicle* as 'the kingdom of the Mercians'.

Moreover, according to post-Conquest sources, in the 970s King Edgar ceded Lothian to King Kenneth II of Scotland. The extent of Anglo-Saxon authority over this region is difficult to reconstruct and Edgar might simply have been formally recognising the fact that it had passed under Scottish control. Nevertheless, Lothian had been part of the kingdom of Northumbria and its inhabitants were considered in some way English long after it was ceded to Scotland. The kingdom of England as it stood at the end of Edgar's reign has to be seen, then, as the product of a series of contingent events, as created by chance and compromise far more than by any overall royal design or strategy.

Ruling the Kingdom in the Tenth Century

Over the course of the tenth century, the descendants of Alfred came to rule what was, by Anglo-Saxon standards, a vast and diverse territory, approximating to something like modern-day England. At the same time, they asserted authority over other kings and peoples in Britain, with kings such as Æthelstan and Edgar claiming to be rulers not just of the English but also of Britain as a whole, utilising titles such as 'emperor' or 'basileus' in their charters. Whatever the validity of such claims to pan-British over-lordship, it is clear that Anglo-Saxon kings could, at times, demand extensive tribute from British client kings and compel such rulers to attend their courts and support their military campaigns.

The tenth century was also a period in which Anglo-Saxon kings formed close ties with Continental rulers, such as the Ottonian emperors of Germany. As the Carolingian Empire fractured, new ruling families emerged, and marriage alliances with the now comparatively venerable house of Wessex was one way for these arriviste dynasties to cement their claims to power. Alongside these marriage alliances, Anglo-Saxon kings were also prepared to intervene more directly in Continental affairs. Æthelstan, for example, aided his nephew Louis IV to gain the throne of West Francia and subsequently provided him with military support.

The symbolic culmination of the ambitions and pretensions of Anglo-Saxon kings in the tenth century was the coronation and anointing of King Edgar and his wife, Ælfthryth, at Bath in 973 – the reasons for the delay between 959 and 973 are unclear. In the coronation order, Edgar was presented as 'above all the kings of Britain' and the ceremony was designed to draw on the Roman and imperial associations of Bath, magnifying Edgar's power and authority. The consecration at Bath was followed by a meeting between Edgar and his sub-kings at Chester, another site redolent of the Roman past. Here he was rowed on the River Dee by these rulers, with himself as the helmsman of the boat – symbolism that needs no further elaboration.

Tenth-century kings were, then, very different from their earlier counterparts, not just in terms of territory but also in their relationships with other kings and peoples. Yet these changing circumstances made new demands on Anglo-Saxon kings. How could a king hope to control a territory that stretched from Scotland to the Channel? How could the loyalties of different regions and aristocracies be cultivated and maintained? How, above all, could a king bring about harmony – the ultimate aim of Christian kingship – in this vastly expanded realm?

Such questions became all the more pressing as the pace of West Saxon conquest slowed. Campaigns in the Danelaw had offered a means of binding together the West Saxon and Mercian nobility, giving them a common purpose and a common foe, as well as holding out the prospect of rich reward for loyal service to the king. The final conquest of Northumbria not only added considerably to the territories under the control of the West Saxon dynasty but it also brought to a close this extended period of expansive warfare. Even before this conquest, however, Anglo-Saxon kings had been seeking out new mechanisms of rule, consolidating and standardising a variety of diverse practices and institutions and attempting to impose an administrative, governmental and judicial uniformity across their kingdom. A central part of this process was the increasing desire and ability of kings to intervene in the lives of their subjects, to stamp their power and authority on society at a local level, and to claim royal control and oversight of a range of customs and practices.

The development of the governance and administration of later Anglo-Saxon England can be traced in some detail, albeit imperfectly, over the course of the tenth century. Such is facilitated by the remarkable upswing in the production of legal texts in this period. Though Alfred had revived the moribund tradition of Anglo-Saxon law codes in the late ninth century, the level of legal activity in the tenth century far outstripped anything that had gone before. The promulgation of law became, if not a routine part of royal business, then at least a frequent activity.

This change is a reflection of the very different conception of law codes in the tenth century to that of earlier periods. A wide range of different types of texts, with different audiences, aims and contexts of production, is included within the broad category of law codes. Some codes represent specific instructions or injunctions to royal agents, while others represent the response of local groups to instances of royal law-giving. Still others include statements issued by the king and his counsellors directed at the whole community, either in response to specific circumstances, such as the outbreak of plague, or to further particular royal agendas. The promulgation of law became a form of communication between the king, his advisors and his subjects. Law codes were a means of demonstrating negotiation, of building consent, of establishing shared aims and of solving problems.

The codes issued in the reign of Æthelstan offer clear insight into these processes at work. The code known as *II Æthelstan* records pronouncements made at a royal council at Grately (Hampshire), covering a wide range of issues from the administration of justice, the apprehension of thieves, the functioning of the ordeal (a test of guilt or innocence), to the minting of coins and the purchasing of livestock. Æthelstan and his counsellors subsequently issued another set of decrees at Exeter (*V Æthelstan)* after the king had learnt 'that public peace has not been kept to the extent, either of my wishes, or of the provisions laid down at Grately'. In response to the failure of the Grately decrees, Æthelstan offered, among other things, an amnesty for wrongdoers, if they would desist from their crimes. A council held at Thundersfield (Surrey, now lost) sometime later, imposed the death penalty on anyone who subsequently committed an act of theft (*IV Æthelstan*).

These codes show Æthelstan and his counsellors responding to the success or otherwise of previous pronouncements in achieving their aims, modifying their positions and changing tack where it proved necessary or likely to produce the right results. The responses of some of Æthelstan's subjects have also survived. *III Æthelstan* is presented as the response of the people of Kent, led by the nobles and bishops, to various of the king's decrees, thanking him for the measures he has enacted, agreeing specifically with certain declarations and offering statements that seem to represent their understanding of the laws that have been promulgated. The document closes with a request that Æthelstan alter the document as he sees fit and underlines the commitment of the people of Kent 'to carry out everything you are willing to order us'.

Likewise, *VI Æthelstan* opens with details of the arrangements for the preservation of order and harmony put in place by the 'Peace Guild' of London, as a supplement to Æthelstan's pronouncements at Grately, Exeter and Thundersfield. The text also includes details of subsequent changes made by Æthelstan to his own judgments, in particular a decision made at Whittlebury (Northamptonshire) to restrict the death penalty to those over the age of 15.

As well as offering insight into the negotiations and compromises that helped to shape the development of the legal framework of England, the tenth-century codes show the establishment of the key administrative and judicial institutions through which kings governed. By the end of the reign of Edgar the most important of these were the shire and the hundred (*wapentake* in the Danelaw). Both were territorial divisions, as well as a grouping of people, a meeting and a court.

The hundred was a subdivision of the shire and varied significantly in area: some hundreds could be as small as 67 square kilometres, others as large as 168 square kilometres. In some parts of the Midlands, they come close to comprising one hundred

6.14 Secklow Mound, Milton Keynes. The low mound may have been specially constructed to serve as the meeting place of the Secklow Hundred

hides but elsewhere, particularly in the south in 'Greater Wessex', hundreds could comprise only two or three settlements. The workings of the hundred are described in some detail in a text known as the *Hundred Ordinance*, dating to the reign of King Edmund or perhaps to the early years of King Edgar. According to this code, the hundred court was to meet every four weeks for the administering of justice; failure to attend resulted in a 30-shilling fine and repeated failure to abide by the judgments of the hundred court led to an escalating series of fines, with the forfeiture of all lands and a sentence of outlawry being the final punishment. The hundred was also responsible for witnessing transactions and pursuing criminals, and if a trail so followed led into another hundred the head of that hundred was to be sought out and he was to join the pursuit.

Debate continues as to the significance of the first appearance of the hundred in texts of the mid-tenth century. Elements of the *Hundred Ordinance* can certainly be found in earlier legislation. The law code of Alfred includes references to public meetings held in the presence of the royal reeve, and one of Edward's codes decrees that such meetings should be held every four weeks. There are also a number of elements common to the *Hundred Ordinance* and the organisation of the London Peace Guild as outlined in *VI Æthelstan*. The meeting sites themselves may suggest the system of hundreds was based on much older and more ancient elements. Meeting sites were most often centred on or near one or more distinctive features in the landscape – linear earthworks, mounds, stones or trees as well as communication nodes such as fords or crossroads. In some cases the features so chosen were ancient or prehistoric. Thus the Guthlaxton *Wapentake* met at a site close to the Fosse Way and the stone of Guthlac that gave the *wapentake* its name may have been a Roman milestone. Ancient or prehistoric features could have been chosen simply because they were prominent in the landscape but some at least are likely to have long been places of assembly. In some cases new mounds may have been specifically constructed – the mound that gave Secklow Hundred its name is certainly of post-Roman date.

If certain aspects that made up the hundredal system were well established by the mid-tenth century, nevertheless the *Hundred Ordinance* marks a significant turning point in the royal oversight of these elements, emphasising the role of royal regulation in determining their functioning and organisation.

Above the hundred was the shire. Territorial divisions of this name are first mentioned in the law code of King Ine of Wessex (d. c. 726). Here they represent the sphere of authority of an ealdorman (probably the same official as the 'shireman' who is also mentioned in the code) and are connected in some way with the administration of justice. In the later eighth and ninth centuries, ealdormen and shires appear in West Saxon sources almost exclusively in military contexts, with ealdormen frequently leading the forces of their shires against the Vikings. References to shires as territorial and administrative divisions continue in tenth-century law codes. Æthelstan, for example, decreed that reeves should obtain pledges from their own shires that they would obey the decrees issued at Grately and elsewhere. The role of the reeve in administering the oath of a shire here adumbrates developments in the late tenth century when the role of the ealdorman as head of the shire was largely replaced by a royal agent, the shire-reeve (whence modern English 'sheriff').

Though meetings under the authority of an ealdorman are referred to in King Alfred's law code and ealdormen were apparently fulfilling some judicial functions already in Ine's reign, it is only in King Edgar's reign that there is the first explicit reference to a shire court presided over by an ealdorman and a bishop. In a code issued at Andover, Hampshire (*III Edgar*) in the early 960s, Edgar decreed that the court should meet twice a year and that the bishop and ealdorman should expound to those present both ecclesiastical and secular law (presumably, respectively, though this is not stated).

The date at which Mercia and the Midlands were divided into shires remains much disputed, with the first references to shires outside 'greater Wessex' occurring only in the final decades of the tenth century. In these regions the shires were based on and named for particular *burhs* – Cheshire from Chester, Staffordshire from Stafford, for example. A notable absence is a shire based on Tamworth, one of the most important centres in Mercia in the eighth and ninth centuries. Indeed, the boundaries of two shires run through the town. This apparent slighting of existing power structures may be evidence that Edward the Elder was responsible for the shiring of Mercia and would make such one of the means by which he asserted his authority over the former kingdom. This would also allow the shiring of Mercia to be part of the defensive arrangements recorded in the *Burghal Hidage*, a text probably dating from Edward's reign. Nevertheless, in the absence of proof, the question remains open, and any date and context from the beginning to the end of the tenth century remain possible.

Institutions such as the hundred and the shire offered a means through which kings could rule, but their proper functioning relied on the cooperation and consent of a network of nobles, royal agents and officials. The power of Anglo-Saxon government rested to a large degree on the coming together of royal power in the centre and noble power in the localities.

The means by which kings could cultivate the loyalties of the nobility were manifold, but central to them was the court as a source of patronage and legitimacy. Lands, wealth and office could be bestowed by rulers on loyal followers, and power already held could be royally sanctioned and acknowledged. Attendances at court and on the king himself could likewise be sources of significant prestige and were rights that were carefully guarded by rulers as well as proudly displayed by recipients.

Written sources also emphasise the importance of royal feasts and celebrations as arenas in which the loyalty of leading nobles could be cultivated and a sense of shared identity and common purpose inculcated. That the king spent most of his time in the heartlands of Wessex meant that the nobility from the farthest reaches of the kingdom had to travel significant distances to take part in such activities. As well as stressing the authority of the king, such meant that the court became a place where local loyalties

6.15 Reform-type penny of King Edgar, minted by Oswulf at Derby

and identities could be broken down to some degree and where nobles from throughout the kingdom could meet. Such meetings also provided a venue for status-affirming displays, such as the ritualised crown-wearing first attested in the reign of King Edgar.

The tenth century also saw the emergence of a number of particularly powerful noble families, members of which held ealdordoms and other offices across a number of different reigns and could at times dominate the upper echelons of royal administration and government. Chief among these was the family of Æthelstan 'Half-King', whose soubriquet gives an indication of the extent of his power. He was the ealdorman of East Anglia – though his authority effectively stretched throughout the eastern Danelaw – between 932 and 957 and was succeeded in this position by his son Æthelwine (see chapter 7). His own father, Æthelfrith, had been an ealdorman in southern Mercia in the early tenth century, and for a time in the 940s Æthelstan's brothers Eadric and Æthelwold were also ealdormen. Æthelstan's importance in this period is underlined by his acting as foster-father to King Edgar and by his role in advising kings Edmund and Eadred.

Though Æthelstan's ealdordom was in the eastern Danelaw, he possessed estates in Somerset and Devon and was a patron of Glastonbury Abbey, where he ultimately retired to become a monk. Given his connections with Wessex and the possibility that he was distantly related to the West Saxon ruling dynasty, Æthelstan may have been seen by successive kings as a loyal agent in the eastern Danelaw to whom power could be safely delegated. On the other hand, Æthelstan's family may already have been prominent in the eastern Danelaw and so was carefully cultivated by the West Saxon royal dynasty. Whatever his origins, Æthelstan's landholdings, like those of other significant nobles, were scattered throughout large parts of England and so must have helped to bind together the newly expanded kingdom and may thus reflect deliberate royal policy.

The tenth century saw, then, the development of a complex and sophisticated system of governance, law and justice in England. If such a process was ongoing across the whole of the tenth century, nevertheless there are signs that the reign of Edgar marked a watershed in royal power and in the growth of the capabilities of the Anglo-Saxon state. The system of hundreds was fully formed only by the middle of the tenth century, and though shires had existed, at least in parts of the kingdom, for a considerable time, only from the reign of Edgar onwards is there clear evidence of the functioning of the shire court, both in law codes and in the records of dispute settlement.

The clearest indication of Edgar's governmental ambitions and capabilities is his reform of the coinage, late in his reign. These reforms ensured that there was a single, uniform coinage, of the same design across the whole of the English kingdom. Die production and distribution were centralised and the numbers of mints in operation were greatly expanded. Edgar's successors would introduce new designs at regular intervals – possibly every six years – accompanied by the recall and recoining of the existing issues in circulation, though such recoinings are unlikely ever to have been comprehensive. Whether Edgar had originally envisaged such periodic recoinages as part of his reform is unclear. Elements of his coinage reforms can be seen earlier – Æthelstan's

'Grately Code' legislated for a uniform coinage throughout 'Greater Wessex' – but Edgar was the first ruler to attempt and to achieve uniformity throughout England.

By the end of the reign of King Edgar, Anglo-Saxon England possessed a sophisticated machinery of rule, capable of significant and, in medieval terms, precocious administrative feats. Some scholars, most notably James Campbell, have not hesitated to label late Anglo-Saxon England a state, even a nation state. Whether such an abstraction would be meaningful or even comprehensible to an Anglo-Saxon audience is unclear. Furthermore, the surviving sources may conspire to overemphasise the abilities and achievements of late Anglo-Saxon kings. The written record is dominated by sources generated at the centre of the royal regime or by religious institutions especially close to the king and his court. Many of the surviving texts set out royal ambition rather than royal achievement or action. The local and regional diversity or the ad hoc and informal qualities of legal and governmental arrangements may be obscured by the normative nature of the sources.

Yet that claims to statehood can even be entertained for late Anglo-Saxon England is in itself significant. If the capabilities of kings such as Edgar never quite reached the heights suggested by the sources, nevertheless it is clear that the tenth century saw fundamental and far-reaching changes in the relationship between ruler and ruled.

Reform and the Church

Under the year 964, the 'A' version of the *Anglo-Saxon Chronicle* records 'Edgar drove the priests in the city [i.e. Winchester] from the Old Minster and from the New Minster, and from Chertsey and from Milton; and replaced them with monks'. Later sources describe how Edgar sent one of his agents, Wulfstan of Dalham, to enforce the expulsion at the Old Minster and that the priests there were stricken with terror. These were among the more dramatic of the religious changes that took place in the middle decades of the tenth century – the 'Benedictine Reforms' as modern scholars have labelled them. Reaching their peak in the reign of Edgar, these reforms sought to replace communities of clerks – that is, members of the clerical orders – with communities of monks, following the monastic rule attributed to St Benedict of Nursia.

The central figures of these reforms were Dunstan, archbishop of Canterbury (959–88), Æthelwold, bishop of Winchester (963–84), and Oswald, bishop of Worcester (c. 961–92) and archbishop of York (c. 971–92). They drew inspiration from Continental monasteries such as Cluny, Fleury and Gorze, while their reading of texts such as Bede's *Ecclesiastical History* encouraged them to see the early Anglo-Saxon Church as dominated by monasteries that had since declined almost to the point of extinction, with religious communities no longer staffed by monks but by clerks owning private property and even with wives and children. Such houses had, they believed, fallen under the control of laymen, who appropriated their estates and sapped their wealth.

The agenda of these reformers dominates texts produced in the later tenth and eleventh centuries, and religious life in this period is seen most often through this reforming lens. Though Æthelwold in particular wrote works describing and justi-fying the reforms that had been attempted, in practice much of what is known about the reforms comes from later writings. Central among these are the earliest biogra-phies of the three central figures – the *Life of Æthelwold* by Wulfstan 'Cantor', the *Life of Dunstan* by a cleric writing on the Continent and known only as 'B', and the *Life of Oswald*, attributable on stylistic grounds to Byrhtferth of Ramsey.

All three of these works derive from the final decade of the tenth or first decade of the eleventh centuries, a time when Anglo-Saxon England was once again under threat from Viking attacks. By this period, Edgar's reign was already being seen as a Golden Age, a moral and spiritual high point from which things had fallen away, a notion that is particularly fostered in these three texts. Unsurprisingly, the biographies tend to amplify the achievements of their subjects as well as their significance, and draw an improbably sharp divide between the pre-reform and reform periods. However, assessing the impact on England of the Benedictine Reforms is problematic, as, for want of evidence, is understanding the nature of religious life away from the institu-tions controlled by the reformers.

Such is the dominance of reform sources that it is difficult to assess the survival of any form of monastic life in Anglo-Saxon England into the tenth century. The impact of Viking attacks and Scandinavian settlement has been explored above and it seems likely that the monastic life was already in decline in the late eighth and ninth centuries. King Alfred established a small number of monasteries, most importantly Athelney (Somerset), but religious foundations in the late ninth and early tenth centuries seem to have been predominantly clerical.

6.16 Opening of the Gospel of Matthew from the *Mac Durnan Gospels*. Produced at Armagh in the late ninth or early tenth century, this Gospel Book was owned by King Æthelstan who gifted it to Christ Church Canterbury

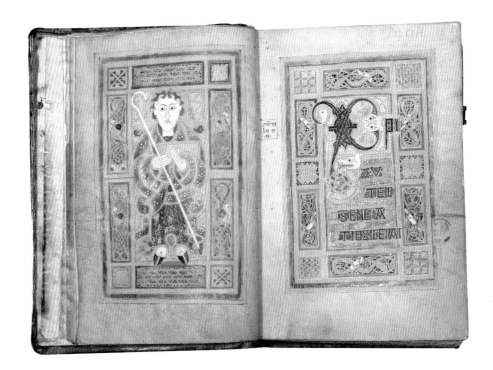

Nevertheless, Byrhtferth's statement that in the 940s there existed no monks or monasteries in England is clearly an exaggeration – indeed, this is contradicted within his own text. Not only were some communities still monastic, or at least housed some monks, but a number of leading Anglo-Saxon churchmen were emphasising their status as professed monks. Cenwald, bishop of Worcester (c. 929–58) attests a series of charters in the late 940s and early 950s as 'monachus' (monk) rather than bishop. Likewise, Oda, archbishop of Canterbury (941–58) is described by Byrhtferth as a professed monk and Ælfheah, bishop of Winchester (934–51) may have been tonsured, for his cognomen was 'the Bald'. The case for early tenth-century monasticism is therefore arguably understated.

The mid-tenth-century monastic revival and the Benedictine Reforms that it inspired originated during the reign of King Æthelstan. The king was himself particularly noted for his piety; he was an avid collector of relics and other sacred items. He also established a significant library, donating some of his books to particular religious institutions, such as the ninth-century *MacDurnan Gospels* gifted to Christ Church Canterbury. Æthelstan's court, like that of his grandfather Alfred, drew scholars from across Britain, Ireland and the Continent. Israel the Grammarian, one of the most learned figures in western Europe at this date and noted particularly for his facility with Greek, spent time in Æthelstan's household, as did a number of Irish and Breton scholars.

Anglo-Saxon churchmen, including Bishop Cenwald, are also known to have travelled extensively on the Continent and visited numerous monasteries and religious houses, particularly in what are now Germany and Switzerland. They would thus be aware of the key developments in Continental monasticism and, in particular, the beginnings of a movement to reform religious houses along Benedictine lines. The monastery at Fleury was emerging as an important centre of this reform movement, and Archbishop Oda of Canterbury certainly had links with this institution, indeed, he may even have taken monastic vows there. Oda also had other Continental contacts, for his name is recorded in the confraternity books of St Gallen and Pfäfers.

A number of texts written by Oda survive and one in particular, the *Constitutions* or *Chapters*, suggests some general concerns with the reform of religious life and observance. One canon specifically stresses the need for monks to engage in reading and continual prayer and to remain in the institutions where they first took monastic vows. Oda also played a role in the drafting of the first of King Edmund's law codes, a code that legislated on a number of ecclesiastical matters including clerical celibacy. His commissioning of a lyrical poem celebrating the translation of the relics of St Wilfrid to Canterbury c. 948 in addition confirms Oda's commitment to and commemoration of early Northumbrian monasticism.

Though Oda would clearly influence the Benedictine Reform movement in England – Oswald was his nephew – it would be wrong to see him simply as a proto-Benedictine Reformer. Though his episcopate featured many elements that would characterise the later reforms, he seems to have had a broader vision of the process, without an exclusively monastic focus, and been prepared to work within the existing religious framework.

By the 930s and 940s there were, then, several leading churchmen in England who were professed monks, reform-orientated, and linked to the Continent. These churchmen were also significant figures at court; it was probably in the royal household that Dunstan and Æthelwold first came into contact with the kinds of ideas about reform and the monastic life that would inform their later activities.

Dunstan's appointment by King Edmund as abbot of Glastonbury is usually seen as the starting point of the Benedictine Reforms proper in England, but the reality is more complex. Dunstan's connections with Glastonbury went back to his childhood; his family owned estates in the vicinity of the abbey and he had received his early religious education there. Indeed, his biographer records that the infant Dunstan had a vision of the great monastic buildings he would one day construct there.

However, the nature of the community that Dunstan took over at Glastonbury is unclear, as is how he subsequently transformed it. His biographer records that he set about managing it according to the precepts of St Benedict but stops well short of stating that Dunstan reformed the community there or imposed strict observance of the Benedictine Rule on all inmates. Certainly, Dunstan encouraged monasticism, for Æthelwold joined the Glastonbury community and was professed as a monk there, but Dunstan's activities may have been more in the spirit of Oda's reforms than later ones.

Such an interpretation may explain why Æthelwold eventually left Glastonbury. Wulfstan records that during the reign of Eadred, Æthelwold formed the desire to go abroad to receive further scriptural education and to gain 'a more perfect grounding in a monk's religious life'. At the behest of his mother, Eadgifu, Eadred prevented Æthelwold's departure and instead gave him a site at Abingdon, which had formerly been a monastery but had fallen into decay with its estates passing into secular hands. There Æthelwold founded – refounded as he saw it – a monastery, staffed by former inmates of Glastonbury and clergy from London and Winchester, and was ordained its abbot. Abingdon subsequently received extensive grants of land from King Eadred and from Eadgifu. Though Æthelwold himself had not been able to travel to the Continent to study monasticism, in the late 950s he sent Osgar, one of the Abingdon monks, to St Benedict's at Fleury in order to learn the Rule that he might teach it to his brethren when he returned.

Oswald similarly spent time at Fleury, having been sent there by his uncle, Archbishop Oda, probably in the late 940s or early 950s (perhaps overlapping with Osgar). Oswald spent a number of years at Fleury, undertaking monastic vows and, according to Byrhtferth, memorising the settings of the liturgy so that he might teach them on his return home. Dunstan also had direct contact with reformed monasticism on the Continent, albeit in less auspicious circumstances than Oswald – he was exiled from England by King Eadwig in 956. According to his biographer, Dunstan earned Eadwig's displeasure when he dragged him away from the embraces of a certain Ælfgifu, and from her mother, to return him to his coronation feast. This story probably hides a more prosaic tale of political factionalism – though Eadwig's marriage to Ælfgifu was later dissolved by Archbishop Oda on grounds of consanguinity.

Dunstan spent his exile in Flanders at the monastery of St Peter's at Ghent, which had recently been reformed along Benedictine lines by Gerhard of Brogne. When

6.17 Frontispiece to New Minster refoundation charter: King Edgar, with the Virgin Mary and St Peter, presents the charter to Christ. A lavish and lengthy document, executed in the Winchester Style and written entirely in gold ink, the charter is testament to royal investment in the Benedictine Reforms

Edgar became king of the Mercians and Northumbrians, he summoned Dunstan back and appointed him bishop of Worcester and then London (the chronology here is obscure), seemingly to hold the two sees in plurality. By the end of 959, Edgar had appointed Dunstan archbishop of Canterbury.

The reign of Edgar was the high point of the Benedictine Reform movement, and there seems little doubt that the king was personally committed to the ideals espoused by the reformers and so occupies a central place in the texts produced by them. Alongside Dunstan at Canterbury, Oswald was appointed to the bishopric of Worcester in 961 and to the archiepiscopal see of York in 971, holding them in plurality, and Æthelwold was appointed to the bishopric of Winchester in 963. Edgar's reign witnessed the establishment of a number of monasteries and the reform of some existing communities along Benedictine lines. Æthelwold founded or refounded a

6.20 Walrus ivory carving of the baptism of Christ, executed in the Winchester Style in the late tenth or early eleventh century. Cut down from a larger panel, the carving may originally have formed part of the cover of a book

The witness lists to these leases show no dramatic changes of personnel, such as would have accompanied an expulsion like that at the New Minster, and although some of the witnesses are described as monks, clerics were clearly still part of the cathedral community. Moreover, at least one of these leases is to a monk, an indication that the ideal of communal property had not been fully introduced at Worcester. From the 970s onwards there is, however, an apparent preference for those who had taken monastic vows to occupy key positions, such as dean, within the community. Rather than expelling clerks from the cathedral and replacing them with monks, Oswald instead constructed a separate monastic foundation, St Mary's, within the cathedral precincts. For Canterbury, the evidence is less straightforward, but a gradualist approach by Dunstan seems most likely; the see was wholly monastic by the early eleventh century.

The different approaches of Dunstan and Oswald to the staffing of their sees may be the result of their direct experiences of the Continental Reform movement. Here, the reorganisation of religious institutions along Benedictine lines did not encompass cathedrals and episcopal churches but was instead restricted to monasteries. By contrast, though Æthelwold had, through Osgar and others, contact with religious developments on the Continent, he may have drawn his inspiration more directly from the Anglo-Saxon past. A number of documents written by Æthelwold show a familiarity with Bede's *Ecclesiastical History*, and he may have taken from this text the model of a Church ruled by monk-bishops (such as Augustine, Aidan or Cuthbert), with sees staffed by monks possessing no personal property.

By the mid-970s there was a significant number of religious institutions following a way of life based on the Rule of St Benedict. Yet the Rule could not on its own offer a complete and comprehensive guide to monastic life, not least because it was originally devised for a large, self-sufficient rural monastery in Italy. As a consequence, the different reformed houses in England were following slightly divergent ways of life, all based on the Rule but interpreting and supplementing it in different ways. Such a situation ran counter to the ideal of uniform observance that underlay the reform movement, and in the early 970s King Edgar summoned a council at Winchester to promulgate a customary (or 'consuetudinary') that would lay out the definitive way of life to be observed by all English houses.

The text issued by this council, known as the *Regularis concordia*, was probably composed by Æthelwold and presented a detailed statement of the aims of the reformers and their vision for religious life in Anglo-Saxon England. It begins by setting out how monasteries had been brought low by neglect and how Edgar sought to restore them to their former state, by driving out 'the negligent clerks with their abominations'. It then explains that members of the council had sought advice from Continental houses – Fleury and St Peter's at Ghent are named specifically – and put together the customary that makes up the bulk of the *Regularis concordia*.

Though the document makes clear the English Reformers' debt to Continental monasticism and, indeed, the *Regularis* resembles in many respects the earliest customary from Fleury, the text nevertheless reflects a distinctively Anglo-Saxon vision of monastic reform. It places royal authority at the centre of the reform process, with the king as patron, protector and overseer of monasteries, whilst the queen fulfilled a similar role for nunneries. Anglo-Saxon texts, including Bede's letter to Bishop Ecgberht of York, were drawn on by the author of the *Regularis*, and such features as the obligation for monasteries to pray for the king can be paralleled in earlier English sources, for example in the canons of the 747 council of *Clovesho*.

Works such as the *Regularis concordia* presented the Benedictine Reforms as initiating fundamental changes in the nature of religious life in Anglo-Saxon England, but it is hard to assess their actual impact. In some respects, the reforms were clearly of immense significance. The more important of the reformed monasteries would become the richest religious institutions in late Anglo-Saxon England and then retain that status even after the Norman Conquest.

The reforms also led to fundamental changes in the urban centres where a number of the foundations were based. At Winchester, for example, the necessity of enclosing the New and Old Minsters and Nunnaminster required the construction of a number of walls or hedges as well as the diverting of streams to provide monastic water supplies. By the end of the tenth century, the construction of monastic precincts had effectively

6.21 Cast of a late tenth-century Winchester Style sculpture of an angel from St Lawrence's Church, Bradford-on-Avon. One of a pair of such angels, this was originally probably part of a larger Crucifixion scene

shut off the south-east part of Winchester from the laity and a number of secular dwellings had been demolished to facilitate the enclosures.

In the cultural sphere, the Benedictine Reforms clearly had a long-lasting and significant effect. Æthelwold, in particular, promoted the use of the vernacular as a means of educating those lacking proficiency in Latin, and his school at Winchester was probably responsible for establishing a standardised form of Old English, with a specific and restricted vocabulary. Such was the success of Æthelwold's activities that the bulk of the surviving Old English literature was produced by disciples of the Benedictine Reformers and was written in this standard Old English or variants thereof.

The reform movement also championed a form of Latin known as the Hermeneutic – that is, glossary-derived – Style. Practitioners of this style employed a self-consciously erudite and obscure vocabulary, using Greek or Greek-derived words and coining neologisms, alongside a complex and sometimes convoluted syntax and sentence structure. This 'Hermeneutic Style' was to dominate English Latin composition throughout the late tenth and eleventh centuries.

The reformed houses cultivated a particular form of manuscript decoration and illumination, the so-called Winchester Style. This drew extensively on earlier

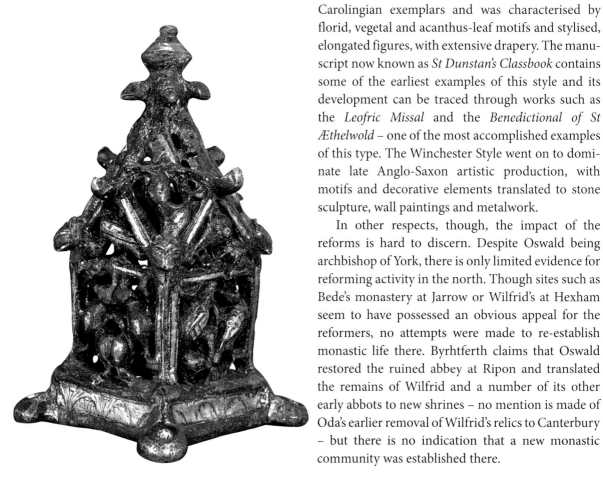

6.22 Mid-tenth-century copper alloy censer cover found in Canterbury. Inlaid with silver and niello, this features acanthus leaf decoration and bird and animal figures typical of early Winchester Style

Carolingian exemplars and was characterised by florid, vegetal and acanthus-leaf motifs and stylised, elongated figures, with extensive drapery. The manuscript now known as *St Dunstan's Classbook* contains some of the earliest examples of this style and its development can be traced through works such as the *Leofric Missal* and the *Benedictional of St Æthelwold* – one of the most accomplished examples of this type. The Winchester Style went on to dominate late Anglo-Saxon artistic production, with motifs and decorative elements translated to stone sculpture, wall paintings and metalwork.

In other respects, though, the impact of the reforms is hard to discern. Despite Oswald being archbishop of York, there is only limited evidence for reforming activity in the north. Though sites such as Bede's monastery at Jarrow or Wilfrid's at Hexham seem to have possessed an obvious appeal for the reformers, no attempts were made to re-establish monastic life there. Byrhtferth claims that Oswald restored the ruined abbey at Ripon and translated the remains of Wilfrid and a number of its other early abbots to new shrines – no mention is made of Oda's earlier removal of Wilfrid's relics to Canterbury – but there is no indication that a new monastic community was established there.

This lack of reforming activity in the north may be an indication of how tightly the reforms were bound up with royal power. The reformers needed the backing of Edgar to make progress, particularly if they wished to expel secular clergy, and his power may simply have been too tenuous to support such activities in the north. Indeed, the Benedictine Reforms as a whole seem to have been court-centred; the leading players were important members of successive royal regimes, and the most intensive reforming activities were focused on the city of Winchester.

Important though the Benedictine Reforms undoubtedly were, other processes underway in the tenth century would eventually prove of greater long-term significance and would ultimately impact upon a far larger segment of society. Both written and archaeological evidence confirm that the tenth and eleventh centuries were a period of extensive church building. Though such activities did include the building or remodelling of large churches and monasteries, such as Christ Church Canterbury or Westminster Abbey (see chapter 8), it was the founding of small, local churches by minor nobles and landholders that made up the majority of these undertakings. The fragmentation of larger estates into small holdings created a class of lesser landowners for whom the foundation and construction of a church on their estate was a key means by which their status could be displayed and confirmed. Such local churches would eventually form the basis of the medieval parochial system, and over the course of the tenth and eleventh centuries these churches increasingly impinged on the rights and obligations of existing churches, modifying the ways in which pastoral care was provided. Pre-Viking sources make references to a range of payments, dues and tithes owed by the laity to the Church for the provision of pastoral care and, as was the case in other areas, these apparently inchoate and local arrangements were standardised through royal law codes over the course of the tenth century.

6.23 Tenth-century reliquary cross from Winchester. Behind the walrus ivory carving of Christ a small recess in the wood originally housed the relic – a human finger, probably female. The cross affords precious insight into the lavish fittings and furnishings of Late Anglo-Saxon churches

Until the reign of Edgar there is no clear indication of to whom or to what institution these dues were to be paid. Æthelstan, for example, simply decreed that church dues and payments for the souls of the dead (probably to be understood as funeral fees) were to be rendered 'at the places to which they are legally due'. In Edgar's law code issued at Andover, however, tithes are ordered to be paid 'to the old churches to which obedience is due' unless a nobleman holds an estate by bookland that has a church on it with a graveyard, in which case he is to pay a third-part of his tithes to that church. If the church does not have a graveyard, the nobleman is to pay for it from the nine-tenths of his income that remain, presumably with the full tithe going to the old church.

6.24 St James' Church,
Selham, West Sussex. A small,
local church of the type that
flourished in the later
Anglo-Saxon period. The nave
and chancel are eleventh-
century, the chapel on the
north side probably
fourteenth-century

By the first decades of the eleventh century, a more complex hierarchy of churches had developed, with King Æthelred II legislating for chief minsters, smaller minsters, even smaller minsters and field churches. The 'old church' of Edgar's code, as well as the chief minsters and smaller minsters of Æthelred's code, are probably those institutions that had originally been pre-Viking monasteries tasked with providing pastoral care to large, extensive 'parishes'. These 'mother parishes' would endure well beyond the Norman Conquest, retaining some of their former rights and importance, but it is clear already from Edgar's code, and perhaps is implied by Æthelstan's, that newly established local churches were increasingly meeting the pastoral needs of the laity. The owners and patrons of these churches, not unreasonably, were seeking to support them and their clergy by diverting tithes and other dues away from the old churches and chief minsters to the newer foundations.

As with the system of hundreds and shires that was established by Edgar's reign, this newer model of pastoral provision, extended and formalised over time, would provide the pattern not just for the Middle Ages but also for the early modern and modern periods. The legacy of the tenth century was a set of surprisingly long-enduring institutions that would shape significantly the subsequent development and history of England. The eleventh century would, however, see the political system of Anglo-Saxon England stretched to breaking point, as the return of the Vikings and internal dispute and division led to the temporary and then permanent eclipse of the house of Wessex.

VILLAGE AND OPEN FIELD

NICHOLAS J. HIGHAM

Across the later nineteenth and early twentieth centuries scholars believed that Anglo-Saxon settlers brought with them the habits of living in villages and cultivating land in open fields – large tracts of arable land without internal divisions which were subject to rotation, ploughed in long, intermingled strips and managed communally. An early study, published in 1915, distinguished six regional field types and explained them on grounds of ethnicity, with 'Celtic' town-fields in the north and west at one extreme contrasting with the 'Midland System' in what is now generally termed the 'central province', from Dorset and Hampshire through the East Midlands northwards, which best exemplified the agricultural practice of Germanic settlers. Here, open fields eventually included most of the lands of a township or manor. Laxton (Nottinghamshire) offers a good example, where the remnants of open fields still operate around a village occupied from the late Anglo-Saxon period.

However, recognition of the open field system throughout Britain, both in 'Celtic' and 'Anglo-Saxon' areas, undermined the assumption that it was linked to Germanic settlement. The 'Midland System' does not correspond well with archaeological evidence for early Anglo-Saxon material culture, which is concentrated in the Upper Thames Valley, East Anglia, Lincolnshire and Kent rather than the 'central province'. Scholars have therefore sought alternative explanations of open fields, arguing that they derive from one or a combination of the following: the sharing of plough-teams by peasant farmers (co-aration); the parcelling out of collectively cleared land (assarting); the subdivision of peasant farms as a result of partible inheritance; primitive shareholding by villagers enjoying common rights, and/or risk aversion encouraging each farmer to spread his arable land across different types of ground. Discussion long focused on the Anglo-Saxon period, but in the 1960s the 'Midland System' was thought a late stage of development, emerging under the pressure of rising population and growing shortages of grazing in the twelfth and thirteenth centuries.

In important respects this case was persuasive. Rising population pushed up grain prices, so encouraged the expansion of cultivation, requiring more ploughs so more oxen, which in turn required larger herds, so more animal feed, at the same time as more land was coming under the plough. It is easy to envisage reorganisation as arable expanded, with close management of meadow and fallow land used for pasture,

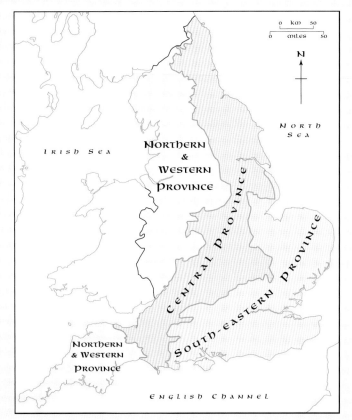

6a.1 The division of England into three landscape provinces. The central province was characterised in the Middle Ages by open fields, nucleated villages and a scarcity of woodland; the other two provinces had less systematic field systems, more dispersed settlement and more woodland

combined with maximal use of plough teams to minimise their number. Strict rotation of the arable was a logical solution to these problems.

However, the assumption that the adoption of a more tightly managed open-field system was driven by rising population is at odds with the distribution of population in Domesday Book, since areas with the highest densities – Sussex and parts of East Anglia – did not use the 'Midland System'. Clearly, an open-field system could not occur without sufficient peasant farmers, but population does not seem to have been the principal driver for its adoption. Indeed, many manors with open fields were 'closed' comparatively early, so the number of shares was fixed, although subdivision of shares might still occur. There is also evidence that suggests an early date: 'shared' lands within collectively maintained boundaries occur in Ine's law code, c. 690, indicating that some at least of the characteristics of open fields were already then in operation in Wessex; increasingly, landscape archaeologists believe that open fields existed at least from the eighth century onwards.

The development of ploughing technology has a bearing on these issues. Although a heavy plough was available, the standard plough in Roman Britain was probably an ard or scratch plough pulled by just two oxen. Concentration of the rural population onto light, well-drained sands and gravels in the fifth and sixth centuries meant that cultivation was focused on easily ploughed land well suited to the ard. By 1066, however, the standard plough was the heavy, mould-board type, capable of turning a furrow and forming ridges. This plough was used to cultivate a wider variety of soils than the ard, including extensive clay lands. It could also plough far more land per year and far more than any one peasant would have needed – 120 acres (48 hectares) is often quoted. In contrast, most Domesday villeins had less than 60 acres (24 hectares, or 2 virgates) and most bordars and cottars just an acre or two. To give an example, on the 12 ploughlands of the royal estate of Keyston (Huntingdonshire), 2 ploughs cultivated the demesne lands of the king while 24 villeins and 8 bordars had another 12 ploughs, suggesting that these 32 tenants shared approximately 1,200 acres between them at an average of less than 40 acres.

A switch occurred, therefore, during the Anglo-Saxon period from a plough suited to the needs of individual farmers to one best used collaboratively with up to eight farmers combining their oxen and cultivating more productive, heavier soils. This switch seems to have occurred not only in areas where large-scale open fields were dominant but elsewhere as well. The advantages of the new technology were consider-

6a.2 Open field still in cultivation at Laxton (Nottinghamshire). Large open fields without internal divisions but with parallel ridges (here ploughed out) were characteristic particularly of the central province

able: the mould-board plough could work a bigger area, cultivate heavier land, and do so with just one ox for every 15 acres of arable. The new arrangements might even reduce the number of cattle the manor needed, so also the area of pasture and hay meadows set aside from cultivation, if peasants with less than 30 acres of arable had hitherto kept their own plough teams.

Adoption of the mould-board plough therefore enabled communities to cultivate a higher proportion of the land available and maximise the area under cereals. There was, however, a need to use it efficiently, establish holdings of the right size, reorganise farms into strips spread evenly across several fields, and impose a system of crop rotation capable of delivering fallow. The presence on some Domesday manors of far more ploughs than ploughlands suggests that these economies were not always realised: at Gunthorpe (Nottinghamshire) land for 6 ploughs supported 4 demesne ploughs and a further 16 ploughs in the hands of the 47 manorial tenants, so a total of 20 ploughs where only 6 were needed.

The shift in plough technology had some potential, therefore, to encourage the adoption of open fields and concentrate farmers so as to facilitate cooperation. The great problem, though, is that the change from one technology to another is not closely dated. All the ploughshares so far identified come from later Anglo-Saxon deposits and have been classified as ards. The impression that adoption of the heavy plough was therefore late has never satisfied archaeologists, who have recognised both nucleation of settlement and the reorganisation of fields occurring in many areas rather earlier. The recent identification of a coulter blade, that is, the upright knife used to cut the sod prior to its being turned by the share and mouldboard, in a seventh-century context at Lyminge in Kent, is therefore significant. This indicates that the new technology was available already in the age of Bede, though ards may certainly have remained in use in some areas

6a.3 Coulter blade for a heavy plough from excavations of a seventh-century monastic site at Lyminge (Kent)

well into the ninth and tenth centuries. The heavy wheeled plough begins to feature in manuscript illustrations from the eleventh century, and plough ridges have been identified beneath late eleventh- and twelfth-century structures, as at Hen Domen castle (Powys), but not under any of the dykes of the early to mid-Anglo-Saxon periods.

Open fields and villages are closely linked, and it was long assumed that neither occurred without the other. Excavations at Wharram Percy (North Yorkshire) from the 1950s onwards revealed that the village did not emerge in a clearly recognisable form until the twelfth century, but the settlement had a long and complex history prior to village formation and the building of a church there marks it as a place of local significance in the Viking Age. Late settlement nucleation has been confirmed by excavation at several other northern sites, such as Thrislington (County Durham), but recent work in Northamptonshire suggests that village formation was already occurring there by the first half of the ninth century. At this stage some pre-existing settlements were abandoned and ploughed over while others expanded; families presumably moved from failing sites to the more successful ones. Clearly, the pace of change varied. Areas of old woodland, wetland and heath were resistant to settlement nucleation even in areas such as the East Midlands where village formation took place comparatively early: recent research on the Whittlewood area (Northamptonshire) reveals that nucleation began in this old woodland region only comparatively late, resulting in a mix of irregular villages, hamlets and isolated farms becoming established from the later Anglo-Saxon period onwards.

A geometric layout is a common feature of villages in some areas of England, encouraging the assumption that they were planned, to an extent at least. Many of those exhibiting this regularity lie in regions where village formation was compara-

6a.4 The heavy plough in use. Redrawn from the illustration for December in an eleventh-century calendar

tively late, as the playing-card-shaped villages of Appleton-le-Moors (North Yorkshire) or Milburn (Cumbria), neither of which is likely to pre-date Norman reorganisation of these areas. Similar developments occurred in the Marcher lordship of Chepstow, for example, and Pembrokeshire, where English colonists settled in newly laid-out villages with small open fields.

By the twelfth century, therefore, regular villages and open fields had become tools of Anglo-Norman colonisation, but it is unclear how much earlier they occurred. In lowland England village streets often have very regular property divisions at right angles, with back lanes dividing the village tofts from open fields. Such need not, however, be planned; recent research in Northamptonshire suggests that it may have resulted from the expansion of settlement onto the ends of open-field strips, which encouraged regularity in the layout. Much village development was, however, broadly contemporary with the ninth- and tenth-century revival of towns, where clear external boundaries, geometric road systems and comparatively standardised tenements were commonplace, so the thinking underlying the new towns may have influenced village formation. Emulation was probably equally a factor in the spread of villages, with the adoption elsewhere of settlement types common in old arable areas. Longer-distance transfers of the village as a settlement type also occurred: the monks of Glastonbury seem to have imported nucleated settlement and open fields to their estates in Somerset, although irregularities in the layout of even neighbouring villages imply that much of the detail was left to local communities.

Much of the countryside of late Anglo-Saxon England was clearly not dominated by either villages or open fields. For example, Devon, Essex and Cheshire were characterised by dispersed farms and hamlets, with few if any large open fields, and many Domesday manors were little more than one large farm. Tom Williamson has

6a.5 Milburn, Cumbria. A green village of the eleventh- to twelfth-century village

argued that the development of open fields was conditioned primarily by environmental factors. Neither villages nor open fields were well developed in areas with extensive woodland in the eleventh century, such as the Lower Thames Basin and large parts of the West Midlands. The 'central province' is characterised by the virtual absence of both woodland place names and Domesday woodland. The basic patterning of the English landscape was clearly already ancient when Domesday Book was compiled, and pre-existing landscapes and social structures certainly influenced the spread of villages and open fields.

There is, therefore, considerable but not uniform evidence of landscape change in the mid–late Anglo-Saxon period. In some areas village formation occurred in combination with the inception of open fields. In the Viking Age numerous large estates were divided to provide holdings for warriors and small estates were increasingly being leased out. These resulting manors were often organised in new ways utilising an open-field economy. Pressure to produce a greater surplus encouraged the expansion of arable production and a spread of cultivation onto new lands. Nucleation of settlement was part and parcel of these processes, although not always synchronous, and was adopted wholeheartedly in some areas, partially in others, but elsewhere barely at all. Alongside, adoption of the mould-board plough enabled the spread of cultivation onto heavier land and encouraged the reorganisation of arable land into long strips which reduced the number of times the team had to be turned in ploughing a specific area. In some sense open-field cultivation had begun by the start of the eighth century but spread more widely across the later Anglo-Saxon period, appearing in different forms and in association with varying settlement patterns. While it is wrong today to suppose that the late Anglo-Saxon landscape was uniformly dominated by open fields and villages, both were important elements of the rural scene and integral to the way that the countryside worked in many parts of England.

VIKING AGE HOARDS

MARTIN J. RYAN

On the evening of 15th May last, a number of workmen, engaged in repairing the southern embankment of the river Ribble, near Cuerdale Hall, and about three miles from Preston, were agreeably surprised by the discovery of a hidden treasure, which had for many centuries lain inhumed in that delightful and secluded vale, within three feet of the surface of the pasture, and about thirty yards from the edge of the river.

So Joseph Kenyon of Preston reported to the *Chronicle* of the Royal Numismatic Society in June of 1840 the discovery of a cache of over 8,500 items of silver, including some 7,500 coins, buried in a lead chest near the banks of the River Ribble in Lancashire. The Cuerdale Hoard, as it is now known, was deposited early in the tenth century and represents one of the largest discoveries of precious metals in Britain. Such hoards have been unearthed from across the whole of the Anglo-Saxon period, with collections stretching from the Patching Hoard (West Sussex), dating to the middle of the fifth century and perhaps buried in response to the threat of Anglo-Saxon attacks, to the Sedlescombe Hoard (East Sussex), dating to around 1066 and one of a number of hoards in Sussex possibly buried in the run-up to, or in the immediate aftermath of, the Battle of Hastings.

Despite this broad chronological range, the deposition of hoards peaked at times of particular upheaval or disruption, such as 1066 or the later ninth to early tenth centuries. In such times some individuals or groups buried their wealth, probably to protect it from the attentions of raiding bands or invading armies (or, perhaps, to avoid it being requisitioned to counter the threat posed by such groups). Raiding bands and armies also in their turn deposited wealth and plunder for safe keeping and to avoid the need to carry it with them: treasure could be heavy – the Cuerdale Hoard weighs some 40 kilograms.

In most cases wealth so buried must have been recovered by its owner or owners sometime after deposition, so the hoards known from the Anglo-Saxon period probably represent only a fraction of what was originally committed to the ground. The *Anglo-Saxon Chronicle* even claimed that when the Romans left Britain 'they collected all the treasures which were in Britain, and hid some in the ground, so that none could

Hoard

Flusco Pike

Silverdale

Harrogate

Cuerdale

Huxley

Patching   Sedlescombe

6b.1 Location of hoards
mentioned in the text

find them afterwards'. Such may have been inspired by the chance discovery of Roman hoards, and we should remember that Roman materials continued to be reused throughout the Anglo-Saxon period. It may also, however, indicate that the burying of hoards was considered a normal strategy in the late ninth century, when this passage of the *Chronicle* was probably written, and might therefore then have been expected to have characterised the Roman departure from Britain.

One particular cluster of hoards occurs in the early decades of the tenth century in Northumbria and northern Mercia – nearly twenty have so far been discovered, with one of the most recent, the Silverdale Hoard (Lancashire), found in the autumn of 2011. The composition of these hoards is typical of known Viking hoards found elsewhere in Britain, Ireland and the Continent; they represent precious evidence for the movements of Scandinavians active in northern England during the momentous but poorly documented period of West Saxon conquest of central and northern England.

The largest of this group of hoards, that discovered near Cuerdale, has already been noted. Alongside the 7,500 coins, the majority of which were minted in England under Viking authority, there was over 35 kilograms of bullion, in the form of ingots and hack silver, that is jewellery and other items of precious metal that have been hacked or broken up into smaller pieces, intended either to be melted down or to have served as bullion. The coins indicate that the hoard was deposited in the first few years of the tenth century, arguably between c. 905 and 910, while analysis of the hack silver suggests provenances from the Baltic and Scandinavia to Scotland and Ireland (both native and Viking), with some material from Anglo-Saxon England and Carolingian Francia as well.

The dating of the hoard and its location on one of the main routes of communication between York and the Irish Sea point to a connection with the Vikings expelled from Dublin in 902 who were subsequently involved in struggles for the control of York and seem to have settled areas of the Wirral and Lancashire. The presence of a large number of apparently freshly minted coins from York in the hoard may suggest it was assembled in that city and was perhaps intended to pay or to recruit forces for an attempt to reconquer Dublin.

The Vale of York Hoard, discovered near Harrogate (North Yorkshire) in 2007, has a composition similar to the Cuerdale Hoard, although it is considerably smaller in size. Some 617 coins, mostly minted in England, one gold and five silver arm-rings and over sixty pieces of hack silver and ingots make up the hoard, along with a silver-gilt cup, approximately 9 centimetres high, adorned with roundels, inscribed animals, and vine-scroll and acanthus-leaf decoration, that contained the bulk of the hoard. The cup was probably produced in the mid-ninth century in Carolingian Francia and has very

6b.2 Items from the Cuerdale Hoard

close affinities with a cup found as part of the eleventh-century Halton Moor Hoard (West Yorkshire), suggesting that such items could be in circulation for centuries.

The coins in the Vale of York Hoard include 106 issued in the name of King Æthelstan, one of which gives his title as 'King of All Britain', a style he adopted c. 927. Given that this style then became common on his coinage, the presence of only one coin with such a style suggests the hoard was probably deposited soon after 927. Another significant coin in the hoard was an anonymous issue of the 'Sword' type, a type minted in the name of a number of Viking rulers in Northumbria and the Midlands in the early tenth century. Though lacking the name of any ruler, this coin bore the mint name 'Rorivascastr', not otherwise attested but probably to be identified with Rocester in Staffordshire.

Not all hoards contain coins. The Huxley Hoard, discovered in 2004 near Huxley in Cheshire, comprises some 20 silver broad-band arm-rings, a number with punched decorations, a twisted silver rod arm-ring and a single silver ingot, all probably buried in a lead container. The arm-rings are of a type found throughout Ireland and Britain (though here concentrated in north Wales and north-west England) and although ultimately based on Scandinavian prototypes were probably produced in Ireland. Given that the broad-band arm-rings had been flattened, and were perhaps never fully finished, and the rod arm-ring had been twisted, they were presumably included in the hoard as bullion rather than jewellery to be worn, gifted or exchanged. The absence of coins makes determining the period of deposition difficult, but the hoard's location near the River Gowy, which flows into the Mersey estuary, may point to a connection

with the settlement of Dublin Vikings in north-west England in the early tenth century. Whether those who buried the Huxley Hoard had any links with those who buried the Cuerdale Hoard is unknowable, but the very different composition of the two deposits may indicate that such a connection is unlikely.

Discovered in 1989, the Flusco Pike Hoard (Cumbria), like the Huxley Hoard, contained no coinage but comprised the remains of at least five silver brooches, two of which were 'thistle-brooches' and three Irish bossed penannular brooches. To these items can probably be added two other thistle-brooches found in the same area in the eighteenth and nineteenth centuries. On stylistic grounds, the hoard can be dated to the 920s–930s; given the general lack of significant damage to the brooches, it was probably the burial of intact jewellery rather than bullion. The historical context of the deposition is unclear but, given the location, it is tempting to link it in some way to the submissions received by King Æthelstan by the River Eamont, near Penrith, in 927.

These hoards, and others like them, are significant for a number of reasons. Firstly, and most simply, they offer clear confirmation of the substantial levels of moveable wealth that could be accrued by individuals and groups, as indicated by the written sources. One of the colloquies of the eleventh-century monk Ælfric Bata, for example, includes a book buyer counting out some 360 coins to pay for the book he is purchasing, while the coins and precious metals bequeathed by King Eadred in his will ran into the thousands of pounds (by weight). Secondly, the quality and craftsmanship of some of the pieces included are reminders of the skills and capabilities of goldsmiths and silversmiths in the Early Middle Ages. Thirdly, the range of material included in the hoards provides an indication of the cultural contacts of the Vikings. As well as coins from the Atlantic Archipelago, the Cuerdale Hoard included coins from the Islamic world, from

6b.4 Thistle brooches from Flusco Pike (Penrith)

Francia and from Byzantium, with a similar range of coins represented in the Vale of York Hoard.

Fourthly, the hoards shed light on the nature of the economy in the Viking-controlled territories in England. The presence of large numbers of coins alongside ingots, hack silver and jewellery points to a dual economy in which both bullion and regulated coinage were in use alongside one another, as the frequent discovery of weights and scales confirms. Likewise, the presence of foreign coins – those produced outside Northumbria – implies that Viking rulers in the north were less able or less inclined to control the circulation of coinage than their Anglo-Saxon counterparts to the south.

Fifthly, hoards are a vitally important source for numismatists. Most obviously, the hoards provide a large sample of coinage and a number of rare or unique types is known only from such contexts – such as the coin minted at Rocester from the Vale of York Hoard or the unique coin from the Silverdale Hoard in the name of King Harthacnut, otherwise unknown unless he is the Harthacnut who was the father of King Guthred mentioned in the tenth-century *History of St Cuthbert*. That hoards can be considered to contain a sample, however imperfect, of coins in circulation together also offers one important means of establishing a relative chronology of coin production. A coin of King Æthelstan, for example, found in hoards alongside coins of his predecessors King Edward the Elder and King Alfred is likely to be an earlier issue than a coin of Æthelstan found together with coins of his successors King Edmund and

6b.5 The Silverdale Hoard

King Eadred. The high number of coins deposited in hoards likewise facilitates more complex methods of dating, such as the establishment of die-linkages between coins. The obverse and reverse dies used to strike a coin tended to wear out at different rates and this, coupled with accidental breakages or other damage, meant that dies were not always replaced in pairs. One die might thus serve as the obverse for two or more reverse dies, again, allowing for a relative chronology of production to be established.

The Old English poem *Beowulf* ends with the burial of treasure recovered from a dragon's lair. The poet describes the treasure as 'gold under ground, where it still lies, useless to men as it ever was'. As should be clear, if hoards from the Anglo-Saxon period are not quite as eloquent witnesses as the *Beowulf* poet, they are nevertheless far from useless to men; indeed, they remain sources of vital importance. Moreover, while another *Beowulf* is most unlikely to be discovered, as recent events have shown more hoards certainly await discovery and each has the potential, in small ways and in large, to reshape our understanding of the Anglo-Saxon past.

The Age of Æthelred

MARTIN J. RYAN

> It is written and was long ago prophesied, 'after a thousand years will Satan be unbound'. A thousand years and more is now gone since Christ was among men in a human family, and Satan's bonds are now indeed slipped, and Antichrist's time is now close at hand. . . . And people will contend and dispute among themselves. There will also break out far and wide dispute and damage, envy and enmity and rapine of robbers, hostility and hunger, burning and bloodshed and distressing disturbances, disease and death, and many misfortunes.

So, shortly after the year 1000, wrote the homilist and statesman Wulfstan. The approach of the millennium had given renewed vigour to the eschatological anxieties that suffused much Christian literature and if the millennium had passed and gone, nevertheless Wulfstan, like other writers of the time, continued to scrutinise current events relentlessly for signs of the End of Days. Wulfstan could be forgiven for thinking he saw them in his own society. Already by this time, the reign of King Edgar was being written of as the culmination of Anglo-Saxon kingship, the high point from which England had fallen, grievously. Edgar's rule had become, and to some extent remains, a byword for peace and prosperity, hence his popular name, 'Edgar the Peaceable'.

In sharp contrast to his father, Edgar's youngest son, King Æthelred (c. 968–1016), appears the archetypal weak king and bad ruler, and his reign the lowest ebb of Anglo-Saxon kingship. His soubriquet 'the Unready' suggests a king ill-prepared for the difficulties he faced. The origin and real meaning of this nickname, already attested in the twelfth century, namely 'Unræd' – that is 'ill-counselled', punning on 'Æthelred' or 'noble counsel' – softens but does not wholly remove such condemnation.

It is not difficult to see why Æthelred gained such a reputation. His reign began with regicide, was halted by exile, and ended in invasion by Cnut of Denmark. Æthelred's rule appears characterised by violence and treachery and the despotic exercise of royal power, and his failure to deal with the renewed Viking threat to England has guaranteed his reputation. After decades of apparent absence, the Vikings returned to England in the 980s and their attacks escalated until the kingdom was overrun and a Danish king was on the throne. Æthelred's inability to stem the flood, even the

7.1 Places mentioned in
chapter 7

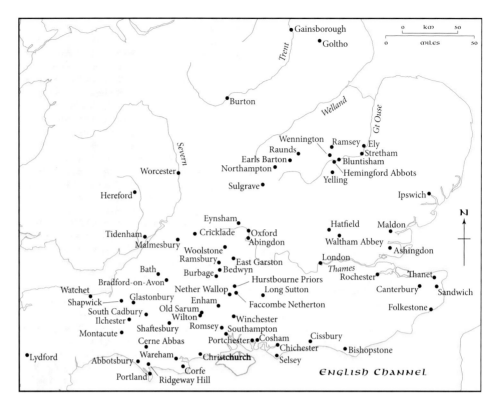

7.1 Places mentioned in chapter 7

methods by which he attempted to do so, drew sharp criticism from contemporaries, and modern scholarship has until recently been only a little less hostile.

Yet the late tenth and eleventh centuries were far more than simply a period of political failure and national disaster. Seemingly paradoxically, this was a time of significant intellectual endeavour and achievement, both in Latin and in Old English. The period likewise saw significant social mobility, with the boundaries between different ranks and statuses seemingly more permeable and surmountable. There is growing evidence for a new class of local, small-scale landowners, enjoying considerable prosperity and affluence. This 'gentry class' was undoubtedly much troubled by the political upheavals that took place in this period, but nevertheless life, and an increasingly comfortable one for some, still went on.

Edgar, Edward and Æthelred

On 8 July 975, King Edgar died, and he was only in his thirties. The consequences of Edgar's early death were far-reaching and dramatic. Around the turn of the millennium, the monk Byrhtferth of Ramsey wrote in his *Life of St Oswald* of the immediate aftermath of Edgar's death:

the commonwealth of the entire realm was shaken: bishops were perplexed, ealdormen were angry, monks were struck with fear, the people were terrified, and the secular clerics were made happy, because their time had come. Abbots are now expelled, together with their monks; clerics are brought in together with their wives; and 'the last error was worse than the first'.

Byrhtferth went on to name Ælfhere, ealdorman of Mercia, as one of the chief agitators, turning the minds of the people against the monks and appropriating monastic lands and income. Dissension spread eastwards through Mercia until it was checked by the party led by Ealdorman Æthelwine of East Anglia, one of the heroes of the *Life of St Oswald* and described therein as 'so excellent in body and bearing that no one more distinguished could be imagined'. The *Anglo-Saxon Chronicle* records similar upheavals, with the 'D' and 'E' versions singling out Ealdorman Ælfhere as a destroyer of monasteries and one who put monks to flight. Likewise, the *Book of Bishop Æthelwold* – a twelfth-century Latin translation of earlier Old English material relating to the abbey of Ely – repeatedly records how dissension arose after the death of King Edgar and how the monastery was again and again despoiled of its properties.

This 'anti-monastic reaction', as it has been labelled by modern scholars, is a reminder of how closely dependent the Benedictine Reformers of the tenth century had been on the power and authority of King Edgar. Yet what occurred after Edgar's death was not a hostile reaction to reformed monasticism per se. Monastic reform had provided a vocabulary with which writers such as Byrhtferth could denigrate opponents, and one that allowed them to depict events not as a competition for power and influence between rival factions but as a battle for the very survival of Christianity and the Church. Despite Byrhtferth's assertions, Ælfhere was not opposed to monasticism for he was a benefactor of Abingdon and Glastonbury and, indeed, was buried at the latter. His actions may have been motivated more by Oswald and the see of Worcester's encroachment upon his powers as an ealdorman, and the concomitant challenges to the long-entrenched interests of his own family.

Material from the *Book of Bishop Æthelwold* shows that many used the opportunity provided by the death of Edgar – and thus Ely's loss of its most powerful patron – to reclaim lands acquired by the monastery or to contest transfers of estates. Some litigation was clearly opportunistic, but other cases suggest genuine grievances about how the monastery had acquired its lands, with accusations of coercion and underhand methods being made by a number of litigants. Thus Ælfwold of Mardleybury (Hertfordshire) attempted to reclaim land at Stretham that he had sold to Bishop Æthelwold on the grounds that he had been forced into the sale 'and that violence and pillage had been inflicted upon him'. Presumably Æthelwold had relied in some way on the coercive power of the king or his agents to effect the sale and the removal of such support left him vulnerable. In other cases the death of Edgar seems to have been the occasion for the reopening of age-old disputes. The sons of Boga of Hemingford claimed an estate at Bluntisham (Cambridgeshire) on the grounds that their uncle's grandmother had petitioned King Edward the Elder (d. 924) for the land.

Ealdorman Æthelwine appears a much more ambiguous figure in the *Book of Bishop Æthelwold* than he does in the *Life of St Oswald*. Sometimes he is shown acting in support of Ely and defending its patrimony, at other times he acts against it. Indeed, Æthelwine was himself accused of laying claim to an estate at Hatfield (Hertfordshire) that had been granted to Ely by King Edgar, and only by giving up land at Hemingford (Hertfordshire), Wennington and Yelling (both Cambridgeshire) was Ely able to regain the estate. The situation was clearly more complex than the simple pro- and anti-monastic division set up by Byrhtferth. Æthelwine's intervention against Ælfhere was as much about regional rivalries between two leading noble families as it was about the defence of monasteries and monastic property.

The 'anti-monastic reaction', however it is understood, was but one part of more widespread upheavals that accompanied Edgar's death, disruptions that brought to the surface tensions and rivalries that had been developing during his reign. Dispute about royal succession was one further arena in which these rivalries were played out. In the later years of his reign Edgar stressed the legitimacy of his marriage to Ælfthryth, privileging the children of that union over his other offspring and marking them out for succession. However, Ælfthryth's elder son, Edmund, died in 971 and her other son, Æthelred, was perhaps eight or nine, possibly younger, when King Edgar himself died. Nevertheless, Æthelred's cause attracted some support: along with his mother Ælfthryth can probably be placed the powerful and influential Bishop Æthelwold and Ealdorman Ælfhere.

Æthelred's older half-brother, Edward, may have appeared a more promising candidate for the throne given his age – perhaps 13 or 14 – at his father's death. Yet

7.2 The shrine of St Edward the Martyr in the church of the St Edward Brotherhood, Brookwood Cemetery near Woking. The relics of Edward were recovered by J. Wilson-Claridge during excavations at Shaftesbury Abbey in the 1930s and were eventually translated to a specially founded monastery in the former London Necropolis in the 1980s

Byrhtferth claimed in his *Life of St Oswald* that Edward struck fear and terror into everyone and 'hounded them not only with tongue-lashings, but even with cruel beatings'. Æthelred, by contrast, 'seemed more gentle to everyone in word and deed'. There may also have been doubts about Edward's legitimacy. Certainly, by the later eleventh century stories were circulating that he was the son of a nun of Wilton who had been seduced by Edgar. Nevertheless, it was Edward who first gained the throne, a succession probably owing much to the support of Archbishop Dunstan of Canterbury and, probably, Ealdorman Æthelwine. Some concessions were made to Æthelred. A number of estates said to be 'lands belonging to kings' sons' were granted to him, these even including lands at Bedwyn (Wiltshire), Hurstbourne (Hampshire) and Burbage (Wiltshire) that had been granted by Edgar to Abingdon.

Whatever factions brought him to the throne, Edward's reign was short-lived. He was murdered in circumstances that remain obscure while visiting Æthelred at the Gap of Corfe on 18 March 979. Æthelred was the most obvious beneficiary of Edward's murder, succeeding to the throne in the same year, but it is unclear what part, if any, he played in the regicide. According to Byrhtferth, whose *Life of St Oswald* provides the most detailed near-contemporary account of events, Edward was dragged from his horse by a number of Æthelred's thegns and died in the process. He was then hastily buried. These men may have been motivated by their own interests, hoping for advancement when Æthelred gained the throne, or may have been encouraged in their actions by Æthelred and/or his mother Ælfthryth – the latter was certainly accused of complicity by later writers. Whatever the causes, the regicide cast a long shadow over Æthelred's reign and he remained a source of suspicion. For the compiler of the 'Northern Recension' of the *Anglo-Saxon Chronicle*, 'no worse deed than this [i.e. Edward's murder] for the English people was committed since first they came to Britain'.

The body of Edward, having been reburied at Shaftesbury, was soon the focus of a cult and he was venerated as a saint and martyr. Æthelred would later legislate for the observance of the feast of St Edward throughout England and was a patron of Shaftesbury Abbey, granting it the monastery of Bradford-on-Avon and confirming other possessions. Whether this is evidence against his involvement in his half-brother's murder or was an attempt to neutralise the potentially damaging effects of Edward's nascent cult on his own reputation is unclear.

The Reign of Æthelred

The lengthy reign of Æthelred (978–1016) has long been seen as the nadir of Anglo-Saxon kingship. Generations of writers and scholars, beginning in the eleventh century itself, characterised the king as weak, ineffective and easily led. The nobility of the period have likewise been presented as treacherous and disloyal, putting self-interest above the safety and security of the kingdom. The verdict of the Victorian scholar Edward Freeman can stand for countless others: 'Under Æthelred nothing was done; or, more truly, throughout his whole reign he left undone those things which he ought to have done, and he did those things which he ought not to have done.'

It is not difficult to find justification for such judgements. Æthelred's reign ended in invasion, with England conquered by Cnut, and this had been preceded by Æthelred's exile on the Continent in 1013–14, during which time Cnut's father, Swein Forkbeard, ruled England. The 'C', 'D' and 'E' versions of the *Anglo-Saxon Chronicle* present Æthelred's reign as a depressing descent into passivity, treachery and dissension in the face of a growing Viking threat. Numerous examples of violence perpetrated in the name of Æthelred likewise feature in the *Chronicle*. Charters from the period include detailed narrative sections describing the histories of the estates being granted, histories that frequently include unjust seizures and forfeitures and feature a cast of criminals and traitors.

Over the past generation, the work of scholars such as Simon Keynes or Pauline Stafford has sought, if not to rescue Æthelred from an ill-deserved reputation, then at least to understand why such a reputation came about and what this might tell us of the nature of Anglo-Saxon kingship in the tenth and eleventh centuries. Central to this process has been the recognition that the most detailed account of Æthelred's reign – that included in the 'C', 'D' and 'E' versions of the *Anglo-Saxon Chronicle* – is not a contemporary, year-by-year record of events. Rather, it was produced by a single author, probably based in London, in the early years of Cnut's reign. The compiler was

7.3 The hanging of Pharoah's baker from the *Old English Hexateuch*, produced at Canterbury in the early to mid-eleventh century

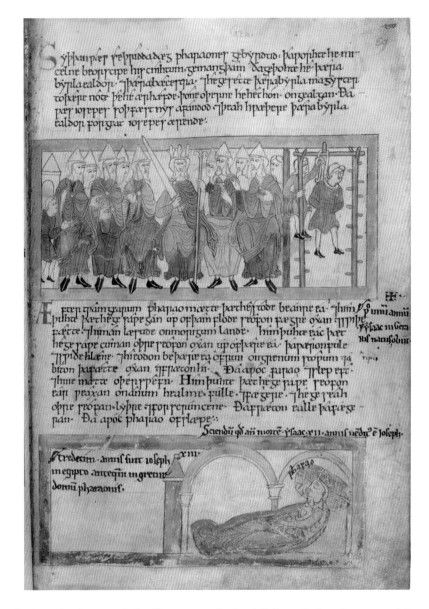

thus looking back on Æthelred's reign with the full knowledge that it would end in disaster, defeat and conquest. The judgements of the narrative, the selection of information, even the connections drawn between different events are all made with this ultimate end in mind. The account is rarely directly critical of Æthelred himself, but nevertheless it gives the overriding impression of a king presiding over the descent of a nation into disaster. The 'A' version of the *Chronicle*, at times a contemporary record for Æthelred's reign, offers a different perspective but is far less detailed and thus hard to use as a counterbalance to the narrative in versions 'C', 'D' and 'E'.

It is also clear that the problems Æthelred faced were far from unique to his reign. Rather, the period was one in which the tensions and compromises inherent in Anglo-Saxon royal government were thrown into sharp relief and the fault lines running through society broke to the surface. The reign of Æthelred marks something of a documentary watershed; far more is known about his rule than about almost any of his predecessors. Such may be a reflection of the upheavals and disorder of the time – detailed written records would be a precious source of security, particularly for those holding estates that had been forfeited by their former owners. Yet the number and the loquacity of the sources can conspire to magnify the problems of the period and to draw particular attention to them. The difficulty is determining whether the differences of Æthelred's reign were new problems or simply old problems newly documented.

7.4 Late tenth-century copper alloy seal matrix bearing the inscription 'SIGILLVM ÆLFRICI' ('the seal of Ælfric'). The design closely resembles King Æthelred's 'First Hand' type coins and it is tempting to associate the seal with the prominent Ealdorman Ælfric of Hampshire, though this is ultimately beyond proof

The well-known case of the crimes of Wulfbald highlights these problems. In 996 Æthelred granted a number of estates in Kent to his mother, Ælfthryth. These estates had formerly belonged to one Wulfbald and had come into Æthelred's hands through forfeiture. However, the charter recording the grant paints a picture of royal powerlessness in the face of repeated wrongdoing. Having twice ignored royal orders to restore goods he had plundered from his stepmother, Wulfbald seized the lands of a kinsman, Brihtmær. He then twice ignored Æthelred's commands to vacate these lands before a royal council at London assigned all his property to the king and 'also placed him at the king's mercy, whether to live or to die'. Despite these judgments Wulfbald retained all his property until he died, and it was only after his death that Æthelred gained control of the lands that had been forfeit. Even this was resisted – after Wulfbald's death, his widow killed a king's thegn and 15 of his companions at one of the contested estates, presumably to prevent its seizure.

Yet if Æthelred did face nobles able to resist his authority and to reject repeatedly his judgments, he was not the first or only Anglo-Saxon ruler to do so. In the 920s King Æthelstan had to legislate for noble families so powerful that they could not be brought to justice for their crimes. If Æthelstan here seems active where Æthelred looks passive, nevertheless it is unclear how such legislation could have been effective. Æthelred's misfortune is that the charters from his reign give colour and detail to the problems that appear abstract or notional in Æthelstan's legislation.

If not all of the problems Æthelred faced were unique, neither were the remedies that he sought. Much has been made of the periodic episodes of violence that mark out his reign: the blinding of Ælfgar, the son of Ealdorman Ælfric, in 993; the killing of Ealdorman Ælfhelm and the blinding of his sons Wulfheah and Ufegeat in 1006; the killing of Sigeferth and Morcar in 1015; and the order to slaughter all Danish men in England in 1002, the infamous 'St Brice's Day Massacre'. Yet even here Æthelred may not have been so different from his predecessors. For all the administrative efficiency and capabilities of the late Anglo-Saxon 'state', it rested, at least in part, on the ability to inflict in the name of justice shocking levels of violence and suffering. Even Edgar, whose reign appears in so many ways the mirror image of Æthelred's, issued a decree that thieves should have their eyes put out, their ears, hands and feet cut off, their nostrils sliced open and, having been scalped as well, should be left in an open field to be devoured by beasts. The terse accounts of royally directed violence in the *Chronicle*, shorn of all context, necessarily look like despotism on Æthelred's part rather than the exercise of a brutal but nevertheless licit justice. Violence, even extreme violence, was but one more tool of governance in the late Anglo-Saxon period.

Particularly early in his reign, Æthelred was operating within a political system that was not of his own making. His ability to transform it and his freedom of movement were restricted by deep-rooted interests as well as by the inherent limitations of royal power. Despite the contentious circumstances surrounding Æthelred's succession, little change was made to the composition of the court: those who had been in office during the reigns of Edgar and Edward remained, for the most part, in office. Ælfthryth is notably prominent in the witness lists of charters from this period and, given Æthelred's age at succession, she probably acted as something approaching a regent. Bishop Æthelwold was also at the centre of Æthelred's regime and received the earliest recorded religious patronage of his reign, a grant of land at Long Sutton (Hampshire).

If the prominence of Ælfthryth and Æthelwold reflects the support they gave Æthelred's candidacy, others at court must have endorsed the claims of Edward and yet were not deprived of office, though they may have been marginalised in other ways. Such reflects the situation that met Æthelred and his party on his accession to the throne. Those in positions of authority were powerful and well entrenched. Of the ealdormen surviving from King Edgar's reign, Æthelwine came from an influential and powerful noble family, whose interests in East Anglia stretched back generations. Ealdorman Ælfhere's lineage was similarly venerable and his family's power in Mercia was as long established as Æthelwine's in East Anglia. Less is known of the family connections of Ealdorman Byrhtnoth, but he had held the ealdordom of Essex since 956 and had ties by marriage to Ælfhere. Those ealdormen appointed during the brief reign of Edward are less well documented, but Æthelweard, ealdorman of the western provinces, was a member of a cadet branch of the royal dynasty, being descended from King Æthelred I, and had strong ties with the Continent. The ability of Æthelred and his supporters to remove from office any or all of these men, even assuming they had wanted to, was severely limited. Likewise, the death of Edward had left Æthelred as the only credible candidate for the English throne. The former supporters of Edward would have had little choice but to acquiesce in Æthelred's succession.

It was in the 980s that Æthelred seems to have fully asserted his independence and begun to pursue new policies and new alliances. His mother, Ælfthryth, disappears from the witness lists of his charters, reappearing again only in the 990s. Given that Ealdorman Ælfhere died in 983 and Bishop Æthelwold in 984, by the second half of the 980s three of the most powerful figures of Æthelred's early reign were out of the picture. Other evidence suggests a new start in this period. The mid-980s probably saw the introduction of a new coinage, the so-called 'Second Hand' type, and a return to the centralised production and distribution of dies, although such centralisation did not last long. It is also likely that Æthelred promulgated his first law code around 985, probably at a meeting of his councillors at *Bromdun*, although only traces of this code now survive.

The period of the late 980s to early 990s was also marked by a number of appropriations by Æthelred of the estates of certain churches and monasteries and the subsequent granting of these lands to his lay followers. These appropriations are known from a remarkable series of charters, beginning in 993, in which the king restored lands so seized to Abingdon, the Old Minster at Winchester and Rochester. These charters describe how the young king had acted unjustly, led astray by the bad advice of his councillors and others close to him – Ealdorman Ælfric of Hampshire, Bishop Wulfgar of Ramsbury and the thegn Æthelsige are among those specifically named. Now, with the wisdom of maturity and better counsel, Æthelred sought to repent and to rectify his errors publicly.

If Æthelred later had cause to regret his actions in this period or, at least, to explain his restoration of ecclesiastical lands through the language of penitence, the seizures of the 980s may have been understood in very different ways at the time. Æthelred is known to have been in serious dispute with Ælfstan, bishop of Rochester, and, indeed, ravaged his diocese in 986. Such fundamental ruptures between king and churchman rather than simple royal or lay avarice may have been the context for other appropriations. Furthermore, Æthelred's decision to restore certain lands came after some of those involved had died or fallen from favour – Bishop Wulfgar died around 986, Æthelsige had been stripped of his office for murder, and Ælfric had been accused of warning a Viking army of plans to entrap them, though he subsequently held onto his office. The make-up of Æthelred's court had also been significantly reorganised in the 990s. Ealdorman Æthelweard and his son Æthelmær were among those who became increasingly prominent in this period. Others included Ealdorman Ælfhelm of Northumbria, his brother Wulfric 'Spot', now best remembered as the founder of a monastery at Burton (Staffordshire), and Wulfheah, the son of Ælfhelm. As noted above, Æthelred's mother Ælfthryth also reappears in charter witness lists around this time. A narrative of bad counsel and youthful inexperience may have been a useful device to explain and to justify fundamental shifts in royal policy and patronage.

The Oncoming Storm

However Æthelred's actions in the 980s and 990s are to be interpreted, they played out against a backdrop of increasing Viking activity in England. The *Chronicle* records the sacking of Southampton by a naval force in 980, with the 'C' version adding the ravaging of Thanet in the same year and an assault on Cheshire by a 'northern naval force'. The pattern of apparently small-scale and localised raiding – albeit sometimes particularly destructive – continues up to 988. Attacks on the coasts of Cornwall and Devon, including the sacking of the monastery of St Petroc, occurred in 981, and Portland was ravaged in 982. Watchet was attacked in 988, with the *Chronicle* noting that the thegn Goda was killed 'and many fell with him'. If this incident is the same as the 'savage battle . . . in the west' recorded in the *Life of Oswald*, then it resulted in a victory for the forces of Devon, despite heavy losses.

It is not clear whether the raid on Southampton represented the recommencing of Viking attacks on England after an extended absence or just the first of such attacks deemed worthy of record. Certainly, the late eighth and ninth centuries witnessed numerous Viking raids that were not recorded in narrative sources. The will of King Eadred (d. 955) included a large sum of money bequeathed to his subjects that they 'may redeem themselves from famine and a heathen army if they need', though no Viking attacks are known from the period. With the possible exception of the raid on

7.5 Site of the Battle of Maldon

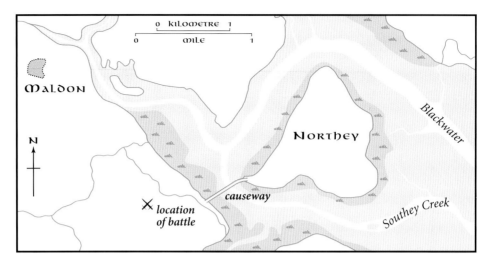

Thanet, it is likely that the attacks of the 980s were undertaken not by raiding parties from Scandinavia but by Viking groups already based in Britain, Ireland and the surrounding seas. Certainly, this period saw attacks on Anglesey, Dyfed and Pembrokeshire from Viking bases on the Isle of Man or the Hebrides.

The Viking attacks escalated dramatically in 991 when a fleet of over ninety ships ravaged Folkestone, Sandwich and Ipswich before coming to Maldon (Essex) where it was met by an army led by the now venerable Ealdorman Byrhtnoth. One of the leaders of this Viking fleet was Olaf Tryggvason, who would become king of Norway in 995. Another leader may have been Swein Forkbeard, king of Denmark and son of Harald Bluetooth, for a certain Æthelric of Bocking was subsequently accused of planning to receive Swein when he arrived in Essex with a fleet, actions that must have taken place in the early 990s.

The force that faced Byrhtnoth at Maldon was, then, a formidable one and led by some of the most powerful figures of the period. The *Chronicle* offers little detail of the battle that ensued, simply recording that Byrhtnoth was killed and the Vikings won the field. A poem in Old English, perhaps though not certainly written soon after the battle, provides more detail and praises the doomed bravery and noble ends of the Anglo-Saxon warriors. According to the poem, the Viking fleet was encamped on Northey Island in the Blackwater Estuary and Byrhtnoth and his warriors held the tidal causeway. The Vikings asked to be let across in order better to engage the Anglo-Saxon forces in battle and Byrhtnoth, 'because of his pride', agreed. Despite such judgement, Byrhtnoth may have had little choice but to acquiesce if he wished to engage the Vikings in open battle. Had they not been able to cross the causeway, the Vikings could easily have taken to their ships and moved elsewhere, forcing Byrhtnoth into a game of cat and mouse in which the Vikings would have had the upper hand. Nor was the battle necessarily the one-sided affair the *Chronicle* and the poem suggest. The *Life of Oswald* describes numerous Viking casualties and claims that after the battle 'they were scarcely able to man their ships'.

Following the defeat at Maldon, the decision was made to pay tribute to the Viking army and a sum of £10,000 was handed over. Despite this payment, in the following year Æthelred was forced to assemble all English ships at London with the intention of trapping the still-active Viking fleet. Beginning a theme that would run through the whole account of Æthelred's later years, the 'C', 'D' and 'E' versions of the *Chronicle* record that through the treachery of Ealdorman Ælfric the Viking fleet was able to escape the trap and continue its destruction. In 994 Olaf and Swein, leading a force of some 94 ships, attacked London and then ravaged and burned their way along the south coast from Essex to Hampshire, before riding inland to continue their destruction. Æthelred and his counsellors finally sued for peace, providing the army with provisions and a payment of £16,000. After this agreement, Olaf was baptised – another well-established strategy for dealing with Viking leaders – and left England promising never to return.

The payments of £10,000 and £16,000 are the first of a series of such tribute payments recorded in the 'C', 'D' and 'E' versions of the *Chronicle*. Amounts of £24,000 (1002), £36,000 (1007), £48,000 (1012), £21,000 (1014) and £72,000 plus £10,500 from the citizens of London (1018, under Cnut) are set out. These figures seem high, astonishingly so when compared with the tax revenues that could be raised by later medieval kings of England. The round numbers and simple arithmetical progression of the figures for 1002–12 in the *Chronicle* likewise invite suspicion. Yet the basic accuracy of the amounts in the *Chronicle* is confirmed by other sources. The text known as *II Æthelred* records the agreement between the king and the Viking forces active in 994 and notes 'twenty-two thousand pounds in gold and silver were paid from England ... for this truce' – higher than the figure of £16,000 given in the *Chronicle*. Similarly, King Harthacnut, son of Cnut, was able to raise £21,099 in 1041 and another £11,048 soon afterwards as payment for his fleet of ships.

If the *Chronicle*'s figures are credible, the amounts paid must nevertheless have put a strain on the resources of England. If the payments of 1012 and 1014 were made solely in coin, they would have accounted for perhaps 55 per cent of the total Late Small Cross issue. In practice, payments were probably made in a mixture of coinage and bullion, but sources still record churches being stripped of precious metals and other wealth, and churchmen having to sell estates to meet their share of the payment. Even Æthelred himself had to go to some lengths to raise money: a number of charters record grants of land made by the king in exchange for bullion to pay the tribute. Not all the money paid to Viking armies would have left England, but the high numbers of Anglo-Saxon coins in Scandinavian hoards of this period suggest a considerable outflow of wealth.

This payment of tribute to the Vikings – often erroneously labelled 'Danegeld' – has contributed considerably to Æthelred's poor reputation. Yet it was a strategy that had long been employed against the Vikings: even Alfred the Great made such payments. Moreover, tribute was not paid solely to make the Vikings go away. *II Æthelred* makes clear that the Viking signatories to the treaty were to defend England against attacks by other Viking groups, effectively becoming mercenary forces. Such a policy would continue throughout Æthelred's reign; indeed, in 1012 he initiated an annual land tax – the *heregeld* – to pay for Viking mercenaries. *II Æthelred* also notes that earlier payments to the Vikings had been made by Archbishop Sigeric of

Canterbury, Ealdorman Æthelweard and Ealdormen Ælfric in order to secure peace in their own territories. The payment of tribute was thus a strategy that had widespread support among Æthelred's councillors, with local initiatives operating alongside national ones. The entry for 1011 in the *Anglo-Saxon Chronicle* even complains not that a tribute had been paid but that it was not offered to the Viking army in time.

The agreement in 994 brought relief from Viking attacks for a few years, but in 997 they resumed again. An army ravaged Devon, Cornwall and parts of Wales, harrying the coasts and then moving inland as far as Lydford in Devon. The following years saw the army moving along the south coast, spending some time on the Isle of Wight in 998, ravaging parts of Kent in 999 before finally heading to Normandy in the summer of 1000. In 1001 a naval force again attacked England, with battles in Sussex, Dorset, Somerset and Devon. From this point until 1007, the Viking attacks on England escalated in severity and scope, with only the devastating famine of 1005 briefly driving Viking armies back to Denmark.

According to the *Chronicle*, some sporadic resistance was offered to the Vikings. Ulfcetel of East Anglia was singled out for praise having fought resolutely, though ultimately in vain, against Swein's forces in 1004. Despite episodes of bravery, the overall story presented by the *Chronicle* is of Viking destruction and English inaction, ineffectiveness or treachery. Thus in 1003, Ealdorman Ælfric, 'up to his old tricks', feigned sickness when facing the Viking army that had sacked Exeter and so the combined forces of Wiltshire and Hampshire were scattered. Ulfcetel himself was undone because the full force of the East Anglian army failed to turn out.

Despite the compellingly gloomy narrative of the *Chronicle*, Æthelred did take further steps to counter the Viking threat. Through papal intervention, in late 990 or early 991 a peace agreement was signed between Æthelred and Duke Richard of Normandy. One of the terms of this agreement was that Richard was to receive none of Æthelred's enemies and it is likely that such was intended to prevent Viking fleets from sheltering in Normandy. This Norman alliance was further strengthened in 1002, when Æthelred married Emma, daughter of Duke Richard. Denial of safe havens and harbours for Viking fleets may also have been behind Æthelred's ravaging of Cumberland and the Isle of Man in the year 1000.

Æthelred also shored up English fortifications. Excavations at a number of *burhs*, such as Cricklade (Wiltshire), or Christchurch (Dorset), have revealed the construction of new stone walls fronting the ditched banks that enclose the sites, while at other *burhs*, such as Hereford and Wareham (Dorset), walls were constructed on top of the enclosing banks. Such refortifications are difficult to date closely but it is likely that this extensive construction programme should be seen as part of Æthelred's response to renewed Viking attacks. In addition, a number of mints were transferred from their existing sites to new, more defensible locations – the so-called 'emergency *burhs*'. The mint at Wilton (Wiltshire) moved to the Iron Age hillfort of Old Sarum, probably soon after Wilton was sacked by Swein's forces in 1003. Limited evidence suggests that the existing Iron Age ramparts were augmented at this time. Sometime early in the second decade of the eleventh century, the mint at Ilchester (Somerset) was similarly moved to the hillfort at South Cadbury, where archaeological excavation has

7.6 Cissbury Ring, near Worthing, from the west. This Iron Age hillfort was one of the so-called 'emergency *burhs*' of the later reign of King Æthelred

uncovered extensive refortification of the site in this period. Around the same time, a new mint was established at Cissbury Ring (West Sussex), another Iron Age hillfort. This apparently worked in close association with the mint at nearby Chichester rather than replacing it.

It is in the context of these active measures against the growing Viking threat that one of the most notorious episodes of Æthelred's reign – the 'St Brice's Day Massacre' – should be understood. On 13 November 1002, Æthelred ordered that 'all the Danish men who were in England' were to be slain as he had learned they were plotting his overthrow and death. Further details are recorded in a charter of 1004 concerning the rebuilding of St Frideswide's church in Oxford. Danes are said 'to have sprung up in this island, sprouting like cockle amongst wheat', and so they 'were to be destroyed by a most just extermination'. When Æthelred's orders were being carried out, the Danes in Oxford sought sanctuary in St Frideswide's; when they could not be forced out, the church was fired.

Æthelred's orders cannot have been directed at the descendants of the Scandinavian settlers of the ninth and early tenth centuries, who were by now well integrated into

7.7 Penny of King Æthelred produced at the Cissbury mint by the moneyer Ceolnoth

7.8 Mass burials at St John's College, Oxford, probably of victims of the St Brice's Day Massacre

English society and could scarcely be presented as new arrivals. Æthelred must instead have been targeting recent settlers, including those he had paid to serve as mercenaries. Certainly, he had reason to fear the loyalty of such individuals: in 1001 Pallig, the brother-in-law of Swein, joined Viking forces attacking Devon, despite the pledges he had given to Æthelred and the treasures and lands he had received in return.

Recent excavations have uncovered the likely remains of some of the victims of the 'St Brice's Day Massacre'. At St Johns College, Oxford, a mass grave of perhaps 35 individuals – all male, with the majority in their twenties and thirties – was discovered in 2008. Most of the skeletons showed injuries to the back or to the skull, consistent with being attacked from behind or while prone; few had wounds typical of battle injuries. A number of the bodies had also been burnt before being dumped in the mass grave – perhaps a consequence of the firing of St Frideswide's church. Carbon-dating of the remains was compatible with a date in the early eleventh century. In 2009 an excavation at Ridgeway Hill (Dorset) uncovered a mass grave of 54 males, all of whom appeared to have been executed in a brutal fashion, with the bodies decapitated and many bearing multiple wounds. Isotope analysis of a number of the skeletons pointed to Scandinavian origins and carbon-dating placed the burials in the tenth to eleventh centuries.

The 'St Brice's Day Massacre' was undoubtedly brutal in its execution and appears in the *Chronicle* as the action of a paranoid ruler, seeing plots and treachery every-where. Æthelred was also no doubt able to call on the hatred and aggression of an English population that had by now endured decades of Viking attacks. Yet the Massacre shows a king who was far from powerless in his own kingdom and far from impotent in the face of the Viking threat. The location of the Ridgeway Hill burial pit is also typical of Anglo-Saxon execution cemeteries, suggesting there was potentially a judicial dimension to the violence here. Moreover, as the St Frideswide's charter makes clear, such violence could be presented as the actions of a just ruler protecting his people rather than as an episode of capricious and paranoid savagery.

Thorkell, Swein and the Ruin of Æthelred

In August 1009 an 'immense raiding army' led by Thorkell – a Dane who had served under Swein – landed at Sandwich. For the compiler of the account in the *Chronicle* it was this army that finally broke the Anglo-Saxon kingdom and paved the way for the conquest by Swein of Denmark. The treachery and disunity that had thwarted previous attempts to drive out the Vikings reach a crescendo as the *Chronicle* sets out a detailed but at times curiously vague or evasive narrative of the collapse of Æthelred's regime. Key moments – the surrender of the north and the Midlands to Swein or the recall of Æthelred from exile – are left largely unexplained and unexplored. The chief dynamic of the account is the personalities, the animosities and the character flaws of those involved, with Ealdorman Eadric the chief villain of the piece. Barely visible beneath this account is a more complex narrative of political factions, rivalries at court, and competitions for power between the sons of Æthelred. Though such a narrative can be only partially reconstructed now, it is clear from Æthelred's charters that the final decade of his reign saw fundamental changes in the composition of his court and in the structure of his regime.

In 1006 Ealdorman Ælfhelm of Northumbria was killed and his sons Wulfheah and Ufegeat were blinded. Such marked the final, bloody end of the dominance at Æthelred's court of the group who had risen to prominence in the 990s. Some members of this group, such as Æthelweard or Wulfric 'Spot', had ceased to attest Æthelred's charters some years before, while others, such as Ealdorman Æthelmær, the son of Æthelweard, disappear around this time. The chief beneficiaries and perhaps architects of this 'palace revolution' – to use Simon Keynes's oft-cited phrase – were the family of Eadric. They had been present at Æthelred's court since the 990s at least but became the dominant group in the final years of his reign. Eadric himself was appointed ealdorman of Mercia in 1007 and by 1011 occupied a position of pre-eminence as Æthelred's chief ealdorman. The final collapse of Æthelred's regime was heavily bound up with the fall-out of this 'palace revolution' and the animosities and rivalries between the factions involved.

The arrival of Thorkell's army or a similar threat had evidently been expected by Æthelred and his advisors. The previous year had seen an unprecedented militarisation of England as well as the promulgation of a law code aimed at religious and moral reform. Æthelred had ordered that ships be built throughout the kingdom, with every 310 hides supplying a warship and every eight hides supplying a helmet and corselet. Despite Æthelred assembling the largest naval force ever seen, the *Chronicle* could still gloomily report failure. At the muster, Brihtric, the brother of Ealdorman Eadric, accused Wulfnoth Cild of unspecified offences and the latter seized 20 ships and ravaged the coasts of Sussex. Brihtric's pursuit with another 80 ships ended in disaster. The ships dispersed and 'the toil of all the nation thus lightly came to naught'. It was then that Thorkell's army arrived at Sandwich and, having been paid tribute by the people of eastern Kent, ravaged along the south coasts.

In 1010 Thorkell and his army were held up for a time in East Anglia but eventually reached the Thames Valley and the heartlands of Wessex. For the compiler of the *Chronicle* by now all English resistance was at an end: 'finally there was no leader who could collect an army but each fled as best he could, and in the end no shire would even help the next'. In the entry for 1011 the compiler resorted to giving a numbered list of the regions overrun by the army, complaining that it was only after the Vikings

7.9 Selection of late tenth- or eleventh-century Viking weaponry recovered from around London Bridge

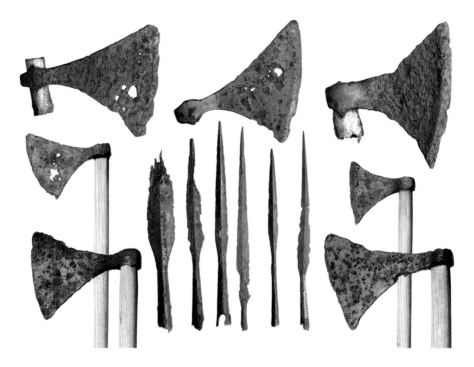

had done great damage that truces were agreed and tribute paid. Even this did not stop the violence and destruction. In the autumn, the army besieged Canterbury and, having got inside the walls through treachery, took prisoner the archbishop of Canterbury, Ælfheah. For the *Chronicle*, this was a devastating blow, a sign of just how bad things now were: 'there could misery be seen where happiness was often seen before, in that wretched city from which first came to us Christianity and happiness in divine and secular things'.

In 1012 a tribute of £48,000 was paid and finally the army dispersed, with Thorkell committing himself and 45 ships to Æthelred. In a last moment of violence, Archbishop Ælfheah was murdered. Having got drunk, his captors pelted Ælfheah with bones and ox heads before one of them killed him with a single blow from the back of an axe. According to the near-contemporary account of Ælfheah's murder in the *Chronicle* of Thietmar of Merseburg, Thorkell himself tried to prevent the killing, promising gold, silver and all of his possessions save his ship, but to no avail. Such a murder was shocking even to a kingdom well used to violence and Ælfheah was soon venerated as a martyr.

The next year, 1013, Swein came again to England with a fleet, sailing first to Sandwich, then up the Humber and the Trent to Gainsborough (Lincolnshire). Such marked the beginnings of Swein's conquest of England. Various motivations have been sought for his actions – revenge for the 'St Brice's Day Massacre', enmity towards Thorkell and numerous others – but Swein probably needed no motivation other than opportunity and capability. England was a rich and prosperous kingdom, capable of raising vast sums to buy peace and pay off armies even after decades of Viking attacks. Moreover, the dispersal of Thorkell's fleet in the previous year would have made considerable additional manpower available to Swein.

Having arrived at Gainsborough, Swein accepted the surrender of Ealdorman Uhtred and the Northumbrians and subsequently that of the people of Lindsey (Lincolnshire), the Five Boroughs and all the forces north of Watling Street. Though these areas had seen some of the most extensive Scandinavian settlement in the ninth and tenth centuries, it is unlikely Swein was looking to capitalise on any latent ethnic sympathies. Rather, the areas first captured by Swein were the heartlands of the party of the late Ealdorman Ælfhelm and the Danish king may have deliberately exploited hostility to Æthelred arising from the events of 1006. Certainly, it is likely to have been at this point that Swein's son, Cnut, married Ælfgifu of Northampton, Ælfhelm's daughter. Leaving the hostages he had received with Cnut, Swein moved south, first unsuccessfully attacking London – where Æthelred and Thorkell were based – and then receiving at Bath the surrender of the western provinces under Ealdorman Æthelmær, who had recently come out of retirement. London finally submitted and Æthelred fled, ultimately to the protection of his brother-in-law, Duke Richard II, in Normandy.

However, although Swein had achieved his rapid conquest, his reign was short-lived: he died on 3 February 1014. The Danish army in England elected Cnut as king and there is a possibility that Swein may also have nominated him earlier as his heir. The Anglo-Saxon nobility, however, invited Æthelred back from Normandy and following negotiations extracted promises from him that he would 'reform all the things which they all hated; and all the things that had been said and done against him should be forgiven'. Though by now Cnut had also secured the support of the men of Lindsey, he was driven from Gainsborough by Æthelred's forces and fled by sea.

If Æthelred was restored to the throne, nevertheless his authority quickly evaporated. In 1015 the thegns Sigeferth and Morcar were killed at an assembly at Oxford, through the treachery of Eadric according to the *Chronicle*. Æthelred then seized their property and had Sigeferth's widow seized and taken to Malmesbury (Wiltshire). Given that Sigeferth and Morcar were based in the Midlands and the north, these actions were probably revenge for the surrender of those regions to Swein – an indication that Æthelred's promises of the previous year would only extend so far. It must also be significant that Sigeferth and Morcar had ties to the faction that had recently fallen from power – the after-effects of the 'palace revolution' were still being felt.

The killing of Sigeferth and Morcar provided the opportunity for Æthelred's son by his first wife Ælfgifu, Edmund 'Ironside', to make a bid for power in 1015. He married Sigeferth's widow and went north, taking control of the estates of the two thegns and receiving the submission of the Five Boroughs. As with Swein, Edmund seems here to have been capitalising on the disaffections of the faction that had lost out to Eadric and his family in 1006. Edmund's ties to this group were probably well established for his brother, Æthelstan (d. c. 1014), had had close links with them and, indeed, Morcar may have been one of his military retainers.

The reasons for Edmund's rebellion against his father are not known but tensions within the royal family must have played a part. Edmund's half-brother Edward, the son of Æthelred by Emma of Normandy, was approaching his teens by this date and already had acted as his father's representative in the negotiations of 1014. Edward's claim to be Æthelred's heir would have been further strengthened by the status and connections of Emma and the fact that, unlike Edmund's mother, she was a consecrated queen. Given that Æthelred's health was already failing, Edmund must have felt the need for urgency.

By this time, Cnut had returned to England and was ravaging Dorset, Wiltshire and Somerset – the heartlands of Wessex. With Æthelred lying ill at Cosham (Portsmouth), Edmund and Ealdorman Eadric raised armies to counter the threat from Cnut. Eventually, Eadric betrayed Edmund and changed sides, taking with him 40 ships. Thorkell probably defected at the same time. In 1016, on 23 April, Æthelred died. Though Edmund for a time offered some resistance to Cnut, after a devastating defeat at Ashingdon (Essex) in which, according to the *Chronicle*, 'all the nobility of England was . . . destroyed', he was forced to accept terms and divide the kingdom. Edmund succeeded to Wessex and the south, Cnut to Mercia and the north. When Edmund died on 30 November, of causes unknown, Cnut succeeded to the whole kingdom of England.

Religion, Repentance and the Renewal of Society

An account of the politics of Æthelred's reign suggests a kingdom descending into anarchy and chaos, with internal dissension, treachery, disloyalty and cowardice leading inexorably to invasion and conquest. Such an account, while not inaccurate, inevitably offers only one perspective on the period. Despite the significant political problems, the reigns of Æthelred and Cnut were times of intense intellectual activity and cultural achievement. Such can be seen across all spheres of creativity. Some of the finest examples of Anglo-Saxon manuscript illumination – such as the *Benedictional of St Æthelwold* or the *Ramsey Psalter* – belong to this period. Innovative and accomplished wall paintings and sculptural programmes – such as the Crucifixion at Romsey Abbey or the Christ in Majesty at Nether Wallop church, both in Hampshire – demonstrate the skills of Anglo-Saxon artists across a variety of media. Likewise, the majority of the surviving Old English poetry, both religious and secular, was written down, though not necessarily composed, in this period. The *Beowulf* manuscript is the most famous example, but the crucially important compilations contained in the *Junius Manuscript*, the *Exeter Book* and the *Vercelli Book* are all products of the late tenth or early eleventh centuries.

In part, this intellectual and cultural flowering was a product of the Benedictine Reforms and the ties with Continental scholarship that had been fostered particularly since the 930s. The immensely learned Abbo of Fleury (c. 945–1004), for example, spent the years 985 to 987 at the newly founded monastery of Ramsey (Cambridgeshire). His pupils there included Byrhtferth, whose *Life of St Oswald* has already been referred to and was only one of a number of highly accomplished works written by him on subjects ranging from computistics to hagiography. The Reforms had also enriched many monasteries, providing them with the resources necessary to sustain large communities of scholars. At the same time, this second generation of Reformers

7.10 Crucifixion or rood on the outside wall of the west transept of Romsey Abbey. The hand of God ('manus dei') descending from the clouds above Christ's head has parallels with tenth- and eleventh-century Anglo-Saxon manuscripts

sought to preserve the legacy and to defend the actions of the founders of the movement – Dunstan, Oswald and Æthelwold – through the production of biographies and other texts.

However, the very disruptions that beset England in this period provoked considerable scholarly enterprise. Churchmen, their patrons and their rulers attempted to understand the causes of these upheavals and to seek out remedies. This led to an urgent cultivation of learning, as writers looked to the Bible and Christian literature, to the Anglo-Saxon past and to their own behaviour and the events around them, for insight and guidance. Added to the problems specific to England was the growing sense of eschatological expectation in the run-up to the year 1000. Though such expectations were far from universal in western Europe, they formed a significant intellectual current, influential on some Anglo-Saxon thinkers.

The writings of two Anglo-Saxon churchmen in particular dominate the intellectual landscape of the late tenth and early eleventh centuries: Archbishop Wulfstan of York (d. 1023) and Ælfric of Eynsham (d. c. 1010). Both produced an extensive and varied corpus of writings and, though Wulfstan was the more conspicuously 'public' figure of the two, both authors sought through their writings to identify and to remedy the problems besetting England.

Ælfric was educated at Bishop Æthelwold's school at Winchester and he retained ties to that community throughout his life. His status as an alumnus of an institution at the heart of the Benedictine Reforms was central to the image of himself which he projected in his writings and was a key source of his authorial authority. Ælfric is unlikely to have joined Winchester as a child oblate for he writes of having once had a teacher who could understand Latin only in part ('*be dæle*') and could read the Old Testament only in a literal sense, suggesting Ælfric received his earliest education outside the cloister.

Though Winchester was central to his intellectual development, Ælfric began writing in earnest only in the later 980s after he was transferred to the community at Cerne Abbas (Dorset) at the request of Æthelmær, son of Ealdorman Æthelweard. It was while at Cerne Abbas that Ælfric produced the bulk of his scholarly output, with

7.11 Walrus ivory carving of Christ in Majesty from the first few decades of the eleventh century. Executed in the Winchester Style, the carving also shows the influence of Carolingian artistic traditions and was probably originally painted and gilded – traces of blue pigment still remain

works including translations and adaptations of the Bible, an Old English grammar and glossary, pastoral letters setting out the responsibilities of secular clergy, a collection of the lives of saints venerated by Anglo-Saxon monks and two collections of sermons or homilies following the order of the liturgical year – the crucially important *Catholic Homilies*. In 1005 Ælfric became abbot of the monastery at Eynsham (Oxfordshire). Apparently intended as a place of retirement or temporary retreat, this community had been founded by Æthelmær after he had fallen from favour at Æthelred's court. The date of Ælfric's death is unknown but should probably be placed around the year 1010.

Ælfric's two series of *Catholic Homilies*, produced initially in the period c. 989–c. 995, offer a convenient distillation in Old English of authoritative Christian teachings. In the first series, Ælfric aimed to provide a complete cycle of homilies for the liturgical year, in which the individual preacher's role was primarily that of a reader. In the second series, Ælfric envisaged a more active role for the preacher in selecting material and shaping and adapting the homilies to his own needs and the needs of his audience. The second series also incorporates more material aimed at the education of the clergy themselves, with references to canonical injunctions concerning clerical celibacy or the avoidance of secular business.

The *Catholic Homilies* presuppose a mixed or changing audience, addressing lay people, the clergy and even monks at different times. The purpose of the *Catholic Homilies* seems to have been to meet the pastoral needs of smaller and less well-resourced religious communities. Ælfric's move from Winchester to Cerne Abbas took him from the intellectual heart of the Anglo-Saxon kingdom not to an intellectual backwater per se but to a community of more limited resources and abilities and one more closely in contact with the small, and sometimes impoverished or underfunded, religious houses and thegnly churches that provided pastoral care for increasing numbers of the population. There was an urgent need for such communities to be provided with the basic intellectual resources that would allow them to fulfil their pastoral obligations.

If the primary purpose of the *Catholic Homilies* was as preaching tools, Ælfric may also have intended them to be suitable for private, personal reading and meditation by clerics and monks and literate members of the lay community. If so, there would be a connection here with his *Lives of the Saints*. In the preface to this work, Ælfric records that not only have Æthelweard and Æthelmær often read his works in Old English but that they have now asked him to provide a translation of the *Lives* of the saints venerated in the monastic liturgy. Such may suggest that Ælfric's lay patrons were actively embracing aspects of monastic piety and religious observance alongside more traditional forms of lay religiosity. Other laymen also requested works from Ælfric, such as the Old English summary and abridgement of the Bible written for Sigeweard of Asthall or the letter concerning clerical celibacy written to Sigefyrth. Ælfric's learning and opinions were clearly much sought after by a religiously engaged and literate lay nobility.

Concern for pastoral care and for the religious needs of the laity was a vital part of Ælfric's engagement with his own society, but his engagement with contemporary issues went beyond this. Particularly in the later years of life, and especially after his move to Eynsham, Ælfric referred both implicitly and explicitly to the political difficulties facing England and to remedies that were required. His homily on the *Prayer of Moses*, for example, explicitly contrasted the current situation – disease, starvation and invasion by a heathen people – with the peace and prosperity that had formerly existed in times when monastic life was respected and the people were vigilant. Through the example of Judas Maccabeus, Ælfric reminded his readers of the need to keep their word and to fight against the enemy. God would reward with victory those who were faithful and steadfast in their resistance. Ælfric even engaged with royal policy. The text known as *Wyrdwriteras* provided biblical and historical exemplars for rulers who had successfully delegated military matters to their noblemen – Ælfric uses the term 'ealdormen'. Given the repeated treachery and failings of ealdormen recorded in the *Chronicle*, such a policy presumably required some defence. Ælfric may also have offered criticism, albeit veiled, of some royal actions. His discussion of the penance performed by the fourth-century Emperor Theodosius following a massacre at Thessalonica may have contained implicit judgement on the morality of the 'St Brice's Day Massacre'.

Little is known of the career of Wulfstan outside of his clerical appointments. He was made bishop of London in 996, archbishop of York in 1002 and at the same time bishop of Worcester, holding the archiepiscopacy until his death in 1023 and the episcopacy of Worcester until at least 1016 and probably for some time afterwards. Wulfstan's earliest writings were homilies, both in Old English and in Latin, but it was as the author of a series of law codes issued in the names of Æthelred and Cnut, as well as treatises on status and the right order of society, that Wulfstan made his mark on eleventh-century society.

Wulfstan's vision of society as explored in his writings, together with the public pronouncements he made in the name of the kings he served, have influenced in highly significant ways modern understanding of the reigns of Æthelred and Cnut. For a long time, such influence was to the detriment of the reputation of Æthelred and his court. The law codes produced by Wulfstan were long seen as one more sign of a fundamental national malaise, indicative of a general failure to adopt appropriate responses in the face of the Viking threat – an attempt to chase off the Vikings with 'pious moans', as Eric John acerbically put it.

Yet such is to misunderstand the thought processes of the tenth and eleventh centuries and to apply anachronistic categories and definitions to the evidence. The law codes associated with Wulfstan do certainly contain elements that read like pious exhortations or homilies rather than law as it might be understood in a modern context. Yet this is precisely because the boundaries between homily and law were, if not meaningless in the tenth and eleventh centuries, then at least difficult to draw precisely. Both genres were concerned with establishing order and harmony in society, and for writers like Wulfstan, law was a continuum, embracing the decrees of God and the decrees of the king. Such was not just because the king was the Lord's anointed but also because a just king would follow the precepts of God and the teachings of the Church. The harmony that flowed from a well-ordered society would further the promotion of Christianity and ensure the stability of the monarch. Nor were there clear distinctions between liturgical ceremonies such as royal consecrations – where the king pledged to uphold justice, to support the Church and to obey the word of God – and the promulgation of royal law, which could also be understood as a series of public undertakings and commitments by the king about the nature of his rule.

Within such a vision of society, the Vikings appeared less the causes of the upheavals and disruptions plaguing England and more the symptoms of fundamental and deep-seated problems. In a sense, the works of Wulfstan are part of the same tradition as those of Alcuin of York and Alfred the Great on the Viking threat in the eighth and ninth centuries – indeed, Wulfstan is known to have studied closely the writings of Alcuin on the Vikings. Such sensibilities were sharpened and refined by the eschatological tensions surrounding the turning of the year 1000. The earliest writings of Wulfstan are shot through with millennial anxiety and with fears about the approaching reign of Antichrist and the times of tribulation that are to come. Wulfstan's early homilies, belonging to the end of the tenth century, note that some of the signs of the coming of Antichrist have already been seen in England and stress the need for men to prepare their minds and souls better to withstand the approaching tribulations.

As the millennial anxieties declined after the year 1000, Wulfstan carried over the sense of the urgent need for action that such fears had provoked into a programme for the reform of Christian society. Such was intended not so much to prepare society for the unavoidable trials that were to come at the end of days as to strengthen it and shore it up against disorder and dissension. The Vikings feature more prominently in Wulfstan's later writings, but they are most often a reflection or a consequence of the problems that beset the English – their sins, their moral cowardice, their debauchery – not the actual cause of these problems.

Wulfstan's thinking exerted a direct and profound influence on royal discourse. The laws promulgated in Æthelred's name at Enham (Hampshire) in 1008 – now surviving in a series of different versions and languages – were the first royal code for which Wulfstan was in large parts responsible. The Enham decrees are among the most homiletic of Wulfstan's codes, offering general principles about what should be done – 'men of every order are each to submit willingly to that duty which befits them both in religious and in secular concerns' – rather than specific and detailed legislation. The intentions were to bring order and harmony to society, to ensure that justice was done and illegal practices abolished. The peace and harmony meant to result from these decrees were not a means to avoid conflict – to chase off the Vikings – but were a way to ensure success in that conflict. As such, these measures should be placed alongside Æthelred's ship-building programme of the same year, designed as preparation for the arrival of Thorkell's army or for a threat of similar magnitude.

When Thorkell's army did arrive in 1009, Wulfstan was again responsible for the production of a law code – now known as *VII Æthelred*. This decreed three days of national fasting, general penance and the giving of alms. Even slaves were to be freed from work to attend Mass during this period. This code has to be seen not as the last desperate measures of a regime that had been overrun but as the amplification and extension of what had been attempted at Enham, given greater urgency and force by the particular circumstances. Moreover, the remedies set out by the law code were long-established responses to Viking attacks and to other calamities and would have been understood as such by contemporaries. Indeed, Æthelred's repentance in the 990s for his youthful misdeeds may have been intended as a programme of public, royal penance aimed at stemming the growing Viking menace. The continuation of such attacks and the crisis of 1009 called for an escalation in response and for the instigation of a national programme of penance.

The ideals of such an endeavour may have been embodied in a new coinage, the 'Agnus Dei' pennies. On these coins, the royal portrait was replaced by the Agnus Dei (the Lamb of God) – perhaps intended here as a symbol of peace – while the reverse featured a bird with wings outspread, either the dove of peace or a symbol of the Holy

7.12 'Agnus Dei'-type penny of King Æthelred, produced by the moneyer Blacaman at Derby

7.13 Opening of the earliest manuscript of the *Sermon of the Wolf to the English*. The Latin rubric includes the date 1014 and the manuscript features a number of annotations, possibly in Wulfstan's own hand

Spirit. Only a small number of these coins has been found, suggesting they were a special issue rather than general currency.

The best-known of Wulfstan's works and one of the few that specifically names him as the author is the *Sermon of the Wolf to the English*. This was probably first delivered in 1014 and now survives in three versions of differing length. The order of these versions remains unclear but it seems likely that the shortest version is the earliest and that Wulfstan returned to the sermon on a number of occasions, adding to it and editing it as the situation changed and his thinking developed.

For a sermon delivered during, and probably again in the aftermath of, Æthelred's exile at the hands of Swein, the virtual absence of references to the Vikings is striking. Instead, the sermon concentrates on the sins committed by the English – despoiling churches, oppressing the poor, denying rights and justice and, greatest of all, treachery to one's lord, under which heading Wulfstan places the murder of King Edward and the driving into exile of Æthelred. Such sins had resulted in numerous disasters and calamities: ruination at the hands of robbers – possibly the Vikings are meant here – famine, the failure of crops, disease, pestilence and oppressive taxation.

The longest version of the sermon closes with a reference to Gildas and his account of how the sins of the Britons 'angered God so excessively that finally he allowed the army of the English to conquer their land and to destroy the host of the Britons entirely'. This offered a dire historical precedent for the worst that could happen if the English did not repent of their sins and reform their ways. It was, of course, exactly what did happen in 1016. Yet Wulfstan's vision of the ordering of Christian society and the obligations of Christian kingship was embraced by Cnut, and the law codes produced in his reign represent the summation of Wulfstan's homiletic and legislative activity. Cnut's codes of 1020, drafted by Wulfstan, were the last royal law codes issued in the Anglo-Saxon period and would subsequently be copied and studied intensely after the Norman Conquest.

The Reign of Cnut

The events of 1066 loom large in the English historical consciousness in a way that the events of 1016 do not. Cnut's conquest is very much the forgotten conquest of the eleventh century. This relative neglect is partly a product of the paucity of the surviving sources. The *Anglo-Saxon Chronicle*, so loquacious for the reign of Æthelred, particularly its final years, has far less to say about the reign of Cnut. Though charters were issued in Cnut's name, only 36 are now extant, and this figure includes numerous forgeries. Moreover, charters are absent for particularly crucial periods of Cnut's reign, most notably the late 1020s to early 1030s. To the charters can be added an additional eight writs – much shorter documents written in Old English – and three law codes, along with two letters written to the people of England in Cnut's name.

Other narrative sources can round out the picture, but such texts bring with them their own particular interpretative difficulties. The most significant of these texts is the so-called *Encomium Emmae Reginae*. Despite the title, this source is less a poem in praise of Queen Emma and more an encomium on the reign of Cnut and his son Harthacnut. Commissioned by Emma, the widow of Æthelred and subsequently wife of Cnut, the *Encomium* was written by a Flemish monk in the 1040s, and though it is a vital source for the events of the eleventh century it is curiously evasive and reticent at times – Emma's marriage to Æthelred is not mentioned, for example. Such surely reflects the complex political situations Emma herself was forced to negotiate throughout her life and the changes of allegiance these shifting circumstances necessitated.

Far more than the exiguous source material, it is the continuity between Cnut's reign and those of his predecessors that explains why his conquest is so little remembered. Compared to the upheavals that were a consequence of the Norman Conquest, the

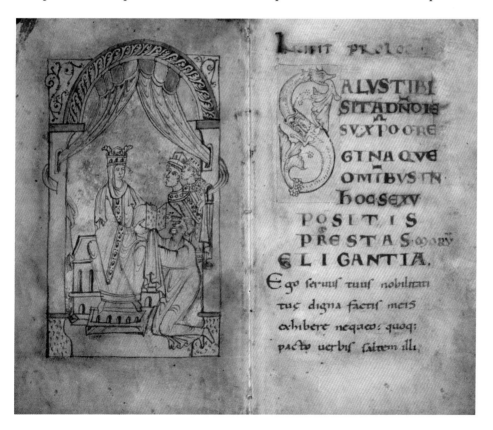

7.14 Opening pages of the *Encomium Emmae Reginae*. Queen Emma receives the manuscript of the poem (left)

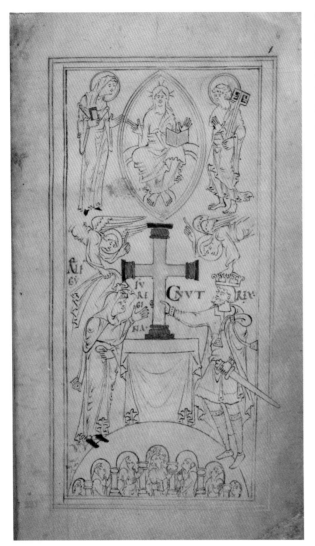

7.15 King Cnut and Queen Ælfgifu in the *New Minster Liber Vitae*. An angel crowns Cnut while pointing to God, indicating Divine approval of Cnut's kingship. Cnut's appearance is reminiscent, probably deliberately so, of manuscript depictions of King Edgar

transition between Æthelred, Edmund and Cnut seems far less dramatic. Changes did take place across a range of areas, but under the influence of figures like Archbishop Wulfstan, Cnut sought to rule England in the style of an English king, presenting himself explicitly as the restorer of the order and justice that had existed during the reign of Edgar.

Though post-Conquest sources would stress that Cnut gained the kingship of the entirety of England under the terms of his agreement with Edmund Ironside and with the consent of the Anglo-Saxon nobility, Cnut's earliest actions suggest an uneasy ruler, uncertain of his position. In 1017 Cnut divided England into four parts, assigning East Anglia to Thorkell, Mercia to Eadric, and Northumbria to Eric – a Norwegian who had played a central role in the campaigns that led to Cnut's conquest. Cnut kept Wessex for himself. This division of power was presumably intended to cement the loyalty of three of the most powerful figures in the kingdom, all of whom were potential rivals to Cnut or, particularly in Eadric's case, possible foci of resistance. How long such an arrangement lasted is unclear. At any rate, Eadric was killed in the same year, in a purge that also saw the deaths of Northman, son of Ealdorman Leofwine, Æthelweard, son of Ealdorman Æthelmær, and Brihtric, son of Ælfheah of Devonshire.

Alongside members of the Anglo-Saxon nobility, Æthelred's sons and grandsons also remained a threat to Cnut's rule. Eadwig, the son of Æthelred by his first consort Ælfgifu of York, was driven into exile in 1017 and probably killed soon afterwards, while Edward and Alfred, Æthelred's sons by Emma, went into exile in Normandy. Edmund Ironside's sons, Edward and Edmund, were likewise exiled to the Continent, ending up eventually in Hungary having escaped attempts by Cnut to have them murdered.

It was also in 1017 that Cnut married Æthelred's widow, Emma. The *Chronicle* simply records Cnut ordering her 'to be fetched as his wife', while the *Encomium* presents a suitable bride for Cnut being sought far and wide until Emma, 'a famous queen', was found in Normandy. Such a marriage would have furthered Cnut's legitimacy as a ruler, as well as countering the danger of Norman support for Emma's sons by Æthelred. Emma's role in all this is difficult to determine. The *Encomium* presents her as refusing marriage to Cnut 'unless he would affirm to her by oath, that he would never set up the son of any wife other than herself to rule after him' and praises her prudency in looking to secure the legacy of future sons. Such may suggest Emma was aware of her value to Cnut and drove a hard bargain. Certainly, she appears as a figure of considerable power and authority in Cnut's reign, with post-Conquest sources even claiming she acted as a regent during Cnut's absence from England. On the other hand, the Encomiast's words may speak more to the struggles between Emma's son Harthacnut and his half-brother Harold Harefoot after Cnut's death than to the circumstances of 1017.

The various events of 1017 look to have left Cnut more secure on his throne and in 1018, having collected a vast tribute of some £82,500, he finally disbanded his army, keeping only 40 ships. In the same year, the *Chronicle* notes that 'the Danes and the English reached an agreement at Oxford'. The text of this agreement or a law code promulgated in its aftermath survives. The work of Archbishop Wulfstan, this text draws extensively on earlier Anglo-Saxon legislation and notes that all have pledged to observe and uphold the laws of King Edgar. This was not simply presenting Cnut's kingship as the continuation of existing practices. Rather it was connecting Cnut's rule directly with the reign of Edgar, a time by then seen as a Golden Age of Anglo-Saxon kingship. Further deliberations were promised by the code and the result of these may inform the two law codes promulgated in the early 1020s, codes that both bear the imprint of Archbishop Wulfstan.

If legal texts stress continuity, nevertheless there were significant changes in royal administration and governance during Cnut's rule. Most notable is a lack of continuity in personnel from Æthelred's reign to Cnut's. Unsurprisingly, at the beginning of his reign, Cnut advanced Scandinavians to positions of authority. Up to the late 1020s, Cnut's ealdormen – or earls, as they were now increasingly known – were almost exclusively Scandinavian. Many, such as Eric or Ulfr, were related to Cnut by marriage and most had presumably played a part in Cnut's conquest of England. A few Anglo-Saxon ealdormen did hold onto their power, albeit mostly briefly. Only Leofwine, ealdorman of the *Hwicce* since the 990s, retained his position into the mid-1020s and this despite the killing of his son, Northman, in 1017.

By the early 1030s, this situation had dramatically altered. The final years of Cnut's reign saw the pre-eminence of Anglo-Saxon earls. Most significant among these was Earl Godwine, whose rise to prominence began in Cnut's reign and whose son Harold would eventually be crowned king of England. Leofwine's son Leofric also rose rapidly in this period and his family would subsequently rival Godwine's in power and influence. The combined effect of the reigns of Æthelred and Cnut was thus to end the power of the old, long-established Anglo-Saxon aristocracy. It was the 'new men' and their families, principally raised up under Cnut, who would dominate the final decades of Anglo-Saxon England.

Lower down the scale, Scandinavians likewise dominated the ranks of thegns and *ministri*, though significant numbers of Anglo-Saxons also held such office. Despite the presence of these Anglo-Saxon thegns it is, again, the lack of continuity that is most striking. Very few can be shown to have survived from Æthelred's reign and such continuity as there is was restricted largely to two particular groups or factions. One centred on Odda of Gloucestershire, whose career stretched from the reign of Æthelred to that of Edward the Confessor. The other was that of the family and associates of

Ælfgar 'Mæw', also based in the south west. Again, the power of this group persisted through the reigns of Æthelred to Edward the Confessor. The survival, indeed, the flourishing of these two groups under Cnut cannot now be easily explained, though presumably they were being rewarded for having transferred their loyalty to Cnut early in his campaigns of conquest. That both groups had links with the faction that fell from power in the final decade of Æthelred's reign may also be of significance.

Though there were significant changes in the make-up of the aristocracy, there is far less evidence for the expropriation of land or for the redistribution of estates – particularly in comparison with the Norman Conquest. Such may be partly explained by Cnut's use of money and treasure – the vast tribute of 1018 – to reward his followers rather than grants of land. Certain areas did, however, see significant settlement of Scandinavians under Cnut and some concomitant changes in land ownership. Settlement seems to have been particularly extensive in the West Midlands. The bishop of Worcester, Lyfing, famously addressed 'all the thegns in Worcestershire, both English and Danish' in a charter of c. 1042, and similar salutations were used in other documents from the region. Expropriations of land by Earl Hakon, both from the monks of Worcester and from laymen in the diocese, are recorded in the late eleventh-century document known as *Hemming's Cartulary* – though such seizures seem to have been on a more limited scale than Hemming's account suggests.

Certain of Cnut's Scandinavian followers are known to have had extensive land-holdings in England. The thegn Tofi, for example, held lands in Berkshire, Hertfordshire,

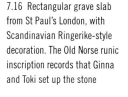

7.16 Rectangular grave slab from St Paul's London, with Scandinavian Ringerike-style decoration. The Old Norse runic inscription records that Ginna and Toki set up the stone

Somerset, Surrey and Essex, and founded or refounded a church at Waltham (Essex), giving to it a stone crucifix said to have been discovered on his estate at Montacute (Somerset). Other followers seem to have been of more local importance but still controlled significant estates in their region, such as Orc, known to have owned a number of estates in Dorset which he subsequently used to endow the monastery at Abbotsbury. Urban areas also saw settlement. A naval garrison, for example, was stationed at Southwark, on the south bank of the Thames, the members of which seem to have played an important role in the governance and administration of London.

The nature and structure of Cnut's regime in England were shaped also by his extensive interests in Scandinavia. Much of his reign was spent consolidating his control over the kingdom of Denmark and expanding his power elsewhere in the region, particularly Norway. Cnut was in Denmark in the winter and spring of 1019–20, probably to secure the throne after the death of his brother Harald, and he returned to Denmark again in 1023 and campaigned repeatedly in Scandinavia in the late 1020s. Cnut also had to deal with the powerful Holy Roman Emperors whose territory bordered Denmark. Cnut's presence in Rome in 1027 when Emperor Conrad II was crowned is unlikely to have been coincidental, although Cnut also used the trip to negotiate the protection of English pilgrims and merchants travelling to the Continent.

The Continental campaigns of Cnut offered an obvious route of advancement for his followers. Godwine, for example, is known to have gained Cnut's particular favour as a result of his service during one of the king's campaigns in Denmark, probably that of 1023. Cnut's repeated absences from England also forced him to rely heavily on a small number of individuals to protect his interests. Thorkell probably acted as regent during Cnut's time in Denmark in 1019–20, and Godwine is likely to have fulfilled a similar role later in Cnut's reign. Even with such regents, Cnut's absences threatened the stability of his rule in England. Some kind of revolt took place in 1019–20, for on his return to England Cnut outlawed Ealdorman Æthelweard and Eadwig, 'king of the *ceorls*' – about whom nothing else is known unless he was the son of Æthelred of the same name. Thorkell may have been implicated in some way for he was outlawed by Cnut the following year, although the two were reconciled in 1023.

The aspect of Cnut's rule that made the greatest impact on the sources was, however, his religious benefaction. Cnut appears in the sources as a particularly generous bene-factor, even for a king, and as a ruler of particular personal piety. The *Encomium Emmae Reginae*, for example, describes the lavish gifts he bestowed on the monastery of St Omer in France and how he approached the altar there kissing the pavement, beating his breast and weeping. The New Minster, Winchester, received a vast cross of gold and silver, containing numerous relics, and other churches and monasteries were similarly enriched.

If Cnut's religious benefaction was lavish, it was not indiscriminate. Christ Church Canterbury and the communities at Winchester, for example, were particularly prominent beneficiaries, while the bishopric of London was one of the notable losers. Not only is Cnut known to have expropriated at least one of its estates – that at Southminster – but he directed his favour and patronage to the neighbouring community at Westminster, bestowing on it a number of important relics. Cnut's treatment of the bishopric of London presumably reflects the support that the city and its bishop had offered to Æthelred and, subsequently, to Edmund. The naval garrison at Southwark may be a further indication of Cnut's uncertainty about the loyalty of London.

Such concerns may be one of the reasons Cnut chose to translate the remains of the martyred Archbishop Ælfheah from London to Canterbury in 1023. The cult of an archbishop murdered by Vikings would form an obvious focus of resistance to Cnut's rule, and this removal not only transferred the body from a city whose loyalty Cnut may have questioned but, by patronising the cult himself, Cnut could potentially also neutralise its damaging connotations. Similar reasons may lie behind Cnut's patronage of the cult of St Edmund, the East Anglian king killed by Vikings in the 860s. The cult of Edward the Martyr was likewise particularly promoted by Cnut, though whether this was to blacken the name of Æthelred – for Æthelred may have been implicated in the murder – or to stress continuity with him – Æthelred was a patron of Edward's cult – is not clear.

Cnut's death on 12 November 1035 precipitated a struggle for the English throne between two of his sons, Harthacnut and Harold Harefoot. The former was supported by his mother Emma, as well as by Godwine, while the latter was supported by his mother Ælfgifu of Northampton and Earl Leofric. Eventually, at a meeting in Oxford, the kingdom was divided between the two brothers, with Harthacnut ruling the south and Harold the north. Such an agreement was, however, reached in Harthacnut's absence – he had not returned from Denmark where he was establishing his power as king. Harthacnut's continued absence in the years following meant Harold became de facto king of the whole of England and Emma fled to Bruges. It was only on Harold's

7.17 St Mary's Church, Breamore. The layout and much of the surviving fabric of the church are late Anglo-Saxon. The porch features a low-relief crucifixion scene, while an archway in the nave bears the Old English inscription 'HER SPUTELAÐ SEO GECPYDRÆDNES ÐE', 'Here is manifested the covenant to you' (or perhaps 'Here is manifested the covenant which…')

death in 1040 that Harthacnut was able to claim the English throne – among his first actions was to have Harold's body dug up and thrown into the marshes.

Wealth, Social Mobility and the Rise of the 'Gentry'

The renewed Viking attacks that culminated in Cnut's conquest were but the most obvious sign of a world that had descended into disorder and sin. Archbishop Wulfstan could discern many others. The social order was coming apart, the boundaries between different ranks and statuses were becoming blurred and difficult to distinguish:

> Once it used to be that people and rights went by dignities, and councillors of the people were then entitled to honour, each according to his rank, whether noble or *ceorl*, retainer or lord.

The text from which this lament comes – *Gethynctho* or *Concerning the Dignities and Laws of the People* – is part of a series of works exploring rank and status that were assembled, edited and extended by Wulfstan. It goes on to set out how a *ceorl* used to attain the status and rights of a thegn if he had five hides of land, a bell-house, church, kitchen, gate-house ('*burhgeat*') and an office at the king's court. A trader was similarly entitled to the rights of a thegn if he undertook three sea crossings at his own expense, while a lengthier list stipulated the requirements for a thegn to achieve the status of an earl. Another text in this collection, *Northleoda laga* or the *Laws of the Northern People*, similarly notes that a *ceorl* who possessed five hides of land was to have the status of a thegn but 'even if he prospers so that he possesses a helmet and a coat of mail and a gold-plated sword, if he has not the land, he is a *ceorl* all the same'.

7.18 Luxuria tempts warriors to abandon their weapons and give themselves over to pleasure and indulgence. From a late-tenth-century manuscript of Prudentius' *Pyschomachia*, a poem describing the battle between the virtues and vices

Wulfstan's compilation on status was a reaction to an increasing social mobility in late Anglo-Saxon England and to a growing tendency for those lower down the social hierarchy to emulate the lifestyles and mores of their supposed social betters. Such was accompanied by a growth in conspicuous consumption and display, with the powerful and socially ambitious expressing their status more and more through ostentatious clothing and feasting. Indeed, it was in the tenth and eleventh centuries that the Old English word 'rice' came to mean not simply 'powerful', as it had done, but also something closer to 'rich' – power and wealth were becoming the same thing. What Wulfstan was seeking to do was to restore a putative former social order, to ensure that only certain routes to advancement were open. His enterprise was as much historical as it was legal.

Though the late tenth and eleventh centuries saw the rise to pre-eminence of a new 'super rich' – particularly the families of Godwine and Leofwine – it was the emergence and growth of a class of lesser, local landowners – a gentry class – that particularly marked out this period. Of the approximately five thousand individuals listed in Domesday Book as owning land in 1066, perhaps only one hundred held lands more extensive than 40 hides and very few held lands throughout the kingdom. The economic base of this emerging gentry class can be explored in some detail through landscape archaeology and the excavation of settlements, along with the written record.

The later Anglo-Saxon period saw the development of new types of estates and landholdings and the formation of new settlement types. In the early and middle Anglo-Saxon periods, estates were large and comprised sometimes widely dispersed

7.19 The Hurbuck Hoard. A late ninth- or tenth-century collection of agricultural and woodworking tools, plus a sword and seax

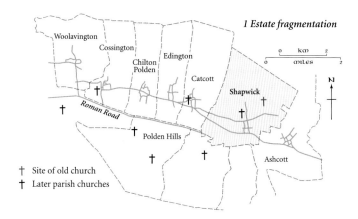

1 Estate fragmentation

† Site of old church
† Later parish churches

7.20 Development of the estate of Shapwick in the later Anglo-Saxon period. Fragmentation of the larger estates (above); process of settlement nucleation at eventual village of Shapwick (below)

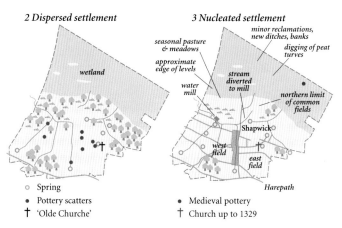

2 Dispersed settlement

○ Spring
● Pottery scatters
† 'Olde Churche'

3 Nucleated settlement

● Medieval pottery
† Church up to 1329

holdings, with resources drawn from a wide area of the landscape – the so-called 'multiple estate' model. Though such estates continued into the later Anglo-Saxon period in certain areas – the north in particular – from the tenth century onwards, and possibly earlier, many of these estates were broken up, with smaller, discrete holdings being carved out of them. In some cases these new holdings were named after their owners, as with Woolstone (Berkshire) named for the thegn Wulfric ('Wulfricestun') or East Garston (Berkshire) named for Esgar ('Esgareston'). The break-up of the multiple estates was frequently accompanied by nucleation, with dispersed farmsteads abandoned and settlement concentrated into new villages, often with regularly laid-out plots, separated by ditches, and the establishment of open fields.

The best understood example of these processes in action is the manor at Shapwick in Somerset. This had been given to Glastonbury in the eighth century as part of a larger 60-hide grant that also included what was to become the manor of Wilton. In the second half of the tenth century, Shapwick was divided up into six separate estates, of around 5 hides each, that became the villages of Woolavington, Cossington, Chilton Polden, Edington, Catcott and Shapwick. The division seems to have been carefully planned and designed to ensure that each of these smaller units had access to water, pasture and the other necessary natural resources. At the same time, numerous scattered settlements were abandoned and new nucleated villages established. In what

7.23 West tower of St Michael
Northgate, Oxford

Churches, as were required of the socially ambitious *ceorl* of *Gethynctho*, have been identified on a number of sites and the tenth and eleventh centuries were, in general, periods of intensive church-building. At some point after 950, a small church was built to the east of the lordly complex at Furnells. The graveyard of this church served the whole of the village but a number of the graves were marked by stone grave-covers – one also originally had a free-standing cross – and were presumably the burials of the lordly proprietor and his family. Other examples of such churches include those at Goltho (Lincolnshire), Faccombe Netherton (Hampshire) and Sulgrave (Northamptonshire); it is possible that the stone tower at Portchester fulfilled a similar role as it was the focus of a number of burials.

Alongside these changes in landscape and settlement, written sources from later Anglo-Saxon England also show a concern for the proper and efficient management of rural estates. Texts set out the roles, duties and obligations of different classes of workers and the qualities that should be looked for in estate managers and other officials. Some texts, such as that known as *Gerefa* (*The Reeve*), seem to be less practical guides and more literary productions. *The Reeve* includes rhyme and alliteration and seems in places simply to be lists of technical vocabulary. Likewise, despite setting out what are claimed to be the appropriate times and seasons for the different agricultural activities, there are numerous omissions and the activities seem to have been selected for stylistic rather than practical reasons. The influence on the text of Classical authors such as Cato and Columella further points to a classroom setting rather than an agricultural one.

Some texts were, however, intended as practical documents. A number of estate surveys survive from the later Anglo-Saxon period, such as those for Tidenham (Gloucestershire) and Hurstbourne Priors (Hampshire) or that now known as the *Rectitudines singularum personarum*, perhaps connected with the abbey of Bath. These record the dues owed by the tenants of the estate and the labour services they must carry out. The *ceorls* at Hurstbourne, for example, paid 40 pence, three sesters of bread wheat and six *mittan* of ale at the autumn equinox. They were also expected to plough and sow 3 acres, mow half an acre of meadow and make a rick, and supply and stack 4 fothers of wood and 16 poles of fencing, as well as to undertake such weekly work as they were bidden (though they did get midwinter, Easter and Rogationtide off). Such texts suggest attempts to record and to regularise disparate practices, presumably to increase the ease and efficiency of estate management. Standardisation could, however, only go so far. The *Rectitudines singularum personarum* noted that specific customs varied from estate to estate and that these long-established practices should continue to be respected.

For Wulfstan, it was the ownership of land and the holding of royal office that were the only legitimate route to social betterment. Unsurprisingly, his treatises on status have little to say about the other, improper ways in which individuals attempted social advancement. Yet, as the *Laws of the Northern People* reject the idea that material possessions alone – gold-plated swords and coats of mail – were sufficient for advancement, such must have been the way many attempted to improve their station in life. Certainly, the theme of ostentatious display runs through much evidence from later Anglo-Saxon England.

Clothing offered one key way in which status could be displayed or claimed. Norman commentators writing after the Conquest were particularly struck by the finery of Anglo-Saxon dress and the wealth invested in costume. There are frequent references in the written sources to cloaks and other items of clothing made of silk, and a small number of silk items have been recovered archaeologically. In other cases, wealth and status were demonstrated through decoration and adornment. Manuscript illustrations show cuffs, hems and trimmings apparently embroidered or brocaded, sometimes with what looks like gold or silver thread. The reputation of English needlework – the *opus Anglicanum* of the later Middle Ages – was already well established in the later Anglo-Saxon period, with Continental commentators noting not just the quality of the work but the amount of it and how extensively it was employed. Such was the investment in dress that clothing could act as a form of moveable wealth. In her will, Wulfwaru, a landowner in Somerset in the late tenth century, left to her daughter a headband worth 30 mancuses and to four of her servants a golden headband worth 20 mancuses. Presumably, the latter could be divided up or the gold braid extracted.

Though the most expensive materials and the most extravagant styles would have been restricted to the very richest, in particular the king and queen, those lower down the social scale sought to emulate as best they could the fashions of the very wealthy. Even minor nobles could, through the finery of their clothing and jewellery, appear to be of much higher status. The best-known example is the thegn Gospatric who was able to trick thieves in Italy into thinking that he was Earl Tostig partly because of the clothes he was wearing.

Though dress had been a marker of wealth and status throughout the Anglo-Saxon period, there is evidence that elite clothing was becoming more elaborate and costly in the eleventh century. Manuscript illustrations, for example, suggest female fashion in this period embraced longer sleeves, with extended cuffs and the pleating and bunching of material. At the same time, male dress was changing, with Byzantine-inspired long robes and gowns being increasingly adopted by the elite. Such clothing was first depicted in the image of King Edgar in the *Regularis concordia* in the later tenth century, with eleventh-century manuscripts suggesting such outfits were subsequently adopted by royal courtiers and officials.

Feasting was another way in which status and wealth could be displayed, both in terms of the quantities eaten – Norman writers commented particularly on the size of English portions – and the types of food consumed. Archaeological evidence indicates a growing divide between the types of food eaten by the powerful and wealthy and those eaten by those lower down the social scale. Whales and porpoises, for example, were particularly prized by the elite, and in the west of England herring was likewise highly valued. Written sources show that lords laid claim to any rare and valuable fish caught in the weirs of their tenants. Thus at Tidenham, the lord could claim every other fish caught in the weirs on the estate as well as any sturgeon, porpoise, herring

7.24 The month of October from an eleventh-century calendar. A nobleman hunts with a falcon

or sea fish – Tidenham is close to the Severn Estuary. The lord could also expect to be informed if anyone sold fish for money on the estate. Deer and other game, especially fowl, were also a prominent part of late Anglo-Saxon aristocratic diets, not least because hunting and hawking were noble pastimes.

If the upheavals and instability of the later tenth and eleventh centuries caused significant problems for Anglo-Saxon England, nevertheless it was a period in which many prospered, enjoying better and more comfortable lives than individuals of their status had hitherto known. Violence and warfare must have undermined feelings of security and stability, yet England, for all its problems, remained a wealthy kingdom and one in which it was possible to thrive and to seek social betterment. Such would reach its apogee, and Anglo-Saxon England its perigee, in 1066, when Harold, son of Cnut's 'new man' Godwine, gained the English throne.

EOFORWIC/*JORVIK*/YORK

NICHOLAS J. HIGHAM

From about 700 onwards, York emerged as the most important centre in northern England. The diocese began in the 620s, ceased abruptly in 633, but was then refounded in the 660s and upgraded as an archdiocese covering all Northumbria in 735. It was significant to the kings as well, the site of their only mint and by far the most important port in eastern Northumbria.

Eighth-century York extended across three sites. The Roman legionary fortress housed the archdiocesan church (though as yet unlocated), the bishop's residence and, probably, a royal palace. Secondly, there was activity in the old Roman *colonia* facing the fortress across the River Ouse, around Holy Trinity/Agia Sophia and along the waterfront – a monastery seems a real possibility. Thirdly, on the east bank of the River Foss over a kilometre from the medieval minster, excavation of 46–54 Fishergate revealed a *wic* – Eoforwic.

The size of Eoforwic is uncertain. Comparison with trading sites at London, Hamwic, Ipswich, Dorestad, Quentovic and Ribe would suggest an area of 30–60 hectares, but excavation around the Barbican found little trace, implying that it was either smaller than these or tightly concentrated along the river; York was at the northern extremity of trade centred on the Channel, which could account for a smaller size. This was, however, an integral part of Anglian York, established in all probability under royal and/or archdiocesan authority. Goods from overseas arrived here and both exports and exchange were managed. Imported pottery came from present-day northern France, Belgium and Rhineland Germany – Mayen ware, for example, accompanied basalt from the Rhineland-Palatinate, used for the manufacture of quernstones. Ipswich Ware and Ipswich-type wares also arrived up the east coast. Three Frisian coins substantiate Alcuin's reference to Frisian traders at York c. 800. Manufacturing waste indicates the production of glass vessels either here or elsewhere in York, alongside metalworking, woodworking, bone and antler comb-making, leather-working and textile production. Pottery was manufactured nearby in two distinct traditions, of which sand-tempered wares were the more abundant; shell-tempered wares were only present in small quantities and finds peter out for the ninth century. Compared with Hamwic, the pottery range is limited, but the proportion derived from overseas is higher, suggesting that locally manufactured wares were in short supply.

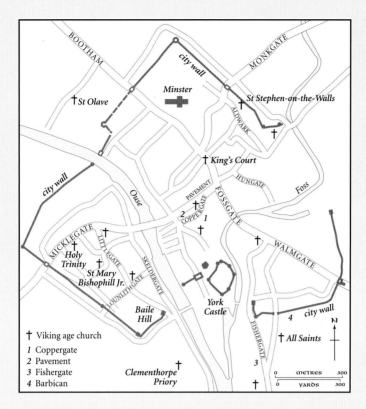

7a.1 Viking Age York. Note the division into three sectors focused on the old Roman legionary fortress, location of the minster, the extra-mural area around the Foss and the old Roman *colonia* west of the Ouse

After shifting fortunes across the earlier ninth century, Fishergate was abandoned quite suddenly in the 860s or 870s: the latest coin find was a West Saxon silver penny of 858–66. This coincides with the *Anglo-Saxon Chronicle* account of the Danish occupation, when the 'great raiding-army' seized then successfully defended the fortress against the Northumbrians in 866, and then Healfdene 'divided up the land of Northumbria' in 876, making himself the ruler of the north. In this time of crisis, 46–54 Fishergate was abandoned and the commercial centre relocated on a low spur of land between the Foss, the Ouse and the fortress. This re-siting differs from that at Winchester or London, where trade and manufacturing actually shifted within the Roman walls. Here continuing commitment to extramural settlement suggests real confidence in the new Viking kingdom.

Excavations in several locations, but most famously at 16–22 Coppergate, have revealed much about the development of York from the late ninth century onwards, when it emerged as the largest settlement in England north of the Wash. Roman sequences at Coppergate ended with a fourth-century cemetery. Thereafter the area was deserted until the ninth century, when an eighth-century Anglian helmet was buried alongside various other artefacts in a wood-lined pit – probably a shallow well. It is tempting to view this in the context of the disastrous attack on York by Northumbrian forces late in 866, but this is only one possible interpretation. More organised use of the site followed soon after. 'The Viking Dig' revealed the first appearance of post/stake and wattle alignments in the later ninth century, following which the road that became Coppergate was laid out. In the period 930/5–c. 975, four tene-

7a.2 Viking Age Coppergate. Early tenth-century wattle-built structures

ments were established fronting Coppergate with buildings constructed with posts in-filled with wattle. These were then replaced c. 975-early/mid-eleventh century by new cellar-type, plank-built structures erected within the same boundaries in a double row along the street frontage.

The Coppergate excavation revealed a congested urban complex in which different tradesmen worked cheek by jowl. The street name derives from cup manufacturing. Ironworking was present on a commercial scale, with techniques ranging from simple welding and hammering through to steeling and decorative work. Large numbers of knives were found, alongside small bells and tools associated with agriculture, and

7a.3 Bone combs from Coppergate. Bone was worked on site to make an array of domestic items

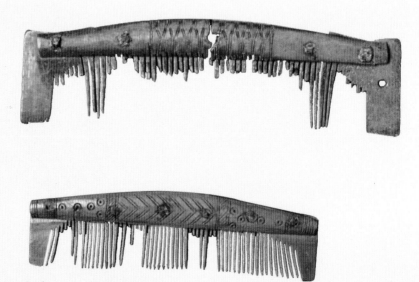

metal-, leather-, textile- and wood-working. Glass-working was also present and finds of coin dies either indicate coining here or a metalworker recycling dies from elsewhere in York. In all some forty thousand finds came from the excavations and Coppergate yielded rich 'waterlogged' deposits which preserved exceptional quantities of organic material, allowing an unusual range of activities to come under the microscope.

York's trade was at its height in the late ninth and early tenth centuries but remained vigorous, with Scandinavian connections dominant, right up to the Norman Conquest. Evidence of trade with the Scandinavian world includes hones of Norwegian schist, Norwegian and/or Shetland soapstone and clubmoss (used for dyeing) from southern Scandinavia, as well as amber, most of which probably derived from the Baltic. It is tempting to see the site as a Scandinavian colony dependent on the new Viking king-ship and drawing on a mixed Danish, Norwegian and Hiberno-Norse heritage, but there are signs too of a local 'native' presence continuing. For example, two different styles of shoe manufacture may reflect two different markets, with incoming Scandinavians and local Northumbrians each preferring the style of footwear with which they were familiar. There were similarly two styles of knife-sheath manufac-tured. Trades that were traditionally male seem to have been more affected by Scandinavian traditions than those that were 'female', suggesting that male incomers may have formed a larger sector of the market than did female. This is best evidenced in cloth manufacturing, which was traditionally women's work.

Evidence relating to textile production was widespread at Coppergate, reflecting both domestic output and more commercial levels of production. Wool, flax, hemp, silk and gold thread were all identified, with silk particularly well represented in comparison with other sites by 22 examples of woven fragments as opposed to 32 of wool. Mid-tenth-century Coppergate yielded evidence of wool-combing, spinning, weaving, dyeing, needlework, flax production and laundering, suggesting that the whole gamut of production was present. Silk, of course, was imported and this more

7a.4 Excavated shoes from Coppergate

expensive textile seems to have been used primarily for small items, particularly head-dresses and ribbons. Prior to the Viking Age silk barely occurs in northern England and was clearly a highly exotic import. However, the Viking expansion into Russia and down to the Black Sea opened up trade with Byzantium, which was both a producer of silk itself and the western end of the Silk Road to China. It is in this context that the amount of silk reaching York expanded, but it remained an expensive textile. Wool and linen cloth were manufactured in much larger quantities, including what may have been local copies of Scandinavian textiles. Most of the Coppergate cloth does, however, belong to northern Anglian cloth-making traditions and should be seen as the work of indigenous Northumbrians aiming at a local market. Only a small minority of the textiles found are likely to have been imports and these were the finer cloths brought in from Frisia and the Rhineland, including linen featuring a honeycomb weave. By the early tenth century, the finishing of cloth on site with teasels and shears had ended, and dyeing was no longer practised by the later eleventh century, when the arrival of the treadle loom initiated major changes in textile manufacture, speeding up the process considerably and encouraging the shift from female workers to the male ones of the post-Conquest period.

Large quantities of bone indicate that cattle were the predominant food animal, perhaps due to the nature of the grazing in the Vale of York, followed rather distantly by sheep and pigs. Pigs, fowl and geese were probably all kept in the town, but the scarcity of goats suggest that milk and cheese came from the surrounding countryside. Hunted game was rare, although the proportion of wild birds (and pigs) rose in the late tenth century. That said, domestic fowl and geese remained the dominant bird species throughout and eggs were consumed widely. Animals seem to have been butchered close by and this may be one reason why such a range of meat cuts was present. Fish were important, particularly eels and herring but also other sea fish and shellfish. Large amounts of flour-based foods were consumed, mostly derived from wheat and rye, while fruit-stones demonstrate the popularity of the plum family and a few fig and grape seeds suggest some imports. Bees were probably kept, judging from the large numbers found dead.

Living conditions clearly left much to be desired, though by the standards of the day they were probably quite good. The identification of numerous parasites suggests that the inhabitants were lousy and flea-ridden, and excrement lay on the ground. Chickens and pigs were kept close by humans and probably played their part in the waste-recycling process.

Similarly rich organic deposits were sampled at 6–8 Pavement and 5–7 Coppergate, the former yielding a complete human coprolite (fossilised excrement) which revealed several parasitic worms. Querns and grindstones, locks and keys, wooden vessels, fragments of one or more soapstone bowls and items of personal wear all imply a domestic setting, while masses of leather offcuts and tools such as awls and a shoe-last indicate leather-working at a commercial level.

Trading and small-scale manufacturing occupied a great swathe of Viking Age York. Large-scale excavations between the fortress and the River Foss centred on Hungate are currently exploring another part of Viking Age York. Here activity is present from the early tenth century and timber-lined cellars indicative of two-storey houses and warehouses some 3 metres below modern street level belong to the mid–late tenth century, comparable to the structures found at Coppergate. Ship timbers that had originated in southern England had been recycled in one building. Although it is at this stage too early to comment fully, finds again imply a vibrant commercial and industrial centre integral to well-used trade routes to other regions of western Europe and even the Islamic world. Numerous cesspits, access ways and regular tenement boundaries suggest a well-organised townscape. While we must await detailed publication of this new excavation and the archaeological riches being exposed, it is already clear that it will take our understanding of Viking Age York to new levels.

The old *colonia* also saw considerable occupation in the Viking Age. The main axis from the fortress was via Micklegate – the 'great street', around which a distorted grid of roads ignored the Roman layout, with Anglo-Scandinavian names implying pre-Conquest foundation (as Skeldergate, Lounlithgate, Littlegate). Excavations at 58–59 Skeldergate revealed a structure of the late ninth/early tenth centuries built on rubble-filled trench foundations, suggesting that the waterfront was occupied by traders. Five of the nine medieval churches or chapels here are demonstrably pre-Conquest, including Clementhorpe Nunnery outside the walls. Research at St Mary Bishophill Junior has revealed eighth/ninth-century stone carving, but it also flourished in the Viking Age: among a group of burials to the north of the church, one was coin-dated 905–30, and a new tower was constructed in the third quarter of the eleventh century from reused masonry, mostly Roman but including fragments of Anglian and Anglo-Scandinavian sculpture.

New church construction was also occurring east of the River Ouse. St Helen-on-the-Walls, for example, was built as a single-cell, near-square church in the later tenth century, subsequently enlarged with a rectangular chancel. The cemetery revealed more than one thousand graves, dating from the tenth century to the sixteenth. Excavation at 1–5 Aldwark revealed reoccupation in the eleventh century. However,

7a.6 Excavation underway at Hungate. A massively-built timber-lined cellar deep beneath current ground level implies a two-storey house, comparable to late tenth-century examples found at Coppergate.

the main cemetery on this side of York remained the minster's, with graves so far dated 850–950.

Viking Age York was exceptionally large by the standard of English towns, with a population numbered in many thousands and with great wealth, but alongside social deprivation and poverty. How should we explain the exceptional rise of Viking York as a manufacturing and commercial settlement? Anglian York lay on the periphery of a trading network centred on the Channel. The Viking Age created a different orbit, centred on Scandinavia but encompassing Ireland, Scotland and the Atlantic as well as the great eastern European river valleys and the eastern Mediterranean. York served as a hub of Viking trade routes in the west. One consequence of successive Viking occupations by armies rich with plunder was the revival of the Northumbrian currency. The Vikings minted silver coins in considerable quantities, as the Cuerdale Hoard indicates. The new elite probably treated the walled city as a quasi-capital. Kings, archbishops and their retinues, and an inflow of taxes and renders from the Viking kingdom, capitalised the markets and attracted imports, encouraging trade and manufacturing. Even after the English conquest in the mid-tenth century, rule of the north centred on York, and earls Siward and Tostig maintained grand establishments and their treasuries there in the eleventh century. York, then, should be viewed both as a centre of manufacturing and commerce and also as a focus of government and elite consumption at the core of a vibrant Viking kingdom, then a vast earldom within the polyfocal kingdom of late Anglo-Saxon England.

BEOWULF

MARTIN J. RYAN

> Listen! We have heard of the glory
> Of the kings of the Spear-Danes in days gone by.
> How those princes performed great deeds.

At the end of the tenth or beginning of the eleventh century a manuscript was compiled containing a *Life* of Christopher, a saint believed by medieval churchmen to have had the head of a dog; a description of the marvellous inhabitants of far-off lands, known as the *Wonders of the East*; a letter supposedly from Alexander the Great to his tutor Aristotle detailing the wonders of India; and a poem of around 3,100 lines recounting a heroic warrior's struggles against various monsters and his death at the hands (claws?) of a dragon. After surviving various vicissitudes, including being severely singed in a fire in the eighteenth century, this compilation now forms part of British Library Cotton Vitellius A. xv and must rank as one of the most studied manuscripts of the Anglo-Saxon period. The reason for this scholarly attention is the poem that was the final text of the original compilation. The poem survives only in this manuscript and although originally untitled is now known as *Beowulf*, undoubtedly the most famous poem in Old English and one of the most famous texts from the Middle Ages as a whole.

Set in Scandinavia in the later fifth century – though the poem locates the events no more precisely chronologically than 'in days gone by' or 'in days of yore' ('*in geārdagum*') – it tells the story of a man called Beowulf, a Geat from what is now southern Sweden. He travels with a band of warriors to Denmark to the court of King Hrothgar whose mighty hall, Heorot, is plagued by a monster called Grendel, 'a grim monster, a wanderer in the borderlands, who held the moors, the fen and the fastness' who comes at night to kill those sleeping in the hall. Beowulf defeats Grendel in hand-to-hand combat, gripping hold of his arm and refusing to let go until 'the loathsome creature was wracked with pain, a great wound appeared on his shoulder. Sinews snapped, joints burst'.

Having torn off his own arm to escape, Grendel returned to his lair at the bottom of a mere: 'doomed to die, in misery he laid down his life, his heathen soul, in his fenland refuge hell claimed him. The rejoicing of Hrothgar and his court is short-lived. The next night another monster – Grendel's mother – comes to the hall to seek venge-

7b 1 Probable locations of
places and peoples in *Beowulf*

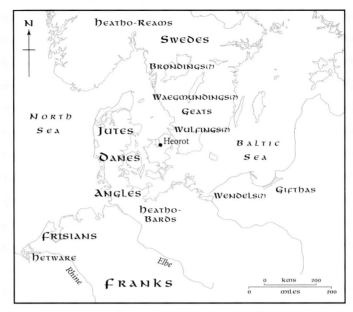

ance and drags off one of Hrothgar's most beloved warriors, Æschere. In the morning, Beowulf tracks Grendel's mother back to the mere and dives to the bottom to kill her. In the ensuing fight, the sword Beowulf is using is unable to wound Grendel's mother – 'the battle light would not bite' – and he is only able to defeat and kill her by using a sword – 'an ancient sword, strong edged, the work of giants' – which, conveniently, he finds nearby.

Having received gifts and great praise from Hrothgar, Beowulf and his warriors return home to their own king in Geatland. The action of the poem then jumps forward some fifty years. Beowulf is now ruler of the Geats, 'a wise king, a guardian of his land', and his own land is being terrorised by a monster, 'the burning thing, the barrow-seeker, the hostile dragon, night-flying, flame enfolded'. Beowulf and a band of his warriors track the dragon to its lair and Beowulf pledges to defeat the dragon alone. When one of his warriors, Wiglaf, sees that the dragon is killing Beowulf, he tries to rally his fellow warriors to support their lord – '"I remember the time, as we drank mead in the hall, that we pledged to our lord, our ring-giver, that we would repay him . . . when such need as this arose"' – but they refuse. Wiglaf goes alone to aid Beowulf and the dragon is killed, though Beowulf has been mortally wounded.

The final scene of the poem is the funeral of Beowulf, who is cremated and then buried beneath a mound on a headland as his people lament his passing and praise his accomplishments: 'They praised his courage, his mighty deeds, extolled his virtue. And it is fitting that a man should honour in words his beloved lord, when he is led forth from his body'.

A summary such as this one does scant justice to the complexity, the subtlety and, indeed, the beauty of the poem: it is a masterpiece. The poem is allusive and evocative. Woven into the narrative are references to other stories, other characters and events, poems are recited and lengthy speeches made. Future happenings are hinted at – Heorot will be destroyed by fire, Geatland will be invaded and conquered after

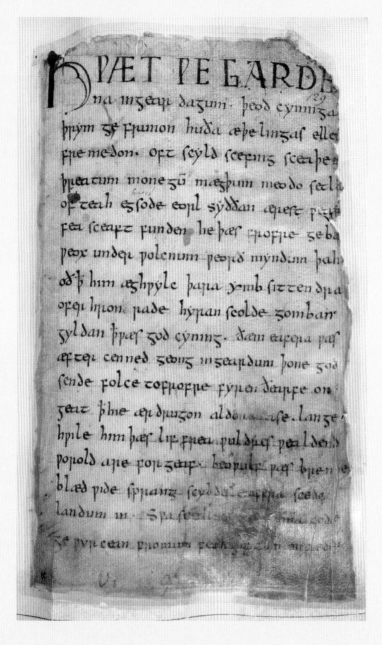

Beowulf's death. Time shifts constantly backwards and forwards, as the histories of
men, monsters, and even swords are traced by the poem. Key events are skilfully structured and described. When Grendel, striding 'from the moors under the misty fells',
approaches Heorot, where Beowulf lies in wait, the action shifts from Heorot to
Grendel, to Heorot again, and back to Grendel until he stands at the doors of the hall.
When Grendel enters the hall and devours a sleeping warrior, there is silence with no
crunching of bones and no cries of terror, but when Beowulf seizes Grendel this silence
is broken by the din of battle and Grendel's own strange cry, 'the song of the defeated,
God's foe, hell's captive, lamenting his pain'. During this passage the poet uses the same

control, let alone hope to stop. The fame Beowulf has won is meaningless; in the end Geatland will be overrun and Beowulf's people scattered. Indeed, rather than seeing the poem as reflecting the ideals of the English aristocracy, with Beowulf himself as an Anglo-Saxon warrior in fifth-century Scandinavian garb, the poet may be describing an alien and confusing world, with Beowulf as strange and unfamiliar as the monsters he defeats.

Another central problem is the religious tone of the poem. It describes a pagan people and yet the scribe, if not the original poet, must have been a member of the Church. Moreover, though characters in the poem sometimes worship idols and are buried with what seem to be pagan ceremonies, they nevertheless show knowledge of the Old Testament, particularly the Book of Genesis, and frequently invoke a singular, seemingly monotheistic, god. Are the biblical elements Christian additions or glosses – Grendel, for example, is described as being of the kin of Cain – or was the poet largely ignorant of paganism and pagan practices, understanding that his characters were non-Christian but having little knowledge of what such peoples were like aside from the example of Israelites in the Old Testament? What would a Christian author or audience have made of the characters in the poem? Could any useful, moral lessons be learnt from a pagan hero or was Beowulf ultimately bound for hell and his life to be seen as at best a warning?

Some Anglo-Saxon churchmen certainly questioned the place of secular poetry in a Christian context, with Alcuin of York famously asking Bishop Unwona of Leicester 'What has Ingeld to do with Christ?' – Ingeld being a character featured in a number of heroic poems, including *Beowulf*. Yet such condemnations, of course, imply that heroic poetry was being read, recited and presumably enjoyed in ecclesiastical contexts. Nor should it be assumed that such pleasures were illicit. Numerous commentators have detected an overall Christian message in *Beowulf* despite its pagan heroes. Some scholars, such as Allen Cabaniss, have even read *Beowulf*, or episodes therein, as an allegory of the life of Christ. Alcuin evoked a narrow house with no room for long-dead pagan kings when he asked his question about Ingeld, but other churchmen may have preferred the many mansions of John 14: 2.

The continuing debates and controversies about almost every facet of *Beowulf* are a testament to the complexities of the poem. *Beowulf* seems to have the potential to shed light on nearly all aspects of Anglo-Saxon society and culture, but its meaning and significance are difficult to pin down. It is perhaps this very elusiveness that is the ultimate message of *Beowulf*; it is a reminder that the values and attitudes of Anglo-Saxon society were no more simple and monolithic than those of modern societies.

CHAPTER 8

The Transformation of Anglo-Saxon England

NICHOLAS J. HIGHAM

While drinking at a wedding celebrated by the families of two of his courtiers, King Harthacnut had a seizure, probably a stroke, from which he never recovered. His death on 8 June 1042 brought to an end the line of direct descendants of Cnut (d. 1035), clearing the way to the throne for Edward 'the Confessor' as he is usually known, Harthacnut's older maternal half-brother and King Æthelred's eldest son by his second marriage.

Thus began one of the least likely reigns of any Anglo-Saxon king and the last considered legitimate by all commentators, for Edward's death in January 1066 sparked dynastic crisis and the Norman Conquest of England. Ever since, that Conquest has overshadowed his kingship. Norman writers looked to him to validate William's candidacy, claiming that Edward had nominated William his heir. Later generations looked back to Edward's reign as a golden era and made the king a saint. Edward himself may actually have promulgated aspects of his saintly reputation while in exile, when it had some potential to further his candidacy as king. He was eventually canonised in 1161.

National prejudices have since clouded discussion of the period. Hostility to 'the Norman Yoke' characterised reactions in nineteenth-century England, when antipathy towards both France and Catholicism was high. Commentators portrayed a legitimate and consensual Anglo-Saxon state tragically overthrown by post-Conquest tyranny, and Harold II was revered as the English patriot heroically resisting invasion. Alongside, Edward was a foolish but saintly weakling and his reign a contest between the loyal Godwinesons and the king's Norman favourites. This nationalistic, 'Germanist' interpretation fell away from the 1890s onwards, as anti-French sentiment declined and Britain and France moved towards alliance against Germany.

The nature of the evidence, however, leaves considerable room for debate: accounts written by the Norman victors dominate near-contemporary narratives and are to a reasonable degree mutually consistent; in important respects, however, they were designed to disguise the poverty of William's claim to the English throne. Their story differs from that in versions 'C', 'D' and 'E' of the *Anglo-Saxon Chronicle*, which cover parts at least of Edward's reign. In turn, the *Chronicle* versions differ one from another. Version 'C', once thought to have been written at Abingdon (Oxfordshire), is now thought to be Mercian and connected with Earl Leofric's family; Version 'E' was written in the south, probably at Canterbury and predominantly from the perspective of

8.1 Places named in chapter 8

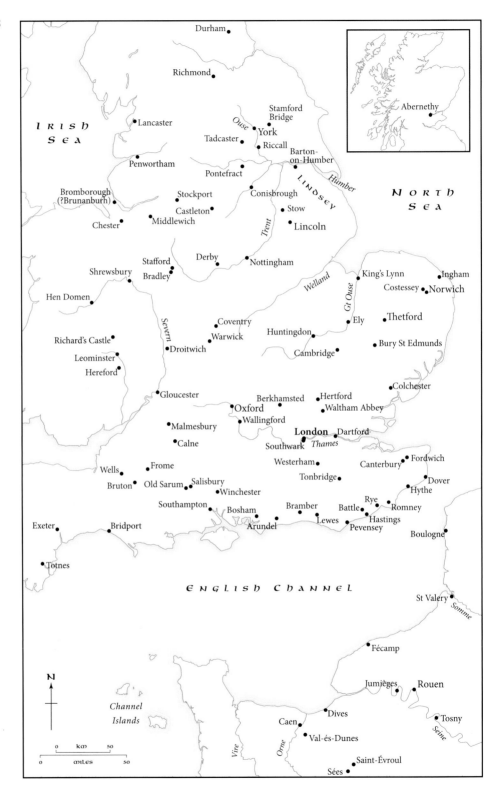

Opposite:

8.2 Simplified genealogies of
the English and Danish royal
families and Norman dukes,
tenth–twelfth centuries

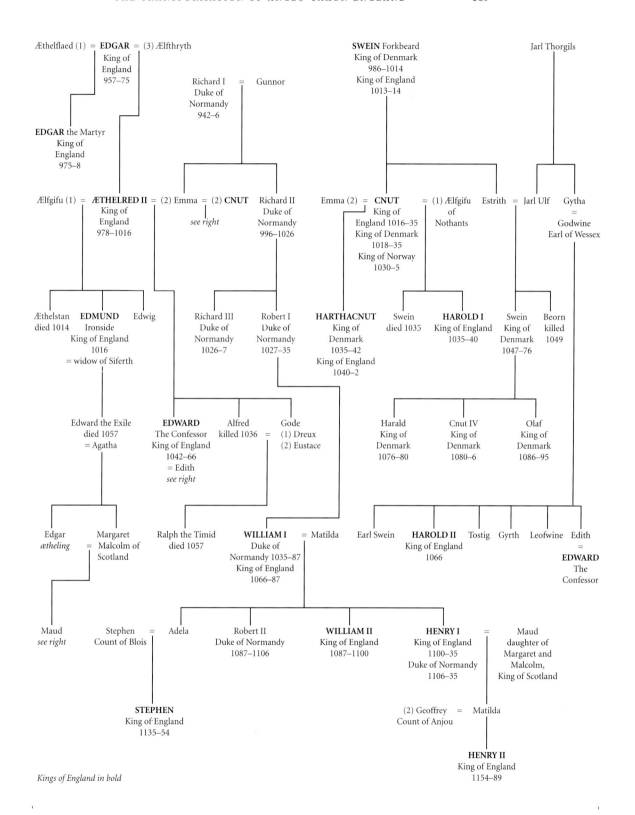

Kings of England in bold

8.3 Atlantic Europe in the mid-eleventh century

8.3 Atlantic Europe in the mid-eleventh century

Godwine and his sons, while 'D' is a later work probably made at Worcester, which seems to have used a northern chronicle connected with Archbishop Ealdred of York (d. 1069).

Nor are these *Chronicle* accounts always consistent with the evidence offered by a work commissioned by Queen Edith (Edward's wife), *The Life of King Edward*, probably in the mid-1060s but then much extended after the Battle of Hastings. The *Life* is a work of two halves, therefore; it opens with a broadly chronological sketch of Edward's life which is friendly to Edith's family, Earl Godwine and his sons, but then closes with dire prophecies of calamity voiced by Edward which were written after the deaths of all Edith's brothers in the autumn of 1066.

An alternative take on the crisis is offered by the Bayeux Tapestry, which although designed and embroidered for a Norman patron was arguably of Kentish workmanship. This hints at alternative perspectives. Finally, yet another viewpoint is offered by Scandinavian saga literature which was written down in the thirteenth century and tells us something of how these events were remembered by the Vikings.

All these works are either biased or propagandist, none more so than the Norman texts. Given the differences of detail and of inclusion, what actually occurred is often unclear, leading to as many accounts as there are historians, even down to the basic sequence of events. It is often far easier to establish what particular individuals wanted on record than what actually occurred.

That said, the period enjoys far greater written sources than any earlier. When Edward came to the throne his mother had just commissioned a eulogy; his reign ends with a *Life* of the old king written for his wife. Never before in Anglo-Saxon England were women so active in commissioning such works. Sources otherwise include about one hundred Old English royal writs from Edward's reign and 67 charters issued in Edward's name (although only 22 of these are certainly genuine), but these documents are dwarfed in scale by Domesday Book, commissioned by William, which looks back from 1086 to the close of Edward's reign in 1066. This near-complete national survey exposes the scale of individual landholdings at the close of Anglo-Saxon England and their transfer to new holders. Taken together with other sources of information, we are looking at a quantitative and qualitative revolution in data, which distinguishes the study of Conquest-period England from preceding eras.

Amidst these riches, a broadly chronological approach is offered here. It covers Edward's 24 years as king, then Harold's brief reign and the crisis of 1066, and finally assesses the impact of Norman government on England.

King Edward: 1042–1066

Edward was born in or before 1005, the eldest son of King Æthelred by his second wife, Emma of Normandy. His childhood was overshadowed by Viking raiding and his family fled England for the second time in 1016 to escape the Danish conquest: Edward spent about 24 years in exile in Normandy (1016/17–1040/1), despite his mother's marriage to Cnut (king of England 1016–35) in 1017. Edward received recognition as king and considerable assistance from his maternal cousin, Duke Robert the Magnificent (1027–35), but the duke died on pilgrimage to the Holy Land, leaving the duchy of Normandy in chaos during the minority of his bastard son, William, born in 1027/8. William's very survival was in doubt until the Battle of Val-ès-Dunes in 1047, won by King Henry of France on his behalf, and William did not gain full control of his duchy for several more years. William of Jumièges reported that Edward sailed to Southampton with 40 ships when Cnut died but withdrew in the face of English opposition; his brother Alfred entered England independently but was taken by Earl Godwine and murdered by the agents of Harold I. The years 1035 to 1036 were therefore a disaster from Edward's perspective. Although the *Life of King Edward* stresses Edward's hereditary right to the throne as his father's heir, it was as Harthacnut's half-brother and at his invitation that Edward returned to England in 1041. His mother, Emma, commissioned the *Encomium* from an author at St Omer, probably while in exile in Flanders in 1040. This centres on her marriage to Cnut but presents a harmonious picture of her two surviving sons. In 1042 Edward was the only royal candidate in England, leaving his closest rival, Harthacnut's cousin Swein Estrithson, to fight the Norwegians for Denmark.

On his return, Edward was virtually unknown, middle-aged yet inexperienced and without following or estates. He brought with him a small band of Norman friends and

and made provision for perhaps two dozen laymen, mostly Norman or northern French, among whom the most important by far was his nephew Ralph, appointed earl in the south-east Midlands after Beorn's death. Robert of Jumièges was made bishop of London in 1044 then promoted to Canterbury in 1051, despite Godwine's opposition. At the same time Edward was pursuing a low-key strategy of establishing loyal allies in Marcher lordships, with Richard fitz Scrob constructing Richard's Castle near Tenbury Wells (Herefordshire), several coastal estates granted to Norman abbeys and the clerk Osbern fitz Osbern established at Bosham (Sussex). Only three castles are known for England before 1066, all associated with Edward's Norman friends. These were unpopular, but Edward courted wider popularity by disbanding the royal fleet, which had long been a drain on English taxes. He also seems to have reinstated Earl Swein: the *Anglo-Saxon Chronicle* clearly implies that he retained his earldom in 1052, so the king had perhaps attempted to placate Godwine in 1050.

Relations between Edward and Godwine reached crisis point in 1051. Robert's appointment to Canterbury may have been the key; he returned to England from Rome with the pallium in this year fired by his contact with the newly reformed and energised papacy. The *Life of King Edward* blamed his influence with the king for the worsening situation, but the final breakdown came when Count Eustace of Boulogne, Edward's brother-in-law, clashed with the men of Dover in Godwine's earldom. Eustace may have expected to take command of a new castle there; whether or not, Godwine refused to punish the townspeople and he and his family were manoeuvred into an armed confrontation. Earls Leofric, Ralph and Siward supported Edward and forced his opponents into exile, the majority seeking shelter with Count Baldwin in Flanders while Harold and Leofwine fled to Ireland. With his in-laws expelled, Edward sent Edith to a nunnery, a strategy often used by Anglo-Saxon kings to rid themselves of unwanted wives.

The short period September 1051–September 1052 provides an opportunity to see what Edward had in mind. His coinage had been traditional across the 1040s but at this point new designs sport a bust and sceptre, with PACX ('peace') on the reverse, signalling the need to calm nerves. Earl Leofric was rewarded: his son Ælfgar received Harold's earldom of East Anglia and Leofric's own authority now perhaps extended into Oxfordshire. Earl Siward probably had authority over Huntingdonshire. Elsewhere Edward advanced new men: Domesday Book records that the Norman Osbern Pentecost gained Burghill (Herefordshire), suggesting that he was given authority over parts at least of Swein's earldom, and Odda, Edward's distant kinsman, was promoted as earl in the south west.

Only the 'D' version of the *Chronicle* records a visit by William, Duke of Normandy, to Edward in 1051:

> Then soon Earl William came from beyond the sea with a great troop of Frenchmen, and the king received him and as many of his companions as suited him, and let him go again.

The silence of Norman commentators regarding such a visit invites extreme caution, but this remains a possibility. William of Jumièges tells a different story, that Edward

8.5 Silver coin of Edward the Confessor. On the obverse, a regally diademed bust of the king with sceptre; on the reverse, a long cross voided with a circle in the centre and a crescent ending each limb; PACX occurs in the angles

'sent Robert archbishop of Canterbury to the duke to nominate him as the heir to the kingdom which God had given him.' Robert is likely to have passed through Normandy to and from Rome, so this meeting is credible. Members of Godwine's family ended up in Normandy as hostages and this is the likeliest time for that to have happened. Edward presumably anticipated Godwine's attempt to return with Flemish help, allied to Harold with Irish-Norse backing. With William now established in Normandy, the duke was potentially a valuable ally and Edward certainly owed debts to his family. Edward was also surely determined to exclude Scandinavian claimants to the English throne. The new hostility of the French king towards his recent ally, William, is difficult to explain without reference to England. Edward may, therefore, have favoured William as his successor and told him so. However, discrepancies in the sources make it impossible to be sure exactly what Edward had in mind and it must be stressed that the succession was not entirely in his gift. No English account makes any reference to William's nomination at this stage.

Whatever occurred, Edward emerges from these events as a king who knew his own mind and was moulding events to his will. The opportunity was brief, however. Godwine and Harold united their forces in the summer of 1052 and, despite efforts to repulse them, were able to recruit ships and raise an army in Sussex and Kent. Edward's supporters were less resolute than previously and at London the two sides agreed peace terms which restored Godwine and his family to all that they had lost. According to the 'C' version of the *Anglo-Saxon Chronicle*:

> They outlawed all the Frenchmen who earlier promoted illegality and passed unjust judgements and counselled bad counsel in this country, except for as many as they decided that the king liked to have about him, who were faithful to him and all his people. And Bishop Robert and Bishop William and Bishop Ulf escaped with difficulty with the Frenchmen who were with them, and thus came away across the sea.

The Anglo-Danish political establishment closed ranks against most of Edward's Norman associates, with Leofric and Siward ultimately preferring Godwine to Archbishop Robert. Edward bowed to the inevitable, took back his wife Edith and abandoned his plans for the succession, whatever those were. Swein Godwineson's death on a pilgrimage to the Holy Land in the autumn of 1052 did, however, remove the most violent member of the Godwine family.

Their reinstatement gave Godwine and Harold collectively earldoms stretching from Cornwall to Norfolk. When united, their influence and resources outweighed those of any other group. Odda's command was reduced to part of the south-west Midlands and Leofric retained only the north-west Midlands. The deaths of Godwine in 1053, Siward in 1055, Odda in 1056 and then Leofric and Ralph in 1057 provided new opportunities for Edward to rebalance the earldoms. Instead, he appointed Harold to Wessex and gave other commands to his brothers Tostig (Northumbria, 1056), Gyrth (East Anglia, by 1059) and Leofwine (south-east Midlands, by 1059), advancing the Godwinesons to authority over some 80 per cent of England. Ælfgar's opposition

8.6 Lands held by Earl Harold in 1066, according to Domesday Book. While clearly concentrated within the expanded earldoms of Wessex and the south-west Midlands, and particularly Sussex whence the family originated, they also include estates in East Anglia, where he ceased to be earl in April 1053, and others in the Midlands and even Northumbria where he had never exercised authority

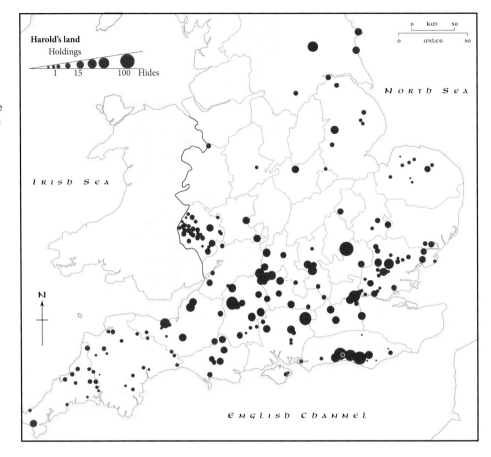

led to his outlawery in 1055 then again in 1058, though he forced his way back each time with Welsh and Norse support. Edward allowed Godwine's sons extraordinary influence in the mid-1050s; the shift from the position he adopted in 1051 is difficult to explain other than by assuming that he felt powerless to prevent it.

The earldoms provide the best key to the power struggles of the period, since they carried with them formal oversight of justice, local government and the power to raise military forces. Late Anglo-Saxon kings granted a substantial proportion of what had originally been royal estates to sustain regional government. Such estates were generally held only so long as the individual remained earl, injecting a degree of insecurity into their tenure. In most shires, the earl would have been one of the greatest landholders and a natural focus for the free community, so many would have commended themselves to him. Earls naturally built up local patronage to entrench their power. Despite the frequency with which earldoms were reorganised and/or redistributed, there was a growing tendency for hereditary tenure, with four generations of Leofric's family controlling the north-west Midlands and Godwine followed by Harold in Wessex. In Northumbria and the north-west Midlands we should think in terms of regional governments, linked to the royal court primarily through the earls themselves and the local bishops but in practice often acting independently. Three incidents illustrate this: the clearest is Ælfgar's Viking mercenaries arriving at Chester for payment in 1055 following their participation in an invasion of Herefordshire from Wales, defeating the king's nephew Earl Ralph and burning Hereford; the others are the undated external marriage alliances made by Godwine and Leofric, with Flanders and Gwynedd respectively. Leofric and Siward both held territories into which Edward never ventured and in some parts of which, such as Cheshire, he had no lands, all having been granted generations earlier to the earls.

In 1066 the landed wealth of the Godwinesons collectively was not much less than that of the king. Much rests on the value of such assets as the 'farm of one night', which was owed by some estates as maintenance to the households of senior figures, often the king's. However, between 1055 and 1065, Tostig's lands as earl of Northumbria should be factored in, boosting the Godwinesons' total significantly, and it is hard to say where we should place Queen Edith's lands in these calculations. Even if we accept that Edward was marginally richer than the principal family from which his earls had been appointed, the margin was narrow and considerable powers had been ceded. Domesday Book demonstrates that not all estates were given up when an earl was deprived. Harold and Tostig acquired vast estates throughout England even outside their own commands. Harold, for example, held land valued at £52 in the East Riding of Yorkshire and Conisbrough in the West Riding valued at 32s yet had never been earl nor is likely to have inherited land in either.

The succession remained an issue. In the mid-1050s, efforts were made to bring Edmund Ironside's son to England from Hungary: Edward the Exile reached England with his wife, son Edgar and daughters in 1057 but died on arrival and was buried at St Paul's, London. This left Edgar, aged about five, as Edward's closest blood relative. That he was placed in the care of Queen Edith and termed *ætheling* in the *Book of Life* of New Minster, Winchester, alongside Edward and Edith's names, suggests recognition as a potential successor. However, there is no evidence that Edgar attended court and the king made no provision for his young kinsman, despite his being about 14 by 1066. Rather, by the late 1050s the king seems to have withdrawn from active politics. It was Harold and Tostig who in 1063 invaded Wales and destroyed King Gruffudd, probably taking advantage of the death of Earl Ælfgar, Gruffudd's father-in-law, c. 1062/3. Edward spent his energies in hunting and in his great building project at Westminster Abbey. Otherwise he left the running of the country to the Godwinesons.

1066

The crisis that broke finally in 1066 developed across the two preceding years. Although the event is not mentioned by any version of the *Anglo-Saxon Chronicle*, Norman sources portray Harold travelling to the Continent about 1064, sailing from Bosham on the Sussex coast. The *Life of King Edward* refers to Harold's involvement in French politics without mentioning this particular journey, but the Bayeux Tapestry makes this the starting point for the struggle for the English Crown.

Assuming that the story has some substance, why Harold made the journey is unclear. He may have been attempting to gain the release of relatives who were hostages at William of Normandy's court, in which case he was intentionally visiting the duke. Alternatively Harold may have been seeking to contact William's rivals in the hope that they might prevent the duke intervening in England at Edward's death. The old ally of

8.7 Natural harbour at Bosham, West Sussex, from which Harold was said to have sailed to France. The church with its tower was built in the second half of the eleventh century, quite possibly under the patronage of Harold and his father

Harold's family, Baldwin V of Flanders, controlled land only a short distance from his landing point, though Baldwin was by now allied by marriage to William. Harold was, however, captured by the Count of Ponthieu and then 'rescued' by William, who prevailed upon him to swear him an oath and receive arms, becoming his man. Norman commentators presented this as rendering Harold's claim to the throne invalid, allowing them to portray him as a perjurer when he accepted the throne. Several also suggested that Harold was betrothed to one of William's daughters, implying that a marriage alliance was negotiated, but they fail to agree on which daughter.

8.8 Harold's oath on relics depicted on the Bayeux Tapestry. Here located at Bayeux but placed at Bonneville-sur-Touques by William of Poitiers

Had Harold been the victor at Hastings these stories would have been forgotten: clearly their propaganda value far outweighed their influence over events, but they do suggest attempts to negotiate a settlement between Harold and William which ulti-

mately foundered on the unwillingness of both to forego the English Crown. That the Bayeux Tapestry designer portrayed Edward as stern towards Harold on his return and depicted the body language of the earl as apologetic undermines any suggestion that Edward had sent Harold to confirm William as his successor, but it is otherwise difficult to interpret the scene.

The northern revolt of autumn 1065 was of more immediate relevance to the succession. Tostig had been earl for ten years, bringing comparative peace to the Scottish frontier, and had been Harold's partner in the Welsh campaign of 1063. He was a powerful figure with military experience and there are signs that he was close to both Edith and Edward. According to Simeon of Durham, Edith had the northern leader Gospatric murdered on Tostig's behalf in December 1064, and Tostig killed two other Northumbrian nobles at York. The earl was also said by the rebels to have demanded excessive taxes and to have manipulated justice. While he was with the king in Dorset, the Northumbrians rebelled, sacking Tostig's headquarters at York. The northerners demanded not independence from England but their own choice as earl, inviting Earl Edwin of Mercia's young brother, Morcar, to take on the role, so ensuring Mercian and Welsh support. Their combined forces ravaged parts of the East Midlands where Tostig had land, causing considerable damage in Northamptonshire. Harold negotiated with the rebels, receiving some credit in the *Chronicle* for his attempts but less so in the *Life of King Edward*, which suggested that Harold was complicit in the uprising. Given the local context, this accusation may go too far, but he likely did steer the outcome to his own advantage, as Tostig believed. Despite wishing to fight, Edward had to acquiesce in the appointment of Morcar and allow Tostig to go into exile in Flanders.

At some point between 1063 and 1066, Harold married Edwin and Morcar's sister, the widowed Ealdgyth, thereby allying himself with the only other English family of real consequence. Late in 1065 he rid himself of a brother who might have held him

8.9 An angry King Edward, seated, receives an abject and apologetic Harold on his return from Normandy

back from the throne, giving his command to his new in-laws instead. Here we see Harold strengthening his candidacy for the throne. The shift in the attitude of Leofric's grandsons is manifest in the enthusiasm for Harold shown in 1066 by the 'C' version of the *Anglo-Saxon Chronicle*, which was normally hostile to Godwine's family:

> However, the wise man [Edward] committed the kingdom
> To a distinguished man, Harold himself,
> A princely earl, who at all times
> Loyally obeyed his superior
> In words and deeds, neglecting nothing
> Of which the nation's king was in need.

The *Life of King Edward*, however, claims that Edward attempted to raise forces to oppose the northerners, his frustration leading to the illness from which he died in January 1066. The king's inability to act without Harold is clear; by this stage it was the premier earl who wielded the greater power. Although several accounts are somewhat guarded, on his deathbed Edward does seem to have nominated Harold as successor, or at least placed the kingdom under his protection. Edward was buried at the hastily consecrated abbey of Westminster on 6 January and Harold's coronation followed on the same day, in the same church.

Harold II was king for less than ten months. Given that he was not himself descended through the male line from previous English kings, his elevation represents a change of dynasty. However, Harold was the old king's brother-in-law and senior earl, so in many respects the obvious candidate. We should recall that Edward had succeeded not his English father but his Danish/Norman half-brother, to whom Harold too was related through his mother. He was clearly an accomplished politician with experience of war. He had an imposing physical presence and brothers and sons capable of ensuring the succession, so was in important ways well qualified. He seems to have been widely supported within England, with nobody standing by Edgar *ætheling*, the only king-worthy figure descended from the old English line. Prompt coronation gave Harold the advantages of being a consecrated king and public recognition of his claim. Excepting only Waltheof's small command in the East Midlands, the earls were either his brothers or brothers-in-law and he himself brought to the kingship the massive resources in land and men of an earldom stretching from Cornwall to Sussex and Herefordshire to the Isle of Wight, so placing the Crown on a completely new footing. The new king had far greater direct power than had Edward since 1052 so was less dependent on his earls.

Harold rapidly took control of royal government; he was issuing writs, though only one survives confirming the privileges of the Lotharingian Bishop Giso of Wells. New silver pennies carrying Harold's portrait were struck throughout England, with Edward's engraver at London still responsible for the dies. The design chosen was unusual: Edward's final issue had him facing right, bearded and helmeted, a sceptre before his face. Harold's kept the sceptre and beard, though the beard made him look much younger than Edward and more stylish, and he adopted a youthful profile facing left

8.10 The king in majesty, crowned and with sceptre. Silver coin of Harold II minted at Wallingford by the moneyer Burewine

and adorned with a crown rather than a helmet. The crown and the PACX motif suggest efforts to calm nerves over the succession and emphasise Harold's legitimacy as king.

William also saw himself as Edward's successor, even though he was no more a descendant of English kings than was Harold. The duke now dominated north-west France, both the King of France and the Count of Anjou having died in recent years leaving minors as heirs. Harold held an army and navy in readiness on the south coast across the summer, but only Tostig arrived with a small force and he was driven off from the south and then from Lindsey (Lincolnshire) and finally fled north to King Malcolm of Scotland. Precisely what Tostig was attempting is unclear, whether he only sought reinstatement or was contesting Harold's kingship. Whichever it was, he did not have the resources necessary to fight either his brother or Edwin and Morcar.

In Normandy, William organised a major shipbuilding programme. His need to transport cavalry mounts in large numbers was something new and the Bayeux Tapestry shows his preparations. William of Poitiers wrote an account of William's deeds modelled in part on Caesar's *Gallic Wars*. He reported wide-scale Norman scepticism, although this was perhaps a rhetorical device to underline William's personal responsibility for his triumph. The duke successfully petitioned the papacy for support, which encouraged wider French participation in his enterprise, the fighting strength of Normandy alone being too small. Even so, the duke's armada was something which he was only likely to be able to stage once. The fleet assembled at the mouth of the Dives in Lower Normandy. There may have been an abortive attempt to make the crossing, but William of Poitiers reported merely that the fleet was blown by westerly winds to St Valery, at the mouth of the Somme, where it then awaited a favourable wind. Having run out of provisions, Harold disbanded his forces on the south coast on 8 September.

Harald Hardrada of Norway also had designs on England, so he gathered a great fleet and set out. Hardrada's claim was flimsy but his reputation and ability to deploy large forces made his challenge very real. Without allies on the east side of the Channel, he took the island route via Orkney. Tostig joined Hardrada in Scotland, providing a much needed English ally. They raided the Northumbrian coast then entered the Humber and the Ouse, coming ashore at Riccal (North Yorkshire) probably on 16 September.

Harold mobilised and marched north in haste. In his absence Edwin and Morcar fought the Vikings at Gate Fulford outside the southern walls of York, but were defeated with heavy losses on 20 September, leaving the city to make terms. Harold reached Tadcaster (North Yorkshire) on 24 September, by which time Hardrada had withdrawn to Stamford Bridge (Yorkshire, East Riding). Harold led his army through York and on to Stamford Bridge on Monday 25 September, where he destroyed the Norwegians. Both Tostig and Hardrada were slain and most of their forces perished, 24 ships sufficing to transport the survivors home.

Stamford Bridge was the greatest victory won by an English king against Viking opponents, certainly since Æthelstan's success at *Brunanburh* in 937. His triumph entirely vindicated the choice of Harold Godwineson as king, conferring upon him the cloak of divine approval. It also, however, drew Harold away from the south of England. In Harold's absence the Norman fleet crossed the Channel to Sussex during the night of 26 September without fear that their horse-laden vessels might be attacked at sea.

8.11 Castle motte at Hastings. The core at least was probably constructed in the autumn of 1066

William arrived initially at Pevensey, where he constructed a castle within the old Roman Saxon Shore Fort, then quickly moved to Hastings, where he again built a castle. The Bayeux Tapestry depicts his forces firing houses in the neighbourhood and they seized supplies at least as far east as Romney. News of the Norman arrival reached Harold within a few days and William, in turn, learned the result of Stamford Bridge from Edward's old Norman courtier, Robert fitz Wimarc. Harold marched south. He did not delay to call out as large an army as he might, instead forcing the pace as had proved so successful at Stamford Bridge. He confronted the invader some 10 kilometres

8.12 Senlac Hill. Visible beyond the wood, a low ridge on top of which the English army was drawn up. William later constructed Battle Abbey there

north of Hastings on Senlac Hill – the site later occupied by Battle Abbey – on 14 October. In a hard-fought battle between armies probably of approximately equal strength, the Anglo-Saxons were eventually overthrown and Harold and his two brothers killed, though whether or not Harold was slain by an arrow in the eye, as often assumed, is far from certain. The defeat became a rout.

William's success at Hastings has been put down to several different factors. In retrospect it is tempting to see Harold as overly impetuous in not waiting for reinforcements. However, following Stamford Bridge and with William ravaging lands held by Harold's family for generations, it is easy to see why he felt haste was paramount. One could argue that the battle showed the advantages of Frankish styles of warfare, with archers supporting cavalry, over English heavy infantry, yet throughout the day the English shield wall also showed its value. Then again it has been suggested that William displayed superior generalship on the day, but since all the extended reports were written by his apologists this is hardly surprising. The battle might have gone either way; the crucial factor was surely the death of Harold, following those of Gyrth and Leofwine, which left the Anglo-Saxons leaderless.

The defeated survivors withdrew to London, where Archbishop Ealdred of York was joined by Edwin and Morcar in throwing their weight behind the claims of Edgar *ætheling*. William moved east to Dover, which he garrisoned, then Canterbury, which

8.13 Battle Abbey. The site of the high altar within the demolished church, traditionally the spot where Harold was slain

surrendered to him. In November, although suffering from dysentery, William marched west, beating back an Anglo-Saxon sally from Southwark and firing the suburb, then crossed the Thames at Wallingford and ravaged the countryside west of London. Despite the large numbers of soldiers available to them, Edgar's party lost their nerve, surrendering to William at Berkhamsted (Berkshire). William was crowned by Archbishop Ealdred at Westminster on Christmas Day 1066.

William of Poitiers's defence of his claim to the throne reveals just how weak was the kinship between himself and Edward, the son of the duke's great-aunt, so his first cousin once removed. William's candidacy was without support from any significant political faction in England and was pressed home primarily through conquest, bringing to an end a year of political and military drama and crisis on a scale unprecedented in Western Europe since Visigothic Spain fell to the Arabs and Berbers in 711. That William was crowned while his guards sacked and fired the suburbs west of London sets the tone.

King William

William saw his coronation as the start of his reign, a novelty given the normal assumption of power by Anglo-Saxon kings months – even years – earlier than their coronation. In this respect Harold's rapid enthronement may provide the precedent William was following. Certainly, it brought him much needed legitimacy and initially he acted with a view to reconcile the English to his rule, leaving those who had not fought against him at Hastings in possession of their lands. Cnut had murdered several key members of the English political classes at the start of his reign; William did not. Instead, he accepted the submission of the leading thegns of Mercia, led by Edwin and Morcar, then presided over a similar event at Pevensey.

There was a price, though: William levied fines for confirmation of tenure, which caused some to contract debts that would cause them to lose their estates. At the same time lands held by the Godwinesons and their followers were confiscated and re-granted. Normans already in England, like Robert of Rhuddlan, and some English members of Edward's household did well, but the vast bulk of these estates went to incomers. In March 1067 the king took Edgar, Edwin, Morcar and other English leaders to Normandy, as virtual hostages by one report. In William's absence, England was ruled by his half-brother Odo, bishop of Bayeux and newly appointed earl of Kent, and William fitz Osbern, earl of Hereford. Both were accused by the English of forcing the marriages of English heiresses to Continental knights; they also levied a heavy geld and pushed forward castle-building. In the south-west Marches for example, Ewias Harold, Chepstow, Clifford, Monmouth and Wigmore were all thrown up at this date, as the earl of Hereford pushed into what had until recently been Welsh territory.

The king granted consolidated estates along the Channel to Continental associates, who built castles at Hastings, Arundel, Lewes and Bramber (all Sussex), and Tonbridge in West Kent. In an atmosphere of growing distrust, a series of local disturbances broke out: Eadric the Wild raised the northern Welsh Marches and Exeter closed its gates, apparently in collusion with Harold's sons and in expectation of a rising. William retook Exeter and built Rougemont Castle to overawe the town. An attack from Ireland

8.14 Stone keep of Rougemont Castle, Exeter. Built by William to overawe the city following revolt, inclusion of windows comparable to those in contemporary insular church towers suggest the employment of Anglo-Saxon masons

by Harold's sons on Devon's north coast was driven off. Castles were constructed as foci for new consolidated estates granted to Normans, for example at Totnes (Devon).

Numerous English thegns were losing their lands through debt, arbitrary eviction or legal process, and a trickle of establishment figures took refuge in flight, such as Mærleswein, who was a significant figure in the East Midlands and the south west (assuming these estates were held by the same individual). Edwin and Morcar fled from court following the coronation of Matilda as queen in May 1068. William may have reneged on an offer to Edwin of his daughter in marriage, but a new earldom at Shrewsbury for Roger of Montgomery, within the heartland of their family's influence, was clearly an issue. A Mercian rebellion was beginning, but William marched north, building castles at Warwick, Nottingham, York, Lincoln, Huntingdon and Cambridge, and nipped it in the bud.

William made Robert de Commines earl of Northumbria but he was killed at Durham in January 1069 and the whole of the north rose in revolt. The rebellion embraced the house of Bamburgh and their kinsman Edgar *ætheling*. Yorkshire thegns were incensed at the oppression carried out by William Malet, the newly appointed sheriff, and the revolt also included Earl Waltheof of the south-east Midlands and such Anglo-Saxon nobles as Siward Barn, whose lands were centred on Nottinghamshire, Derbyshire and Warwickshire. William's rapid march north and the building of a second castle at York did not end the matter, and rebellion rekindled later in the year with the backing of a Danish fleet. The Northumbrians took control of York, killing William's appointees and overthrowing their castles, but the whole city burnt. Archbishop Ealdred died there in 1069 and with him ended any chance of reconciliation.

William put down the rebellion with extraordinary violence across the winter. There have been efforts to reinterpret the so-called 'Harrying of the North' as less brutal than hitherto imagined, but refugees were reported begging as far south as Evesham (Worcestershire). Domesday Book reveals that in 1086 manors without value or even inhabitants were numerous in the north and the north-west Midlands. William now began to reorganise Northumbria and northern Mercia into great lordships and grant them to his henchmen. The Breton Count Alan's fief focused on Richmond (North Yorkshire) comprised 199 manors in the eastern Pennines; Pontefract went to Ibert de Lacy and Chester to Earl Hugh Lupus, while William also built the Castle of the Peak in Derbyshire.

It was probably the northern revolt that convinced William to remove the English from all positions of power. In 1070 he replaced several bishops, including Stigand as archbishop of Canterbury with Lanfranc, an elderly native of Pavia (northern Italy) who had long been an enthusiastic reformer and close ally. By 1087, when William died, there was only one English bishop left, Wulfstan at Worcester, plus Bishop Giso, the elderly Lotharingian who had been appointed by King Edward to Wells. At the same time, English landholders in the Midlands and the north were stripped of their lands.

Resistance to William did not cease immediately, but the end was in sight. The Danish fleet overwintered in the Humber and was reinforced in 1070, but with Northumbria devastated it moved south to East Anglia. Hereward was leading resistance at Ely but the Danes merely raided then returned home. Edwin and Morcar escaped from court in 1071 but were too late to join the northern revolt. Edwin was quickly slain. Morcar joined Hereward 'the Wake', but was captured and imprisoned for the remainder of the reign.

By 1072 William felt sufficiently free of English unrest to campaign in Scotland, where Malcolm had married Edgar's sister, Margaret. At Abernethy, King Malcolm did homage and agreed no longer to support the dissidents: Edgar and Gospatric of Bamburgh fled to Flanders and William appointed Waltheof, who as Earl Siward's son was related to Gospatric, as earl of Bamburgh. But Waltheof was implicated in the so-called 'revolt of the three earls' in 1076 and was executed for his part despite having betrayed the plot to Lanfranc. In his place William made Bishop Walcher of Durham earl of Northumberland, but he was caught up in a blood feud and murdered.

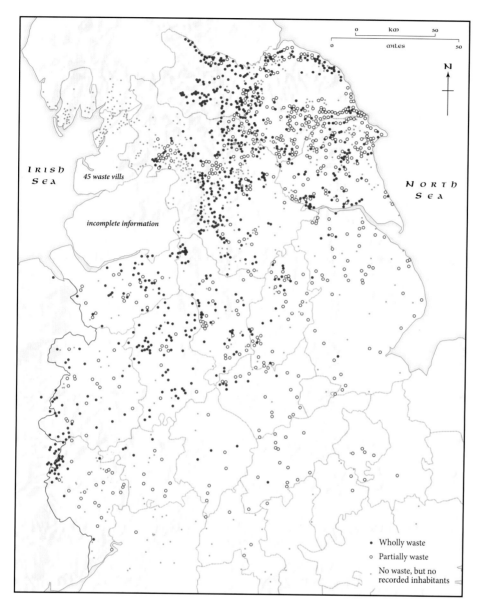

IRISҺ
SEA

45 waste vills

incomplete information

NORTҺ
SEA

8.15 Distribution of estates described as 'waste' in Domesday Book, 1086. Concentration in southern Northumbria and north-west Mercia suggests this was largely the result of Norman devastation to put down the northern revolt of 1069/70, although individual instances may have had several different causes

- • Wholly waste
- ◦ Partially waste
- . No waste, but no recorded inhabitants

That was not the last opposition to William, however, since the Danish King Cnut, Swein's son and successor, formed a marriage alliance in 1085 with Flanders with the intention of attacking England. The expected invasion fleet did not sail in 1085, however, and the king was murdered on 10 July 1086 immediately prior to departure. But this grand venture demonstrates just how insecure William's conquest was in his lifetime. It was with that threat in mind that William commissioned Domesday Book, set in train at the council meeting held at Gloucester at Christmas 1085. After the folios were delivered to him at an extraordinary meeting the following August at Old Sarum, William left England for the last time to fight his overlord, the king of France.

The absence of serious rivals in northern France in the late 1060s was a major factor enabling William's invasion of England. Had Edward died before 1062 or after

number of English landholders remains very low. The Norman court was predominantly immigrant in composition and French speaking, as were elite households throughout the land.

Taking the Leicestershire folios of Domesday Book as an example, the only English names occurring among 44 landholders in 1086 are the almsman, Godwine the Priest, whose holding was paltry, and two widows – countesses Godiva and Ælfeva. All others were incomers. Clearly there was a much higher survival rate among elite women than men and many of the next generation's aristocrats were born of English women and learnt English at home, but the changes were nevertheless profound. Among the elite, by 1100, Norman and French personal names had virtually swept away the Old English and Old Norse which had predominated in 1065.

In many shires a small proportion of named 1066 holders appear in 1086 with much reduced holdings and as tenants of Norman lords, so as subtenants. Other unnamed tenants in 1086 may have been the named freeholders of 1066 or their heirs but in that case they had suffered even greater loss of status, while some unnamed free tenants in 1066 had probably joined the ranks of the manorial peasantry by 1086. However, the majority of 1066 holders are simply untraceable. In 1086 the king held approximately 20 per cent of the land of England and the Church another 25 per cent. Of the remainder, incoming secular lords held some 50 per cent, leaving a mere 5 per cent or less in the hands of English landholders.

Alongside the shift from English to Norman tenure, there were major changes in the balance of elite society. The upper tier of late Anglo-Saxon landholders centred on the king and queen, the wealthier bishops and religious houses and the earls, but there were also numerous thegns with estates in excess of 50 hides. Some of these were wealthy men with large landholdings, such as Edric of Laxfield, with extensive estates in Norfolk and Suffolk. Most of the more substantial were king's thegns, owing service to no one except the king. Others had commended themselves to another lord but the choice was generally their own to make, irrespective of whether or not they held land of another. In contrast, tenure of land and commendation were closely linked under the Norman king and land-tenure was far more tightly structured, with William at the apex of a landholding system of a type which had not existed either in England or Normandy before 1066. This was perhaps the most fundamental structural change consequent on William's seizure of the throne, applied not just to incomers but also to existing holders, be they clerical or lay. Fewer than 150 lay tenants-in-chief held substantial estates from William and others held lands of and owed service to these new barons.

There was massive shrinkage, therefore, in the ranks of landholders immediately below the king. The great Anglo-Saxon earldoms were likewise dissolved, with individuals holding the title of earl now linked with specific shires rather than whole regions (much as ealdormen in ninth-century Wessex), and the title was largely honorary. The earl's duties in most respects passed to sheriffs whose actions frequently attracted complaints. The result was a far narrower hierarchy. The king sat at the apex of a society characterised by duties defined in terms of military service and other feudal obligations, which flowed upwards from subtenant to king via a comparatively small number of intermediaries.

Anglo-Saxon thegns and others holding bookland (land which had been granted by charter into private ownership) had long owed military service to the Crown, but the frequent military crises of William's reign led to these obligations being institutionalised at inflated levels. Religious houses and others fulfilled their quotas by granting lands in return for military service. For many churches and monasteries, the difficulties were exacerbated by the losses which they suffered as incomers took over the portion of their lands that had previously been leased to Anglo-Saxon thegns. Efforts to defend and regain such estates encouraged a new emphasis on pre-Conquest land documentation. This in turn led to the forging of charters where existing documentation was found wanting and generally encouraged a renewed interest in the English past, which led to the histories of Eadmer at Canterbury and William of Malmesbury.

Royal grants of lands to lay supporters took several different forms. A minority received adjacent estates forming a compact block, normally for strategic purposes and mostly on the edges of England, as in Sussex, the north or the Welsh Marches. Others were granted all the lands held by one or more Anglo-Saxon landholder, so that the spread depended on previous patterns. In most cases, however, the process was less tidy and there often seems little logic to the bundles of manors and other assets held by a particular individual in 1086. William intentionally rewarded supporters in different regions but rarely gave individuals predominance in any particular locality. This led to a bundling of estates.

Clearly there was also confusion regarding the tenure of some manors, with conflicting claims. On occasion William had inadvertently granted the same land to different recipients, but more often land had been acquired through coercion by powerful incomers, often including sheriffs. The forcible marriage of an heiress was just one means of securing property. It should also be remembered that numerous transactions which are undocumented or at best only partially documented may separate information relating to 1066 and 1086. In some areas, the process of the granting out of land by tenants-in-chief was still very much in process in 1086. Occasionally the claims of the dispossessed occur in Domesday Book, but Domesday juries were highly susceptible to pressure and few wrongs were righted. Only very rarely did English plaintiffs have their grievances heard, given that the courts were dominated by the incomers who had taken over their lands. To deter the waylaying and murder of Frenchmen, William's regime introduced a novel fine, *murdrum*, which was imposed on any community where a French corpse was found.

The Conquest also resulted in wholesale appointments of incomers to senior religious positions, and in this it contrasts with Cnut's practice of appointing Englishmen to the Church. By William's death, numerous senior positions in the monasteries had gone to Frenchmen, although most monks and parish priests were still natives. Another outcome was the transfer of English resources to continental abbeys. The granting of estates to Norman houses had begun under Edward, with gifts of substantial lands in Sussex to Fécamp Abbey, for instance, but this escalated post-1066, as numerous newly rich landholders made gifts to abbeys 'back home', and looked to them to provide clergy for their new estates. This continued for some decades: Roger of Poitou, for

8.16 Jumièges Abbey, by the Seine in Normandy. Construction began just prior to Edward's departure for England, under the supervision of that Robert of Jumièges whom he made archbishop of Canterbury. The abbey was arguably the inspiration for the king's own new work at Westminster, which would have looked similar

example, granted the parish church of Lancaster to the Norman abbey of Sées in 1094, along with a further nine churches in Lancashire.

There was also profound change as regards the weight of governmental demands. While Edward had shown a reluctance to levy land tax, William demanded ever more and heavier gelds. The new regime had not only to pay significant numbers of troops after the 1066 campaign but also raised mercenaries thereafter. William encountered far more challenging circumstances than Edward, both in terms of internal disaffection and overseas commitments, so his government was far more expensive.

William clearly wished to be considered Edward's legitimate heir, governing in traditional ways. However, his regime instituted a revolution in terms of who held land and how. Behind the rhetoric, the Normans had imposed an alien regime on an unwilling people by force, rewriting the immediate past as they did so and constructing a racially structured state in which the minority treated the majority with contempt. The Conquest was not just about the transfer of power, it was also about marking that transfer, for there was nothing self-effacing about the Norman incomers. A new 'colo-nial' architecture differentiates William's reign. This is visible primarily in two areas, churches and castles.

Virtually every major church in England was rebuilt in the late eleventh century, leaving intact very few front-rank Anglo-Saxon buildings. Of course, there are hints of this pre-Conquest in Edward's rebuilding of Westminster Abbey in the new Romanesque style. His close associate, Robert of Jumièges, was instrumental in rebuilding Nôtre-Dame at Jumièges and this was probably the trigger for Edward's initiative. Indeed, he may even have employed a mason from there. Before 1066, though, in England the new architecture was confined to this one site, and Westminster Abbey survived because Edward's tomb was of too much value to the new regime for it to be disturbed.

Elsewhere church rebuilding spread across England, with wholesale replacement of Anglo-Saxon cathedrals and abbeys, as well as of more local churches. The new struc-tures were generally much larger. At Canterbury, however, the cathedral had already been rebuilt following its destruction in 1011, and here Lanfranc's replacement was not so very different in size from the late Anglo-Saxon church which burnt down in December 1067. Of England's great churches, Durham Cathedral is today the most complete survival of early Norman church-building, but the cathedrals of Ely and Winchester also retain much early Norman work.

Not only were numerous Anglo-Saxon churches replaced by the new elite but a critical light was shed on their traditions as well. Local minster churches often retained in their dedications a memory of their founders or early champions. Since the tenth century, the reformed monasteries had been replacing such cults with more universal

8.17 Canterbury Cathedral
Reconstruction of the late
Anglo-Saxon cathedral
following destruction of the
earlier building in 1011

8.18 Canterbury Cathedral.
Reconstruction of the new
Norman cathedral built after
destruction by fire of the
previous church in 1067

8.19 Development of a thegnly
residence at Goltho
(Lincolnshire): (a) modest farm
within field ditches, c. 800–50;
(b) more substantial 'hall' type
building, c. 850–950, with
possible kitchen to east and
weaving sheds to north of
courtyard; (c) basic plan
through second half of tenth
century, but hall and kitchen
expanded; (d) eleventh-century
settlement surrounded by a
defensive ditch and bank and
with a far more massive hall, its
timber uprights capable of
supporting an upper storey.
Construction of a Norman motte
later eclipsed the site

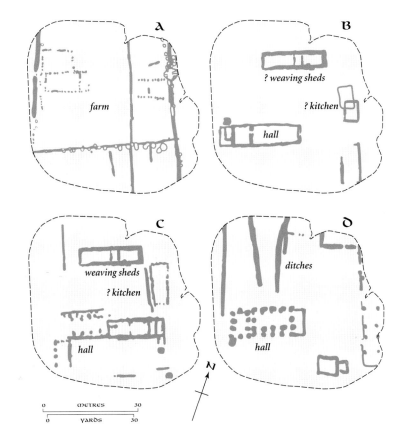

saints. In the late eleventh century the influx of Continental clerics and monks further accelerated this process. They repressed local cults of obscure saints whose deeds were not properly authenticated, and rededicated their new churches. The result was a dramatic loss of collective memories, leaving just a few remaining, as St Bertolin (Beorhthelm) at Stafford and various sites in the north-west Midlands, St Eadburh at Pershore, and St Pega at Peakirk.

Castles were also archetypal monuments to Norman colonialism, providing elite residences with an inbuilt military capability not hitherto common in England. Some late Anglo-Saxon thegnly residences, such as those excavated at Portchester (Hampshire), Goltho (Lincolnshire) and Sulgrave (Northamptonshire), boasted a defensive capability, with a substantial bank and ditch around residential buildings, but none really matched the Norman castle and many remained undefended. Hitherto most defences had been communal and urban, providing a strongpoint for the whole community. Castles provided private rather than public security, featuring ring-works, mottes or even stone keeps.

William's campaigning earth and timber castles at Pevensey and Hastings mark the inception of a phase of castle-building which then spread across England and on into Wales, Scotland and ultimately Ireland. New Norman, Breton or French landholders constructed mottes and/or ring-works as the foci for their estates, as Robert did at Rhuddlan for his new barony in North Wales. William himself used castles to impose his rule at important centres: three castles were built on the edges of London – the White Tower (later known as the Tower of London), Baynard's Castle and Montfichet Castle, two in York and at least one in most other major towns, often causing the destruction of existing housing. At Canterbury, a motte called the Dane John (from

8.20 The great earthen motte at Rhuddlan. The caput of a major group of estates in North Wales held by Robert of Rhuddlan variously of the king and his kinsman, Hugh of Avranches, earl of Chester. By 1086 Robert and the earl had founded a new borough nearby; the site had earlier been an Anglo-Saxon *burh* then King Gruffudd's palace

8.21 The Dane John (foreground). An early Norman motte built immediately inside the walls of Canterbury, it was replaced later in William's reign by a stone keep, visible at Worthgate (to the left)

Norman French *donjon*) was thrown up immediately inside the walls in 1066, then a stone keep was built at Worthgate later in the reign, dispossessing townsfolk and destroying 32 houses. The abbot of St Augustine's was compensated with 14 properties in the town.

While it has become fashionable in recent years to think of medieval castles underpinning elite status with symbolic power, there can be no doubting their role as a practical weapon of colonisation in the Norman period and they were seen as such by Anglo-Saxon commentators. As the author of the 'E' version of the *Anglo-Saxon Chronicle* put it when recording William's death:

> He had castles built and wretched men oppressed. The king was so very stark and seized from his subject men many a mark of gold, and many more hundreds of pounds of silver that he took by weight and with great injustice from his land's nation with little need.

The castle was, therefore, a major weapon in the arsenal of the Norman elite. Castle walls secured their households and treasuries while prisons and towers served to overawe a conquered land. Many, like Pilsbury Castle, are undocumented, so it is not even clear whether they were constructed in the context of the Conquest or later in the troubles of Stephen's reign (1135–54). Extensive excavations at Hen Domen (Montgomeryshire) have demonstrated that a timber castle was capable of providing comparatively sophisticated accommodation for a family of the highest status, in this case that of the earls of Shrewsbury, who commissioned its construction.

We might reasonably conclude from this that the impact of the Normans was both extraordinarily deep and long-lasting. However, if we shift our attention away from the elite, the Conquest becomes somewhat less visible. New church-building was not

8.22 Pilsbury Castle, near Hartington (Derbyshire), overlooking the river Dore. The motte and twin baileys were built by the de Ferrers family to protect their local estates against insurgents or other Norman lords. Whether the castle is a late eleventh-century castle or mid-twelfth century is unclear

entirely a product of the Conquest, for both the replacement of old churches with new stone structures and the proliferation of manorial churches with parishes carved out of those of the old minsters were underway already in later Anglo-Saxon England, as across much of contemporary Europe. Some of this was, of course, sponsored by the elite, such as the church of St Mary at Stow (Lincolnshire) and Coventry Abbey (Warwickshire), both commissioned by Earl Leofric and his wife Godiva, or Tovi the Proud's development of Waltham Abbey (Essex), where he relocated a black cross recently found on his estates. Often we do not know who commissioned new work, but

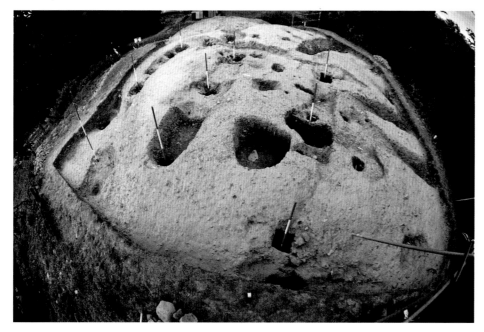

8.23 Hen Domen (Montgomeryshire). A late eleventh-century timber motte and bailey castle constructed by the earls of Shrewsbury and the most extensively excavated Norman example of its type. At the apex of the motte are post-holes for a defensive timber structure

8.24 The late Anglo-Saxon tower of the church of St Mary's, Sompting (West Sussex). The 'Rhenish helm' style of the roof and Romanesque architectural details suggest that the upper parts predate the Conquest by only a generation or so

numerous parish churches in such areas as coastal Sussex retain elements of late Anglo-Saxon fabric (as at Selham), with the occasional survival of virtually complete examples, at Sompting for example. New churches were increasingly constructed alongside elite residences in the countryside and that was probably the origin of Earls Barton church (Northamptonshire), which is adjacent to extensive earthworks of a defensive, high-status complex.

Domesday Book records numerous churches in parts of East Anglia by 1066, suggesting that manorial parishes had proliferated there; poor recording may mask densities elsewhere. Small, one-village parishes became commonplace across the south and east of England, even while parishes in the outer edges of England often remained very extensive. Although the earliest stonework in many parish churches is Norman and the network of England's parish churches continued to evolve into the early thirteenth century and beyond, the impetus had clearly begun before 1066.

Estimates of England's population in the eleventh century have risen from the 1.2–1.5 million proposed in the mid-twentieth century to 2–2.5 million today, following a re-evaluation of Domesday Book. To put this in perspective, the recent estimates approximate to those for England and Wales around 1500. Norman immigration had little impact on the total, numbering only perhaps some twenty thousand, so barely 1 per cent of the overall population, and far more English were

8.25 West tower of All Saints Church, Earls Barton. Constructed in the later tenth century, this is one of the best preserved Anglo-Saxon tower churches. Immediately behind the church are massive Conquest-period earthworks, remains of a manorial complex held by Earl Waltheof and his wife Judith, William's niece. Pairing of a high-status residence with a manorial church was commonplace in later Anglo-Saxon England

either killed or expelled. The English population remained very much 'English' in genetic terms, therefore, despite the Conquest.

Eleventh-century England was predominantly rural, with perhaps 90 per cent of the population engaged in farming. Very few incomers became farmers. Over a third of the Domesday population was classified as (villeins *villani*), with small family farms subject to the manorial court, and other large categories were all sections of the rural workforce – bordars (literally, men who ate at the lords table), cottars (cottagers, often with a few acres) and slaves. None of these are likely to have been immigrants from France. Settlement nucleation was well underway pre-1066 and was not dependent on the Conquest, although incoming Norman lords probably introduced it to new areas. In most places rural settlements were not much affected by the Conquest beyond increased demands for rent, services and produce, and the incorporation of new castles into some villages.

There was considerable continuity too in methods of agriculture. The Domesday Inquest assumed use of the heavy plough throughout Anglo-Saxon England, capable of cultivating around 120 acres (49 hectares) each year. Difficulties of interpreting Domesday Book make it impossible to provide a firm estimate of the total area under the plough, but there were over 70,000 plough teams at work in 28 Domesday shires (excluding Middlesex and the northern counties). It seems reasonably safe to assume an arable area roughly comparable to the 3.1 million hectares under the plough in 1914, although the distribution was radically different. The countryside was hit hard for a generation in parts of northern England due to the 'Harrying of the North' by which William suppressed the Northumbrian rebellion of 1069/70; to a lesser extent other regions suffered similarly, particularly northern and north-western Mercia, but elsewhere expansion of ploughing at the expense of pasture, woodland and heath probably continued across the Conquest period little affected by the politics of the age.

Although most of the population lived off food they produced themselves, eleventh-century England had an increasingly monetised economy with a proportion of agricultural production going to markets. Most of those which we can identify were in towns. Domesday York, for example, had a meat market and larger towns generally had several specialised markets. Local markets are problematic at this period, becoming far more recognisable as borough charters proliferated in the twelfth and thirteenth centuries, but such place name elements as 'port' ('market', as Stockport, Bridport, and see 'Hugh of the port' in Domesday Dartford) imply their presence. Archaeological evidence sometimes suggests that the layout of a later medieval town may pre-date 1066, as at Barton-on-Humber, for example, where Domesday Book records a market and ferry. A key indicator is the presence of burgesses – individuals holding by the burgage tenure characteristic of a town: over one hundred places had burgesses in Domesday Book, although some, such as Penwortham (Lancashire), had only a handful.

Particular concentrations of small towns occur in Domesday Wiltshire (as Calne and Malmesbury), Somerset (as Bruton and Frome), and around the south-east seaways (as Fordwich, Hythe). Other market centres are somewhat speculative: King's Lynn (Norfolk), for example, although not formally founded until 1090, may already have been operative in William's reign. Given that most medieval markets were not in

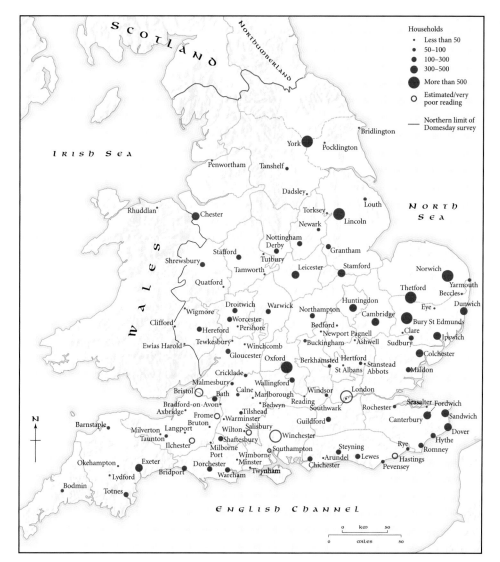

the larger towns, it seems likely that we are missing numerous examples, even despite
the limitation of trade to *burhs* in the tenth century. Some new towns were founded
between 1066 and 1086, for example at Rye (East Sussex), where the abbot of Fécamp
established a town and harbour, but again this may have merely formalised an existing
market. Sites on the south coast received an impetus from new cross-Channel interests
whereas markets that depended on trade with Scandinavia experienced a recession.

In most areas the larger towns were the shire boroughs, where mints were
concentrated, administration centred and the more important defences maintained,
although some others, such as Thetford (Norfolk), with its long-sustained mint and
943 burgesses in 1066, were also sizeable. A handful of Domesday towns were clearly
exceptional: in 1066 York had 1,418 houses as well as those held of the archbishop, so
probably some eight thousand residents; Lincoln, Norwich and Oxford were not much
smaller, but all four suffered population reduction by 1086, in York's case dramatically.

London was clearly by far the largest late Anglo-Saxon town but its omission from Domesday Book makes it difficult to assess. Archaeological finds of the period are mainly limited to the Roman walled area, plus Southwark on the southern side of the river, which had expanded down Borough High Street. Southwark, though, was fired by the Normans in 1066. The waterfront between London Bridge and Billingsgate was regularly rebuilt and has produced quantities of imported pottery from the mid-eleventh century onwards, suggesting a vibrant community with strong links to the Continent as well as coastal England, exporting wool, cloth and lead.

In Edward's reign all England's mints received their dies from London, and its mint was by far the most productive. Edward's development of Westminster reflects the expansion of London's suburbs; the foundation of several new priories around the City followed in the Norman period. Whether London's experience of the Norman Conquest was negative even in the short term is unclear: the literary evidence for burning and looting is to an extent contradicted by the demolition of the riverside wall in the late eleventh century which implies expansion, suggesting that any downturn was short-lived.

Most towns, even shire towns, were far smaller and many had shrinking populations during William's reign: Stafford had only 179 dwellings in 1086 of which 41 were unoccupied and/or derelict, suggesting a loss since 1066 in excess of 20 per cent. There is some evidence of castle-building but Stafford's castle was eventually resited at some distance from the town. Many of the houses here were attached to rural estates: for example, 13 were linked with Robert of Stafford's nearby manor of Bradley, so probably included his lodgings and others for his men. Such towns had highly fluctuating populations, rising when the shire court, fair, market or some major social event was in progress, then dropping away.

Many even of the shire towns embraced farming alongside more 'urban' activities: at Derby, 41 burgesses cultivated 8 ploughlands in 1086; the 243 burgesses of 1066 had declined to 140 by then, so almost 30 per cent of the townsfolk were farming. Its 10 mills suggest that the town was also a focus for producing flour. At Colchester (Essex), a detailed list of the king's burgesses in 1086 entered into Little Domesday Book reveals that many held a few acres of land, so were both tradesmen and small-scale farmers. At Bury St Edmunds (Suffolk) bakers, brewers, tailors, washers, shoemakers, robemakers, cooks, porters and bursars are all noted. Numerous buildings in England's southern towns had tiled roofs and there were large-scale ceramics industries in the immediate vicinity of some, as at Canterbury. Bone, ivory, metal and textile-working were commonplace; some towns offered specialised marketing of local products (as salt at Droitwich in Worcestershire and Middlewich in Cheshire). Some burgesses were clearly literate, and written records played an increasing role in commerce, estate management and government.

Despite the reduced numbers of inhabitants, towns owed greater revenues in 1086 than they had in 1066: Hertford, for example, paid £7 10s in 1066 but £20 in 1086. Many towns both lost population and faced greater demands after the Conquest, suggesting that incomes declined noticeably. Much the same can be said of great swathes of the countryside, where values were reckoned to have increased between

1066 and 1086 despite static or declining assets. Assuming these figures were based on lordly income, landholders were necessarily exacting a higher share of the yield than in the past. To take a few examples, the 36 estates of Count Alan in Norfolk for which we have 1066 and 1086 values show an overall rise of around 40 per cent (£96 17s to £133 19s), with increases recorded in 16 instances and falls in just 5. Some of these rises are extreme, as at Costessey, for example, where the valuation rose from £20 to £45 and Ingham from £2 to £9.

Warwickshire was a shire where between 1066 and 1086 warfare is not recorded. Taking the estates held of the king by Earl Roger, Earl Aubrey and the Count of Meulan as a sample, the 68 estates where the calculation can be made were valued on average around 30 per cent higher in 1086 than 1066. If we break this down there is some variability, with Earl Roger's showing only a 14 per cent rise (£28 to £32 10s) while Earl Aubrey's lands, which were being farmed short term while in the king's hands, show a 77 per cent increase (£9 5s to £16 5s 4d). The much larger holdings of the Count of Meulan rose in value closer to the overall average of 30 per cent. Lords were, therefore, exacting an increased share of the proceeds of farming compared to 1066, most markedly when they had only temporary control of the land, a process we might liken to asset stripping.

If we look at the estates of Thorkell of Warwick, a comparable overall increase in values is present, but it is noticeable that his estates were generally far poorer than those of the incomers, valued at a mere 34s each on average compared to Roger's 72s, Aubrey's 65s and the Count of Meulan's 67s. Many of Thorkell's tenants were incomers and most of his more profitable manors were sublet to the new aristocracy. He had been unable to protect his pre-existing Anglo-Saxon tenants, therefore, even supposing he had wished to.

Conclusion

There are considerable continuities to set beside the discontinuities of the Conquest period which we need to bear in mind as we review the political history. Overall, the impact was less likely to be personal and more likely to be financial the further down the social scale we look, with numerous hitherto prosperous families driven into poverty. At whatever level of society, however, the Conquest was a major watershed. By the twelfth century, even the peasantry were abandoning Anglo-Saxon naming habits and calling many of their sons William, Henry and Robert, their daughters Matilda, Emma and Eleanor, although this was delayed somewhat in parts of the north, where Scandinavian personal names still remained in use.

Its extraordinary success meant that the story of the Norman Conquest was told on William's terms and it is Norman accounts that underpin attempts to write a history of 1066 and its immediate aftermath. By the time of Domesday Book, Harold's reign had been virtually erased from the record and William was presenting himself as Edward's heir. A generation further on, Harold had become little more than a symbol of misrule. Writing in 1127 at Saint-Évroul, the Anglo-Norman Orderic Vitalis remarked of 1066:

In England there was great disorder after the death of King Edward, when the perjured Harold, son of Godwin, who was not of royal stock, seized the kingdom by force and fraud.

Had the Battle of Hastings turned out differently then chroniclers may have referred to William in similar terms, with as much justification. That said, although there were frequent divisions within the English establishment, it is worth stressing that from the close of 1066 onwards William always had some English support and never faced a truly national rebellion. The northern revolt was by far the most dangerous but it was unsupported in southern England. The backing of several ecclesiasts appointed during Edward's reign was unwavering: these naturally included men like the Lotharingian Giso, bishop of Wells, the Norman William, bishop of London, and Baldwin, abbot of Bury St Edmunds, but they also included such Englishmen as Bishop Wulfstan and Archbishop Ealdred. Numerous thegns also stood by William and he still counted on Anglo-Saxon contingents in the latter part of his reign when fighting in Normandy. Indeed, when William was unhorsed and struck down in a melee against his rebellious son Robert a few days after Christmas 1078, it was an English thegn, Toki, son of Wigot, who shielded him at the cost of his own life. The rebellions which William did confront were generally ill-focused and poorly led. His victory at Hastings gave William an aura of invincibility which discouraged insular opponents from confronting him. It has often been suggested that his use of heavy cavalry and archers was crucial, bringing new dimensions to English warfare which had to that point been comparatively traditional in style. That the great expansion of Norman power into England and southern Europe coincided with the adoption of both castles and heavy cavalry is pertinent. Normans had established control of southern Italy by 1066; four years later Sicily fell as well. The energy of William himself, his determination and his self-belief also played their part in his victory, although much the same might have been said of either Harold Godwineson or Harald Hardrada had they won.

Most Norman landholders in 1086 were named for their places of origin on the Continent (as Berengar de Tosny, Hugh de Grandmesnil), but a few were identified via places in England (as Robert de Romney, Roger de Westerham) and this would spread as the insular Norman elite increasingly saw themselves and were viewed by others as 'English' Normans or the 'Norman' English, as distinct from 'Norman' Normans and the 'English' English. There can be no doubting that the England which emerged into the twelfth century was a markedly different place to that which had existed in 1065, with a new elite, a new architecture, new cultural conventions and usage and a different style of warfare. For centuries to come, overseas commitments would shape royal policy. Indeed, the English state over which Edward the Confessor had ruled would not finally re-emerge divested of Continental territory until Queen Mary lost Calais in 1558, and even then the acquisition of Wales seriously weakens the comparison.

At the last we should acknowledge that the late Anglo-Saxon state was part of a world which was fast disappearing. Cnut's conglomerate Viking Empire strung out along the Atlantic coastline of northern Europe disintegrated even before his death through infighting, regional particularism and the problems of maintaining the neces-

THE TRANSFORMATION OF ANGLO-SAXON ENGLAND

sary contact between its several parts. Edward's reign was played out against a back-drop of ambitious Viking and Anglo-Scandinavian warlords whom only good fortune kept away from England's shores. His own sympathies were always with Normandy, and it was arguably its preferred candidate, though not necessarily the candidate to whom he ultimately lent his support, who eventually prevailed.

Anglo-Saxon England may not have died on the field of Hastings but it certainly changed radically over the following few years. William crushed his northern opponents, dispossessed others who had turned against him, progressively ceased patronising or employing Anglo-Saxons and turned instead to French-speaking incomers. The Anglo-Saxon elite was variously destroyed, driven abroad or slain, with groups dispersing to Ireland, Scotland, Scandinavia and the Continent, often to join Viking forces. A substantial fleet made up of English and Danes reached the eastern Mediterranean in 1088, many taking service in the imperial Varangian Guard at Byzantium and fighting the Normans in Sicily. In Atlantic Europe, the Viking Age was ending and Scandinavian influence in England was in steep decline.

In the late eleventh century, the new Norman aristocracy of England pushed forward into Wales, with Scotland and Ireland also in their sights. The Norman Conquest should be remembered as the most brutal land grab in English history and the changes that it brought about serve as a fitting point at which to close this new introduction to Anglo-Saxon England.

Yet despite the traumas of the Norman Conquest, much of the Anglo-Saxon world survived. Anglo-Norman and Latin became the languages of the royal court, of justice

8.27 Circular walrus-ivory seal die with projecting handle. On the face (right) God the Father and Son sit enthroned over a prostrate human figure, the damaged symbol of the Holy Ghost above. Within the circular frame a bearded man holds a sword in his right hand, with the inscription 'THE SEAL OF GODWIN THE THEGN'. On the reverse (left) a woman seated on a cushion holds a book with the secondary inscription 'THE SEAL OF GODGYTHA A NUN GIVEN TO GOD'; she may be his relative. Found at Wallingford and made around 1040, the seal demonstrates the workmanship and wide-ranging contacts of eleventh-century Anglo-Saxon craftsmen

and administration, and of learning and culture, but nevertheless English continued to be spoken as a mother tongue by the majority of the population. By the end of the fourteenth century, English – Middle English – had reasserted itself as the dominant vernacular literary language, sidelining the hitherto pre-eminent Anglo-Norman. Now in the twenty-first century, English in its many forms and dialects is one of the great global languages and the vernacular of the Internet.

The English kingdom which forms such a central part of the United Kingdom of Great Britain and Northern Ireland was brought into existence by Anglo-Saxon kings over the tenth and eleventh centuries. If little of the governmental apparatus of the late Anglo-Saxon 'state' survived long after the Conquest, nevertheless the basic structures of England owe much to the Anglo-Saxon past. England's counties and shires, its parishes and dioceses, its main administrative towns and many of its historic ports are in origin or development Anglo-Saxon. The agrarian landscape that emerged across the Middle and Late Saxon periods dominated England for much of the medieval and early modern periods, only finally giving way in the Enclosure Acts of the modern era.

It is not just the fabric of Anglo-Saxon England that has continued to exert an influence – so too has the idea of the Anglo-Saxons. In contexts as diverse as the Reformation and the American Revolutionary Wars, the Anglo-Saxon past has served as a justification and template for change. At the height of Britain's imperial power in the nineteenth century, many commentators attributed its greatness to its Anglo-Saxon inheritance and these roots were celebrated and embraced enthusiastically. The revival of Anglo-Saxon personal names – as Alfred, Edgar, Ethel, Edwina – illustrates the point. Through to the twentieth century, the English, together with many of the other English-speaking peoples, saw themselves as a part of a wider Germanic world. While the two world wars of the twentieth century weakened and devalued this perceived common bond, the story of England's origins via migration from Germanic homelands in the fifth and sixth centuries still retains some traction.

Origins are tricky things. Historical debts that seem self-evident to one generation are rejected and repudiated by the next. Yet it is clear that the Anglo-Saxons do still matter. For whether we know it or not their shadow still lies long over England itself, and, too, over the whole English-speaking world. We tread where those ancestors trod, in a world which still bears the imprint of their decisions, their deeds, their wants and their needs.

THE BAYEUX TAPESTRY

NICHOLAS J. HIGHAM

The Bayeux Tapestry was commissioned and produced only a few years after the Battle of Hastings. It offers a unique and visually arresting account of the Norman Conquest. Whenever we call to mind the persons of Edward, Harold or William, the Tapestry images dominate, inevitably. Who commissioned it, though, why it was made, and where, are all debated.

So who did commission it? For a long time Queen Matilda was the prime suspect but that theory now has virtually no support. A recent suggestion was that Edward's widow Edith was responsible, but by far the strongest candidate has long been William's half-brother Odo, bishop of Bayeux and earl of Kent. He is the only figure named more than once other than King Edward (3 times), Harold (20), Count Guy (6), William (18) and Count Conan (2). He appears in at least three scenes, invariably with his influence and power emphasised, and the Tapestry tells a version of the Conquest very close to the Norman narrative accounts but stages the oath-taking at Bayeux, Odo's see, rather than at Bonneville, as the narratives suggest.

8a.1 Bishop Odo (far left) on horseback wields a mace in the midst of battle, rallying the young Norman cavalry in support of Duke William (visor raised) at a moment of crisis

.

UBI:UNUS:CLERICUS: ÆLFGYVA

8a.2 An unarmed Harold in the presence of Duke William, seated, with armed men in the background. The naked figure beneath serves as a warning that Harold's speech is not to be trusted

Whoever commissioned it, the Tapestry had a designer of genius and numerous craftsmen or women working under close supervision. Although some have argued that it was undertaken in Normandy, the majority favour manufacture in south-east England, most probably at Canterbury where the church libraries contained manuscript illustrations to which the design seems indebted. Odo was earl of Kent.

What is it? Strictly speaking this is not a tapestry at all, but an embroidery stitched on a long strip made up of sections of bleached linen sewn together. Late Anglo-Saxon England had great expertise in embroidery and this is its finest product, made probably by English needlewomen. The strip is around 50 centimetres wide and, at 70.34 metres long, is by far the largest work of its kind from the period, although it is unclear whether or not it was exceptional then. Eleventh-century art is predominantly on religious themes, but this is a work of contemporary history. Though it is not clear whether it had been there since the late eleventh century, the Tapestry was one of the treasures of Bayeux Cathedral by the early fifteenth. Later in that century it was exhibited annually in the nave. Today it is on permanent display in the city in a specially constructed exhibition centre.

It has often been suggested that the Tapestry was commissioned to grace the new cathedral which Odo consecrated in 1077. However, the theme seems improbable for such a purpose. An alternative is that it was designed for a square room, so perhaps for the banqueting hall of a castle. If so, then images of Harold's feast at Bosham confront across the room the feast at Hastings presided over by Odo, while the others have Harold's oath at Bayeux opposite the image of Odo on a stallion at full gallop.

The narrative is made up of panels each depicting a particular scene or event. How many there were is unclear since the final sections of the Tapestry are lost. The story currently closes as the English flee from the battlefield following Harold's death but probably originally continued to William's coronation, on Christmas Day 1066. Panels are separated by buildings and trees with interlaced foliage, or simply by abrupt scene changes. In some parts there is such fluidity that adjacent elements of the story flow together and are difficult to section off, so the division into panels is not always clear. The emphasis on human interactions within settings which are barely sketched in and often stereotypical has some parallels with modern cartoons.

The audience gains most from the Tapestry when accompanied by a commentary. A running text in Latin along the top provides some guidance and identifies some individuals, but many contemporary viewers may well have been illiterate. The skeletal nature of the text may imply that it was intended as a prompt for a guide to offer a much fuller explanation.

The main panels account for about 60 per cent of the total height of the Tapestry, with the remainder taken up by running borders at top and bottom. These are used for a variety of small-scale figures: most are animals, either real or mythical, apparently included as decoration. However, the borders also provide a commentary on parts of the main story which can be judgemental.

Harold is the principal victim of this process. The main panels and commentary treat him comparatively well, recognising his status at key points. The marginalia tell a different story: the two wolves licking their paws beneath Harold's feasting at Bosham, for example, associate him with their cunning; a series of rural scenes – ploughing, sowing, harrowing, hunting birds with slingshot and hunting with hounds – accompany the to and fro of messengers regarding transfer of Harold from Guy's custody to William's, but beneath the figure of Harold as he actually meets William is a nude man using an adze. The next panel continues the same theme, with a squatting nude male. Numerous references to Aesop's fables inject warnings which undermine the apparently honourable Harold presented in the main panels. While the Tapestry is generally viewed as a commentary on the Norman Conquest, its focus is better described as the rise and fall of Harold Godwineson, who appears in the very first panel, whose trip to France is

8a.3 Harold seated in majesty, crowned and with orb and sceptre, with lay representatives offering a sword. The commentary reads 'HAROLD KING OF THE ENGLISH'. Archbishop Stigand's presence threatens the event's legitimacy. In the next scene (right) courtiers are alarmed by the sight of Halley's comet, harbinger of calamity. Below, dogs, their tongues extended, undermine the scene

8a.4 Harold hears news of the comet, visible above, and takes counsel. The phantom fleet in the lower border suggests the threat from Normandy is the subject of their discussion. Harold's twisted body reflects his illegitimacy

covered in some detail, and whose brief kingship and subsequent death are the main story. Harold was not, the marginalia are telling us, quite the noble figure that he seemed.

The story divides loosely into four main sections, sometimes separated by just one or two scenes. First is Harold's journey to and from the Continent. This visit was widely reported in Norman texts and served as the basis for the Conqueror's case against him. The detail offered is exceptional. Following a cordial meeting with Edward, Harold and his companions ride to Bosham and take ship across the Channel, caste anchor and wade ashore. There Harold is captured by men of Guy of Ponthieu, taken to him at Beaurain but then surrendered to Duke William, whom he accompanies on campaign against Conan of Brittany. Harold distinguishes himself at the crossing of the River Couesnon, and at the close William gives him arms in a ceremony that implies vassalage, following which Harold swears an oath to the duke on holy relics before returning to England.

The precise nature of this oath is not recorded, but the audience was expected to share the view that these acts undermined Harold's claim on the kingship. The Tapestry displays exceptional interest in this story, which accounts for over a third of the surviving length. Care was taken to frame it effectively: a scene centred on the old king opens the sequence and it closes with the seated Edward berating an obsequious Harold. That no other events prior to Edward's death were included emphasises just how important this story was in legitimising the Conquest.

Edward's death and Harold's coronation follow. The death is told in reverse order, the first panel depicting the funeral cortege followed by the second in which two scenes are superimposed, the upper depicting the dying king addressing 'his faithful followers', the lower his body being prepared for burial while a clergyman prays. Harold is offered the crown and then enthroned and crowned, an orb and sceptre in hand, with laymen proffering the sword of state and Archbishop Stigand enrobed on his left. Stigand's presence undermines the legitimacy of the event, given that his elevation to the archbishopric was considered uncanonical. Halley's Comet then appears, to the consternation of the English, a portent of terrible things to come.

This warning, in the upper border, confirms what the audience already know, that divine retribution will fall on Harold through God's agent, William. Here the second main sequence begins: Harold, crowned and seated on his throne, is seen in whispered consultation with an armed retainer, bending uncomfortably to his right: a fleet in the lower margin suggests the subject under discussion. His contorted figure symbolises the illegitimacy of the king's position. An English messenger then brings news to William and a tonsured figure beside him (almost certainly Odo). They begin building and equipping an invasion fleet. Trees are cut down, timbers worked and ships built and equipped, men ride down to the ships and embark, and the fleet sails to Pevensey. The main theme is preparation, pushed through resolutely. This sequence is much shorter than the first, at less than 20 per cent of the surviving tapestry, but is notable as much for what is omitted as for what is included; neither the long delay on the French coast nor the Norwegian invasion is mentioned. The appearance of phantom ships in the lower margin opens this sequence. It closes with the beaching of the Norman fleet on the Sussex coast; the fears of the crooked king, Harold, have become reality.

The third section opens with the Norman cavalry riding out from Pevensey and closes with their departure from Hastings, once again on horseback, for battle. This is the prequel to battle: much space is taken up by the preparation and consumption of food and the building of Hastings Castle, but the Normans are also ravaging the countryside, burning and looting, much as the narratives suggest. Harold is absent from this sequence, though there is news of him. William is the focal figure but shares this role with Odo: 'the bishop' blesses food and drink as the feast begins and the man beside him obligingly points to the words above the next panel, 'ODO: EPS:' ('Bishop Odo'); we see him seated on William's right in discussion with the duke, with Robert, William's other half-brother, unregarded on the duke's left; 'HERE IS WADARD' appears over the figure of a mounted Norman in full armour, who is probably Odo's tenant of the same name. Odo serves, therefore, as an agent of God, preparing for what is to come and legitimising William's candidacy. At only 10 per cent of the surviving Tapestry, this is the shortest section.

The final section centres on the battle of Hastings; at over a third of the surviving length, this is the longest. It opens with William receiving his horse and leading his troops out of Hastings and closes with the flight of the English from the field, pursued by mounted Normans (where the damaged Tapestry now ends). Above the marching army, the figure of a naked lewd man reappears, yet this time the naked female is not resistant but is inviting him into her arms. Again, this is best read as a comment on Harold; the moustache proclaims the man to be English. William heads the column to speak to Vital, who may be equated with one of Odo's Domesday tenants in Kent, bringing news of Harold's approach. Behind the duke rides a second figure with a mace (or similar) rather than a spear, who, like William, exceptionally has mail leggings: this is probably Odo.

The armies locate each other, William makes a speech, then the two forces come together, most of the space being given over to the Norman cavalry, with a scattering

of archers. The lower border now begins to fill with the dead and dying, with broken weapons and dismembered bodies. The battle is condensed and simplified, though the deaths of Leofwine and Gyrth are recorded. Bishop Odo plays a vital role rallying the Norman youths at a moment of crisis, as William bares his head to demonstrate that he has not been slain, so the two half-brothers once again share the scene. The lower border is given over to archers as the assault is launched in which Harold is killed, then gives way to naked bodies being stripped of their armour. The English who flee in the last, truncated scene are neither armoured nor armed, so probably non-combatants from the English camp. Neither William nor Odo appears in these final scenes but of course either or both presumably reappeared in later ones.

The Bayeux Tapestry is a unique document, therefore, which sheds light not just on the politics of the day but also on many aspects of visual culture. It opens windows on such things as castle-building, military preparation, tools, shipbuilding, clothing and the depiction of elite status. It is, however, far from realistic: buildings and trees, in particular, are contrived and stereotypical representation is used, for example to distinguish English from Normans and in portraying horses, which closely reflect the status of their riders. Some of the internal conventions weaken as the scenes progress, suggesting that time pressures caused the embroiderers to streamline some aspects.

At the last, though, it must be remembered that this extraordinary work of art was a piece of propaganda, designed to tell the story of the passage of the Crown from Edward to William in ways that lay blame squarely on Harold's shoulders. It is, therefore, a partial story, told at several levels simultaneously. Harold is the victim of this work, being presented as an outwardly heroic but inwardly flawed character whose failings brought divine retribution upon his countrymen. Of course, William is ultimately the victor but his success is often shared with Odo. If he habitually interpreted the Tapestry for guests, Odo would have had no difficulty depicting himself as one of its heroes.

DOMESDAY BOOK

NICHOLAS J. HIGHAM

Domesday Book is unique: written with sharpened goose quills in heavily abbreviated Latin on parchment (sheepskin), at around 2 million words it is the oldest public record in Europe on anything like this scale. It lists manorial assets at over 13,000 different named places spread across 34 English shires; it provides oversight of England's land tenure not just for 1086 but also 'when King Edward was alive' (at the start of 1066) and for some shires when the current holder obtained the manor (although inclusion of this data is very variable).

The shires provide the principal internal divisions, serving rather like chapters in a book. Each shire is structured internally by reference to land held of the king by particular tenants-in-chief. Within each such lordship estates are subdivided by the hundred (or equivalent) in which they lie, often in a repeating sequence. The structure reflects, therefore, both land tenure and the organs of local government and justice. Most shires

8b.1 Domesday Book. The five Domesday texts in their modern binding, with Great Domesday Book open at the back and Little Domesday Book at the front

8b.2 Opening page of Great Domesday Book for Northamptonshire (folio 219a). A list of landholders in descending order of importance follows a brief description of the shire town

begin with a record of the shire town (or towns), followed by a listing of holdings: these occur in order of seniority, with the king's estates followed by those of senior churchmen, rich abbeys and churches, then those of secular lords in approximate order of status. The Northamptonshire folios, for example, open with an account of Northampton, then the king's estates followed by those of four bishops, ten abbeys or churches and a few lesser clerics, then some 43 secular lords, headed by the king's half-brother and ending with the king's thanes, the last of whom was Oslac, who held just [East] Farndon.

Domesday Book is not the original name of this great work but one which it acquired from its use in law as a record of land tenure of last resort. Otherwise it was known as the *Book of Winchester*, the *Description of England*, the *King's Book* and the *Book of the Treasury*. Nor was it a single volume, though that may have been the original intention. Little Domesday Book comprises Essex, Norfolk and Suffolk. Great Domesday Book covers the rest of England, excluding only northern areas outside the direct control of the English king and London and Winchester, for which entries were never inserted.

Great Domesday Book was almost certainly the intended outcome and the first volume written. It was in the more condensed style, with a greater burden placed on the clerks responsible – it has often been asserted that a single scribe wrote the whole but there may have been several with very similar hands. Two stages of preparation have been identified. First the primary data were collected and verified, shire by shire, by teams of royal agents appointed to probably seven regional circuits, the geography of which suggests they were influenced to some extent by the late pre-Conquest earldoms. Then a synthesis was made, probably circuit by circuit: if abbreviation had not already occurred, then it was introduced at this point, though differences between shires and even individual hundreds remained. Finally the data were collected and integrated into the master work.

The south-eastern and south-western circuits make up the first ten shires, working east–west, but thereafter the circuits were not retained, the scribes instead organising their material in east to west transepts, Middlesex to Herefordshire and Cambridgeshire to Shropshire. They then abandoned this ordering principle in turn in favour of a west–east organisation of the northern shires, from Cheshire across the northern Midlands, then Yorkshire and finally Lincolnshire. Essex, Suffolk and Norfolk were not included; instead the preparatory materials were copied into a separate volume, called Little Domesday Book, without final editing and abbreviation, so retaining much additional information, regarding livestock for example. In this sense, Little Domesday Book is closer to the materials from which Great Domesday Book was compiled. A comparable survivor from this stage is provided by the Exon Book, covering the south west, preserved at Exeter Cathedral. The process seems to have been completed in 1086, when the colophon (closing statement) of Little Domesday Book was written:

IN THE YEAR ONE THOUSAND AND EIGHTY SIX FROM THE INCARNATION OF THE LORD AND IN THE TWENTIETH OF THE REIGN OF WILLIAM THIS SURVEY WAS MADE NOT ONLY FOR THESE THREE COUNTIES BUT ALSO FOR THE OTHERS.

The obituary of William offered by the *Anglo-Saxon Chronicle*, 'E' version, written by an Old English speaker with experience of William's court, clearly refers to the Domesday Survey as complete by his death in 1087, 'all set down in his record'.

What precisely is Domesday Book, why was it made and in what context? While the document itself is comparatively easy to understand, there is much regarding its purpose which is not. The Inquest was clearly commissioned in a time of crisis. The 'E' version of the *Chronicle* reported that invasion from Denmark was imminent in 1085. In expectation, William brought to England 'a larger raiding-army of cavalry and foot soldiers from France and Brittany than has ever sought out this land before, such that

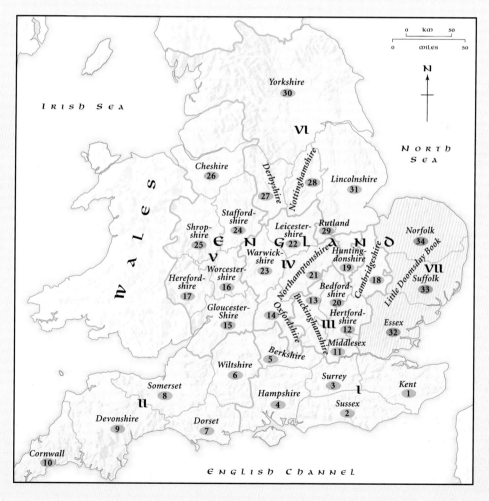

8b.3 Probable Domesday Inquest Circuits (I–VI) and eventual ordering of shires in Great Domesday Book (1–31) and Little Domesday Book (32–4)

men wondered how this land could feed all that force'. The Viking fleet never actually sailed, so William released some of these mercenaries but he retained many. At midwinter, King William was at Gloucester where he

> had great thought and very deep conversation with his Council about this land, how it was occupied, or with which men. Then he sent out his men all over England into every shire to ascertain how many hundreds of hides there were in the shire, or what land and livestock the king himself had in the land, or what dues he ought to have in a twelve-month from the shire. Also he had it written down how much land his archbishops had, and his diocesan bishops, and his abbots and his earls, and – though I tell it at too great length – what or how much each man had who was occupying land in England, in land or livestock, and how much money it was worth. He had it audited so very thoroughly that there was not a single hide, not a yard of land, not even (it is shameful to say – though it seemed to him no shame to do it) one ox, one cow, one pig that was omitted, that was not set down in his record. And afterwards all the records were brought to him.

Agents went into the shires armed with a standardised list of questions, a copy of which has survived at Ely, asking:

> The name of the place. Who held it, before 1066, and now?
> How many hides? How many ploughs, both those in lordship and the men's?
> How many villeins, cottagers and slaves, how many free men and sokemen [that is, men under the jurisdiction of another]?
> How much woodland, meadow and pasture? How many mills and fishponds?
> How much has been added or taken away? What the total value was and is?
> How much each free man or sokeman had or has? All threefold, before 1066, when King William granted it, and now; and if more can be had than at present.

William's commissioners took evidence on oath 'from the sheriff, from all the barons and their Frenchmen, and from the whole hundred, the priests, the reeves and six villeins from each vill', which was then verified by local witnesses. In total, some sixty thousand testimonies were taken.

Domesday Book's retention in the Exchequer, the political context in which the Inquest was instigated and the primacy within each entry of geld information, all encouraged early commentators to interpret Domesday Book as a geld book. Its value to tax collectors has since been questioned because the information is organised by tenants-in-chief within the shire, rather than by taxpayers or manors listed according to proximity. That said, if tenants-in-chief were held responsible for the taxation owed by their tenants to each shire court, then Domesday Book would have been an effective instrument of taxation. Given the amount of additional information, however, other explanations are needed, for Domesday Book is not just a geld book.

Another explanation has focused on the feudal organisation of Domesday Book, seeing it as a means by which William gained legitimacy as Edward's heir, airbrushing Harold II from the record. But again, this fails to account for the detail offered.

Domesday Book necessarily had more complex purposes. It was a composite tool of government, providing William with information regarding important dues, a coherent account of the tenure and value of estates and the means of managing vacancies and wardships. It brought together notices of disputes relating to tenure, offered an opportunity to resolve those, and a clear statement of geld liability, manor by manor, across the estates held by an individual or institution.

The speed and ease of compilation imply that the principal landholders also benefited, perhaps through the recording of their tenure. There was probably far more documentation available at the shire court and on individual estates than now survives, which provided the basis. The 'if more can be had than at present' at the close of the questions implies that William's need for resources was a major driver: both 1086 and 1087 saw poor harvests, so the provisioning of mercenaries was an issue. The oath of allegiance taken by William in August 1087 of his tenants, and even their tenants, before returning to the Continent suggests the settlement of deep divisions. Domesday Book was clearly an important part of this process.

It has been suggested that Domesday Book was compiled as a new database for the geld, revenues from which had probably fallen across the eleventh century, but to see ploughlands as the basis of a new assessment seems counter-intuitive; they were never used for this purpose and they do seem to just measure arable land, as the term suggests. The emphasis on agricultural production implies that foodstuffs were an issue. Though information regarding numerous towns was included, it is probably significant that no questions on the subject occur in the original list, placing the emphasis on the countryside.

Today Domesday Book provides us with invaluable data. It is Domesday information regarding land tenure which underpins histories of the Crown, the greater nobility, the gentry, the shire and baronies, and allows us an unprecedented understanding of the relationship between social and economic power. The data have been mapped in some detail, providing the distribution of ploughs, ploughlands, woodland, pasture, meadow and mills, as well as regional differences in the status of sections of the population. Free men and sokemen were concentrated in the old Danelaw, villeins in the 'central province' and slaves predominantly in western Britain, where they were agricultural labourers on the lords' demesnes.

Differences between the two volumes and some of these regional variations are best illustrated by examples. Starting with Little Domesday Book, an entry from the Chelmsford hundred section of the barony of Ranulph Peverel in the Essex folios (75b) reads as follows:

> Thorold holds *Cice* [St Osyth] from Ranulph, which Siward held as a manor for 2 and a half hides.
> Then and later 9 villeins, now 6. Then and later 12 bordars, now 11. Always 7 slaves. Then and later 4 ploughs in lordship, now 3. Then and later 7 ploughs of the men, now 5. Woodland for 800 pigs, 4 acres of meadow. Pasture for 200 sheep, always 1 mill. Then 6 cobs, 50 cattle, 300 sheep, 40 pigs, 6 beehives. Now 4 cobs, 4 cattle, 68 sheep, 37 pigs, 18 goats. Then and later £9, now £8.

8b.4 Little Domesday Book
entry for *Cice* (St Osyth), Essex

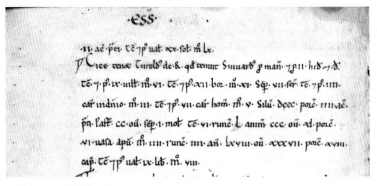

8b.4 Little Domesday Book
entry for *Cice* (St Osyth), Essex

Unlike many manors in Great Domesday Book, this deals with three points in time: 1066, when Thorold received the estate, and the present. There is much information about livestock, which tallies with the *Chronicle*'s comment but not the questions listed in the *Inquisition of Ely*. Clearly the estate had deteriorated since Ranulph was granted it, though revenues remained high, suggesting his take represented a higher proportion of the output than his predecessor had enjoyed.

Compare this with an entry from Great Domesday Book, from the estates of Goisfrid [Geoffrey] Alselin in southern Nottinghamshire. Here Scandinavian terminology was dominant, settlement was more nucleated and open fields more extensive:

> In *Laxintune* [Laxton] Toki had 3 carucates of land to the geld.
> Land for 6 plougths. There Walter the man of Goisfrid Alselin has 1 plough[,] and 22 villeins and 7 bordars have 5 ploughs. And [there are] 5 slaves and 1 female slave and 40 acres of meadow. Wood pasture 1 league long and a half wide. Time of King Edward value £9, now £6. The Jurisdiction of this Manor:
>
> In *Schidrinctune* [Kirton] 2 bovates of land to the geld. Land for 4 oxen. 3 sokemen have 1 plough . . . [several other outlying assets follow]

8b.5 Laxton (Nottinghamshire), an 'L'-shaped village at the heart of the central province in the Danelaw

Goisfrid was a major tenant-in-chief in the Midlands and this was the first named of his six manors in Nottinghamshire, but it was sublet to Walter, whose sole manor this was in the shire and who was therefore probably resident here. Although it is not mentioned so perhaps was not yet built in 1086, a substantial motte and bailey castle lies to the north of the village. This description has only two dates for information, 1066 and 1086, and data concerning livestock are omitted. Although both these manors probably had churches, recording was poor in both shires and neither is mentioned.

Bosham in Sussex offers a very different type of manor, on an altogether different scale:

King William holds Bosham in lordship.
Earl Godwin held [it] and then there were 56 and a half [hides] and it paid geld for 38 hides and now similarly. Land for [. . .]
In lordship there are 6 ploughs and 39 villeins with 50 bordars who have 19 ploughs. There [is] a church and 17 slaves and 8 mills at £4 less 30d. There are 2 fisheries bringing in 8s 10d.
Wood for 6 pigs.
To this manor [were attached] 11 enclosures in Chichester which paid 7s 4d in 1066. Now the bishop has 10 of them from the king and 1 is now in the manor. The whole manor in King Edward's day and after was valued at £40. Now similarly £40. However it renders £50 assayed and weighed, which is valued at £65.

From this manor Engelhere has 2 hides from the king and he has 1 plough and 1 bordar.

8b.6 Great Domesday Book entry for the king's manor of Bosham, Sussex

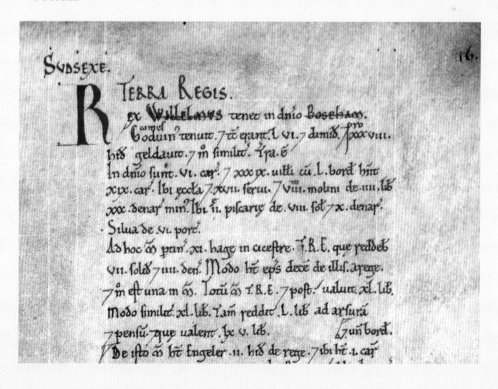

This was the first recorded of the king's manors in Sussex and its appearance on the Bayeux Tapestry implies considerable importance. It is common for urban property to be attached to an important rural manor. Again, there was strong upward pressure on rents.

These three manors of varying scale and located in different parts of England offer insights into the complexities attending any effort to generalise on the basis of Domesday data across England. Clearly, the terms used and practices adopted are more consistent regionally than nationally. Despite such differences, however, Domesday Book was a great achievement, demonstrating the extraordinary capacities of the early Norman state. It remains today the foundational work of English administrative history.

BIBLIOGRAPHY

Abbreviations

A.S.E. – *Anglo-Saxon England* (journal)
A.S.S.A.H. – *Anglo-Saxon Studies in Archaeology and History*
E.H.R. – *English Historical Review*
E.M.E. – *Early Medieval Europe*
M.A. – *Medieval Archaeology*
T.R.H.S. – *Transactions of the Royal Historical Society*

Bibliographies

The journal *Anglo-Saxon England* publishes a bibliography of all aspects of Anglo-Saxon studies, the *Old English Newsletter* similarly publishes a guide, 'The Year's Work in Old English Studies' and a bibliography. The journal *Medieval Archaeology* offers a report of recent archaeological discoveries: 'Medieval Britain and Ireland'. The British Numismatic Society publishes an annual *Journal* that frequently includes information about new coin finds, as does the *Spink Numismatic Circular*, and the annual *Numismatic Chronicle* of the Royal Numismatic Society. The most detailed single-volume bibliography is Simon Keynes, *Anglo-Saxon England: A Bibliographical Handbook for Students of Anglo-Saxon History*, 7th edn (Cambridge, 2006), which is copiously annotated and authoritative.

Select Bibliography

General Works

J. Blair, *The Anglo-Saxon Age: A Very Short Introduction* (Oxford, 2000): offers a very brief history covering the key events and people.
J. Campbell, ed., *The Anglo-Saxons* (London, 1982): a multi-authored, richly illustrated history of the whole period.
T. Charles-Edwards, ed., *After Rome* (Oxford, 2003): thematic essays by leading scholars exploring pre-Viking Britain and Ireland.
W. Davies, ed., *From the Vikings to the Normans* (Oxford, 2003): part of the same series as Charles-Edwards, above, and offering the same width and depth.
R. Fleming, *Britain after Rome: The Fall and Rise, 400 to 1070* (London, 2010): a lively and engaging study, drawing particularly on material culture and primarily focusing on the Anglo-Saxon kingdoms.
D. Hill, *An Atlas of Anglo-Saxon England* (London, 1981): maps illustrating key areas, events and themes.
E. James, *Britain in the First Millennium* (London, 2001): particularly strong on the pre-Viking period, offering an island-wide perspective.
M. Lapidge, J. Blair, S. Keynes and D. Scragg, eds, *The Blackwell Encyclopaedia of Anglo-Saxon England* (Oxford, 1999): short essays on all aspects of Anglo-Saxon studies by many of the top scholars.
H. Loyn, *The Governance of Anglo-Saxon England 500–1087* (London, 1984): a detailed but readable administrative history.
The New Cambridge Medieval History (Cambridge, 1995–2004): essays exploring the whole of medieval Europe; volumes 1–4 cover the Anglo-Saxon period and include authoritative discussions of the material.
P. Stafford, *Unification and Conquest: A Political and Social History of England in the Tenth and Eleventh Centuries* (London, 1989): combines an insightful political narrative with thematic sections exploring the later Anglo-Saxon period.
P. Stafford, ed., *A Companion to the Early Middle Ages: Britain and Ireland c. 500–1100* (Oxford, 2009): a series of important essays that sets Anglo-Saxon England in its wider context.
F. M. Stenton, *Anglo-Saxon England*, 3rd edn (Oxford, 1971): first published in 1943, this classic account shows its age but is still a rewarding read.
A. Williams, *Kingship and Government in Pre-Conquest England* (Basingstoke, 1999): a narrative history focusing on royal authority and government.
B. Yorke, *The Anglo-Saxons* (Sutton, 1999): a 'Pocket History' of the Anglo-Saxon period; brief but eminently readable.

Handbooks and Guides

J. Backhouse, D. H. Turner and L. Webster, eds, *The Golden Age of Anglo-Saxon Art, 966–1066* (London, 1984): extended catalogue of an exhibition by the British Museum and British Library, richly illustrated.

M. Brown, *Manuscripts from the Anglo-Saxon Age* (London, 2007): 140 plates of the most important manuscripts plus expert commentary.

J. Crick and E. van Houts, eds, *A Social History of England, 900–1200* (Cambridge, 2011): learned but readable essays discussing areas all too easily overlooked.

R. Gameson, ed., *The Cambridge History of the Book in Britain: Volume 1, c. 600–1100* (Cambridge, 2011): essays covering book production, ownership and use, with studies of particular types.

M. Gelling, *Signposts to the Past*, 3rd edn (Chichester, 1997): the best guide to place names in England, focuses on the Anglo-Saxon period.

M. Godden and M. Lapidge, eds, *The Cambridge Companion to Old English Literature* (Cambridge, 1991): insightful thematic essays covering Old English literature and its place in Anglo-Saxon society.

A. Gransden, *Historical Writing in England: c. 550–c. 1307*, 2nd edn (London, 1997): arranged chronologically, with chapters on key texts and genres.

P. Grierson and M. Blackburn, *Medieval European Coinage: With a Catalogue of the Coins in the Fitzwilliam Museum, Cambridge, 1: The Early Middle Ages (5th to 10th Centuries)* (Cambridge, 1986): illustrated chronological surveys of the key developments, arranged according to peoples/kingdoms.

H. Hamerow, D. A. Hinton and S. Crawford, eds, *The Oxford Handbook of Anglo-Saxon Archaeology* (Oxford, 2011): essays covering all aspects of the archaeological record.

R. M. Hogg, ed., *The Cambridge History of the English Language, 1: the Beginnings to 1066* (Cambridge, 1992): learned but suitable for the non-specialist.

R. Horsman, *Race and Manifest Destiny: The Origins of American Racial Anglo-Saxonism* (Cambridge, MA, 1981): the classic study of the roles played by the Anglo-Saxon past in the shaping of identity in the United States.

H. A. MacDougall, *Racial Myth in English History: Trojans, Teutons and Anglo-Saxons* (Montreal, 1982): concise, readable guide to changing attitudes to the English past.

H. C. G. Matthew and B. Harrison, eds, *Oxford Dictionary of National Biography*, 60 vols (Oxford, 2004): scholarly biographies of many of the people discussed in this book.

J. J. North, *English Hammered Coinage, Volume 1: Early Anglo-Saxon to Henry III, c. 650 – 1272*, 3rd edn (London, 1994): reference work with illustrations of all the major types.

P. Pulsiano and E. Treharne, eds, *A Companion to Anglo-Saxon Literature* (Oxford, 2008): engaging chronological and thematic essays that cover literature in Latin and the vernacular languages.

P. Sawyer, *Anglo-Saxon Charters: An Annotated List and Bibliography* (London, 1968): fundamental starting point, now updated by S. Kelly and R. Rushforth at http://www.esawyer.org.uk.

H. M. Taylor and J. Taylor, *Anglo-Saxon Architecture*, 3 vols (Cambridge, 1965–78): the focus is predominantly ecclesiastical, the coverage is comprehensive.

L. Webster, *Anglo-Saxon Art* (London, 2012): an up-to-date and authoritative survey.

L. Webster and J. Backhouse, eds, *The Making of England: Anglo-Saxon Art and Culture, AD 600–900* (London, 1991): another lavishly illustrated exhibition catalogue, with detailed commentary.

Chapter 1

For varying approaches to Roman Britain, see R. G. Collingwood and J. N. L. Myres, *Roman Britain and the English Settlements* (Oxford, 1936); S. S. Frere, *Britannia: A History of Roman Britain* (London, 1967); P. Salway, *Roman Britain* (Oxford, 1981); M. Millett, *The Romanization of Britain* (Cambridge, 1990) and *Roman Britain* (London, 1995); A. Woolf, *Roman Britain* (London, 2006); D. J. Mattingly, *An Imperial Possession* (London, 2006), and M. Russell and S. Laycock, *UnRoman Britain* (London, 2010). R. Collins and J. Gerrard, eds, *Debating Late Antiquity in Britain, 300–700* (Oxford, 2004), highlights current research directions. An excellent atlas is provided by B. Jones and D. Mattingly, *An Atlas of Roman Britain*, 2nd edn (Oxford, 2002).

For the environment, see P. Dark, *The Environment of Britain in the First Millennium AD* (London, 2000), and P. Fowler, *Farming in the First Millennium AD* (Cambridge, 2002). For population, see P. Slack and R. Ward, eds, *The Peopling of Britain: The Shaping of a Human Landscape* (Oxford, 2002).

For settlements, see D. Perring, *The Roman House in Britain* (London, 2002); R. Hingley, *Rural Settlement in Roman Britain* (London, 1989); K. and P. Dark, *The Landscape of Roman Britain* (Stroud, 1997); J. Taylor, *An Atlas of Roman Rural Settlement in England* (York, 2007); D. S. Neal and S. R. Cosh, *Roman Mosaics of Britain*, 4 vols (London 2002–10), and J. Wacher, *The Towns of Roman Britain*, 2nd edn (London, 1995). For coinage, see R. Reece, *The Coinage of Roman Britain* (Stroud, 2002). For place names, language and personal names, see A. L. F. Rivet and C. Smith, *The Place-Names of Roman Britain* (London, 1979); S. Laker and P. Russell, eds, 'Languages of Early Britain', *Transactions of the Philological Society*, 109.2 (2011), and A. Mullen and P. Russell, *Celtic Personal Names of Roman Britain* at www.asnc.cam.ac.uk/personalnames/.

For Christianity, see C. Thomas, *Christianity in Roman Britain to AD 500* (London, 1981); D. J. Watts, *Christians and Pagans in Roman Britain* (London, 1991); A. Thacker and R. Sharpe, eds, *Local Saints and Local Churches* (Oxford, 2002); D. Petts, *Christianity in Roman Britain* (Stroud, 2003).

For the end of the Western Roman Empire, see J. K. Knight, *The End of Antiquity: Archaeology, Society and Religion* AD *235–700* (Stroud, 1999); J. Moorhead, *The Roman Empire Divided* (Harlow, 2001); P. Heather, *The Fall of the Roman Empire: A New History* (London, 2005); B. Ward-Perkins, *The Fall of Rome and the End of Civilization* (Oxford, 2005); C. Wickham, *Framing the Early Middle Ages: Europe and the Mediterranean, 400–800* (Oxford, 2005); M. Innes, *Introduction to Early Medieval Western Europe, 300–900* (London, 2007).

For the end of Roman Britain, see S. Esmonde Cleary, *The Ending of Roman Britain* (London, 1989); N. J. Higham, *Rome, Britain and the Anglo-Saxons* (London, 1992); K. Dark, *Civitas to Kingdom: British Political Continuity 300–800* (Leicester, 1994), and *Britain and the End of the Roman Empire* (Stroud, 2000); M. E. Jones, *The End of Roman Britain* (New York, 1996); C. A. Snyder, *An Age of Tyrants: Britain and the Britons* AD *400–600* (University Park, PA, 1998); N. Faulkner, *The Decline and Fall of Roman Britain* (Stroud, 2000); T. Charles-Edwards ed., *After Rome* (Oxford, 2003); R. White, *Britannia Prima: Britain's Last Roman Province* (Stroud, 2007), and S. Laycock, *Britannia: The Failed State* (Stroud, 2008). For late Roman Britain's defences, see D. J. Breeze and B. Dobson, *Hadrian's Wall*, 4th edn (London, 2000); A. Pearson, *The Roman Shore Forts. Coastal Defences of Southern Britain* (Stroud, 2002). For the north, see T. Wilmot and P. Wilson, eds, *The Late Roman Transition in the North: Papers from the Roman Archaeology Conference, Durham 1999* (Oxford, 2000). For the final events, see J. F. Drinkwater, 'The Usurpers Constantine III (407–411) and Jovinus (411–413)', *Britannia*, 29 (1998), 269–98; M. Kulikowski, 'Barbarians in Gaul, Usurpers in Britain', *Britannia*, 31 (2000), 325–45.

For late Roman towns, see A. Rogers, *Late Roman Towns in Britain: Rethinking Change and Decline* (Cambridge, 2011). For the Hoxne Hoard, see P. S. W. Guest, *The Late Roman Gold and Silver Coins from the Hoxne Treasure* (London, 2005). For Germanus, see F. R. Hoare, *The Western Fathers* (London, 1954), 283–320; A. A. Barrett, 'Saint Germanus and the British Missions', *Britannia*, 40 (2010), 197–217. For Patrick, see A. B. E. Hood, *St Patrick: His Writings and Muirchu's Life* (London, 1978); D. R. Howlett, *The Book of Letters of Saint Patrick the Bishop* (Blackrock, Dublin, 1994), and D. Dumville, ed., *Saint Patrick* A.D. *493–1993* (Woodbridge, 1993).

Sources and Issues 1a
See M. Winterbottom's edition and translation, *Gildas: The Ruin of Britain and Other Works* (London, 1978). Then M. Lapidge and D. Dumville, eds, *Gildas: New Approaches* (Woodbridge, 1984); N. J. Higham, *The English Conquest: Gildas and Britain in the Fifth Century* (Manchester, 1994); D. Dumville, 'Post-Colonial Gildas: A First Essay', *Quaestio Insularis*, 7 (2006), 1–21; K. George, *Gildas's De Excidio Britonum and the Early British Church* (Woodbridge, 2009); L. Larpi, *Prolegomena to a New Edition of Gildas Sapiens 'De Excidio Britaniae'* (Florence, 2012).

Sources and Issues 1b
For early literary sources, see J. Morris, ed. and trans., *Nennius: British History and the Welsh Annals* (London, 1980); R. Bromwich and D. Simon Evans, eds and trans., *Culhwch and Olwen: An Edition and Study of the Oldest Arthurian Text* (Cardiff, 1992), and A. O. H. Jarman, ed. and trans., *Aneirin. Y Gododdin* (Llandysul, 1988). For the 'historical Arthur', see G. Ashe, *The Quest for Arthur's Britain* (London, 1968); L. Alcock, *Arthur's Britain: History and Archaeology* AD *367–634* (Harmondsworth, 1971); J. Morris, *The Age of Arthur* (London, 1973), and C. Gidlow, *The Reign of Arthur* (Stroud, 2004). Opposed are D. Dumville, 'Sub-Roman Britain: History and Legend', *History*, 62 (1977), 173–92, and 'The Historical Value of the *Historia Brittonum*', *Arthurian Literature*, 6 (1986), 1–26; O. Padel, 'The Nature of Arthur', *Cambrian Medieval Celtic Studies*, 27 (1994), 1–31; N. J. Higham, *King Arthur: Myth-Making and History* (London, 2002), and T. Green, *Concepts of Arthur* (Stroud, 2007). Recent scholarly collections of essays include R. Bromwich et al., eds, *The Arthur of the Welsh* (Cardiff, 1991); H. Fulton, ed., *A Companion to Arthurian Literature* (Oxford, 2009), and S. Echard, ed., *The Arthur of Medieval Latin Literature* (Cardiff, 2011).

Chapter 2
For Tacitus, see H. Mattingly, trans., *Tacitus on Britain and Germany* (Harmondsworth, 1948). For Bede, see J. McClure and R. Collins, *Bede: The Ecclesiastical History of the English People* (Oxford, 1994). For early literary sources, see P. Sims-Williams, 'The Settlement of England in Bede and the Chronicle', *A.S.E.*, 12 (1983), 1–41; B. Yorke, 'Fact or Fiction? The Written Evidence for the Fifth and Sixth Centuries AD', *A.S.S.A.H.*, 6 (1995), 45–50, and eadem, 'The Origins of Anglo-Saxon Kingdoms: The Contribution of the Written Sources', *A.S.S.A.H.*, 10 (1999), 25–9.

For archaeological approaches, see H. Hamerow, 'The Earliest Anglo-Saxon Kingdoms', in P. J. Fouracre, ed., *The New Cambridge Medieval History I, c. 500–c. 700* (Cambridge, 2005), 263–88. For burials, the indispensable guide is S. Lucy, *The Anglo-Saxon Way of Death* (Stroud, 2000), but see also S. Lucy and A. Reynolds, eds, *Burial in Early Medieval England and Wales* (London, 2002), and M. Welch, *Anglo-Saxon England* (London, 1992).

For cemetery archaeology, see J. N. L. Myres, *Anglo-Saxon Pottery and the Settlement of England* (Oxford, 1969) and *The English Settlements* (Oxford, 1986); V. I. Evison, *The Fifth-Century Invasions South of the Thames* (London, 1965); S. C. Hawkes, 'Anglo-Saxon Kent c. 425–725', in P. Leach, ed., *Archaeology in Kent to* AD *1500* (London, 1982), 64–78; J. Hines, *The Scandinavian Character of Anglian England in the pre-Viking Period* (Oxford, 1984), and idem, 'Philology, Archaeology and the *adventus Saxonum vel Anglorum*', in A. Bammesberger and A. Wollmann, eds, *Britain 400–600: Language and History* (Heidelberg, 1990), 17–36.

For the quoit-brooch style, see S. Suzuki, *The Quoit Brooch Style and Anglo-Saxon Settlement* (Woodbridge, 2000); P. Inker, 'Technology as Active Material Culture: The Quoit-brooch Style', *M.A.*, 44 (2000), 25–52. For clothing, see G. R. Owen-Crocker, *Dress in Anglo-Saxon England*, revised edn (Woodbridge, 2004), and P. W. Rogers, *Cloth and Clothing in Early Anglo-Saxon England: AD 450–700* (York, 2007).

Cemetery studies include: J. N. L. Myres and B. Green, *The Anglo-Saxon Cemeteries of Caistor-by-Norwich and Markshall, Norfolk* (London, 1973); J. N. L. Myres and W. H. Southern, *The Anglo-Saxon Cemetery at Sancton, East Yorkshire* (Hull, 1973); C. J. Arnold, *The Anglo-Saxon Cemeteries of the Isle of Wight* (London, 1982); V. I. Evison, *Dover: The Buckland Anglo-Saxon Cemetery* (London, 1987), and *An Anglo-Saxon Cemetery at Alton, Hampshire* (Gloucester, 1988); A. Down and M. Welch, *Chichester Excavations VII: Apple Down and the Mardens* (Chichester, 1990); V. Evison, *An Anglo-Saxon Cemetery at Great Chesterford, Essex* (York, 1994); J. R. Timby, *The Anglo-Saxon Cemetery at Empingham II, Rutland* (Oxford, 1996); V. I. Evison and P. Hill, *Two Anglo-Saxon Cemeteries at Beckford, Hereford and Worcester* (York, 1996); K. Parfitt and B. Brugmann, *The Anglo-Saxon Cemetery on Mill Hill, Deal, Kent* (London, 1997); S. J. Lucy, *The Early Anglo-Saxon Cemeteries of East Yorkshire: An Analysis and Reinterpretation* (Oxford, 1998); G. Drinkall and M. Foreman, *The Anglo-Saxon Cemetery at Castledyke South, Barton-on-Humber* (Sheffield, 1998); T. Malim and J. Hines, *The Anglo-Saxon Cemetery at Edix Hill (Barrington A), Cambridgeshire* (York, 1998); C. Haughton and D. Powlesland, *West Heslerton: The Anglian Cemetery*, 2 vols (Yedingham, 1999); A. Richardson, *The Anglo-Saxon Cemeteries of Kent* (Oxford, 2005); S. C. Hawkes and G. Grainger, *The Anglo-Saxon Cemetery at Finglesham, Kent* (Oxford, 2006); K. Leahy, *'Interrupting the Pots': The Excavation of Cleatham Anglo-Saxon Cemetery* (York, 2007); M. Carver, C. Hills and J. Scheschkewitz, *Wasperton: A Roman, British and Anglo-Saxon Community in Central England* (Woodbridge, 2009); C. Hills and T. O'Connell, 'New Light on the Anglo-Saxon Succession: Two Cemeteries and their Dates', *Antiquity*, 83 (2009), 1,096–1,108; K. Annable and B. Eagles, *The Anglo-Saxon Cemetery at Blacknall Field, Pewsey, Wiltshire* (Devizes, 2010).

For ethnicity, see R. Jenkins, *Rethinking Ethnicity: Arguments and Explorations* (London, 1997); P. J. Geary, 'Ethnic Identity as a Situational Construct in the Early Middle Ages', *Mitteilungen der Anthropologischen Gesellschaft in Wien*, 113 (1983), 15–26; G. Ausenda, ed., *After Empire: Towards an Ethnology of Europe's Barbarians* (Woodbridge, 1995), 75–94; J. Hines, ed., *The Anglo-Saxons from the Migration Period to the Eighth Century: An Ethnographic Perspective* (Woodbridge, 1997); W. Pohl with H. Reimitz, ed., *Strategies of Distinction: The Construction of Ethnic Communities, 300–800* (Leiden, 1998); H.-W. Goetz, J. Jarnut and W. Pohl, eds, *Regna and Gentes: The Relationship between Late Antique and Early Medieval Peoples and Kingdoms in the Transformation of the Roman World* (Leiden, 2003); H. Härke, 'Anglo-Saxon Immigration and Ethnogenesis', *M.A.*, 55 (2011), 1–28.

For the scale of the Anglo-Saxon settlement, see C. J. Arnold, *From Roman Britain to Saxon England* (London, 1984) and *An Archaeology of the Early Anglo-Saxon Kingdoms* (London, 1988); R. Hodges, *The Anglo-Saxon Achievement* (London, 1989); N. J. Higham, *Rome, Britain and the Anglo-Saxons* (London, 1992); H. Hamerow, 'Migration Theory and the Migration Period', in B. Vyner, ed., *Building on the Past* (London, 1994), 164–77, and J. Chapman and H. Hamerow, eds, *Migrations and Invasions in Archaeological Explanation* (Oxford, 1997). For Kent, see M. Welch, 'Anglo-Saxon Kent to AD 800', in J. H. Williams, ed., *The Archaeology of Kent to AD 800* (Woodbridge, 2007), 187–248.

For the environment, see P. Dark, *The Environment of Britain in the First Millennium AD* (London, 2000). For the 530s climatic crisis, see M. Baillie, *Exodus to Arthur: Catastrophic Encounters with Comets* (London, 1999).

For isotopic studies, see J. Montgomery, P. Budd and J. Evans, 'Reconstructing the Lifetime Movements of Ancient Peoples', *European Journal of Archaeology*, 3 (2000), 370–85; P. Budd, A. Millard, C. Chenery, S. Lucy and C. Roberts, 'Investigating Population Movement by Stable Isotope Analysis: A Report from Britain', *Antiquity*, 78 (2004), 127–41; H. Eckardt, C. Chenery, P. Booth, G. Müldner, J. A. Evans and A. Lamb, 'Oxygen and strontium isotope evidence for mobility in Roman Winchester', *Journal of Archaeological Science*, 36 (2009), 2,816–25; S. Marzinzik, 'Ringlemere in Reference to Early Cross-Channel Relations', in S. Brookes, S. Harrington and A. Reynolds, eds *Studies in Early Anglo-Saxon Art and Archaeology: Papers in Honour of Martin G. Welch* (Oxford, BAR BS, 2011), 55–61.

For archaeogenetics, see L. Cavalli-Sforza, P. Menozzi and A. Piazza, *The History and Geography of Human Genes* (Princeton, NJ, 1994), and L. Cavalli-Sforza, *Genes, Peoples and Languages* (London, 2001). Then J. F. Wilson, D. A. Weiss, M. Richards, M. G. Thomas, N. Bradman and D. B. Goldstein, 'Genetic Evidence for Different Male and Female Roles during Cultural Transitions in the British Isles', *Proceedings of the National Academy of Science USA*, 98 (2001), 5,078–83; M. E. Weale, D. A. Weiss, R. F. Jager, N. Bradman and M. G. Thomas, 'Y Chromosome Evidence for Anglo-Saxon Mass Migration', *Molecular Biological Evolution*, 19 (2002), 1,008–21; C. Capelli, N. Redhead and F. Graix, 'A Y Chromosome Census of the British Isles', *Current Biology*, 13 (2003), 979–84; B. McEvoy, M. Richards, M. Forster and D. G. Bradley, 'The *Longue Durée* of Genetic Ancestry: Multiple Genetic Marker Systems and Celtic Origins on the Atlantic Façade of Europe', *American Journal of Human Genetics*, 75 (2004), 693–702; S. Oppenheimer, *The Origins of the British* (London, 2006); M. G. Thomas, M. P. Stumpf and H. Härke, 'Evidence for an Apartheid-like Social Structure in Early Anglo-Saxon England', *Proceedings of the Royal Society B*, 273 (2006), 2,651–7.

For buildings, see S. James, A. Marshall and M. Millett, 'An Early Medieval Building Tradition', *Archaeological Journal*, 141 (1984), 182–215; S. West, *West Stow: The Anglo-Saxon Village* (Ipswich, 1985); P. Rahtz, 'Buildings and Rural Settlement', in D. M. Wilson, ed., *The Archaeology of Anglo-Saxon England* (London, 1976),

49–98; H. Hamerow, *Excavations at Mucking, Vol. 2, The Anglo-Saxon Settlement* (London, 1993), and *Early Medieval Settlements: The Archaeology of Rural Communities in North-West Europe 400–900* (Oxford, 2002); S. Losco-Bradley and G. Kinsley, *Catholme: An Anglo-Saxon Settlement on the Trent Gravels in Staffordshire* (Nottingham, 2002); J. Tipper, *The Grubenhaus in Anglo-Saxon England* (Yedingham, 2004).

For the Celtic/Latin–Anglo–Saxon linguistic interface, see K. H. Jackson, *Language and History in Early Britain* (Edinburgh, 1953); K. Cameron, 'Eccles in English Place-Names', in M. W. Barley and R. P. C. Hanson, eds, *Christianity in Britain 300–700* (Leicester, 1968), 87–92; M. Gelling, *Signposts to the Past*, 3rd edn (Chichester, 1997), and 'Why Aren't We Speaking Welsh?', *A.S.S.A.H*, 6 (1993), 51–6; A. Wollmann, 'Early Latin Loan-words in Old English', *A.S.E.*, 22 (1993), 1–26; R. Coates and A. Breeze, *Celtic Voices, English Places: Studies of the Celtic Impact on Place-Names in England* (Stamford, 2000); P. Cavill and G. Brodrick, eds, *Language Contact in the Place-Names of Britain and Ireland* (Nottingham, 2007); N. J. Higham, ed., *Britons in Anglo Saxon England* (Woodbridge, 2007). For Language and society, see D. H. Green, *Language and History in the Early Germanic World* (Cambridge, 1998).

For regional studies, see B. Eagles, 'Anglo-Saxon Presence and Culture in Wiltshire c. AD 450–c. 675', in P. Ellis, ed., *Roman Wiltshire and After: Papers in Honour of Ken Annable* (Devizes, 2001), 199–233; S. Draper, *Landscape, Settlement and Society in Roman and Early Medieval Wiltshire* (Oxford, 2006); D. Rudling, ed., *The Archaeology of Sussex to AD 2000* (King's Lynn, 2003); J. T. Baker, *Cultural Transition in the Chilterns and Essex Region, 350 AD to 650 AD* (Hatfield, 2006); M. Dawson, *Archaeology in the Bedford Region* (Oxford, 2004); B. Eagles, 'The Archaeological Evidence for Settlement in the Fifth to Seventh Centuries AD', in M. Aston and C. Lewis, eds, *The Medieval Landscape of Wessex* (Oxford, 1994), 13–32, and 'Britons and Saxons on the Eastern Boundary of the *Civitas Durotrigum*', *Britannia*, 35 (2004), 234–40; K. Leahy, *The Anglo-Saxon Kingdom of Lindsey* (Stroud, 2007); T. Green, 'The British Kingdom of Lindsey', *Cambrian Medieval Celtic Studies*, 56 (2008), 1–44, and *Britons and Anglo-Saxons in Lincolnshire: AD 400–650* (Lincoln, 2012). For the underlying cultural geography, see T. Williamson, 'The Environmental Contexts of Anglo-Saxon Settlement', in N. J. Higham and M. J. Ryan, eds, *Landscape Archaeology of Anglo-Saxon England* (Woodbridge, 2010), 133–56. For the formation of an Anglo-Saxon people, see J. Hines, 'The Becoming of the English: Identity, Material Culture and Language in Early Anglo-Saxon England', in *A.S.S.A.H.*, 7 (1994), 49–59; P. Wormald, 'Bede, the *Bretwaldas* and the Origins of the *Gens Anglorum*', in P. Wormald et al., eds, *Ideal and Reality in Frankish and Anglo-Saxon Society* (Oxford, 1983), 99–129. For processes of anglicisation, see A. Woolf, 'The Britons: From Romans to Barbarians', in H. W. Goetz, J. Jarnintt and W. Pohl, eds, *Regna and Gentes* (Leiden, 2003), 345–80. For parallels with the Balkans, see P. Fouracre, 'Britain, Ireland and Europe, c. 500–c. 750', in P. Stafford (ed.) *A Companion to the Early Middle Ages* (Oxford, 2009), 126–42.

Sources and Issues 2a
C. Hills, *The Anglo-Saxon Cemetery at Spong Hill, North Elmham, Part I: Catalogue of Cremations Nos. 20–64 and 1000–1690* (Gressenhall, 1977); C. Hills and K. Penn, *The Anglo-Saxon Cemetery at Spong Hill, North Elmham, Part II* (Gressenhall, 1981); C. Hills, K. Penn and R. Rickett, *The Anglo-Saxon Cemetery at Spong Hill, North Elmham, Part III: Catalogue of Inhumations* (Gressenhall, 1984); C. Hills, K. Penn and R. Rickett, *The Anglo-Saxon Cemetery at Spong Hill, North Elmham, Part IV: Catalogue of Cremations* (Gressenhall, 1987); J. I. McKinley, *The Anglo-Saxon Cemetery at Spong Hill, North Elmham Part VIII: The Cremations* (Gressenhall, 1994); R. Rickett, *The Anglo-Saxon Cemetery at Spong Hill, North Elmham, Part VII: The Iron Age, Roman and Early Saxon Settlement* (Gressenhall, 1995); K. Penn and B. Brugmann, with Karen Høilund Nielsen, *Aspects of Anglo-Saxon Burial: Morning Thorpe, Spong Hill, Bergh Apton and Westgarth Gardens* (Gressenhall, 2007); C. Hills and S. Lucy, *Spong Hill IX: Chronology and Synthesis* (Cambridge 2012).

Sources and Issues 2b
The Prittlewell Prince: The Discovery of a Rich Anglo-Saxon Burial in Essex, Museum of London Archaeological Service (London, 2004); S. Tyler, 'The Anglo-Saxon Cemetery at Prittlewell, Essex: An Analysis of the Grave Goods', *Essex Archaeology and History*, 19 (1988), 91–116.

Chapter 3

For Bede, see J. McClure and R. Collins, eds, *Bede: The Ecclesiastical History of the English People* (Oxford, 1994).

For burial archaeology, see S. Lucy, *The Anglo-Saxon Way of Death* (Stroud, 2000); H. Geake, *The Use of Grave-Goods in Conversion-Period England, c. 600–c. 850* (Oxford, 1997); N. Stoodley, *The Spindle and the Spear: A Critical Enquiry into the Construction and Meaning of Gender in the Early Anglo-Saxon Burial Rite* (Oxford, 1999); S. Lucy and A. Reynolds, eds, *Burial in Early Medieval England and Wales* (London, 2002), and H. Williams, *Death and Memory in Early Medieval Britain* (Cambridge, 2006). For specific cemeteries, see chapter 2 or Lucy, above, but for St Peter's Tip, Broadstairs, see A. C. Hogarth, 'Structural Features in Anglo-Saxon Graves', *Archaeological Journal*, 130 (1973), 104–19.

For 'princely burial', see R. L. S. Bruce-Mitford, *The Sutton Hoo Ship-Burial*, 3 vols (London, 1975–83); A. C. Evans, *The Sutton Hoo Ship Burial* (London, 1986); M. Carver, *The Age of Sutton Hoo* (Woodbridge, 1992) and *Sutton Hoo: Burial Ground of Kings?* (London, 1998), and W. Filmer-Sankey and T. Pestell, *Snape Anglo-Saxon Cemetery: Excavations and Surveys 1824–1992* (Ipswich, 2001);

For 'princely settlements', see B. Hope-Taylor, *Yeavering: An Anglo-British Centre of Early Northumbria* (London, 1977); M. Millett with S. James, 'Excavations at Cowdery's Down, Basingstoke, Hants.', *Archaeological Journal*, 140 (1983), 151–279; J. Hinchcliffe, 'An Early Medieval Settlement at Cowage Farm, Foxley, near Malmesbury', *Archaeological Journal*, 143 (1986), 240–59;

B. J. Philp, *The Discovery and Excavation of Anglo-Saxon Dover: The Detailed Report on Fourteen of the Major Anglo-Saxon Structures and Deposits Discovered in the Centre of Ancient Dover, during Large-Scale Rescue-Excavation 1970–1990* (Dover, 2003); P. Frodsham and C. O'Brien, *Yeavering: People, Power and Place* (Stroud, 2005).

For kingdom and kingship formation, see J. Campbell, *Bede's Reges and Principes* (Jarrow, 1979); S. Bassett, ed., *The Origins of Anglo-Saxon Kingdoms* (Leicester, 1989); B. Yorke, *Kings and Kingdoms of Early Anglo-Saxon England* (London, 1990) and *Wessex in the Early Middle Ages* (London, 1995); D. P. Kirby, *The Earliest English Kings* (London, 1991); T. Dickinson and D. Griffiths, eds, *The Making of Kingdoms*, A.S.S.A.H., 10 (1999); D. Rollason, *Northumbria 500–1100: Creation and Destruction of a Kingdom* (Cambridge, 2003).

For 'overkingship', see B. A. E. Yorke, 'The Vocabulary of Anglo-Saxon Overlordship', A.S.S.A.H., 2 (1981), 171–200; P. Wormald, 'Bede, the *Bretwaldas* and the Origins of the *Gens Anglorum*', in P. Wormald et al., eds, *Ideal and Reality in Frankish and Anglo-Saxon Society* (Oxford, 1983), 99–129; S. Fanning, 'Bede, *Imperium* and the *Bretwaldas*', *Speculum*, 66 (1991), 1–26.

For ships, see S. McGrail, *Ancient Boats in North-West Europe: The Archaeology of Water Transport to AD 1500* (Harlow, 1987). For trade and industry, see D. M. Wilson, ed., *The Archaeology of Anglo-Saxon England* (London, 1976); J. W. Huggett, 'Imported Grave Goods and the Early Anglo-Saxon Economy', *M.A.*, 32 (1988), 63–96; M. Anderton, ed., *Anglo-Saxon Trading Centres: Beyond the Emporia* (Glasgow, 1999); I. L. Hansen and C. Wickham, eds, *The Long Eighth Century: Production, Distribution and Demand* (Leiden, 2000); D. Hill and R. Cowie, *Wics: The Early Medieval Trading Centres of Northern Europe* (Sheffield, 2001); M. McCormick, *Origins of the European Economy: Communications and Commerce AD 300–900* (Cambridge, 2001); T. Pestell and K. Ulmschneider, eds, *Markets in Early Medieval Europe: Trading and 'Productive' Sites, 650–850* (Macclesfield, 2003).

For coinage, see S. E. Rigold, 'The Two Primary Series of English Sceattas', *British Numismatic Journal*, 30 (1960), 6–53, and 'The Primary Series of English Sceattas', *British Numismatic Journal*, 47 (1977), 21–30; D. Hill and D. M. Metcalf, eds, *Sceattas in England and on the Continent* (Oxford, 1984); M. A. S. Blackburn, ed., *Anglo-Saxon Monetary History* (Leicester, 1986); A. Gannon, *The Iconography of Early Anglo-Saxon Coinage, Sixth to Eighth Centuries* (Oxford, 2003). For recent coin finds see the *Early Medieval Corpus of Single Finds in the British Isles*, at *http://www.medievalcoins.org.*, B. Cook and G. Williams, eds, *Coinage and History in the North Sea World c. 500–1250* (Leiden, 2006), and G. Williams, *Early Anglo-Saxon Coins* (Botley, 2008).

The earliest law codes are translated by F. L. Attenborough, ed., *The Laws of the Earliest English Kings* (Cambridge, 1922), L. Oliver, *The Beginnings of English Law* (Toronto, 2002), and in D. Whitelock, ed., *English Historical Documents*, vol. 1 (London, 1955).

For Anglo-Saxon paganism, see G. R. Owen, *Rites and Religions of the Anglo-Saxons* (Newton Abbot, 1981); D.

M. Wilson, *Anglo-Saxon Paganism* (London, 1992); T. Dickinson, 'An Anglo-Saxon "Cunning Woman" from Bidford-on-Avon', in M. O. H. Carver, ed., *In Search of Cult: Archaeological Investigations in Honour of Philip Rahtz* (Woodbridge, 1993), 45–54; T. Hofstra, L. Houwen and A. MacDonald, eds, *Pagans and Christians: The Interplay between Christian Latin and Traditional Germanic Cultures in Early Medieval Europe* (Groningen, 1995), 99–130; K. L. Jolly, *Popular Religion in Late Anglo-Saxon England* (Chapel Hill, NC, 1996); S. D. Church, 'Paganism in Conversion-Age Anglo-Saxon England: The Evidence of Bede's *Ecclesiastical History* Reconsidered', *History*, 93 (2008), 162–80.

For the Conversion, see H. Mayr-Harting, *The Coming of Christianity to Anglo-Saxon England*, 3rd edn (University Park, PA, 1991); M. Dunn, *The Christianization of the Anglo-Saxons, c. 597–700: Discourses of Life, Death, and Afterlife* (London, 2009). James Campbell, *Essays in Anglo-Saxon History* (London, 1986); P. Sims-Williams, *Religion and Literature in Western England, 600–800* (Cambridge, 1990); N. J. Higham, *The Convert Kings: Power and Religious Affiliation in Early Anglo-Saxon England* (Manchester, 1997); S. Hollis, *Anglo-Saxon Women and the Church: Sharing a Common Fate* (Woodbridge, 1992); R. Fletcher, *The Conversion of Europe from Paganism to Christianity 371–1386 AD* (London, 1997); R. Gameson, ed., *St Augustine and the Conversion of England* (Stroud, 1999); M. Carver, ed., *The Cross Goes North: Processes of Conversion in Northern Europe, AD 300–1300* (Woodbridge, 2003); B. Yorke, *The Conversion of Britain, 600–800* (Harlow, 2006). For Augustine, see N. Brooks, *The Early History of the Church of Canterbury* (Leicester, 1984); I. Wood, 'The Mission of Augustine of Canterbury to the English', *Speculum*, 69 (1994), 1–17; R. Meens, 'A Background to Augustine's Mission to Anglo-Saxon England', *A.S.E.*, 22 (1994), 5–17. For Anglo-Saxon saints, see F. P. Webb and D. Farmer, eds and trans, *The Age of Bede* (Harmondsworth, 1983); G. Bonner, D. Rollason and C. Stancliffe, eds, *St Cuthbert, His Cult and His Community* (Woodbridge, 1989), and C. F. Battiscombe, ed., *The Relics of St Cuthbert* (Oxford, 1956); C. Stancliffe and E. Cambridge, eds, *Oswald: Northumbrian King to European Saint* (Stamford, 1995); B. Colgrave, ed. and trans., *The Life of Bishop Wilfrid* (Cambridge, 1927); W. T. Foley, *Images of Sanctity in Eddius Stephanus' 'Life of Wilfrid', an Early English Saint's Life* (Lampeter, 1992); N. J. Higham, ed., *Wilfrid, Abbot, Bishop, Saint* (Donnington, 2013). For the penitentials, see J. T. McNeill and H. M. Gamer, *Medieval Handbooks of Penance: A Translation of the Principal Libri Poenitentiales* (New York, 1938). For monasteries, see S. Foot, *Monastic Life in Anglo-Saxon England* (Cambridge, 2006); for nunneries, see idem, *Veiled Women*, 2 vols (Aldershot, 2000), and B. Yorke, *Nunneries and the Anglo-Saxon Royal Houses* (London, 2003). For church councils, see C. Cubitt, *Anglo-Saxon Church Councils, c. 650–c. 850* (London, 1995). J. Blair and R. Sharpe, eds, *Pastoral Care before the Parish* (Leicester, 1992).

Sources and Issues 3a
S. DeGregorio, ed., *The Cambridge Companion to Bede* (Cambridge, 2010), contains essays on Bede's writings, context and later reception. G. H. Brown, *A Companion to Bede* (Woodbridge, 2009), surveys Bede's writings, usefully arranged by genre and subject. Important essay collections include S. DeGregorio, ed., *Innovation and Tradition in the Writings of the Venerable Bede* (Morgantown, 2006); S. Lebecq et al., eds, *Bède le Vénérable entre Tradition et Postérité* (Villeneuve d'Ascq, 2004), with essays in both French and English; L. A. J. R. Houwen and A. A. Macdonald, eds, *Beda Venerabilis: Historian, Monk and Northumbrian* (Groningen, 1996); R. T. Farrell, ed., *Bede and Anglo-Saxon England* (Oxford, 1978); and G. Bonner, ed., *Famulus Christi* (London, 1976). The annual Jarrow Lectures, on subjects relating to Bede and his world, are published individually; those from 1958–93 are collected in M. Lapidge, ed., *Bede and His World*, 2 vols (Aldershot, 1994). The most accessible translation of the *Ecclesiastical History* is in J. McClure and R. Collins, *Bede: The Ecclesiastical History of the English People* (Oxford, 1994), which also includes a number of other texts. There are numerous studies of the *Ecclesiastical History*: see W. Goffart, *The Narrators of Barbarian History* (Princeton, NJ, 1988); J. M. Wallace-Hadrill, *Bede's Ecclesiastical History of the English People: A Historical Commentary* (Oxford, 1988); and N. J. Higham, *(Re-) Reading Bede: The Ecclesiastical History in Context* (London, 2006).

Sources and Issues 3b
This hoard, discovered only in 2009, has not yet been sufficiently studied for there to be much literature. See the beautifully illustrated booklet by K. Leahy and R. Bland, *The Staffordshire Hoard* (London, 2009), and S. Dean, D. Hooke and A. Jones, 'The "Staffordshire Hoard": The Fieldwork', *Antiquaries Journal*, 90 (2010), 139–52.

Chapter 4
For William of Malmesbury's thoughts on Offa, see R. A. B. Mynors, R. M. Thomson and M. Winterbottom, *William of Malmesbury: Gesta Regum Anglorum*, 2 vols (Oxford, 1998–9). For the Mercian Supremacy, see F. M. Stenton, 'The Supremacy of the Mercian Kings', *E.H.R.*, 33 (1918), 433–52, and *Anglo-Saxon England*, 3rd edn (Oxford, 1971); M. Brown and C. Farr, eds, *Mercia: An Anglo-Saxon Kingdom in Europe* (London, 2001); D. Hill and M. Worthington, eds, *Æthelbald and Offa: Two Eighth-Century Kings of Mercia* (Oxford, 2005). Other useful surveys include D. Kirby, *The Earliest English Kings*, rev. edn (London, 2000), and B. Yorke, *Kings and Kingdoms of Early Anglo-Saxon England* (London, 1990).
  Boniface's letter to Æthelbald is translated in E. Emerton, *The Letters of Saint Boniface* (New York, 1940). See also N. Brooks, 'The Development of Military Obligations in Eighth- and Ninth-Century England', in P. Clemoes and K. Hughes, eds, *England before the Conquest* (Cambridge, 1971), 69–84, and P. Stafford, 'Political

Women in Mercia, Eighth to Early Tenth Centuries', in M. Brown and C. A. Farr, eds, *Mercia*, 35–49.
  For Offa's involvement in Kent, see N. Brooks, *The Early History of the Church at Canterbury: Christ Church from 597–1066* (Leicester, 1984). Offa's Dyke is explored in D. Hill and M. Worthington, *Offa's Dyke: History and Guide* (Stroud, 2003); for a critique of the 'truncated' Dyke see I. Bapty, 'The Final Word on Offa's Dyke?', A review of *Offa's Dyke: History and Guide* at www.cpat.org.uk/offa/offrev.htm. For Offa's Continental connections, see J. Nelson, 'Carolingian Contacts', in M. Brown and C. A. Farr, eds, *Mercia*, 126–43, and J. Story, *Carolingian Connections: Anglo-Saxon England and Carolingian Francia, c. 750–870* (Aldershot, 2003). The letters from Charlemagne to Offa are translated in H. Loyn and J. Percival, *The Reign of Charlemagne* (London, 1975). For Cynethryth, see Stafford, 'Political Women in Mercia'; for Offa's coinage see R. Naismith, *Money and Power in Anglo-Saxon England: The Southern English Kingdoms, 757–865* (Cambridge, 2012), and also the entries on coinage below. The nature of Cenwulf's hegemony over Kent is explored in S. Keynes, 'The Control of Kent in the Ninth Century', *E.M.E.*, 2 (1993), 111–31, and Brooks, *Early History*. For Essex, see B. Yorke, 'The Kingdom of the East Saxons', *A.S.E.*, 14 (1985), 1–36.
  For trading and 'productive sites', see chapter 3, above. In addition, for *Lundenwic* see, for example, L. Blackmore, 'The Origins and Growth of *Lundenwic*, a Mart of Many Nations', in B Hårdh and L. Larsson, eds, *Central Places in the Migration and Merovingian Periods* (Stockholm, 2002), 273–301, J. R. Maddicott, 'London and Droitwich, c. 650–750: Trade, Industry and the Rise of Mercia', *A.S.E.*, 34 (2005), 7–58, and G. Malcolm, D. Bowsher and R. Cowie, *Middle Saxon London: Excavations at the Royal Opera House, 1989–99* (London, 2003). For the high-status site at Whitehall, see R. Cowie and L. Blackmore, *Early and Middle Saxon Rural Settlement in the London Region* (London, 2008). For Sandtun, see M. Gardiner, 'Continental Trade and Non-Urban Ports in Middle Anglo-Saxon England: Excavations at Sandtun, West Hythe, Kent', *Archaeological Journal*, 158 (2001), 161–290. For toll exemptions, see S. Kelly, 'Trading Privileges from Eighth-Century England', *E.M.E.*, 1 (1992), 3–23, and for trading more generally, N. Middleton, 'Early Medieval Port Customs, Tolls and Controls on Foreign Trade', *E.M.E.*, 13 (2005), 313–58. For 'productive sites' see G. Davies, 'Early Medieval "Rural Centres" and West Norfolk: A Growing Picture of Diversity, Complexity and Changing Lifestyles', *M.A.*, 54 (2010), 89–122.
  For rural settlements and the landscape, see R. Faith, *The English Peasantry and the Growth of Lordship* (London, 1997); H. Hamerow, *Early Medieval Settlements: The Archaeology of Rural Communities in North-West Europe, 400–900* (Oxford, 2002); J. Moreland, 'The Significance of Production in Eighth-Century England', in I. Hansen and C. Wickham, eds, *The Long Eight Century: Production, Distribution and Demand* (Leiden, 2000), 69–104; A. Reynolds, 'Boundaries and Settlements in Later Sixth- to Eleventh-Century England', *A.S.S.A.H.*, 12 (2003), 97–139, and S. Rippon, 'Landscape Change

During the "Long Eighth Century" in Southern England', in N. J. Higham and M. J. Ryan, eds, *Landscape Archaeology of Anglo-Saxon England* (Woodbridge, 2010), 39–64. For marine resources see, for example, P. Murphy, 'The Landscape and Economy of the Anglo-Saxon Coast: New Archaeological Evidence', in Higham and Ryan, eds, *Landscape Archaeology*, 211–21.

In addition to the items under chapter 3, above, see for the coinage M. M. Archibald, 'Beonna and Alberht: Coinage and Historical Context', in Hill and Worthington, eds, *Æthelbald and Offa* 123–132, 1–74; D. Chick, 'The Coinage of Offa in the Light of Recent Discoveries', in Hill and Worthington, eds, *Æthelbald and Offa*, 111–22; idem, *The Coinage of Offa and His Contemporaries* (London, 2010), 1–33; Naismith, *Money and Power*, and idem, 'Kings, Crisis and Coinage Reforms in the Mid-Eighth Century', *E.M.E.*, 20 (2012), 291–332, and G. Williams, 'Mercian Coinage and Authority', in Brown and Farr, eds, *Mercia*, 210–28.

For the 'common burdens', see R. Abels, *Lordship and Military Obligation in Anglo-Saxon England* (Berkeley, CA, 1988); Brooks, 'The Development of Military Obligations', G. Williams, 'Military Institutions and Royal Power', in Brown and Farr, eds, *Mercia*, 295–309, and idem, 'Military Obligations and Mercian Supremacy in the Eighth Century', in Hill and Worthington, eds, *Æthelbald and Offa*, 103–10. For Abbess Eangyth, see B. Yorke, *Nunneries and the Anglo-Saxon Royal Houses* (London, 2003).

For the pre-Viking Church, see J. Blair, *The Church in Anglo-Saxon Society* (Oxford, 2005), supplemented with S. Foot, *Monastic Life in Anglo-Saxon England, c. 600–900* (Cambridge, 2006). For use of the term 'minster', see S. Foot, 'Anglo-Saxon Minsters: A Review of the Terminology', in J. Blair and R. Sharpe, eds, *Pastoral Care before the Parish* (Leicester, 1992), 212–25. Bede's letter to Ecgberht is translated in J. M. McClure and R. Collins, *Bede: The Ecclesiastical History of the English People* (Oxford, 1994). The councils of *Clovesho* and Chelsea as well as the *Dialogue* of Ecgberht and the report of the papal legates can be found in J. Johnson, *A Collection of the Laws and Canons of the Church of England*, 2 vols, new edn (London, 1850). For the issue of secularisation and disputes between Mercian kings and archbishops of Canterbury, see Blair, *Church in Anglo-Saxon Society*, and Brooks, *Early History*. For the councils themselves, see C. Cubitt, *Anglo-Saxon Church Councils, c.650–c.850* (London, 1995), and S. Keynes, *The Councils of Clofesho* (Leicester, 1994). The fate of female houses is explored by S. Foot, *Veiled Women: The Disappearance of Nuns from Anglo-Saxon England*, 2 vols (Aldershot, 2000), and Yorke, *Nunneries*. For Worcester, see P. Sims-Williams, *Religion and Literature in Western England, 600–800* (Cambridge, 1990).

For the 'Tiberius Style' see, for example, by M. Brown, 'Mercian Manuscripts? The "Tiberius" Group and Its Historical Context', in Brown and Farr, eds, *Mercia*, 278–90. For Mercian sculpture, see the essays by Hawkes and Jewell in Brown and Farr, eds, *Mercia*; R. N. Bailey, *The Meaning of Mercian Sculpture* (Leicester, 1988); R. Cramp, 'Schools of Mercian Sculpture', in A. Dornier, ed., *Mercian Studies* (Leicester, 1977), 191–231. For Brixworth, R. Gem, 'Architecture of the Anglo-Saxon

Church, 735–870: From Archbishop Ecgberht to Archbishop Ceolnoth', *Journal of the British Archaeological Association*, 146 (1993), 29–66, idem, *Architecture, Liturgy and Romanitas at All Saints' Church, Brixworth* (Leicester, 2011). For Cædmon's hymn see, for example, D. P. O'Donnell, *Cædmon's Hymn: A Multi-Media Study, Edition and Archive* (Cambridge, 2005).

For pastoral care and lay religiosity, see Blair, *The Church in Anglo-Saxon Society*, and the essays in Blair and Sharpe, *Pastoral Care*. The role of monasteries in the provision of pastoral care is debated by J. Blair, 'Debate: Ecclesiastical Organization and Pastoral Care in Anglo-Saxon England', *E.M.E.*, 4 (1995), 193–212, and E. Cambridge and D. Rollason, 'The Pastoral Organization of the Anglo-Saxon Church: A Review of the "Minster Hypothesis"', *E.M.E.*, 4 (1995), 87–104. For Alcuin's letters, see S. Allott, *Alcuin of York* (York, 1974).

Sources and Issues 4a
The key sources are translated in C. Talbot, *The Anglo-Saxon Missionaries in Germany* (London, 1954), and E. Emerton, *The Letters of Saint Boniface* (New York, 1940). R. McKitterick, 'Eighth-Century Foundations', in R. McKitterick, ed., *The New Cambridge Medieval History, II, c. 700–c. 900* (Cambridge, 1995), 681–94, introduces the religious and intellectual currents of this period. W. Levison, *England and the Continent in the Eighth Century* (Oxford, 1946), is the classic study. Other insightful contributions include R. McKitterick, *Anglo-Saxon Missionaries in Germany* (Leicester, 1990); J. Palmer, *Anglo-Saxons in a Frankish World, 690–900* (Turnhout, 2009), and I. Wood, *The Missionary Life: Saints and the Evangelisation of Europe 400–1050* (Harlow, 2001). D. Bullough, *Alcuin: Achievement and Reputation* (Leiden, 2002), is heavy-going but comprehensive and authoritative.

Sources and Issues 4b
C. Loveluck and D. Atkinson, *The Early Medieval Settlement Remains from Flixborough, Lincolnshire: The Occupation Sequence, c. AD 600–1000* (Oxford, 2007); D. H. Evans and C. Loveluck, eds, *Life and Economy at Early Medieval Flixborough, c. AD 600–1000: The Artefact Evidence* (Oxford, 2007); K. Dobney, D. Jaques, J. Barrett and C. Johnstone, *Farmers, Monks and Aristocrats: The Environmental Archaeology of Anglo-Saxon Flixborough* (Oxford, 2007); C. Loveluck, *Rural Settlement, Lifestyles and Social Change in the Later First Millennium AD: Anglo-Saxon Flixborough in its Wider Context* (Oxford, 2007). For a critique, see J. Blair, 'Flixborough Revisited', *A.S.S.A.H.*, 17 (2011), 101–7.

Chapter 5
Ealhburg's charter is translated in F. Harmer, *Select English Historical Documents of the Ninth and Tenth Centuries* (Cambridge, 1914), and her family is reconstructed in N. Brooks, *The Early History of the Church at Canterbury: Christ Church from 597–1066* (Leicester, 1984).

Alcuin's letters are translated in S. Allott, *Alcuin of York* (York, 1974). For Viking activity, see C. Downham, 'Vikings in England', in S. Brink and N. Price, eds, *The Viking World* (London, 2008), 341–9, and S. Keynes, 'The Vikings in England, c. 790–1016', in P. Sawyer, ed., *The Oxford Illustrated History of the Vikings* (Oxford, 1997), 48–82. For Peter Sawyer's thinking on the nature of the Vikings, see his *The Age of the Vikings*, 2nd edn (London, 1971). N. Brooks, 'England in the Ninth Century: The Crucible of Defeat', *T.R.H.S.*, 5th series, 29 (1979), 1–20, critiques some of Sawyer's ideas and explores many of the themes of this chapter. For discussion of the term 'Viking', and much else, see C. Downham, *Viking Kings of Britain and Ireland: The Dynasty of Ívarr to A.D. 1014* (Edinburgh, 2007). Reasons for Scandinavian expansion are explored by J. Barrett, 'What Caused the Viking Age?', *Antiquity*, 82 (2007), 671–85.

Mercian overlordship in Kent is explored in S. Keynes, 'The Control of Kent in the Ninth Century', *E.M.E.*, 2 (1993), 111–31, see also idem, 'Mercia and Wessex in the Ninth Century', in M. Brown and C. Farr, eds, *Mercia: An Anglo-Saxon Kingdom in Europe* (London, 2001), 310–28. For the lack of landed resources, P. Wormald, 'The Ninth Century', in J. Campbell, ed., *The Anglo-Saxons* (London, 1982), 132–57. For the expansion of Wessex, see B. Yorke, *Wessex in the Early Middle Ages* (London, 1995), and for the 'Bretwalda' see, for example, S. Keynes, 'Rædwald the Bretwalda', in C. B. Kendall and P. S. Wells, eds, *Voyage to the Other World: The Legacy of Sutton Hoo* (Minneapolis, MN, 1992), 103–23. Eardwulf's exile is discussed in J. Nelson, 'England and the Continent in the Ninth Century: I, Ends and Beginnings', *T.R.H.S.*, 6th series, 12 (2002), 1–21, and Northumbria's involvement with northern Britain by A. Woolf, *From Pictland to Alba: Scotland, 789–1070* (Edinburgh, 2007). For differing structures of governance in Wessex and Mercia, see Keynes, 'Mercia and Wessex' and D. Pratt, *The Political Thought of King Alfred the Great* (Cambridge, 2007).

For the material evidence, see D. Hinton, *Gold, Gilt, Pots and Pins: Possessions and People in Medieval England*, new edn (Oxford, 2005). For coinage, additional to the entries under chapter 4, above, see E. J. Pirie, 'Contrasts and Continuity within the Coinage of Northumbria', in B. Cook and G. Williams, eds, *Coinage and History in the North Sea World c. 500–1250* (Leiden, 2006), 211–39. For the *emporia* see chapters 3 and 4 above; for the Continental context, see M. Costambeys, M. Innes and S. MacLean, *The Carolingian World* (Cambridge, 2011). See also J. D. Richards, 'Cottam: An Anglo-Scandinavian Settlement on the Yorkshire Wolds', *Archaeological Journal*, 156 (1999), 1–111, J. D. Richards, and J. Naylor, 'A "Productive Site" at Bidford-on-Avon, Warwickshire: Salt, Communication and Trade in Anglo-Saxon England', in S. Worrel, ed., *A Decade of Discovery* (Oxford, 2010), 193–200, and G. Beresford, *Goltho: The Development of an Early Medieval Manor, c. 850–1150* (London, 1987). The evidence from Canterbury is explored by Brooks, *Early History*, and for Winchester see Sources and Issues 5b, below.

For manuscripts, see M. Lapidge, *The Anglo-Saxon Library* (Oxford, 2006), and for scriptoria see Brooks, *Early History*. For West Saxon charters see S. Keynes, 'The

West Saxon Charters of King Æthelwulf and His Sons', *E.H.R.*, 109 (1994), 1,109–49. For the 'Sunday Letter', see D. Whitelock, 'Bishop Ecgred, Pehtred and Niall', in D. Whitelock, R. McKitterick and D. Dumville, eds, *Ireland in Early Medieval Europe* (Cambridge, 1982), 47–68. For Lupus, see J. Story, *Carolingian Connections: Anglo-Saxon England and Carolingian Francia, c. 750–870* (Aldershot, 2003), and for church-building, see R. Gem, 'Architecture of the Anglo-Saxon Church, 735–870: From Archbishop Ecgberht to Archbishop Ceolnoth', *Journal of the British Archaeological Association*, 146 (1993), 29–66. For the Vikings and monasticism, see J. Blair, *The Church in Anglo-Saxon Society* (Oxford, 2005), and D. Hadley, *The Vikings in England: Settlement, Society and Culture* (Manchester, 2006); for Peterborough, see S. Kelly, *Charters of Peterborough Abbey* (Oxford, 2009).

The movements and campaigns of the Great Army are explored in detail by R. Abels, *Alfred the Great: War, Kingship and Culture in Anglo-Saxon England* (London, 1998), and Hadley, *Vikings in England*. For Repton, see M. Biddle and B. Kjølbye-Biddle, 'Repton and the Vikings', *Antiquity*, 66 (1992), 36–51.

The literature on King Alfred is vast. Important studies include Abels, *Alfred*, A. J. Frantzen, *King Alfred* (Boston, MA, 1986), Pratt, *Political Thought*, and P. Wormald, 'Living with Alfred', *Haskins Society Journal*, 15 (2004), 1–39. Many aspects of Alfred's life and reign are explored in the essays in T. Reuter, ed., *Alfred the Great* (Aldershot, 2003). For Alfred's subsequent reputation, see S. Keynes, 'The Cult of King Alfred the Great', *A.S.E.*, 28 (1999), 225–356, and J. Parker, *England's Darling: The Victorian Cult of Alfred the Great* (Manchester, 2007).

In addition: key sources for Alfred's reign are translated in S. Keynes and M. Lapidge, *Alfred the Great: Asser's Life of King Alfred and Other Contemporary Sources* (London, 1983). Alfred's authorship, or otherwise, of texts is explored by M. Godden, 'Did King Alfred Write Anything?', *Medium Aevum*, 76 (2007), 1–23, and D. Pratt, 'Problems of Authorship and Audience in the Writings of King Alfred the Great', in P. Wormald and J. Nelson, eds, *Lay Intellectuals in the Carolingian World* (Cambridge, 2007), 162–91. For Alfredian 'propaganda', see R. H. C. Davies, 'Alfred the Great: Propaganda and Truth', *History*, 56 (1971), 169–82. For Æthelwulf's marriage to Judith, see M. J. Enright, 'Charles the Bald and Aethelwulf of Wessex: The Alliance of 856 and Strategies of Royal Succession', *Journal of Medieval History*, 5 (1979), 291–302. For Alfred's journey to Rome, see S. Keynes, 'Anglo-Saxon Entries in the "Liber Vitae" of Brescia', in J. Roberts, J. L. Nelson and M. Godden, eds, *Alfred the Wise* (Cambridge, 1997), 99–119.

For illness and spirituality, see P. Kershaw, 'Illness, Power and Prayer in Asser's Life of King Alfred', *E.M.E.*, 10 (2001), 201–24, J. L. Nelson, 'Monks, Secular Men and Masculinity, c. 900', in D. Hadley, ed., *Masculinity in Medieval Europe* (Harlow, 1999), 121–42, D. Pratt, 'The Illnesses of King Alfred the Great', *A.S.E.*, 30 (2001), 39–90, and M. Wood, 'Alfred the Great: The Case of the Fenland Forger', in idem, *In Search of England* (London, 1999), 125–48. For Asser's *Life* as a forgery, see A. Smyth, *King Alfred the Great* (Oxford, 1995), and for a response

S. Keynes, 'On the Authenticity of Asser's Life of King Alfred', *Journal of Ecclesiastical History*, 47 (1996), 529–51.

Relations between Wessex and Mercia are explored in S. Keynes, 'King Alfred and the Mercians', and M. Blackburn, 'The London Mint in the Reign of Alfred', both in M. Blackburn and D. Dumville, eds, *Kings, Currency and Alliances: History and Coinage of Southern England in the Ninth Century* (Woodbridge, 1998). For London, J. Clark, 'King Alfred's London and London's King Alfred', *London Archaeologist*, 9 (1999), 35–8, and J. Haslam, 'King Alfred, Mercia and London, 874–86: A Reassessment', *A.S.S.A.H.*, 17 (2011), 120–46. For English identity, see S. Foot, 'The Making of *Angelcynn*: English Identity before the Norman Conquest', *T.R.H.S.*, 6th series, 6 (1996), 25–49; for a critique, see, G. Molyneaux, 'The *Old English Bede*: English Ideology or Christian Instruction?', *E.H.R.*, 124 (2009), 1,289–1,323.

For military reforms, see R. Abels, *Lordship and Military Obligation in Anglo-Saxon England* (Berkeley, CA, 1988), G. Halsall, *Warfare and Society in the Barbarian West, 450–900* (London, 2003), and, more generally, R. Lavelle, *Alfred's Wars: Sources and Interpretations of Anglo-Saxon Warfare in the Viking Age* (Woodbridge, 2010). For the *burhs* see Sources and Issues 5b, below. For literacy and reform see, for example, S. Kelly, 'Anglo-Saxon Lay Society and the Written Word', in R. McKitterick, ed., *The Uses of Literacy in Early Mediaeval Society* (Cambridge, 1990), 36–62. For Alfred's laws, P. Wormald, *The Making of English Law: King Alfred to the Twelfth Century. Volume 1: Legislation and Its Limits* (Oxford, 2001). For artistic production in Alfred's reign, see D. A. Hinton, *The Alfred Jewel and Other Late Anglo-Saxon Decorated Metalwork* (Oxford, 2008).

Sources and Issues 5a
J. Stodnick, 'Second-Rate Stories? Changing Approaches to the Anglo-Saxon Chronicle', *Literature Compass*, 3 (2006), 1,253–65, provides a stimulating survey of approaches to the *Chronicle*, with a useful bibliography. The most recent complete translation is M. J. Swanton, *The Anglo-Saxon Chronicles* (London, 1996). S. Keynes, 'Manuscripts of the *Anglo-Saxon Chronicle*', in R. Gameson, ed. *The Cambridge History of the Book in Britain: Volume 1, c. 600–1100*, (Cambridge, 2011), 537–52, offers the ideal starting point. Recent important studies include N. Brooks, 'Why Is the Anglo-Saxon Chronicle about Kings?', *A.S.E.*, 39 (2010), 43–70; S. Baxter, 'MS C of the Anglo-Saxon Chronicle and the Politics of Mid-Eleventh-Century England', *E.H.R.*, 122 (2007), 1,189–227; P. Stafford, '"The Annals of Æthelflæd": Annals, History and Politics in Tenth-Century England', in J. Barrow and A. Wareham, eds, *Myth, Rulership, Church and Charters* (Aldershot, 2008), 101–16; and eadem, 'The Anglo-Saxon Chronicles: Identity and the Making of England', *Haskins Society Journal*, 19 (2007), 28–50.

Sources and Issues 5b
There is a vast amount written on early medieval towns, of which only a small fraction can be named here. For an overview, see J. Haslam, *Anglo-Saxon Towns in Southern England* (Chichester, 1984); P. Ottaway, *Archaeology in British Towns* (London, 1992); D. M. Palliser, ed., *The Cambridge Urban History of Britain, vol. I, 600–1540* (Cambridge, 2000).

For *Hamwic*, see A. D. Morton, ed., *Excavations at Hamwic*, vol. 1 (London, 1992), and P. Andrews, ed., *Excavations at Hamwic*, vol. 2 (York, 1997). For Hereford, see R. Shoesmith, *Hereford City Excavations*, vol. *2* (London, 1982), and A. Thomas and A. Boucher, eds, *Hereford City Excavations, Volume 4: Further Sites and Evolving Interpretations* (Almeley, 2002); for Winchester see M. Biddle, ed., *Winchester in the Early Middle Ages* (Oxford, 1976). For the Burghal Hidage, see D. H. Hill and A. R. Rumble, eds, *The Defence of Wessex: The Burghal Hidage and Anglo-Saxon Fortifications* (Manchester, 1996); for later developments, see D. Hill, 'Athelstan's Urban Reforms', in *A.S.S.A.H.*, 11 (2000), 173–85. The case for ninth-century Mercian boroughs is made by S. Bassett, 'The Middle and Late Anglo-Saxon Defences of Western Mercian Towns', *A.S.S.A.H.*, 15 (2008), 180–239, and for a long process of development of the West Saxon *burhs* by J. Baker and S. Brookes, 'From Frontier to Border: The Evolution of Northern West Saxon Territorial Delineation in the Ninth and Tenth Centuries', *A.S.S.A.H.*, 17 (2011), 109–23.

Chapter 6
For Scandinavian settlement in England, see D. Hadley, *The Vikings in England: Settlement, Society and Culture* (Manchester, 2006); J. D. Richards, *Viking Age England* (Stroud, 2004); J. Graham-Campbell, R. Hall, J. Jesch and D. Parsons, eds, *Vikings and the Danelaw* (Oxford, 2001), and D. Hadley and J. D. Richards, eds, *Cultures in Contact: Scandinavian Settlement in England in the Ninth and Tenth Centuries* (Turnhout, 2000).

For Scandinavians in the north-west, see F. Edmonds, 'History and Names', in J. Graham-Campbell and R. Philpott, eds *The Huxley Hoard: Scandinavian Settlement in the North West* (Liverpool, 2009), 3–12, and N. J. Higham, 'Viking Age Settlement in the North-Western Countryside: Lifting the Veil?', in J. Hines, A. Lane and M. Redknap, eds, *Land, Sea and Home: Settlement in the Viking Period* (London, 2004), 297–311. For York, see Sources and Issues 7a, below; for the Midlands, see R. Hall, 'The Five Boroughs of the Danelaw: A Review of Present Knowledge', *A.S.E.*, 18 (1989), 149–206. The *History of St Cuthbert* is translated in T. Johnson South, *Historia de Sancto Cuthberto* (Cambridge, 2002).

For the place name evidence, see L. Abrams and D. N. Parsons, 'Place-Names and the History of Scandinavian Settlement in England', in Hines, Lane and Redknap, eds, *Land, Sea and Home*, 379–431; K. Cameron, *Place-Name Evidence for the Anglo-Saxon Invasion and Scandinavian Settlements: Eight Studies* (Nottingham, 1975), and G. Fellows-Jensen, *The Vikings and Their Victims: The Verdict of the Names* (London, 1995). For Amounderness see R. Watson, 'Viking Age Amounderness: A Reconsideration', in N. J. Higham and M. J. Ryan, eds, *Place-Names, Language and the Anglo-Saxon Landscape* (Woodbridge, 2011), 125–42.

R. N. Bailey, *Viking Age Sculpture in Northern England* (London, 1980), offers a detailed overview of the evidence. For hogbacks, see J. Lang, 'The Hogback: A Viking Colonial Monument', *A.S.S.A.H.*, 3 (1984), 83–174. The sculpture is catalogued, discussed and illustrated in the relevant volumes of the *Corpus of Anglo-Saxon Stone Sculpture* (Oxford, 1984–). For rural settlement, see D. Coggins, 'Simy Folds: Twenty Years On', in Hines, Lane and Redknap, eds, *Land, Sea and Home*, 326–34, and J. D. Richards, 'The Anglo-Saxon and Anglo-Scandinavian Evidence', in P. Stamper and R. Croft, eds, *Wharram: A Study of Settlement in the Yorkshire Wolds. VIII: The South Manor Area* (York, 2000), 195–200. For burial, see D. Hadley, 'Burial Practices in Northern England in the Later Anglo-Saxon Period', in S. Lucy and A. Reynolds, eds, *Burial in Early Medieval England and Wales* (London, 2002), 209–28, eadem, 'Warriors, Heroes and Companions: Negotiating Masculinity in Viking-Age England', *A.S.S.A.H.*, 15 (2008), 270–84, and J. D. Richards, 'The Case of the Missing Vikings: Scandinavian Burial in the Danelaw', in Lucy and Reynolds, eds, *Burial*, 156–70. For archaeogenetics and other scientific data, see P. Budd et al., 'Investigating Population Movement by Stable Isotope Analysis: A Report from Britain', *Antiquity*, 78 (2004), 127–41, C. Capelli et al., 'A Y Chromosome Census of the British Isles', *Current Biology*, 13 (2003), 979–84, S. Harding, M. Jobling and T. King, *Viking DNA: The Wirral and West Lancashire Project* (Nottingham, 2010), and S. S. Mastana and R. J. Sokol, 'Genetic Variation in the East Midlands', *Annals of Human Biology*, 25 (1998), 43–68.

The politics of the tenth century are now best approached via three books: S. Foot, *Æthelstan: The First King of England* (London, 2011), N. J. Higham and D. Hill, eds, *Edward the Elder, 899–924* (London, 2001), and D. Scragg, ed., *Edgar: King of the English, 959–975* (Woodbridge, 2008).

For Æthelflæd, see P. Stafford, 'Political Women in Mercia, Eighth to Early Tenth Centuries', in M. Brown and C. Farr, eds, *Mercia: An Anglo-Saxon Kingdom in Europe* (London, 2001), 35–49, eadem, ' "The Annals of Æthelflæd": Annals, History and Politics in Tenth-Century England', in J. Barrow and A. Wareham, eds, *Myth, Rulership, Church and Charters* (Aldershot, 2008), 101–16. For *Brunanburh*, see S. Foot, 'Where English Becomes British: Rethinking Contexts for *Brunanburh*', in Barrow and Wareham, eds, *Myth, Rulership, Church and Charters*, 127–44, and M. Livingstone, ed., *The Battle of Brunanburh: A Casebook* (Exeter, 2011). For relationships between Wessex and the north, see C. Downham, 'The Chronology of the Last Scandinavian Kings of York', *Northern History*, 40 (2003), 25–51; D. Rollason, 'St Cuthbert and Wessex: The Evidence of Cambridge, Corpus Christi College MS 183', in G. Bonner, D. Rollason and C. Stancliffe, eds, *St Cuthbert: His Cult and His Community* (Woodbridge, 1989), 413–24, and D. Whitelock, 'The Dealings of the Kings of England with Northumbria in the Tenth and Eleventh Century',

in P. Clemoes, ed., *The Anglo-Saxons* (London, 1959), 70–88.

For interactions between Anglo-Saxon kings and Scottish and Welsh rulers, see H. Loyn, 'Wales and England in the Tenth Century: The Context of the Æthelstan Charters', in his *Society and Peoples* (London, 1992), 173–99, and G. Molyneaux, 'Why Were Some Tenth-Century English Kings Presented as Rulers of Britain?', *T.R.H.S.*, 6th series, 21 (2011), 59–91. For Continental connections see the essays by Foot and Ortenberg in D. Rollason, C. Leyser and H. Williams, eds, *England and the Continent in the Tenth Century: Studies in Honour of Wilhelm Levison (1876–1947)* (Turnhout, 2011), and K. Leyser, 'The Ottonians and Wessex', in his *Communications and Power in Medieval Europe: The Carolingian and Ottonian Centuries* (London, 1994), 73–104. For Edgar and Chester, see J. Barrow, 'Chester's Earliest Regatta? Edgar's Dee-Rowing Re-Visited', *E.M.E.*, 10 (2001), 81–93.

For law codes see P. Wormald, *The Making of English Law: King Alfred to the Twelfth Century. Volume 1: Legislation and Its Limits* (Oxford, 2001); C. Cubitt, ' "As the Lawbook Teaches": Reeves, Lawbooks and Urban Life in the Anonymous Old English Legend of the Seven Sleepers', *E.H.R.*, 124 (2009), 1,021–49; S. Keynes, 'Royal Government and the Written Word in Late Anglo-Saxon England', in R. McKitterick, ed., *The Uses of Literacy in Early Mediaeval Europe* (Cambridge, 1990), 226–57, and D. Pratt, 'Written Law and the Communication of Authority in Tenth-Century England', in Rollason, Leyser and Williams, eds, *England and the Continent*, 331–50. For the specific examples from Æthelstan's law explored in this chapter, see Foot, *Æthelstan*. The codes themselves are translated in F. L. Attenborough, *The Laws of the Earliest English Kings* (Cambridge, 1922), and A. J. Robertson, *The Laws of the Kings of England from Edmund to Henry I*, 2 vols (Cambridge, 1925).

Governance and administration are explored by J. Campbell in a series of important essays collected in his *Essays in Anglo-Saxon History* (London, 1986) and *The Anglo-Saxon State* (London, 2000). See also H. Loyn, 'The King and the Structure of Society in Late Anglo-Saxon England' and 'The Hundred in England in the Tenth and Early Eleventh Centuries', both in his *Society and Peoples*, and Molyneaux, 'Tenth-Century English Kings'. For meeting sites, see A. Pantos, 'The Location and Form of Anglo-Saxon Assembly Places: Some "Moot Points" ', in A. Pantos and S. Semple, eds, *Assembly Places and Practices in Medieval Europe* (Dublin, 2004), 155–80, and for a sample of the long history of some moot sites, see A. Meaney, 'Pagan English Sanctuaries, Place-Names and Hundred Meeting Places', *A.S.S.A.H.*, 8 (1997), 29–42. For feasting and itinerant kingship, see L. Roach, 'Hosting the King: Hospitality and the Royal *Iter* in Tenth-Century England', *Journal of Medieval History*, 37 (2011), 34–46.

For the late Anglo-Saxon aristocracy, see C. Hart, 'Athelstan "Half King" and His Family', *A.S.E.*, 2 (1973), 115–44, and A. Williams, '*Princeps Merciorum gentis*: The Family, Career and Connections of Ælfhere, Ealdorman of Mercia, 956–83', *A.S.E.*, 10 (1981), 143–72. More generally see S. Baxter, *The Earls of Mercia: Lordship and*

Power in Late Anglo-Saxon England (Oxford, 2007); R. Fleming, *Kings and Lords in Conquest England* (Cambridge, 1991), and A. Williams, *The World before Domesday: The English Aristocracy, 871–1066* (London, 2008).

C. E. Blunt, B. H. I. H. Stewart and C. S. S. Lyon, *Coinage in Tenth-Century England: From Edward the Elder to Edgar's Reform* (Oxford, 1989), is the most comprehensive guide. For Æthelstan's coinage, see M. Blackburn, 'Mints, Burhs and the Grately Code, Cap. 14.2', in D. Hill and A. Rumble, eds, *The Defence of Wessex* (Manchester, 1996), 160–75. For the maximalist view of Edgar's reforms, see R. H. M. Dolley, 'Roger of Wendover's Date for Eadgar's Coinage Reform', *British Numismatic Journal*, 49 (1979), 1–11, and for reservations see I. Stewart, 'Coinage and Recoinage after Edgar's Reforms', in K. Jonsson, ed., *Studies in Late Anglo-Saxon Coinage in Memory of Bror Emil Hildebrand* (Stockholm, 1990), 455–85.

For discussion of the meaning and suitability of the term 'State', see S. Baxter, 'The Limits of the Late Anglo-Saxon State', in W. Pohl, ed., *Der frühmittelalterliche Staat – europäische Perspektiven* (Vienna, 2009), 503–14, and the essays by Foot and Wormald in L. Scales and O. Zimmer, eds, *Power and Nation in European History* (Cambridge, 2005).

The lives of the three central figures of the Benedictine Reforms are translated in M. Lapidge, *Byrhtferth of Ramsey: The Lives of St Oswald and St Ecgwine* (Oxford, 2008); M. Winterbottom and M. Lapidge, *Wulfstan of Winchester: Life of St Æthelwold* (Oxford, 1991), and M. Winterbottom and M. Lapidge, *The Early Lives of St Dunstan* (Oxford, 2011). For a translation of the New Minster refoundation charter and a discussion of the topography of Winchester, see A. Rumble, *Property and Piety in Early Medieval Winchester* (Oxford, 2002); for the *Regularis Concordia*, see T. Symons, *The Monastic Agreement of the Monks and Nuns of the English Nation* (London, 1953). Each of the three central figures is the subject of a volume of studies; these form the ideal introduction to the Reforms: N. Brooks and C. Cubitt, eds, *Oswald of Worcester: Life and Influence* (Leicester, 1996); N. Ramsay, M. Sparks and T. Tatton-Brown, eds, *St Dunstan: His Life, Times and Cult* (Woodbridge, 1992), and B. Yorke, ed., *Bishop Æthelwold: His Career and Influence* (Woodbridge, 1988). These volumes are usefully reviewed by C. Cubitt, 'Review Article: The Tenth-Century Benedictine Reform in England', *E.M.E.*, 6 (1997), 77–94. For the Hermeneutic Style, see M. Lapidge, *Anglo-Latin Literature, 900–1066* (London, 1993), and for Standard Old English see, for example, M. Gretsch, *Winchester Vocabulary and Standard Old English* (Manchester, 2001). The Winchester Style is discussed in M. Brown, *Manuscripts from the Anglo-Saxon Age* (London, 2007), and L. Webster, *Anglo-Saxon Art* (London, 2012). For the wider context, see R. Gameson, *The Role of Art in the Late Anglo-Saxon Church* (Oxford, 1995).

The significance of the Benedictine Reforms is assessed by J. Blair, *The Church in Anglo-Saxon Society*

(Oxford, 2005), which also discusses the development of new models of pastoral care in the late Anglo-Saxon period. On this subject see also the essays in J. Blair, ed., *Minsters and Parish Churches: The Local Church in Transition, 950–1200* (Oxford, 1998), and F. Tinti, ed., *Pastoral Care in Late Anglo-Saxon England* (Woodbridge, 2005).

Sources and Issues 6a
For an overview, see S. Rippon, *Beyond the Medieval Village: The Diversification of Landscape Character in Southern Britain* (Oxford, 2008); H. Hamerow, *Rural Settlements and Society in Anglo-Saxon England* (Oxford, 2012). Key works include C. Lewis, P. Mitchell-Fox and C. Dyer, *Village, Hamlet and Field: Changing Medieval Settlements in Central England* (Manchester, 1997); B. K. Roberts and S. Wrathmell, *An Atlas of Rural Settlement in England* (London, 2000); T. Williamson, *Shaping Medieval Landscapes: Settlement, Society, Environment* (Macclesfield, 2004). For village formation, see J. G. Hurst, ed., *Wharram: A Study of Settlement on the Yorkshire Wolds. Volume 1. Domestic Settlement, 1: Areas 10 and 6* (Leeds, 1979); B. K. Roberts, *The Making of the English Village* (Harlow, 1987); R. Jones and M. Page, *Medieval Villages in an English Landscape: Beginnings and Ends* (Macclesfield, 2006).

Discussion of open fields begins with H. Gray, *English Field Systems* (Cambridge, MA, 1915); then on to C. S. Orwin and C. S. Orwin, *The Open Fields* (Oxford, 1938); J. Thirsk, 'The Origins of the Common fields', *Past and Present*, 33 (1966), 142–7; T. Rowley, ed., *The Origins of Open-Field Agriculture* (London, 1981); R. Dodgshon, *The Origins of British Field Systems: An Interpretation* (London, 1980); T. Brown and G. Foard, 'The Saxon Landscape: A Regional Perspective', in P. Everson and T. Williamson, eds, *The Archaeology of Landscape: Studies Presented to Christopher Taylor* (Manchester, 1998), 67–94. Now, see N. J. Higham and M. J. Ryan, eds, *Landscape Archaeology of Anglo-Saxon England* (Woodbridge, 2010). For the plough, see G. Astill and L. Langdon, eds, *Medieval Farming and Technology: The Impact of Agricultural Change in Northwest Europe* (Leiden, 1997); P. J. Fowler, *Farming in the First Millennium AD* (Cambridge, 2002).

Sources and Issues 6b
For a useful overview see J. Graham-Campbell, 'The Northern Hoards from Cuerdale to Bossall/Flaxton', in N. J. Higham and D. Hill, eds, *Edward the Elder, 899–924* (London, 2001), 212–29. For the individual hoards: J. Graham-Campbell, ed., *Viking Treasures from the North-West: The Cuerdale Hoard in its Context* (Liverpool, 1992), G. Williams and B. Ager, *The Vale of York Hoard* (London, 2010), J. Graham-Campbell and R. Philpott, eds, *The Huxley Hoard: Scandinavian Settlement in the North West* (Liverpool, 2009), for Flusco-Pike/Penrith see Graham-Campbell, 'Northern Hoards'. The Silverdale Hoard has not yet been fully published.

Chapter 7

For Millennial thought, see M. Godden, 'Apocalypse and Invasion in Late Anglo-Saxon England' in M. Godden, D. Gray and T. Hoad, eds, *From Anglo-Saxon to Early Middle English* (Oxford, 1994), 130–62, idem, 'The Millennium, Time, and History for the Anglo-Saxons' in R. Landes, A. Gow and D. C. Van Meter, eds, *The Apocalyptic Year 1000* (Oxford, 2003), 155–80. The translation at the head of this chapter is taken from P. Wormald, *The Making of English Law: King Alfred to the Twelfth Century. Volume 1: Legislation and Its Limits* (Oxford, 2001).

For the 'Anti-monastic reaction', see S. Jayakumar, 'Reform and Retribution: The "Anti-Monastic Reaction" in the Reign of Edward the Martyr', in S. Baxter, C. E. Karkov, J. L. Nelson and D. Pelteret, eds, *Early Medieval Studies in Memory of Patrick Wormald* (Farnham, 2009), 337–52. The *Life of Oswald* is translated in M. Lapidge, *Byrhtferth of Ramsey: The Lives of St Oswald and St Ecgwine* (Oxford, 2008); there is no translation of the *Book of Bishop Æthelwold* but it was incorporated into the *Liber Eliensis*, see J. Fairweather, *Liber Eliensis: A History of the Isle of Ely from the Seventh to the Twelfth Centuries* (Woodbridge, 2005); for discussion, see A. Kennedy, 'Law and Litigation in the *Libellus Æthelwoldi episcopi*', *A.S.E.*, 24 (1995), 131–83. For the cult of King Edward, in addition to the studies of Æthelred, below, see C. Cubitt, 'Sites and Sanctity: Revisiting the Cults of Murdered and Martyred Anglo-Saxon Royal Saints', *E.M.E.*, 9 (2000), 53–83; C. E. Fell, *Edward, King and Martyr* (Leeds, 1971); S. J. Ridyard, *The Royal Saints of Anglo-Saxon England* (Cambridge, 1988), and D. Rollason, 'The Cult of Murdered Royal Saints in Anglo-Saxon England', *A.S.E.*, 11 (1982), 1–22.

For Æthelred the fundamental study is S. Keynes, *The Diplomas of King Æthelred 'the Unready', 978–1016: A Study in their Use as Historical Evidence* (Cambridge, 1980); R. Lavelle, *Aethelred II: King of the English 978–1016*, rev. edn (London, 2008), and A. Williams, *Æthelred the Unready: The Ill-Counselled King* (London, 2003), offer useful and complementary introductions. S. Keynes, 'Re-Reading King Æthelred the Unready' in D. Bates, J. Crick and S. Hamilton, eds, *Writing Medieval Biography* (Woodbridge, 2006), 77–97, is a masterful survey. D. Hill, ed., *Ethelred the Unready: Papers from the Millenary Conference* (Oxford, 1978), likewise contains important material, particularly the papers by Keynes, Stafford and Wormald. For the violence of Æthelred's reign, see S. Keynes, 'Crime and Punishment in the Reign of King Æthelred the Unready', in I. Wood and N. Lunds, eds, *People and Places in Northern Europe* (Woodbridge, 1991), 67–81. For Æthelred's appropriations of land, see P. Stafford, 'Political Ideas in Late Tenth-Century England: Charters as Evidence' in P. Stafford, J. L. Nelson and J. Martindale, eds, *Law, Laity and Solidarities* (Manchester, 2001), 68–82; for Æthelred's repentance, C. Cubitt, 'The Politics of Remorse: Penance and Royal Piety in the Reign of Æthelred the Unready', *Historical Research*, 85 (2012), 179–92; more generally, L. Roach, 'Public Rites and Public Wrongs: Ritual Aspects of Diplomas in Tenth- and Eleventh-Century England', *E.M.E.*, 19 (2011), 182–203.

For the return of the Vikings, see the general studies listed under chapter 5 above. See also D. Scragg, ed., *The Battle of Maldon, AD 991* (Oxford, 1991), and J. Cooper, ed., *The Battle of Maldon: Fiction and Fact* (London, 1993). For the levels of tribute, see the debate between J. Gillingham and M. K. Lawson in the *E.H.R.*; M. K. Lawson, 'Danegeld and Heregeld Once More', *E.H.R.*, 105 (1990), 951–61, summarises the debates and references the other articles. For the scale of the coinage, see M. Allen, 'The Volume of the English Currency, c. 973–1158', in B. Cook and G. Williams, eds, *Coinage and History in the North Sea World* (Leiden, 2006), 487–523. For a translation of *II Æthelred* see A. J. Robertson, *The Laws of the Kings of England from Edmund to Henry I*, 2 vols (Cambridge, 1925).

J. Haslam, 'The Early Development of Late Saxon Christchurch, Dorset, and the Burghal Hidage', *M.A.*, 53 (2009), 95–118, surveys later Anglo-Saxon defences, although questioning the attribution of such works to Æthelred. For the traditional approach, see D. Hill, 'Trends in the Development of Towns during the Reign of Ethelred II', in idem, ed., *Ethelred the Unready*, 213–26; this also includes information on the 'emergency *burhs*'. In addition, see R. H. M. Dolley, 'Three Late Anglo-Saxon Notes', *British Numismatic Journal*, 28 (1955–7), 88–105, and idem and F. Elmore Jones, 'The Mints "Æt Gothabyrig" and "Æt Sith(m)estebyrig" ', *British Numismatic Journal*, 28 (1955–7), 270–82. For discussion of fortifications, see R. Lavelle, *Alfred's Wars: Sources and Interpretations of Anglo-Saxon Warfare in the Viking Age* (Woodbridge, 2010). The Ridgeway Hill and St John's College burial pits have not yet been fully published; for initial discussion of the Oxford evidence, see A. M. Pollard et al., ' "Sprouting like cockle amongst the wheat": The St Brice's Day Massacre and the Isotopic Analysis of Human Bones from St John's College, Oxford', *Oxford Journal of Archaeology*, 31 (2012), 83–102.

For the ending of the tenth-century aristocracy, see S. Baxter, *The Earls of Mercia: Lordship and Power in Late Anglo-Saxon England* (Oxford, 2007), and R. Fleming, *Kings and Lords in Conquest England* (Cambridge, 1991). For the impact of this on Swein's and Cnut's conquests, see C. Insley, 'Politics, Conflict and Kinship in Early Eleventh-Century Mercia', *Midland History*, 25 (2000), 28–42. For conflict between Æthelred's sons, see P. Stafford, *Unification and Conquest: A Political and Social History of England in the Tenth and Eleventh Centuries* (London, 1989), and idem, *Queen Emma and Queen Edith: Queenship and Women's Power in Eleventh-Century England* (Oxford, 2001). For the martyrdom of Ælfheah, N. Brooks, *The Early History of the Church at Canterbury: Christ Church from 597–1066* (Leicester, 1984).

The literature on Wulfstan and, particularly, Ælfric is extensive. For Ælfric the best starting point is H. Magennis and M. Swan, eds, *A Companion to Ælfric* (Leiden, 2009), with the essay by Hill offering an excellent introduction. For the composition of the *Catholic*

Homilies, see M. Godden, 'The Development of Aelfric's Second Series of Catholic Homilies', *English Studies*, 54 (1973), 209–16, and for Ælfric's monasteries M. Lapidge, 'Ælfric's Schooldays', in E. Treharne and S. Rosser, eds, *Early Medieval English Texts and Interpretations* (Tempe, AZ, 2002), 301–9; K. Barker, ed., *The Cerne Abbas Millenary Lectures* (Cerne Abbas, 1988), and C. A. Jones, *Ælfric's Letter to the Monks of Eynsham* (Cambridge, 1998). For Wulfstan, start with M. Townend, ed., *Wulfstan: Archbishop of York* (Turnhout, 2004). For Ælfric's and Wulfstan's engagement with their society, see also M. Clayton, 'Of Mice and Men: Ælfric's Second Homily for the Feast of a Confessor', *Leeds Studies in English*, n.s., 24 (1993), 1–26; Godden, 'Apocalypse and Invasion'; S. Keynes, 'An Abbot, an Archbishop, and the Viking Raids of 1006–7 and 1009–12', *A.S.E.*, 36 (2007), 151–220; M. K. Lawson, 'Archbishop Wulfstan and the Homiletic Elements in the Laws of Æthelred II and Cnut', *E.H.R.*, 107 (1992), 565–86, and J. Wilcox, 'Ælfric in Dorset and the Landscape of Pastoral Care' in F. Tinti, ed., *Pastoral Care in Late Anglo-Saxon England* (Woodbridge, 2005), 52–62, Wormald, *The Making of English Law*.

For Cnut, see M. K. Lawson, *Cnut: The Danes in England in the Early Eleventh Century* (London, 1993); T. Bolton, *The Empire of Cnut the Great: Conquest and Consolidation of Power in Northern Europe in the Early Eleventh Century* (Leiden, 2009), and A. R. Rumble, ed., *The Reign of Cnut: King of England, Denmark and Norway* (London, 1994). For Emma, see Stafford, *Queen Emma and Queen Edith*, and for the *Encomium*, see A. Campbell, ed., *Encomium Emmae Reginae*, reprinted with a new introduction (Cambridge, 1998). For changes to the Anglo-Saxon aristocracy, see also K. Mack, 'Changing Thegns: Cnut's Conquest and the English Aristocracy', *Albion*, 16 (1984), 375–87; for Godwin and Leofric, see F. Barlow, *The Godwins* (Harlow, 2002); Baxter, *Earls of Mercia*; Fleming, *Lordship and Conquest*; C. Insley, 'Where Did All the Charters Go? Anglo-Saxon Charters and the New Politics of the Eleventh Century', *Anglo-Norman Studies*, 24 (2002), 109–28, and E. Mason, *The House of Godwin* (London, 2004). For Scandinavian settlement, see P. Nightingale, 'The Origin of the Court of Husting and Danish Influence on London's Development as a Capital City', *E.H.R.*, 102 (1987), 559–78, and A. Williams, '"Cockles amongst the wheat": Danes and English in the Western Midlands in the First Half of the Eleventh Century', *Midland History*, 11 (1986), 1–22.

For social changes in the later Anglo-Saxon period, see R. Fleming, 'The New Wealth, the New Rich and the New Political Style in Late Anglo-Saxon England', *Anglo-Norman Studies*, 23 (2001), 1–22. The main sources are translated in D. Whitelock, *English Historical Documents, I: c. 500–1042*, 2nd edn (London, 1979). For the meaning of 'rice', see M. Godden, 'Money, Power and Morality in Late Anglo-Saxon England', *A.S.E.*, 19 (1990), 41–65; for social mobility and the rise of the gentry J. Gillingham, 'Thegns and Knights in Eleventh-Century England: Who Was Then the Gentleman?', *T.R.H.S.*, 6th series, 5 (1995), 129–53, W. G. Runciman, 'Accelerating Social Mobility: The Case of Anglo-Saxon England', *Past*

and Present, 104 (1984), 3–30; F. M. Stenton, 'The Thriving of the Anglo-Saxon Ceorl', in *Preparatory to Anglo-Saxon England*, ed. D. M. Stenton (Oxford, 1970), 383–93, and A. Williams, *The World Before Domesday: The English Aristocracy, 871–1066* (London, 2008).

For Shapwick, see M. D. Costen, *The Origins of Somerset* (Manchester, 1992); C. M. Gerrard and M. Aston, eds, *The Shapwick Project, Somerset* (London, 1997), and, for the wider context, F. Pryor, *The Making of the British Landscape* (London, 2010). For Raunds, see M. Audouy and A. Chapman, *Raunds: The Origin and Growth of a Midland Village AD 450–1500: Excavations in North Raunds, Northamptonshire 1977–87* (Oxford, 2009).

For thegnly residences, see A. Williams, 'A Bell-House and a Burh-geat: Lordly Residences in England before the Norman Conquest', in R. Liddiard, ed., *Anglo-Norman Castles* (Woodbridge, 2003), 23–40, and G. Beresford, *Goltho: The Development of an Early Medieval Manor, c. 850–1150* (London, 1987); B. Cunliffe, *Excavations at Portchester Castle: Volume II, Saxon* (London, 1975); J. Fairbrother, *Faccombe Netherton: Excavations of a Saxon and Medieval Manorial Complex*, 2 vols (London, 1990), and G. Thomas, *The Later Anglo-Saxon Settlement at Bishopstone: A Downland Manor in the Making* (London, 2010). For the church at Furnells, see A. Boddington, *Raunds, Furnells, the Anglo-Saxon Church and Churchyard* (London, 1996), and for the complex at Sulgrave, B. K. Davison, 'Excavations at Sulgrave, Northamptonshire', *Archaeological Journal*, 134 (1977), 105–14. For *The Reeve* and similar texts, see P. D. A. Harvey, '*Rectitudines Singularum Personarum* and *Gerefa*', *E.H.R.*, 108 (1993), 1–22, and M. Gardner, 'Implements and Utensils in *Gerefa* and the Organisation of Segneurial Farmsteads in the High Middle Ages', *M.A.*, 50 (2006), 260–70. For translations, see M. Swanton, trans., *Anglo-Saxon Prose*, new edn (London, 1995), and for estate surveys A. J. Robertson, ed. and trans., *Anglo-Saxon Charters* (Cambridge, 1939). For clothing, see G. Owen-Crocker, *Dress in Anglo-Saxon England*, rev. edn (Woodbridge, 2004), and C. R. Dodwell, *Anglo-Saxon Art: A New Perspective* (Manchester, 1982); for silk, specifically, R. Fleming, 'Acquiring, Flaunting and Destroying Silk in Late Anglo-Saxon England', *E.M.E.*, 15 (2007), 127–58. For a useful introduction to the later Anglo-Saxon diet, see N. Sykes, 'Woods and the Wild', in H. Hamerow, D. A. Hinton, and S. Crawford, eds, *The Oxford Handbook of Anglo-Saxon Archaeology* (Oxford, 2011), 327–45.

Sources and Issues 7a

For an oversight, see R. Hall, ed., *Viking Age York and the North* (London, 1978), *The Viking Dig* (London, 1984) and *Viking Age York* (London, 1994); for the detail, see *The Archaeology of York, Anglo-Scandinavian York*, published in fascicles by The Council of British Archaeology. Otherwise, see D. Rollason, *Northumbria, 500–1100: The Creation and Destruction of a Kingdom* (Cambridge, 2003), and R. A. Hall et al., *Aspects of Anglo-Scandinavian York* (York, 2004).

Sources and Issues 7b

The literature is, as might be expected, vast. One of the most evocative translations is S. Heaney, trans., *Beowulf: A New Verse Translation* (London, 1999); the Norton Critical Edition of this translation, ed. D. Donoghue (New York, 2002), also includes important scholarly studies on the poem. There are many other very good translations available, for details see the chapter by Osborn in *A Beowulf Handbook* (below). R. D. Fulk, trans., *The Beowulf Manuscript* (Cambridge, MA, 2010), uniquely translates *Beowulf* and the four other works from the original manuscript; some of the insights that might be gained from reading the poem in its manuscript context are explored by A. Orchard, *Pride and Prodigies: Studies in the Monsters of the Beowulf-Manuscript* (Cambridge, 1995). For key issues and debates see R. E. Bjork and J. D. Niles, eds, *A Beowulf Handbook* (Lincoln, NE, 1996), and A. Orchard, *A Critical Companion to Beowulf* (Cambridge, 2003). A number of important studies are usefully reprinted in L. E. Nicholson, ed., *An Anthology of Beowulf Criticism* (Notre Dame, IN, 1971); R. D. Fulk, ed., *Interpretations of Beowulf: A Critical Anthology* (Bloomington, IN, 1991); and P. S. Baker, ed., *Beowulf: Basic Readings* (London, 1994).

Chapter 8

An excellent new collection on Edward the Confessor is R. Mortimer, ed., *Edward the Confessor: The Man and the Legend* (Woodbridge, 2009); see particularly the essay by S. Baxter. The first major history of the period was that of E. A. Freeman, *The History of the Norman Conquest of England*, 6 vols (Oxford, 1867); F. M. Stenton, *Anglo-Saxon England*, 3rd edn (Oxford, 1971), offers a balanced view but see also D. C. Douglas, *William the Conqueror* (Berkeley, CA, 1964). The 'Norman' case for the succession was argued by E. John: 'Edward the Confessor and the Norman Succession', *E.H.R.*, 94 (1979), 241–67, in 'The End of Anglo-Saxon England', in J. Campbell, ed., *The Anglo-Saxons* (London, 1982), 214–39, and *Reassessing Anglo-Saxon England* (Manchester, 1996). G. Garnett offers an opposing view: *Conquered England: Kingship, Succession and Tenure, 1066–1166* (Oxford, 2007) and *The Norman Conquest: A Very Short Introduction* (Oxford, 2009). For wider discussion, see M. Chibnall, *The Debate on the Norman Conquest* (Manchester, 1999).

For the political narrative, see B. Golding, *Conquest and Colonisation: The Normans in Britain, 1066–1100* (Basingstoke, 1994); N. J. Higham, *The Death of Anglo-Saxon England* (Stroud, 1997), and *The Norman Conquest* (Stroud, 1998), and/or R. Huscroft, *The Norman Conquest: A New Introduction* (Harlow, 2009). For a more structural approach, see J. Campbell, *Essays in Anglo-Saxon History* (London, 1986); F. Barlow, *The Feudal Kingdom of England 1042–1216*, 4th edn (Harlow, 1988), and C. Hicks, ed., *England in the Eleventh Century* (Stamford, 1992). For Normandy, see D. Bates, *Normandy before 1066* (London, 1982), and D. Bates and A. Curry, eds, *England and Normandy in the Middle Ages* (London,

1994). For warfare, see M. Strickland, *Anglo-Norman Warfare* (Woodbridge, 1992), and S. Morillo, *The Battle of Hastings: Sources and Interpretations* (Woodbridge, 1996); for the north the best study remains W. E. Kapelle, *The Norman Conquest of the North: The Region and its Transformation, 1000–1135* (London, 1979). 'Waste' in Domesday Book is mapped by H. C. Darby, *Domesday England* (Cambridge, 1977), 232–59; for whether most should be ascribed to Norman activity, see D. Palliser, 'Domesday Book and the Harrying of the North', *Northern History*, 29 (1993), 1–23.

For the literary sources, see D. C. Douglas and G. W. Greenaway, eds, *English Historical Documents, vol. II, 1042–1189* (London, 1953). For the *Anglo-Saxon Chronicle*, see S. Baxter, 'MS C of the Anglo-Saxon Chronicle and the Politics of Mid-Eleventh-Century England', *E.H.R.*, 122 (2007), 1,189–227. For other sources, see A. Campbell, ed., *Encomium Emmae Reginae*, reprinted with a new introduction (Cambridge, 1998); F. Barlow, ed., *The Life of King Edward Who Rests at Westminster*, 2nd edn (London, 1992); D. W. Rollason, ed., *Simeon of Durham, Libellus de Exordio atque Procursu Istius, hoc est Dunhelmensis, Ecclesie: Tract on the Origins and Progress of this the Church of Durham* (Oxford, 2000). The Norman sources are collected in R. A. Brown, *The Norman Conquest* (London, 1984); see also M. Chibnall, ed., *The Ecclesiastical History of Orderic Vitalis*, 6 vols (Oxford, 1968–80); R. H. C. Davis and M. Chibnall, eds, *The 'Gesta Guillelmi' of William of Poitiers* (Oxford, 1998), and F. Barlow, ed., *The Carmen de Hastingae Proelio of Guy, Bishop of Amiens* (Oxford, 1999).

For the principal leaders, see F. Barlow, *Edward the Confessor* (London, 1970); I. Walker, *Harold: The Last Anglo-Saxon King* (Stroud, 1997); P. Stafford, *Queen Emma and Queen Edith: Queenship and Women's Power in Eleventh-Century England* (Oxford, 1997); D. Bates, *William the Conqueror* (Stroud, 2001); G. R. Owen-Crocker, ed., *King Harold II and the Bayeux Tapestry* (Woodbridge, 2005). For the aristocracy, see R. Fleming, *Kings and Lords in Conquest England* (Cambridge, 1991); A. Williams, *The English and the Norman Conquest* (Woodbridge, 1995) and *The World before Domesday: The English Aristocracy, 900–1066* (London, 2008); F. Barlow, *The Godwins* (Harlow, 2002); E. Mason, *The House of Godwine* (London, 2004), and S. Baxter, *The Earls of Mercia* (Oxford, 2007). For Edward's Normans, see C. P. Lewis, 'The French in England before the Norman Conquest', *Anglo-Norman Studies*, 17 (1994), 123–44.

Studies of early castles include R. A. Brown, *English Castles*, 3rd edn (London, 1976); D. J. Cathcart King, *The Castle in England and Wales: An Interpretative History* (London, 1988), and P. Barker and R. Higham, *Timber Castles* (London, 1992). A reappraisal of the castle was offered by C. L. H. Coulson, *Castles in Medieval Society* (Oxford, 2003), and R. Liddiard, *Castles in Context: Power, Symbolism and Landscape, 1066 to 1500* (Macclesfield, 2005), but see C. Platt, 'Revisionism in Castle Studies: A Caution', *M.A.*, 51 (2007), 83–102. For churches, see H. M. Taylor and J. Taylor, *Anglo-Saxon*

Architecture, 3 vols (Cambridge, 1965–78); E. Fernie, *The Architecture of the Anglo-Saxons* (London, 1983); J. Blair, ed., *Minster and Parish Churches: The Local Church in Transition* (Oxford, 1988), 21–30. For patronage, see E. Cownie, *Religious Patronage in Anglo-Norman England* (Woodbridge, 1998); more generally, see H. Mayr-Harting, *Religion, Politics and Society in Britain, 1066–1272* (Harlow, 2011). For the archaeology of later Anglo-Saxon England, see J. D. Richards, *Viking Age England* (London, 1994), and A. Reynolds, *Later Anglo-Saxon England: Life and Landscape* (Stroud, 1999). For high-status sites, see particularly G. Beresford, *Goltho: The Development of an Early Medieval Manor c. 850–1150* (London, 1987). A magisterial overview of Domesday England is Darby, *Domesday England*. For the broader landscape, see G. J. White, *The Medieval English Landscape 1000–1540* (London, 2012). For Conquest-period towns, see J. Schofield and A. Vince, *Medieval Towns* (London, 1994); D. Palliser, ed., *The Cambridge Urban History of Britain, I, 600–1540* (Cambridge, 2000), and see chapter 7 above.

Sources and Issues 8a
For a high-quality photographic reproduction, see M. Parisse, *La Tapisserie de Bayeux* (Paris, 1983); L. Musset, *La Tapisserie de Bayeux* (Bayeux, 1989); W. Grape, *The Bayeux Tapestry: Monument to a Norman Triumph* (Munich, 1994), M. Rud, trans. C. Ejlers, *The Bayeux Tapestry and the Battle of Hastings 1066*, 5th edn (Copenhagen, 2004); M. K. Foys, *Bayeux Tapestry, Digital Edition* (2003), or D. M. Wilson, *The Bayeux Tapestry: The Complete Tapestry in Colour* (London, 2004). N. Brooks and the late H. E. Walker, 'The Authority and Interpretation of the Bayeux Tapestry', *Proceedings of the Battle Conference*, 1 (1979), 1–34; D. M. Wilson, *The Bayeux Tapestry* (London, 1985); G. R. Owen-Crocker, ed., *King Harold II and the Bayeux Tapestry* (Woodbridge, 2005). For the later history of the Tapestry, see C. Hicks, *The Bayeux Tapestry: The Life Story of a Masterpiece* (London, 2006). For recent discussion, see M. J. Lewis, *The Real World of the Bayeux Tapestry* (Stroud, 2008).

Sources and Issues 8b
Domesday Book was edited by A. Farley (London, 1783); this then formed the basis for translation, shire by shire under the editorship of John Morris for Phillimore (London and Chichester) in the 1980s. A photographic facsimile was produced in the late 1980s, again shire by shire, by Alecto Historical Editions, prefaced by *Domesday Book Studies*, ed. A. Williams and R. W. H. Erskine (London, 1987): see particularly H. Loyn, 'A General Introduction to Domesday Book', 1–24.

For varying interpretations, see J. H. Round, *Feudal England* (Cambridge, 1895); F. W. Maitland, *Domesday Book and Beyond* (Cambridge, 1897); A. Ballard, *The Domesday Inquest* (London, 1906); V. H. Galbraith, *The Making of Domesday Book* (Oxford, 1961) and *Domesday Book: Its Place in Administrative History* (Oxford, 1974); R. W. Finn, *Domesday Book: A Guide* (London, 1973). Two collections of essays celebrated the 900th anniversary: P. H. Sawyer, ed., *Domesday Book: A Reassessment* (London, 1985), and J. C. Holt, ed., *Domesday Studies* (Woodbridge, 1987); see also E. M. Hallam, *Domesday Book through Nine Centuries* (New York, 1986); D. Roffe, *Domesday: The Inquest and the Book* (Oxford, 2000) and *Decoding Domesday* (Woodbridge, 2007).

INDEX